C000149701

1 MONTH OF
FREE
READING

at

www.ForgottenBooks.com

By purchasing this book you are eligible for one month membership to ForgottenBooks.com, giving you unlimited access to our entire collection of over 1,000,000 titles via our web site and mobile apps.

To claim your free month visit:
www.forgottenbooks.com/free149382

ISBN 978-1-5280-8524-3
PIBN 10149382

NAPOLEON

A Sketch of

HIS LIFE, CHARACTER, STRUGGLES, AND ACHIEVEMENTS

BY

THOMAS E. WATSON

AUTHOR OF "THE STORY OF FRANCE," ETC.

ILLUSTRATED WITH PORTRAITS AND FACSIMILES

New York

THE MACMILLAN COMPANY

LONDON: MACMILLAN & CO., Ltd.

1910

Norwood Press
J. S. Cushing & Co. — Berwick & Smith
Norwood Mass. U.S.A.

TO MY WIFE

Georgia Durham Watson

PREFACE

IN this volume the author has made the effort to portray Napoleon as he appears to an average man.   Archives have not been rummaged, new sources of information have not been discovered; the author merely claims to have used such authorities, old and new, as are accessible to any diligent student.   No attempt has been made to give a full and detailed account of Napoleon's life or work. To do so would have required the labor of a decade, and the result would be almost a library.   The author *has* tried to give to the great Corsican his proper historical position, his true rating as a man and a ruler, — together with a just estimate of his achievements.

THOMSON, GEORGIA,
    Dec. 24, 1901.

CONTENTS

LIST OF ILLUSTRATIONS

xi

NAPOLEON

CHAPTER I

CORSICA, an island in the Mediterranean Sea, has an extreme width of 52 miles and length of 116. It is within easy reach of Italy, France, Spain, Sardinia, and the African coast. Within 54 miles lies Tuscany, while Genoa is distant but 98, and the French coast at Nice is 106. Across the island strides a chain of mountains, dividing it into two nearly equal parts. The slopes of the hills are covered with dense forests of gigantic pines and chestnuts, and on their summits rests eternal snow. Down from these highlands rapid streams run to the sea. There are many beautiful valleys and many fine bays and harbors.

The population of the island was, in the eighteenth century, about 130,000. The Italian type predominated. In religion it was Roman Catholic.

The history of Corsica has been wonderfully dramatic. Peopled originally by the Celts, perhaps, the island has been so often war-swept, so often borne down under the rush of stronger nations, that the native race almost disappeared. The Greeks from Asia Minor, back in the dim ages, seized upon a part of the coast and colonized it. Carthage, in her day of greatness, was its mistress; and then came Rome, whose long period of supremacy left its stamp upon the people, bringing as it did multitudes of Italians, with their language, customs, and religion.

After the day of Rome came Germans, Byzantine Greeks, Moors, Goths, Vandals, and Longobards. For centuries the island was torn by incessant war, the Corsicans doing their utmost to keep themselves free from foreign masters. The feudal system was fastened upon the struggling people by the chiefs of the invaders. The crags were crowned with castles, and half-savage feudal lords ruled by the law of their own fierce lusts. They waged war upon each other, they ground down the native races. Unable to defend themselves, miserably poor, but full of desperate courage, the Corsicans fled from the coasts to escape the pirate, and to the mountains to resist the feudal robber. In their distress the peasants found a leader in Sambuccio, who organized them into village communities, — a democratic, self-ruling confederation. There were no serfs, no slaves, in Corsica; freedom and equality the people claimed and fought for; and under Sambuccio they totally routed the barons.

The great leader died; the barons took up arms again; the peasants appealed to the margrave of Tuscany for aid ; an army came from Italy, the barons were beaten, and the village confederation restored. From A.D. 1020 to A.D. 1070, Tuscany protected the Corsicans; but the popes, having looked upon the land with eyes of desire, claimed it for the Church, and, through skilful manipulations (such as are common in cases of that kind), the people were persuaded to submit. In the year 1098 Pope Urban II. sold the island to Pisa, and for one hundred years Corsica remained under the dominion of that republic.

Genoa, however, envied Pisa this increase of territory,

claimed the island for herself, and backed her claim by arms. Corsica was rent by the struggle, and the Corsicans themselves were divided into hostile camps, one favoring Pisa, the other Genoa.

The leader of the Pisan faction, Guidice della Rocca, kept up, for many years, an unequal struggle, showing wonderful courage, fertility of resource, rigorous justice, and rare clemency. He killed his own nephew for having outraged a female prisoner for whose safety he, Della Rocca, had given his word. Old and blind, this hero was betrayed by his bastard son, delivered to the Genoese, and died in a wretched Genoese dungeon; and with his downfall passed away the Pisan sovereignty.

A period of anarchy followed the death of Della Rocca. The barons were unmerciful in their extortions, and the people were reduced to extreme misery. After many years appeared another valiant patriot of the Rocca race, Arrigo della Rocca (1392). He raised the standard of revolt, and the people rallied to him. He beat the Genoese, was proclaimed Count of Corsica, and ruled the land for four years. Defeated at length by the Genoese, he went to Spain to ask aid. Returning with a small force, he routed his enemies and became again master of the island. Genoa sent another army, Arrigo della Rocca was poisoned (1401), and in the same year Genoa submitted to France.

Corsica kept up the struggle for independence. Vincentello, nephew of Arrigo della Rocca, was made Count of Corsica, and for two years maintained a gallant contest. Genoa poured in more troops, and the resistance was crushed. Vincentello left the island. Soon returning with help from Aragon, he reconquered the county with the exception of the strongholds of Calvi and Bonifaccio. Inspired by the success of Vincentello, the young king of Aragon, Alfonso, came in person with large forces to complete the conquest. Calvi was taken, but Bonifaccio resisted all efforts. The place was strongly Genoese, and for months the endurance of its defenders was desperately heroic. Women and children and priests joined with those who manned the walls, and all fought together. Spanish courage was balked, Spanish pride humbled, and Alfonso sailed away. Vincentello, bereft of allies, lost ground. He gave his own cause a death-blow by abusing a girl whose kinsmen rose to avenge the wrong. The guilty man and indomitable patriot determined to seek aid once more in Spain; but Genoa captured him at sea, and struck off his head on the steps of her ducal palace (1434).

Then came anarchy in Corsica again. The barons fought, the peasants suffered. Law was dead. Only the dreaded vendetta ruled — the law of private vengeance. So harried were the people by continued feuds, rival contentions, and miscellaneous tumult, that they met in general assembly and decided to put themselves under the protection of the bank of St. George of Genoa. The bank agreed to receive this singular deposit (1453). The Corsican nobles resisted the bank, and terrible scenes followed. Many a proud baron had his head struck off, many of them left the country. Aragon favored the nobles, and they came back to renew the fight, defeat the forces of the bank, and reconquer most of the island.

In 1464 Francesco Sforza of Milan took Genoa, and claimed Corsica as a part of his conquest. The islanders preferred Milan to Genoa, and but for an accidental brawl, peaceful terms might have been arranged. But the brawl occurred, and there was no peace. Years of war, rapine, and universal wretchedness followed. Out of the murk appears a valiant figure, Giampolo, taking up with marvellous tenacity and fortitude the old fight of Corsica against oppression. After every defeat, he rose to fight again. He never left the field till Corsican rivalry weakened and ruined him. Then, defiant to the last, he went the way of the outlaw to die in exile.

Renuccio della Rocca's defection had caused Giampolo to fail. After a while Rocca himself led the revolt against Genoa, and was overthrown. He left the island, but came again, and yet again, to renew the hopeless combat. Finally his own peasants killed him to put an end to the miserable war, there being no other method of turning the indomitable man (1511).

Resistance over, the bank of Genoa governed the island. The barons were broken, their castles fell to ruin. The common people kept up their local home-rule, enjoyed a share in the government, and were in a position much better than that of the common people in other parts of Europe. But the bank was not satisfied to let matters rest there; a harsh spirit soon became apparent; and the privileges which the people had enjoyed were suppressed.

Against this tyranny rose now the strongest leader the Corsicans had yet found, Sampiero. Humbly born, this man had in his youth sought adventures in foreign lands. He had served the House of Medici, and in Florence became known for the loftiness and energy of his character. Afterward he served King Francis I., of France, by whom he was made colonel of the Corsican regiment which he had formed. Bayard was his friend, and Charles of Bourbon said of him, " In the day of battle

the Corsican colonel is worth ten thousand men"; just
as another great warrior, Archduke Charles of Austria,
said of another great Corsican, serving then in France
(1814), "Napoleon himself is equal to one hundred
thousand men."

In 1547 Sampiero went back to Corsica to select a wife.
So well established was his renown that he was given the
only daughter of the Lord of Ornano, the beautiful Vannina. The bank of Genoa, alarmed by the presence of
such a man in the island, threw him into prison. His
father-in-law, Francesco Ornano, secured his release.

Genoa, since her delivery from French dominion by
Andrea Doria, was in league with the Emperor of Germany, with whom the French king and the Turks were
at war. Hence it was that Sampiero could induce France
and her allies to attack the Genoese in Corsica. In 1553
came Sampiero, the French, and the Turks; and all Corsica, save Calvi and Bonifaccio, fell into the hands of the
invaders. Bonifaccio was besieged in vain, until, by a
stratagem, it was taken. Then the Turks, indignant that
Sampiero would not allow them to plunder the city and
put all the Genoese to the sword, abandoned the cause,
and sailed away. Calvi still held out. The Emperor sent
an army of Germans and Spaniards; Cosmo de Medici
also sent troops; Andrea Doria took command, and the
French were everywhere beaten. Sampiero quarrelled
with the incapable French commander, went to France
to defend himself from false reports, made good his purpose, then returned to the island, where he became the lion
of the struggle. He beat the enemy in two pitched battles, and kept up a successful contest for six years. Then
came a crushing blow. By the treaty of Cambray, France

agreed with Spain that Corsica should be given back to Genoa.

Under this terrible disaster, Sampiero did not despair. Forced to leave the island, he wandered from court to court on the continent, seeking aid. For four years he went this dreary round, — to France, to Navarre, to Florence. He even went to Algiers and to Constantinople. During this interval it was that Genoa deceived and entrapped Vannina, the wife of the hero. She left her home and put herself in the hands of his enemies. One of Sampiero's relatives was fool enough to say to him, " I had long expected this."—" And you concealed it !" cried Sampiero in a fury, striking his relative to the heart with a dagger. Vannina was pursued and caught, Sampiero killed her with his own hand.

Failing in his efforts to obtain foreign help, the hero came back to Corsica to make the fight alone (1564). With desperate courage he marched from one small victory to another until Genoa was thoroughly aroused. An army of German and Italian mercenaries was sent over, and the command given to an able general, Stephen Doria. The war assumed the most sanguinary character. Genoa seemed bent on utterly exterminating the Corsicans and laying waste the entire country. Sampiero rose to the crisis ; and while he continued to beseech France for aid, he continued to fight with savage ferocity. He beat Doria in several encounters, and finally, in the pass of Luminada, almost annihilated the enemy. Doria, in despair, left the island, and Sampiero remained master of the field. With his pitifully small forces he had foiled the Spanish fleet, fifteen thousand Spanish soldiers, and an army of mercenaries; and had in succession beaten the

best generals Genoa could send. All this he had done
with half-starved, half-armed peasants, whose only strength
lay in the inspiration of their patriotism and the unconquerable spirit of their leader. Few stronger men have
lived and loved, hoped and dared, fought and suffered,
than this half-savage hero of Corsica. With all the world
against him Sampiero fought without fear, as another
great Corsican was to do.

In open fight he was not to be crushed : on this his enemies were agreed, therefore treachery was tried. Genoa
bribed some of the Corsican chiefs ; Vannina's cousins
were roused to seek revenge ; Vittolo, a trusted lieutenant, turned against his chief ; and a monk, whom Sampiero could not suspect, joined the conspirators. The
monk delivered forged letters to Sampiero, which led him
to the ambuscade where his foes lay in wait. He fought
like the lion he was. Wounded in the face, he wiped the
blood out of his eyes with one hand while his sword was
wielded by the other. Vittolo shot him in the back, and
the Ornanos rushed upon the dying man, and cut off his
head (1567).

The fall of Sampiero created intense satisfaction in
Genoa, where there were bell-ringings and illuminations.
In Corsica it aroused the people to renewed exertions;
but the effort was fitful, for the leader was dead. In
a great meeting at Orezzo, where three thousand patriots
wept for the lost hero, they chose his son Alfonso their
commander-in-chief.

After a struggle of two years, in which the youth bore
himself bravely, he made peace and left the country.
Accompanied by many companions in arms, he went to
France, formed his followers into a Corsican regiment,

of which Charles the Ninth appointed him colonel.
Other Corsicans, taking refuge in Rome, formed themselves into the Pope's Corsican guard.

Thrown back into the power of Genoa, Corsica suffered all the ills of the oppressed. Wasted by war,
famine, plague, misgovernment, a more wretched land
was not to be found. Deprived of its privileges, drained
of its resources, ravaged by Turks and pillaged by Christians, it bled also from family feuds. The courts being
corrupt, the vendetta raged with fury. In many parts
of the country, agriculture and peaceful pursuits were
abandoned. And this frightful condition prevailed for
half a century.

The Genoese administration became ever more unbearable. A tax of twelve dollars was laid on every hearth.
The governors of the island were invested with the power
to condemn to death without legal forms or proceedings.

One day, a poor old man of Bustancio went to the
Genoese collector to pay his tax. His money was a
little short of the amount due — a penny or so. The
official refused to receive what was offered, and threatened to punish the old man if he did not pay the full
amount. The ancient citizen went away grumbling.
To his neighbors, as he met them, he told his trouble.
He complained and wept. They sympathized and wept.
Frenzied by his own wrongs, the old man began to
denounce the Genoese generally, — their tyranny, cruelty,
insolence, and oppression. Crowds gathered, the excitement grew, insurrectionary feelings spread throughout
the land. Soon the alarm bells were rung, and the war
trumpet sounded from mountain to mountain. This was
in October, 1729.

A war of forty years ensued. Genoa hired a large
body of Germans from the Emperor, and eight thousand
of these mercenaries landed in Corsica. At first they
beat the ill-armed islanders, who marched to battle bare
of feet and head. But in 1732 the Germans were almost
destroyed in the battle of Calenzala. Genoa called on
the Emperor for more hirelings. They were sent; but
before any decisive action had taken place, there arrived
orders from the Emperor to make peace. Corsica had
appealed to him against Genoa, and he had decided that
the Corsicans had been wronged. Corsica submitted to
Genoa, but her ancient privileges were restored, taxes
were remitted, and other reforms promised.

No sooner had the Germans left the island than Genoese and Corsicans fell to fighting again. Under Hya-
cinth Paoli and Giafferi, the brave islanders defeated the
Genoese, at all points; and Corsica, for the moment, stood
redeemed.

In 1735 the people held a great meeting at Corte
and proclaimed their independence. A government was
organized, and the people were declared to be the only
source of the laws.

Genoa exerted all her power to put down the revolt.
The island was blockaded, troops poured in, the best
generals were sent. The situation of the Corsicans was
desperate. They stood in need of almost everything
requisite to their defence, except brave men. The
blockade cut off any hope of getting aid from abroad.
English sympathizers sent two vessels laden with supplies, and keen was the joy of the poor islanders. With
the munitions thus obtained they stormed and took
Alesia.

But their distress was soon extreme again, and the struggle hopeless. At this, the darkest hour, came a very curious episode. A German adventurer, Theodore de Neuhoff, a baron of Westphalia, entering the port with a single ship, under the British flag, offered himself to the Corsicans as their king. Promises of the most exhilarating description he made as to the men, money, munitions of war he could bring to Corsican relief. Easily believing what was so much to their interest, and perhaps attaching too much importance to the three English ships which had recently brought them supplies, the Corsican chiefs actually accepted Neuhoff for their king.

The compact between King Theodore and the Corsicans was gravely reduced to writing, signed, sealed, sworn to, and delivered. Then they all went into the church, held solemn religious services, and crowned Theodore with a circlet of oak and laurel leaves. Theodore took himself seriously, went to work with zeal, appointed high diguitaries of the crown, organized a court, created an order of knighthood, and acted as if he were a king indeed. He marched against the oppressors, fought like a madman, gained some advantages, and began to make the situation look gloomy to the Genoese.

Resorting to a detestable plan, they turned loose upon the island a band of fifteen hundred bandits, galley-slaves, and outlaws. These villains made havoc wherever they went. In the meantime, the Corsican chiefs began to be impatient about the succors which Theodore had promised. Evasions and fresh assurances answered for a while, but finally matters reached a crisis. Theodore was told, with more or less pointedness, that either the succors must come or that he must go. To avoid a storm, he went,

saying that he would soon return with the promised relief.
Paoli and the other Corsican chiefs realized that in catch‐
ing at the straw this adventurer had held out to them, they
had made themselves and Corsica ridiculous.   They ac‐
cordingly laid heavy blame on Theodore.

Cardinal Fleury, a good old Christian man, who was at
this time (1737) minister of France, came forward with a
proposition to interfere in behalf of Genoa, and reduce the
Corsicans to submission.   Accordingly French troops were
landed (1738), and the islanders rose *en masse* to resist.
Bonfires blazed, bells clanged, war trumpets brayed.   The
whole population ran to arms.   The French were in no
haste to fight, and for six months negotiations dragged
along.   Strange to say, the Corsicans, in their misery, gave
hostages to the French, and agreed to trust their cause
to the king of France.   At this stage who should enter
but Theodore !   The indefatigable man had ransacked
Europe, hunting sympathy for Corsica, and had found it
where Americans found it in a similar hour of need — in
Holland.   He had managed to bring with him several
vessels laden with cannon, small arms, powder, lead,
lances, flints, bombs, and grenades.   The Corsican peo‐
ple received him with delight, and carried him in triumph
to Cervione, where he had been crowned ; but the chiefs
bore him no good-will, and told him that circumstances
had changed.   Terms must be made with France; Corsica
could not at this time accept him as king — oaths, religious
services, and written contract to the contrary notwith‐
standing.   Theodore sadly sailed away.

The appeal to the French king resulted in the treaty of
Versailles, by whose terms some concessions were made
to the Corsicans, who were positively commanded to lay

down their arms and submit to Genoa. Corsica resisted, but was overcome by France. In 1741 the French withdrew from the island, and almost immediately war again raged between Corsican and Genoese.

In 1748 King Theodore reappeared, bringing munitions of war which the island greatly needed. He seems to have succeeded in getting the Corsicans to accept his supplies, but they showed no inclination to accept himself. Once again he departed — to return no more. The gallant, generous adventurer went to London, where his creditors threw him into prison. The minister, Walpole, opened a subscription which secured his release. He died in England, and was buried in St. Anne's churchyard, London, December, 1756.

Peace was concluded between Genoa and Corsica, whose privileges were restored. For two years quiet reigned. Family feuds then broke out, and the island was thrown into confusion. Following this came a general rising against the Genoese, in which the English and Sardinians aided the Corsicans. Genoa applied to France, which sent an army. Dismayed by the appearance of the French, the island came to terms. Cursay, the commander of the French, secured for the unfortunate people the most favorable treaty they had ever obtained. Dissatisfied with Cursay, the Genoese prevailed on France to recall him. Whereupon the Corsicans rose in arms, Gaffori being their chief. He displayed the genius and the courage of Sampiero, met with the success of the earlier hero, and like him fell by treachery. Enticed into an ambuscade, Gaffori was slain by Corsicans, his own brother being one of the assassins. The fall of the leader did not dismay the people. They chose other leaders,

and continued the fight. Finally, in July, 1755, the celebrated Paschal Paoli was chosen commander-in-chief.
At this time he was but twenty-four years old. Well
educated, mild, firm, clear-headed, and well balanced, he
was very much more of a statesman than a warrior. His
first measure, full of wisdom, was the abolition of the
vendetta.

Mainly by the help of his brother Clemens, Paoli
crushed a rival Corsican, Matra, and established himself
firmly as ruler of the island. Under his administration
it flourished and attracted the admiring attention of all
European liberals. Genoa, quite exhausted, appealed to
France, but was given little help. As a last resort,
treachery was tried: Corsican was set against Corsican.
The Matra family was resorted to, and brothers of him
who had led the first revolt against Paoli took the field
at the head of Genoese troops. They were defeated.

Genoa again turned to France, and on August 6, 1764,
was signed an agreement by which Corsica was ceded to
France for four years. French garrisons took possession
of the few places which Genoa still held. During the four
years Choiseul, the French minister, prepared the way for
the annexation of Corsica to France. As ever before,
there were Corsicans who could be used against Corsica.
Buttafuoco, a noble of the island, professed himself a convert to the policy of annexation. He became Choiseul's
apostle for the conversion of others. So adroitly did he
work with bribes and other inducements, that Corsica
was soon divided against herself. A large party declared
in favor of the incorporation of the island with France.
In 1768 the Genoese realized that their dominion was gone.
A bargain was made between two corrupt and despotic

powers by which the one sold to the other an island it did not own, a people it could not conquer, — an island and a people whose government was at that moment a model of wisdom, justice, and enlightened progress. Alone of all the people of Europe, Corsica enjoyed self-government, political and civil freedom, righteous laws, and honest administration. Commerce, agriculture, manufactures, had sprung into new life under Paoli's guidance, schools had been founded, religious toleration decreed, liberty of speech and conscience proclaimed. After ages of combat against awful odds, the heroic people had won freedom, and, by the manner in which it was used, proved that they had deserved to win it. Such were the people who were bargained for and bought by Choiseul, the minister of France, at and for the sum of $400,000. The Bourbons had lost to England an empire beyond seas — by this act of perfidy and brutality they hoped to recover some of their lost grandeur.

Terrible passions raged in Corsica when this infamous bargain became known. The people flew to arms, and their wrongs sent a throb of sympathy far into many lands. But France sent troops by the tens of thousands; and while the Corsicans accomplished wonders, they could not beat foes who outnumbered them so heavily. Paoli was a faithful chief, vigilant and brave, but he was no Sampiero. His forces were crushed at Ponte Nuovo on June 12, 1769, and Corsica laid down her arms. The long chapter was ended, and one more wrong triumphant.

Chief among the painful features of the drama was that Buttafuoco and a few other Corsicans took service with France, and made war upon their own people.

Paoli with a band of devoted supporters left the island.

From Leghorn, through Germany and Holland, his journey was a triumphal progress. Acclaimed by the liberals, honors were showered upon him by the towns through which he passed; and in England, where he made his home, he was welcomed by the people and pensioned by the government.

The French organized their administration without difficulty. The Buttafuoco element basked in the warmth of success and patronage. For a while all was serene. Later on the French grip tightened, the Corsican time-honored privileges were set aside, the old democracy was no longer the support of a government which relied more and more on French soldiers. Power, taken from the village communities, was placed entirely in the hands of a military governor and a council of twelve nobles. Frenchmen filled all the important offices. The seat of government was moved from Corte to Bastia and Ajaccio. The discontent which these changes caused broke into open rebellion. The French crushed it with savage cruelty. After that Corsica was a conquered land, which offered no further resistance; but whose people, excepting always those who had taken part with France, nursed intensely bitter feelings against their conquerors.

Of this fiery, war-worn, deeply wronged people, Napoleon Bonaparte was born; and it must be remembered that before his eyes opened to the light his mother had thrilled with all the passions of her people, her feet had followed the march, her ears had heard the roar of battle. As Dumas finely says, "The new-born child breathed air that was hot with civil hates, and the bell which sounded his baptism still quivered with the tocsin."

CHAPTER II

"FROM St. Charles Street you enter on a very small square. An elm tree stands before a yellowish gray plastered house, with a flat roof and a projecting balcony. It has six front windows in each of its three stories, and the doors look old and time-worn. On the corner of this house is an inscription, *Letitia Square*. The traveller knocks in vain at the door. No voice answers."

Such is the picture, drawn in 1852, of the Bonaparte mansion in Ajaccio. Few tourists go to see it, for Corsica lies not in the direct routes of the world's trade or travel. Yet it is a house whose story is more fascinating, more marvellous, than that of any building which cumbers the earth this day.

We shut our eyes, and we see a picture which is richer than the richest page torn from romance. We see a lean, sallow, awkward, stunted lad step forth from the door of the old house and go forth into the world, with no money in his pocket, and no powerful friends to lift him over the rough places. He is only nine years old when he leaves home, and we see him weep bitterly as he bids his mother good-by. We see him at school in France, isolated, wretched, unable at first to speak the language, fiercely resenting the slights put upon his poverty, his ignorance, his family, his country — suffering, but never subdued.

We see him rise against troubles as the eagle breasts the storm. We see him lay the better half of the civilized world at his feet. We see him bring sisters and brothers from the island home, and put crowns on their heads. We see him shower millions upon his mother ; and we hear him say to his brother on the day he dons the robes of empire, " Joseph, suppose father were here — ! "

As long as time shall last, the inspiration of the poor and the ambitious will be the Ajaccio lawyer's son : not Alexander, the born king; not Cæsar, the patrician; but Napoleon, the moneyless lad from despised Corsica, who stormed the high places of the world, and by his own colossal strength of character, genius, and industry took them !

As long as time shall last his name will inspire not only the individual, but the masses also. Wherever a people have heard enough, read enough, thought enough to feel that absolutism in king or priest is wrong ; that special privilege in clan or clique is wrong; that monopoly of power, patronage, wealth, or opportunity is wrong, there the name of Napoleon will be spoken with reverence, despot though he became, for in his innermost fibre he was a man of the people, crushing to atoms feudalism, caste, divine right, and hereditary imposture.

As early as the year 947 there had been Bonapartes in Corsica, for the name of one occurs as witness to a deed in that year. There were also Bonapartes in Italy ; and men of that name were classed with the nobles of Bologna, Treviso, and Florence. It is said that during the civil wars of Italy, members of the Bonaparte family took refuge in Corsica, and that Napoleon's origin can be traced to this source. It is certain that the Bonapartes of Corsica continued to claim kindred with the Italian family, and to class themselves as patricians of Italy ; and both these claims were recognized. In Corsica they ranked with the nobility, a family of importance at Ajaccio.

At the time of the French invasion the representatives of the family were Lucien, archdeacon of Ajaccio, and Charles Bonaparte, a young man who had been left an orphan at the age of fourteen.

Born in 1746, Charles Bonaparte married, in 1764, Letitia Ramolino, a Corsican girl of fifteen. She was of good family, and she brought to her husband a dowry at least equal to his own estate. Beautiful, high-spirited, and intelligent, Madame Letitia knew nothing of books, knew little of the manners of polite society, and was more of the proud peasant than of the grand lady. She did not know how to add up a column of figures ; but time was to prove that she possessed judgment, common sense, inflexible courage, great loftiness and energy of character. Misfortune did not break her spirit, and prosperity did not turn her head. She was frugal, industrious, strong physically and mentally, "with a man's head on a woman's shoulders," as Napoleon said of her.

Charles Bonaparte was studying law in Italy when the war between France and Corsica broke out. At the call of Paoli, the student dropped his books and came home to join in the struggle. He was active and efficient, one of Paoli's trusted lieutenants. After the battle of Ponte Nuovo, realizing that all was lost, he gave in his submission (May 23, 1769) to the French, and returned to Ajaccio.

The policy of the French was to conciliate the leading Corsicans, and special attention seems to have been given to Charles Bonaparte. His mansion in Ajaccio, noted for its hospitality, became the favorite resort of General Marbeuf, the bachelor French governor of the island. With an ease which as some have thought indicated suppleness or weakness of character, Bonaparte the patriot became Bonaparte the courtier. He may have convinced himself that incorporation with France was best for Corsica, and that his course in making the most out of the new order of things was wisdom consistent with patriotism.

Resistance to France having been crushed, the policy of conciliation inaugurated, and the Corsicans encouraged to take part in the management of their own affairs, subject to France, one might hesitate before condemning the course of Charles Bonaparte in Corsica, just as we may hesitate between the policies of Kossuth and Déak in Hungary, or of Kosciusko and Czartoryski in Poland. We may, and do, admire the patriot who resists to the death; and, at the same time, respect the citizen who fights till conquered, and then makes the best of a bad situation.

In 1765 Madame Letitia Bonaparte gave birth to her first child; in 1767, to her second, both of whom died while infants. In 1768 was born Joseph, and on August 15, 1769, Napoleon.[1]

---

[1] During the period of this pregnancy, Corsica was in the storm of war; and Madame Bonaparte, following her husband, was in the midst of the sufferings, terrors, and brutalities which such a war creates. The air was still electrical with the hot passions of deadly strife when

Other children came to the Bonapartes in the years following, the survivors of these being: Elisa, Lucien, Louis,
Pauline, Caroline, and Jerome. To support this large
family, and to live in the hospitable fashion which custom
required of a man of his rank, Charles Bonaparte found a
difficult matter, especially as he was a pleasure-loving, extravagant man whose idea of work seemed to be that of
a born courtier. He returned to Italy after the peace;
spent much of his patrimony there; made the reputation
of a sociable, intelligent, easy-going gentleman; and took
his degree of Doctor of Laws, at Pisa, in November,
1769.

It was his misfortune to be cumbered with a mortgaged
estate and a hereditary lawsuit. Whatever surplus the
mortgage failed to devour was swallowed by the lawsuit.
His father had expensively chased this rainbow, pushed
this hopeless attempt to get justice; and the steps of the
father were followed by the son. It was the old story of
a sinner, sick and therefore repentant; a priest holding
the keys to heaven and requiring payment in advance; a
craven surrender of estate to purchase the promise of salvation. Thus the Jesuits got Bonaparte houses and lands,

the young wife's time came. On the 15th of August, 1769, Madame
Bonaparte, a devout Catholic, attended service at the church; but feeling labor approaching, hastened home, and was barely able to reach her
room before she was delivered of Napoleon on a rug upon the floor.

The authority for this statement is Madame Bonaparte herself, who
gave that account of the matter to the Permons in Paris, on the 18th of
Brumaire, the day on which the son thus born was struggling for
supreme power in France.

The story which represents the greatest of men and warriors as having
come into the world upon a piece of carpet, or tapestry, upon which the
heroes of the "Iliad" were represented, is a fable, according to the express statement made by Madame Bonaparte to the American General
Lee, in Rome, in 1830.

in violation of the terms of an ancestor's will, the lawsuit being the effort of the legal heirs to make good the testament of the original owner.

In spite of all they could do, the Bonapartes were never able to recover the property.

Charles Bonaparte, a man of handsome face and figure, seems to have had a talent for making friends, for he was made assessor to the highest court of Ajaccio, a member of the council of Corsican nobles, and later, the representative of these nobles to France. With the slender income from his wife's estate and that from his own, aided by his official earnings, he maintained his family fairly well; but his pretensions and expenditures were so far beyond what he was really able to afford that, financially, he was never at ease.

It was the familiar misery of the gentleman who strives to gratify a rich man's tastes with a poor man's purse. There was his large stone mansion, his landed estate, his aristocratic associates, his patent of nobility signed by the Duke of Florence; and yet there was not enough money in the house to school the children.

The widowed mother of Madame Letitia had married a second husband, Fesch, a Swiss ex-captain of the Genoese service, and by this marriage she had a son, Joseph Fesch, known to Napoleonic chronicles as "Uncle Fesch." This eleven-year-old uncle taught the young Napoleon the alphabet.

In his sixth year Napoleon was sent to a dame's school. For one of the little girls at this school the lad showed such a fondness that he was laughed at, and rhymed at, by the other boys.

Napoleon di mezza calzetta
Fa l'armore a Giacominetta.[1]

The jeers and the rhyme Napoleon answered with sticks and stones.

It is not very apparent that he learned anything here, for we are told that it was the Abbé Recco who taught him to read; and it was this Abbé whom Napoleon remembered in his will. As to little Giacominetta, Napoleonic chronicles lose her completely, and she takes her place among the "dream children" of very primitive poesy.

Just what sort of a boy Napoleon was at this early period, it is next to impossible to say. Perhaps he did not differ greatly from other boys of his own age. Probably he was more fractious, less inclined to boyish sports, quicker to quarrel and fight. But had he never become famous, his youthful symptoms would never have been thought to indicate anything uncommon either for good or evil.

At St. Helena, the weary captive amused himself by picturing the young Napoleon as the bad boy of the town. He quarrelled, he fought, he bit and scratched, he terrorized his brothers and sisters, and so forth. It may be true, it may not be; his mother is reported as saying that he was a "perfect imp of a child," but the authority is doubtful.

The Bonaparte family usually spent the summer at a small country-seat called Milleli. Its grounds were beautiful, and there was a glorious view of the sea. A large granite rock with a natural cavity, or grotto, offered a cool, quiet retreat; and this is said to have been Napoleon's favorite resort. In after years he improved the spot, built

[1] Napoleon with his stockings half off
Makes love to Giacominetta.

a small summer-house there, and used it for study and meditation.

It is natural to suppose that Napoleon as a child absorbed a good deal of Corsican sentiment. His wet-nurse was a Corsican peasant, and from her, his parents, his playmates, and his school companions he probably heard the story of Corsica, her wrongs, her struggles, and her heroes. Della Rocca, Sampiero, Gaffori, and Paoli were names familiar to his ears. At a very early age he had all the.passions of the Corsican patriot. The French were masters, but they were hated. While the Bonapartes had accepted the situation, they may not have loved it. The very servants in the house vented their curses on " those dogs of French."

General Marbeuf, the warm friend of the family, encouraged Charles Bonaparte to make the attempt to have the children educated at the expense of France. In 1776 written application was made for the admission of Joseph and Napoleon into the military school of Brienne. At that time both the boys were on the safe side of the age-limit of ten years. But the authorities demanded proofs of nobility, — four generations thereof, — according to Bourbon law; and before these proofs could be put into satisfactory shape, Joseph was too old for Brienne.

Chosen in 1777 by the nobles of Corsica as their deputy to France, Charles Bonaparte set out for Versailles in 1778, taking with him his sons Joseph and Napoleon. Joseph Fesch accompanied the party as far as Aix, where he was to be given a free education for the priesthood by the seminary at that place. Joseph and Napoleon both stated in after years that their father visited Florence on

the way to France, and was given an honorable reception
at the ducal court.

The Bishop of Autun, nephew of General Marbeuf, had
been interested in behalf of the Bonapartes; and it was
at his school that Joseph was to be educated for the
Church.   Napoleon was also placed there till he could
learn French enough for Brienne.   On January 1, 1779,
therefore, he began his studies.

The Abbé Chardon, who was his teacher, says that he
was a boy of thoughtful and gloomy character.   " He
had no playmate and walked about by himself."   Very
naturally.   He was a stranger to all the boys, he was in
a strange country, he could not at first speak the language,
he could not understand those who did speak it — how
was the homesick lad to be sociable and gay under such
conditions ?   Besides, he was Corsican, a despised representative of a conquered race.   And the French boys
taunted him about it.   One day, according to the teacher,
the boys threw at him the insult that " the Corsicans
were a lot of cowards."   Napoleon flashed out of his reserve and replied, " Had you been but four to one you
would never have conquered us, but you were ten to one."
To pacify him the teacher remarked, " But you had a good
general — Paoli." — " Yes," answered the lad of ten, " and
I would like to resemble him."

According to the school register and to Napoleon's own
record, he remained at Autun till the 12th of May, 1779.
He had learned " enough French to converse freely, and
to make little themes and translations."

In the meantime, Charles Bonaparte had been attending
his king, the young Louis XVI., at Versailles.   Courtier
in France as in Ajaccio, the adroit lawyer had pleased.

A bounty from the royal purse swelled the pay of the
Corsican delegates, a reward for "their excellent behavior"; and for once Charles Bonaparte was moderately
supplied with funds.

On May 19, 1779, Napoleon entered the college of
Brienne.   Its teachers were incompetent monks.   The
pupils were mainly aristocratic French scions of the privileged nobility, proud, idle, extravagant, vicious.   Most of
these young men looked down upon Napoleon with scorn.
In him met almost every element necessary to stir their
dislike, provoke their ridicule, or excite their anger.   In
person he was pitifully thin and short, with lank hair
and awkward manners; his speech was broken French,
mispronounced and ungrammatical; it was obvious that
he was poor; he was a Corsican; and instead of being
humble and submissive, he was proud and defiant.   During the five years Napoleon spent here he was isolated,
moody, tortured by his own discontent, and the cruelty
of his position.   He studied diligently those branches he
liked, the others he neglected.   In mathematics he stood
first in the school, in history and geography he did fairly
well; Latin, German, and the ornamental studies did not
attract him at all.   The German teacher considered him
a dunce.   But he studied more in the library than in the
schoolroom.   ᐧWhile the other boys were romping on the
playground, Napoleon was buried in some corner with a
book.

On one occasion Napoleon, on entering a room and seeing a picture of Choiseul which hung therein, burst into a
torrent of invective against the minister who had bought
Corsica.   The school authorities punished the blasphemy.

At another time one of the young French nobles scornfully said to Napoleon, "Your father is nothing but a wretched tipstaff." Napoleon challenged his insulter, and was imprisoned for his temerity.

Upon another occasion he was condemned by the quartermaster, for some breach of the rules, to wear a penitential garb and to eat his dinner on his knees at the door of the common dining-room. The humiliation was real and severe; for doubtless the French lads who had been bullying him were all witnesses to the disgrace, and were looking upon the culprit with scornful eyes, while they jeered and laughed at him. Napoleon became hysterical under the strain, and began to vomit. The principal of the school happening to pass, was indignant that such a degradation should be put upon so dutiful and diligent a scholar, and relieved him from the torture.

"Ah, Bourrienne! I like you: you never make fun of me!" Is there nothing pathetic in this cry of the heartsick boy?

To his father, Napoleon wrote a passionate appeal to be taken from the school where he was the butt of ridicule, or to be supplied with sufficient funds to maintain himself more creditably. General Marbeuf interfered in his behalf, and supplied him with a more liberal allowance.

The students, in turn, were invited to the table of the head-master. One day when this honor was accorded Napoleon, one of the monk-professors sweetened the boy's satisfaction by a contemptuous reference to Corsica and to Paoli. It seems well-nigh incredible that the clerical teachers should have imitated the brutality of the supercilious young nobles, but Bourrienne is authority for the incident. Napoleon broke out defiantly against the

teacher, just as he had done against his fellow-students :
"Paoli was a great man; he loved his country; and I
will never forgive my father for his share in uniting
Corsica to France. He should have followed Paoli."
Mocked by some of the teachers and tormented by the
richer students, Napoleon withdrew almost completely
within himself. He made no complaints, prayed for no
relief, but fell back on his own resources. When the
boys mimicked his pronunciation, turned his name into an
offensive nickname, and flouted him with the subjection
of his native land, he either remained disdainfully silent,
or threw himself single-handed against his tormentors.

To each student was given a bit of ground that he
might use it as he saw fit. Napoleon annexed to his own
plat two adjacent strips which their temporary owners
had abandoned; and by hedging and fencing made for
himself a privacy, a solitude, which he could not otherwise get. Here he took his books, here he read and
pondered, here he indulged his tendency to day-dreaming,
to building castles in the air.

His schoolmates did not leave him at peace even here.
Occasionally they would band together and attack his
fortress. Then, says Burgoing, one of his fellow-students, "it was a sight to see him burst forth in a fury
to drive off the intruders, without the slightest regard
to their numbers."

Much as he disliked his comrades, there was no trace
of meanness in his resentments. He suffered punishment
for things he had not done rather than report on the real
offenders. Unsocial and unpopular, he nevertheless en_
joyed a certain distinction among the students as well
as with the teachers. His pride, courage, maturity of

thought, and quick intelligence arrested attention and compelled respect.

When the students, during the severe winter of 1783–84, were kept within doors, it was Napoleon who suggested mimic war as a recreation. A snow fort was built, and the fun was to attack and defend it with snow-balls. Then Napoleon's natural capacity for leadership was seen. He at one time led the assailants, at another the defenders, as desperately in earnest as when he after-ward attacked or defended kingdoms. One student refusing to obey an order, Napoleon knocked him down with a chunk of ice. Many years after this unlucky person turned up with a scar on his face, and reminded the Emperor Napoleon of the incident; whereupon Napoleon fell into one of his best moods, and dealt liberally with the petitioner.

During the whole time Napoleon was at Brienne he remained savagely Corsican. He hated the French, and did not hesitate to say so. Of course the French here meant were the pupils of the school — the big boys who jeered at his poverty, his parentage, his countrymen. It is worth notice that he never by word or deed sought to disarm his enemies by pandering to their prejudices. He made no effort whatever to ingratiate himself with them by surrendering any of his own opinions. He would not even compromise by concealing what he felt. He was a Corsican to the core, proud of his island heroes, proud of Paoli, frankly detesting those who had trampled upon his country. It must have sounded even to the dull ears of ignorant monks as something remarkable when this shabby-looking lad, hardly in his teens, cried out, defiantly, " I hope one day to be able to give Corsica her freedom!" He had drunk in the wild stories the peasants told of Sampiero; he had devoured the vivid annals of Plutarch, and his hopes and dreams were already those of a daring man.

During these years at Brienne, General Marbeuf continued to be Napoleon's active friend. He seems to have regularly supplied him with money, and it was the General's interference which secured his release from imprisonment in the affair of the duel. Through the same influence Napoleon secured the good-will of Madame de Brienne, who lived in the château near the school. This lady warmed to the lad, took him to her house to spend holidays and vacations, and treated him with a motherly kindness which he never forgot.

The character which Napoleon established at Brienne varied with the point of view. To the students generally he appeared to be unsocial, quarrelsome, and savage. To some of the teachers he seemed to be mild, studious, grateful. To others, imperious and headstrong. M. de Keralio reported him officially as submissive, upright, thoughtful, "conduct most exemplary." On all he made the impression that he was inflexible, not to be moved after he has taken his stand. Pichegru, afterward conqueror of Holland, and after that supporter of the Bourbons, was a pupil-teacher to Napoleon at Brienne, and is thought to have been the quartermaster who put upon him the shame of eating on his knees at the dining-room door. Bourbon emissaries were eager to win over to their cause the brilliant young general, Bonaparte, and suggested the matter to Pichegru. "Do not try it," said he. "I knew him at Brienne. His character is inflexible. He has taken his side, and will not change."

When Napoleon, in his last years, came to speak of his school days, he seemed to have forgotten all that was unpleasant. Time had swept its effacing fingers over the actual facts, and he had come to believe that he had not only been happy at Brienne, but had been a jolly, frolicksome fellow — a very cheerful, sociable, popular lad. It was some other youth who had shunned his fellows, fenced himself within a garden wall, combated all intruders with sticks and stones, and hated the French because they teased him so. The real Napoleon, according to the captive Emperor, was a boy like other boys, full of fun, frolic, tricks, and games. One of the sportive tricks of the merry and mythical Bonaparte was this : An old commandant, upward of eighty, was practising the boys at target-shooting with a cannon. He complained that the aim was bad, none of the balls hit the target. Presently, he asked of those near him if they had seen the ball strike. After half a dozen discharges, the old general bethought himself of counting the balls. Then the trick was exposed — the boys had slipped the balls aside each time the gun was loaded.

Another anecdote told by the Emperor brings him more immediately within the circle of our sympathies. Just above his own room at the college was a fellow-student who was learning to play on the horn. He practised loudly, and at all hours. Napoleon found it impossible to study. Meeting the student on the stairs, Napoleon feelingly remonstrated. The horn player was in a huff at once, as a matter of course. His room was his own, and he would blow horns in it as much as he pleased. "We will see about that," said Napoleon, and he challenged the offender to mortal combat. Death could have no terrors compared to the incessant tooting in the room above, and Napoleon was determined to take his chances on sudden sword thrust rather than the slow tortures of the horn practice. Fellow-students interfered, a compromise was reached, and the duel did not come off. The student who roused the ire of Napoleon in this extreme manner was named Bussey, and in the campaign of 1814 Napoleon met him again, received offers of service from him, and named him aide-de-camp. It is a pleasure to be able to record that this fellow-student of Brienne remained faithful to Napoleon to the very last, in 1814 and again in 1815.

In the year 1810 the Emperor Napoleon, divorced from Josephine, was spending a few days in seclusion in the Trianon at Versailles, awaiting the coming of the Austrian wife, " the daughter of the Cæsars." Hortense and Stephanie Beauharnais were with him, and Stephanie mischievously asked him if he knew how to waltz. Napoleon answered : —

" When I was at the military school I tried, I don't know how many times, to overcome the vertigo caused by waltzing, without being able to succeed. Our dancing-master had advised us when practising to take a chair in our arms instead of a lady. I never failed to fall down with the chair, which I squeezed affectionately, and to break it. The chairs in my room, and those of two or three of my comrades, disappeared one after another."

The Emperor told this story in his gayest manner, and the two ladies laughed, of course ; but Stephanie insisted that he should even now learn to waltz, that all Germans waltzed, that his new wife would expect it, and that as the Empress could only dance with the Emperor, he must not deprive her of such a pleasure.

"You are right," exclaimed Napoleon. "Come! give me a lesson."

Thereupon he rose, took the merry Stephanie in his arms, and went capering around the room to the music of his own voice, humming the air of *The Queen of Prussia*. After two or three turns, his fair teacher gave him up in despair ; he was too hopelessly awkward ; and she flattered him, while pronouncing him a failure, by saying that he was made to give lessons and not receive them.

Toward the close of 1783 a royal inspector of the military schools, Keralio by name, examined the students at Brienne for the purpose of selecting those who were to be promoted to the higher military school at Paris. M. de Keralio was greatly impressed by Napoleon, and emphatically recommended his promotion. This inspector having died, his successor examined Napoleon the second time, and passed him on to the Paris school, which he entered on October 30, 1784. On the certificate which went with him from Brienne were the words, "Character masterful, imperious, and headstrong."

When Napoleon alighted from the coach which brought him from Brienne to Paris, and stood, a tiny foreign boy, in the midst of the hurly-burly of a great city, he must have felt himself one of the loneliest and most insignificant of mortals. Demetrius Permon found him in the Palais Royal, "where he was gaping and staring with wonder at everything he saw. Truly, he looked like a fresh importation." M. Permon invited the lad to dine, and found him "very morose," and feared that he had

D

"more self-conceit than was suitable to his condition."
Napoleon made this impression upon Permon by declaim-
ing violently against the luxury of the young men at the
military school, denouncing the system of education which
prevailed there, comparing it unfavorably to the system
of ancient Sparta, and announcing his intention of memo-
rializing the minister of war on the subject.

Napoleon, at the military school of Paris, continued to
be studious, and to read almost constantly. He was obedient to the authorities, and defiant to the young aristocrats who surrounded him and looked down on him. The
extravagance, indolence, and superciliousness of the noble
students, together with the general luxury which prevailed in the establishment, disgusted and enraged a
scholar who had no money to spend, and who had come
there to study. When he, as head of the State, came to
reorganize the educational system of France, he did not
forget the lessons taught by his own experience. As a
man he adopted a system which avoided all the abuses
which as a boy he had denounced.

During this period he may have occasionally visited
the Permons in Paris and his sister Elisa, who had been
admitted into the State school at St. Cyr. Madame
D'Abrantes so relates in her *Memoirs;* and while there
is a difficulty about dates, her narrative is, perhaps,
substantially correct. It is a lifelike picture she paints
of Napoleon's gloom at Paris and Elisa's sorrow at St. Cyr :
Napoleon wretched because he could not pay his way
among the boys; Elisa miserable because she could not
keep step with the girls. Napoleon sulked and denounced
luxury; Elisa wept and bewailed her poverty. Elisa
was consoled by a tip given by Madame Permon. As

for Napoleon, he refused to borrow: "I have no right to add to the burdens of my mother."

On final examination, August, 1785, Napoleon stood forty-second in his class — not a brilliant mark, certainly, but it sufficed. He received his appointment of sub-lieutenant with joy unbounded. His days of tutelage were over: henceforth he was a man and an officer. Having chosen the artillery service, he set out with Des Mazis, a friend he had made at the military school, to join the regiment of La Fère, which was stationed at Valence. According to one account, Napoleon borrowed money from a cloth merchant to make this journey; according to another, Des Mazis paid the way of both. However that may be, it seems that when the young officers reached Lyons, a gay city of the south, they relaxed the rigors of military discipline to such an extent that their money all vanished. The remainder of the distance to Valence was made on foot.

Those biographers who devote their lives to defaming Napoleon, lay stress on the alleged fact that he was educated by the King. In becoming an adherent of the Revolution, these writers say that he betrayed an amount of moral obliquity quite appalling. Louis XVI. was king while Napoleon was at Brienne, and the suggestion that Napoleon owed a debt of gratitude to Louis XVI. is amusing. The tax-payers, the people, educated Napoleon; and whatever debt of gratitude he owed, he owed to them. In going with the Revolution, he went with those who had paid his schooling. He himself drew this distinction at the time. When M. Demetrius Permon rebuked him for criticising royalty, throwing the alleged debt of gratitude in his teeth, the boy replied, "The State educates me; not the King."

Of course Permon could not admit the distinction, he being a noble of the Old Order; nor can biographers who write in the interest of modern Toryism admit it. But the distinction is there, nevertheless; the boy saw it, and so does impartial history.

CHAPTER III

NAPOLEON carried with him to his new home a letter of introduction from the Bishop of Autun to the ex-Abbot of St. Ruffe, and with this leverage he made his way into the best society of Valence. For the first time circumstances were favorable to him, and the good effects of the change were at once evident. Occupying a better place in life than before, he was more contented, more sociable. He mingled with the people about him, and made friends. No longer a waif, a charity boy from abroad, thrust among other boys who looked down upon him as a social inferior, he was now an officer of State, housed, fed, clothed, salaried at the public expense. No longer under the wheels, he held a front seat in that wondrous vehicle which men call government, and in which a few so comfortably ride while the many so contentedly wear harness and pull. No longer subject to everybody's orders, Napoleon had become one of the masters in God's world here below, and could issue orders himself. Glorious change! And the sun began to look bright to "Lieutenant Bonaparte of the King's Royal Academy." He cultivated himself and others socially. He found some congenial spirits among the elderly men of the place; also some among the young women. In the hours not spent in study, and not claimed by his duties, he

could be found chatting at the coffee-house, strolling with
brother officers, dancing at the neighborhood balls, and
playing the beau amid the belles of this high provincial
circle.

To one of these young ladies, according to tradition
and his own statement, he lost his heart. But when we
seek to know something more definite, tradition and his
own statements differ. If we are to accept his version,
the courtship led to nothing beyond a few promenades,
and the eating of cherries together in the early morning.
According to the local tradition, however, he proposed
and was rejected. Her parents were local aristocrats,
and had so little confidence in the future of the little
officer that they married their girl by preference to a
M. de Bressieux — a good, safe, commonplace gentleman
of the province. In after years the lady reminded Napoleon of their early friendship, and he at once made
generous provision for both herself and husband.

If possible, Napoleon studied more diligently at Valence
than at Brienne. Plutarch's *Lives* and Cæsar's *Commen-
taries* he had already mastered while a child ; Rousseau
had opened a new world of ideas to him in Paris : he now
continued his historical studies by reading Herodotus,
Strabo, Diodorus. Anything relating to India, China,
Arabia, had a peculiar charm for him. Next he learned
all he could of Germany and England. French history
he studied minutely, striving to exhaust information on
the subject. In his researches he was not content merely
with ordinary historical data : he sought to understand the
secret meaning of events, and the origin of institutions.
He studied legislation, statistics, the history of the Church,
especially the relation of the Church to the State. Like.

wise he read the masterpieces of French literature and the critical judgments which had been passed upon them. Novels he did not disdain, and for poetry of the heroic cast he had a great fondness.

He read also the works of Voltaire, Necker, Filangieri, and Adam Smith. With Napoleon to read was to study. He made copious notes, and these notes prove that he bent every faculty of his mind to the book in hand. He analyzed, commented, weighed statements in the balance of his own judgment — in short, doing everything necessary to the complete mastery of the subject. A paper on which he jotted down at that time his ideas of the relations between Church and State appear to show that he had reached at that time the conclusions he afterward embodied in the Concordat. Rousseau he studied again, but the book which seems to have taken his fancy more than any other was the Abbé Raynal's famous *History of the Institutions and Commerce of the Europeans in the Two Indies.* This book was a miscellany of essays and extracts treating of superstition, tyranny, etc., and predicting that a revolution was at hand in France if abuses were not reformed.

How was it that Napoleon, with his meagre salary, could command so many costly books? A recent biographer patly states that be "subscribed to a public library." This may be true, but Napoleon himself explained to an audience of kings and princes at Erfurth, in 1808, that he was indebted to the kindness of one Marcus Aurelius, a rich bookseller, "a most obliging man who placed his books at my service."

The personal appearance of the young lieutenant was not imposing. He was short, painfully thin, and awkward. His legs were so much too small for his boots that he looked ridiculous — at least to one young lady, who nick-named him "Puss in Boots." He wore immense "dog's ears," which fell to his shoulders, and this style of wearing the hair gave his dark Italian face a rather sinister look, impressing a lady acquaintance with the thought that he would not be the kind of man one would like to meet near a wood at night. Generally he was silent, wrapped in his own thoughts; but when he spoke, his ideas were striking and his expressions energetic. He rather affected the laconic, oracular style, and his attitude was somewhat that of a man posing for effect. In familiar social intercourse he was different. His smile became winning, his voice soft and tender, and his magnetism irresistible. He loved to joke others and play little pranks with them; but he could not relish a joke at his own expense, nor did he encourage familiarity. He had none of the brag, bluster, or roughness of the soldier about him, but in a quiet way he was imperious, self-confident, self-sufficient. So little did his appearance then, or at any other time, conform to the popular ideal of the soldier, that one old grenadier of the Bourbon armies, on having Napoleon pointed out to him, after the Italian campaign, could not believe such a man could possibly be a great warrior. "That a general!" said the veteran with contempt; "why, when he walks he does not even step out with the right foot first!"

Extremely egotistic he was, and so remained to his last hour. He had no reverence, looked for fact in all directions, had almost unerring judgment, and believed himself superior to his fellow-students, to his teachers, and to his brother officers. At the age of fifteen he was giving advice to his father — very sound advice, too. At that early age he had taken family responsibilities upon his shoulders, and was gravely disposing of Joseph and Lucien. In a remarkable letter he elaborately analyzed Joseph's character, and reached the conclusion that he was an amiable nonentity, fit only for society. It had been well for Napoleon if he had always remembered this, and acted upon it.

In August, 1786, Napoleon spent a short time in Lyons. After this he was perhaps sent to Douay in Flanders, though he himself has written that on September 1, 1786, he obtained leave of absence and set out for Corsica, which he reached on the fifteenth of the same month.

*

Napoleon found the condition of the family greatly changed. Charles Bonaparte had died in France in February, 1785. General Marbeuf, also, was dead. The French officials were not now so friendly to the Bonapartes. Madame Letitia had been growing mulberry trees in order to obtain the governmental bounty — the government being intent upon building up the silk industry. Madame Bonaparte had apparently been giving more thought to the bounty than to the trees, and the result was that the officials had refused payment. Hence the supply of cash in the household was cut down to Napoleon's salary (about $225), and such sums as could be teased out of the rich uncle — the miserly archdeacon. Desperately worried as he must have been by the condition of the family finances, Napoleon put a bold face upon it, strutting about town so complacently that he gave much offence to the local magnates — the town oracles whose kind words are not easily won by the neighborhood boys who have

gone to distant colleges for an education and have returned
for inspection and approval.　To the sidewalk critics, who
only nine years ago had jeered at the slovenly lad and his
girl sweetheart, Napoleon's style of walk and talk may
have seemed that of inflated self-conceit.

Like a good son, Napoleon exerted himself to the utmost
in behalf of his mother, making every effort to have the
mulberry bounty paid, and to wring revenue out of the
family property.　He met with no success in either direction, though it appears that he prevailed upon the local
authorities to grant some slight favor to the family.　At
one time Madame Letitia was reduced to the necessity of
doing all her housework with her own hands.

At Elba, the Emperor related a story which belongs to
this period of his life.　He said that one day his mother's
mother was hobbling along the street in Ajaccio, and that
he and Pauline followed the old lady, and mimicked her.
Their grandmother, happening to turn, caught them in
the act.　She complained to Madame Letitia.　Pauline was
at once " spanked" and disposed of ; Napoleon, who was
rigged out in regimentals, could not be handled.　His
mother bided her time.　Next day, when her son was off
his guard, she cried, "Quick, Napoleon!　You are invited
to dine with the governor !"　He ran up to his room to
change clothing—she quietly followed.　When she judged
that the proper time had come, she rushed into the room,
seized her undressed hero before he guessed her purpose,
laid him across the maternal knees, and belabored him
earnestly with the flat of her hand.

In October, 1787, Napoleon was again in Paris, petition-
ing the government in behalf of his mother, and seeking
to have his furlough extended.　Failing as to his mother,

succeeding as to himself, he was back home in January, 1788, and remained there until June of the same year. While in Corsica, Napoleon frequently dined with brother officers in the French army. Between him and them, however, there was little congeniality. He was hotly Paolist, and his talk was either of Corsican independence or of topics historical and governmental. His brother officers did not enjoy these conversations. His patriotism offended ; his learning bored them. What did the average French officer of that day know or care about history and the science of government? The upshot of such a dinner-party usually was that Napoleon got into a wrangle with that one of the officers who imagined he knew something of the subject, while the others, who honestly realized that they did not, would walk off in disgust. "My comrades, like myself," says M. de Renain, one of the officers in question, "lost patience with what we considered ridiculous stuff and pedantry."

So far did Napoleon carry his patriotic sentiments that he rather plainly threatened to take sides with the Corsicans if any collision should occur between the French and his countrymen. Upon this, one of the officers who disliked him asked sharply, "Would you draw your sword against the soldiers of the King?"

Napoleon, dressed in the King's uniform, had the good sense to remain silent. The officers were offended at his tone, and, says Renain, "This is the last time he did me the honor of dining with me."

Not for a day had Napoleon neglected his books. To escape the household noises, he went to the attic, and there pursued his studies. Far and wide ranged his restless mind, from the exact sciences, dry and heavy, to Plato and Ossian, rich in suggestions to the most opulent imagination nature ever gave a practical man. To the very last, Napoleon remained half mystic; and when he stood in the storm the night before Waterloo, and cast into the darkness the words, " We are agreed"; or when he remained silent for hours at St. Helena watching the vast wings of the mist whirl, and turn, and soar around the summit of the bleak, barren mountain of rock, we feel that if pens were there to trace his thought, Ossian would seem to live again. From his youth up the most striking characteristic of his mind was its enormous range; its wide sweep from the pettiest, prosiest details of fact to the sublimest dreams and the most chimerical fancies. Not wholly satisfied with reading and commentary, he strove to compose. Under the Bourbons, his outlook in the army was not promising. He might hope, after many tedious years of garrison service, to become a captain; after that it would be a miracle if he rose higher. Hence his lack of interest in the routine work of a soldier, and hence his ambition to become an author. He wrote a story called *The Count of Essex*, also a novel founded on Corsican life, and pulsing with hatred of France. Another story which he called *The Masked Prophet*, is the same which Moore afterward used in *The Veiled Prophet of Khorassan*.

His greatest exertions, however, were spent upon the *History of Corsica*. To this work he clung with a tenacity of purpose that is touching. All the long, tragic story of Corsica seems to have run like fire in the boy's veins, and the heroes of his country — Paoli, Sampiero, Della Rocca — seemed to him to be as great as the men of antiquity, as perhaps they were. There-

fore, the young man wrote and rewrote, trying to get
the book properly written, his thoughts properly expressed. He had turned to Raynal, as we have seen,
and the abbé had kindly said, "Search further, and
write it over." And Napoleon had done so. At least
three times he had recast the entire book. He sought'
the approval of a former teacher, Dupuy; he sent "copy"
to Paoli. Dupuy had a poor opinion of the performance;
and Paoli told him flatly he was too young to write history. But Napoleon persevered, finished the work, and
eagerly sought publishers. Alas! the publishers shook
their heads. Finally, at Paris was found a bold adventurer
in the realm of book-making, who was willing to under-
take half the cost if the author would furnish the other
half. But for one reason or another the book was never
published.

The passionate earnestness with which Napoleon toiled
at his book on Corsican history, the intense sympathy
with which he studied the lives of Corsican heroes, the
fiery wrath he nursed against those who had stricken
down Corsican liberties, were but so many evidences of
the set purpose of his youth — to free his country, to
give it independence. There is no doubt that the one
consuming ambition of these early years was as pure as
it was great: he would do what Sampiero and Paoli
had failed to do — he would achieve the independence
of Corsica!

Napoleon rejoined his regiment at Auxonne at the end
of May, 1788. That he did so with reluctance is apparent from the manner in which he had distorted facts
to obtain extension of his furlough. Garrison duty had
no charms for him; the dull drudgery of daily routine

became almost insupportable. It appears that he was put under arrest for the unsatisfactory manner in which he had superintended some work on the fortifications. When off duty he gave his time to his books. He became ill, and wrote to his mother, " I have no resource but work. I dress but once in eight days. I sleep but little, and take but one meal a day." Under this regimen of no exercise, hard work, and little sleep he came near dying.

In September, 1789, came another furlough, and the wan-looking lieutenant turned his face homeward. In passing through Marseilles he paid his respects to the Abbé Raynal.

CHAPTER IV

THE French Revolution was now (1789–90) getting under full headway. The States-General had met on May 5, 1789; the Third Estate had asserted and made good its supremacy. The King having ordered up troops and dismissed Necker, riots followed; the Bastille was taken and demolished. The nobles who had persuaded Louis XVI. to adopt the measures which provoked the riots, fled to foreign lands. Louis was brought from Versailles to Paris, Bailly was made mayor of the city, Lafayette commander of the National Guard, and on the night session of August 4, feudalism, losing hope, offered itself up as a sacrifice to the Revolution.

Liberty, fraternity, equality, freedom of conscience, liberty of the press, were proclaimed; and the mighty movement which was shaking down the Old Order was felt at Auxonne as in Paris. The officers, as a rule, were for the King; the soldiers for the nation. Society ladies and governmental officials were royalists, generally; so, also, the higher clericals. The curés and the masses of the people were for the Revolution.

Instinctively, and without the slightest hesitation, Napoleon took sides with the nation. He needed no coercion, no change of heart; he was already an enemy of the Ancien Régime, and had been so from his first years in France.

"How does it happen that you, Napoleon, favor democracy? You are a noble, educated at a school where none but nobles can enter; you are an officer, a position none but nobles may hold; you wear the King's livery; you are fed on his bounty: where did you get your republican principles?"

Supposing such a question to have been put, we can imagine the answer to have been something like this: —

"I go with the reformers partly because I hate the Old Order, partly because I see in the coming changes a chance for me to rise, and partly because I believe the reformers are right. I have read books which gave me new ideas; I have thought for myself, and reached conclusions of my own. The stupid monk who threw my schoolboy essay into the fire at Brienne because it criticised royalty, only stimulated my defiance and my independence. I have seen what your system of education is, and condemn it; have learnt what your nobles are, and detest them. I have seen the Church, which preaches the beauties of poverty, rob my family of a rich inheritance, and I loathe the hypocrisy. I have read Rousseau, and believe in his gospel; have studied Raynal, and agree that abuses must be reformed. I have looked into the conduct of kings, and believe that there are few who do not deserve to be dethroned. The privileged have combined, have closed the avenues of progress to the lower classes, have taken for a few what is the common heritage of all. The people are the source of power — those below not those above. I am poor, I hate those above me, I long to be rich, powerful, admired. If things remain as they are, I shall never be heard of: revolution will change all. New men will rise to make the most of new opportunities.

Hence I am a Jacobin, a democrat, a republican — call it what you will. I am for putting the premium on manhood. The tools to him who can use them! As to the King's uniform and bounty — bah! — you must take me for a child. The King gives nothing, is nothing; the nation gives all, and is everything. I go with the nation!"

With such thoughts fermenting in his head, Napoleon reached home, and at once began to agitate the politics of the island. Corsica was far out of the track of the Revolution, and the people had not been maddened by the abuses which prevailed in France. The one great national grievance in Corsica was French domination. Therefore to arouse the island and put it in line with revolutionary France, was a huge task. Nevertheless Napoleon and other young men set about it. Copying the approved French method, he formed a revolutionary committee, and began to organize a national guard. He became a violent speaker in the Jacobin club, and a most active agitator in the town. Soon the little city of Ajaccio was in commotion.

Paoli's agents bestirred themselves throughout the island. In some towns the patriot party rose against the French authorities. In Ajaccio the royalist party proved the stronger. The French commandant, De Barrin, closed the democratic club and proclaimed martial law. The patriots met in one of the churches, on the night of October 31, 1789, and signed a vigorous protest and appeal to the National Assembly of France. This paper was written by Napoleon, and he was one of those who signed.

Baulked in Ajaccio, Napoleon turned to Bastia, the capital. Agitating there and distributing tricolored cockades

which he had ordered from Leghorn, he soon got matters
so well advanced that he headed a deputation which waited
upon the royal commandant and demanded that he, too,
should adopt the national cockade.   De Barrin, the commandant, refused.   A riot broke out, and he consented.
Napoleon agitated for a national guard.   Deputations
sought the governor and requested his sanction.   He refused.   One morning the streets were thronged with
patriots, armed, marching to one of the churches to be
enrolled.   De Barrin called out his troops, trained cannon
on the church, and set his columns in motion to attack.
Shots were exchanged, two French soldiers killed, two
wounded, and an officer got a bullet in the groin.   Several
Bastians, including two children, were wounded.   De
Barrin lost his head, yielded at all points, and ordered six
hundred guns delivered to the insurgents.   Prompt obedience not having been given to his order, the Bastians
broke into the citadel, armed themselves, and insisted that
they, jointly with the French, should garrison the fortress.
When quiet was restored, the governor ordered Napoleon
to leave, and he did so.

This episode in Napoleon's career is related by an enemy
of Napoleon, and it is to be received with caution.   Yet as
it is a companion piece to what he had attempted at Ajaccio,
there is nothing violently incredible about it.   It is certain he was very active at that time, and that he was often
at Bastia.   What was his purpose, if not to foment revolutionary movements ?

On November 30, 1789, the National Assembly of France
decreed the incorporation of Corsica with France, and
amnesty for all political offenders, including Paoli.   Bonfires in Corsica and general joy greeted the news.   The

triumph of the patriots was complete. A democratic town
government for Ajaccio was organized, a friend of Napoleon was chosen mayor, and Joseph was put in place as
secretary to the mayor. A local guard was raised, and
Napoleon served as private member of it. At the club
and on the streets he was one of the loudest agitators.

Paoli, now a hero in France as well as in Corsica, was
called home by these events, received a magnificent ovation from the French, and reached Corsica, July, 1790.
When he landed, after an exile of twenty-one years, the
old man knelt to the ground and kissed it.

Supported by the town government, Napoleon renewed
his activity, the immediate object aimed at being the capture of the citadel. He made himself intensely disagree-
able to the royalists. Upon one occasion, during a
religious procession, he was attacked by the Catholics, as
an enemy of the Church. His efforts to seize the citadel
came to nothing. There was an uprising of the revolutionists in the town, but the French officials fled into the
citadel and prepared to defend it. Napoleon advised an
attack, but the town authorities lost heart. They decided
not to fight, but to protest; and Napoleon drew up the
paper.

The people of Corsica met in local district meetings and
chose delegates to an assembly which was to elect departmental and district councils to govern the island. This
general assembly met at Orezzo, September 9, 1790, and
remained in session a month. Among the delegates were
Joseph Bonaparte and Uncle Fesch. Napoleon attended
and took an active part in the various meetings which
were held in connection with the work of the assembly.
He was a frequent speaker at these meetings, and, while

timid and awkward at first, soon became one of the most popular orators.

It was while he was on his way to Orezzo, that Napoleon first met Paoli. The old hero gave the young man a distinguished reception. Attended by a large cavalcade, the two rode over the fatal field of Ponte Nuovo. Paoli pointed out the various positions the troops had occupied, and related the incidents of that lamentable day. Napoleon's comments, his peculiar and original thought and speech, struck Paoli forcibly ; and he is said to have remarked that Napoleon was not modern, but reminded him of Plutarch's heroes. Napoleon himself, when at St. Helena, represents Paoli as often patting him on the head and making the remark above mentioned.

The assembly at Orezzo voted that Corsica should constitute one department, and that Paoli should be its president. He was also made commander-in-chief of the National Guard. The conduct of Buttafuoco and Peretti who had been representing Corsica in France, was condemned. Pozzo di Borgo and Gentili were chosen to declare to the National Assembly the loyalty of Corsica to the principles of the French Revolution.

Napoleon had endeavored to secure the election of Joseph Bonaparte to the general directory of the department. In this he failed, but Joseph was chosen as one of the district directory for Ajaccio.

During the sitting of the convention Napoleon wiled away many an hour in familiar intercourse with the peasantry. He visited them at their huts, made himself at home by their firesides, and interested himself in their affairs. He revived some of the old Corsican festivals, and the target practice which had long been forbidden.

Out of his own purse he offered prizes for the best marksmen. In this manner he won the hearts of the mountain-
eers — a popularity which was of value to him soon
afterward.

Returned to Ajaccio, Napoleon continued to take prominent part in the debates of the club, and he also continued
his efforts at authorship. He threw off an impassioned
" open letter " to Buttafuoco. This was his first successful writing. With imperial pride, it is dated "from my
summer house of Milleli." Stimulated perhaps by the
applause with which young Corsican patriots hailed his
bitter and powerful arraignment of a traitor, Napoleon
ventured to compete for the prize which Raynal, through
the Academy of Lyons, had offered for the best essay on
the subject *"What truths and ideas should be inculcated in
order best to promote the happiness of mankind."* His essay
was severely criticised by the learned professors, and its
author, of course, failed of the prize.

It was on the plea that his health was shattered, and
that the waters of Orezzo were good for his complaint, that
Napoleon had been enabled to prolong his stay in Corsica.
In February, 1791, he rejoined his regiment at Auxonne.
His leave had expired long since, but his colonel kindly
antedated his return. Napoleon had procured false certificates, to the effect that he had been kept in Corsica by
storms. To ease his mother's burden, he brought with him
his little brother Louis, now twelve years old, whose support and schooling Napoleon proposed to take upon himself. To maintain the two upon his slender pay of
lieutenant required the most rigorous economy. He
avoided society, ate often nothing but bread, carried on
his own studies, and taught Louis. The affectionate,

fatherly, self-denying interest he took in the boy beautifully illustrates the better side of his complex character.

During the Empire an officer, whose pay was $200 per
month, complained to Napoleon that it was not enough.
The Emperor did not express the contempt he felt, but
spoke of the pittance upon which *he* had been made to
live. "When I was lieutenant, I ate dry bread; but I
shut the door on my poverty."

It was at Dôle, near Auxonne, that the letter to Buttafuoco was printed. Napoleon used to rise early, walk to
Dôle, correct the proofs, and walk back to Auxonne, a distance of some twenty miles, before dinner.

In June, 1791, Napoleon became first lieutenant, with a
yearly salary of about $260, and was transferred to the,
Fourth Regiment, stationed at Valence. Glad of the promotion and the slight increase in salary, he did not relish
the transfer, and he applied for leave to remain at Auxonne.
Permission was refused, and he quitted the place, owing
(for a new uniform, a sword, and some wood) about $23.
Several years passed before he was able to pay off these
debts.

Back in Valence, he again lodged with old Mademoiselle
Bou, he and Louis. He continued his studies, and continued to teach Louis. His former friends were dead, or
had moved away, and he did not go into society as he had
done before; his position was too dismal, his poverty too
real. He lived much in his room, reading, studying, com-
posing. Travels, histories, works which treated of politics, of ecclesiastical affairs and institutions, attracted him
specially. No longer seen in elegant drawing-rooms, he
was the life of the political club. He became, successively,
librarian, secretary, and president.

All this while the Revolution had been rolling on. The wealth of the Church was confiscated. Paper money was issued. The Festival of the Federation was solemnized. Necker lost his grip on the situation, and fled. Mirabeau became the hope of the moderates. Danton, Robespierre, Marat, became influential radicals. The Jacobin club rose to power. There developed the great feud between the Church and the Revolution, and factions began to shed blood in many parts of France. The old-maid aunts of the King fled the realm, causing immense excitement.

In April, 1791, Mirabeau died. His alliance with the court not being then known, his death called forth universal sorrow and memorial services. At Valence the republican club held such a service, and Napoleon is said to have delivered an address. Then came the flight of the King to Varennes. Upon this event also the club at Valence passed judgment, amid excitement and violent harangues.

In July, 1791, the national oath of allegiance to the new order of things was taken at Valence with imposing ceremony, as it was throughout the country. The constitution had not been finished; but the French of that day had the faith which works wonders, and they took the oath with boundless enthusiasm.

There was a monster meeting near Valence: a huge altar, a grand coming together, on common ground, of dignitaries high and low, officials of Church and State, citizens of all degrees. Patriotism for one brief moment made them all members of one fond family. "We swear to be faithful to the Nation, the law, and the King; to maintain the constitution; and to remain united to all Frenchmen by the bonds of brotherhood." They all swore it, amid patriotic shouts, songs, cannon thunder, band music, and uni-

versal ecstasy.   Mass had begun the ceremony, a *Te Deum*
ended it.   At night there was a grand banquet, and one
of those who proposed a toast was Napoleon.   Of course
he was one of those who had taken the oath.

"Previous to this time," said he, later, "had I been
ordered to fire upon the people, habit, prejudice, education,
and the King's name would have induced me to obey.
With the taking of the national oath it was otherwise;
my instinct and my duty were henceforth in harmony."

Kings and aristocrats throughout the world were turning black looks upon France, and an invasion was threatened.   The Revolution must be put down.   It was a fire
which might spread.   This threat of foreign intervention
had an electrical effect upon the French, rousing them to
resistance.

Paris was the storm centre, Napoleon was highly excited, and to Paris he was most eager to go.   Urgently
he wrote to his great-uncle, the archdeacon, to send him
three hundred francs to pay his way to Paris.   "There
one can push to the forefront.   I feel assured of success.
Will you bar my road for the lack of a hundred crowns?"
The archdeacon did not send the money.   Napoleon also
wrote for six crowns his mother owed him.   The six
crowns seem not to have been sent.

This anecdote of Napoleon's sojourn at Valence is preserved by the local gossips: Early one morning the
surgeon of the regiment went to Napoleon's room to
speak to Louis.   Napoleon had long since risen, and was
reading.   Louis was yet asleep.   To arouse the lad, Napolcou took his sabre and knocked with the scabbard on
the ceiling above.   Louis soon came down, rubbing his

eyes and complaining of having been waked in the midst
of a beautiful dream — a dream in which Louis had fig-
ured as a king. "You a king!" said Napoleon; "I
suppose I was an emperor then."

The keenest pang Napoleon ever suffered from the
ingratitude of those he had favored, was given him by
this same Louis, for whom he had acted the devoted,
self-denying father. Not only was Louis basely ungrateful in the days of the Napoleonic prosperity, but he
pursued his brother with vindictive meanness when that
brother lay dying at St. Helena, publishing a libel on
him so late as 1820.

A traveller in Corsica (Gregorovius, 1852) writes:
"We sat around a large table and regaled ourselves
with an excellent supper. . . . A dim olive-oil lamp
lit the Homeric wanderers' meal. Many a bumper was
drunk to the heroes of Corsica. We were of four nations, — Corsicans, French, Germans, and Lombards. I
once mentioned the name of Louis Bonaparte, and asked
a question. The company suddenly became silent, and
the gay Frenchman looked ashamed."

In August, 1791, Napoleon obtained another furlough,
and with about $80, which he had borrowed from the
paymaster of his regiment, he and Louis set out for
home. Again he left debts behind him, one of them
being his board bill.

CHAPTER V

SOON after Napoleon reached home, the rich uncle, the archdeacon, died, and the Bonapartes got his money. The bulk of it was invested in the confiscated lands of the Church. Some of it was probably spent in Napoleon's political enterprises.

Officers of the Corsican National Guard were soon to be elected, and Napoleon formed his plans to secure for himself a lieutenant colonelship. The leaders of the opposing faction were Peraldi and Pozzo di Borgo.

Three commissioners, appointed by the Directory of the Island, had the supervision of the election, and the influence of these officers would have great weight in deciding the contest. Napoleon had recently been over the island in company with Volney, inspector of agriculture and manufactures, and had personally canvassed for votes among the country people. He had made many friends; and, in spite of powerful opposition in the towns, it appeared probable that he would win. It is said that he resorted to the usual electioneering methods, including bribes, threats, promises, and hospitality. Napoleon made a good combination with Peretti and Quenza, yielding to that interest the first lieutenant colonelship. The second was to his own. But one of the commissioners, Murati, took up lodgings with Bonaparte's rival candidate, Pe.

raldi. This was an ominous sign for Napoleon. On the night before the election, he got together some of his more violent partisans, sent them against the house of Peraldi, and had Murati seized and brought to the house of the Bonapartes. "You were not free at Peraldi's," said Napoleon to the amazed commissioner; "here you enjoy liberty." Murati enjoyed it so much that he was afraid to stir out of the house till the election was over.

Next morning Pozzo di Borgo commenced a public and violent harangue, denouncing the seizure of the commissioner. He was not allowed to finish. The Bonaparte faction rushed upon the speaker, knocked him down, kicked him, and would have killed him had not Napoleon interfered. In this episode is said to have originated the deadly hatred with which Pozzo ever afterward pursued Napoleon, who triumphed over him in the election.

Ajaccio was torn by revolutionary passion and faction. Resisting the decrees of the National Assembly of France, the Capuchin friars refused to vacate their quarters. Riotous disputes between the revolutionists and the partisans of the Old Order ensued. The public peace was disturbed. The military ousted the friars, and took possession of the cloister. This added fuel to the flames, and on Easter day there was a collision between the factions. One of the officers of the militia was killed. Next morning, reënforcements from outside the town poured in to the military. Between the volunteer guards on the one hand, the citadel garrison and the clerical faction on the other, a pitched battle seemed inevitable. Commissioners, sent by Paoli, arrived, dismissed the militia, and restored quiet by thus virtually deciding in favor of the Capuchins.

Napoleon was believed by the victorious faction to have

been the instigator of all the trouble. The commander
of the garrison bitterly denounced him to the war office
in Paris. Napoleon, on the contrary, published a manifesto in his own defence, hotly declaring that the whole
town government of Ajaccio was rotten, and should have
been overthrown. Unless Ajaccio differed radically from
most towns, then and now, the indictment was well
founded.

At all events, his career in Corsica was at an end, for
the time. He had strained his relations with the French
war office, had ignored positive orders to rejoin his command, had been stricken off the list for his disobedience,
had exhausted every resource on his Corsican schemes,
and was now at the end of his rope. And what had he
gained ? He had squandered much money, wasted much
precious time, established a character for trickiness, violence, and unscrupulous self-seeking ; and had aroused
implacable enmities, one of which (that of Pozzo) had no
trifling share in giving him the death-wound in his final
struggles in 1814–15. What, after it all, must he now
do ? He must get up a lot of certificates to his good conduct during the long time he had been absent from France ;
he must go to Paris and petition the central authority to
be taken back to the French army. There was no trouble
in getting the certificates. Paoli and his party, the priests
and the wealthy towns-people, were so eager to get rid of
this dangerous young man that they were ready to sign
any sort of paper, if only he would go away. Armed with
documentary evidence of his good behavior, Napoleon left
Corsica in May, 1792, and reached Paris on the 28th of
that month.

Things were in a whirl in France. War had been

declared against Austria. Officers of royalist principles were resigning and fleeing the country. Excitement, suspicion, alarm, uncertainty, were everywhere. No attention could be given to Napoleon and his petition just then. He saw that he would have to wait, be patient and persistent, if ever he won reinstatement. Meanwhile he lived in great distress. With no money, no work, no powerful friends, Paris was a cold place for the suppliant. He sauntered about with Bourrienne, ate at the cheapest restaurants, discussed many plans for putting money in his purse — none of which put any there. He pawned his watch to get the bare necessaries of life.

Bearing in mind that Napoleon had been so active in the republican clubs at Valence and Ajaccio, and recalling the urgent appeal for three hundred francs which he had made to his great-uncle in order that he might go to Paris and push himself to the front, his attitude now that he was in Paris is a puzzle. According to his own account and that of Bourrienne, he was a mere spectator. A royal officer, he felt no inclination to defend the King. A violent democratic agitator, he took no part in the revolutionary movements. Seeing the mob marching to the Tuileries in June, his only thought was to get a good view of what was going on; therefore he ran to the terrace on the bank of the river and climbed an iron fence. He saw the rabble burst into the palace, saw the King appear at the window with the red cap on his head. " The poor driveller ! " cried Napoleon. And according to Bourrienne he said that four or five hundred of the mob should have been swept away with cannon, and that the others would have taken to their heels.

During the exciting month of July, Napoleon was still

in Paris. He was promenading the streets daily, mingling
with the people; he was idle, discontented, ambitious; he
was a violent revolutionist, and was not in the habit of
concealing his views : therefore the conclusion is well-nigh
irresistible that he kept in touch with events, and knew
what was in preparation. Where was Napoleon when the
battalion from Marseilles arrived? What was his attitude
during Danton's preparation for the great day on which
the throne was to be overturned? Was an ardent, intensely active man like Napoleon listless and unconcerned,
while the tramp of the gathering thousands shook the city?
He had long since written "Most kings deserve to be
dethroned": did he by any chance hear what Danton
said at the Cordeliers, — said with flaming eyes, thundering voice, and wild gesticulation, — " Let the tocsin sound
the last hour of kings. Let it peal forth the first hour of
vengeance, and of the liberty of the people! To arms!
and it will go!"

However much we may wish for light on this epoch
of Napoleon's career, we have no record of his movements.
We only know that on the 10th of August he went to see
the spectacle, and saw it. From a window in a neighboring house, he looked down upon the Westermann attack
and the Swiss defence. He saw the devoted guards of
the palace drive the assailants out, doubtless heard Wes-
termanu and the brave courtesan, Théroigne de Méricourt,
rally their forces and renew the assault; was amazed
perhaps, when the Swiss ceased firing; and looked on
while the triumphant Marseillaise broke into the palace.
After the massacre, he walked through the Tuileries,
piled with the Swiss dead, and was more impressed by
the sight than he ever was by the dead on his own fields

of battle. He sauntered through the crowds and the neighboring cafés, and was so cool and indifferent that he aroused suspicion. He met a gang of patriots bear-ing a head on a pike. His manner did not, to this gang, indicate sufficient enthusiasm. "Shout, 'Live the nation,'" demanded the gang; and Napoleon shouted, "Live the nation!"

He saw a man of Marseilles about to murder a wounded Swiss. He said, "Southron, let us spare the unfortunate." — "Art thou from the South?" — "Yes." — "Then we will spare him."

According to Napoleon, if the King had appeared on horseback, — that is, dared to come forth and lead the defence, — he would have won the day.

Other days of wrath Napoleon spent in Paris — the days of the September massacres. What he saw, heard, and felt is not known. Only in a general way is it known that during the idle summer in Paris, Napoleon lost many of his republican illusions. He conceived a horror of mob violence and popular license, which exerted a tremendous influence over him throughout his career. He lost faith in the purity and patriotism of the revolutionary leaders. He reached the conclusion that each man was for himself, that each one sought only his own advantage. For the people themselves, seeing them so easily led by lies, preju-dices, and passions, he expressed contempt. The Jacobins were, he thought, a "parcel of fools"; the leaders of the Revolution "a sorry lot."

This sweepingly severe judgment was most unfortu-nate; it bore bitter fruit for Napoleon and for France. He never ceased to believe that each man was governed by his interest — an opinion which is near the truth, but is not the truth. If the truth at all, it is certainly not the whole truth.

Napoleon, with the independence of his native land ever in mind, wrote to his brother Joseph to cling to Paoli; that events were tending to make him the all-powerful man, and might also evolve the independence of Corsica.

During this weary period of waiting, Napoleon was often at the home of the Permons. On the 7th or 8th of August an emissary of the revolutionary government made his way into the Permon house without a warrant, and, because M. Permon refused to recognize his authority and threatened to take a stick to him, left in a rage to report against Permon. Napoleon, happening to call at this time, learned the fact, and hurried off to the section where he boldly denounced the illegal conduct of the officer. Permon was not molested further.

The King became a prisoner of the revolutionists, the moderates fell from power, the radicals took the lead. Napoleon's case had already received attention, he had already been pronounced blameless, and he was now, August 30, 1792, restored to his place in the army, and promoted. He was not only made captain, but his commission and pay were made to date from February 6, 1792, at which time he would have been entitled to his promotion had he not fallen under official displeasure. Such prompt and flattering treatment of the needy officer by the radicals who had just upset the monarchy, gives one additional cause to suspect that Napoleon's relation to current events and Jacobin leaders was closer than the record shows.

It became good policy for him in after years to suppress the evidence of his revolutionary period. Thus he burnt the Lyons essay, and bought up, as he supposed, all copies of *The Supper of Beaucaire*. The conclusion is irresistible that the efforts to suppress have been more successful as to the summer of 1792 than in the other instances. It is impossible to believe that Napoleon, who had been so hot in the garrison towns where he was stationed in France, and who had turned all Corsica topsy-turvy with democratic harangues and revolutionary plots, should have become a passionless gazer at the show in Paris.

Whatever share he took, or did not take, in the events of the summer, he now turned homeward. The Assembly having abolished the St. Cyr school, where his sister Elisa was, Napoleon asked and was given leave to escort her back to Corsica. Travelling expenses were liberally provided by the State. Stopping at Valence, where he was warmly greeted by local friends, including Mademoiselle Bou to whom he owed a board bill, Napoleon and Elisa journeyed down the Rhone to Marseilles, and sailed for Corsica, which they reached on the 17th of September, 1792.

The situation of the Bonaparte family was much improved. The estate was larger, the revenues more satisfactory. Joseph was in office. Lucien was a leading agitator in the Jacobin club. The estate of the rich uncle had helped things wonderfully. It must have been from this source that Napoleon derived the fine vineyard of which he spoke to Las Cases, at St. Helena, as supplying him with funds — which vineyard he afterward gave to his old nurse. The position which his promo-

tion in the army gave him ended the persecution which
had virtually driven him from home; and a reconciliation
was patched up between him and Paoli.

Napoleon insisted upon holding both his offices, — the
captaincy in the regular army and the lieutenant colonelship
in the Corsican National Guard.   Paoli strongly objected;
but the younger man, partly by threats, carried his point.
It may have been at this period that Paoli slightly modi-
fied the Plutarch opinion; he is said to have remarked:
"You see that little fellow?   Well, he has in him the
making of two or three men like Marius and one like
Sulla ! "

During his sojourn in Corsica, Napoleon took part in
the luckless expedition which the French government sent
against the island of Sardinia.   The Corsican forces were
put under the command of Paoli's nephew, Colonna-Cæsari,
whose orders, issued to him by Paoli, who strongly opposed the enterprise, were, "See that this expedition ends in
smoke."   The nephew obeyed the uncle to the letter.   In
spite of Napoleon's good plan, in spite of his successful
attack on the hostile forts, Colonna declared that his
troops were about to mutiny, and he sailed back home.

Loudly denouncing Colonna as a traitor, Napoleon bade
adieu to his volunteers, and returned to Ajaccio.

There was great indignation felt by the Jacobins against
Paoli.   He was blamed for the failure of the Sardinian
expedition, for his luke-warmness toward the French Revolution, and for his alleged leaning to England.   The
September massacres, and the beheading of the King, had
been openly denounced by the old hero, and he had exerted
his influence in favor of conservatism in Corsica.   The
Bonaparte faction was much too rabid, and the Bonaparte

brothers altogether too feverishly eager to push themselves forward. The friendship and mutual admiration which Napoleon and Paoli had felt for each other had cooled. Paoli had thrown ice water on the *History of Corsica*, and had refused to supply the author with certain documents needed in the preparation of that work. Neither had he approved the publication of the *Letter to Buttafuoco*; it was too bitter and violent. Again, his influence seems to have been thrown against the Bonapartes at the Orezzo assembly. All these things had doubtless had their effect; but the radical difference between the two men, Napoleon and Paoli, was one of Corsican policy. Napoleon wished to revolutionize the island, and Paoli did not. If Corsican independence could not be won, Napoleon favored the French connection. Paoli, dismayed by the violence of the Revolution in France, favored connection with England.

It is said that Lucien Bonaparte, in the club at Ajaccio, denounced Paoli as a traitor. The club selected a delegation to go to Marseilles and denounce the old hero to the Jacobin clubs there. Lucien was a member of the delegation; but after delivering himself a wild tirade against Paoli in Marseilles, he returned to Corsica. The delegation went on to Paris. In April, 1793, Paoli was formally denounced in the National Convention, and summoned to its bar for trial.

At first Napoleon warmly defended Paoli, and drew up an impassioned address to the Convention in his favor. In this paper he expressly defends his old chief from the accusation of wishing to put Corsica into the hands of the English.

Within two weeks after writing the defence of Paoli,

Napoleon joined his enemies. What brought about this sudden change is not certain. His own excuse was that Paoli was seeking to throw the island to England. As a matter of fact, however, Napoleon's course at this period seems full of double dealing. For a time he did not have the confidence of either faction.

Sémonville, one of the French commissioners then in Corsica, related to Chancellor Pasquier, many years later, how Napoleon had come and roused him, in the middle of the night, to say: " Mr. Commissioner, I have come to say that I and mine will defend the cause of the union between Corsica and France. People here are on the point of committing follies; the Convention has doubt-less committed a great crime " — in guillotining the King — " which I deplore more than any one; but whatever may happen, Corsica must always remain a part of France."

As soon as this decision of the Bonapartes became known, the Paolists turned upon them savagely, and their position became difficult. The French commis-sioners, of whom the leader was Salicetti, appointed Napoleon inspector general of artillery for Corsica. He immediately set about the capture of the citadel of Ajaccio, the object of so much of his toil. Force failed, stratagem availed not, attempted bribery did not succeed; the citadel remained untaken. Ajaccians bitterly resented his desertion of Paoli, and his life being in danger, Napoleon in disguise fled to Bastia. Indomitable in his purpose, he proposed to Salicetti's commission another plan for the seizure of the coveted citadel. Some French war vessels then at St. Florent were to surprise Ajaccio, land men and guns, and with the help of some Swiss troops, and of such Corsicans as felt disposed to help, the citadel was to be taken.

Paoli was warned, and he prepared for the struggle. The French war vessels sailed from St. Florent, Napoleon on board, and reached Ajaccio on May 29. It was too late. The Paolists, fully prepared, received the assailants with musketry. Napoleon captured an outpost, and held it for two days; but the vessels could not coöperate effi. ciently, and the assailants abandoned the attempt. Napoleon joined his family at Calvi. They had fled from Ajaccio as Napoleon sailed to the attack, and the Paolists were so furiously enraged against them that their estates were pillaged and their home sacked. Paoli had made a last effort to conquer the resolution of Madame Letitia, but she was immovable. On June 11 the fugitives left Corsica for France, escaping from their enemies by hiding near the seashore till a boat could approach in the darkness of night and take them away. Jerome and Caroline were left behind, concealed by the Ramolinos.

Napoleon himself narrowly escaped with his life. He was saved from a trap the Peraldis had set by the faithfulness of the Bonaparte tenants. He was forced to disguise himself, and lay concealed till arrangements could be made for his flight. Far-seeing was the judgment and inflexible the courage which must have sustained him in cutting loose entirely from his first love, Corsica, and casting himself upon revolutionary France. For it would have been an easy matter for him to have gone with the crowd and been a great man in Corsica.

In his will Napoleon left 100,000 francs to Costa, the loyal friend to whom he owed life at the time the Paolists were hounding him down as a traitor.

CHAPTER VI

THE French revolutionists had overturned the absolute monarchy of the Bourbons, but they themselves had split into factions. The Moderates who favored constitutional monarchy had been trodden under foot by the Girondins who favored a federated republic; and the Girondins, in their turn, had been crushed by the Jacobins who favored an undivided republic based upon the absolute political equality of all Frenchmen. To this doctrine they welded State-socialism with a boldness which shocked the world at the time, and converted it a few years later. The Girondins did not yield without a struggle, drawing to themselves all disaffected elements, including the royalists; and the revolt which followed was supported by the English. Threatened thus from within and without, the Revolution seemed doomed to perish.

It was in the midst of this turmoil that the Bonapartes landed at Toulon in June, 1793. In a short while they removed to Marseilles. Warmly greeted by the Jacobins, who regarded them as martyrs to the good cause, the immediate necessities of the family were relieved by a small pension which the government had provided for such cases. Still, as they had fled in such haste from their house in Ajaccio that Madame Letitia had to snatch up the little Jerome and bear him in her arms, their condition upon reaching France was one of destitution.

NAPOLEON

From an engraving by Tomkins of a drawing from life during the campaign in Italy. In the collection of Mr. W. C. Crane

"One of the liveliest recollections of my youth," said Prince Napoleon, son of Jerome Bonaparte, "is the account my father gave of the arrival of our family in a miserable house situated in the lanes of Meilhan," a poor district of Marseilles. "They found themselves in the greatest poverty."

Having arranged for the family as well as he could, Napoleon rejoined his regiment at Nice. To shield himself from censure, on account of his prolonged absence, he produced Salicetti's certificate to the effect that the Commissioner had kept him in Corsica. The statement was false, but served its purpose. So many officers had fled their posts, and affairs were so unsettled, that it was no time to reject offers of service; nor was it a good time to ride rough-shod over the certificate of so influential a Jacobin as Salicetti.

Napoleon's first service in France was against the Girondin revolt. At Avignon, which the insurgents held, and which the Convention forces had invested, Napoleon, who had been sent from Nice to secure necessary stores, was appointed to the command of a battery. Mr. Lanfrey says, "It is certain that with his own hands he pointed the cannons with which Carteaux cleared Avignon of the Marseilles federates."

About this time it was that Napoleon came in contact with Augustin Robespierre, brother of the great man in Paris. The Convention had adopted the policy of sending commissioners to the armies to stimulate, direct, and report. Robespierre was at the head of one of these formidable delegations, and was now at Avignon in his official capacity. With him, but on a separate commission, were Salicetti and Gasparin.

To these gentlemen Napoleon read a political pamphlet he had just finished, and which he called *The Supper of Beaucaire*. The pamphlet was a discussion of the political situation. The author threw it into the attractive and unusual form of a dialogue between several guests whom he supposed to have met at an inn in the town of Beaucaire. An actual occurrence of the sort was doubtless the basis of the pamphlet.

A citizen of Nismes, two merchants of Marseilles, a manufacturer of Montpellier, and a soldier (supposed to be Napoleon), finding themselves at supper together, fell naturally into conversation and debate, the subject being the recent convulsions. The purpose of the pamphlet was to demonstrate the weakness of the insurgent cause, and the necessity of submission to the established authorities at Paris.

The Commissioners were so well pleased with Napoleon's production that they ordered the work published at the expense of the government. Exerting himself in behalf of his family, Napoleon secured positions in the public service for Lucien, Joseph, and Uncle Fesch.

Into the great seaport town of Toulon, thousands of the Girondin insurgents had thrown themselves. The royalists and the Moderates of the city made common cause with the revolting republicans, and England was ready to help hold the place against the Convention.

The royalists, confident the counter-revolution had come, began to massacre the Jacobins in the town. The white flag of the Bourbons was run up, displacing the red, white, and blue. The little boy, son of Louis XVI.,

who was lying in prison at Paris, was proclaimed king
under the name of Louis XVII. Sir Samuel Hood, commanding the British fleet, sailed into the harbor and took
possession of about twenty-five French ships, "in trust"
for the Bourbons; General O'Hara hurried from Gibraltar
with troops to aid in holding this "trust"; and to the
support of the English flocked Spaniards, Sardinians, and
Neapolitans. Even the Pope could not withhold his helping hand; he sent some priests to lend their prayers and
exhortations.

When it became known throughout France that Toulon had revolted, had begun to exterminate patriots, had
proclaimed a Bourbon king, had surrendered to the British the arsenal, the harbor, the immense magazines, and
the French fleet, a tide of furious resentment rose against
the town. There was but one thought: Toulon must
be taken, Toulon must be punished. The hunger for
revenge said it; the promptings of self-preservation
said it; the issue was one of life or death to the Revolution.

The Convention realized the crisis; the Great Committee realized it; and the measures taken were prompt.
Commissioners hurried to the scene, and troops poured in.
Barras, a really effective man in sudden emergencies,
Fréron, Salicetti, Gasparin, Ricord, Albitte, and Robespierre the Younger were all on hand to inspirit the army
and direct events. Some twenty odd thousand soldiers
soon beleagured the town. They were full of courage,
fire, and enthusiasm; but their commander was a painter,
Carteaux, whose ideas of war were very primitive. To
find where the enemy was, and then cannonade him vigorously, and then fall on him with muskets, was about the

substance of Carteaux' military plans. At Toulon, owing
to peculiarities of the position, such a plan was not as
excellent as it might have been at some other places.
Besides, he had no just conception of the means needed
for such a work as he had undertaken. Toulon, with its
double harbor, the inner and the outer, its defences by
land and by sea, to say nothing of the fortresses which
Lord Mulgrave had constructed on the strip of land
which separated and commanded the two harbors, presented difficulties which demanded a soldier. Carteaux
was brave and energetic, but no soldier ; and week after
week wasted away without any material progress having
been made in the siege.

Near the middle of September, 1793, Napoleon appeared
at Toulon, — at just the right moment, — for the artillery
service had well-nigh broken down. General Duteuil,
who was to have directed it, had not arrived ; and Dommartin had been disabled by a wound. How did Napoleon, of the army of Italy, happen to be at Toulon at
this crisis ? The question is one of lasting interest,
because his entire career pivots on Toulon. Mr. Lanfrey
states that, on his way from Avignon to Nice, Napoleon
stopped at Toulon, was invited by the Commissioners to
inspect the works, and so won upon them by his intelligent comments, criticisms, and suggestions, that they
appointed him at once to a command.

Napoleon's own account of the matter was that the
Minister of War sent him to Toulon to take charge of
the artillery, and that it was with written authority that
he confronted Carteaux, who was not at all pleased to see
him. " This was not necessary ! " exclaimed Carteaux.
" Nevertheless, you are welcome. You will share the

glory of taking the town without having borne any of the toil ! "

But the biographers are almost unanimous in refusing to credit this account. Why Napoleon should have falsified it, is not apparent. Mr. Lanfrey says that Napoleon's reason for not wishing to admit that the Commissioners appointed him was that he was unwilling to own that he had been under obligations to Salicetti. But Salicetti was only one of the Commissioners; he alone could not appoint. So far was Napoleon from being ashamed to acknowledge debts of gratitude that he never wearied of adding to the list. In his will he admits what he owed to the protection of Gasparin at this very period, and left a legacy of $20,000 to that Commissioner's son. Hence Mr. Lanfrey's reasoning is not convincing. Napoleon surely ought to have known how he came to be at Toulon, and his narrative is natural, is seemingly truthful, and is most positive.

But these recent biographers who dig and delve, and turn things over, and find out more about them a century after the occurrences than the men who took part in them ever knew, assert most emphatically that both Mr. Lanfrey and Napoleon are wrong. They insist that the way it all happened was this : After Dommartin was wounded, Adjutant General Cervoni, a Corsican, was sent to Marseilles to hunt around and find a capable artillery officer. Apparently it was taken for granted by whoever sent Cervoni, that capable artillery officers were straggling about at random, and could be found by diligent searchers in the lanes and by-ways of towns and cities. We are told that Cervoni, arrived in Marseilles, was strolling the streets, his eyes ready for the capable artillery officer, — when, who should he see coming down the road, dusty

and worn, but his fellow-Corsican, Napoleon Bonaparte !
Here, indeed, was a capable artillery officer, one who had
just been to Avignon, and was on his way back to Nice.

That Cervoni should at once invite the dusty Napoleon
into a café to take a drink of punch was quite as natural
as any other part of this supernatural yarn.   While drinking punch, Cervoni tells Napoleon his business, and urges
him to go to Toulon and take charge of the artillery.
And this ardently ambitious young man, who is yearning
for an opening, is represented as at first declining the
brilliant opportunity Cervoni thrusts upon him !   But at
length punch, persuasion, and sober second thought soften
Napoleon, and he consents to go.

All this you may read in some of the most recent works
of the diggers and delvers ; and you may believe it, if
you are very, very credulous.

The arrival on the scene of an educated artillery officer
like Napoleon, one whose handling of his guns at Avignon
had achieved notable success, was a welcome event.   His
friends, the Commissioners, took him over the field of
operations to show him the placing and serving of the
batteries.   He was astonished at the crude manner in
which all the arrangements had been made, and pointed
out the errors to the Commissioners.   First of all, the
batteries were not in range of the enemy ; the balls fell
into the sea, far short of the mark.   " Let us try a proof-
shot," said Napoleon ; and luckily he used a technical term,
coup d'épreuve.   Favorably impressed with this scientific
method of expression, the Commissioners and Carteaux
consented.   The proof-shot was fired, and the ball fell

harmlessly into the sea, less than halfway to its mark. "Damn the aristocrats!" said Carteaux; "they have spoilt our powder."

But the Commissioners had lost faith in Carteaux' management of the artillery; they determined to put Napoleon in charge of it.

On the 29th of September, Gasparin and Salicetti recommended his promotion to the rank of major, and on the next day they reported that Bonaparte was "the only artillery captain able to grasp the operations."

From the first Napoleon threw his whole heart into his work. He never seemed to sleep or to rest. He never left his batteries. If exhausted, he wrapped himself in his cloak, and lay down on the ground beside the guns.

From Lyons, Grenoble, Briançon, he requisitioned additional material. From the army of Italy he got more cannon. From Marseilles he took horses and workmen, to make gabions, hurdles, and fascines. Eight bronze guns he took from Martigues; timbers from La Seyne; horses from Nice, Valence, and Montpellier. At the ravine called Ollioules he established an arsenal with forty workmen, blacksmiths, wheelwrights, carpenters, all busy making those things the army needed; also a gunsmith's shop for the repair of muskets; and he took steps to reëstablish the Dardennes gun foundry.

Thus he based his hopes of success upon *work*, intense, well-directed, comprehensive work. All possible precautions were taken, all possible preparations made, every energy bent to bring to bear those means necessary to the end. Nothing was left to chance, good luck, providence, or inspiration. Cold calculation governed all, tireless labor provided all, colossal driving force moved it all. In

ever so short a time, Napoleon was felt to be "the soul of
the siege." In November he was made acting commander
of the artillery. Carteaux had been dismissed, and to the
painter succeeded a doctor named Doppet. The physician
had sense enough to soon see that an easier task than the
taking of Toulon would be an agreeable change, and he
asked to be sent elsewhere. To him succeeded Dugommier, an excellent soldier of the old school. Dutiel, official commander of the artillery, at length arrived, and he
was so well pleased with Napoleon's work that he did not
interfere.

The Committee of Public Safety, sitting in Paris, had
sent a plan of operations, the main idea of which was a
complete investment of the town. This would have required sixty thousand troops, whereas Dugommier had
but twenty-five thousand. But he dared not disobey the
terrible Committee. Between the loss of Toulon and his
own head he wavered painfully. A council of war met.
The Commissioners of the Convention were present, among
them Barras, Ricord, and Fréron. Officers of the army
thought the committee plan bad, but hesitated to say so in
plain words. One, and the youngest, spoke out; it was
Napoleon. He pointed to the map lying unrolled on the
table, explained that Toulon's defence depended on the
British fleet, that the fleet could not stay if a land battery
commanded the harbor, and that by seizing a certain point,
the French would have complete mastery of the situation.
On that point on the map he put his finger, saying,
"There is Toulon."

He put his plan in writing, and it was sent to the war
office in Paris. A second council of war adopted his
views, and ordered him to put them into execution.

The English had realized the importance of the strategic point named by Napoleon, and they had already fortified it. The redoubt was known as Fort Mulgrave; also as Little Gibraltar.

On the 30th of November the English made a desperate attempt to storm Napoleon's works. They were repulsed, and their leader, General O'Hara, was taken prisoner. At St. Helena Napoleon said that he himself had seized the wounded Englishman and drawn him within the French lines. This statement appears to have been one of his fancy sketches. Others say that General O'Hara was taken by four obscure privates of Suchet's battalion.

A cannoneer having been killed by his side, Napoleon seized the rammer and repeatedly charged the gun. The dead man had had the itch; Napoleon caught it, and was not cured until he became consul.

Constantly in the thick of the fighting, he got a bayonet thrust in the thigh. He fell into the arms of Colonel Muiron, who bore him to a place of safety. Napoleon showed the scar to O'Meara at St. Helena.

It was at Toulon that fame first took up that young dare-devil, Junot, whom Napoleon afterward spoiled by lifting him too high.

Supping with some brother officers near the batteries, a shell from the enemy fell into the tent, and was about to burst, when Junot rose, glass in hand, and exclaimed, "I drink to those who are about to die!" The shell burst, one poor fellow was killed, and Junot drank, "To the memory of a hero!"

Some days after this incident Junot volunteered to make for Napoleon a very dangerous reconnoissance. "Go in civilian's dress; your uniform will expose you to too much

risk." — "No," replied Junot, "I will not shrink from the
chance of being shot like a soldier; but I will not risk
being hanged like a spy." The reconnoissance made,
Junot came to Napoleon to report. " Put it in writing,"
said Napoleon ; and Junot, using the parapet of the battery
as a desk, began to write. As he finished the first page, a
shot meant for him struck the parapet, covering him and
the paper with earth. " Polite of these English," he cried,
laughing, " to send me some sand just when I wanted it."
Before very long Napoleon was a general, and Junot was
his aide-de-camp.

On December 17 everything was ready for the grand
assault on the English works. Between midnight and
day, and while a rainstorm was raging, the forts, which
for twenty-four hours had been bombarded by five batteries, were attacked by the French. Repulsed at the first
onset, Dugommier's nerve failed him, and he cried, " I am
a lost man," thinking of that terrible committee in
Paris which would cut off his head. Fresh troops were
hurried up, the attack renewed, and Little Gibraltar
taken. Thus Napoleon's first great military success was
won in a fair square fight with the English.

Assaults on other points in the line of defence had also
been made, and had succeeded ; and Toulon was at the
mercy of Napoleon's batteries. The night that followed
was one of the most frightful in the annals of war. The
English fleet was no longer safe in the harbor, and was
preparing to sail away. Toulon was frantic with terror.
The royalists, the Girondins, the refugees from Lyons and
Marseilles, rushed from their homes, crowded the quays,
making every effort to reach the English ships. The
Jacobins of the town, now that their turn had come, made

Instruits de la couverture

J'ai travaillé enchemin dans les hommes
sont fatigués veuillez general pourrais je vous envoyer
400 hommes pour travailler — le plus tôt possible la
enfin quelque-quatre depuis le chemin de
fait
j'aurai faire placer le plein de canons
sur la gauche aujourd'hui le plus avancé
le courant comme vous faire avancer.

LETTER FROM BONAPARTE, COMMANDANT OF ARTILLERY, TO GENERAL CARTEAUX.

the most of it, and pursued the royalists, committing every
outrage which hate and lust could prompt. Prisoners
broke loose, to rob, to murder, to ravish. The town became a pandemonium. Fathers, mothers, children, rushed ⸱
wildly for safety to the quays, screaming with terror, and
plunging into the boats in the maddest disorder. And all
this while the guns, the terrible guns of Napoleon, were
playing on the harbor and on the town, the balls crashing
through dwellings, or cutting lanes through the shrieking
fugitives on the quays, or sinking the boats which were
carrying the wretched outcasts away. The English set
fire to the arsenal, dockyard, and such ships as could not
be carried off, and the glare shone far and wide over the
ghastly tumult. Intensifying the horror of this hideous
night came the deafening explosion of the magazine ships,
and the rain of the fragments they scattered over all the
surrounding water.

Some fourteen thousand of the inhabitants of Toulon
fled with the English; some other thousands must have
perished in the bombardment and in the butcheries of
the days that followed. Toulou's baseness had aroused
the ire, the diabolism of the Revolution, and the vilest
men of all her ravening pack were sent to wreak revenge.
There was Barras, the renegade noble; Fréron, the Marat
in ferocity without Marat's honesty or capacity; Fouché,
the renegade priest. And the other Commissioners were
almost as ferocious; while from the Convention itself
came the voice of Barère demanding the total destruction of Toulon. Great was the sin of the doomed city;
ghastly was its punishment. Almost indiscriminately
people were herded and mown down with musketry.

On one of the days which ensued, Fouché wrote to his

friend, Collot d'Herbois : " We have sent to-day 213 rebels
to hell fire.   Tears of joy run down my cheeks and flood
my soul."   Royalist writers do not fail to remind the
reader that this miscreant, Fouché, became minister of
police to Napoleon.   They omit the statement that he
was used by Louis XVIII. in the same capacity.

Napoleon exerted himself to put a stop to these atrocities, but he was as yet without political influence, and
he could do nothing.   Some unfortunates he rescued
from his own soldiers, and secretly sent away.   He was
forced to witness the execution of one old man of eighty-
four, whose crime was that he was a millionnaire.   " When
I saw this," said Napoleon afterward, " it seemed to me
that the end of the world had come."

In his spiteful *Memoirs*, Barras labors hard to draw a
repulsive portrait of the Napoleon of Toulon.   The
young officer is represented as bustling about with a
bundle of his *Supper of Beaucaire*, handing copies
right and left to officers and men.   He is made to pro-
fess rank Jacobinism, and to allude to Robespierre and
Marat as "my saints."   He pays servile court to the
wife of Commissioner Ricord, and to the Convention
potentates generally.   Of course he was on his knees to
Barras.   That lofty magnate stoops low enough to mention, as a matter detrimental to Napoleon, that his uniform
was worn out and dirty — as if a tattered and soiled uniform at the close of such a siege, such herculean work,
could have been anything but a badge of honor to
the soldier who wore it ! Dugommier's official report
on the taking of Toulon contains no mention of Napoleon by name, but he uses this expression, " The fire
from our batteries, directed with the greatest talent,"

etc. This allusion could have been to no other than to Napoleon.

To the minister of war Duteil wrote on December 19, 1793, "I cannot find words to describe the merit of Bonaparte; a considerable amount of science, just as much intelligence, and too much bravery, such is a feeble outline of the virtues of that rare officer."

The Commissioners themselves, whose names crowded the name of Bonaparte out of the official report, recognized his services by at once nominating him to the post of general of brigade.

English authors dwell extensively on Napoleon's hatred of their country : do they never recall the origin of the feeling ? Had not England deceived old Paoli, crushed the opposite faction, and treated Corsica as a conquest? Was it not the English faction which had sacked the home, confiscated the property, and sought the lives of the Bonaparte family ? Had not England been striving to force the Bourbons back on France ; had it not seized the French ships at Toulon " in trust "; had it not then given to the flames not only the ships, but dockyards, arsenals, and magazines ? Did not William Pitt, in the King's speech of 1794, include among the subjects of con-gratulation "the circumstances attending the evacuation of Toulon " ? Had not England, in 1793, bargained with Austria to despoil France and divide the booty : Austria to have Alsace and Lorraine ; and England to have the foreign settlements and colonies of France ? " His Majesty " (of England) " has an interest in seeing the house of Austria strengthen itself by acquisitions on the

French frontier ; the Emperor " (of Austria) " must see with pleasure the relative increase of the naval and commercial resources of this country " (England) " over those of France."

Historians have long said that England's war with France was forced upon her, that it was defensive. Does the language just quoted (official despatches) sound like the terms of self-defence? It is the language of aggression, of unscrupulous conquest ; and the spirit which dictated this bargain between two powers to despoil a third is the same which gave life to each successive combination against the French Republic and the Napoleonic Empire.

Like master, like man : the British ministry having adopted the policy of blind and rancorous hostility in dealing with France, the same fury of hatred pervaded the entire public service. Edmund Burke and William Pitt inoculated the whole nation. "Young gentlemen," said Nelson to his midshipmen, "among the things you must constantly bear in mind is to hate a Frenchman as you would the devil." At another time, the same illustrious Englishman declared, " I hate all Frenchmen ; they are equally the object of my detestation, whether royalists or republicans." Writing to the Duke of Clarence, he stated: " To serve my king and to destroy the French, I consider the great order of all. . . . Down, down with the damned French villains ! My blood boils at the name of Frenchman ! " At Naples he exclaimed, " Down, down with the French ! is my constant prayer."

I quote Nelson simply because he was a controlling factor in these wars, a representative Englishman, a man in full touch with the policy, purpose, and passion of his government.

Consider England's bargain with Austria ; consider her
bribes to Prussia to continue the struggle when even
Austria had withdrawn ; consider the animus of such leading actors as Burke and Nelson — is it any wonder that
Napoleon regarded Great Britain as the one irreconcilable
and mortal enemy of France ?

And what was England's grievance ?   Her rival across
the Channel had overturned a throne, slain a king, and
proclaimed principles which were at war with established
tyranny.   But had England never upset a throne, slain a
king, and proclaimed a republic ?

Was it any matter of rightful concern to Great Britain
that France had cast out the Bourbons, and resorted to
self-government ?   Did England, by any law human or
divine, have the right to impose her own will upon a
sister state ?   Was she right in seizing and destroying the
French fleet at Toulon, which she had accepted as a trust ?
Unless all these can be answered Yes, Napoleon deserves
no deep damnation for his hatred of Great Britain.

CHAPTER VII

THE Mediterranean coast of France being almost at the mercy of the English fleet, Napoleon was sent, immediately after the fall of Toulon, to inspect the defences and put them into proper condition. He threw into this task the same activity and thoroughness which had marked him at Toulon, and in a short while the coast and the coasting trade were secure from attack.

His duties carried him to Marseilles, where he found that a fortress necessary to the defence of the harbor and town had been dismantled by the patriots, who detested it as a local Bastille. Napoleon advised that the fortifications be restored " so as to command the town." This raised a storm. The Marseilles Jacobins denounced Bonaparte to the Convention. By that body he was summoued to appear at its bar. He had no inclination to take such a risk, and hastened to Toulon, where he put himself under the protection of Salicetti and Augustin Robespierre. At their instance he wrote to the Paris authorities an exculpatory letter, and the storm blew over.

In March, 1794, Napoleon returned to headquarters at Nice. By his influence over the Commissioners of the Convention, young Robespierre in particular, he became the dominant spirit of the army of Italy.

General Dumerbion, commander-in-chief, a capable officer but too old, had been wasting time, or the strength of his troops, for several months, in attacks upon the enemy (Piedmontese and Austrians) who were intrenched at the foot of the maritime Alps. Despondent after repeated failures, officers and men were contenting themselves with holding their positions, and conducting such operations as were consistent with extreme prudence. Napoleon had no sooner made a careful study of the positions of the opposing forces, than he drew up a plan of campaign, and submitted it to the commander-in-chief and the Commissioners. In a council of war it was discussed and approved. Early in April, the army was in motion ; the position of the enemy was to be turned. Masséna led the corps which was to do what fighting was necessary. The enemy was beaten in two engagements, and Piedmont entered by the victorious French, who then turned back toward the Alps. The communications between Piedmont and the fortified camps of the enemy being thus endangered, they abandoned them without a fight; and thus in a campaign of a month the French won command of the whole range of the Alps, which had so long resisted every attack in front.

At this time the Bonaparte family was living in Nice, and Napoleon, during the months of May and June, 1794, spent much of his time with his mother and sisters. Uncle Fesch, Joseph, and Lucien were in good positions ; and Napoleon secured for Louis, by the telling of some falsehoods and the use of the influence of Salicetti, the rank of lieutenant in the army. Louis was represented as having served as a volunteer at Toulon, and as having been wounded there. As a matter of fact, Louis had visited Napoleon during the siege, but had not served, and had not been wounded.

Joseph Bonaparte was made war commissioner of the first class. Napoleon, in securing him the place, represented Joseph as being the holder of the commission of lieutenant colonel of Corsican volunteers, the commission which Napoleon had won for himself at such a cost in his native land. The fraud was discovered later on; but, for the present, his brother Joseph was snugly berthed.

In July, 1794, Napoleon went to Genoa on a twofold mission. That republic, which was wholly controlled by a few rich families, had been giving aid and comfort to the enemies of republican France. The English and the Austrians had been allowed to violate Genoa's neutrality. Also, the English had been permitted to set up an establishment for the manufacture of counterfeit assignats — that peculiar policy of the British ministry which had been used with good effect against the revolted American colonies. Besides, there was a complaint that certain stores bought from Genoa, and paid for, had not been delivered to the French.

Ostensibly, therefore, Napoleon's mission was about the stores which Genoa withheld, and about the neutrality which she was allowing to be violated. But within this purpose lay another. Genoa, and her neutrality was an obstacle to French military plans ; she was weak, and the temptation to seize upon her was strong. Napoleon while at Genoa was to look about him with the keen eyes of a military expert, and to form an opinion as to the ease with which the little republic could be made the victim of a sudden spring.

This mission, which bears an unpleasant resemblance to that of a spy, was undertaken at the instance of the younger Robespierre.   Salicetti and Albitte had not been consulted, and knew nothing of the secret instructions given to Napoleon.   Suddenly recalled to Paris by his brother, Robespierre wished to take with him the young officer whose "transcendent merit" he had applauded. With Napoleon to command the Paris troops, instead of Henriot, the Robespierres might confidently expect victory in the crisis they saw coming.   But it was a part of Napoleon's "transcendent merit" to possess excellent judgment, and he declined to go to Paris.   So the friends parted : the one to visit little Genoa and bully its feeble Doge, the other to return to the raging capital and to meet sudden death there in generous devotion to his brother.

Napoleon reached Nice again, July 21, 1794, after his successful mission to Genoa, and in a few days later came the crash.   The Robespierres were overthrown, and the Bonapartes, classed with that faction, fell with it.   Napoleon was put under arrest ; his brothers thrown out of employment.   For some reason Salicetti and Albitte, previously so friendly to Napoleon, had turned upon him, had denounced him to the Convention, and had signed the order of arrest — an order almost equivalent to a death warrant.

It was a stunning, unexpected blow.   Madame Junot, in her *Memoirs*, hints that the traditional woman was at the bottom of it ; that the younger man, Napoleon, had found favor in the eyes of a lady who looked coldly upon the suit of Salicetti.   But this explanation does not explain the hostility of other commissioners, for members of two separate commissioners signed against Napoleon.   Surely he had not cut them all off from the smiles of their ladies.

No ; it would seem that Napoleon owed his tumble to the
fact that he was standing upon the Robespierre scaffold-
ing when it fell.   He merely fell with it.

He was known as a Robespierre man, and to a very
great extent he was.   He had been put under heavy
obligations by the younger brother whom he liked, and
he did not believe that the elder was at heart a bad man.
He had seen private letters which the elder brother had
written to the younger, in which letters the crimes of the
more rabid and corrupt revolutionists were deplored,
and the necessity for moderation and purity expressed.
Among those who befouled the names of the Robespierres,
either then or afterward, Napoleon is not to be found.
He understood well enough that the convulsion of July
27, 1794 (Thermidor), was the work of a gang of scoundrels (Barras, Fouché, Carrier, Tallien, Billaud, Collot),
who took advantage of circumstances to pull down a man
who had threatened to punish them for their crimes.
Napoleon believed then and afterward that Robespierre
had been a scapegoat, and that he had not been responsible for the awful days of the Terror in June and July
1794.   The manly constancy with which he always clung
to his own estimates of men and events is shown by the
way in which he spoke well of the Robespierre brothers
when all others damned them, and by his granting Char-
lotte Robespierre a pension at a time when the act could
not have been one of policy.   Marvellous was the com-
plexity of Napoleon's character ; but like a thread of gold
runs through all the tangled warp and woof of his life
the splendid loyalty with which he remembered those
who had ever been kind to him.   Not once did he ever
pursue a foe and take revenge so far as I can discover ;

not once did he ever fail to reward a friend, so far as the record is known.

Napoleon's arrest created such indignation among the young officers of the army of Italy that a scheme for his forcible release was broached. Junot, Marmont, and other ardent friends were to take him out of prison and flee with him into Genoese territory. Napoleon would not hear of it. "Do nothing," he wrote Junot. "You would only compromise me."

Junot the hot-headed, Junot the tender-hearted, was beside himself with grief; and he wept like a child as he told the bad news to Madame Letitia.

But Napoleon himself was not idle. He knew that to be sent to Paris for trial at that time was almost like going to the scaffold, and he made his appeal directly to the Commissioners. By name he addressed Salicetti and Albitte, in words manly, bold, and passionate, protesting against the wrong done him, demanding that they investigate the case, and appealing to his past record and services for proofs of his republican loyalty. This protest had its effect. Salicetti himself examined Napoleon's papers, and found nothing against him. The suspicious trip to Genoa was no longer suspicious, for his official instructions for that trip were found.

After an imprisonment of about two weeks, he was released, but his employment was gone. He still held his rank in the army, but he was not on duty. It was only as an adviser and spectator that he remained, and, at the request of Dumerbion, furnished a plan of campaign, which was successful to the extent that Dumerbion pushed it. He did not push it far enough to gain any very solid advantages, much to Napoleon's disgust.

It was at this time that the incident occurred which he related at St. Helena. He was taking a stroll with the wife of the influential Commissioner Turreau, when it occurred to him to divert and interest her by giving her an illustration of what war was like. Accordingly he gave orders to a French outpost to attack the Austrian pickets. It was a mere whim; the attack could not lead to anything. It was done merely to entertain a lady friend. The soldiers could but obey orders. The attack was made and resisted. There was a little battle, and there were soldiers wounded, there were soldiers killed. And the entertainment which the lady got out of it was the sole other result of the attack.

It was Napoleon who told this story on himself : he declared that he had never ceased to regret the occurrence.

Corsican affairs now claimed attention for a moment in the counsels of the government at Paris (September, 1794). For after the Bonapartes had fled the island, Paoli had called the English in. The old hero intended that there should be a protectorate, thought that England would be satisfied with an arrangement of that sort, and that he, Paoli, would be left in control as viceroy or something of the kind. But the English had no idea of putting forth their strength for any such halfway purpose. They intended that Corsica should belong to England, and that an English governor should rule it. They intrigued with Paoli's stanch friend, Pozzo di Borgo, and Pozzo became a convert to the English policy. King George III. of England wrote Paoli a polite and pressing invitation to visit England, and Paoli accepted.

England bombarded and took the remaining French strongholds (February, 1794), went into quiet and peaceable possession of the island, and appointed Sir Gilbert Elliott, governor. Of course Paoli's stanch friend, Pozzo di Borgo, was not forgotten; he was made president of the state council under Elliott.

When commissioners from Paris came to the headquarters of the army of Italy, instructed to suspend the operations of the army and to prepare for an expedition against Corsica, Napoleon saw an opportunity to get back into active service again. He sought and obtained, perhaps by the favor of Salicetti, command of the artillery for the expedition. Great preparations were made at Toulon to organize the forces and to equip the fleet. In this work Napoleon was intensely engaged for several months. His mother and the younger children took up their residence in pleasant quarters near Antibes, and he was able to enjoy the luxury of the home circle while getting ready to drive the English out of Corsica. In due time the French fleet set sail; in due time it did what French fleets have usually done — failed dismally. The English were on the alert, swooped down, and captured two French vessels. The others ran to shelter under the guns of shore forts. The conquest of Corsica was postponed.

CHAPTER VIII

IT must have been a sadly disappointed young man who rejoined his family, now at Marseilles, in the spring of 1795. Gone was the Toulon glory; gone the prestige of the confidential friend of commissioners who governed France. Barely escaping with his life from the Robespierre wreck, here he now was, stranded by the failure, the miserable collapse, of an expedition from which so much had been expected. Very gloomy must have been Napoleon's "yellowish green" face, very sombre those piercing eyes, as he came back to his seat at the hearth of the humble home in Marseilles. Ten years had passed since he had donned his uniform; they had been years of unceasing effort, painful labor, and repeated failure. A demon of ill-luck had dogged his footsteps, foiled him at every turn, made null all his well-laid plans. Even success had come to him only to mock him and then drop him to a harder fall. Not only had he lost ground, but his brothers had been thrown out of the places he had obtained for them. In the midst of these discouragements came another: Lacombe St. Michel, a commissioner who bore him no good-will, urged the government to remove him from the army of Italy and to transfer him to the West. An order to that effect had been issued. This transfer would take him away from an army where he had made some reputation and some friends, and

from a field of operations with which he was thoroughly
familiar. It would put him in La Vendée, where the war
was the worst of all wars,—civil strife, brother against
brother, Frenchman against Frenchman,—and it would
put him under the command of a masterful young man
named Hoche.

Absolutely determined not to go to this post, and yet
desperately tenacious in his purpose of keeping his feet
upon the ladder, Napoleon set out for Paris early in May,
1795, to exert himself with the authorities. In the capital
he had some powerful friends, Barras and Fréron among
them. Other friends he could make. In a government
where committees ruled, and where the committees were
undergoing continual changes, everything was possible to
one who could work, and wait, and intrigue. Therefore
to Paris he hastened, taking with him his aides Junot and
Marmont, and his brother Louis.

Lodged in a cheap hotel, he set himself to the task
of getting the order of transfer cancelled. A general
overhauling of the army list had been going on recently,
and many changes were being made. Napoleon's was
not an isolated case. The mere transfer from one army
to the other, his rank not being lowered, was, in itself, no
disgrace; but Aubrey, who was now at the head of the
war committee, decided upon a step which became a real
grievance. The artillery service was overstocked with
officers; it became necessary to cut down this surplus;
and Napoleon, as a junior officer, was ordered to the army
of the West as general of a brigade of infantry.

Napoleon regarded this as an insult, a serious injury,
and he never forgave the minister who dealt him the blow.
Aubrey had been a Girondin, and was at heart a royalist

He knew Napoleon to be a Jacobin, if not a Terrorist. Without supposing that there were any causes for personal ill-will, here were sufficient grounds for positive dislike in times so hot as those. In vain Napoleon applied in person, and brought to bear the powerful influence of Barras, Fréron, and the Bishop of Marboz. Either his advocates were lukewarm, or his cause was considered weak. Neither from the full committee nor from Aubrey could any concession be wrung. Aubrey, himself a soldier of the perfunctory, non-combative sort, believed that Napoleon had been advanced too rapidly. "You are too young to be commander-in-chief of artillery," he said to the little Corsican. "Men age fast on the field of battle," was the retort which widened the breach; — for Aubrey had not come by any of his age on fields of battle.

Foiled in his attempt on the committees as then constituted, Napoleon's only hope was to wait until these members should go out and others come in by the system of rotation.

In the meantime he stuck to Paris with supple tenacity. By producing certificates of ill-health, he procured and then lengthened leave of absence from this obnoxious post in the West. He clung to old friends, and made new ones. Brother Lucien having been cast into prison as a rabid Jacobin, Napoleon was able to secure his release. Peremptory orders were issued that Napoleon should go to his post of duty, but he succeeded, through his friends, in evading the blow. Louis, however, lost his place as lieutenant, and was sent back to school at Châlons.

In spite of all his courage and his resources, Napoleon became, at times, very despondent. He wrote his brother Joseph that "if this continues, I shall not care to get out

of the way of the carriages as they pass." The faithful
Junot shared with his chief the money he received from
home, and also his winnings at the gaming table; — for
Junot was a reckless gambler, and, being young, sometimes
had good luck. Bourrienne and Talma may also have
made loans to Napoleon in these days of distress, but this
is not so certain. There is a letter which purports to have
been from Napoleon to Talma, asking the loan of a few
crowns, and offering repayment " out of the first kingdom
I win with my sword." But Napoleon himself declared
that he did not meet Talma before the time of the
consulate.

Idle, unhappy, out of pocket, Napoleon became morose
and unsocial. If he seemed gay, the merriment struck his
friends as forced and hollow. At the theatre, while the
audience might be convulsed with laughter, Napoleon was
solemn and silent. If he was with a party of friends, their
chatter seemed to fret him, and he would steal away, to be
seen later sitting alone in some box of an upper tier, and
" looking rather sulky."

Pacing the streets from day to day, gloomy, empty of
pocket, his career seemingly closed, his thoughts were
bitter. He envied and hated the young men who dashed
by him on their fine horses, and he railed out at them and
at fate. He envied his brother Joseph, who had married
the daughter of a man who had got rich in the business of
soap-making and soap-selling. " Ah, that lucky rogue,
Joseph ! " But might not Napoleon marry Désirée, the
other daughter of the soap man? It would appear that
he wished it, and that she was not unwilling, but the
soap-boiler objected. " One Bonaparte in the family is
enough."

Napoleon traced his misfortunes back to the date of his arrest: "Salicetti has cast a cloud over the bright dawn of my youth. He has blighted my hopes of glory." At another time he said mournfully, striking his forehead, "Yet I am only twenty-six." Ruined by a fellow-Corsican! Yet to all outward appearance Salicetti and Napoleon continued to be good friends. They met at Madame Permon's from time to time, and Salicetti was often in Napoleon's room. Bourrienne states that the two men had much to say to each other in secret. It was as though they were concerned in some conspiracy.

On May 20, 1795 (1st of Prairial), there was a riot, formidable and ferocious, directed by the extreme democrats against the Convention and its moderates. The Tuileries was forced by the mob, and a deputy killed. Intending to kill Fréron, the crowd slew Ferraud. The head of the deputy was cut off, stuck on a pike, and pushed into the face of Boissy d'Anglas, the president. Gravely the president took off his hat and bowed to the dead. The Convention troops arrived, cleared the hall, and put down the riot.

Napoleon was a witness to this frightful scene. After it was over, he dropped in at Madame Permon's to get something to eat. The restaurants were all closed, and he had tasted nothing since morning. While eating, he related what had happened at the Tuileries. Suddenly he inquired, "Have you seen Salicetti?" He then went on to complain of the injury Salicetti had done him. "But I bear him no ill-will." Salicetti was implicated in the revolt, and the conspiracy which preceded it may have been the subject of those private conversations he had been having at Napoleon's room — conversations which, according to Bourrienne, left Napoleon "pensive, melancholy, and anxious."

The conspiracy had ripened, had burst into riot, and the riot had been crushed. "Have you seen Salicetti?" A very pertinent inquiry was this, for Salicetti was being hunted, and in a few days would be proscribed. If caught, he would probably be executed. Madame Junot says that while Napoleon spoke of Salicetti he "appeared very abstracted." Briefly to conclude this curious episode, Salicetti was proscribed, fled for refuge to Madame Permon's house, was hidden by her, and was finally smuggled out of Paris disguised as her valet. Napoleon had known where Salicetti lay concealed, but did not betray him. Was his conduct dictated by prudence or by generosity? There was something generous in it, no doubt; but the conclusion is almost unavoidable that there was policy, too. If driven to the wall, Salicetti could have disclosed matters hurtful to Napoleon. Those private interviews, secret conferences, daily visits to Napoleon's room on the days the conspiracy was being formed — would they not look bad for a young officer who was known to have a grievance, and who had been heard frequently and publicly to denounce the government? This may have been what was on Napoleon's mind while he was so much buried in thought at Madame Permon's.

It was fine proof of Napoleon's judgment that he did not allow himself to be drawn into the conspiracy. Angered against the government, despising many of the men who composed it, restlessly ambitious, and intensely yearning for action, the wonder is that he came within the secrets of the leaders of the revolt and yet kept his skirts clear.

Napoleon at this period was sallow and thin ; his chest-nut hair hung long and badly powdered. His speech was generally terse and abrupt. He had not yet developed grace of speech and manner. When he came to present Madame Permon a bunch of violets, he did it awkwardly — so much so that his ungainly manner provoked smiles. His dress was plain. A gray overcoat buttoned to the chin; a round hat pulled over his eyes, or stuck on the back of his head; no gloves, and a black cravat, badly tied ; boots coarse, and generally unclean. When the weather was bad, these boots would be muddy and wet, and Napo-leon would put them on the fender to dry, to the irritation of those who had exacting noses. Madame Permon's being a nose of that class, her handkerchief rose to her nose whenever the Bonaparte boots rose to the fender. Napoleon, an observant man, took the hint, and got into the habit of stopping in the area for the chambermaid to clean his boots with her broom. His clothes had become threadbare, his hat dilapidated. The bootmaker who gave him credit in this dark hour was never forgotten. The Emperor Napoleon persisted in patronizing the clumsy cobbler whose heart had not hardened itself against the forlorn brigadier.

One night at St. Helena, when Napoleon, unable to sleep, was trying to rob time of its tedium by recalling the vicissitudes of his past, he related this incident : " I was at this period, on one occasion, suffering from that extreme depression of spirits which renders life a burden too great to be borne. I had just received a letter from my mother, revealing to me the utter destitution into which she was plunged. My own salary had been cut off, and I had but five francs in my pocket. I wandered along the banks of the river, tempted to commit suicide. In a few moments I should have thrown myself into the water, when I ran against a man dressed like a mechanic. 'Is that you, Napoleon?' and he threw himself upon my neck. It was my old friend, Des Mazis, who had emigrated, and who had now returned in disguise to visit his mother. 'But what is the matter, Napoleon? You do not listen to me! You do not seem to hear me!'

"I confessed everything to him.

"'Is that all?' said he, and unbuttoning his coarse waistcoat and taking off a belt which he handed me, 'Here are 30,000 francs which I can spare; take them and relieve your mother.'"

Napoleon told how he was so overjoyed that he rushed away to send the money to his mother, without having waited to thank his friend. Ashamed of his conduct, he soon went back to seek Des Mazis, but failed to find him anywhere. It was under the Empire that the two again met. Napoleon forced ten times the amount of the loan upon Des Mazis, and appointed him to a position which paid him 30,000 francs per year.

Low as he was in purse and spirit, Napoleon was too young, too strong, too self-reliant to yield to despair for any length of time. His active brain teemed with schemes for the future. His airy fancy soared all the way from plans which involved a book store, and a leasing and sub-letting of apartment houses, to service in Turkey and an empire in the East. Sometimes his friends thought him almost crazy. Going with Bourrienne, who was looking about for a suitable house, Napoleon took a fancy to the house opposite, and thought of hiring it for himself, Uncle Fesch, and his old Brienne teacher, Patrault:

"With that house, my friends in it, and a horse and cabriolet, I should be the happiest fellow in the world."

Junot relates that one evening when the two were walking in Jardin des Plantes, Napoleon appeared to be overcome by the beauties of his surroundings and the charms of the night. He made Junot his confidant — he was in love, and his affection was not returned. Junot listened, sympathized, condoled, and then made Napoleon *his* confidant. Junot was also in love — he loved Pauline Bonaparte, and wished to wed her. At once Napoleon recovered himself. Firmly he rejected the proposition: Junot had no fortune, Pauline had none — marriage was out of the question.

"You must wait. We shall see better days, my friend. — Yes! We shall have them even should I go to seek them in another quarter of the world!"

But where should he go? This question he put to himself and to the few friends who felt interest in his fate. One of his former teachers at Brienne, D'Harved, met him at this time in Paris, and was struck by his dejected appearance. "Chagrin and discontent were vividly painted on his face. He broke out into abuse of the government." D'Harved was afraid that such talk would endanger listener as well as speaker, and at his instance they retired into the garden of the Palais Royal, accompanied by an Englishman named Blinkam or Blencowe. Napoleon continued to complain of the manner in which the authorities had treated him, and he declared his purpose of leaving the country. The Englishman proposed that they enter a restaurant. There the conversation was resumed. Napoleon did not favor D'Harved's suggestion, that he offer his services to England. Nor did

Germany attract him.   Spain might do, for " there is not a single warrior in that country."

Then the Englishman proposed Turkey, promising to write letters which would favorably dispose certain influential persons in Constantinople to the luckless adventurer.   Napoleon jumped at the idea.   " His countenance beamed with delight and hope."   He exclaimed, " I shall at once solicit permission to depart to Constantinople."   And he did so.

At the end of July, Aubrey went out of office, and was succeeded in the war committee by Doulcet de Pontécoulant.   One of the first matters which engaged his attention was the condition of the army of Italy.   It had been losing ground.   Doulcet needed the advice of some one who was familiar with the situation there ; and Boissy d'Anglas recommended Napoleon.   Summoned to the war office, Napoleon answered all questions promptly, and made suggestions as to what ought to be done, which so dazzled the minister that he said to Napoleon, " General, take time and write out what you propose, so that it may be laid before the Committee."

" Time! " cried Napoleon, " give me a couple of sheets of paper and a pen.   In half an hour I will have the plan of campaign ready."   He sat down and wrote, but who could read that awful writing ?   Taking it home with him, he made Junot copy it, and the plan was submitted to the full committee, which sent it on to the army. Doulcet, favorably impressed by Napoleon, retained him in the topographical bureau, where he and three others drew up plans and directions for all the armies.

On the 16th of August the order was issued peremptorily, that Napoleon should proceed to the post assigned

him in the army of the West. He did not obey, and
powerful friends screened him. On August 30 he applied
to be sent to Turkey to increase the military resources of
the Sultan. On September 15 or 25 (for authorities
differ painfully on the date), a report signed by Cambacérès and others decreed that his name be stricken from
the list of generals in active service.

One reason given for the sudden harshness of the Committee in striking his name off the list is that he had
pressed for payment of fraudulent accounts. He had
claimed and received mileage from Nice to Paris, when he
had come from Marseilles only. He had also claimed pay
for horses sold by him according to orders, when he set
forth on the Corsican expedition. The authorities had no
faith in these horses, considered them purely imaginary ;
and, in consequence, Napoleon was spoken of very harshly
by government officials. Letourneur, who had succeeded
Doulcet on the Committee, was one of those who disliked
and opposed him.

On September 15 a subcommittee reported to the full
committee in favor of the proposition, that Napoleon be
sent, with officers of his suite, to reorganize the military
system of the Turks. Only in government by committee
could such a contradictory series of orders and resolutions
be possible. Napoleon had seriously canvassed the officers
who were to compose his suite on the mission to Turkey,
when symptoms of another revolutionary convulsion attracted his notice and halted his preparations.

The Convention, which had reeled and rocked along for
three years, was now about to adjourn. It felt that it
must, and yet it did not wish to do so. They therefore
decreed that two-thirds of the next legislature should be

composed of themselves. The other third, the people might elect. One reason for this strange law was that the royalist reaction had become extremely threatening. The Count of Artois was said to be hovering on the coast, ready to land an expedition from England, and to march on Paris. The army of Condé was expecting to coöperate from the Rhine. Paris was to give the signal by a revolt which should upset the Convention.

Besides the royalists, there were other formidable malcontents. There were the poorer classes, who had been deprived of their votes by the property qualification of the new constitution. In the revolt which ensued, however, the royalists were the soul of the movement. The extreme democrats, though hotly opposed to the property qualification, hated royalism worse. Santerre was ready to sustain the Convention, and did so. The very prisoners who had been lying in chains since the democratic revolt of May (1st of Prairial) were now willing to fight for the Convention, and did fight for it.

The centre of the insurrection against the Convention, its new constitution, and its decrees was the Section Lepelletier, the home of the rich men of the middle class. The National Guards from this section, it will be remembered, had fought in defence of the King on the famous 10th of August. It was now ready to fight for royalty again.

On the 4th of October (12th of Vendémiaire) the Section Lepelletier declared itself in insurrection, and it became the rallying-point for insurgents from all the sections of Paris. The National Guard, forty thousand strong, had been so reorganized that it was now with the insurgents. To the royalists the situation seemed full of promise, for

the Convention had but seven or eight thousand troops
upon which it could rely. General Dumas was selected
by the Convention to take command of its forces, but he
had left town three days before.

General Menou, in command of the Convention forces,
was ordered to go and disarm and disperse the insurgents.
For some reason, either because he failed to realize the
gravity of the crisis, or because he was unnerved by it, he
did the worst thing possible. He parleyed, and compro-
mised. He agreed to withdraw his troops on the promise
of the insurgents to withdraw theirs. He then retreated,
and the insurgents held their ground and their arms,
loudly proclaiming their triumph.

As the nerveless and witless Menou was drawing off
his men, a young officer, on the steps of the Feydau
Theatre, exclaimed to his companion, "Where can that
fellow be going?" It was Napoleon speaking to Junot.
And he continued : " Ah, if the sections would only let
me lead them, I would guarantee to place them in the
Tuileries in two hours, and have all those Convention rascals driven out ! " Then he hurried to the Tuileries to see
what the Convention would do next.

It was evident that on the morrow the insurgents would
attack. They proclaimed their intention of doing so, and
they were confident of success.

The Convention removed Menou from command, and
placed him under arrest. They then chose Barras commander-in-chief, remembering his vigor and success in
July, 1794, when Robespierre fell. Napoleon was made
second in command.

Just how this appointment came to be made, will always
be a matter of dispute. It is certain that Barras suggested

Bonaparte's name to the Committee in the words: "I have precisely the man we want. It is a little Corsican officer, who will not stand on ceremony." Baron Fain states that Napoleon was at this time in the topographical office, that he was sent for, and sworn in by the Committee in the committee-room. Napoleon himself, in one of his different versions, relates that he was at the Feydau Theatre, was told what was happening at the Lepelletier section, left the theatre, witnessed Menou's retreat, and then hurried to the Convention to see how the news would be received. Arrived at the Tuileries, he mixed with the crowd in the galleries, and heard his name called. Announcement was made that he had been appointed as aide to Barras.

Barras, in his turn, says that on this fateful evening Bonaparte could not be found at any of his usual haunts, that he came to the Tuileries late, looking confused, and that in answer to sharp questions he admitted that he had come from the section Lepelletier, where he had been reconnoitring the enemy. Barras charges that he had been dickering with the other side.

By whatever means it came about, Napoleon Bonaparte was acting chief in the famous 13th of Vendémiaire (5th of October, 1795). It was he whose genius converted the Tuileries, which the Parisian mobs had time and again stormed, into a fortress an army could not have taken. Cannon were at Sablons, cannon he must have, and Murat at the head of three hundred horse went in a gallop to bring the guns. In the nick of time the order was given, for the insurgents had sent also. Murat's mounted men reached Sablons in advance of the unmounted insurgents, and the cannon were whirled away

to the Tuileries. Planted so as to command all avenues
of approach, they made the position invulnerable, for the
insurgents had no cannon.

General Thiébault says: "From the first, his activity
was astonishing: he seemed to be everywhere at once, or
rather he only vanished at one point to reappear instantly.
He surprised people further by his laconic, clear, and
prompt orders, imperative to the last degree. Everybody
was struck also by the vigor of his arrangements, and
passed from admiration to confidence, and from confidence
to enthusiasm."

Morning came, and with it the insurgents ; but at sight
of the formidable defences which had been the work of
the night, they halted. Hour after hour passed away in
hoots, yells, threats, negotiation. Toward evening it
seemed that the Convention troops might be brought to
fraternize with the insurgents. Suddenly a musket was
fired, and the battle opened ; or rather the cannonade
commenced, for battle it could not be called. The insurgents showed courage, but had no chance of success whatever. It was cannon against muskets, an army intrenched
against a packed mob in the streets. The firing commenced at about four in the evening. By six all was over.

A few attempts to rally the insurgents were made, but
were easily frustrated. The Convention forces carried out
the orders Menou had received by disarming the turhu-
lent sections. A few of the ringleaders of the revolt were
tried and punished, but only one, Lafond, was executed.

During this disarmament, which recent writers say
never happened, but which Menou had been officially
instructed to effect, and which both Napoleon and Barras
say they *did* effect, the victorious conventionals made one

of those mistakes incident to the prevailing darkness and confusion. The house of Madame de Beauharnais was entered, the sword of her late husband, the Viscount Beauharnais, was carried off. In a day or so the son of the widow Beauharnais went to Napoleon and asked for the return of his dead father's sword. His request immediately granted, and the sacred relic being placed in his hands, the boy covered the handle of the weapon with kisses, and burst in tears. Napoleon's interest was deeply aroused, and he treated the lad with that winning kindness which fascinated all who came within its influence. Such report did Eugène Beauharnais carry home that his mother felt bound to call upon the General, and thank him in person ; and it was thus, perhaps, that these two first met.

Later biographers scout this story as a romance fashioned by Napoleon himself, and they say that (1) no disarmament took place ; and (2) that if such disarmament did take place, Madame Beauharnais, a friend of Barras, would not have been molested. To say nothing of further proof, the contemporaneous letter of Napoleon to Joseph shows that the sections *were* disarmed ; and as to Madame Beauharnais being screened by her friendly relations with Barras, *that* presupposes every soldier in the Convention army to have known all about Barras's private affairs. How could the thousands of Convention troops, fifteen hundred of whom were democrats just out of jail, know who was or was not a personal friend of Barras ? The Convention was in the minority ; it had less than eight thousand troops : would it have left arms in the hands of the majority and the forty thousand National Guards?

Captious critics call attention to the fact that Napoleon elsewhere stated that he met his future wife at the house of Barras. This assertion does not necessarily conflict with the other. A call at the office of an official does not constitute a social meeting. When Napoleon said he met Madame Beauharnais at the house of Barras, his meaning probably was that he there first knew her socially. And why should a man like Napoleon, who could lie so superbly when he tried, invent so bungling a hoax as one which involved a disarmament of Paris which did not take place, and the return of a sword which had never been seized?

General Thiébault says: "A few days after the 13 of Vendémiaire I happened to be at the office of the general staff when General Bonaparte came in. I can still see his little hat surmounted by a chance plume badly fastened on, his tricolor sash more than carelessly tied, his coat cut anyhow, and a sword which did not seem the kind of weapon to make his fortune. Flinging his hat on a large table in the middle of the room, he went up to an old general, named Krieg, a man of wonderful knowledge of military detail and author of a soldier's manual. He made him take a seat beside him at the table, and began questioning him, pen in hand, about a host of facts connected with the service and discipline. Some of his questions showed such complete ignorance of some of the most ordinary things that several of my comrades smiled. I was myself struck by the number of his questions, their order, and their rapidity, no less than by the way in which the answers were caught up, and often found to resolve themselves into new questions, which he deduced as consequences from them. But what struck me still more was the sight of a commander-in-chief perfectly indifferent about showing his subordinates how completely ignorant he was of various points of the business which the junior of them was supposed to know perfectly, and this raised him a hundred cubits in my eyes."

Here we see Napoleon drawn to the life. Instead of sitting down to gloat over his recent brilliant success, he had gone to work with the devouring zeal of a man who had done just enough to encourage him to do more. He did not idle away any time listening to congratulations. His cannon having opened one door in his advance, his eager eyes were already fixed far ahead on another, and his restless feet were in the path. In his garrison days he had not loved the details of his profession. Dull routine had been hateful, keeping him away from his books and his solitary musings. Now it was different. He saw the need of mastering everything which related to war, and, before he had even arrayed himself in new uniform, he had sought the old officer, Krieg, and was exhausting that source of information. In such direct, honest, practical way he came by that knowledge of war which justified him in saying in later years: " I know my profession thoroughly. Everything which enters into war I can do. If there is no powder, I can make it. If there are no cannon, I will cast them." He knew better how to construct a road or a bridge than any engineer in the army. He had the best eye for ground, could best estimate distances, could best tell what men could do on the march or in the field. Down to the pettiest details, he studied it all. " Do you know how the shirts which come in from the wash should be placed in the drawer? No? Then I will tell you. Put them always at the bottom of the drawer, else the same shirts will be constantly in use."

This advice he volunteered to the astonished matron who had charge of the soldiers' linen at the Invalides.

On October 12, 1795, Napoleon was restored to his grade in the artillery, and was named second commandant in the Army of the Interior. Ten days later, Barras having resigned his generalship, Napoleon became general of division and commander-in-chief of the Army of the Interior.

On October 26, 1795, the Convention finally adjourned; and on the next day it began to govern the country again with its two-thirds of the new legislatures (councils of Ancients and of Five Hundred) and its five regicide directors, — Barras, Carnot, Rewbell, Letourneur, and Larévellière-Lépaux.

Napoleon had become one of the dominant men of the State. In his every movement was the sense of his power. His position good, he lost no time in making it better. He took up suitable quarters in the *Rue des Capuchines*, surrounded himself with a brilliant staff, donned a handsome uniform, sported carriages and fine horses, and appeared in society.

He did not narrow himself to any clique or faction, but sought friends in all parties. He protected and conciliated royalists, called back to the service officers who had been retired, found good places for his friends, sent bread and wood to famishing families in the districts of the poor. At the same time he held down lawless outbreaks with a hand of iron, and wênt in person to close the great club of the Panthéon, the hot-bed of political agitation. He thoroughly reorganized the Army of the Interior and the National Guard, formed guards for the legislative councils and for the Directory, acting almost always on his own responsibility, and consulting his superiors but little.

Uncle Fesch came to town to be nominally Napoleon's secretary. Joseph received money and the promise of a consulship. Lucien was reinstalled in the fruitful commissary. Louis was once more lieutenant, and Jerome was placed in school in Paris. Of course Madame Letitia and the sisters basked in the sunshine also; for Napoleon could never do too much for his family. Nor did he overlook the Permons. According to Madame Junot, he had always liked them in the days of his poverty. Now that prosperity had come, he loved them better than ever: so much so indeed that he proposed that the Bonapartes should matrimonially absorb the entire Permon family. Jerome was to be married to Laura Permon, Pauline to Albert Permon, and Napoleon, himself, was to wed the widow Permon. According to Laura (afterward Madame Junot), this proposition was formally made by Napoleon, and laughed out of court by Madame Permon. The baffled matchmaker continued his visits, however, and frequently came to the house, accompanied by members of his staff.

One day as he stepped from his carriage, a poor woman held out toward him a dead child in her arms — the youngest of her six children. It had died of starvation, and the others would die if she could not get help. Napoleon was deeply moved, gave the woman kind words and money, and followed the matter up by getting her pensioned.

There was widespread squalor and misery in Paris during the winter of 1795, and Napoleon showed tact as well as kindness and firmness in preventing tumult.

Consider that little picture which is usually passed over so lightly: an angry mob of the unemployed, hungry, desperate, threatening, and on the brink of violence. They suffer, their wives starve, their children die in the garrets. Of course they blame the government. How could such misery exist where there was so much wealth and food, if the government was treating all fairly? Furious women stir about in the crowd lashing the upper classes with bitter tongues, and goading the men on to the point of rioting. Napoleon and his escort arrive. One fat fisherwoman bustles and bawls: "Don't mind these dandies in uniform with epaulettes on their shoulders! Don't disperse! They care not if the poor people starve, if they can but eat well and grow fat."

Think of Napoleon, the leanest of all lean men, "the thinnest and oddest object I ever laid eyes on," sitting there on his horse representing the unpopular "they"! "Madame, pray look at me: tell us which of us two is the fatter." The paunchy fisherwoman was stunned; the crowd laughed, and fell to pieces.

CHAPTER IX

THE young Republic found itself beset by the old governments of Europe. Because the Revolution proclaimed a new gospel, because it asserted the divine right of the people to govern themselves, because it made war upon caste and privilege, because it asserted the equal right of every citizen to take his share in the benefits as well as the burdens of society, because it threatened the tyranny of both Church and State, it was hated with intense bitterness by the kings, the high-priests, and the aristocracy of Europe.

In 1793 the first great league was formed to crush it, and to restore the Old Order in France. The strong member of this combination against human progress was Great Britain. Rendered secure from attack by her ocean girdle and her invincible fleets, she nevertheless dreaded what were called " French principles." In these principles she saw everything to dread ; for they were most insidious, and few were the men of the masses who, having learned what the new doctrine was, did not embrace it.

The common man, the average man, the full-grown man, the man who had not been stunted by the Orthodox pedagogue or priest, could not listen to the creed of the French republicans without feeling in his heart of hearts that it offered to the world an escape from the system which then enslaved it. Into Great Britain, in Germany, in Italy, in the Netherlands, in Russia itself, the shock with which the Old Order had fallen in France sent its vibrations — tremors which made the kings, princes, and privileged who dwelt in the upper stories of the social fabric quake with terror for the safety of the entire building.

The controlling man in England was William Pitt, able, proud, cold, ambitious. Personally honest, his policy sounded the deepest depravities of statecraft. Under his administration India was looted, ravaged, enslaved; Ireland coerced and dragooned; France outlawed because she dared to kill a king and call into life a republic; Europe bribed to a generation of war; freedom of thought, and speech, and conduct denied, and the cause of feudalism given a new lease of life. The aims and ends of this man's statesmanship were eternally bad; his methods would have warmed the heart of a Jesuit. He would not stoop to base deeds himself, would not speak the deliberately false word, would not convey the bribe, would not manufacture counterfeit money, would not arm the assassin, would not burn cities nor massacre innocent women and children. No, no! — he belonged to what Lord Wolseley complacently calls "the highest type of English gentleman," and his lofty soul would not permit him to do things like these himself. He would not corrupt Irish politicians to vote for the Union; but he would supply Castlereagh with the money from which the bribes were paid. He would not himself debauch editor or pamphleteer to slander a political foe, and deceive the British nation; but he supplied funds to those who did. Nor would he have put daggers into the hands of fanatics that they might do murder; but he protected and aided in England those who did. Not a political criminal himself, he used criminals and garnered the harvest of their crimes. Not himself capable of political theft, he countenanced the political thief, approved his success, and as a receiver of stolen goods, knowing them to have been stolen, haughtily added huge gains to his political wealth.

The same lofty-minded minister who had debauched Ireland — an enemy to Irish independence — made war upon free speech and political liberty in England, and exhausted the resources of diplomacy and force to stamp out the revolutionary movement of France. Under his sanction, his emissaries attacked the French Republic by forging and counterfeiting her paper currency; by arming her factions the one against the other; by corrupting her trusted leaders; by nerving the hand of the assassin when the corruptionist could not prevail. That London harbored the Bourbon and his paid assassin was due to the influence of William Pitt. That the Bourbon could land on the French coast the emissaries who came to rouse Vendeans to revolt, or to murder Bonaparte in Paris, was due to the position of William Pitt.

To the same eminent statesman was due the fact that for a whole generation British newspapers were so filled with falsehoods against France and Napoleon that an Englishman could not know the truth without leaving his country to hear it. To the same cause was due the league after league of Europe against France, which, beginning in 1793, reunited and renewed the struggle as often as opportunity offered until France was crushed, and the hands upon the clock of human progress put back a hundred years.

Without England, the coalitions against republican France would have had trifling results. It was England which furnished inexhaustible supplies of money; England which scoured the ocean with her fleets and maintained the blockade.

There had been a time when the French Revolution was not unpopular in Great Britain. This was when the reform movement was under the control of leaders who proclaimed their purpose to be to model the monarchy in France upon that of England. So long as professions of this sort were made, there was nothing to awaken distrust in staid, conservative England. Even aristocracy loves a fettered king. But when more radical men wrested leadership from the constitutionals, and boldly declared that the work of reform must strike deeper, must destroy feudalism root and branch, must consign a corpulent Church to the poverty whose beauties it preached, the lords and the bishops of Great Britain realized that the time had come when they must legislate, preach, pray, and fight against inovations which, if successful in France, would inevitably cross the narrow Channel.

All the machinery of repression was put to work. Books were written against the Revolution, and paid for by pensions drawn from the common treasury. Sermons were preached against the Revolution, and paid for in salaries drawn from the State funds. Parliament was set in motion to enact rigorously oppressive laws, and courts were set in motion to enforce the statutes. The political system in England might be ever so bad, but the people should not discuss it. Public meetings became criminal; public reading rooms, unlicensed, were criminal.

By the plain letter of the law of Christian England, if any citizen opened his house or room "for the purpose of reading books, or pamphlets, or newspapers," such citizen became a criminal and such house "a disorderly house." Before the citizen could permit others to use his books for pay, he must secure the approval and the license of bigoted Tory officials. No public meeting at all could be held unless a notice of such meeting signed by a householder, and stating the object of the meeting, should be inserted in a newspaper at least five days previous to the meeting. And even then the Tory justice of the peace was empowered to break up the meeting and imprison the persons attending it, if he thought the language held by the speaker of the meeting was calculated to bring the King or the government into contempt. Not even in the open fields could any lecture, speech, or debate be had without a license from a Tory official.

The government spy, the paid informer, went abroad, searching, listening, reporting, persecuting, and prosecuting. No privacy was sacred, no individual rights were respected, terrorism became a system. Paine's *Rights of Man* threw the upper classes into convulsions; his *Common Sense* became a hideous nightmare. Men were arrested like felons, tried like felons, punished like felons for reading pamphlets and books which are now such commonplace exponents of democracy that they are well-nigh forgotten. It was a time of misrule, of class legislation, of misery among the masses. It was a time when the laborer had almost no rights, almost no opportunities, almost no inducement to live, beyond the animal instinct which preserves the brute. It was a time when the landlord was almost absolute master of land and man; when the nobleman controlled the King, the House of Lords, and the House of Commons. It was a time when a duke might send half a dozen of his retainers to take seats in Parliament, or when he might advertise the seats for sale and knock them down to the highest bidder. It was a time when a close corporation of hereditary aristocrats controlled England like a private estate, taxed her people, dictated her laws, ruled her domestic and foreign policies, and made war or peace according to their own good pleasure. It was a time when it might have been said of most English towns as the town-crier reported to his Tory masters in reference to the village of Bolton — that he had diligently searched the place and had found in it neither *The Rights of Man* nor *Common Sense*.

There was one class which shared with the nobles the control of English national policies, and this was that of the great merchants and manufacturers. The exporter, The Prince of Trade, was a power behind the throne, and in foreign affairs his selfish greed dominated England's policy.

This governing class, as Napoleon said, looked upon the public, the people, as a milch cow; the only interest which they had in the cow was that it should not go dry. Offices, dignities, salaries, were handed down from sire to son. By hereditary right the government, its purse and its sword, belonged to these noble creatures whose merit frequently consisted solely in being the sons of their sires. To fill the ships which fought for the supremacy of this oligarchy, press-gangs prowled about the streets on the hunt for victims. Poor men, common laborers, and people of the lowlier sort were pounced upon by these press gangs, and forcibly carried off to that " hell on earth," a

British man-of-war of a century ago. One instance is recorded of a groom coming from the church where he had just been married, and who was snatched from the arms of his frantic bride and borne off — to return after many years to seek for a wife long since dead, in a neighborhood where he had long been forgotten.

In the army and in the fleet soldiers and sailors were lashed like dogs to keep them under ; and it was no uncommon thing for the victims to die from the effects of the brutal beating.

Considering all these things, the reader will understand why England made such determined war upon republican France. Against that country she launched armies and fleets, bribed kings and ministers, subsidized coalitions, straining every nerve year in and year out to put the Bourbons back on the throne, and to stay the advance of democracy. She temporarily succeeded. Her selfish King, nobles, and clericals held their grip, and postponed the day of reform. But the delay was dearly bought. The statesmanship of Pitt, Canning, Castlereagh, and Burke strewed Europe with dead men, and loaded nations with appalling debts. Upon land and sea, in almost every clime, men of almost every race were armed, enraged, and set to killing each other in order that the same few might continue to milk the cow.

In forming an opinion about Napoleon, it must be remembered that when he first came upon the scene he found these conditions already in existence, — Europe in league against republican France. With the creation of those conditions he had had nothing to do. Not his was the beginning of the Revolution ; not his the execution of Louis XVI. ; not his the quarrel with England. If

Great Britain and her allies afterward concentrated all their abuse, hatred, and hostility upon him, it was because he had become France; he had become, as Pitt himself said, "the child and champion of democracy"; he had become as Toryism throughout the world said, the "embodiment of the French Revolution."

This is the great basic truth of Napoleon's relations with Europe; and if we overlook it, we utterly fail to understand his career. In an evil hour for France, as well as for him, the allied kings succeeded in making the French forget her past. It was not till the Bourbons had returned to France, to Spain, to Italy; it was not till feudalism had returned to Germany with its privilege, its abuses, its stick for the soldier, its rack and wheel for the civilian; it was not till Metternich and his Holy Alliance had smashed with iron heel every struggle for popular rights on the Continent; it was not till Napoleon, dead at St. Helena, was remembered in vivid contrast to the soulless despots who succeeded him, that liberalism, not only in France, but throughout the world, realized how exceeding great had been the folly of the French when they allowed the kings to divorce the cause of Napoleon from that of the French people.

CHAPTER X

THE French Revolution was no longer guided by the men of ideals. With the downfall of Robespierre had come the triumph of those who bothered themselves with no dreams of social regeneration, but whose energies were directed with an eye single to their own advantage. Here and there was left a relic of the better type of revolutionist, " a rose of the garden left on its stalk to show where the garden had been"; but to one Carnot there were dozens of the brood of Barras.

The stern, single-minded, terribly resolute men of the Great Committee, who had worked fourteen hours a day in a plainly furnished room of the Tuileries, taking their lunch like common clerks as they stood about the table at which they wrote, — smiling perhaps, as they ate, at some jest of Barère, — with no thought of enriching themselves, intent only upon working out the problems of the Revolution in order that France might find her way to a future of glory and happiness — these men were gone, to come no more. Fiercely attached to variant creeds, they had warred among themselves, destroying each other, wearying the world with violence, and giving the scoundrels the opportunity to cry " Peace ! " and to seize control. True, the work of the Revolution had been done too well to be wholly undone. Feudalism had been torn up root and

branch; it could never be so flourishing again. Absolutism, royal and papal infallibility, had been trodden into
the mire where they belonged; they might be set in place
again, but they would never more look quite so dazzling,
nor be worshipped with quite such blindness of devotion.
Great principles of civil and religious liberty had been
planted; they could never be wholly plucked out. The
human race had for once seen a great people fill its lungs
and its brain with the air and the inspiration of absolute
freedom from priest, king, aristocrat, precedent, conven-
tionality, and caste-made law; the spectacle would never
be forgotten, nor the example cease to blaze as a beacon,
lighting the feet and kindling the hopes of the world.

But, for the time, the triumph of the venal brought with
it shame and disaster to the entire body politic. The
public service corrupt, the moral tone of society sank.
Ideals came into contempt, idealists into ridicule. The
"man of the world," calling himself practical, and prid-
ing himself on his ability to play to the baser passions
of humanity, laughed revolutionary dogmas aside, put
revolutionary simplicity and honesty out of fashion, made
a jest of duty and patriotism, and prostituted public office
into a private opportunity.

Hordes of adventurers, male and female, stormed the
administration, took it, and looted it. The professional
money-getter controlled the Directory: the contractor,
stock-jobber, fund-holder, peculator, and speculator. In
all matters pertaining to finance, the Bourse was the
government. The nobility of the Old Order had monop-
olized the State's favors under the kings; the rich men
of the middle class, the Bourgeoisie, did so now. The
giver and the taker of bribes met and smiled upon each

other ; the lobbyist hunted his prey and found it. Once again the woman, beautiful, shrewd, and unchaste, became greater than the libertine official who had surrendered to her charms ; and she awarded fat contracts, trafficked in pardons and appointments, and influenced the choice of army chiefs.

The government no longer concerned itself with chimeras, dreams of better men and methods, visions of beneficent laws dealing impartially with an improving mass of citizenship. Just as the Grand Monarch's court had revelled in the fairyland of joy and light and plenty at Versailles while peasants in the provinces fed on grass and roots, dying like flies in noisome huts and garrets ; just as the Pompadour of Louis the XV. had squandered national treasures upon diamonds, palaces, endless festivities, while the soldiers of France starved and shivered in Canada, losing an empire for want of ammunition to hold it ! so, under the Directory, Barras held court in splendor, while workmen died of want in the garrets of Paris ; and he feasted with his Madame Tallien or his Josephine Beauharnais, while the soldiers on the Rhine or on the Alps faced the winter in rags, and were forced to rob to keep from starvation.

This wretched state of things had not reached its climax at the period I am treating, but the beginnings had been made, the germs were all present and active.

In this revival of mock royalty, Barras outshone his peers. He was of most noble descent, his family " as old as the rocks of Provence "; his manners redolent of the Old Régime, and much more so his morals. His honesty, like his patriotism, delighted in large bribes ; and he never by any chance told the truth if a lie would do as well. His person was tall and commanding; his voice, in a crisis, had sometimes rung out like a trumpet and rallied the wavering, for the man was brave and capable of energetic action. But he was a sensualist, base to the core, vulgar in mind and heart, true to no creed, and capable of no high, noble, strenuous rôle. Rotten himself, he believed that other men were as degraded. As to women, they never stirred a thought in him which would not, if worded in the ears of a true woman, have mantled her cheek with shame.

This was the man to whom Napoleon had attached himself; this was the man in whose house Josephine was living when Napoleon met her. Barras was the strong man of the hour; Barras had places to give and favors to divide; Barras was the candle around which fluttered moths large and small; and to this light had come the adventurer from Corsica, and the adventuress from Martinique. Usually it is the candle which singes the moth; in this case it was the moths which put out the candle.

Napoleon had become a thorough man of the world. Hard experience had driven away sentimental illusions. The visionary of the Corsican sea-lulled grotto, the patriotic dreamer of the Brienne garden-harbor, had died some time ago. The man who now commanded the Army of the Interior was different altogether. Reading, experience, observation, the stern teachings of necessity, had taught him to believe that the Italian proverb was true, "One must not be too good, if one would succeed." He believed now that rigid principles were like a plank strapped across the breast: not troublesome when the path led through the open, but extremely detrimental to speed in going through a wood. He had studied the lives of great men, — Alexander, Cæsar, Richelieu, Frederick, Cromwell, — and the study had not tended to his elevation in matters of method. He had studied the politics of the world, the records of national aggrandizement, the inner secrets of government, and his conceptions of public honor had not been made more lofty. He had come to believe that interest governed all men; that no such things as disinterested patriotism, truth, honor, and virtue existed on earth. He believed that life was a fight, a scramble, an unscrupulous rush for place, power, riches; and that the strongest, fleetest, most artful would win — especially if they would take all the short cuts. Idealogists he despised.

Cold, calculating, disillusioned, he took the world as he found it. New men and women he could not create, nor could he create other conditions, moral, social, political, or material. He must recognize facts, must deal with actualities. If bad men alone could give him what he wanted, he must court the bad men. If bad men only could do the work he wanted done, he must use the bad men. Barras, Fréron, Tallien, being in power, he would get all he could out of them, just as he had exhausted the friendship of Robespierre and Salicetti, and just as he afterward used Fouché and Talleyrand.

Nor was he more scrupulous in his relations with women. He must have known the character of Madame Tallien, mistress and then wife of the man of July, and now mistress of Barras; but nevertheless he sought her acquaintance, and cultivated her friendship. Knowing the character of Madame Tallien, he must have felt that her bosom friend, Madame Beauharnais, could not be wholly pure. He saw them together night and day, he witnessed their influence with Barras; it is impossible that he did not hear some of the talk which coupled their names with that of the libertine Director. He must have heard of the early life of this creole widow, whose husband, the Viscount Beauharnais, had separated from her, accusing her of scandalous immorality. He must have heard that after her husband had been guillotined, and she herself released from prison by the overthrow of Robespierre, she had begun a life of fashionable dissipation. He must have heard the talk which coupled her name with that of such women as Madame Tallien, Madame Hamelin, and a dozen other Aspasias of like kind. The names of her lovers were bruited about like those of Madame Tallien, one of these lovers having been General Hoche. Now that she, a widow just out of prison, having no visible income or property, and whose children had been apprenticed at manual labor, sported a magnificent establishment, wore most expensive toilets, led the life of the gayest of women,—the favorite of those who had recently beheaded her husband,—the world classed her with those with whom she was most intimate, and thought her morals could not be purer than those of her associates. Justly or unjustly, she was regarded as one of the lights of the harem of Barras; and people were beginning to hint that she and her extravagance had become a burden of which the Director would gladly be rid.

Napoleon had never come under the spell of such society as that which he had now entered. That fleeting glimpse of polite society which he had caught at Valence bore no comparison to this. In his limited experience he had not met such women as Madame Tallien and Josephine. He moved in a new sphere. Around him was the brilliance of a court. In apartments adorned with every ornament and luxury, night was turned into day; and with music, the dance, the song, the feast, men and women gave themselves to pleasure. He, the unsocial man of books and camps, was not fitted to shine in this social circle. He was uncouth, spoke the language with an unpleasant accent, had no graces of manner or speech, had nothing imposing in figure or bearing, and he felt almost abashed in the high presence of these elegant nullities of the drawing-room.

Shy, ill at ease, he was not much noticed and not much liked by the ladies of the directorial court, with one exception — Josephine. Either because of the alleged return of the sword, and the good impression then made, or because of her natural tact and kindness of heart, Madame Beauharnais paid the uncouth soldier those little attentions which attract, and those skilful compliments which flatter, and almost before he was aware of it Napoleon was fascinated. Here was a woman to take a man off his feet, to inflame him with passion. She was no longer young, but she was in the glorious Indian summer of her charms. Her perfect form was trained in movements of grace. Her musical voice knew its own melody, and made the most of it. Her large, dark eyes with long lashes were soft and dreamy. Her mouth was sweet and sensuous. Her chestnut hair was elegantly disordered, her shoulders and bust hid behind no covering, and of her little feet and shapely ankles just enough was seen to please the eye and stimulate the imagination.

As to her costume and her general toilet, it was all that studied art and cultivated taste could do for generous nature. Madame Tallien was more beautiful and more queenly than Josephine, many others excelled her in wit, accomplishments, and mere good looks ; but it may be doubted whether any lady of that court, or other courts, ever excelled the gentle Josephine in the grace, the tact, the charm, which unites in the make-up of a fascinating society woman.

Add to this that she was sensual, elegantly voluptuous, finished in the subtle mysteries of coquetry, fully alive to the power which the physically tempting woman exerts over the passions of men, and it can be better understood how this languishing but artful widow of thirty-three intoxicated Napoleon Bonaparte, the raw provincial of twenty-seven.

That he *was* madly infatuated, there can be no doubt. He loved her, and he never wholly ceased to love her. Never before, never afterward, did he meet a woman who inspired him with a feeling at all like that he felt for her. If he did not know at that time what she had been, he knew after the marriage what she continued to be, and he made a desperate effort to break the spell. He could not completely do so. She might betray his confidence, laugh at his love-letters, neglect his appeals, squander his money, sell his secrets, tell him all sorts of falsehoods, underrate his value, misconceive his character, and befoul his honor with shameless sin ; but against her repentance and her childlike prayers for pardon, the iron of his nature became as wax. Before those quivering lips, before those tear-filled eyes, before that tenderly sweet voice, all broken with grief, he could rarely stand. "I will divorce her!" he said fiercely to his brothers, when they put before him proofs of her guilt, after the

Egyptian campaign. But through the locked door came the sobs of the stricken wife, came her plaintive pleadings. "*Mon ami!*" she called softly, called hour after hour, piteously knocking at the door. It was too much; the cold resolution melted; the soldier was once more the lover, and the door flew open. When the brothers came next day to talk further about the divorce, they found little Josephine, happy as a bird, sitting on Napoleon's knee, and nestling in his arms.

"Listen, Bourrienne!" exclaimed Napoleon, joyously, on his return to Paris from Marengo, "listen to the shouts of the people! It is sweet to my ears, this praise of the French — as sweet as the voice of Josephine!"

Even when cold policy demanded the divorce, it was he who wept the most. "Josephine! my noble Josephine! The few moments of happiness I have ever enjoyed, I owe to you!"

And in the closing scene at St. Helena it was the same. The dying man thought no more of the Austrian woman. Even in his delirium, the wandering memory recalled and the fast freezing lips named "Josephine!"

Yet calculation played its part in Napoleon's marriage, as it did in everything he undertook. He was made to believe that Josephine had fortune and high station in society. He weighed these advantages in considering the match. Both the fortune and the social position would be valuable to him. In fact, Josephine had no fortune, nor any standing in society. Men of high station were her visitors; their wives were not. All the evidence tends to show that Barras arranged the match between his two hangers-on, and that the appointment to the command of the Army of Italy became involved in the negotiation. Napoleon received this coveted commission March 7, 1796; two days later the marriage occurred.

On the register both Napoleon and Josephine misrepresented their ages. He had made himself one year older, and she three years younger, than the facts justified. There was a difference of six years between them, and Madame Letitia angrily predicted that they would have no children.

In forty-eight hours after the marriage, Napoleon set out for Italy. At Marseilles he stopped, spending a few days with his mother and sisters. On March 22, 1796, he was at Nice, the headquarters of the army with which he was to win immortality.

Almost at every pause in his journey Napoleon had dashed off hot love-letters to the languid Josephine whom he left at Paris. The bride, far from sharing the groom's passion, did not even understand it — was slightly bored by it, in fact. Now that he had gone off to the wars, she relapsed into her favorite dissipations, she and her graceful daughter Hortense.

Madame Junot gives an account of a ball at the banker Thellusson's, which not only illustrates the social status of Josephine, but also the mixed conditions which the Revolution had brought about in society.

Thellusson was a rich man, and not a nobleman; one of those unfortunate creatures who, in the eyes of lank-pursed aristocrats, have more money than respectability. In our day he would be called a plutocrat, and he would hire some bankrupt imbecile with a decayed title to marry his idiotic daughter. For Thellusson, just like a plutocrat with more money than respectability, craved what he did not have, and was giving entertainments to foist himself up the social height. Of course he crowded his sumptuous rooms with a miscellany of people, most of whom despised him, while they feasted with him. It was one of these entertainments, a ball, at which took place the incidents Madame Junot relates.

It seems that a captious, querulous, nose-in-the-air *Grand Dame*, Madame de D., had been decoyed to this Thellusson ball by the assurance of the Marquis de Hautefort that she would meet none but the best people — her friends of the Old Régime. Very anxious to see former glories return, and very eager to meet her friends of this bewitching Old Régime, Madame de D. not only came to the ball herself, but consented to bring her daughter, Ernestine. As all high-born people should, Madame de D. and her daughter Ernestine arrived late. The ballroom was brilliant, but crowded. The high-born late comers could find no seats, an annoyance which the Marquis de Hautefort, who was on the lookout for them, at once tried to remedy.

A sylph-like young lady, who had been divinely dancing, was being led to her place beside another beautifully dressed woman who seemed to be an elder sister. So charming was the look of these seeming sisters that even Madame de D. admired.

"Who are those persons?" she inquired of the Marquis, before the seats had been brought.

"What!" he exclaimed, "is it possible that you do not recognize Viscountess Beauharnais, now Madame Bonaparte, and her daughter Hortense? Come, let me seat you beside her ; there is a vacant place by her, and you can renew your acquaintance."

Madame de D. stiffened with indignation and made no reply. Taking the old Marquis by the arm, she led him to a side room and burst forth : "Are you mad? Seat me beside Madame Bonaparte ! Ernestine would be obliged to make the acquaintance of her daughter. I will never connect myself with such persons — people who disgrace their misfortunes ! "

Presently there entered the ballroom a woman, queen-like, lovely as a dream, dressed in a plain robe of Indian muslin, a gold belt about her waist, gold bracelets on her arms, and a red cashmere shawl draped gracefully about her shoulders.

"Eh ! my God ! who is that ? " cried Madame de D.

"That is Madame Tallien," quoth the Marquis.

The high-born relic of the Old Régime flamed with wrath, and was beginning a tirade against the Marquis for having dared to bring her to such a place, when the door flew open, and in burst a wave of perfume and — Madame Hamelin, the fastest woman of the fastest set in Paris. All the young men crowded around her.

" And now in heaven's name, Marquis, who may *that* be ? "

At the words demurely uttered, " It is Madame Hamelin," the high-born Madame de D. unfurled the red banner of revolt. It was the one shock too much.

"Come, Ernestine ! Put on your wrap ! We must go, child. I can't stand it any longer. To think that the Marquis assured me I should meet my former society here ! And for the last hour I have been falling from the frying-pan into the fire ! Come, Ernestine ! "

And out they went.

CHAPTER XI

THE year 1796 found the Republic in sorry plight. The treasury was empty, labor unemployed, business at a standstill. So much paper money, genuine and counterfeit, had been issued, that it almost took a cord of assignats to pay for a cord of wood. Landlords who had leased houses before the Revolution, and who had now to accept pay in paper, could hardly buy a pullet with a year's rental of a house. There was famine, stagnation, maladministration. The hope of the Republic was its armies. Drawn from the bosom of the aroused people at the time when revolutionary ardor was at its height, the soldiers, after three years of service, were veterans who were still devoted to republican ideals. Great victories had given them confidence, and they only needed proper equipment and proper direction to accomplish still greater results. At the end of 1795, Moreau commanded the army of the Rhine, Jourdan that of the Sambre and Meuse, Hoche that of the West. Schérer commanded the Army of Italy, where, on November 24, 1795, he beat the Austrians and Sardinians in the battle of Loano. He did not follow up his victory, however, and the Directory complained of him. On his part he complained of the Directory. They sent him no money with which to pay his troops, no clothing for them, and only bread to feed

135

them on. The commissary was corrupt; and the Directory, which was corrupt, winked at the robbery of the
troops by thievish contractors. Schérer, discouraged,
wished to resign. It was to this ill-fed, scantily clothed,
unpaid, and discouraged army that Napoleon was sent;
and it was this army which he thrilled with a trumpet-
like proclamation.

"Soldiers! You are naked, badly fed. The government owes you much; it can give you nothing. Your
endurance, and the courage you have shown, do you credit,
but gain you no advantage, get you no glory. I will lead
you into the most fertile plains in the world. Rich provinces, great cities, will be in your power ; and there you
will find honor, glory, and riches. Soldiers of Italy, can
you be found wanting in courage?"

The army was electrified by this brief address, which
touched masterfully the chords most likely to respond.
Courage, pride, patriotism, and cupidity were all invoked
and aroused. For the first time the soldiers of the Revolution were tempted with the promise of the loot of the
vanquished. "Italy is the richest land in the world; let
us go and despoil it." Here, indeed, was the beginning
of a new chapter in the history of republican France.

Not without a purpose did Napoleon so word his proclamation. There had been an understanding between
himself and the Directory that his army must be self-
sustaining; he must forage on the enemy as did Wallen-
stein in the Thirty Years' War. The government had
exerted itself to the utmost for Napoleon, and had supplied
him with a small sum of specie and good bills; but, this
done, he understood that the Directors could do no more.
As rapidly as possible he put his army in marching order,

NAPOLEON

From a print in the collection of Mr. W. C. Crane. The original engraving by G. Fiesinger, after a miniature by Jean-Baptiste-Paulin Guerin. Deposited in the National Library, Paris, 1799

and then marched. From the defensive attitude in which Schérer had left it, he passed at once to the offensive. The plan of campaign which Napoleon, the year before, had drawn up for the revolutionary committee, and which, when forwarded to the army, Kellermann had pronounced "the dream of a madman," was about to be inaugurated by the lunatic himself.

The generals of division in the Army of Italy were older men, older officers than Napoleon, and they resented his appointment. Masséna, Augereau, Sérurier, Laharpe, Kilmaine, Cervoni, but especially the two first, murmured discontentedly, calling Napoleon, "one of Barras's favorites," a "mere street general," a "dreamer" who had "never been in action."

Napoleon, aware of this feeling, adopted the wisest course. He drew around himself the line of ceremony, repelled with steady look all inclination toward familiarity, abruptly cut short those who ventured to give advice, adopted a stern, imperative, distant manner, took the earliest opportunity of showing his absolute self-confidence and his superiority, indulged in no levity or dissipatiou, and issued his orders in a tone so laconic and authoritative that, after his first formal interview with his division commanders at Albenga, his power over them was established. On leaving the tent of the new chief, Augereau remarked to Masséna, "That little —— of a general frightened me," and Masséna confessed to the same experience.

The military plans of the Directory, emanating from such men as Carnot and Bonaparte, were bold and practical. Austria, which had invaded France from the Rhine, was to be held in check there by Moreau and Jourdan at the same time that she was assailed by way of Italy. The three armies of the republic, operating far apart, were to coöperate in general design, and were finally to converge upon Vienna. Incidentally to this plan of campaign, Genoa was to be brought to terms for violations of neutrality; the Pope was to be punished for his constant encouragement to La Vendée and the royalists generally; and also because he had screened the assassins of the French ambassador, Basseville. Sardinia (whose king was father-in-law to the Counts of Provence and Artois, afterward respectively Louis XVIII. and Charles X.) was to be humbled for its alliance with Austria against France.

The armies opposed to Napoleon were commanded by old men, excellent officers so long as war was conducted with a sword in one hand and a book of etiquette in the other. Opposed to a man like Napoleon, who set all rules at naught, and put into practice a new system, they were sadly outclassed and bewildered.

Napoleon intended to force his way into Italy at the point where the Alps and the Apennines join. From Savona on the Mediterranean to Cairo it is about nine miles by a road practicable for artillery. From Cairo carriage roads led into Italy. At no other point could the country be entered save by crossing lofty mountains. Therefore Napoleon's plan was to turn the Alps instead of crossing them, and to enter Piedmont through the pass of Cadibona.

Putting his troops in motion, he threw forward toward Genoa a detachment under Laharpe. The Austrian commander, thinking that Bonaparte's plan was to seize Genoa, divided his forces into three bodies, — the Sardinians on the right at Ceva, the centre under D'Argenteau marching toward Montenotte, and the right under Beaulieu himself moved from Novi upon Voltri, a town within ten miles of Genoa. Between these three divisions there was no connection; and, on account of the mountainous country, it was difficult for them to communicate with each other, or be concentrated.

On April 10, 1796, Beaulieu attacked Cervoni, leading the van of the French in their march toward Genoa, and drove him.

But D'Argenteau, who had advanced on Montenotte, was less fortunate. Colonel Rampon, who commanded twelve hundred Frenchmen at this point, realized the immense importance of checking the Austrian advance, to prevent it from falling upon the flank of Napoleon's army as it moved along the Corniche road. Throwing himself into the redoubt of Montelegino, Rampon barred the way of the Austrians with heroic gallantry. Three times he threw back the assault of the entire Austrian-Sardinian division. During the combat he called upon his little band to swear that they would die in the redoubt rather than give it up, and the oath was taken with the greatest enthusiasm.

Had D'Argenteau continued his efforts, the oath-bound defenders would probably have been exterminated, but he did not persevere. He drew off his forces in the evening, to wait till next morning, and then renew the attack. Morning came, but so did Napoleon. D'Argenteau looked around him, and lo! he was a lost man. Three French divisions enveloped the one division of their foe, and to the discomfited Austrians was left the dismal alternative of surrender or a desperate fight against overwhelming odds. The battle was fought, and Napoleon won his first individual and undivided triumph, the victory of Montenotte. The enemy lost colors and cannon, a thousand slain, and two thousand prisoners.

Napoleon had kept the divisions of his army so skilfully placed that each could support the other, and all could concentrate. Thus he crushed the Austrian centre, which could get no support from its two wings, and with his small force triumphed over the larger armies opposed to him.

But in this his first campaign, Napoleon's tactics presented that weak point which was in the end to be his ruin ; he risked so much that one slip in his combination was too likely to bring about a Waterloo. Had Rampon been merely an average officer, or had D'Argenteau been a Rampon, or had the gallant twelve hundred been merely average soldiers, the road through the pass at Montenotte would have been cleared, the Austrians would have been on Napoleon's flank, and only a miracle could have saved him from disaster. But Napoleon was young, and luck was with him : the time was far distant when he himself was to be angrily amazed at seeing Fortune mock his best combinations, and trivial accidents ruin his campaigns.

Swiftly following up his advantage, Napoleon pushed forward to Cairo, to wedge his army in between the separated wings of the enemy. At Dego, lower down the valley of the Bormida, in which the French were now operating, were the rallying Austrians, guarding the road from Acqui into Lombardy. To the left of the French were the Sardinians in the gorges of Millesimo, blocking the route from Ceva into Piedmont. It was necessary for Napoleon to strike the enemy at both points, drive them farther apart, so that he might combat each in detail.

On April 13 the French moved forward, Augereau to
the attack of the Sardinians, Masséna and Laharpe against
the Austrians. The Sardinians were strongly posted on
high ground, but the onset of the French carried all before it. So impetuous had been the rush of Augereau,
that one of the divisions of the enemy under General Provera was cut off. That brave soldier threw himself into
the old castle of Cossario, and could not be dislodged.
Napoleon in person came up and directed three separate
assaults, which were heavily repulsed. Provera was then
left in possession, the castle blockaded, and the strength
of the French reserved for the remaining divisions of the
Sardinian army. On the next day (April 14) General
Colli, commander-in-chief of the Sardinian army, made
every effort to relieve Provera, but was repulsed and
driven back upon Ceva, farther than ever from the Austrians. Provera then surrendered.

While the battle raged at Millesimo, Laharpe had
crossed the Bormida, his troops wading up to their waists,
and attacked the Austrian flank and rear at Dego ; at the
same time Masséna struck the line of communication between the two armies on the heights of Biastro. Both
attacks succeeded ; and as Colli retreated on Turin, Beaulieu drew off toward Milan.

On the morning after these victories a fresh Austrian
division, which had come from Voltri on the seacoast to
join the main army, reached Dego, and drove out the
few French they found there. The appearance of this
force in his rear gave Napoleon a surprise, and a feeling of alarm ran through his army. He immediately
marched upon the town, and gave battle. The French
were twice beaten off. A third charge led by Lanusse,

waving his hat on the point of his sword, carried all before it.

For his gallantry in this action, Lanusse was made brigadier general on the recommendation of Napoleon, under whose eyes the splendid charge had been made. Lieutenant Colonel Lannes distinguished himself greatly also, and Napoleon made him colonel on the field.

The result of these battles were nine thousand of the enemy taken prisoners, other thousands killed, besides thirty cannon taken, and a great quantity of baggage. Napoleon was now master of the valley of the Bormida, and of all the roads into Italy. It was his duty, for Carnot had so ordered, to leave the Sardinians and pursue the Austrians. He took just the opposite course. Turning to his left, he entered the gorges of Millesimo, and followed the road to Piedmont. Laharpe's division was left to watch the Austrians. On April 28 the French were in full march upon Mondovi. When they reached the height of Mount Lemota, " the richest provinces in the world" lay beneath them, stretching from the foot of the height as far as eye could reach. The troops, so wonderfully led and so daringly fought, were in raptures with themselves and their chief.

As they looked down upon the lovely Italian plains, dotted with towns and silvered with rivers, they broke into enthusiastic cheers for the young Napoleon. For him and for them it was a proud moment. " Hannibal forced the Alps; we have turned them."

Passing the Tanaro, the French entered the plains, and for the first time cavalry was in demand. On April 22 the Sardinians made a stubborn fight at Mondovi. They had repulsed Sérurier with heavy loss on the day before;

but now Sérurier was joined by Masséna and the Sardinians routed.   The Piedmontese cavalry, however,
turned upon the French horse, which had pursued too far,
and General Stengel, its commander, was killed.   Murat,
at the head of three regiments, dashed against the Sardinian cavalry with such reckless courage that they broke.
The Sardinians, defeated at all points, lost three thousand,
slain or prisoners, eight cannon, ten stand of colors.   Colli
requested an armistice which Napoleon refused to grant.
The French continued their advance upon Turin.   The
king of Sardinia, Amadeus, wished to prolong the
struggle ; but his courtiers clamored for peace, and prevailed.   Overtures were made, Napoleon gladly accepted.
Such terror had Napoleon inspired by his rapid and
brilliant victories that he practically dictated his own
terms to the king.   The "Keys of the Alps," Coni and
Tortona, besides Alessandria and other fortresses, were
surrendered to him pending negotiations, and the immense
magazines they contained were appropriated to the use
of the French army.   The Sardinian army was to be
retired from the field, and the roads of Piedmont were to
be opened to the French.   The Austrian alliance should
cease, and the royalist émigrés from France should be
expelled.   This armistice was signed April 29, 1796.   As
to a definitive peace, plenipotentiaries were to be sent at
once to Paris to conclude it.

Napoleon had violated both the letter and the spirit of
his instructions in virtually making peace with the king
of Sardinia.   The Directory, many republicans in France,
and many in the army maintained that Amadeus, a kins-
man of the Bourbons, should have been dethroned, and
his country revolutionized.   Augereau and others boldly

declared their disapproval of Napoleon's course. He himself was serenely certain that he had done the proper thing, and he gave himself no concern about the grumblers.

To Paris he sent his brilliant cavalry-officer, Murat, with twenty-one flags taken from the enemy. To his troops he issued a stirring address, recounting their great achievements, and inspiring them to still greater efforts.

With hands freed, Napoleon turned upon the Austrians. Deceiving them as to the point at which he would cross the Po, they prepared for him at one place while he dashed at another. While Beaulieu waited at Valenza, Napoleon was crossing at Placenza, May 7, 1796. On the next day an Austrian division arrived at Fombio, a league from Placenza. Napoleon attacked and routed it, taking two thousand prisoners and all their cannon. Beaulieu put his troops in motion, hoping to catch the French in the act of crossing the river.

As the Austrians, preceded by a regiment of cavalry, approached, they struck the advance posts of Laharpe. That general rode forward to reconnoitre, and, returning by a different road, was fired upon and killed by his own troops, in almost precisely the same manner as the great Confederate soldier, Stonewall Jackson, was slain at Chancellorsville.

The Austrians, realizing that they were too late, drew off toward Lodi. On May 10, Napoleon overtook them there. The town was on that side of the river Adda on which were the French, and Napoleon drove out the small detachment of Austrians which held it.

On the opposite side of the river Beaulieu had stationed twelve thousand infantry, two thousand horse, and twenty

cannon to dispute the passage. A single wooden bridge,
which the retreating Austrians had not had time to burn,
spanned the river.   In the face of an army sixteen thousand strong, and twenty pieces of artillery ready to rain
a torrent of iron on the bridge, Napoleon determined to
pass.   Behind the walls of the town of Lodi the French
army was sheltered. Napoleon, under fire, went out to
the bank of the river to explore the ground and form his
plan.   Returning, he selected six thousand grenadiers, and
to these he spoke brief words of praise and encouragement, holding them ready, screened behind the houses of
the town, to dash for the bridge at the word.   But he
had also sent his cavalry up the stream to find a ford to
cross, and to come upon the Austrian flank.   Meanwhile
his own artillery rained a hail of deadly missiles upon the
Austrian position, making it impossible for them to approach the bridge.   The anxious eyes of Napoleon at last
saw that his cavalry had forded the river, and were turning the Austrians' flank.   Quick as a flash the word went
to the waiting grenadiers, and with a shout of " Live the
Republic," they ran for the bridge.   A terrific fire from
the Austrian batteries played upon the advancing column,
and the effect was so deadly that it hesitated, wavered,
seemed about to break.   The French generals sprang to
the front, — Napoleon, Lannes, Masséna, Berthier, Cervoni, — rallied the column, and carried it over the bridge.
Lannes was the first man across, Napoleon the second.
The Austrian gunners were bayoneted before the infantry
could come to their support.   In a few minutes the Austrian army was routed.

The moral effect of this victory, " the terrible passage
of the bridge of Lodi," as Napoleon himself called it,

was tremendous. Beaulieu afterward told Graham that
had Napoleon pushed on, he might have taken Mantua
without difficulty — no preparations for its defence having then been made. The Austrians lost heart, uncovered Milan in their retreat ; and, five days after the
battle, Napoleon entered the Lombard capital, under a
triumphal arch and amid thousands of admiring Italians.

It was after this battle that some of the soldiers got
together and gave Napoleon the name of the " Little
Corporal," an affectionate nickname which clung to him,
in the army, throughout his career. His personal bravery
at Lodi, and his readiness to share the danger, made a
profound impression on his troops, and when he next
appeared he was greeted with shouts of " Live the Little
Corporal."

Napoleon asked a Hungarian prisoner, an old officer,
what he now thought of the war. The prisoner, not
knowing that Napoleon himself was the questioner, replied : " There is no understanding it at all. You
French have a young general who knows nothing about
the rules of war. To-day he is in your front, to-morrow
in the rear. Now he is on your left, and then on your
right. One does not know where to place one's self.
Such violation of the rules is intolerable."

Upon the victor himself Lodi made a lasting impression ; it was the spark, as he said afterward, " which
kindled a great ambition." Already Napoleon had begun
to levy contributions and to seize precious works of art.
The Duke of Parma, pleading for peace and protection,
had been required to pay $400,000, to furnish sixteen
hundred horses and large quantities of provisions. His
gallery was stripped of twenty of its best paintings, one of

which was the "Jerome" of Correggio. The Duke offered
$200,000 to redeem this painting, but Napoleon refused.
The offence which this duke had committed was his
adhesion to the coalition against France, and his con-
tributing three thousand soldiers to aid in the glorious
work of maintaining feudalism.

In France the effect of Napoleon's victories upon the
excitable, glory-loving people was prodigious. His name
was on every tongue. Crowds gathered around the
bulletins, and the streets rang with acclamations. Murat
and Junot, bringing to Paris the captured colors, were
given enthusiastic ovations by government and people.
But the Directors began to be uneasy. They would have
been more or less than human had they relished the
autocratic manner in which Napoleon behaved. He had
ignored their plans and their instructions. He had
developed an imperiousness which brooked no control.
His fame was **dwarfing** all others to an extent which gave
rise to unpleasant forebodings. All things considered,
the Directors thought it would be a good idea to divide
the Italian command. To that effect they wrote Napoleon. In reply he offered to resign. A partner he
would not have: he must be chief, or nothing. The Directors dared not make such an issue with him at a time
when all France was in raptures over his triumphs; and
they yielded.

Napoleon has been heartily abused because he stripped the art galleries of Italy of their gems — statuary and paintings. French writers of the royalist school swell the cry and emphasize the guilt. Lanfrey, particularly, calls the world to witness the fact that he hangs his head in shame, so much is his conscience pricked by Napoleon's seizure of pictures. How absurd is all this! If to the victor belong the spoils, where is the line to be drawn? If one may take the purse of the vanquished, his jewels, his house, his lands, why are his pictures sacred? If the civilized world insists upon maintaining the trained soldier, and continues to hunger after the alleged glories of wars of conquest, we must get accustomed to the results. Wars of conquest are waged for very practical purposes. We combat the enemy because he happens to be in possession of something which we want and which we mean to have. When we have taken the trouble to go up against this adversary, prepared to smite him hip and thigh, in robust, Old-Testament style, and have prevailed against him by the help of the Lord, shall we not Biblically despoil him of all such things as seem good in our own eyes? Are we to allow the vanquished heathen — heathen because vanquished — to choose for us those things which we shall take with us when we go back home? If mine enemy has a golden crown, or a golden throne, the appearance and the weight and the fineness of which please me exceedingly, shall I not take it? If I happen to be a king, shall I not include such trophies among my "crown jewels" in my strong "Tower of London"?

And if by chance there should be in the land of mine enemy, the land which the Lord has given me as the con-

quest of my sword, a diamond of surpassing size and
purity, — a gem so rich and rare that the mouth of the
whole world waters at the mere mention of Kohinoor —
the heathen name thereof, — shall I not take this rare gem
from among unappreciative heathen, and carry it to my
own land, where people worship the only true and living
God and cultivate ennobling fondness for the best diamonds? If I should chance to be king of my native land,
shall I not gladden the heart of my queen by the gift of
the marvellous gem, so that she may wear it upon her
royal brow, and so outshine all royal ladies whomsoever?

Between such trophies as these and paintings, Napoleon
could see no difference in principle. Numerous are the
historians, tracking dutifully after other historians, who
have been, these many years, heaping abuse upon Napoleon concerning those Italian paintings. It so happens
that while the present chronicler has been engaged with
this book, the world has witnessed quite a variety of warfare. There has been battle and conquest in China, South
Africa, the Philippines; and the Christian soldiers of
Europe and America have prevailed mightily against the
heathen and the insurgent. There has been much victory
and much loot; and with the record of what our Christian soldiers took in Africa, Asia, and the islands of the
sea fresh in mind, it seems to me that we might all become silent about Napoleon's Italian "works of art."

Lombardy, in 1796, was a possession of the house of
Austria, and was nominally ruled by the Archduke Ferdinand, who lived at Milan in magnificent state. The victorious approach of the French filled him and his court

with terror, and he called on the Church for help. The
priests aroused themselves, put forth the arm ecclesiastic,
and endeavored to avert the storm by religious ceremonies. The bones of the saints were brought out, processions formed, and street parades held. Also there were
chants, prayers, mystical invocations. Heaven was implored to interfere and save the city. Heaven, as usual,
had no smiles for the weak; the angels, who save no
doves from hawks, no shrieking virgin from the ravisher,
concerned themselves not at all (so far as any one could
see) with the terrors of the priests and the nobles of
Milan. The Archduke with his Duchess, and the ever
faithful few, deserted his beautiful capital; and Count
Melzi went forth with a deputation to soften the wrath
of the conqueror.

Napoleon's terms were not hard. Money he needed to
pay his troops, also provisions, clothing, munitions of war.
These he must have, and these Milan could supply. About
$4,000,000 was the sum demanded, but he allowed this to
be reduced by payments in such things as the army needed.
The conquered province was reorganized on a liberal basis,
a national guard enrolled, new officials appointed, and a
constitution framed for it — all this being provisional, of
course.

The Duke of Modena sued for peace, and was made to
pay $2,000,000, furnish provisions and horses, and to give
up many precious works of art.

During the negotiations with Modena, Salicetti came
into Napoleon's room one day and said: "The brother of
the Duke is here with four coffers of gold, 4,000,000
francs. He offers them to you in his brother's name, and
I advise you to accept them."

"Thank you," answered Napoleon, "I shall not for
that sum place myself in the power of the Duke of
Modena."

Such rivulets of gold as Napoleon had set flowing into
the army chest had far-reaching influence. First of all,
the army itself was put into first-class condition. The
troops were newly clothed, well fed, punctually paid.
The pockets of the generals were filled with coin. The
cavalry was splendidly mounted ; the artillery brought to
perfection. As a war machine, the Army of Italy was
now one of the best the world ever saw. The Directors
were not forgotten. Napoleon gladdened the souls of
Barras and his colleagues with $1,000,000 in hard cash.
Other millions followed the first, Napoleon doling out
the sums judiciously, until his contributions exceeded
$4,000,000.

To Moreau, sitting idly on the Rhine, purse empty and
spirit low, Napoleon sent a million in French money.
To Kellermann, commanding in Savoy, he sent 1,200,000
francs. It is hardly necessary to add that he kept the
lion's share of all his booty for his own army chest.
Austria was rousing herself to renew the struggle, France
could send him no supplies, and it would have been
lunacy for him to have emptied his pockets at the opening of another campaign.

After a rest of a week in Milan, the French army was
pushed forward toward Austria. Napoleon advanced his
headquarters to Lodi on the 24th of May, 1796. Shortly
after his arrival, he learned that a revolt had broken out
behind him, that the French garrison at Pavia had surrendered, and that insurrection had spread to many towns
of Lombardy, and that in Milan itself there was revolt.

He immediately turned back with a small force, re-entered Milan, fought the insurgents at Binasco, where Lannes took and burned the town, and then with fifteen hundred men stormed Pavia, defended by thirty thousand insurgents, forced his way in, and gave it over to pillage, butchery, and the flames. The French officer who had signed the order of capitulation was court-martialled and shot.

Why had the Italians risen against their liberator? There are those who say that his exactions in money, provisions, horses, paintings, and so forth caused it. This could hardly have been the sole cause, for Napoleon's exactions did not directly reach the peasants. His heavy hand was felt by the rich men of the Church and the State; but upon the poor he laid no burden. A more reasonable explanation seems to be that the priests, encouraged by aristocrats, preached a crusade against the French marauders, who looted rich temples, and made spoil of things that were believed to be holy. Besides, these marauders were infidel French who had trampled upon the Church in France, confiscating the riches thereof, and ousting fat clericals from high, soft places. The Pope knew that his turn would come, — Basseville's ghost not yet being laid, — and that he would have to suffer for all the cruel blows he had aimed at republican France. Therefore as Napoleon marched off to meet the Austrians, who were reported to be mustering in overwhelming numbers, it was thought to be a good time to kindle flames in his rear. Priests rushed frantically to and fro, the cross was lifted on high, church bells pealed from every steeple, and the ignorant peasants flew to arms to win a place in heaven by shedding the blood of heretics.

The insurrection stamped out, Napoleon proved what *he* thought of its origin. He demanded hostages, not from the peasants, but from the nobles. The hostages were given, and there was no further revolt.

The Austrian army, in its retreat from Lodi, had taken up the line of the Mincio, its left at Mantua and its right at Peschiera, a city belonging to Venice. This violation of neutral ground by Beaulieu gave Napoleon an excuse, and he seized upon the Venetian town of Brescia. He proclaimed his purpose to do nothing against Venice, to preserve strict discipline, and to pay for whatever he might take. Pursuing his march, he again deceived the aged Beaulieu as to the place where he meant to cross the river; and he was over the Mincio before the Austrians could mass sufficient troops to make any considerable resistance. On the other side of the river, Napoleon, in passing with a small escort from the division of Augereau to that of Masséna, narrowly missed falling into the hands of an Austrian corps which was hastening up the river to join Beaulieu. Napoleon, after having ridden some distance with Augereau, had returned to Valeggio, where he stopped to get a foot-bath to relieve a headache. At this moment the light cavalry of the enemy dashed into the village. There was barely time to sound the alarm, close the gates of the carriage-way, and to post the escort to defend the place. Napoleon ran out the back way with only one boot on, made his escape through the garden, jumped on his horse, and galloped as hard as he could to Masséna, whose troops, near by, were cooking their dinner. Masséna promptly aroused his men, rushed them against the enemy — and then it was the turn of the Austrians to run.

The danger which he had incurred caused Napoleon to

form a personal guard for his own protection. Called by the modest name of *Guides* at first, the force swelled in numbers and importance until it became the immortal Imperial Guard. Its commander was Bessières, a young officer of humble birth, who had attracted Napoleon's notice during the campaign by his coolness and courage. He became Marshal of France and Duke of Istria.

In the fighting which took place at Borghetta, the cavalry began to show its capacity for achieving brilliant results. It was young Murat, the innkeeper's son, who inspired, led it, and impetuously fought it. A finer cavalier never sat a horse. A better leader of cavalry never headed a charge. It was a sight to see him, — brilliantly dressed, superbly mounted, on fire with the ardor of battle, leading his magnificent squadrons to the charge. Even Napoleon thrilled with unwonted admiration in looking upon Murat in battle. "Had I been at Waterloo," said Murat, the outcast, in 1815, with a flash of his old pride, "the day had been ours."

And the sad, lonely man of St. Helena assented : —

"It is probable. There were turning-points in that battle when such a diversion as Murat could have made might have been decisive."

Beaulieu fell back to the Tyrol, and Napoleon occupied Peschiera. He was furiously angry with Venice because she had allowed Beaulieu to take possession of this town, which cost the lives of many Frenchmen before it was retaken. The Venetian Senate, bewildered and dismayed, sent envoys to propitiate the terrible young warrior. Napoleon assumed his haughtiest tone, and threatened vengeance.

Finally, when the Venetians had opened to him the

gates of Verona, and had agreed to supply his army, he
began to soften, and to talk to the envoys of a possible
alliance between Venice and France.

On June 5, 1796, one of these envoys wrote of Napoleon,
in a letter to Venice, " That man will some day have great
influence over his country."

The French were now masters of the line of the Adige,
which Napoleon considered the strongest for the defence
of Italy. This line was of vast importance to him, for he
knew that Austria was recruiting her strength and preparing to retrieve her losses. He had won Italy; could
he hold it ? That was now the issue.

Before reënforcements from Austria could arrive, Napoleon calculated that he would have time to punish the
Pope and to humble Naples. Leaving Mantua invested,
and the line of the Adige well defended, he took one division and turned to the South. There were many reasons
why he should do so. The Bourbons of Tuscany had
welcomed the English to Leghorn, and in Naples preparations were being made to equip a large force to act against
the French. Genoa was giving trouble, her nobles being
very unfriendly to France. In Genoese territories troops
of disbanded Piedmontese soldiers, escaped Austrian prisoners and deserters, infested the Apennine passes, stopped
couriers, plundered convoys, and massacred French detachments.

Reaching Milan, Napoleon directed Augereau upon
Bologna, and Vaubois on Modena. To the Senate of
Genoa was sent a haughty letter demanding to know
whether that state could put down the disorders of
which the French complained. Murat, the bearer of the
message, read it to the trembling Senate. It had the

effect desired : Genoa promised, and did all that was asked.

Lannes, with twelve hundred men, sent to chastise the feudatory families of Austria and Naples, resident in Genoese territories, did the work with energy and success. Châteaux of conspiring nobles were burnt; and wherever any of the bands which had been molesting the French could be found, they were summarily shot down.

Naples was cowed before she had been struck, and she sent in her submission to the conqueror. He dealt with her leniently. She must abandon the coalition against France, open all her ports to the French, withdraw her ships from England, and deliver to Napoleon the twenty-four hundred cavalry which she had furnished to Austria. This armistice signed, he turned his attention and his troops in the direction of Rome. Bologna, a papal fief, was seized. Ferrara, another papal domain, threw off the papal yoke.

The Pope, smitten with fear, sent Azara, the ambassador of Spain, to negotiate terms ; and again Napoleon was mild. He required that Ancona should receive a French garrison, that Bologna and Ferrara should remain independent, that an indemnity of 21,000,000 francs should be paid, that one hundred statues and paintings should be given up, besides grain and cattle for the army. The Pope consented. Here again Napoleon gave great offence to the Directory, and to many republicans in France, as well as in the army.

The Pope had been the centre of the hostility against the Revolution and its principles. He had actively coöperated with the enemies of France, had torn her with civil strife, had suffered her ambassador to be brutally murdered, and had given aid, comfort, blessings, and pontifical inspiration to her enemies wherever he could. The Directory wished that the papal power should be totally destroyed. Napoleon had no such intention. Catholicism was a fact, a power, and he proposed to deal with it accordingly. He accepted the money and the paintings and the marbles: Basseville's ghost being left to lay itself as best it could. In delicate compliment to the Pope, the young conqueror did not enter Rome. In all his passings to and fro, this modern Cæsar, this restorer of the Empire of the West, never set his foot in the Sacred City.

On June 26, 1796, Napoleon crossed the Apennines into Tuscany. By forced marches, a division was thrown forward to Leghorn, where, it was hoped, the English ships would be taken. Warned in time, they had sailed away, but the French seized large quantities of English goods. Leaving a garrison at Leghorn, Napoleon proceeded to Florence, where the grand-duke fêted him royally. The grand-duchess did not appear at the banquet: she was "indisposed." Italy having been pacified in this swift manner, Napoleon returned to his army headquarters near Mantua.

CHAPTER XIII

EVEN Austria could now see that Beaulieu was no match for Napoleon. In his place the Emperor sent the aged Wurmser, another officer excellent in the old leisurely cut-and-dried style of campaigning. If Napoleon would rest satisfied to wage war according to the rules laid down in the books, Wurmser would perhaps crush him, for to the 34,000 French there would be 53,000 Austrians in the field, not counting the 15,000 Austrians who were blockaded in Mantua by 8000 French.

Napoleon was at Milan when news came that Wurmser had issued from the mountain passes and was in full march to envelop the French below Lake Garda. Hastening back to the front, Napoleon established headquarters at Castel-Nuovo. Wurmser was confident; Napoleon anxious, watchful, and determined. The Austrians were divided into three columns, — one came down the western bank of Lake Garda, and the other two down the eastern shore. At first the Austrians drove the French at all points, and Napoleon's line was broken, July 30, 1796. This brought on the crisis in which it is said that he lost his nerve, threw up the command, and was saved by doughty Augereau. The evidence upon which this alleged loss of nerve is based is of the frailest, and the undisputed record of the campaign discloses Napoleon's plan, Napoleon's orders, and Napoleon's presence throughout. His only hope was to prevent the junction of the Austrian divisions. Could he hold two off while he concentrated on the third? Practically the same tactics which won at Montenotte prevailed again. While Wurmser was passing forward to Mantua by forced marches, Napoleon had already called in Sérurier; and when the Austrians arrived, expecting to capture the besiegers, no besiegers were there. They had spiked their siege guns, destroyed surplus ammunition, and gone to join the main army of Napoleon, and to aid in crushing one of Wurmser's lieutenants while Wurmser was idling uselessly at Mantua. Almost identically the same thing had occurred at Montenotte, where Beaulieu had rushed upon Voltri to capture French who had been withdrawn, and who were destroying Colli at Montenotte while Beaulieu at Voltri talked idly with Lord Nelson of the English fleet, devising plans whereby Napoleon was to be annihilated. Napoleon struck the first blow at Quasdanovitch, who led the Austrian division which had come down the western side of the lake. At Lonato, July 31, 1796, the French beat the Austrians, driving them back, recovering the line of communication with Milan which had been cut. Then Napoleon hastened back to confront the Austrian centre. Twenty-five thousand Austrians, marching to join Quasdanovitch, reached Lonato. On August 3, Napoleon threw himself upon this force, and almost destroyed it. So demoralized were the Austrians that a force of four thousand surrendered to twelve hundred French.

Next day Wurmser came up offering battle. Stretching his line too far and leaving his centre weak, Napoleon struck him there, beat him with heavy loss, and sent him

ARMÉE
D'ITALIE

LIBERTÉ,

ÉGALITÉ.

RÉPUBLIQUE FRANÇAISE

Au Quartier-Général de *Archi*

le

an 4.me de la République Française.

flying back toward the mountains. In these various operations, Austria had lost about forty thousand men ; France about ten thousand. Mantua had been revictualled, and the French now invested it again. Their siege outfit having been destroyed, they could only rely upon a blockade to starve the enemy out.

Both armies were exhausted, and there followed a period of rest. Reënforcements were received by Wurmser, and by Napoleon also. The Austrians still outnumbered him, but Napoleon took the offensive. Wurmser had committed the familiar mistake of dividing his forces. Napoleon fell upon Davidovitch at Roveredo and routed him. Then turning upon Wurmser, who was advancing to the relief of Mantua, Napoleon captured at Primolano the Austrian advance guard. Next day, September 8, 1796, he defeated the main army at Bassano.

Wurmser was now in a desperate situation. Shut in by the French on one side and the river Adige on the other, his ruin seemed inevitable. By the mistake of a lieutenant colonel, Legnano had been left by the French without a garrison, and the bridge not destroyed. Here Wurmser crossed, and continued his retreat on Mantua. He gained some brilliant successes over French forces, which sought to cut him off, and he reached Mantua in such good spirits that he called out the garrison and fought the battle of St. George. Defeated in this, he withdrew into the town. He had lost about twenty-seven thousand men in the brief campaign.

At length the armies on the Rhine had got in motion. Moreau crossed that river at Kehl, defeated the Austrians, and entered Munich. Jourdan crossed at Dusseldorf, and won the battle of Alten Kirchen. Then the young

M

Archduke Charles, learning a lesson from Napoleon, left a small force to hold Moreau in check, and massed his strength against Jourdan. The French were badly beaten, and both their armies fell back to the Rhine. The original plan of a junction of Jourdan, Moreau, and Bonaparte for an advance upon Vienna was, for the present, frustrated.

Encouraged by the success, Austria sent a new army of fifty-three thousand men, under **Alvinczy**, to recover the lost ground in Italy. Napoleon had about forty thousand troops, several thousand of whom were in hospitals, and once more his safety depended upon preventing the concentration of the enemy.

As in the former campaign, Austria won the first encounters. Vaubois was driven to Trent, and from Trent to Roveredo, and from thence to Rivoli. **Masséna** fell back, before superior numbers, from Bassano. Napoleon, with the division of Augereau, went to Masséna's support. All day, November 6, 1796, Augereau fought at Bassano, and Masséna at Citadella. Alvinczy gave ground, but the French retreated, because of the defeat of **Vaubois**. It seemed now that the two Austrian divisions would unite, but they did not. At Rivoli a French division, eager to win back the respect of their chief, who had publicly reproved them and degraded their commander, held **Davidovitch** in check, and prevented his junction with **Alvinczy**. Fearful that Rivoli might be forced, and the Austrian divisions united, Napoleon again attacked Alvinczy. This time the French were repulsed with heavy loss, some three thousand men (November 13, 1796). Napoleon now had a fresh Austrian army on each flank, **and Wurmser** on his rear.

Should the three Austrian commanders coöperate, the French were lost. But Napoleon calculated upon there being no coöperation, and he was correct. Nevertheless, he almost desponded, and in the army there was discouragement.

As night closed round the dejected French, Napoleon ordered his troops to take up arms. Leaving a garrison to hold the town, he led his troops out of Verona, and crossed to the right side of the Adige. Apparently he was in retreat upon the Mincio. Down the Adige he marched as far as Ronco. There he recrossed the river on a bridge of boats which he had prepared. On this march the French had followed the bend which the river here makes to the Adriatic. Therefore he had reached the rear of the enemy simply by crossing the Adige and following its natural curve. Arrived at Ronco and crossing the river again, the troops saw at a glance the masterly move their chief had made; their gloom gave way to enthusiastic confidence.

It is a marshy country about Ronco, and the roadways are high dikes lifted above the swamp,—one of these raised roads leading to Verona in Alvinczy's front, another leading from Ronco to Villanova in the Austrian rear. Early in the morning, November 15, 1796, Masséna advanced from Ronco on the first of these roads, and Augereau on the other. Masséna passed the swamp without opposition, but Augereau met an unforeseen and bloody resistance at the bridge of Arcole, a town between Ronco and Villanova, where the little river Alpon crosses the road on its way to the Adige. Two battalions of Croats with two pieces of artillery defended this bridge, and so bravely was their task done that Augereau's column was thrown

back in disorder. There was no better soldier in the
army than he, and Augereau seized the standard himself,
rallied his men, and led them to the bridge. Again the
Croats drove them back with enfilading fire. The bridge
must be taken ; it was a matter of vital necessity, and
Napoleon dashed forward to head the charge. Seizing
the colors, he called upon the troops to follow, and with
his own hands planted the flag on the bridge. But the
fire of the enemy was too hot, their bayonets too determined : the Croats drove the French from the bridge, and
in the confusion of the backward struggle, Napoleon got
pushed off the dike into the swamp where he sank to his
waist. " Forward ! forward ! To save our general ! "

With this cry the French grenadiers rallied their broken
line, made a desperate rush, drove back the Croats, and
pulled Napoleon out of the mud.

It was in the charge led by Napoleon that Muiron, his
aide, threw himself in front of his chief, as a shield, saved
Napoleon's life, and lost his own.

It was not till a French corps, which had crossed the
Adige lower down at a ferry, came upon the Austrian
flank, that the French were able to carry the bridge and
take Arcole. By this time, owing to stubborn fight at the
bridge, Alvinczy had had time to get out of the trap which
Napoleon had planned. The Austrians took up a new
position farther back, and were still superior in numbers
and position to the French. If Davidovitch would only
brush Vaubois out of his way and come upon Napoleon's
flank, and if Wurmser would only bestir himself against
the weakened blockading force at Mantua and make trouble in Napoleon's rear, it would be the French, not the
Austrians, who would feel the inconvenience of the trap !

But Davidovitch did nothing; Wurmser did nothing; and Alvinczy continued to make mistakes. For when Napoleon, after the first day's fighting before Arcole, fell back to Ronco in fear that Davidovitch might come, Alvinczy took up the idea that the French were in full retreat, and he started in pursuit, using the raised roads for his march. On these dikes only the heads of columns could meet, the Austrian superiority in numbers was of no advantage, and Napoleon could not have been better served than by the offer of battle under such conditions. Again there was a day of fighting. Napoleon attempted to get to Alvinczy's rear by crossing the Alpon, but failed. Night came, both armies drew off, and nothing decisive had been done.

Again Napoleon fell back to Ronco to be prepared for Davidovitch, and again the son of David was not at hand. Neither was Wurmser doing anything in the rear. In front, Alvinczy, stubbornly bent on staying just where Napoleon wanted him, came upon the narrow dikes again. Once more it was a battle between heads of columns, where the veteran French had the advantage of the recent recruits of Austria. For a moment the giving way of part of the bridge the French had made over the Adige threatened them with disaster. The Austrians came forward in force to cut off a demi-brigade left on their side of the broken bridge. But the bridge was repaired, French troops rushed over, and threw the Austrians back on the marsh. Napoleon laid an ambuscade in some willows bordering the Alpon, and when the enemy, in retreat, passed along the dike, the soldiers in the ambuscade poured a deadly fire on their flank, and then charged with the bayonet. Taken by

surprise, assailed on front of flank, some three thousand
Croats were thrown into the swamp, where most of them
perished.

Calculating that in the battles of the last three days
Alvinczy had lost so many men that his army did not now
outnumber the French, Napoleon determined to leave
the swamps, advance to the open, dry ground, and beat
the Austrians in pitched battle. Crossing the Alpon by
a bridge built during the night, the French fought a
sternly contested field on the afternoon of the 17th of
November, 1796, and finally won it. Napoleon had sent
about twenty-five mounted guides with four trumpets to
the swamp on which rested the Austrian left, and this
trifling force breaking through the swamp, and making a
tremendous noise with their trumpets, caused the Austrians
to think that another ambuscade was being sprung. This
fear, falling upon them at a time when they were almost
overcome by the stress of actual battle, decided the day.
Alvinczy retreated on Montebello, and the long struggle
was ended. It is said that Napoleon, who had not taken
off his clothes for a week, and who for nearly three days
had not closed his eyes, threw himself upon his couch
and slept for thirty-six hours.

At last Davidovitch roused himself, swept Vaubois
out of his path, and came marching down to join Alvinczy.
There was no Alvinczy to join; Davidovitch was some
three or more days too late. And Wurmser down at
Mantua made brilliant sally, to create apprehension in
the rear. The old man was a week or so behind time.
The grip of Napoleon still held; the line of the Adige
was intact.

But while Napoleon had succeeded in holding his own,

he had done so by such desperate straits and narrow margins, leaving the Austrian armies unbroken, that the Emperor decided on another great effort. Recruits and volunteers were enrolled to reënforce Alvinczy, and hurried forward, bearing a banner embroidered by the Empress. Once more the Austrians took the field with superior numbers; once more these forces were divided; once more Napoleon beat them in detail by skilful concentration.

General Provera was to lead a division to the relief of Mantua; Alvinczy was to overwhelm Napoleon. Provera was to follow the Brenta, pass the Adige low down, and march across to Mantua. Alvinczy was to move along the Adige from Trent, and fall upon the main French army, which it was hoped would have been drawn to the lower Adige by the demonstration of Provera.

The heights of Rivoli on Monte Baldo command the valley of the Adige; and no sooner had the preliminary movements of the enemy revealed their plan of campaign, than Napoleon sent orders to Joubert to seize and fortify the plateau of Rivoli, and to hold it at all hazards. This was on January 13, 1797. That night Napoleon himself marched to Rivoli with twenty thousand men, reaching the heights by a forced march at two in the morning.

Alvinczy felt so confident of enclosing and capturing the small force of Joubert that he had gone to sleep, ranging his army in a semicircle below to await the dawn, when Joubert was to be taken immediately after breakfast.

When Napoleon arrived, between midnight and day, he looked down from the heights, and there below, peacefully snoring and bathed in moonlight, were the confident Austrians — five divisions strong. Leaving them to slumber, he spent the balance of the wintry night get-

ting ready for the battle that would come with the day.
As morning broke, the Austrians attacked the French
right at St. Mark, and the contest soon raged along the
whole line as far as Caprino, where the French left was
driven.   Berthier and Masséna restored order, and repulsed every charge.   Strongly posted on the heights,
the French had all the advantage.   Alvinczy found it
impossible to use his cavalry or artillery with effect, and
many of his troops could not be brought into action.   In
relative position, Napoleon held the place of Meade at
Gettysburg, and Alvinczy that of Lee.   Perhaps Napoleon
was even better intrenched than Meade, and Alvinczy less
able to bring his forces up the heights than Lee.   The result was what it was almost bound to be — the Austrians
were routed with terrible loss, and fled in disorder.   So
great was the panic that a young French officer, René, in
command of fifty men at a village on Lake Garda, successfully " bluffed " and captured a retreating body of fifteen
hundred Austrians.   Joubert and Murat pursued vigorously, and in two days they took thirteen thousand prisoners.   It was not till the battle of Rivoli had raged for
three hours that Alvinczy realized that he was attempting
the foolhardy feat of storming the main French army,
posted by Napoleon himself, in almost impregnable positions.

Leaving Joubert and Murat to follow up the victory,
Napoleon went at full speed to head off Provera.   That
gallant officer had fought his way against Augereau and
Guieu, and had reached the suburb of St. George, before
Mantua, with six thousand men.   He had lost the remainder on the way — some twelve thousand.   Throughout the day of January 15, 1797, he was held in check by

Sérurier. Next morning the battle was renewed; but Napoleon had arrived. Provera attacked the French in front; Wurmser in the rear. Sérurier threw Wurmser back into Mantua; and Victor, who had come with Napoleon, vanquished Provera so completely that he laid down his arms. This action is known as that of La Favorita (the name of a country-seat of the Dukes of Mantua near by), and threw into the hands of the French six thousand prisoners, including the Vienna volunteers and many cannon. One of the trophies was the banner embroidered by the Empress of Austria.

A few days later Mantua capitulated, and the last stronghold of the Austrians in Italy was in the hands of the French.

Critics who understand all the mysteries of Napoleon's character say that there was not a trace of chivalry or generosity in him. Yet at Mantua he, a young soldier, would not stay to gloat over the humiliation of the veteran Wurmser. He praised that old man by word and by letter, he granted him liberal terms, and he left the older Sérurier to receive Wurmser's sword. Was not this delicate, even chivalrous to Wurmser? Was it not even more generous to Sérurier? Mr. Lanfrey hints "No"; but Wurmser thought "Yes," for he warmly expressed his admiration for Napoleon; and out of gratitude warned him, while he was at Bologna, of a plot the papal party had made to poison him — a warning which probably saved his life.

The Pope, believing that Napoleon could not possibly escape final defeat at the hands of Austria, had broken their friendly compact. A crusade had been preached against the French, sacred processions paraded, and mira-

cles worked. The bones of martyrs bled, images of the
Virgin wept. Heaven was outspoken on the side of Rome
beyond all doubt. Aroused by these means, the peasants
flocked to the standard of the Pope; and an army, formidable in numbers, had been raised.

Leaving Sérurier to receive the capitulation of Mantua,
Napoleon hastened to Bologna, and organized a force of
French, Italians, and Poles to operate against the papal
troops. Despatching the greater part of his little army
to Ancona, he advanced with about three thousand men
into the States of the Church. Cardinal Busca with an
army of mercenaries, fanatical peasants, and miscellaneous
Italian recruits was intrenched on the banks of the Senio
to dispute its passage. The French came marching up in
the afternoon of a pleasant spring day; and the Cardinal,
with a solicitude which did honor to his conscience, sent a
messenger, under flag of truce, to notify Napoleon that if
he continued to advance, he would be fired upon. Greeting this as the joke of the campaign, the French became
hilarious; but Napoleon gravely returned a polite answer
to the Cardinal, informing him that as the French had been
marching all day, were tired, and did not wish to be shot
at, they would stop. Accordingly, camp was struck for
the night. Before morning, Lannes had taken the cavalry, crossed the river above, and got in the Cardinal's
rear. Day broke, and there was some fighting. In a short
while the Cardinal fled, and the greater part of his motley
army were prisoners. Advancing on Faenza, which had
closed its gates and manned its ramparts, the French battered their way in with cannon, and routed the defenders.
Napoleon's policy with the Pope was not that of the Directory; it was his own, and it was subtle and far-sighted.

Prisoners were kindly treated and released. Cardinals and influential priests were caressed. Papal officers recently captured were visited, soothed by conciliatory speech, assured that the French were liberators and desired only the welfare of a regenerated Italy — redeemed from papal thraldom and rusty feudalism. For the first time modern Italians heard a great man outlining the future of a united Italy.

⁓ At Loretto were found the relics which made that place one of the holiest of shrines. The very house in which Mary, the mother of Jesus, had received the visit of Gabriel was at Loretto. Had you asked how came it there, the answer would have been that the angels carried it from Nazareth to Dalmatia to keep the Saracens from getting it. From Dalmatia the angels, for reasons equally good, had carried it to Loretto. Within this holy hut was a wooden image of Mary, old, blackened, crudely carved. The angels had carved it. In times of clerical distress this image of Mary was seen to shed tears. As there had been quite an access of clerical woe recently, in consequence of Napoleon's brutal disregard of papal armies led by priests with crucifixes in their hands, the wooden Virgin had been weeping profusely.

Napoleon had doubtless familiarized himself with the methods by which pagan priests had kept up their stupendous impostures, and he had a curiosity to see the old wooden doll which was worshipped by latter-day pagans at Loretto. He found a string of glass beads so arranged that they fell, one after another, from the inside, athwart the Virgin's eyes, and as she was kept at some distance from the devotees, and behind a glass case, the optical illusion was complete. Napoleon exposed the trick, and imprisoned the priests who had caused the recent tears to flow.

To add to the sanctity of the shrine at Loretto, there was a porringer which had belonged to the Holy Family, and a bed-quilt which had belonged to Mary, the mother of Jesus. Thousands of devout Catholics prostrated themselves every year before these relics, and countless were the rich offerings to the shrine.

Napoleon took from the church pretty much all the treasure which the priests had not carried off; and the wooden Madonna was sent to Paris. In 1802 he restored it to the Pope, and it was put back in its old place in the Virgin's hut.

Many of the French priests who had refused the oath of allegiance to the new order of things in France had taken refuge in the papal States. The Directory wished Napoleon to drive these men out of Italy. He not only refused to do that, but he gave them the benefit of his protection. In a proclamation to his troops he directed that the unfortunate exiles should be kindly treated; and he compelled the Italian monasteries, which had indeed grown weary of these come-to-stay visitors, to receive them and supply all their wants.

The breadth and depth of Napoleon's liberalism was also shown by the protection he gave to the Jews. These people had, at Ancona, been treated with mediæval barbarity. Napoleon relieved their disabilities, putting them upon an exact political equality with other citizens. In favor of certain Mohammedans, who resided there, he adopted the same course.

Capturing or dispersing the Pope's troops as he went, and winning by his clemency the good-will of the people,

Napoleon drew near Rome. The Vatican was in dismay, and the Pontiff listened to those who advised peace. The treaty of Tolentino was soon agreed upon, and the papal power once again escaped that complete destruction which the Directory wished. A mere push then, an additional day's march, the capture of another priest-led mob, would have toppled the sovereignty which was at war with creed, sound policy, and common sense. It cost torrents of blood, later, to finish the work which Napoleon had almost completed then.

By the treaty of Tolentino, February 19, 1797, the Pope lost $3,000,000 more by way of indemnity; the legations of Bologna and Ferrara, together with the Romagna, were surrendered; papal claims on Avignon and the Venaisson were released, and the murder of Basseville was to be formally disavowed. To his credit be it said that Napoleon demanded the suppression of the Inquisition; to his discredit, that he allowed the priests to wheedle him into a waiver of the demand.

"The Inquisition was formerly a bad thing, no doubt, but it is harmless now — merely a mild police institution. Pray let it be." Napoleon really was, or pretended to be, deceived by this assurance, and the Inquisition remained to purify faith with dungeon, living death in foul tombs, torture of mind and of body in Italy, in Spain, in South America, in the far Philippines.

"Most Holy Father," wrote Bonaparte to the Pope; "My Dear Son," wrote the Pope to Bonaparte; and so they closed *that* lesson.

Amid all the changes made and to be made in Italy there was one government Napoleon did not touch. This was the little republic of San Marino, perched upon the

Apennines, where from its rain-drenched, wind-swept heights it had for a thousand years or more looked tranquilly down upon troubled Italy. Governed by a mixed council of nobles, burgesses, and farmers, it was satisfied with itself, and asked only to be let alone. Now and then a pope had shown a disposition to reach out and seize the little republic, but it had always managed to elude the fatherly clutch. Napoleon respected the rights of San Marino, and offered to increase its territory. San Marino declined ; it had enough. More would bring trouble. Presenting it with four cannon as a token of his esteem, the great Napoleon got out of the sunshine of this Italian Diogenes, and left it in peace. In 1852 the Pope again hungered for San Marino ; but Napoleon III. interfered, and the smallest and oldest republic in the world was left to its independence in its mountain home.

CHAPTER XIV

THE hope of Austria was now the Archduke Charles, who had so brilliantly forced the two French armies on the Rhine to retreat. He was a young man, younger even than Napoleon, being but twenty-five years of age. The Aulic Council at Vienna decided to pit youth against youth, and the Archduke was ordered to take chief command in Italy. Aware of the fact that the Archduke was waiting for reënforcements from the army of the Rhine, Napoleon decided to take the initiative, and strike his enemy before the succors arrived.

Masséna was ordered up the Piave, to attack a separate division under Lusignan, while Napoleon moved against the Archduke on the Tagliamento. By forced marches, the French reached the river before they were expected (March 16, 1797). Making as if they meant to force a passage, they opened upon the Austrians, who awaited them upon the other side, and gave them a soldierly reception. Then, as if he had suddenly changed his mind and meant to bivouac there, Napoleon drew back his troops, and preparations for a meal were made. The Archduke, deceived by this, drew off also, and returned to his tent. Suddenly the French sprang to arms, and dashed for the fords. Bernadotte's division led, and before the Austrians could get into line, the French were safely over, and prepared for action. The Austrians fought, and fought well; but they were outnumbered, as they had been outgeneralled, and they were beaten, losing prisoners and cannon. Masséna, equally successful, had defeated and captured Lusignan, and was nearing the Pass of Tarvis, which leads into Germany from the Italian side. The Archduke hurried to the defence of this vital point, gathering in all his forces as he went. Taking position in front of the pass, he awaited Masséna. By forced marches that intrepid soldier, " the pet child of victory," came up, battle was joined, and desperately contested. Masséna won ; and the road to Vienna was cleared. The Archduke fell back to Villachi ; Masséna waited at Tarvis, hoping to capture an Austrian division which was advancing to the pass, pursued by General Guieu. Not till the Austrians reached Tarvis did they perceive that they were enclosed, front and rear. Demoralized, they surrendered after feeble resistance.

Bernadotte and Sérurier took Gradisca and its garrison, after the former had sacrificed several hundred men in reckless assault upon the ramparts.

On March 28, 1797, Napoleon, with the main body of his army, passed into Corinthia by the Col de Tarvis. Pressing on, he reached Klagenfurth, from which he wrote to the retreating Archduke a letter suggesting peace, March 31, 1797. In reply, the Austrian commander stated that he had no authority to treat. The French continued a vigorous advance, and near Newmarket the Archduke, having received four battalions of the long-expected reënforcements, stood and fought. He was beaten with a loss of three thousand men. He then asked for an armistice, which was refused. Napoleon would treat for peace, but

a truce he would not grant. At Unzmark the Archduke
was again worsted, and his retreat became almost a rout.
On April 2, 1797, the advance guard of Napoleon was at
Leoben, and the hills of Vienna were in sight from the
outposts.   Then came officers to ask a suspension of arms
to treat for peace ; and the preliminaries of Leoben, after
some delays, were signed.

Many reasons have been suggested for Napoleon's
course in tendering peace when he was apparently carrying all before him.   It is said that he became alarmed at
non-coöperation of the armies of the Rhine ; again, that
he was discouraged by Joubert's want of success in the
Tyrol ; again, that he feared insurrection in his rear.
Whatever the motive, it is difficult to avoid the conclusion
that he made a huge mistake.   The French on the Rhine
had moved.   Desaix was driving one Austrian army
through the Black Forest ; Hoche had beaten and was
about to surround the other.   Austria's situation was
desperate, and Vienna must have fallen.   There are those
who suggest that Napoleon hastened to suspend the war
to deprive rival generals, Hoche especially, of a share in
his glory.   This is far-fetched, to say the least of it.
Month after month he had done all in his power to get
those rival generals to move.   To the Directory he sent
appeals, one after another, to order the Rhine armies to
cross and coöperate.   He even sent money from his own
army chest ; and for fear the funds might lodge somewhere
in Paris, he sent them directly to the Rhine.

Bourrienne is not an authority friendly to Napoleon,
and yet Bourrienne states that when Napoleon, after the
truce, received the despatches announcing the progress of
Desaix and Hoche, he was almost beside himself with cha-

grin. He even wanted to break the armistice, and his generals had to remonstrate. This testimony would seem to conclusively prove that Napoleon offered peace because he had lost hope in the coöperation which had been promised him, and which was necessary to his triumph. Singly he was not able to hold disaffected Italy down, guard a long line of communications, and overthrow the Austrian Empire. The preliminaries of Leoben and the treaty of Campo Formio will always be subject of debate. The part which Venice was made to play — that of victim to the perfidy of Napoleon and the greed of Austria — aroused pity and indignation then, and has not ceased to be a favorite pivot for Napoleonic denunciation. Austria was very anxious to hold Lombardy. Napoleon was determined to hold both Lombardy and Belgium. Venice was coldly thrown to Austria as compensation, because it was easier to seize upon decrepit Venetia than to meet another effort of the great Empire whose courage and resources seemed inexhaustible. Perhaps a clearer case of political hard-heartedness had not been seen since Russia, Prussia, and Austria cut up Poland and devoured it.

But after this has been said, let the other side of the picture be viewed. Venice had undertaken to maintain neutrality, and had not maintained it. She had allowed both belligerents to take her towns, use her fortresses, eat her supplies, and pocket her money. Trying to please both, she pleased neither ; and they united to despoil her.

Again, there was the quarrel between the city of Venice and the Venetian territories on the mainland. Venice had its Golden Book in which were written the names of her nobles. Aristocrats on the mainland craved the writing of their names in this Golden Book, and were refused that bliss; hence heartburnings, which were referred to Napoleon. He advised the Venetian Senate to write the names in the book, and the Senate refused. Venice had long been governed by a few families, and these few had the customary obstinacy and prejudice of a caste. They treated Venetia simply as a fief — an estate belonging to the nobles.

Again, republican leaven had been at work throughout Venetia, and Napoleon had advised the Senate to remodel its mediæval institutions. Other states in Italy were yielding to the trend of the times, and Venice should do likewise. The Senate refused, until its consent came too late to avert its doom.

Again, Napoleon had warned Venice that she was too weak to maintain neutrality, and had advised her to make an alliance with France. She had refused.

Again, as Napoleon was about to set out to join his army for the invasion of Germany, he warned Venice to make no trouble in his rear. Things he might forgive were he in Italy, would be unpardonable if done while he was in Germany. Venetia could not, or would not, profit by this warning. While Napoleon was in Germany, tumults arose in the Venetian states, and the French in considerable numbers were massacred. At Verona the outbreak was particularly savage, three hundred of the French have been butchered, including the sick in the hospitals. To leave nothing undone which could be done to give Napoleon the excuses he wanted, a French vessel, which, chased by two Austrian cruisers, had taken refuge in the harbor at Venice, was ordered to leave (according to the law of the port), and when she refused, was fired upon.

Her commander and others were killed, and some horrible
details aggravated the offence.

Napoleon may have had his intentions from the first
to sacrifice Venetia. He may have been insincere in
offering the weak old oligarchy the protection of liberal
institutions and a French alliance. Letters of his, inconsistent with each other, have been published. They
prove his duplicity, his craft, his cunning, his callousness ;
but this was long after Venice had provoked him.

However cold-blooded Napoleon's treatment of Venice
may have been, the European conscience could not have
been as much shocked as royalist writers pretend, for
after Napoleon's overthrow, Venice, which he had reformed and regenerated, was thrown back as a victim to
Austria.

It was a brilliant gathering which surrounded Napoleon and Josephine in the summer of 1797. Diplomats,
statesmen, adventurers, soldiers, men of science and literature, thronged Milan, and paid court at beautiful
Montebello, the palatial country-seat where Napoleon had
taken up his residence after the preliminaries of Leoben.
Many subjects of importance needed his thought, his
fertile resources, his ready hand. His republics needed
guidance, the affairs of Genoa and Venice were unsettled,
German princelets from along the Rhine had a natural
curiosity to know just who they belonged to, and details
of the coming treaty of Campo Formio needed to be worked
out. It was a busy and a glorious season for Napoleon.
He stood on the highest of pinnacles, his renown blazing
to the uttermost parts of Europe ; and to him was drawn

the enthusiastic admiration which turns so warmly to
heroes who are young.   He had, as yet, made few enemies.
All France was in raptures over him; even Austrians
admired him.   The aristocrats, lay and clerical, in Italy
doubtless wished him dead; but the masses of the people
looked up to him in wonder and esteem.   Of Italian ex-
traction, he spoke their language, knew their character,
despised it, imperiously dominated it, and was therefore
loved and obeyed.

Miot de Melito, an unfavorable witness, declares that
Napoleon already harbored designs for his own sovereignty, and made no secret thereof.   " Do you think I am
doing all this for those rascally lawyers of the Directory ? "
He may possibly have said so, but it is not probable.   A
man like Napoleon, meditating the seizure of power and
the overturn of government, does not, as a rule, talk it to
the Miots de Melito.   Had Napoleon had any such clear-
cut design as Miot records, he would not have allowed
the wealth of Italy to roll through his army chest, while
he himself was left poor.   Like Cæsar, he would have
returned laden with spoil, to be used in furthering his
plans.   Napoleon doubtless took something for Napoleon
out of the millions which he handled, but the amount was
so inconsiderable that he keenly felt the burden of debt
which Josephine had made in furnishing his modest home
in Paris.   And when the time *did* come to overturn the
"rascally lawyers," he had to borrow the money he
needed for that brief campaign.   No ; the simple truth is
that Napoleon indulged no sordid appetites in his Italian
campaign.   He made less money out of it than any of his
lieutenants, than any of the army contractors, than any of
the lucky spoilsmen who followed in his wake.   If he had

harbored the designs attributed to him by Miot, it was
obviously a mistake for him to have declined the $800,000
in gold secretly offered him by the Duke of Modena.   At
St. Helena he uttered something which sounds like an
admission that, in view of his subsequent necessities in
Paris, he should have accepted the money.   For wealth
itself Napoleon had no longing — glory, power, fame, all
these stood higher with him.   The 7,000,000 francs Venice
offered were as coolly refused as the smaller sum tendered
by Modena, and the principality offered by the Emperor
of Germany.

The elections of 1797 were not favorable to the Directory.   Many royalists found seats in the Assembly, and
the presiding officer of each legislative body was an oppo-
nent to the government.   Two of the Directors, Carnot
and Barthélemy, joined the opposition.

Openly and boldly, the malcontents, including royalists,
constitutionals, and moderates, declared their purpose of
upsetting the Directory.   Barras, Rewbell, and Larévellière were united, and Barras still retained sufficient
vigor to act promptly at a crisis.   Seeing that bayonets
were needed, he called on Hoche for aid.   Hoche was
willing enough, but he involved himself in a too hasty
violation of law, and became useless.   Then Barras turned
to Napoleon, and Napoleon was ready.   Angry with the
legislative councils for having criticised his high-handed
conduct in Italy, and feeling that for the present his own
interest was linked with that of the Directory, he did not
hesitate.   He sent Augereau to take command of the
government forces at Paris, and Augereau did his work

with the directness of a bluff soldier. "I am come to kill the royalists," he announced by way of public explanation of his presence in town. "What a swaggering brigand is this!" cried Rewbell when he looked up from the directorial chair at Augereau's stalwart, martial figure. Augereau marched thousands of troops into Paris at night, seized all the approaches to the Tuileries where the councils sat, and to the guard of the councils he called out through the closed gates, "Are you republicans?" and the gates opened. Augereau broke in upon the conspirators, seized with his own hand the royalist commander of the legislative guard, tore the epaulettes from his shoulders, and threw them in his face. Roughly handled like common criminals, the conspirators were carted off to prison. Carnot fled; Barthélemy was arrested at the Luxembourg palace. With them fell Pichegru, the conqueror of Holland. While still in command of the republican army, he had entered into treasonable relations with the royalists, and had agreed to use his republican troops to bring about a restoration of the monarchy. This plot, this treason, had not been known when Pichegru, returned from the army, had been elected to one of the councils and made its president. Moreau had captured the correspondence from the Austrians, and had concealed the facts. After Pichegru's arrest by Augereau, the secret of the captured despatches came to light. Moreau himself made the report, and the question which sprang to every lip was, Why did he not speak out before? This universal and most natural query became the first cloud upon the career of the illustrious Moreau. As Napoleon tersely put it, "By not speaking earlier, he betrayed his country; by speaking when he did, he struck a man who was already down." After having saved the government, as Augereau fancied he alone had done, that magnificent soldier's opinion of himself began to soar. Why should he not become a director, turn statesman, and help rule the republic? Very influential people, among them Napoleon and all the Directors, were able to give good reasons to the contrary, and Augereau was compelled to content himself with remaining a soldier. Although he bragged that he was a better man than Bonaparte, he yielded to the silent, invisible pressure of the little Corsican, and he went to take command of the unemployed army of the Rhine. In a few months the same fine, Italian hand transferred him to the command of the tenth division in Perpignan, where he gradually, if not gracefully, disappeared from the political horizon.

The negotiation for final peace between Austria and France continued to drag its slow length along. Diplomats on either side exhausted the skill of their trade, each trying to outwit the other. How many crooked things were done during those weary months, how many bribes were offered and taken, how many secrets were bought and sold, how much finesse was practised, how many lies were told, only a professional and experienced diplomatist would be competent to guess. Into all these wire-drawn subtleties of negotiation Napoleon threw a new element, — military abruptness, the gleam of the sword. Not that he lacked subtlety, for he was full of it. Not that he was unable to finesse, for he was an expert. Not that he scorned to lie, for he delighted in artistic deception. But on such points as these the veteran Cobentzel and the other old-time diplomats could meet him on something like an equality. To throw in a new element altogether, to hide his perfect skill as a machinator under the brusque manners of a rude soldier, was to take the professionals at a disadvantage. Just as the Hungarian veteran had complained that Napoleon would not fight according to rule, Cobentzel and his band were now embarrassed to find that he would not treat by established precedent. Wearied with delays, indignant that they should threaten him with a renewal of the war, and determined to startle the antiquated Austrian envoys into a decision, Napoleon is said to have sprung up from his seat, apparently in furious wrath, exclaiming, "Very well, then! Let the war begin again, but remember! I will shatter your monarchy in three months, as I now shatter this vase," dashing to the floor a precious vase which Catherine II. of Russia had given Cobentzel.

This story, told by so many, is denied by about an equal number. Cobentzel himself contradicted it, but he makes an admission which almost amounts to the same thing. He says that Napoleon became irritated by the delays, worked himself into a passion, tossed off glass after glass of punch, became rude to the negotiators, flung out of the room, and required a good deal of pacification at the hands of his aides. Says Cobentzel: "He started up in a rage, poured out a flood of abuse, put on his hat in the conference room itself" (an awful thing to do!), "and left us. He behaved as if he had just escaped from a lunatic asylum."

Between this Austrian admission and the Austrian denial the substantial difference is not great. Reading between Cobentzel's lines, one sees that the brutal young soldier ran over Austria's delicate old diplomat just as he had been running over a lot of Austria's delicate old generals.

. The next day after this violent scene, the treaty of Campo Formio was signed. By its terms Austria ceded Lombardy, Belgium, and the German principalities on the Rhine. It recognized the Italian republic; the Cisalpine, composed of Lombardy, Modena, Ferrara; the Romagna, Mantua, Massa-e-Carrara; the Venetian territory, west of the Adige and the Valtelline. It also recognized the Ligurian republic, recently formed by Napoleon out of Genoa and its states. France kept the Ionian Isles, and the Venetian factories opposite on the mainland. To Austria was given the Italian lands eastward from the Adige. Within this concession was embraced the venerable city of Venice.

In the treaty of Campo Formio, Napoleon insisted that Austria should liberate the prisoner of Olmutz, Lafayette, who had been lying in a dungeon since 1793.

To regulate the redistribution of German territory, made necessary by the treaty, a congress was to be convened at Rastadt. It may as well be stated in this place that the congress met, remained in session a long while, and could not reach an agreement. Napoleon having gone to Egypt, Austria renewed the war, broke up the congress, and murdered the French envoys.

The Directors were strongly opposed to the terms of the Campo Formio treaty, but they were powerless. Napoleon disregarded their positive instructions, relying for his support upon the enthusiasm with which the French would hail peace. His calculations proved correct. The nation at large welcomed the treaty as gladly as they had done his victories. It seemed the final triumph and permanent establishment of the new order. Against so strong a current in Bonaparte's favor, the Directory did not venture to steer.

Setting out for Paris, November 17, 1797, Napoleon passed through a portion of Switzerland, where he was encouraging the democratic movement which led to the formation of the Helvetian republic. At Geneva and Lausanne he was given popular and most hearty ovations. He put in appearance at Rastadt, where the congress was in session, and remained just long enough to exchange ratifications of the Campo Formio treaty with Cobentzel; and to hector, insult, and drive away Count Fersen, the old friend of Marie Antoinette. Count Fersen had come as Swedish envoy; and to Napoleon his presence seemed improper, as perhaps it was.

CHAPTER XV

MILITARY critics agree that the Italian campaign was a masterpiece; and many say that Napoleon himself never surpassed it. At no other time was he perhaps quite the man he was at that early period. He had his spurs to win, his fame to establish. Ambition, the thirst for glory, his youth, his intense activity of mind and body, the stimulus of deadly peril, formed a combination which did not quite exist again. To the last a tremendous worker, he probably never was on the rack quite as he was in this campaign. In Italy he did all the planning, and saw to all the execution. He marched with his troops night and day, fair weather and foul. He shared the dangers like a common soldier, pointing cannon, leading charges, checking retreat, taking great risks in reconnoitring. He went without food, sleep, or shelter for days at a time. Horses dropped under him, some from wounds, some from fatigue. He marched all night before the battle of Rivoli, directed his forces during the battle, galloped himself to bring up support at critical points; and then, at two or three in the afternoon, when Alvinczy was beaten, he set out to the relief of Sérurier, marched again all night, and again directed a battle — that of La Favorita. This was but one instance; there were dozens of others, some even more remarkable. For Napoleon never seemed to tire: mind and body were like a machine. He was thin, looked

JOSEPHINE in 1800

From a pastel by P. P. Prud'hon

sickly, and indeed suffered from the skin disease caught from the dead cannoneer at Toulon ; but his muscles were of steel, his endurance phenomenal, his vitality inexhaustible. The impression he made upon one close observer at this period was condensed in the words, "the little tiger."

Inexorably as he marched and fought his men, he as carefully looked after their proper treatment. He was tireless in his efforts to have them shod, clothed, fed as they should be ; when sick or wounded, he redoubled his attention. Oppressed as he was by work and responsibility, he found time to write letters of condolence to the bereaved, those who had lost husbands, sons, or nephews in his service. Quick to condemn and punish negligence, stupidity, or cowardice, he was as ready to recognize and reward vigilance, intelligence, and courage. He cashiered General Vallette in the field, but Rampon, Murat, Junot, Marmont, Bessières, Lannes, and hundreds of others he picked out of the ranks and put in the lead. "I am ashamed of you. You no longer deserve to belong to the army. Let it be written on your colors, 'They no longer belong to the army of Italy.'" Thus in stern tones he spoke to Vallette's troops, who had done too much running as compared to their fighting. The soldiers were in despair. Some groaned; some wept; all were ashamed. "Try us again, General. We have been misrepresented. Give us another chance, General!" Napoleon softened, spoke as his matchless tact suggested, and in the battles that followed no troops fought better than these.

Complete genius for war Napoleon displayed in the campaign : masterly plans, perfection of detail, penetra-

tion of the enemy's plan, concealment of his own, swift
marching, cautious manœuvring, intrepidity in fighting,
absolute self-possession, sound judgment, inflexible will-
power, capacity to inspire his own army with confidence
and the enemy with almost superstitious terror.[1] An
incident occurred after the battle of Lonato, attested
by Marmont and Joubert, which reads like fiction.
Napoleon with twelve hundred men was at Lonato
making arrangements for another battle. An Austrian
column of four thousand, bewildered in the general
confusion, strayed into the neighborhood, and were told
by some peasants that only twelve hundred French
were in the place. The Austrians advanced to capture
this band and sent a summons. Napoleon ordered that
the herald should be brought in blindfolded. When
the bandage was removed, the herald found himself
in the presence of Napoleon, around whom stood his
brilliant staff. " What means this insolence ? Demand
my surrender in the midst of my army ? Go tell your
commander that I give him eight minutes to lay down
his arms." And the Austrian commander had time to
his credit when his surrender of his four thousand had
been made.

It was at this period that Napoleon developed his wonderful fascination of manner. As he could intimidate
by frowns, harsh tones, fierce looks, and cutting words,
he could charm with the sweetest of smiles, the kindest
of glances, the most caressing words. If he wished to

---

[1] It was a curious remark Napoleon made at St. Helena, that his whole
military career had taught him nothing about a battle which he did not
know at the time he fought his first ; subsequent campaigns taught him
no more than the first.

please, he could, as a rule, do so ; if he wished to ter-
rify, it was rarely he failed. Already there were hundreds of young officers who swore by him, lived for his
praise, and were ready to die for him. Muiron had
done so ; Lannes, Junot, Marmont, Bessières, Berthier,
Murat, were as ready. As to the army itself, Cæsar had
never more completely the heart of the Tenth Legion
than the young Napoleon that of the army of Italy. No
higher reward did his soldiers crave than his words of
praise. His proclamations intoxicated them like strong
wine. They were ready to dare all, endure all, to
please him, win his smile, wear his splendid tribute. "I
was at ease; the Thirty-second was there;" and the delighted regiment embroidered the words on its flag.
"The terrible Fifty-seventh" were proud to see on their
banner that battle name given them by their "Little
Corporal"; just as, at Toulon, he had kept the most exposed of the batteries filled with men by posting the
words, "The Battery of those who are not afraid."

Planning, executing, marching, fighting, organizing new
states, Napoleon was still the ardent lover. Josephine
he never neglected. Courier sped after courier, bearing
short, hasty, passionate love-letters to Josephine. He was
in all the stress and storm, often cold, drenched by wintry
rains, pierced by wintry winds, hungry, overwhelmed with
work and care, yet not a day did he forget his bride. She
was lapped in luxury at Paris, — warmth, light, pleasure,
joyous ease, and companionship about her; and she laughed
at the love-letters, thinking them wild, crude, extravagant.
"Bonaparte is so queer ! "

In June, 1796, Napoleon was made to believe that
Josephine was in a fair way to become a mother. His

raptures knew no bounds.   The letter which he then
wrote her is certainly the most ardently tender, furiously
affectionate scrawl ever penned.   It drives in upon the
impartial reader the conviction that this strange man
possessed the uxorious and paternal spirit in its most
heroic form ; and that had he been fitly mated, his devel-
oping character would have reached a perfect harmony
and equilibrium.   It was in him to have found exquisite
enjoyment in home-life ; it was in him to have bent
caressingly over wife and child, to have found at the fireside repose and happiness.   As it was, his marriage was
one source of his ruin.   In Josephine he found no loyalty,
no sympathy of the higher sort, and she bore him no children.   She froze his hot affection with that shallow amiability which smiled on him as it smiled on all the others.
She outraged his best feelings by her infidelities.   She
destroyed his enthusiasm, his hopes, his ideal of pure and
lofty womanhood.   He waited on her too long for children.   His character, undeveloped on that side, hardened
into imperial lines, until he himself was the slave of
political necessities.   The second marriage, and the son
he idolized, came too late.

Napoleon, the lover-husband, who had quitted his bride
in forty-eight hours after the marriage, repeatedly implored her to join him at headquarters.   Josephine had no
inclination to obey : Paris was too delightful.   Upon
various excuses she delayed, and it was not till July,
1796, that she reached Italy.

Arrived in Milan, she was rapturously welcomed by
Napoleon, and found herself treated by the Italians almost
as a queen.   She was lodged in a palace, surrounded with
luxury, and flattered by the attentions of thronging court-

iers. She moved from place to place as the months passed on, shared some of the dangers of the campaign, and by her grace, amiability, and tact made many a conquest useful to her many-sided lord. One conquest she made for herself, and not for her lord. A certain officer named Hypolite Charles, attached to Leclerc's staff, was young, handsome, gallant, — *such* a contrast to the wan, wasted, ungainly, skin-diseased Napoleon! Josephine looked upon Charles and found him pleasing. The husband, engrossed by war and business, was often absent. Charles was not engrossed with war, was present, and was not a Joseph. Here was youth, inclination, opportunity — and the old result. Scandal ensued, Napoleon's sisters made shrill outcry, the husband heard the story, and Charles joined the absent. It was thought for a while that Napoleon would have him shot, but apparently there was some invincible reason to the contrary. He went to Paris and obtained a good position — rumor said by the influence of Josephine.

If Napoleon was imperious at school, a tyrant in his childhood, self-willed and indomitable when out of employment and threatened with starvation, how were the Directors to curb him now? Just as natural as it seemed to be for him to command when among soldiers, it was for him to treat king, duke, and pope as equals, lay down the law of national relations, and create new governments in Italy. He assumed the power as a matter of course, and his assumption of authority was nowhere questioned. "Bless me! I was made that way," exclaimed Napoleon. "It is natural for me to command."

The Directors would gladly have dismissed him, for they doubted, disliked, and feared him; but they dared not face

o

him and France on such an issue. He rode rough-shod over their policies and their instructions, and they could do nothing. They had thought of sending Kellermann, had actually appointed him to share the command ; Napoleon flatly said the command could not be shared, and Kellermann had to go elsewhere.

They sent General Clarke as agent to manage negotiations, treaties, and to supervise matters generally. Napoleon said to Clarke, " If you have come here to obey me, well and good ; but if you think to hamper me, the sooner you pack up and leave, the better." Clarke found himself completely set aside and reduced to nothing. The Directory itself, overawed by Napoleon's tone, wrote Clarke, in effect, that he must not oppose the imperious commander-in-chief.

There were official commissioners in the field, Salicetti and others. How powerful and dreaded these commissioners had formerly been ! Had not Napoleon courted them and their wives with all the haughty cajolery of a proud nature which stoops to conquer ? Now he would stoop no more ; he had conquered. Salicetti and company did the stooping ; and when, at length, their doings displeased the conqueror of Italy, he ordered them off.

The Milanese, historic Lombardy, was the first province which he fashioned into a republic. Here he met Count Melzi, almost the only *man* Italy could boast. Working with Melzi and others, the Transpadane republic was established — the child of Napoleon's brain and energy.

Afterward as liberalism spread, and the papal yoke was thrown off, Bologna, Reggio, Ferrara, clamored for republican institutions. The dream of Italian unity began to be a reality.

Modena caught the infection; its miserly duke had already run away, carrying his treasure. He had failed to pay 500,000 francs of his fine; and, seizing upon this pretext, Napoleon granted the petitions of the people, grouped Modena with the papal legations, and gave organization under a liberal constitution to the Cispadane republic. At a later day the two republics were united into one, and became the Cisalpine.

In the wake of the victorious army skulked the hungry civilian, the adventurer seeking gain, the vultures grouping to the carcass. It was feast-day for the contractor, the speculator, the swindler, the robber, the thief. It threw Napoleon into rage to see himself surrounded by a horde of imitators, puny plunderers doing on a small scale, without risking battle, what he did in grand style, after a fair fight. Soldiers who brought scandal on the army by too notorious pillage he could shoot, and did shoot; he resented the limitations of power which kept the civilian buccaneers from being shot.

An indirect result of Napoleon's victories in Italy was the loss of Corsica to England. The rule of Britannia had not pleased the Corsicans, nor been of any special benefit to England. Toward the close of 1796 the islanders revolted, and the English withdrew. Corsica became again a province of France.

CHAPTER XVI

ON December 5, 1797, Napoleon returned to Paris. With studious eye for effect, he adopted that line of conduct most calculated, as he thought, to preserve his reputation and to inflame public curiosity. He was determined not to stale his presence. Making no display, and avoiding commonplace demonstrations, he doffed his uniform, put on the sober dress of a member of the Institute, to which he was elected in place of Carnot, screened himself within the privacy of his home, and cultivated the society of scholars, authors, scientists, and non-combatants generally. When he went out, it was as a private citizen, his two-horse carriage unattended by aides or escort. He demurely attended the meetings of the Institute, and on public occasions was to be found in his place, in his class, among the savants, just as though he had set his mind now on literary matters and was going to write a book. His brother Joseph gave it out that Napoleon's ambition was to settle down and be quiet, to enjoy literature, friends, and, possibly, the luxuries of the office of Justice of the Peace. It must have been a queer sight to have seen the little Corsican dress-parading as a guileless man of letters; it is very doubtful whether many were deceived by his exaggerated modesty. Those who were in place and power, the men whom he would have to combat and overcome, were not for a moment duped. They suspected, dreaded, and watched him. Prepare for him they could not, for they had not the means. He had said nothing and done nothing which they had not indorsed; with hearts full of repugnance, with faces more or less wry, they had sanctioned even when their instructions had been disobeyed. They could not seize him by brute force, or put him out of the way. They were too weak; he too strong. He was the idol of soldiers and civilians alike; the Directors were not the idols of anybody. They could not even have him poisoned, or stabbed, for he was on his guard against that very thing. Soon after his return to Paris he had received warning of a plot to poison him; he had caused the bearer of the note to be accompanied by a magistrate to the house of the woman who had furnished the information, and she was found lying dead on the floor, her throat cut and her body mutilated. The would-be murderers had, doubtless, discovered her betrayal of them, and had in this manner taken vengeance and assured their own safety. After such an occurrence, Napoleon was not the man to be caught napping; and it was noticed that at the official banquets to which he was invited he either ate nothing, or slightly lunched on wine and bread brought by one of his aides.

The Directory gave him, in due time, a grand public reception at the Luxembourg, which was attended by immense numbers, and which was as imposing as the pomp of ceremony and the genuine enthusiasm of the people could make it. But the part played by the Directory and Talleyrand was theatrically overdone, and gave a tone of bombast and insincerity to the whole.

What now must Napoleon do? There was peace on the Continent; he was too young for a place in the Directory,

and if he remained in Paris too long, France would forget
him. This was the reasoning of Napoleon, the most impatient of men. Evidently the reasoning was unsound ;
it was dictated only by his feverish, constitutional need
of action. There was no danger of his sinking out of
notice or importance in France. There was the danger
of his being identified with a party, but even this peril
has been exaggerated. Astute and coldly calculating as
he was, the party he would have chosen, had he seen fit to
choose one at all, would probably have been the strongest,
and political success comes to that in the long run.

He had been too impatient in Corsica in his earlier
struggles ; he had there alienated the wise and lovable
Paoli, who wanted to be his friend, but could not sympa-
thize with his too violent, too selfishly ambitious character.
He had been too impatient to get on in France, and had
been perilously near losing his head as a terrorist in the
fall of Robespierre. Too anxious for social recognition
and independent military command, he had fallen into
the snares of Barras and the shady adventuress of whom
the libertine Director was tired, and had rushed into a
marriage which proved fatal to him as a man and a
monarch. The same feverish haste was again upon him,
and was to continue to be upon him all the days of his
life, until his final premature rush from Elba was to lead
him, through the bloody portals of Waterloo, to his prison
on the bleak rock of St. Helena.

How could a few months of quiet in Paris have tar-
nished his fame ? Had he not seen the heart of liberalism
throughout all Europe warm to Paoli, — the time having
come,— although the patriot exile had been sitting quietly
at English firesides for twenty-one years ?

Who in France was likely to outstrip Napoleon in one
year, two years, ten years? Hoche was dead, Moreau in
disgrace, Jourdan under the cloud of defeat, Augereau
on the shelf, Carnot an exile, Pichegru banished. In
the Directory there was not a man who could give him
the slightest concern.

But to Napoleon it seemed absolutely necessary that
he must be actively engaged — publicly, and as master.
He could not get the law changed so that he could become a director ; he could not quite risk an attack in
the Directory. *That* pear was not yet ripe. He had
wished to be sent to Rastadt to straighten matters there,
but the Directory chose another man. Napoleon, resenting the slight, threatened, once too often, to resign. A
Director (some say Rewbell, others Larévellière) handed
him a pen, with the challenge, " Write it, General ! "
Moulins interposed, and Napoleon beat a retreat, check-
mated for the time.

Apparently, as a last resort, the expedition to Egypt
was planned, both Napoleon and the Directory cordially
agreeing upon one thing — that it was best for him to
leave France for a while.

The attack on Egypt suggested itself naturally enough
as a flank movement against England. The idea did not
originate with Napoleon ; it was familiar to the foreign
policy of France, and had been urged upon the Bourbon
kings repeatedly. With his partiality for the East, whose
vague, mysterious grandeurs and infinite possibilities never
ceased to fascinate him, the oft-rejected plan became to
Napoleon a welcome diversion. Veiling his design under
the pretence of a direct attack upon England, he bent all
his energies to the preparations for the invasion of Egypt.

Nominally belonging to Turkey, the ancient ally of France, Egypt was in fact ruled by the Mamelukes, a military caste which had, in course of time, evolved from the personal body-guard of Saladin. The reign of the Mamelukes was harsh and despotic ; they paid little respect to religion, and none to law ; and Napoleon thought that by telling the Sultan he would overthrow the Mamelukes in the Sultan's interest, while he assured the subject Egyptians that he came to liberate them from Mameluke tyranny, he would deceive both Sultan and Egyptians. As it happened, he deceived neither.

It was a part of the scheme agreed on by Napoleon and the Directors that Talleyrand should go to Constantinople and gain over the Sultan to neutrality, if to nothing more favorable. With this understanding, Napoleon gathered up the best generals, the best troops, the best vessels, swept the magazines, cleaned out the directorial treasury, and even borrowed from the Institute its best savants, and weighed anchor at Toulon, May 18, 1798, for Alexandria. The wily Talleyrand did not go to Turkey, had apparently never intended to go, and that part of the plan failed from the beginning. English diplomats took possession of the Sultanic mind; and what they saw, the heir of the Prophet saw. To save herself from a movement which threatened her in the East, Great Britain warmed to the infidel, forgot crusading vows and traditions, guided infidel counsels, supplied infidel needs, and aimed infidel guns. So that from the day he set sail, Napoleon had against him all the resources of England, all the power of Ottoman arms, all the strength of Mameluke resistance, all the discouragement of native Egyptian hostility.

NAPOLEON

From the painting by Paul Delaroche entitled "General Buonaparte
crossing the Alps"

To reach Egypt at all it was necessary that he should run the extreme risk of encountering the British fleet. By the victory England had won over the Spanish allies of France off Cape St. Vincent (February, 1797), and over the Dutch at Camperdown (October, 1797), France was left without naval support. In a sea-fight between herself and England, all the advantage would have been with her foe. Conscious of this, Nelson did his utmost to come upon Napoleon during his voyage, and the two fleets passed each other once in the night ; but Napoleon's rare luck favored him, and Nelson missed his prey.

The capture of Malta was a part of Napoleon's plan. This island fortress belonged to the Knights of St. John, a belated remnant of the ancient orders of chivalry, created for the purpose of retrieving Palestine from the infidel. These soldiers of the Cross had fallen upon evil days and ways ; their armor very rusty indeed, their banners covered with dust, their spurs very, very cold. In a world which had seen a new dispensation come, the knights were dismally, somewhat ludicrously, out of place. Asked, What are you doing here ? What do you intend to do ? What is your excuse for not being dead ? the knights would have been stricken dumb. No intelligible reply was possible. Camped there upon a place of strength and beauty, a fortress girdled by the Mediterranean, they were, in theory, Christendom's outpost against the infidel. Christendom, in theory, was yet intent upon raising up champions who would tread in the steps of Godfrey, of Tancred, of Richard Cœur de Lion. In theory, Christendom was never going to rest till the tomb of Jesus had been redeemed, till the shadow of Mahomet should be lifted from the Holy Land. And so it happened that the knights had stopped at Malta, long ages ago, resting upon their arms, until such time as Christendom should rouse itself and send reënforcement. The time had never come. The knights, they waited; but the crusader of Europe had gone home to stay. Once and again, as the centuries crept slowly by, the Church had turned in its sleep and mumbled something about the tomb of Christ; but the Church was only talking in its sleep, and the knights had continued to wait. A king, now and then, suddenly awakened to the fact that he was a very great scoundrel, must finally die, would probably go to hell, and therefore needed to redeem himself at the expense of the infidel, swore a great oath to renew the crusades; but such vows bore no fruit; the spasm of remorse passed over, and the knights continued to wait. Really, it was not so hard upon them. They had a royal home, a royal treasury, a royal standing and a sacred. They lived a pleasant life; they doffed iron armor, and wore silks, velvets, and other precious stuffs more congenial to the flesh than metallic plates. They came to love such things as good eating, joyous entertainments, the smiles and the favors of fair ladies, and the sweetness of doing nothing generally.

Malta being defended by such decadent champions, it was easily captured by such a man as Napoleon Bonaparte. There was, perhaps, bribery; there was, certainly, collusion, and the resistance offered was but nominal. General Caffarelli probably voiced the general sentiment when he said, looking around at the vast strength of the fortress, "It is lucky we had some one to let us in."

Leaving a garrison under Vaubois to hold the place, Napoleon again set sail for Egypt.

Nelson was flying hither and thither, on the keenest of hunts, hoping to pounce upon the crowded vessels of the French, and to sink them. Storms, fog, bad guessing, and Napoleonic luck fought against the English, and they missed the quarry completely. Napoleon hastily landed near Alexandria, July 2, 1798, marched upon the city, and easily took it. After a short rest, the army set out by the shortest route for Cairo. The sun was terribly hot, the desert a burning torment, water it was almost impossible to supply, food failed, and the skirmishes of the enemy from behind sandhills, rocks, or scraggy bushes harassed the march, cutting off every straggler. Bitterly the soldiers complained, contrasting this torrid wilderness to the fertile beauty of Italian plains. Even the generals became disheartened, indignant, almost mutinous. Men like Murat and Lannes dashed their plumed and braided hats on the ground, trampled them, and damned the day that had brought them to this barren Hades.

The common soldiers bitterly recalled Napoleon's promise that each of them should make enough out of the campaign to buy seven acres of land. Was this desert a fair sample of the land they were to get? If so, why the limit of seven acres?

The trying march was over at last, the Nile was reached, and then came the relief of battle and easy victory. The Mamelukes were great horsemen, the best in the world, perhaps; but they had no infantry and no artillery worth the name. In the hands of Napoleon they were children. Battle with Mamelukes was target practice, during which French marksmen, in hollow square, shot out of their saddles the simple-minded Mamelukes, who fancied that they could do everything with horses.

In all of the battles which took place, the tactics of the French were the same : " Form square : savants and asses to the centre." Then, while the baggage, the learned men, and the long-eared donkeys rested securely within the lines, a steady fire of musketry and cannon emptied the saddles of the heroes of the desert.

To see the Mamelukes come thundering on to the attack, was magnificent ; to see them drop in the sand without having been able to reach the French, was pitiful.

After a skirmish at Shebreis, in which the Mamelukes were driven off without any difficulty (July 13), came the encounter known as the Battle of the Pyramids (July 21), chiefly remembered now as that in which Napoleon dramatically exclaimed to his troops as they were being made ready for the struggle, " Soldiers, from yonder pyramids forty centuries look down upon you ! " The telescope had revealed to him the fact that the artillery of the enemy consisted of guns taken from their flotilla on the river. These guns were not on carriages, like field artillery, and therefore they could not be moved at will during battle. This suggested to him a change in his own dispositions. A portion of his army being left to deal with the stationary artillery and the infantry which manned the feeble, sand-bank intrenchments, he directed the other to march out of the range of the guns, for the purpose of throwing against the Mameluke horse his own cavalry, supported by infantry and artillery. Murad Bey, the commander-in-chief of the opposing army, seized the moment when this change was being made by Napoleon to launch against him a mass of seven thousand Mameluke horse. This mighty host struck the division of Desaix when it was in motion, and therefore unprepared for cavalry. For an instant the French, at least of that column, were in peril. So quickly, however, did the veterans of Desaix form squares, so quickly did Napoleon see the point of danger and send relief, that the battle was never in real doubt. The camp of the Arabs was stormed, the Mameluke cavalry slaughtered ; and, inflicting a loss computed at ten thousand on the enemy, the French had but a score or two killed and one hundred and twenty wounded.

The Mameluke power was shattered by the Battle of the Pyramids, and the conquest of Egypt was practically achieved. For some days Frenchmen fished the Nile for dead Mamelukes, to secure the wealth which those warriors carried on their persons.

Arrived in Cairo, Napoleon did his utmost to assure the permanence of his triumph. He caused the religion, the laws, the customs of the country, to be respected. Pursuing his policy of trying to deceive the Mahometans, he proclaimed that the French were the true champions of the Prophet ; that they had chastised the Pope, and conquered the Knights of Malta ; therefore the people of Egypt should be convinced that they were the enemies of the Christians.

" We are the true Mussulmans ! " read the proclamation. " Did we not destroy the Pope because he had preached a crusade against the Mahometans ? Did we not destroy the Knights of Malta because they said that God had directed them to fight the followers of Mahomet ? "

He cultivated the influential men of the country, and

encouraged the belief that he himself might become a Mussulman. In truth, Napoleon admired Mahomet greatly, and he never shrank from saying so, then or afterward. In the classification of the books of his private library, made in his own writing, he grouped under the same head the Bible, the Koran, the Vedas, and Mythology, and Montesquieu's *Spirit of Laws.* These he enumerated in the class of *Politics and Morals.* He reminded his soldiers that the Roman legions had respected all religions. He did not remind them that Roman rulers had considered all religions as equally useful for purposes of government; nor that Roman philosophers had regarded them all as equally sons and daughters of that primeval pair, Fear and Fraud — fear of the unknown, and the fraud which practises upon it.

Napoleon found that Mahometan priests were as eager to convert him as Christian priests had been to capture Constantine and Clovis. In the one case as in the other, the priests were willing to compromise the creed to gain the convert. Napoleon did not quite join the faithful himself, but he approved of General Menou's apostasy, and he ostentatiously observed the Mahometan festivals.

Both Napoleon and Bourrienne denied, as others assert, that he went into the mosque, sat cross-legged on the cushion amid the faithful, muttered Koran verses as they did, and rolled head and body about as a good Mussulman should. If he did not do so it was because he thought, as a matter of policy, that the act would not compensate him for the trouble and the ridicule. He afterward did just about that much for the Christian religion; and faith had no more to do with his conduct in the one case than in the other.

As he went farther with the Jacobins than it was pleasant to remember, so he probably went farther with the
Mahometans than he cared to admit; for he certainly prevailed upon the priesthood to do that which was forbidden
by the Koran unless he was a convert. They officially
directed the people to obey him and pay him tribute.
Nor is there any doubt that the leaders among the priests
liked him well enough, personally, to watch over his personal safety. General Kleber, who succeeded him in command, neglected to pay the chiefs those attentions Napoleon
had lavished upon them, and in turn they neglected him.
To this, perhaps, his assassination was due.

Regarding Egypt as a colony to be developed, rather
than a conquest to be despoiled, Napoleon devoted every
attention to civil affairs. He reorganized the administration, conforming as nearly as possible to established customs. He set up a printing-press, established foundries
and manufactories, planned storage dams and canals to
add to the cultivable soil, organized an institute, and
started a newspaper. He sent his savants abroad to dig,
delve, excavate, explore, map the present and decipher the
past of Egypt. Napoleon himself used his leisure in visiting historic places and making plans for the material
progress of the benighted land. He discovered traces of
the ancient canal connecting the Nile with the Red Sea,
and formed the resolution of reopening it. He himself
located the lines for new canals. He crossed the Red Sea
ford which the Israelites used in fleeing from bondage,
and, staying too long on the opposite shore, was caught
by the rising tide, and came near meeting the fate of
Pharaoh and his host. More self-possessed than Pharaoh,
Napoleon halted when he realized his peril, caused his

escort to form a circle around him, and each to ride outward. Those who found themselves going into deeper
water drew back, followed those who had found fordable
places ; and, by this simple manœuvre, he deprived needy
Christendom of a new text and a modern instance.

While on the farther shore Napoleon visited the Wells
of Moses, and heard the petition of the monks of Sinai.
At their request, he confirmed their privileges, and put
his name to the charters which bore the signature of
Saladin.

A terrible blow fell upon him in August when Nelson
destroyed the French fleet in the famous battle of the
Nile. There is doubt as to who was to blame for this
calamity. Napoleon cast it upon Brueys, the French
admiral who lost the battle ; and Brueys, killed in the
action, could not be heard in reply. He had drawn up
his ships in semicircle so close to the shore that he considered himself comparatively safe, protected as he was
by land batteries at the doubtful end of his line.

But Nelson, on the waters, was what Bonaparte was on
land — the boldest of planners and the most desperate of
fighters. He came up at sunset, and did not wait till
morning, as Brueys expected. He went right to work,
reconnoitred his enemy, conceived the idea of turning his
line, getting in behind with some of his ships, and thus
putting the French between two fires. The manœuvre was
difficult and dangerous, but succeeded. Nelson rammed
some of his ships in on the land side of the amazed Brueys, who had made no preparations for such a manœuvre.
Caught between two terrible fires, Brueys was a lost
man from the beginning. It was a night battle, awful
beyond the power of description. When it ended next

day, the English had practically obliterated the French fleet; Napoleon was cut off from Europe. When the news reached him, he was stunned, almost crushed; but rallying immediately, he wrote to Kleber, "The English will compel us to do greater things in Egypt than we had intended."

Desaix conquered Upper Egypt; organized resistance to the invaders ceased for the time, and from the cataracts to the sea Napoleon held the valley down. The administration began to work smoothly, taxes seemed lighter because more equitably distributed, and the various enterprises Napoleon had set on foot began to show some life. He enrolled natives in his army, and formed a body of Mamelukes which afterward appeared so picturesquely in France. Two young Mamelukes, Roustan and Ibrahim, given him by one of the pachas, became his personal attendants, and served him faithfully till his power was broken in 1814.

The ruin of the fleet was not the only grief of Napoleon in the months which followed. Junot had acted the part of the candid friend, and had revealed to Napoleon the secret of Josephine's infidelities. Captain Hypolite Charles had reappeared in the absence of the husband, and was now living with the wife at Malmaison. So openly was this connection kept up that the Director, Gohier, a friend of Josephine, advised her to divorce Napoleon and marry Charles. The first shock of Junot's revelation threw Napoleon into a paroxism of wrath, then into a stupor of despair and dull disgust with everything. Then, by a reaction, natural, perhaps, to a man of his temperament, he threw himself into libertine excesses. Prior to this period his morals, considering the times and

the temptations, had been remarkably pure.   Henceforth
he was occasionally to give himself a license which scandalized even the French officers.   Scorning subterfuge
and concealment, he became as bold as any born king, a
rake by divine right, in the shamelessness of his amours.
He appeared in public at Cairo with Madame Foures, his
mistress, riding in the carriage by his side ; and if Bourrienne tells the truth on Napoleon, and Carlyle tells no lie
on Peter the Great, the one was about as obscene as the
other while the lustful impulse prevailed.

CHAPTER XVII

ÇAREFULLY as Napoleon had cultivated the native authorities, deferred to prejudice and custom, and maintained discipline, native opposition to French rule seems to have been intense. A revolt in Cairo took him by surprise. It had been preached from the minaret by the Muezzins in their daily calls to prayer. It broke out with sudden fury, and many Frenchmen were slaughtered in Cairo and the surrounding villages. Napoleon quelled it promptly and with awful severity. The insurrection, coming as it did upon the heels of all his attempts at conciliation, filled him with indignant resentment, and, in his retaliation, he left nothing undone to strike terror to the Arab soul. Insurgents were shot or beheaded without mercy. Donkey trains bearing sacks were driven to the public square, and the sacks being untied, human heads rolled out upon the ground — a ghastly warning to the on-looking natives. Such is war; such is conquest. The conquered must be tamed. Upon this principle acted the man of no religion, Napoleon, in Egypt, and the Christian soldier, Havelock, in Hindustan. The Christian Englishmen who put down the Indian mutiny were as deaf to humanity as was the Deist who quelled the revolt in Cairo. Like all the cruelty whose injury society really feels, the crime is in the system, not the individual. War is war; and as long as Christendom must have war to work out the mysterious ways of God, we must be content with the thorns as well as the fruits. If it be a part of the white man's burden to exterminate black and brown and yellow races to clear the way for the thing we call Christian civilization, Napoleon's course in Egypt was temperate and humane. Upon all his deeds a blessing might be asked by the preachers who incited the soldiers of America, Great Britain, Germany, Russia, in the wars of the year 1900; and the chaplains who went, on good salaries, to pray for those who shot down Filipinos, Chinamen, or even South African Boers could just as easily have given pious sanction to the murders-in-mass committed by Bonaparte.

Inspired by the result of the battle of the Nile, England, Turkey, the Mamelukes, and the Arabs made great preparations to drive Napoleon out of Egypt. A Turkish army was to be sent from Rhodes; Achmet, Pacha of Acre, surnamed Djezzar, the Butcher, was raising forces in Syria, and Commodore Sir Sidney Smith was cruising on the coast ready to help Turks, Mamelukes, and Arabs against the French. Sir Sidney had been a political prisoner in Paris, had recently made his escape, and had been assisted in so doing by Napoleon's old schoolmate, Phélippeaux. Following Sir Sidney to the East, Phélippeaux, a royalist, was now at hand eager to oppose the republican army of Napoleon, and capable of rendering the Turks valuable service. There is no evidence that he was actuated by personal hatred of Napoleon. They had not liked each other at school, and had kicked each other's shins under the table; but, as men, they had taken different sides as a matter of policy or principle, and it was this which now arrayed them against each other.

Napoleon's invariable rule being to anticipate his enemy, he now marched into Syria to crush Djezzar before the Turkish army from Rhodes could arrive. Leaving Desaix, Lanusse, and other lieutenants to hold Egypt, he set out with the main army February 11, 1799. El Arish was taken February 20, 1799, and Gaza followed. Jaffa, the ancient Joppa, came next (March 6), and its name will always be associated with a horrible occurrence. Summoned to surrender, the Arabs had beheaded the French messenger. The place was stormed, and the troops gave way to unbridled license and butchery. The massacre went on so long and was so hideous that Napoleon grew sick of it, and sent his step-son, Eugène, and another aide, Croisier, to put a stop to it. He meant, as he claimed, that they were sent to save the non-combatants, — old men, women, and children. He did not mean them to save soldiers, for, by the benign rules of war, all defenders of a place taken by assault could be slain. Misunderstanding Napoleon, or not knowing the benign rules, Eugène and Croisier accepted the surrender of three or four thousand Arab warriors, and brought them toward headquarters. As soon as Napoleon, walking in front of his tent, saw these prisoners coming, he exclaimed, in tones of grief: "Why do they bring those men to me? What am I to do with them?" Eugène and Croisier were severely reprimanded, and he again asked: "What am I to do with these men? Why did you bring them here?"

Under the alleged necessity of the case, want of food to feed them, or vessels to send them away, a council of war unanimously decided that they should be shot.

With great reluctance, and after delaying until the murmurs of the troops became mutinous, Napoleon yielded, and the prisoners were marched to the beach and massacred. That this was a horribly cruel deed no one can deny; but the barbarity was in the situation and the system, not the individual. Napoleon himself was neither blood-thirsty nor inhumane. The last thing he had done before quitting France had been to denounce the cruelty of the authorities in dealing with émigrés who were non-combatants. His proclamation, which really invited soldiers to disobey a cruel law, closed with the ringing statement, " The soldier who signs a death-warrant against a person incapable of bearing arms is a coward ! "

In passing judgment upon Napoleon, we must adopt some standard of comparison; we must know what military precedents have been, and what the present practice is. Three days after the battle of Culloden the Duke of Cumberland, being informed that the field was strewn with wounded Highlanders who still lived, — through rain and sun and the agony of undressed wounds, — marched his royal person and his royal army back to the field and, in cold blood, butchered every man who lay there. A barn, near the battle-field, was full of wounded Scotchmen; the royal Duke set it on fire, and all within were burned to death.

During the conquest of Algiers, in 1830, a French commander, a royalist, came upon a multitude of Arabs — men, women, children — who had taken refuge in a cave. He made a fire at the cavern's mouth and smoked them all to death.

In the year 1900, Russians, Germans, and other Christians invaded China to punish the heathen for barbarities practised upon Christian missionaries. A German emperor (Christian, of course) said, "Give no quarter." Germans and Russians killed everything that was Chinese — men and women and children. Armed or not armed, working in fields or idle, walking in streets or standing still, giving cause or giving none, the heathen were shot and bayoneted and sabred and clubbed, until the streets were choked with dead Chinese, the rivers were putrid with dead Chinese, the very waters of the ocean stank with dead Chinese. Prisoners were made to dig their own graves, were then shot, tumbled into the hole, and other prisoners made to fill the grave. Girls and matrons were outraged in the presence of brothers, sons, husbands, fathers ; and were then shot, or stabbed to death with swords or bayonets.

Were it not for examples such as these, the reader might feel inclined to agree with the anti-Bonaparte biographers who say that the Jaffa massacre was the blackest in the annals of civilized warfare.

Rid of his prisoners, Napoleon moved forward on the Syrian coast and laid siege to St. Jean d'Acre. The town had strong, high walls, behind which were desperate defenders. The lesson from Jaffa had taught the Arab that it was death to surrender. To him, then, it was a stern necessity to conquer or die. The English were there to help. Sir Sidney Smith furnished guns, men to serve them, and skilled engineers.

Napoleon was not properly equipped for the siege, for his battering train, on its way in transports, was stupidly lost by the captain in charge. Sir Sidney took it and appropriated it to the defence. In vain Napoleon lin-

gered till days grew into weeks, weeks into months. He
was completely baffled. There were many sorties, many
assaults, dreadful loss of life, reckless deeds of courage done
on both sides. Once, twice, the French breached the walls,
made good their assault, and entered the town, once reaching Djezzar's very palace. It was all in vain. Every
house was a fortress, every street an ambuscade, every Arab
a hero, — the very women frantically screaming "Fight!"

With bitterness in his soul, Napoleon turned away:
"that miserable hole has thwarted my destiny!" And
he never ceased to ring the changes on the subject. Had
he taken Acre, his next step would have been to the Eu-
phrates; hordes of Asiatics would have flocked to his
banner; the empire of Alexander would have risen again
under his touch; India would have been his booty; Constantinople his prize; and then, from the rear, he would
have trodden Europe into submission. He saw all this
on the other side of Acre, or thought he saw it. But the
town stood, and the château in Spain fell.

Once he had been drawn from the siege to go toward
Nazareth to the aid of Kleber, who was encompassed by
an army outnumbering his own by ten to one. As Napoleon came within sight, he could see a tumultuous host of
cavalry enveloping a small force of infantry. The throngs
of horsemen surged and charged, wheeled and turned, like
a tossing sea. In the midst was an island, a volcano
belching fire. The tossing sea was the Mameluke cavalry; the island in the midst of it was Kleber. Forming
so that his line, added to Kleber's, would envelop the
enemy, Napoleon advanced; and great was the rout and
the slaughter of the foe. No organized force was left
afield either in Syria or Egypt.

Now that the siege of Acre was abandoned, the army must be got back to Cairo, and the country laid waste to prevent Djezzar from harassing the retreat. What could not be moved, must be destroyed. The plague, brought from Damietta by Kleber's corps, had stricken down almost as many as had perished in the siege. To move the wounded and the sick was a heavy undertaking, but it was done. On the night of May 20, 1799, Napoleon began his retreat. A terrible retreat it was, over burning sands, under brazen skies, amid stifling dust, maddening thirst — and over all the dread shadow of the plague. In their selfish fears, the French became callous to the sufferings of the wounded and the sick. The weak, the helpless, were left to die in the desert. Every hamlet was fired, the fields laden with harvest were in flames, desolation spread far and wide. "The whole country was in a blaze."

Napoleon doggedly kept his course, full of dumb rage — seeing all, feeling all, powerless in the midst of its horrors. At Tentoura he roused himself to a final effort to save the sick and the wounded. "Let every man dismount; let every horse, mule, camel, and litter be given to the disabled; let the able go on foot." The order so written, despatched to Berthier, and made known through the camp, Vigogne, groom to the chief, came to ask, "What horse shall I reserve for you, General?"

It was the touch that caused an explosion. Napoleon struck the man with his whip! "Off, you rascal! Every one on foot, I the first. Did you not hear the order?"

The hungry desert swallowed horses and men. The heavy guns were abandoned. The army pressed on in sullen grief, anger, despondency. The chief trudged heavily forward, in grim silence.

On May 24, the French were at Jaffa again. Here
the hospitals were full of the plague-stricken and the
wounded. Napoleon visited these men, spoke encouraging words to them, and, according to Savary, touched one
of the victims of the plague in order to inspire confidence
— the disease being one with whose spread imagination is
said to have much to do. Bourrienne denies this story;
but according to a report written by Monsieur d'Ause,
administrator of the army of the East, and dated May 8,
1829, Napoleon not only touched the afflicted, but helped
to lift one of them off the floor. Substantially to the same
effect is the testimony of the chief surgeon of the army,
Desgenettes. Bourrienne also denies that the sick were
taken away by the retreating French. Monsieur d'Ause
reports that the wounded and the sick were put on board
seven vessels (he names the vessels), and sent by sea to
Damietta. This statement is corroborated by Grobert,
Commissioner of War, who gives the names of the officers
placed in charge of the removal. A few of the plague-
stricken were so hopelessly ill that Napoleon requested
the surgeon to administer opium. It would put the poor
creatures out of their misery, and prevent them from falling into the hands of the enemy. Desgenettes made the
noble reply which Napoleon himself quoted admiringly,
"My duty is to cure, not to kill." But Napoleon's suggestion was really humane; as he says, any man in the
condition of these hopeless, pain-racked invalids would
choose the painless sleep of opium rather than the prolonged agony of the disease.

In the year 1900 the Europeans, beleaguered by the
Chinese in Tien-Tsin, adopted the view of Napoleon.
They killed their own wounded to prevent them from fall-

ing into the hands of the heathen. According to reports published throughout Christendom and not contradicted, Admiral Seymour of the British Navy issued orders to that effect. And when the barbarities which the Christians inflicted upon the heathen became worse than death, Chinamen did as Seymour had done — killed their own friends to escape the torture.

Napoleon not insisting on poison, the few invalids who could not be moved were left alive, and several of these yet breathed when Sir Sidney Smith took possession of Jaffa.

After another dreadful desert-march, in which Napoleon tramped in the sand at the head of his troops, the army reached Cairo, June 14, 1799. With all his art, Napoleon only partially made the impression that he had returned victorious. During his absence there had been local revolts, soon repressed, and he found the country comparatively quiet. It was probably a relief to him when news came that the expected Turkish army had arrived at Aboukir. In open fight on fair field he could wipe out the shame of Acre. With all his celerity of decision, movement, and concentration, he was at Aboukir on July 25, 1799, where the Turkish army had landed. But for an accident, he would have taken it by surprise. In the battle which followed, the Turks were annihilated. Out of a force of twelve thousand scarce a man escaped. Its commander, Mustapha, was taken prisoner by Murat, after he had fired his pistol in the Frenchman's face, wounding him in the head. A blow of Murat's sabre almost severed the Turk's hand. Carried before Napoleon, the latter generously said, "I will report to the Sultan how bravely you have fought." — "You may save yourself the trouble," the proud Turk answered; "my master knows me better than you can."

The aid, counsel, and presence of Sir Sidney Smith had not availed the enemy at Aboukir as at Acre. It was with difficulty that he escaped to his ships. As to Phélippeaux, he had been stricken by the plague and was mortally ill, or already dead.

On his return to Alexandria, Napoleon sent a flag of truce to Sir Sidney, proposing an exchange of prisoners. During the negotiations, the English commodore sent Napoleon a file of English newspapers and a copy of the *Frankfort Gazette*. Throughout the night Napoleon did not sleep; he was devouring the contents of these papers. The story which they told him was enough to drive sleep away.

It is possible that Talleyrand, by way of Tripoli, may have been corresponding with Napoleon; and it seems that a letter from Joseph Bonaparte had also reached him; but Bourrienne, his private secretary, positively denies that he knew of conditions in France prior to the battle of Aboukir. Although it is possible he may have received letters which his private secretary knew nothing about, it is not probable. It would seem, therefore, that his knowledge of the situation in Europe was derived from the newspapers sent him by Sir Sidney Smith.

CHAPTER XVIII

WITH the first coming of the armies of revolutionary France to Italy, the establishment of republics in the peninsula, and the talk of Italian unity, even Rome and Naples began to move in their shrouds. Probably two systems of government more utterly wretched than those of the Pope and the Neapolitan Bourbons never existed. While changes for the better were taking place in the immediate neighborhood of these misruled states, it was natural that certain elements at Rome and Naples should begin to hope for reforms.

The support of the Pope and of the Bourbons was the ignorance of the lowest orders and the fanaticism of the priests. The middle classes, the educated, and even many of the nobles favored more liberal principles. In December, 1797, the democratic faction at Rome came into collision with the papal mob ; and the papal troops worsted in the riot, the democrats sought shelter at the French embassy, Joseph Bonaparte being at that time the minister of France. The papal faction, pursuing their advantage, violated the privilege of the French ministry, and General Duphot, a member of the embassy, was killed. .This was the second time a diplomatic agent of France had been slain by the Pope's partisans in Rome. Joseph Bonaparte left the city, and General Berthier marched in at

the head of a French army. The Pope was removed, and
finally sent to Valence, where he died in 1799. His temporal power having been overthrown, the liberals of Rome,
including many clericals who were disgusted with the
papal management of political affairs, held a great meeting in the forum, renounced the authority of the Pope,
planted a liberty tree in front of the Capitol, and declared
the Roman republic, February 15, 1798.

In the spring of 1798 the democratic cantons in Switzerland had risen against the aristocracy of Berne, had
called in the French, and on April 12, 1798, the Helvetic
republic had been proclaimed.

This continued and successful advance of republican
principles profoundly alarmed the courts and kings of
Europe. Great Britain, having failed in her efforts to
make favorable terms of peace with the French Directory,
and having gained immense prestige from the battle of
the Nile, organized a second great coalition in the
autumn of 1798. Russia, Turkey, Naples, and England
combined their efforts to crush republican France.

A Neapolitan army, led by the Austrian general, Mack,
marched upon Rome for the purpose of restoring the temporal power of the Pope. Its strength was overwhelming,
the French retreated, and Ferdinand of Naples made his
triumphant entrance into Rome in November, 1798. The
liberty tree was thrown down, an immense cross set up in
its place, many liberals put to death in spite of Ferdinand's pledge to the contrary, and a few Jews baptized
in the Tiber. The French, having left a garrison in the
castle of St. Angelo, General Mack issued a written
threat to shoot one of the sick French soldiers in the hos-
pital for every shot fired from the castle.

Ferdinand gave the credit of his victory to "the most miraculous St. Januarius." To the King of Piedmont, who had urged Ferdinand to encourage the peasants to assassinate the French, he wrote that the Neapolitans, guided by Mack, had "proclaimed to Europe, from the summit of the Capitol, that the time of the kings had come."

We do not know of any incident which more fully illustrates the meaning of the gigantic efforts made by Europe against France and Napoleon than this. Ferdinand called to the Pope to return, to sweep away all reforms, to restore all abuses, to become master again of life, liberty, and property : " The time of the kings has come! " And back of the Bourbon king, back of these efforts of Naples to inaugurate the return of the Old Order and all its monstrous wrongs, was Nelson and the English government.

If "the most miraculous St. Januarius" had joined Ferdinand in his Roman campaign, the saint soon wearied of it, for the conquest was lost as soon as made. The Neapolitan forces were badly handled, and the favorites of the saint fell easy prey to the heretic French. King Ferdinand, losing faith in Januarius, fled, the French reëntered Rome, the republic was set up again ; and Championnet, the French general, invaded Neapolitan territory. In December, 1798, the royal family of Naples took refuge on Nelson's ship, and soon sailed for Sicily. The republicans of Naples rose, opened communications with the French, who entered the city, January 23, 1799 ; and the Parthenopean republic was proclaimed. Representative government took the place of intolerant priest-rule and feudalism. Against this new order of things the clergy preached a crusade. The ignorant peasants of the rural districts and the lowest rabble of the city flew to

arms, and civil war in its worst form was soon raging
between the two factions— that which favored and that
which opposed the republic.

In the meantime the forces of the great coalition were
getting under way. A Russian army, led by the celebrated Suwarow, was on the march toward Italy. Austria
had recuperated her strength, and the Archduke Charles
beat the French, under Jourdan, at the battle of Stockach,
March 25, 1799. On the 28th of April of the same year, as
the French envoys to the Congress of Rastadt were leaving that place, they were assailed by Austrian hussars,
two of them killed, and the third left for dead. The
Archduke Charles commenced an investigation of this
crime, but was stopped by the Austrian Cabinet. The
evidence which he collected was spirited away, and has
never since been found.

On April 5, 1799, the army of Italy, under Schérer,
was defeated by the Austrians, who recovered at one blow
Italian territory almost to Milan. In June, Masséna was
beaten by the Archduke Charles at Zurich, and fell back
to a strong position a few miles from that city.

Suwarow having reached Italy in April, 1799, began
a career of victory which would have been followed by
momentous results had not Austrian jealousy marred the
campaign. His impetuous valor overwhelmed Schérer;
and, by the time Moreau was put in command of the
French, the army was too much of a wreck for even that
able officer to stand the onset of the Russians. General
Macdonald, hastening to Morean's aid, was not quite quick
enough. The dauntless and vigilant old Russian commander made a dash at Macdonald, struck him at the
Trebbia, and well-nigh destroyed him, June 18, 1799.

Southern Italy rose against the French. Cardinal Ruffo, at the head of an army of peasants, ravaged Calabria and Apulia. On the 15th of June, 1799, this army, assisted by the lazzeroni of Naples, attacked the republican forces in the suburbs of that city, and for five days there was a carnival of massacre and outrage. On the 19th the Cardinal proposed a truce. The republicans who remained in possession of the forts agreed; negotiations followed, and on the 23d terms of peace were signed by Ruffo on behalf of the King of Naples, and guaranteed by the representatives of Russia and Great Britain. It was agreed that the republicans should march out with the honors of war, that their persons and property should be respected, and that they should have the choice of remaining, unmolested at home, or of being safely landed at Toulon. On the faith of this treaty the democrats yielded up the forts, and ceased all resistance. At this juncture, Nelson sailed into the harbor and annulled the treaty. A reign of terror followed.

The Queen of Naples was the sister of Marie Antoinette, — a violent, cruel, profligate woman. She and her friend, Lady Hamilton, wife of the English minister and mistress of Lord Nelson, hounded on the avengers of the republican revolt, and Naples became a slaughter-pen. Perhaps the blackest of all the black deeds done in that revel of revenge was the murder of Admiral Carraccioli.

This man was a prince by birth, a member of one of the noblest Italian houses ; his character was as lofty as his birth, and he was seventy years old. He had joined the republicans, and had commanded their naval forces. Involved in the failure of his cause, he was entitled to the protection of the treaty of capitulation.

Q

Nelson, returning from his Victory of the Nile, and inflated with pride and political rancor, annulled the terms which Cardinal Ruffo had accepted — doing so over the Cardinal's protest, be it said to his honor. The republican garrisons of the castles were delivered by Nelson to the vengeance of their enemies. As to Prince Carraccioli, Nelson himself took charge of his case. The gray-haired man, who had honorably served his country for forty years, was brought on board the English vessel, with hands tied behind him, at nine o'clock in the forenoon. By ten his trial had begun ; in two hours it was ended. Sentenced to death immediately, he was, at five o'clock in the afternoon of the same day, hanged at the yard-arm, his body cut down at sunset, and thrown into the sea. In vain the old man had pleaded that the president of the court-martial was his personal enemy. In vain he had asked for time, a rehearing, a chance to get witnesses. Nelson was unrelenting. Then the victim of this cold-blooded murder begged that he might be shot. "I am an old man, sir. I leave no family to grieve for me, and therefore cannot be supposed to be very anxious to live ; but the disgrace of being hanged is dreadful to me ! " And again Nelson refused all concession.

Lady Hamilton, Nelson's mistress, looked on with unconcealed satisfaction as the prince-republican was choked to death with a rope ; and if ever Nelson felt a pang because of his shocking inhumanity, it has escaped the record.

Who has not had his ears deafened by royalist diatribes concerning the murder of the Duke d'Enghien ? And how silent are the same royalist authors concerning the murder of the Prince Carraccioli!

The closer the facts of history are studied and com-pared, the less certain the reader will be that Napoleon Bonaparte was a whit worse in any respect than the average public man of his time.

From the newspapers which Napoleon read at Alex-andria during the night of July 25, 1799, he first learned the full extent of the disasters which had be-fallen France in his absence.

" Great heavens, the fools have lost Italy! I must re-turn to France ! "

In the East his work was done. He had crushed organ-ized resistance. From the cataracts to the sea all was quietude. True, he had not conquered Syria, but he had broken Djezzar's strength, and destroyed the relieving army of Turks. What remained? What more had he to do in Egypt? Was he, when France was in such dire distress, to stay at Cairo running the newspaper, making pencils, supervising canals and schools, and dawdling along the Nile as local governor?

In France itself there was no division of sentiment on the subject. All felt that the best soldier of the Republic was needed at home. " Where is Bonaparte? " was the cry throughout the country. The need for him was felt in Italy as well as France, on the Rhine as on the Seine.

Even the Directory realized the necessity for the presence of the one Frenchman who could restore courage, inspire confidence, assure victory. They despatched a special messenger to call him home (September, 1799). This courier did not reach Egypt, and the order of recall

was revoked; but the fact that it was issued, proves that
Napoleon, in returning to France, obeyed an impulse which
even his enemies shared.

Hastily and secretly making the necessary arrangements, and taking with him a chosen few of his soldiers
and his savants, Napoleon embarked in four small vessels,
August 23, 1799, and next morning made sail for France.

In the army left behind there was a wail of despair,
a burst of wrath. Napoleon's name was cursed, — the
traitor, the deserter, the coward! This was very natural,
and very unjust. Kleber himself, to whom Napoleon had
delegated the chief command, was as indignant as the
rest. In bitter, unmeasured terms he denounced Bonaparte
in letters to the Directory — despatches which, when
opened, were opened by Bonaparte, First Consul. Kleber
had grossly exaggerated the difficulties of his situation,
and soon gave proof of that fact. He was in no real
danger. .When other armies were thrown against him,
he gloriously defeated them, and held his ground.

Uncontrollable circumstances, the continued hostility of
England, the unforeseen inability of Napoleon to throw succors into Egypt, alone defeated his plans, finally. Never
did a man strive harder to send relief to a lieutenant.
There is something positively pathetic in the strenuous
and fruitless efforts made by Napoleon to triumph over
the incompetence of his naval commanders, and to compel
them to exhibit enterprise, courage, and zeal in the relief
of Egypt. It was all in vain. " I cannot create men,"
he said sadly. He certainly never was able to find
effective aid in his navy, and Egypt was finally lost, in
spite of all he could do.

That he was correct in his judgment in attaching so

much importance to the conquest of Egypt, subsequent events have proved. In seizing upon the exhaustless granary of the East, the enormously important midway station on the road to India, his was the conception of a far-sighted statesman. It was his fate to teach the world, England especially, the vital importance of Malta and of Egypt, and to lose both.

CHAPTER XIX

THE seas were infested with hostile ships, and a more perilous voyage than Napoleon's from Egypt few men ever risked. His little sailing vessels had but one element of security — their insignificance. They could hope to slip by where larger ships would be sighted; and they could retreat into shoal water where men-of-war could not follow. Napoleon had with him some four or five hundred picked troops and a few cannon; his plan was to run ashore on the African coast, and make his way overland, if he should find his escape cut off on the ocean by English ships. Keeping close to the shore, he made tedious progress against contrary winds, and did not arrive off Corsica till the last days of September, 1799. He had not intended to land on his native soil, but the adverse gales made it necessary to put into the harbor of Ajaccio. Sending ashore for fruit and the latest journals, he sat up all night on board reading. He now learned that the battle of Novi had been fought, and Joubert killed.

The presence of Napoleon in the harbor of Ajaccio created a sensation on shore, and the people thronged the streets and the quays, eager for a sight of the hero of Italy and of Egypt. His victories in the East were known, for he himself had dictated the reports, and had not weakened them with any dashes of modesty. Around his name, therefore, had formed a halo, and even those Corsicans who had scorned him when feeble, admired him now that he was strong. Yielding to popular pressure, Napoleon landed. His reception was enthusiastic. The square was filled with shouting multitudes, the windows and the roofs crowded with the curious, everybody wanting to catch sight of the wondrous little man who had so quickly become the first soldier of the world. Crowds of admiring islanders remembered that they were his cousins. The number of god-children laid to him was immense. His old nurse hobbled to him, hugged him, gave him a blessing, and a bottle of goat's milk.

He walked St. Charles Street, into the little square, and into the old Bonaparte home, which the English troops had used as a barrack. He visited the country-seat, the grotto of Milleli, all the old familiar scenes. He showed his staff, with some pride, the estates of his family ; and to the tenants and the herdsmen he gave cattle and land. The soldiers of the garrison, drawn up to receive him, were in a wretched condition ; they had received no pay for more than a year. Napoleon gave them $8000, all he had, saving necessary travelling expenses. To his nurse he gave a vineyard and a house in Ajaccio.

The Corsicans tell the story that during the time when the young Lieutenant Bonaparte was trying to revolutionize the island, a priest, standing at the window of a house overlooking the street, aimed a gun at the little Jacobin's head. Napoleon, ever watchful, saw the movement just in time to dodge. The bullet struck the wall, and Napoleon scurried off.

This priest, having remained in Ajaccio, and the situation having undergone a change, was very uncomfortable; for Napoleon now had it in his power to make his old enemy do the dodging. But he bore no malice. He offered the embarrassed priest his hand, made a joke of the shot out of the window, and put the good man quite at his ease.

It was while attending a ball given in his honor in Ajaccio that Admiral Ganteaume sent word that the wind had changed, and the voyage could be resumed. Hurriedly bidding adieu to friends, he quitted Corsica for the last time.

On October 8, 1799, the four vessels entered the roads of Fréjus, and immediately upon its becoming known that Napoleon was on board, the water was covered with the boats of hundreds crowding to meet him. It was in this spontaneous rush of the people to greet the returning hero that the quarantine law was violated. The joy of the people was unbounded. They rang the bells, they filled the streets with shouting multitudes, they hailed him as the deliverer of France. A king in the best of Bourbon days had never drawn a warmer welcome. On his way from the coast he met with a prolonged ovation. At Lyons it was as though Napoleon had already become the ruler of France.

General Marbot, late commander of Paris, now passing through Lyons on his way to Italy, was somewhat scandalized and offended to see that Bonaparte was treated like a sovereign. Says his son in his *Memoirs:* —

" The houses were all illuminated, and decorated with flags, fireworks were being let off; our carriage could hardly make its way through the crowd. People were dancing in the open spaces, and the air rang with cries of : 'Hurrah for Bonaparte !   He will save the country ! '"

The hotel keeper had given to Napoleon the rooms for which General Marbot had spoken, and Napoleon was in them. Learning how General Marbot had been treated, Napoleon invited him to come and share the rooms comrade-like. Marbot went to another hotel, rather in a huff, it would seem; and Napoleon, determined not to make an enemy out of such an occurrence, went on foot and at once to apologize and express his regrets to General Marbot in his rooms at the other hotel. As he passed along the street he was followed by a cheering crowd.

"General Marbot," says his son, "was so shocked at the manner in which the people of Lyons were running after Napoleon, as though he were already king, that the journey to Italy was resumed as speedily as possible."

Napoleon's route led him through Valence, where there was not only the miscellaneous crowd to cheer him, but some true and tried personal friends. For example, there was old Mademoiselle Bou, who had credited him for board. Napoleon greeted her affectionately and made her some valuable presents, which are now to be seen in the museum of the town. Indeed, the news, flashed to all parts of France, "Bonaparte has come!" created a kind of universal transport. One deputy, Baudin by name, died of joy. Chancellor Pasquier relates that he was at the theatre one evening in Paris, when he saw two very pretty women, sitting in the box next to him, receive a message. They rose in excitement and hurried away. These very pretty women, as Pasquier learned, were the sisters of Bonaparte. A courier had brought the news that their brother had landed at Fréjus. Béranger says in his autobiography : "I was sitting in our reading room with thirty or forty others, when suddenly the news was brought in that Bonaparte had returned from Egypt. At the words every man in the room started to his feet, and burst into one long shout of joy ! "

By the signal telegraph of that day, the news had flown to the capital, and in a short while carriages were rumbling along the road out of Paris toward Lyons, bearing relatives and friends to meet the returning hero. One of these lumbering vehicles bore the uneasy Josephine. At Lyons, Napoleon, suspicions of political foes perhaps, changed his course, and hastened toward Paris by a different road. Would-be assassins, if there were any, as well as faithful friends, would fix their plans for nothing.

When Napoleon got down from his carriage before his house in the street which was called, in compliment to him, the street of Victory, there was no wife, no relative, no friend to greet him. His home was a dismal picture of darkness, silence, desertion ; and it chilled him with a painful shock which he never ceased to remember. The anxious Josephine, the faithless wife, had gone to meet him, to weep away her sins on his breast, had missed him because of his change of route ; and Napoleon, not knowing this, believed she had fled his home to escape his just anger. Bitter days and nights this eminently human Bonaparte had known ; bitter days and nights he was to know again ; but it may be doubted whether any of them gave to him a bitterer cup to drink than this of his return from Egypt.

Josephine came posting back as fast as she could, worn out with fear and fatigue. Napoleon refused to see her. Locked in his room, he paced the floor, his mind in a tempest of wrath, grief, mortification, wounded love. The guilty wife grovelled at the door, assaulting the barriers with sobs, plaintive cries, soft entreaties. Her friends, Madame Tallien, the Director Gohier, her children, Eugène and Hortense, and some of Napoleon's friends, besieged the infuriated husband, appealing to his pride, his generosity, his self-interest, his fondness for the children, — in short, using every conceivable inducement, — and at length Napoleon, worn out and softened, allowed Eugène and Hortense to put Josephine into his arms.

Bourrienne relates that many years afterward, strolling along the boulevard with Napoleon, he felt the Emperor's hand suddenly close on his arm with spasmodic grip. A carriage had just passed, and within it Napoleon had recognized Hypolite Charles, Josephine's old-time paramour. That this coxcomb still lived, is proof enough that Napoleon the Great scorned personal revenge.

While the hope of the Bonaparte family was in the East, its interest had not been neglected in France. Joseph had been established in state at Paris (town house, country house, etc.) and had cultivated influential men of all parties. Lucien had been elected in Corsica as deputy to the Council of Five Hundred. Bold, and gifted with eloquence, he had become a power in the council, and had been elected its president. Josephine herself had been effective, so splendid had been her establishment, so charming her tact and gracious ways. Therefore, when the returning soldier cast his eye over the political field, there was much to give him satisfaction. He was committed to no party; he was weighed down by no record; he was held in no rigid grooves. Towering above all other heads, he alone could draw strength from all parties. As he himself said, in his march to power he was marching with the nation. Barras admits that all France was rushing to him as to a new existence. That he would become the ruler was expected, was desired; it was only a question of when and how. The almost unanimous voice of the people would have made him Director. Details alone caused differences of opinion. Should the constitution be set aside? Should Bonaparte be one of five Directors? Or should he be vested with a virtual dictatorship? Should the powers of government be distributed, as under the Directory, or should they be concentrated? It was on details like these that differences arose; but as to the importance of having the benefit of Napoleon's services, the great mass of Frenchmen were agreed. True, the brilliant triumphs of Masséna around Zurich, and the overthrow of the English and Russians in Holland, by Brune, had saved the Republic from the pressing dangers of foreign invasion; but the foreign invasion was not the only cause of disquiet in France. The root of the evil was thought to be weakness of the government. The constitution had been violated by the Directors in Fruetidor when Augereau had broken in upon the councils and arrested so many members. Three Directors, it will be remembered, had driven out two, Carnot and Barthélemy. Afterward, in Floréal (May 11, 1798), the elections had been set aside to get rid of objectionable members. In each of these cases the vacancies made by force had been filled by the victors.

Then, finally, the reaction had become too strong, and in Prairial (June 18, 1799) the Fructidorians had in turn been beaten, and the Directory changed by the putting in of Sieyès, Gohier, Moulins, and Roger-Ducos.

People grew weary of so many convulsions, so much uncertainty, so much vacillation, so much disorder. Besides, the finances were in hopeless confusion. National bankruptcy virtually existed, and a forced loan of 100,000,000 francs, the law of hostages, and the vexatious manner in which the new Sunday law was enforced gave offence in all classes. Barras had managed to keep his place in the Directory, but not his power. Sieyès had entered the Directory, but wished to overthrow it. Even had there been no Bonaparte to plan a change, a change was inevitable. Sieyès had said, "France needs a head and a sword." With Sieyès present, only the sword was lacking, and he had tried to find one. Joubert was chosen, but got killed. Bernadotte was mentioned, but he would not take the risk. Moreau was sounded, but would not agree to act. Nevertheless, it was but a question of time when the man and the opportunity would meet. It might possibly have happened that Sieyès with his new constitution and his new executive would have saved the Republic. Better men, coming to the front and casting out the scum which had floated to the top of the revolutionary current, might have established the Republic on a solid basis, and saved the world from the hideous revel of blood and carnage which marked the era of Napoleon. No one can tell. It is easy to say that the directorial régime had failed; it is no less easy to say that a change could have been made without rushing into imperialism. Republics, being merely human, cannot be perfected in a day; and there is some injustice in cutting down the tree because it is not laden with fruit as soon as it is planted.

While Napoleon was exploring the ground and selecting his point of attack, the Directory adopted no measures of self-defence. In a general way they suspected Bonaparte and dreaded him; but they had no proofs upon which they could act. Their minister of war, Dubois de Crancé told them a plot was brewing, and advised the arrest of Napoleon. "Where are your proofs?" demanded Gohier and Moulins. The minister could not furnish them. Then a police agent warned them. Locking the informer in a room, the Directors began to discuss the matter. The agent became alarmed for his own safety, and escaped through a window.

Anxious to get Napoleon away from Paris, the Direcetors offered him his choice of the armies. He pleaded shattered health, and declined. There were two parties, possibly three, with the aid of either of which Napoleon might have won his way to power. There were the Jacobins, the remnants of the thorough-going democrats, who had made the Revolution. These were represented in the Directory by Gohier and Moulins, men of moderate capacity and fine character. But Napoleon had been cured of his youthful Jacobinism, and believed that if he now conquered with the democrats, he would soon be called on to conquer against them. Again, there were the moderates, the politicians, who were sincere republicans, but who opposed the radicalism of the democrats on the one hand, and the weakness of the Directory on the other. Sieyès and Roger-Ducos represented these in the Directory, and their following among the rich and middle-class republicans was very large. Lastly came the Barras following, the Rotten, as Napoleon called them, who would agree to pretty much any change which would not take from them the opportunities of jobbery.

Each of these parties courted Napoleon, who listened to

them all, used them all, and deceived them all. Barras he despised, yet lulled to the last moment. Gohier and Moulins were carefully manipulated and elaborately duped. Sieyès and his associates were used as tools, and then, after the bridge had been crossed, thrown over.

Even the royalists were taken in; they were beguiled with hints that Napoleon was preparing a way for the return of the Bourbons — he to act the part of Monk to the exiled King.

Napoleon's first plan was to oust from the Directory the hateful Sieyès, — "that priest sold to Prussia," and this proposition he urged upon Gohier and Moulins. As there were no legal grounds upon which the election of Sieyès could be annulled, and as Napoleon himself had not reached the age of forty, required by the constitution, Gohier and Moulins refused to have anything to do with the scheme. Its mere mention should have put them on guard; but it did not. Then Napoleon seemed, for a moment, to consider an alliance with Barras. Fouché and other friends of that Director brought the two together, and there was a dinner which was to have smoothed the way to an agreement. Unfortunately for Barras he blundered heavily in proposing an arrangement which meant that he should have the executive power, while Napoleon should merely be military chief. Napoleon, in disgust, looked the Director out of countenance, and, taking his carriage, returned home to tell Fouché what a fool Barras had made of himself. The friends of the Director, going to him at once, were able to convince even him that he had bungled stupidly; and next day he hastened to Bonaparte to try again. He was too late. Napoleon, upon leaving Barras the day before had called in to see Sieyès, and to tell him that the alliance of the Bonapartes would be made with him alone.

Naturally these two men were antagonistic. When Napoleon, quitting the army without orders, had landed at Fréjus, Sieyès had proposed to his colleagues in the Directory to have the deserter shot. The weak Directory had no such nerve as such a plan required, and the advice was ignored. Sieyès detested the abrupt, imperious soldier; and Napoleon despised the ex-priest as a confirmed, unpractical, and conceited visionary. Before he had failed with Gohier and Moulins, Napoleon had treated Sieyès with such contempt as to ignore his presence, when they were thrown together at one of the official banquets. The enraged ex-priest exclaimed to his friends, "See the insolence of that little fellow to a member of the government which ought to have had him shot!" Napoleon, intent upon the plan of ousting Sieyès from the Directory, asked *his* friends, "What were they thinking about to put into the Directory that — priest sold to Prussia?"

Powerful as were these feelings of reciprocal dislike, they were overcome. Talleyrand, Joseph Bonaparte, Cabanis, and others plied both the warrior and the priest with those arguments best suited to each. The promptings of self-interest, as well as the necessities of the case, drew them together. With Sieyès — jealous, irritable, suspicious, impracticable — the task had been most difficult. He knew he was being ensnared, — emphatically said so, — but yielded.

"Once Napoleon gets in he will push his colleagues behind him, like this," and Sieyès forcibly illustrated what he meant by bustling between Joseph and Cabanis, and then thrusting them back. Among the civilians the

Bonaparte campaign at this crisis was actively aided by Talleyrand, Cambacérès, Roger-Ducos, Roederer, Boulay, Regnier, Cabanis, the friend of Mirabeau. Among the soldiery the leading canvassers were Sébastiani, Murat, Leclerc, Marmont, Lannes, Macdonald.

The plan agreed on was that the Council of Ancients, a majority having been gained over, should decree the removal of the legislative sessions to St. Cloud, name Napoleon commander of all the troops in Paris, appoint a provisional consulate (Napoleon, Sieyès, and Roger-Ducos), during which the councils should stand adjourned and a new constitution be framed. The day fixed upon was the 18th of Brumaire (November 9, 1799), and the Ancients were to meet at seven and pass the decrees agreed on by the Bonaparte steering committee. The Five Hundred, a majority of which had not been won, were to meet *after* the Ancients should have voted the removal of the councils to St. Cloud. Hence they would be powerless to prevent Napoleon from doing what he proposed for the 18th. Whether they would be able to resist him after they formed themselves at St. Cloud on the 19th, was another matter.

R

CHAPTER XX

THERE were in Paris at this time certain battalions which had served under Napoleon in Italy; also the directorial, legislative, and national guards, which he had organized. Naturally these troops were all favorably disposed toward him. They had been urging the great soldier to review them. The officers of the garrison and of the National Guard who had not been presented to him had asked him to receive them. Napoleon had postponed action on these requests, thereby increasing the eagerness of officers and men. Now that his plans were matured, he named the 18th of Brumaire (November 9, 1799) for the review, and invited the officers to call upon him early in the morning. His excuse for this unusual hour was that he would have to leave town. Other appointments of interest Napoleon made at about the same time. He had agreed to have a conference with Barras on the night of the 17th of Brumaire, and the Director had caught at the promise as the drowning catch at anything within reach. When Bourrienne went, about midnight, to plead headache for the absent Napoleon, he saw Barras's face fall as soon as the door opened. The worn-out debauchee had no faith in the headache of Napoleon; but yet he had lacked the wish, or the energy, or the influence, to oppose the plot which he now felt sure was aimed at him as well as the others.

Gohier also had his appointments with Bonaparte. The Director was to breakfast, he and wife, with Napoleon on the 18th of Brumaire, and Napoleon was to dine with Gohier on the same day. The minister of war, Dubois de Crancé, had warned both Gohier and Moulins ; but it was not till this late day that Gohier became suspicions enough to stay away from Bonaparte's house on the morning of the 18th. His wife went, found the place thronged with officers in brilliant uniform, and soon left.

In this assembly of soldiers stood the conspicuous figure of Moreau. Discontented with the government, and without plan of his own, he had allowed Napoleon to win him by flattering words, accompanied by the complimentary gift of a jewelled sword. He had joined the movement with his eyes shut. He did not know the plan, and would not listen when Napoleon offered to explain it.

Bernadotte, the jealous, had stood aloof. Inasmuch as he was, in some sort, a member of the Bonaparte family (he and Joseph having married sisters), earnest efforts had been made to neutralize him, if nothing more. Napoleon afterward stated that Bernadotte would have joined him, had he been willing to accept Bernadotte as a colleague.

Whatever efforts were made to gain this inveterate enemy of Napoleon had no other result than to put him in possession of the secret, and to fill him with a cautious desire to defeat the plot. Augereau and Jourdan, both members of the Five Hundred, and known Jacobins, were not approached at all. General Beumonville, the ex-Girondin, had joined.

Meanwhile the conspiracy was at work from the Sieyès-Talleyrand end of the line. The Council of Ancients, convoked at seven in the morning in order that unfriendly and unnotified deputies might not be present, voted that the councils should meet at St. Cloud, and that Napoleon should be invested with command of all the troops in Paris. This decree, brought to him at his house, was immediately read by him from the balcony, and heard with cheers by the officers below.

The Napoleonic campaign was based upon the assumption that the country was in danger, that the Jacobins had made a plot to overthrow everything, and that all good citizens must rush to the rescue. Upon this idea the council had voted its own removal to a place of safety, and had appointed Napoleon to defend the government from the plotters who were about to pounce upon it. Therefore when Napoleon read the decree, he called aloud to the brilliant throng of uniformed officers, " Will you help me save the country? " Wildly they shouted " Yes," and waved their swords aloft. Bernadotte and a few others did not like the looks of things, and drew apart; but, with these exceptions, all were enthusiastic; and when Napoleon mounted his horse, they followed. He went to the Council of Ancients, where he took the oath of office, swearing not to the constitution then in existence, but that France should have a republic based on civil liberty and national representation.

The councils stood adjourned to St. Cloud, and Napoleon went into the gardens of the Tuileries to review the troops. He briefly harangued them, and was everywhere hailed by them with shouts of " Long live Bonaparte ! " So strong ran the current that Fouché volunteered aid that had not been asked, and closed the city gates. "My God! what is that for?" said Napoleon. "Order the gates opened. I march with the nation, and I want nothing done which would recall the days when factious minorities terrorized the people."

Augereau, seeing victory assured, regretted that he had not been taken into the confidence of his former chief, "Why, General, have you forgotten your old comrade, Augereau?" (Literally, "Your little Augereau.") Napoleon had no confidence in him, no use for him, and virtually told him so.

The Directory fell of its own weight; Sieyès and Roger-Ducos, as it had been agreed, resigned. Gohier and Moulins would not violate the constitution, which forbade less than three Directors to consult together; and the third man, Barras, could not be got to act. The plot had caught him unprepared. He knew that something of the kind was on foot, and had tried to get on the inside; but he did not suspect that Napoleon would spring the trap so soon. He had forgotten one of the very essential elements in Napoleonic strategy. Barras bitterly denies that the calamity dropped upon him while he was in his bath. He strenuously contends that he was shaving. When Talleyrand and Bruix came walking in with a paper ready-drawn for him to sign, he signed. It was his resignation as Director. Bitterly exclaiming, "That — Bonaparte has fooled us all," he made his swift preparations, left the palace, and was driven, under Napoleonic escort, to his country-seat of Gros-Bois. His signature had been obtained, partly by threats, partly by promises. He was to have protection, keep his ill-gotten wealth, and, perhaps, finger at least one more bribe. It is said that

Talleyrand, in paying over this last, kept the lion's share for himself.

The minister of war, Dubois de Crancé, had been running about seeking Directors who would give him the order to arrest Napoleon. How he expected to execute such an order if he got it, is not stated. As Napoleon was legally in command of eight thousand soldiers, who were even then bawling his name at the top of their voices, and as there were no other troops in Paris, it may have been a fortunate thing for the minister of war that he failed to get what he was running after.

From this distant point of view, the sight of Dubois de Crancé, chasing the Napoleonic programme, suggests a striking resemblance to the excitable small dog who runs, frantically barking, after the swiftly moving train of cars. "What would he do with it if he caught it?" is as natural a query in the one case as in the other.

So irresistible was the flow of the Bonaparte tide that even Lefebvre, commander of the guard of the Directory, a man who had not been taken into the secret, and who went to Bonaparte's house in ill-humor, to know what such a movement of troops meant, was won by a word, a magnetic glance, a caressing touch, and the tactful gift of the sabre "which I wore at the Battle of the Pyramids." "Will you, a republican, see the lawyers ruin the Republic? Will you help me?" "Let us throw the lawyers into the river!" answered the simple-minded soldier, promptly.

According to Fouché, it was about nine o'clock in the morning when Dubois found the two Directors, Gohier and Moulins, and asked for the order to arrest Bonaparte. While they were in doubt and hesitating, the secretary

of the Directory, Lagarde, stated that he would not countersign such an order unless three Directors signed it.

"After all," remarked Gohier, encouragingly, "how
can they have a revolution at St. Cloud when I have the
seals of the Republic in my possession?" Nothing legal
could be attested without the seals. Gohier had the
seals; hence, Gohier was master of the situation. Of
such lawyers, in such a crisis, well might Lefebvre say,
"Let us pitch them into the river."

Quite relieved by the statement about the seals, Moulins
remembered another crumb of comfort: he had been
invited to meet Napoleon at dinner that very day at
Gohier's. Between the soup and the cheese, the two
honest Directors would penetrate the designs of the
schemer, Napoleon, and then checkmate him.

Moreau had already been commissioned to keep these
confiding legists from running at large. However, it
was not a great while before they realized the true situation, and then they came to a grotesque conclusion. They
would go to Napoleon and talk him out of his purpose.
Barras had already sent Bottot, his private secretary, to
see if anything could be arranged. Napoleon had sternly
said, "Tell that man I have done with him." He had
also addressed the astonished Bottot a short harangue intended for publication: "What have you done with that
France I left so brilliant? In place of victory, I find
defeat." — and so forth.

Gohier and Moulins were civilly treated, but their pro-
tests were set aside. They reminded Napoleon of the
constitution, and of the oath of allegiance. He demanded
their resignations. They refused, and continued to
remonstrate. At this moment word came that Santerre

was rousing the section St. Antoine. Napoleon said to
Moulins, " Send word to your friend Santerre that at the
first movement St. Antoine makes, I will have him shot."
No impression having been made by the Directors on
Napoleon, nor by him on them, they went back to their
temporary prison in the Luxembourg.

Thus far there had been no hitch in the Bonaparte programme.   The alleged Jacobin plot nowhere showed head;
the Napoleonic plot was in full and peaceable possession.
There was no great excitement in Paris, no unusual
crowds collecting anywhere.   Proclamation had been
issued to put the people at ease, and the attitude of the
public was one of curiosity and expectancy, rather than
alarm.   Not a single man had rallied to the defence of
the Directory.   Their own guard had quietly departed
to swell the ranks which were shouting, " Hurrah for
Bonaparte ! "   Victor Grand, aide-de-camp to Barras, did
indeed wait upon that forlorn Director at seven o'clock
in the morning of the 18th, and report to him that one
veteran of the guards was still at his post.   " I am here
alone," said the old soldier; " all have left."

Here and there were members of the councils and
generals of the army who were willing enough to check
the conspiracy of Napoleon, if they had only known how.
With the Directory smashed, the councils divided and
removed, the troops on Napoleon's side, and Paris indifferent, how could Bernadotte, Jourdan, and Augereau
do anything ?

They could hold dismal little meetings behind closed
doors, discuss the situation, and decide that Napoleon must
be checked.   But who was to bell the cat ?   At a meeting
held by a few deputies and Bernadotte in the house of

Salicetti, it was agreed that they should go to St. Cloud next morning, get Bernadotte appointed commander of the legislative guard, and that he should then combat the conspirators. Salicetti betrayed this secret to Napoleon; and, through Fouché, he frustrated the plan by adroitly detaining its authors in Paris next morning.

To make assurance doubly sure, orders were issued that any one attempting to harangue the troops should be cut down.

Sieyès advised that the forty or fifty members of the councils most violently opposed to the Bonaparte programme be arrested during the night. Napoleon refused. "I will not break the oath I took this morning."

By noon of the 19th of Brumaire (November 10, 1799) the members of the councils were at St. Cloud, excited, suspicious, indignant. Even among the Ancients, a reaction against Napoleon had taken place. Many of the members had supported him on the 18th of Brumaire because they believed he would be satisfied with a place in the Directory. Since then further conferences and rumors had convinced them that he aimed at a dictatorship. Besides, those deputies who had been tricked out of attending the session of the day before, resented the wrong, and were ready to resist the tricksters. During the couple of hours which (owing to some blunder) they had to wait for their halls to be got ready, the members of the two councils had full opportunity to intermingle, consult, and measure the strength of the opposition. When at length they met in their respective chambers, they were in the frame of mind which produces that species of disturbance known as a parliamentary storm. Napoleon and his officers were grimly waiting in another room of the palace for the cut-and-dried programme to be proposed and voted. Sieyès had a coach and six ready at the gates to flee in case of mishap.

In the Five Hundred the uproar began with the session. The overwhelming majority was against Bonaparte — this much the members had already ascertained. But the opposition had not had time to arrange a programme. Deputy after deputy sprang to his feet and made motions, but opinions had not been focussed. One suggestion, however, carried; they would all swear again to support the constitution: this would uncover the traitors. It did nothing of the kind. The conspirators took the oath without a grimace — Lucien Bonaparte and all. As each member had to swear separately, some two hours were consumed in this childish attempt to uncover traitors and buttress a falling constitution.

In the Ancients, also, a tempest was brewing. When the men, selected by the Bonaparte managers, made their opening speeches and motions, opposition was heard, explanations were demanded, and awkward questions asked. Why move the councils to St. Cloud? Why vest extraordinary command in Bonaparte? Where was this great Jacobin plot? Give facts and name names!

No satisfaction could be given to such demands. The confusion was increased by the report made to the body that four of the Directors had resigned. Proceedings were suspended until the Council of Five Hundred could receive this report, and some action be suggested for filling the places thus made vacant.

At this point Napoleon entered the hall. He could hear the wrangle going on in the Five Hundred, but he had not expected trouble in the Ancients. The situation had begun to look dangerous. Augereau, thinking it safe to vent his true feeling, had jeeringly said to Napoleon, "Now you are in a pretty fix."

"It was worse at Arcole," was the reply.

Napoleon had harangued sympathetic Jacobins in small political meetings ; but to address a legislative body was new to him. His talk to the Ancients was incoherent and weak. He could not give the true reasons for his conduct, and the pretended reason could not be strengthened by explanation or fact. He was asked to specify the dangers which he said threatened the Republic, asked to describe the conspiracy, and name the conspirators. He could not do so, and after rambling all round the subject, his friends pulled him out of the chamber. Notwithstanding his disastrous speech, the conspiracy asserted its strength, and the Council of Ancients was held to the Bonaparte programme. Napoleon at once went to the Council of Five Hundred, and his appearance, accompanied by armed men, caused a tumult. "Down with the Dictator ! For shame ! Was it for this you conquered. Get out ! Put him out !" Excited members sprang to their feet shouting, gesticulating, threatening. Rough hands were laid upon him. Knives may have been drawn. The Corsican, Peretti, had threatened Mirabeau with a knife in the assembly hall : Tallien had menaced Robespierre with a dagger ; there is no inherent improbability in the story that the Corsican, Arena, a bitter enemy of Napoleon, now struck at him with a knife. At all events, the soldiers thought Napoleon in such danger that they drew him out of the press, General Gardanne (it is said) bearing him backward in his arms.

"*Hors la loi!*" was shouted in the hall — the cry before

which Robespierre had gone down. " Outlaw him ! Outlaw him ! "

Lucien Bonaparte, president of the body, refused to
put the motion. The anger of the Assembly then vented
itself upon Lucien, who vainly attempted to be heard in
defence of his brother. " He wanted to explain," cried
Lucien, " and you would not hear him ! " Finding the
tumult grow worse, and the demand that he put the motion
grow more imperative, he stripped himself of the robe of
office, sent for an escort of soldiers, and was borne out by
Napoleon's grenadiers.

While the council chamber rang with its uproar, there
had been consternation outside. For a moment the Bonaparte managers hesitated. They had not foreseen such a
check. Napoleon himself harangued the troops; and telling them that an attempt had been made on his life, was
answered by cries of " Long live Bonaparte ! " It was
noticed that he changed his position every moment, zigzagging as much as possible, like a man who feared some
assassin might aim at him from a window in the palace.
He said to Sieyès, " They want to outlaw me ! " Seated
in his carriage, ready to run, but not yet dismayed, the
ex-priest is said to have answered : " Then do you outlaw
them. Put them out." Napoleon, reëntering the room
where the officers were sitting or standing, in dismay and
inaction, struck the table with his riding-whip, and said,
" I must put an end to this." They all followed him out.
Lucien, springing upon a horse, harangued the troops,
calling upon them to drive out from the hall the factious
minority which was intimidating the virtuous majority of
the council. The soldiers hesitated. Drawing his sword,
Lucien shouted, " I swear that I will stab my brother to

the heart if ever he attempt anything against the liberties of the people ! ''

This was dramatic, and it succeeded. The troops responded with cheers, and Napoleon saw that they were at length ready. "*Now* I will soon settle those gentlemen ! '' He gave Murat the signal; Murat and Le Clerc took the lead; and to the roll of drums the file advanced. The legislators would have spoken to the troops, but the drums drowned the protest. Before the advancing line of steel, the members fled their hall, and the Bonaparte campaign was decided.

But once more Sieyès was the giver of sage advice. Legal forms must be respected. France was not yet ready for the bared sword of the military despot. The friendly members of the Council of Five Hundred must be sought out and brought back to the hall. The deputies were not yet gone, were still lingering in astonishment and grief and rage about the palace. Lucien Bonaparte, the hero of this eventful day, contrived to assemble about thirty members of the Council of Five Hundred who would vote the Bonaparte programme through. They spent most of the night adopting the measures proposed. It was past midnight when the decrees of this Rump Parliament were presented to the Ancients for ratification. In that assembly the Bonaparte influence was again supreme, and no bayonets were needed there. Napoleon, Sieyès, and Roger-Ducos having been named provisional consuls, appeared before the Five Hundred between midnight and day to take the oath of office.

The legislative councils then stood adjourned till February 19, 1800. Commissions had been selected to aid in framing the constitution. Lucien made the last speech of the Revolution, and, according to Mr. Lanfrey, it was the most bombastic piece of nonsense and falsehood that had been uttered during the entire period. He compared the Tennis Court Oath to the work just done, and said that, as the former had given birth to liberty, this day's work had given it manhood and permanence.

Not until the last detail of the work had been finished and put in legal form, did Napoleon quit St. Cloud. He had even dictated a proclamation in which he gave to the public his own account of the events of the day, He again laid stress on the Jacobin plot which had threatened the Republic, he again renewed his vows to that Republic, he praised the conduct of the Ancients, and claimed that the violence used against the Five Hundred had been made necessary by the factious men, would-be assassins, who had sought to intimidate the good men of that body. This proclamation was posted in Paris before day.

To humor the fiction, if it was a fiction, that Napoleon had been threatened with knives, a grenadier, Thomas Thomé, was brought forward, who said that he had warded off the blow. He showed where his clothes had been cut or torn. As soon as the stage could be properly arranged for the scene, the amiable and grateful Josephine publicly embraced Thomé and made him a present of jewels. Napoleon promoted him later to a captaincy.

The men who stood by Napoleon in this crisis left him under a debt which he never ceased to acknowledge and to pay. With one possible exception, he loaded them with honors and riches. The possible exception was Collot, the banker, who, according to Fouché, supplied the campaign fund. The bare fact that Napoleon did not at any time treat Collot with favor, is strong circumstantial evidence that he rendered no such aid at this crisis as created a debt of gratitude.

It was morning, but before daybreak, when Napoleon, tired but exultant, reached home from St. Cloud. As he threw himself upon the bed by the side of Josephine, he called out to his secretary : —

"Remember, Bourrienne, we shall sleep in the Luxembourg to-morrow."

CHAPTER XXI

0N Sunday evening, Brumaire 19, Napoleon had been
a desperate political gambler, staking fortune and life
upon a throw; on Monday morning following he calmly
seated himself in the armchair at the palace of the Luxembourg and began to give laws to France. He took the
first place and held it, not by any trick or legal contrivance, but by his native imperiousness and superiority. In
genius, in cunning, in courage, he was the master of the
doctrinaire Sieyès, and of the second-rate lawyer, Roger-
Ducos; besides, he held the army in the hollow of his
hand.

The sad comfort of saying "I told you so," was all that
was left to Sieyès. "Gentlemen, we have a master," said
he to his friends that Monday evening; and the will of
this imperious colleague he did not seriously try to oppose.
In the very first meeting of the consuls, Napoleon had won
the complete supremacy by refusing to share in the secret
fund which the Directors had hidden away for their
own uses. They had emptied the treasury, and had spent
$15,000,000 in advance of the revenues, yet they had laid
by for the rainy day which might overtake themselves
personally the sum of 800,000 francs or about $160,000.
Sieyès blandly called attention to this fact, and proposed
that he, Ducos, and Napoleon should divide the fund.

NAPOLEON

As First Consul, at Malmaison. From a painting by J. B. Isabey

"Share it between you," said Napoleon, **who** refused to touch it.

Without the slightest apparent effort, Napoleon's genius expanded to the great work of reorganizing the Republic. Heretofore he had been a man of camps and battle-fields; but he had so completely mastered everything connected with the recruiting equipment and maintenance of an army, had served so useful an apprenticeship in organiz ing the Italian republics, and had been to school to such purpose in dealing with politicians of all sorts, negotiat- ing treaties, and sounding the secrets of parties, that he really came to his great task magnificently trained by actual experience.

In theory the new government of the three consuls was only experimental, limited to sixty days. The two coun- cils had not been dissolved. Purged of about sixty vio- lently anti-Bonaparte members, the Ancients and the Five Hundred were but adjourned to the **19th** of February, **1800.** If by that time the consuls had not been able to offer to France a new scheme of government which would be accepted, the councils were to meet again and decide what should be done. On paper, therefore, Napoleon was a consul on probation, a pilot on a trial trip. In his own eyes he was permanent chief of the State; and his every motion was made under the impulse of that conviction.

Determined that there should be no reaction, that the scattered forces of the opposition should have no common cause and centre of revolt, **he** stationed **his** soldiers at threatened points ; and then used all the art of the fin- ished politician to deceive and divide the enemy. To the

royalists he held out the terror of a Jacobin revival ; to
the Jacobin, the dread of a Bourbon restoration. To the
clergy he hinted a return of the good old days when no
man could legally be born, innocently married, decently
die, or be buried with hope of heaven, unless a priest had
charge of the functions. But above all was his pledge of
strong government, one which would quell faction, restore
order, secure property, guarantee civil liberty, and make
the Republic prosperous and happy. The belief that he
would make good his word was the foundation of the
almost universal approval with which his seizure of power
was regarded. He was felt to be the one man who could
drag the Republic out of the ditch, reinspire the armies,
cleanse the public service, restore the ruined finances,
establish law and order, and blend into a harmonious
nationality the factions which were rending France. Besides, it was thought that a strong government would be
the surest guarantee of peace with foreign nations, as it
was believed that the weakness of the Directory was an
encouragement to the foreign enemies of the country.

One of Napoleon's first acts was to proclaim amnesty
for political offences. He went in person to set free the
hostages imprisoned in the Temple. Certain priests and
émigrés who had been cast into prison, he released. The
law of hostages, which held relatives responsible for the
conduct of relatives, he repealed.

The victims of Fructidor (September, 1797) who had
been banished, he recalled — Pichegru and Aubrey
excepted.

Mr. Lanfrey says that this exception from the pardon
is proof of Napoleon's "mean and cruel nature." Let us
see. Pichegru, a republican general, in command of

a republican army, had taken gold from the Bourbons, and had agreed to betray his army and his country. Not only that, he had purposely allowed that army to be beaten by the enemy. As Desaix remarked, Pichegru was perhaps the only general known to history who had ever done a thing of the kind. Was Napoleon mean and cruel in letting such a man remain in exile? Had Washington captured and shot Benedict Arnold, would that have been proof that Washington's nature was mean and cruel? In leaving Pichegru where he was, Napoleon acted as leniently as possible with a self-convicted traitor.

As to Aubrey, he had held a position of the highest trust under the Republic, while he was at heart a royalist; he had used that position to abet royalist conspiracies; he had gone out of his way to degrade Napoleon, had refused to listen to other members of the government in Napoleon's favor, and had urged against Napoleon two reasons which revealed personal malice, — Napoleon's youth, and Napoleon's politics. To pardon such a man might have been magnanimous; to leave him under just condemnation was neither mean nor cruel.

Under the law of that time, there were about 142,000 émigrés who had forfeited life and estate. They had staked all in opposition to the Revolution, had lost, and had been put under penalty. Almost immediately, Napoleon began to open the way for the return of these exiles and for the restoration of their property. As rapidly as possible, he broadened the scope of his leniency until all émigrés had been restored to citizenship save the very few (about one thousand) who were so identified with the Bourbons, or who had so conspicuously made war on France, that their pardon was not deemed judicious.

Priests were gradually relieved from all penalties and allowed to exercise their office. Churches were used by Christians on the seventh-day Sabbath, and by Theophilanthropists on the Decadi — the tenth-day holiday. The one sect came on the seventh day with holy water, candles, holy image, beads, crucifix, song, prayer, and sermon on faith, hope, and charity, — with the emphasis thrown on the word, Faith. The other sect came on the tenth day with flowers for the altar, hymns and addresses in honor of those noble traits which constitute lofty character, and with the emphasis laid upon such words as Brotherhood, Charity, Mercy, and Love.

It was not a great while, of course, before the Christians (so recently pardoned) found it impossible to tolerate the tenth-day people; and they were quietly suppressed in the Concordat.

One of the Directors, Larévellière, was an ardent Theophilanthropist, and he had made vigorous effort to enroll Napoleon on that side, soon after the Italian campaign. The sect, being young and weak, found no favor whatever in the eyes of the ambitious politician; and he who in Egypt sat cross-legged among the ulemas and muftis, demurely taking lessons from the Koran, had no hesitation in repelling the advances of Theosophy.

Going, perhaps, too far in his leniency to the émigrés (Napoleon said later that it was the greatest mistake he ever made!), the new government certainly erred in its severity toward the Jacobins. Some fifty-nine of these were proscribed for old offences, and sentenced to banishment. Public sentiment declared against this arbitrary *ex post facto* measure so strongly that it was not enforced. The men of the wealthy class were drawn to the government by the repeal of the law called the Forced Loan. This was really an income tax, the purpose of which was to compel the capitalists to contribute to the support of the State. The Directors, fearing that the rich men who were subject to the tax might not make true estimates and returns, assessed it by means of a jury. Dismal and resonant wails arose from among the stricken capitalists.

Although the government created the tax as a loan, to be repaid from the proceeds of the national domain, the antagonism it excited was intense. In England, Mr. Pitt had (1798) imposed a tax upon incomes, — very heavy in its demands, and containing the progressive principle of the larger tax for the larger income, — but the Directors were too feeble to mould the same instrument to their purpose in France. Faultily assessed, stubbornly resisted, irregularly collected, it yielded the Directory more odium than cash.

The five per cent funds which had fallen to one and a half per cent of their par value before the 18th of Brumaire, had risen at once to twelve per cent, and were soon quoted at seventeen.

Confidence having returned, Napoleon was able to borrow 12,000,000 francs for the immediate necessities of the State. The income tax having been abolished, an advance of twenty-five per cent was made in the taxes on realty, personalty, and polls. Heretofore, these taxes had been badly assessed, badly collected, imperfectly paid into the treasury. Napoleon at once remodelled the methods of assessment, collection, and accounting. Tax collectors were required to give bonds in cash; were made responsible for the amount of the taxes legally assessed; were given a certain time within which to make collection, and were required to give their own bills for the amount assessed. These bills, backed by the cash deposit of the collectors, became good commercial paper immediately, and thus the government was supplied with funds even before the taxes had been paid.

It was with this cash deposit of the collectors that Napoleon paid for the stock which the government took in the Bank of France which he organized in January, 1800.

There yet remained in the hands of the government a large amount of the confiscated land, and some of this was sold. To these sources of revenue were soon added the contributions levied upon neighboring and dependent states, such as Genoa, Holland, and the Hanse towns.

Under the Directory, tax-collecting and recruiting for the army had been badly done because the work had been left to local authorities. The central government could not act upon the citizen directly; it had to rely upon these local authorities. When, therefore, the local authorities failed to act, the machinery of administration was at a standstill. Napoleon changed all this, and devised a system by which the government dealt directly with the citizen. It was a national officer, assisted by a council, who assessed and collected taxes. The prefects appointed by Napoleon took the place of the royal intendants of the Bourbon system. Holding office directly from the central government, and accountable to it alone, these local authorities became cogs in the wheel of a vast, resistless machine controlled entirely by the First Consul. So perfect was the system of internal administration which he devised, that it has stood the shock of all the changes which have since occurred in France.

Keeping himself clear of parties, and adhering steadily

to the policy of fusion, Napoleon gave employment to
men of all creeds. He detested rogues, speculators, em-
bezzlers. He despised mere talkers and professional orators. He wanted workers, strenuous and practical. He
cared nothing for antecedents, nor for private morals.
He knew the depravity of Fouché and Talleyrand, yet
used them. He gave employment to royalists, Jacobins,
Girondins, Deists, Christians, and infidels. "Can he do
the work, and will he do it honestly?" these were the
supreme tests. No enmity would deprive him of the service of the honest and capable. No friendship would
tolerate the continuance in office of the dishonest or incompetent. Resolute in this policy of taking men as he
found them, of making the most of the materials at hand,
he gave high employment to many a man whom he personally disliked. He gave to Talleyrand the ministry of
foreign affairs, to Fouché that of the police, to Carnot
that of war. To Moreau he gave the largest of French
armies; Augereau, Bernadotte, Jourdan, he continued to
employ. "I cannot create men; I must use those I find."
Again he said, "The 18th of Brumaire is a wall of brass,
separating the past from the present."

If they were capable, if they were honest, it did not
matter to Napoleon whether they had voted to kill the
King or to save him; he put them to work for France.
Once in office, they must work. No sinecures, no salaries
paid as hush money, or indirect bribe, or pension for past
service, or screen for the privileged; without exception
all must earn their wages. "Come, gentlemen!" Napoleon would say cheerfully to counsellors of State who had
already been hammering away for ten or twelve hours,
"Come, gentlemen, it is only two o'clock! Let us get

on to something else ; we must earn the money the State
pays us." He himself labored from twelve to eighteen
hours each day, and his activity ran the whole gamut of
public work, — from the inspection of the soldier's outfit, the planning of roads, bridges, quays, monuments,
churches, public buildings, the selection of a sub-prefect,
the choice of a statue for the palace, the review of a regiment, the dictation of a despatch, or the details of a tax-
digest, to the grand outlines of organic law, national policy, and the movements of all the armies of the Republic.

Under the Directory, the military administration had
broken down so completely that the war office had lost
touch with the army. Soldiers were not fed, clothed, or
paid by the State. They could subsist only by plundering
friends and foes alike. Frightful ravages were committed
by civil and military agents of the French Republic in Italy,
Switzerland, and along the German frontier. When Napolcou applied to the late minister of war, Dubois de
Crancé, for information about the army, he could get
none. Special couriers had to be sent to the various commands to obtain the most necessary reports. Under such
mismanagement, desertions had become frequent in the
army, and recruiting had almost ceased. The old patriotic enthusiasm had disappeared ; the " Marseillaise " performed at the theatres, by order of the Directory, was
received with hoots. To breathe new life into Frenchmen, to inspire them again with confidence, hope, enthusiasm, was the great task of the new government. The Jacobin was to be made to tolerate the royalist, the Girondin, the
Feuillant, and the priest. Each of these in turn must be
made to tolerate each other and the Jacobin. The noble
must consent to live quietly within the Republic which

had confiscated his property, and by the side of the man who now owned it. The republican must dwell in harmony with the emigrant aristocracy which had once trodden him to the earth, and which had leagued all Europe against France in the efforts to restore old abuses. In the equality created by law, the democrat must grow accustomed to the sight of nobles and churchmen in office ; and the man of the highest birth must be content to work with a colleague whose birth was of the lowest. Ever since the Revolution began, there had been alternate massacres of Catholics by revolutionists, and of revolutionists by Catholics. It is impossible to say which shed the greatest amount of blood — the Red Terror of the Jacobins, or the White Terror of the Catholics. Fanaticism in the one case as in the other had shown a ferocity of the most relentless description. The cruel strife was now to be put down, and the men who had been cutting each other's throats were to be made to keep the peace.

Napoleon, in less than a year, had completely triumphed over the difficulties of his position. The machinery of state was working with resistless vigor throughout the realm. The taxes were paid, the laws enforced, order reëstablished, brigandage put down, La Vendée pacified, civil strife ended. The credit of the government was restored, public funds rose, confidence returned. Men of all parties, of all creeds, found themselves working zealously to win the favor of him who worked harder than any mortal known to history.

Meanwhile Sieyès and the two commissions had been at work on the new constitution. Dreading absolute monarchy on the one hand, and unbridled democracy on the other, Sieyès had devised a plan of government which, as he believed, combined the best features of both systems. There was to be universal suffrage. Every tax-paying adult Frenchman who cared enough about the franchise to go and register should have a vote. But these voters did not choose office-holders. They simply elected those from whom the office-holders should be chosen. The great mass of the people were to elect one-tenth of their number, who would be the notables of the commune. These would, in turn, elect one-tenth of their number, who would be the notables of the department. These again would elect one-tenth, who would be the national notables. From these notables would be chosen the office-holders, — national, departmental, and communal. This selection was made, not by the people, but by the executive. There was to be a council of state working immediately with the executive by whom its members were appointed. This council acting with the executive would propose laws to the tribunate, an assembly which could debate these prepared measures and which could send three of its members to the legislative council to favor or oppose the law. This legislature could hear the champions of the tribunate, and also the delegates from the council of state; and after the speeches of these advocates, pro and con, the legislature, as a constitutional jury which heard debate without itself debating, could vote on the proposed law. Besides, there was to be a Senate, named by the executive, holding office for life. This Senate was to choose the members of the legislative council and of the tribunate, as well as the judges of the high court of appeals. In the Senate was lodged the power of deciding whether laws were constitutional.

According to the Sieyès plan, there were to have been two consuls, of war and of peace respectively; and these consuls were to have named ministers to carry on the government through their appointees. Above the two consuls was to be placed a grand elector, who should be lodged in a palace, maintained in great state, magnificently salaried, but who should have no power beyond the choice of the consuls. If the Senate should be of the opinion, at any time, that the grand elector was not conducting himself properly, it could absorb him into its own body, and choose another.

Sieyès had been one of the charter members of the revolutionary party, had helped to rock the cradle when the infant was newly born, had lived through all the changes of its growth, manhood, madness, and decline. Much of the permanent good work of the Revolution was his. He now wished to frame for the French such a fundamental law as would guard their future against the defects of their national character, while it preserved to them what was best in the great principles of the Revolution.

Once a churchman himself, he knew the Church and dreaded it. He feared that the priests, working through superstitious fears upon the minds of ignorant masses, would finally educate them into hostility to the new order — train them to believe that the Old Régime had been the best, and should be restored. To get rid of this danger (the peril of royalists and priests from above acting upon the ignorant masses below), the far-sighted statesman, dealing with France as it was, did not favor popular sovereignty. Only by indirection were the masses to be allowed to choose their rulers. The people could choose the local notables from whom the local officers must be taken; and

these local notables could vote for departmental notables
from whom departmental officers should be chosen; and
those departmental notables would select from their own
numbers the national notables from whom holders for
national positions must be taken.

These electoral bodies grew smaller as they went upward.   The 5,000,000 voters of the nation first elected
500,000 local notables; these chose from themselves 50,000
departmental electors; and these in turn took by vote
5000 of their own number to constitute the electoral class
for national appointments.   The executive filled all offices
from these various groups.   From below, the masses
furnished the material to be used in governing; from
above, the executive made its own selection from that
material.

This was far from being representative government;
but it was far from being mere despotism, military or
otherwise.   It was considered as free a system as France
was then prepared for; and he is indeed a wise man who
knows that she would have done better under a constitution which granted unlimited popular control.   The French
had not been educated or trained in republican government,
and the efforts which had been made to uphold a republic
in the absence of such education and experience had resulted in the dictatorship of the Great Committee and of
the Directory.

Napoleon and Sieyès were agreed on the subject of
popular suffrage; they were far apart on the question of
the executive.   By nature "imperious, obstinate, masterful," the great Corsican had no idea of becoming a fatu-
ous, functionless elector.   "What man of talent and honor
would consent to such a rôle, — to feed and fatten like a

pig in a stye on so many millions a year?" Before this scornful opposition the grand elector vanished. In his place was put a First Consul, in whom were vested all executive powers. Two associate consuls were given him, but their functions in no way trenched upon his.

The constitution, rapidly completed, was submitted to the people by the middle of December, 1799. It was adopted by three million votes — the negative vote being insignificant.

"This constitution is founded on the true principles of representative government, on the sacred rights of property, equality, and liberty." "The Revolution is ended." So ran the proclamation published by the provisional government.

It was a foregone conclusion that Napoleon would be named First Consul in the new government which the people had ratified. It is no less true that he dictated the choice of his two colleagues, — Cambacérès and Lebrun. These were men whose ability was not of the alarming kind, and who could be relied upon to count the stars whenever Napoleon, at midday, should declare that it was night. Sieyès was soothed with the gift of the fine estate of Crosne, and the presidency of the Senate. Roger-Ducos also sank peacefully into the bosom of that august, well-paid Assembly.

It was on Christmas Eve of 1799 that the government of the three permanent consuls began ; by the law of its creation it was to live for ten years.

This consular government was a magnificent machine, capable of accomplishing wonders when controlled by an able ruler. The gist of it was concentration and uniformity. All the strength of the nation was placed at the dis-

posal of its chief. He could plan and execute, legislate
and enforce legislation, declare war and marshal armies,
and make peace. He was master at home and abroad.
In him was centred France. He laid down her laws,
fixed her taxes, dictated her system of schools, superintended her roads and bridges, policed her towns and
cities, licensed her books, named the number of her
armies; pensioned the old, the weak, and the deserving ;
censored her press, controlled rewards and punishments,
— his finger ever on the pulse-beat of the nation, his will
its master, his ideals its inspiration.

No initiative remained with the people. Political
liberty was a reminiscence. The town bridge could not
be rebuilt or the lights of the village changed without
authority granted from the Consul or his agents. " Confidence coming from below; power descending from
above," was the principle of the new Sieyès system.
Under just such a scheme it was possible that it might
happen that the power of the ruler would continue to
come down long after the confidence of the subject had
ceased to go up.

The Revolution had gone to the extreme limits of
popular sovereignty by giving to every citizen the ballot,
to every community the right of local self-government ;
and to the masses the privilege of electing judicial and
military as well as political officers. France was said to
be cut up into forty thousand little republics. The central authority was almost null ; the local power almost
absolute. It was this federative system carried to excess
(as under the Articles of the Confederation in our own
country) which had made necessary the despotism of
the Great Committee. The consular constitution was

the reverse of this. Local government became null, the
central authority almost absolute. Prefects and sub-
prefects, appointed by the executive, directed local affairs,
nominally assisted by local boards, which met once a year.
Even the mayors held their offices from the central
power. From the lowest round of the official ladder to
the highest, was a steady climb of one rung above the
other. The First Consul was chief, restrained by the
constitution; below him, moving at his touch, came all
the other officers of state.

Under Napoleon the burden of supporting the State
rested on the shoulders of the strong. Land, wealth,
paid the direct taxes; the customs duties were levied
mainly upon luxuries, not upon the necessaries of life.
Prior to the Revolution the taxes of the unprivileged had
amounted to more than three-fourths of the net produce
of land and labor. Under the Napoleonic system the
taxes amounted to less than one-fourth of the net income.

Before the Revolution the poor man lost fifty-nine days
out of every year in service to the State by way of tax.
Three-fifths of the French were in this condition. After
the Revolution the artisan, mechanic, and day laborer lost
from nine to sixteen days per year. Before the Revolution Champfort could say, " In France seven millions of
men beg and twelve millions are unable to give anything."
To the same purport is the testimony of Voltaire that
one-third of the French people had nothing.

Under Napoleon an American traveller, Colonel Pink-
ney could write, " There are no tithes, no church taxes,
no taxation of the poor. All the taxes together do not
go beyond one-sixth of a man's rent-roll."

Before the Revolution the peasant proprietor and

small farmer, out of 100 francs net income, paid 14
francs to the seigneur, 14 to the Church, and 53 to
the State.   After Napoleon's rise to power, the same
farmer out of the same amount of income paid nothing
to the seigneur, nothing to the Church, very little to the
State, and only 21 francs to the commune and department.   Under the Bourbons such a farmer kept for his
own use less than 20 francs out of 100 ; under Napoleon
he kept 79.

Under the Bourbons the citizen was compelled to buy
from the government seven pounds of salt every year at
the price of thirteen sous per pound, for himself and each
member of his family.   Under Napoleon he bought no
more than he needed, and the price was two sous per
pound.

Under the Bourbons the constant dread of the peasant,
for centuries, had been Famine — national, universal, horribly destructive Famine.   With Napoleon's rise to power,
the spectre passed away ; and, excepting local and accidental dearths in 1812 and 1817, France heard of Famine
no more.

Napoleon believed that each generation should pay
its own way.   He had no grudge against posterity,
and did not wish to live at its expense.   Hence he
"floated" no loans, issued no bonds, and piled up no
national debt.

The best of the Bourbon line, Henry IV., lives in
kindly remembrance because he wished the time to come
when the French peasant might, once a week, have a fowl
for the pot.   Compare this with what Lafayette writes
(in 1800): "You know how many beggars there were,
people dying of hunger in our country.   We see no more

of them. The peasants are richer, the land better tilled, and the women better clad."

Morris Birkbeck, an English traveller, writes, "Everybody assures me that the riches and comfort of the farmers have been doubled in twenty-five years.

"From Dieppe to this place, Montpellier, we have not seen among the laboring people one such famished, worn-out, wretched object as may be met in every parish in England, I had almost said on almost every farm. . . . A really rich country, and yet there are few rich individuals."

As one reads paragraphs like these, the words of John Ruskin come to mind, "Though England is deafened with spinning-wheels, her people have no clothes ; though she is black with digging coal, her people have no fuel, and they die of cold ; and though she has sold her soul for gain, they die of hunger ! "

How the government which was overthrown by Napoleon could have gone on much longer even Mr. Lanfrey does not explain. It had neither money nor credit ; the very cash box of the opera had been seized to obtain funds to forward couriers to the armies. It had neither honesty nor capacity. Talleyrand, treating with the American envoys, declined to do business till his hands had been crossed, according to custom ; brigands robbed mail coaches in the vicinity of Paris ; the public roads and canals were almost impassable ; rebellion defied the government in La Vendée. The Directory did not even have the simple virtue of patriotism ; Barras was sold to the Bourbons, and held in his possession letters-patent issued to him by the Count of Provence, appointing him royal commissioner to proclaim and reëstablish the monarchy. "Had I known of the letters-patent on the 18th of Brumaire," exclaimed Napoleon afterward, "I would have pinned them upon his breast and had him shot."

CHAPTER XXII

ALL honor to the ruler who commences his reign by words and deeds which suggest that he has somewhere heard and heeded the golden text, "Blessed are the peacemakers!"

There had been riots in France and the clash of faction; there had been massacre of Catholic by Protestant and of Protestant by Catholic; there had been civil war in La Vendée. Napoleon had no sooner become master than his orders went forth for peace, and a year had not passed before quiet reigned from Paris to all the frontiers. Royally he pardoned all who would accept his clemency, giving life and power to many a secret foe who was to help pull him down in the years to come. France tranquillized within, the First Consul turned to the enemies without, — to the foreign powers which had combined against her.

On Christmas Day, December 25, 1799, Napoleon wrote to the King of England and to the Emperor of Austria nobly worded letters praying that the war might cease. Written with his own hand, and addressed personally to these monarchs, the question of etiquette is raised by royalist writers. They contend that letters, so addressed, were improper. Think of the coldness of nature which would make the lives of thousands of men turn on a piti-

275

ful point like that! These letters were not sincere,
according to Napoleon's detractors. How they come to
know this, they cannot explain; but they know it. The
average reader, not gifted with the acumen of the professional detractor, can only be certain of the plain facts of
the case, and those are, that Napoleon made the first overtures for peace; that his words have the ring of sincerity,
and the virtue of being positive; and that his conciliatory
advances were repelled, mildly by Austria, insolently by
Great Britain.

So arrogant was the letter of reply which Grenville,
the English minister, sent to the French foreign office
that even George III. disapproved of it. With incredible
superciliousness the French were told by the English
aristocrat that they had better restore the Bourbons
under whose rule France had enjoyed so much prosperity
at home and consideration abroad. Inasmuch as England
had but recently despoiled Bourbon France of nearly every
scrap of territory she had in the world, — Canada, India,
etc., — Grenville's letter was as stupidly scornful of fact as
it was of good manners. The Bourbon "glory" which had
sunk so low that France had not even been invited to the
feast when Poland was devoured; so low that the French
flag had been covered with shameful defeat on land and
sea, was a subject which might have made even a British
cabinet officer hesitate before he took the wrong side
of it.

The honors of the correspondence remained with Napoleon; and by way of retort to Grenville's plea, that the
Bourbons were the legitimate rulers of France, whom the
people had no right to displace, the surly Englishman
was reminded that the logic of his argument would bring

the Stuarts back to the throne of England, from which a revolting people had driven them. The truth is that Pitt's ministry believed France exhausted. Malta and Egypt were both coveted by Great Britain, and it was believed that each would soon be lost by France. It was for reasons like these that Napoleon's overtures were rejected.

With the Emperor of Russia the First Consul was more fortunate. The Czar had not liked the manner in which he had been used by his allies, England and Austria. In fact, he had been shabbily treated by both. Added to this was his dissatisfaction with England because of her designs on Malta, in whose fate he took an interest as protector of the Knights of St. John.

Napoleon cleverly played upon the passions of the Czar (who was more or less of a lunatic), flattered him by releasing the Russian prisoners held by France, and sending them home in new uniforms. Soon Napoleon had no admirer more ardent than the mad autocrat Paul, who wrote him a personal letter proposing a joint expedition against India.

Prussia had declared her neutrality. Napoleon sent Duroc and a letter to the young King urging an alliance, Hamburg being the bait dangled before the Prussian monarch's eyes. He was gracious, and he was tempted, but he did not yield : Prussia remained neutral.

Great Britain had good reasons for wishing for the restoration of the Bourbons, from whose feeble hands so much of the colonial Empire of France had dropped ; she had good reason to believe that a continuation of the war would increase her own colonial empire, but the manner in which she repelled Napoleon's advances gave to France just the insult that was needed to arouse her in passionate support of the First Consul.

Forced to continue the war, his preparations were soon made.

It may be doubted whether any victory that he ever won held a higher place in the memory of the great captain than that of Marengo. He never ceased to recall it as one of the most glorious days of his life. We see a proof of this in the Memoirs of General Marbot. The year was 1807, the battle of Eylau had been fought, the armies were in motion again; and Lannes, hard-pressed by the Russian host at Friedland, had sent his aide-de-camp speeding to the Emperor to hurry up support.

"Mounted on my swift Lisette, I met the Emperor leaving Eylau. His face was beaming. He made me ride up by his side, and as we galloped I had to give him an account of what had taken place on the field of battle before I had left. The report finished, the Emperor smiled, and asked, "Have you a good memory?"—"Pretty fair, sire."—"Well, what anniversary is it to-day, the 14th of June?"—"Marengo."—"Yes," replied the Emperor, "and I am going to beat the Russians to-day as I beat the Austrians at Marengo." And as Napoleon reached the field, and rode along the lines, he called out to his troops, "It is a lucky day, the anniversary of Marengo!" The troops cheered him as he rode, and they won for him the great battle of Friedland.

The old uniform, sabre, spurs, hat, he had worn on that sunny day in Italy, in 1800, he scrupulously kept.

In the year he was crowned Emperor he carried Josephine to see the plain he had immortalized, fought again in sham fight the battle of Marengo, wearing the faded uniform he had worn on that eventful day.

Even on his last journey to dismal St. Helena, it seems that these relics of a glorious past were not forgotten. We read that when the dead warrior lay stark and stiff in his coffin on that distant rock, they spread over his feet " the cloak he had worn at Marengo."

It was indeed a brilliant campaign, great in conception, execution, results.

Morean's army lay upon the Rhine, more than one hundred thousand strong. Masséna with the army of Italy guarded the Apennines, facing overwhelming odds. From Paris the First Consul urged Masséna to hold his ground, and Moreau to advance. Against the latter was a weak Austrian commander, Kray, and forces about equal to the French. Much time was lost, Napoleon proposing a plan which Moreau thought too bold, and was not willing to risk. Finally the First Consul yielded, gave Moreau a free hand, and the advance movement began. The Rhine was crossed, and Moreau began a series of victories over Kray which brought him to the Danube. But the Austrians, taking the offensive against the army of Italy, cut it in two, and shut up Masséna in Genoa, where the English fleet could coöperate against the French.

It was then that Napoleon, almost by stealth, got together another army, composed partly of conscripts, partly of veterans from the armies of La Vendée and Holland, and hurried it to the foot of the Alps. The plan was to pass these

mountains, fall upon the Austrian rear, and redeem Italy
at a blow.   His enemies heard of the Army of the Reserve
which he was collecting at Dijon.   Spies went there, saw
a few thousand raw recruits, and reported that Napoleon
had no Army of Reserve — that he was merely trying to
bluff old Melas into loosening his grip on Genoa.   It
suited Napoleon precisely to have his new army treated
as a joke.   With consummate art he encouraged the jest
while he collected, drilled, and equipped at different
points the various detachments with which he intended
to march.

Under the constitution the First Consul could not
legally command the army.   He was not forbidden, however, to be present as an interested spectator while some
one else commanded.   So he appointed Berthier, General-
in-chief.

Early in May, 1800, all was ready, and the First Consul
left Paris to become the interested spectator of the movements of the Army of the Reserve.   At the front, form and
fiction gave way to actuality, and Napoleon's word was
that of chief.   At four different passes the troops entered
the mountains, the main army crossing by the Great St.
Bernard.

Modern students, who sit in snug libraries and rectify
the arduous campaigns of the past, have discovered that
Napoleon's passage of the Alps was no great thing after
all.   They say that his troops had plenty to eat, drink,
and wear; thousands of mules and peasants to aid in the
heavy work of the march; no foes to fight on the way;
and that his march was little more than a military parade.
Indeed, it was one of those things which looked a deal easier
after it had been done than before.   And yet it must have

been a notable feat to have scaled those mighty barriers on which lay the snow, to have threaded those paths up in the air over which the avalanche hung, and below which the precipice yawned — all this having been done with such speed that the French were in Italy before the Austrians knew they had left France. Much of the route was along narrow ledges where the shepherd walked warily. To take a fully equipped army over these rocky shelves, — horse, foot, artillery, ammunition, supplies, — seems even at this admire-nothing day to have been a triumph of organization, skill, foresight, and hardihood. Only a few months previously a Russian army, led by Suwarow, had ventured to cross the Alps — and had crossed; but only half of them got out alive.

In less than a week the French made good the daring attempt, and were in the valleys of Italy marching upon the Austrian rear. They had brought cavalry and infantry almost without loss. Cannon had been laid in hollowed logs and pulled up by ropes. The little fort of Bard, stuck right in the road out of the mountains, had, for a moment, threatened the whole enterprise with ruin. Napoleon had known of the fortress, but had underrated its importance. For some hours a panic seemed imminent in the vanguard, but a goat-path was found which led past the fort on rocks higher up. The cannon were slipped by at night, over the road covered with litter.

Remaining on the French side to despatch the troops forward as rapidly as possible, Napoleon was one of the last to enter the mountains. He rode a sure-footed mule, and by his side walked his guide, a young peasant who unbosomed himself as they went forward. This peasant, also, had his eyes on the future, and wished to rise in the world. His heart yearned for a farm in the Alps, where he might pasture a small flock, grow a few necessaries, marry a girl he loved, and live happily ever afterward. The traveller on the mule seemed much absorbed in thought; but, nevertheless, he heard all the mountaineer was saying.

He gave to the young peasant the funds wherewith to buy house and land; and when Napoleon's empire had fallen to pieces, the family of his old-time guide yet dwelt contentedly in the home the First Consul had given.

So completely had Napoleon hoodwinked the Austrians that the Army of the Reserve was still considered a myth. Mountain passes where a few battalions could have vanquished an army had been left unguarded; and when the French, about sixty thousand strong, stood upon the Italian plains, Melas could with difficulty be made to believe the news.

Now that he was in Italy, it would seem that Napoleon should have relieved Genoa, as he had promised. Masséna and his heroic band were there suffering all the tortures of war, of famine, and of pestilence. But Napoleon had conceived a grander plan. To march upon Genoa, fighting detachments of Austrians as he went, and going from one hum-drum victory to another was too commonplace. Napoleon wished to strike a blow which would annihilate the enemy and astound the world. So he deliberately left Masséna's army to starve while he himself marched upon Milan. One after another, Lannes, leading the vanguard, beat the Austrian detachments which opposed his progress, and Napoleon entered Milan in triumph.

Here he spent several days in festivals and ceremonials,

lapping himself in the luxury of boundless adulation. In the meantime he threw his forces upon the rear of Melas, spreading a vast net around that brave but almost demoralized commander.

On June 4 Masséna consented to evacuate Genoa. His troops, after having been fed by the Austrians, marched off to join the French in Italy. Thus, also, a strong Austrian force was released, and it hastened to join Melas.

When Bourrienne went into Napoleon's room late at night, June 8, and shook him out of a sound sleep to announce that Genoa had fallen, he refused at first to believe it. But he immediately rose, and in a short while orders were flying in all directions, changing the dispositions of the army.

On June 9, Lannes, with the aid of Victor, who came up late in the day, won a memorable victory at Montebello.

Napoleon, who had left Milan and taken up a strong position at Stradella, was in a state of the utmost anxiety, fearing that Melas was about to escape the net. The 10th and 11th of June passed without any definite information of the Austrian movements. On the 12th of June his impatience became so great that he abandoned his position at Stradella and advanced to the heights of Tortona. On the next day he passed the Scrivia and entered the plain of Marengo, and drove a small Austrian force from the village. Napoleon was convinced that Melas had escaped, and it is queer commentary upon the kind of scouting done at the time that the whereabouts of the Austrian army was totally unknown to the French, although the two were but a few miles apart. Leaving Victor in possession of the village of Marengo, and plac-

ing Lannes on the plain, Napoleon started back to headquarters at Voghera. By a lucky chance the Scrivia had
overflowed its banks, and he could not cross. Thus he
remained near enough to Marengo to repair his terrible
mistake in concluding that Melas meant to shut himself
up in Genoa. Desaix, just returned from Egypt, reached
headquarters June 11, and was at once put in command
of the Boudet division. On June 13 Desaix was ordered
to march upon Novi, by which route Melas would have
to pass to Genoa.

Thus on the eve of one of the most famous battles in
history, the soldier who won it was completely at fault as
to the position and the purpose of his foe. His own army
was widely scattered, and it was only by accident that he
was within reach of the point where the blow fell. The
staff-officer whom he had sent to reconnoitre, had reported
that the Austrians were not in possession of the bridges
over the Bormida. In fact they were in possession of
these bridges, and at daybreak, June 14, they began to
pour across them with the intention of crushing the weak
French forces at Marengo and of breaking through Napoleon's net. About thirty-six thousand Austrians fell upon
the sixteen thousand French. Victor was driven out of the
village, and by ten o'clock in the morning his troops were
in disorderly retreat. The superb courage of Lannes stayed
the rout. With the utmost firmness he held his troops in
hand, falling back slowly and fighting desperately as he
retired. At full speed Napoleon came upon the field,
bringing the consular guard and Monnier's division.
Couriers had already been sent to bring Desaix back to
the main army ; but before these messengers reached him,
he had heard the cannonade, guessed that Melas had

struck the French at Marengo, and at once set his columns in motion toward the field of battle.

Napoleon's presence, his reënforcements, his skilful dispositions, had put new life into the struggle; but as the morning wore away, and the afternoon commenced, it was evident that the Austrians would win. The French gave way at all points, and in parts of the field the rout was complete. Napoleon sat by the roadside swishing his riding-whip and calling to the fugitives who passed him to stop; but their flight continued. A commercial traveller left the field and sped away to carry the news to Paris that Napoleon had suffered a great defeat.

Melas, oppressed by age and worn out by the heat and fatigue of the day, thought the battle won; went to his headquarters to send off despatches to that effect, and left to his subordinate, Zach, the task of the pursuit. But Desaix had come — "the battle is lost, but there is time to gain another."

Only twelve pieces of artillery were left to the French. Marmont massed these, and opened on the dense Austrian column advancing *en échelon* along the road. Desaix charged, and almost immediately got a ball in the breast and died "a soldier's beautiful death." But his troops pressed forward with fury, throwing back in confusion the head of the Austrian column. At this moment, "in the very nick of time" as Napoleon himself admitted to Bourrienne, Kellermann made his famous cavalry charge on the flank of the Austrian column, cut it in two, and decided the day. The French lines everywhere advanced, the Austrians broke. They were bewildered at the sudden change: they had no chief, Zach being a prisoner, and Melas absent. In wildest confusion they fled toward the bridges over the Bormida, Austrian horse trampling Austrian foot, and the French in hot pursuit.

Some sixteen thousand men were killed or wounded in this bloody battle, and very nearly half of these were French. But the Austrians were demoralized, and Melas so overcome that he hastened to treat. To save the relics of his army, he was willing to abandon northern Italy, give up Genoa, and all fortresses recently taken.

From the field of Marengo, surrounded by so many dead and mangled, Napoleon wrote a long letter to the Emperor of Austria, urgently pleading for a general peace.

Returning to Milan, he was welcomed with infinite enthusiasm. He spent some days there reëstablishing the Cisalpine republic, reorganizing the administration, and putting himself in accord with the Roman Catholic Church. Just as earnestly as he had assured the Mahometans in Egypt that his mission on earth was to crush the Pope and lower the Cross, he now set himself up as the restorer of the Christian religion. He went in state to the cathedral of Milan to appear in a clerical pageant; and he took great pains to have it published abroad that the priests might rely upon him for protection.

Leaving Masséna in command of the army of Italy, Napoleon returned to Paris by way of Lyons. The ovations which greeted him were as spontaneous as they were hearty. Never before, never afterward, did his presence call forth such universal, sincere, and joyous applause. He was still young, still the first magistrate of a republic, still conciliatory and magnetic, still posing as a public servant who could modestly write that " he hoped France would be satisfied with its army." He was not yet the all-absorbing egotist who must be everything. Moreau was still at the head of an army, Carnot at the war office, there was a tribunate which could debate governmental policies; there was a public opinion which could not be openly braved.

Hence it was a national hero whom the French welcomed home, not a master before whom flatterers fawned. All Paris was illuminated from hut to palace. Thousands pressed forward but to see him; the Tuileries were surrounded by the best people of Paris, all eager to catch a glimpse of him at a window, and greeting him wherever he appeared with rapturous shouts. He himself was deeply touched, and said afterward that these were the happiest days of his life. The time was yet to come when he would appear at these same windows to answer the shouts of a few boys and loafers, on the dreary days before Waterloo.

With that talent for effect which was one of Napoleon's most highly developed traits, he had ordered the Consular Guard back to France almost immediately after Marengo, timing its march so that it would arrive in Paris on the day of the great national fête of July 14. On that day when so many thousands of Frenchmen, dressed in gala attire, thronged the Field of Mars and gave themselves up to rejoicings, the column from Marengo, dust-covered, clad in their old uniform, and bearing their smoke-begrimed, bullet-rent banners, suddenly entered the vast amphitheatre. The effect was electrical. Shout upon shout greeted the returning heroes; and with an uncontrollable impulse the people rushed upon these veterans from Italy with every demonstration of joy, affection, and wild enthusiasm. So great was the disorder that the regular programme of the day was thrust aside; the men of Marengo had dwarfed every other attraction.

About this time the Bourbons made efforts to persuade Napoleon to play the part of Monk in restoring the monarchy. Suasive priests bearing letters, and lovely women bearing secret offers, were employed, the facile Josephine lending herself gracefully to the intrigue. The First Consul was the last of men to rake chestnuts out of the fire for other people, and the Bourbons were firmly advised to accept a situation which left them in exile.

Failing in their efforts to bribe him, the monarchists determined to kill him; and the more violent Jacobins, seeing his imperial trend, were equally envenomed. It was the latter faction which made the first attempt upon his life. The Conspiracy of Ceracchi, Arena, and Topino-Lebrun was betrayed to the police. Ceracchi was an Italian sculptor who had modelled a bust of Napoleon. Arena was a Corsican whose brother had aimed a knife at Napoleon on the 19th of Brumaire. Topino-Lebrun was the juryman who had doubted the guilt of Danton, and who had been bullied into voting death by the painter David. They were condemned and executed.

A yet more dangerous plot was that of the royalists. An infernal machine was contrived by which Napoleon was to have been blown up while on his way to the opera. The explosion occurred, but a trifle too late. Napoleon had just passed. The man in charge of the machine did not know Josephine's carriage from Napoleon's, and approached too near in the effort to make certain. A guard kicked him away, and while he was recovering himself Napoleon's coachman drove furiously round the corner. A sound like thunder was heard, many houses were shattered, many people killed and wounded.

"Drive on !" shouted Napoleon; and when he entered his box at the opera, he looked as if nothing had occurred. "The rascals tried to blow me up," he said coolly as he took his seat and called for an opera-book. But when he returned to the Tuileries he was in a rage, and violently accused the Jacobins of being the authors of the plot. Fouché in vain insisted that the royalists were the guilty parties; the First Consul refused to listen. Taking advantage of the feeling aroused in his favor by the attempts to assassinate him, he caused a new tribunal to be created, composed of eight judges, who were to try political offenders without jury, and without appeal or revision. By another law he was empowered to banish without trial such persons as he considered "enemies of the State." One hundred and thirty of the more violent republicans were banished to the penal colonies.

For the purpose of feeling the public pulse, a pamphlet was put forward by Fontanes and Lucien Bonaparte, called a "Parallel between Caesar, Cromwell, Monk, and Bonaparte." It was hinted that supreme power should be vested in Napoleon, that he should be made king. The pear was not quite ripe, the pamphlet created a bad effect. Napoleon, who had undoubtedly encouraged its publication, promptly repudiated it; and Lucien, dismissed from his office as Secretary of the Interior, was sent to Spain as ambassador.

However willing Austria might be for peace, she could

U

not make it without the consent of England, her ally. The British ministry viewed with the spirit of philosophy the crushing blows which France had dealt Austria, and, secure from attack themselves, encouraged Austria to keep on fighting. Not able to send troops, England sent money. With $10,000,000 she bought the further use of German soldiers to keep France employed on the Continent, while Great Britain bent her energies to the capture of Malta and of Egypt. Thus it happened that the armistice expired without a treaty having been agreed on ; and the war between the Republic and the Empire recommenced (November, 1800). Brune defeated the Austrians on the Mincio ; Macdonald made the heroic march through the Splügen Pass ; Moreau won the magnificent victory of Hohenlinden (December 4, 1800).

It seems that, with a little more dash, Moreau might have taken Vienna, exposed as it was to the march of three victorious armies. But Austria asked for a truce, gave pledges of good faith, and the French halted. On February 9, 1801, the Peace of Lunéville put an end to the war. France had won the boundary of the Rhine ; and, in addition to the territory made hers by the treaty of Campo Formio, gained Tuscany, which Napoleon had promised to Spain, in exchange for Louisiana.

Napoleon's position on the Continent was now very strong. Prussia was a friendly neutral; Spain an ally ; Italy and Switzerland little more than French provinces ; the Batavian republic and Genoa submissive subjects; Portugal in his power by reason of his compact with Spain ; and the Czar of Russia an enthusiastic friend. England was shut out from the Continent almost completely.

Her insolent exercise of the right of search of neutral vessels on the high seas, a right which had no basis in law or justice, had provoked the hatred of the world, and Napoleon took advantage of this feeling and of Russia's friendship to reorganize the armed neutrality of the northern powers for the purpose of bringing England to reason. Her reply was brutal and effective. She sent her fleet, under Parker and Nelson, to bombard Copenhagen and to destroy the Danish navy. The work was savagely done, and the northern league shattered. The English party at St. Petersburg followed up this blow by the murder of the Czar Paul. Hardly had the young Alexander been proclaimed before he announced his adhesion to the English and his antagonism to the French. He may, possibly, have been free from the guilt of conniving at his father's murder; but it is not to be denied that he continued to reward with the highest offices the chief assassins — Bennigsen, for example.

Kléber, who had gloriously maintained himself in Egypt, was assassinated on the day of Marengo. It is one of the mysteries of Napoleon's career that he allowed the incompetent Menou to succeed to a command where so much executive and administrative ability was required. One is tempted to think that even at this early date the genius of Napoleon was overtaxed. In trying to do so many things, he neglected some. Egypt he certainly tried to relieve by sending reënforcements; but he slurred all, neglected all, and lost all, by allowing so notorious an imbecile as Menou to remain in chief command. Why he

did not appoint Reynier or Lanusse, both of whom were
already in Egypt, or why he did not send some good officer from France, can only be explained upon the theory
that his mind was so much preoccupied with other matters
that he failed to attach due importance to the situation of
the Army of the East.

Menon's administration was one dreary chapter of stu-
pidities ; and when the English landed at Alexandria,
they found an easy conquest.   With little effort and little
bloodshed the French were beaten in detail, and agreed
to quit the country.

When the tidings reached Napoleon, his anger and
chagrin were extreme.   He jumped upon his horse and
dashed off into the forest of Bougival as if the furies
were after him.   Hour after hour he rode frantically in
the wood, to the wonder of his staff, who could not guess
what it was all about.   At last, when the storm had
spent itself, he unbosomed himself to the faithful Junot.
That night Junot said to his wife, " Ah, my General suffered cruelly to-day : Egypt has been taken by the English ! "

Malta having been captured also, Napoleon had the
mortification of realizing that his expedition to the East
had had no other result than to sow seed for an English
harvest.

However, Great Britain was dismayed at the increase .
of her public debt, oppressed by the load of taxation,
and somewhat intimidated by the energy which Napoleon
began to show in building up the French navy.   A monster demonstration at Boulogne, — where he gathered an
immense number of armed sloops, apparently for the purpose of invading England, — and the failure of an attack

which Nelson made on this flotilla, had an effect; and
in March, 1802, to the joy of the world, the Peace of
Amiens was signed.

For the first time since 1792 universal peace prevailed
in Europe.

CHAPTER XXIII

NOTHING but memories now remains to France, or to the human race, of the splendors of Marengo, of Austerlitz, Jena, and Wagram ; but the work which Napoleon did while Europe allowed him a few years of peace will endure for ages. Had the Treaty of Amiens been lasting, had England kept faith, had the old world dynasties been willing to accept at that time those necessary changes which have since cost so much labor, blood, and treasure, Napoleon might have gone down to history, not as the typical fighter of modern times, but as the peerless developer, organizer, administrator, and lawgiver. In his many-sided character there was the well-rounded man of peace, who delighted in improvement, in embellishment, in the growth of commerce, agriculture, and manufactures ; in the progress of art, science, and literature ; in the thorough training of the young, the care of the weaker members of society, the just administration of wise laws, the recognition of merit of all kinds. The orderly march of the legions of industry was no less satisfying to him than the march of armies. We have read so much of his battles that we have come to think of him as a man who was never so happy as when at war. This view is superficial and incorrect. It appears that he was never more energetic, capable, effective, never more at ease, never

more cheerful, contented, kind, and magnetic than in the
work connected with his schools, hospitals, public monuments, public improvements of all sorts, the codification of
the laws, the encouragement and development of the
various industries of France.   No trophy of any of his
campaigns did he exhibit with more satisfaction than he
took in showing to visitors a piece of sugar made by
Frenchmen from the beet — a triumph of home industry
due largely to his stimulating impulse.

In all such matters his interest was intelligent, persistent, and intense.   Few were the months given to him
in which to devote himself to such labor; but he took
enormous strides in constructing a new system for France
which worked wonders for her, and which has had its
influence throughout the civilized world.

The men of the Revolution had sketched a grand
scheme of state education, but it remained a sketch.
Napoleon studied their scheme, improved it, adopted it,
and put it into successful operation.   His thorough system
of instruction, controlled by the State, from the primary
schools to the Lyceums and the Technological Institute
remain in France to-day substantially as he left them.

Under the Directory society had become disorganized
and morals corrupt.   Napoleon, hard at work on finance,
laws, education, military and civil administration, inaugurated the reform of social abuses also.   With his removal
to the Tuileries, February 1800, may be dated the recon-
struction of society in France.   The beginnings of a court
formed about him, and into this circle the notoriously
immoral women could not enter.   It must have been a
cruel surprise to Madame Tallien — coming to visit her old
friend Josephine — when the door was shut in her face

by the usher. Of course it was by Napoleon's command that this was done, never by Josephine's. Applying similar rules to the men, Napoleon compelled Talleyrand to marry the woman with whom he openly lived; and even the favorite Berthier, too scandalously connected with Madame Visconti, was made to take a wife. Sternly frowning upon all flaunting immoralities, the First Consul's will power and example so impressed itself upon the nation that the moral tone of society throughout the land was elevated, and a loftier moral standard fixed.

Under the Directory the material well-being of the country, internally, had been so neglected that even the waterways fell into disuse. Under the consular government the French system of internal improvements soon began to excite the admiration of Europe. Englishmen, coming over after the peace, and expecting to see what their editors and politicians had described as a country ruined by revolution, were amazed to see that in many directions French progress could give England useful lessons. Agriculture had doubled its produce, for the idle lands of former grandees had been put into cultivation. The farmer was more prosperous, for the lord was not on the lookout to seize the crop with feudal dues as soon as made. Nor was the priest seen standing at the gate, grabbing a tenth of everything. Nor were state taxes levied with an eye single to making the burden as heavy as peasant shoulders could bear.

Wonder of wonders! the man in control had said, and kept saying, "Better to let the peasant keep what he makes than to lock it up in the public treasury!" The same man said, "Beautify the markets, render them clean, attractive, healthy — they are the Louvres of the common people." It was such a man who would talk with the poor whenever he could, to learn the facts of their condition. In his stroll he would stop, chat with the farmer, and, taking the plough in his own white hands, trace a wobbly furrow.

Commerce was inspired to new efforts, for the First Consul put himself forward as champion of liberty of the seas, combatting England's harsh policy of searching neutral vessels and seizing goods covered by the neutral flag.

Manufactures he encouraged to the utmost of his power, by shutting off foreign competition, by setting the example of using home-made goods, and by direct subsidies. He even went so far as to experiment with the government warehouse plan, advancing money out of the treasury to the manufactures on the deposit of products of the mills.

No drone, be he the haughtiest Montmorency, whose ancestor had been in remote ages a murderer and a thief, could hold office under Napoleon. Unless he were willing to work, he could not enter into the hive. For the first time in the political life of the modern French, men became prouder of the fact that they were workers, doers of notable deeds, than that they were the fifteenth cousin of some spindle-shanked duke whose great-great-grandfather had held the stirrup when Louis XIII. had straddled his horse.

Having founded the Bank of France, January, 1800, Napoleon jealously scrutinized its management, controlled its operations, and made it useful to the State as well as to the bankers. He watched the quotations of government securities, took pride in seeing them command high prices, and considered it a point of honor that they should not

fall below eighty. When they dropped considerably
below that figure, some years later, the Emperor went
into the market, made " a campaign against the Bears,"
and forced the price up again — many a crippled bear
limping painfully off the lost field.

The First Consul also elaborated a system of state education. Here he was no Columbus, no creator, no original
inventor. His glory is that he accomplished what others
had suggested, had attempted, but had not done. He
took hold, gave the scheme the benefit of his tremendous
driving force, and pushed it through. It will be his glory
forever that in all things pertaining to civil life he was
the highest type of democrat. Distinctions of character,
merit, conduct, talent, he could understand ; distinctions
of mere birth he abhorred. The very soul of his system
was the rewarding of worth. In the army, the civil service, the schools, in art and science and literature, his
great object was to discover the real men, — the men of
positive ability, — and to open to these the doors of pre-
ferment.

Remembering the sufferings he and his sister had
endured at the Bourbon schools where the poor scholars
were cruelly humiliated, he founded his training-schools,
military and civil, upon the plan which as a boy he had
sketched. The young men at his military academies
kept no troops of servants, and indulged in no hurtful
luxury. They not only attended to their own personal
needs, but fed, curried, and saddled their own horses.

It was such a man as Napoleon who would turn from
state business to examine in person an ambitious boy
who had been studying at home for admission into one
of the state schools, and who had been refused because

he had not studied under a professor. " This boy is competent ; let him enter the school," wrote Napoleon after the examination : and the young man's career was safe.

It was such a man who would invite the grenadiers to the grand banquets at the palace, and who would direct that special courtesies should be shown these humblest of the guests.

It was such a man who would read every letter, every petition addressed to him, and find time to answer all. Never too proud or too busy to hear the cry of the humblest, to reward the merit of the obscurest, to redress the grievance of the weakest, he was the man to make the highest headed general in the army — Vandamme himself, for instance, — apologized to the obscure captain who had been wantonly insulted. Any private in the ranks — the drummer boy, the grenadier — was free to step out and speak to Napoleon, and was sure to be heard as patiently as Talleyrand or Murat or Cambacérès in the palace. If any difference was made, it was in favor of the private soldier. Any citizen, male or female, high or low, could count with absolute certainty on reaching Napoleon in person or by petition in writing, and upon a reply being promptly given. One day a careless secretary mislaid one of these prayers of the lowly, and the palace was in terror at Napoleon's wrath until the paper was found. Josephine might take a petition, smile sweetly on the supplicant, forget all about it, and suavely assure the poor dupe when meeting him next that his case was being considered. Not so Napoleon. He might not do the sweet smile, he might refuse the request, but he would give the man his answer, and if his prayers were denied, would tell him why.

The Revolution having levelled all ranks, there were
no visible marks of distinction between man and man.
Napoleon was too astute a politician not to pander to
mankind's innate craving for outward tokens of superiority.   The Legion of Honor was created against stubborn opposition, to reward with ribbons, buttons, and
pensions those who had distinguished themselves by
their own efforts in any walk of life.   It embraced
merit of every kind, — civil, military, scientific, literary,
artistic.   Men of all creeds, of every rank, every calling,
were eligible.   The test of fitness for membership was
meritorious service to the State.   Such at least was
Napoleon's theory : whether he or any one else ever
strictly hewed to so rigid a line may be doubted.   His
order of nobility had this merit : it was not hereditary,
it carried no special privileges, it could not build up a
caste, it kept alive the idea that success must be founded
upon worth, not birth.   In theory such an order of
nobility was democratic to the core.   Lafayette, whom
Napoleon had freed from captivity, recalled to France,
and reinstated in his ancestral domain, scornfully declined to enter this new order of nobility.   So did many
others — some because they were royalists, some because
they were republicans.   In a few years the institution
had become so much a part of national life that the
restored Bourbons dared not abolish it.

"I will go down to posterity with the Code in my
hand," said Napoleon with just pride, for time has proven
that as a lawgiver, a modern Justinian, his work has
endured.

Early in his consulate he began the great labor of codifying the laws of France, — a work which had often been suggested, and which the Convention had partially finished, but which had never been completed.

To realize the magnitude of the undertaking, we must bear in mind that, under the Old Order, there were all sorts of law and all kinds of courts. What was right in one province was wrong in another. A citizen who was familiar with the system in Languedoc would have found himself grossly ignorant in Brittany. Roman law, feudal law, royal edicts, local customs, seigniorial mandates, municipal practices, varied and clashed throughout the realm. The Revolution had prostrated the old system and had proposed to establish one uniform, modern, and equitable code of law for the whole country; but the actual carrying out of the plan was left to Napoleon.

Calling to his aid the best legal talent of the land, the First Consul set to work. Under his supervision the huge task was completed, after the steady labor of several years. The Civil Code and the Code of Civil Procedure, the Criminal Code and the Code of Criminal Procedure, were the four parts of the completed system, which, adopted in France, followed the advance of the Empire and still constitutes the law of a large portion of the civilized world.

Every statute passed under Napoleon's eye. He presided over the meetings when the finished work of the codifiers came up for sanction, and his suggestions, reasoning, experience, and natural wisdom left their impress upon every page. "Never did we adjourn," said one of the colaborers of Napoleon, "without learning something we had not known before."

It is the glory of this Code that it put into final and
permanent shape the best work of the Revolution. It
was based upon the great principle that all citizens were
legally equals ; that primogeniture, hereditary nobility,
class privileges, and exemptions were unjust ; that property
was sacred ; that conscience was free ; that state employment should be open to all, opportunities equal to all,
state duties and state burdens the same to all; that laws
should be simple, and legal proceedings public, swift, cheap,
and just ; and that personal liberty, civil right, should be
inviolable.

Recognizing his right as master-builder, his persistence,
zeal, active coöperation in the actual work, and the
modern tone which he gave to it, the world does him no
more than justice in calling it the Code Napoléon.

Another great distinctive work of the First Consul is
the Concordat ; and here his claim to approval must ever
remain a question. Those who believe that the State
should unite with the Church and virtually deny to posterity the right to investigate the most important of subjects, will always strain the language of praise in giving
thanks to Napoleon for the Concordat. On the contrary,
those who believe that the State should not unite with the
hierarchy of any creed, but should let the question of
religion alone,— leave it to be settled by each citizen for
himself,— will forever condemn the Concordat as the colossal mistake of Napoleon's career.

It will be remembered that the Revolution had confiscated the enormous, ill-gotten, and ill-used wealth of the
Catholic Church, but in lieu of this source of revenue
had provided ample salaries to the clergy, to be paid from
the public treasury. It is not true that the Christian

worship was forbidden or religion abolished. Throughout the Reign of Terror the Catholic Church continued to be a state institution. Only those priests who refused to take the oath of allegiance to the New Order were treated as criminals. It was not till September, 1794, that the Convention abolished the salaries paid by the State, thus separating Church and State. After this all creeds were on a level, and each citizen could voluntarily support that which he preferred,— Catholic, Protestant, or the Theophilanthropist.

It was the princely bishop, archbishop, and cardinal who had brought reproach upon the Church under the Old Régime; it was the humble parish priest who had maintained some hold upon the love and the respect of the people. When the Revolution burst upon the land, it was the prince of the Church who fled to foreign shores; it was the parish priest who remained at the post of duty. Bravely taking up the cross where the cardinals and bishops had dropped it, the curés reorganized their Church, pledged themselves to the new order of things, and throughout France their constitutional Church was at work — a voluntary association, independent of Rome, and supporting itself without help from the State. In one very essential particular it stood nearer to the Christ standard than the Church it replaced — it charged no fees for administering the sacraments.

This revived Gallican Church was distasteful to Napoleon, for he wished the State, the executive, to be the head, centre, and controlling power of everything. Voluntary movements of all sorts were his aversion.

To the Pope this independent Gallican Church was a menace, an impertinence, a revolt. Catholicism, be it never so pure in creed, must yield obedience and lucre to Rome, else it savors of heresy, schism, and dire sinfulness.

Again, to the Pope and to the princes of the Church this equality among the denominations in France was a matter that was almost intolerable. Where creeds stand on the same footing, they will compete for converts; where there is room for competition, there is license for investigation, debate, reason, and common sense. And we have the word of Leo XIII., echoing that of so many of his predecessors, that religion has no enemy so subtle, so much to be dreaded, so much needing to be ruthlessly crushed, as reason, investigation.

The Pope of Napoleon's day held this view, as a matter of course; and in order to bring about a renewal of the union between the Catholic Church and the government of France he was ready to concede almost anything Napoleon might demand. Once the union had been accomplished, no matter on what terms, the papacy would feel safe. Evolution and time would work marvels; the essential thing was to bring about the union. Napoleon was mortal, he would die some day, and weaker men would succeed him — a stronger would never appear. Let the Pope bend a little to that imperious will, let concessions be made while the Church was getting fulcrum for its lever. Once adjusted, the lever would do the rest. So it appeared from the point of view of the Pope: time has proven him right.

On the part of Napoleon there were reasons of policy which lured him into the toils of Rome. Immense results, immediate and personal, would follow his compact with the Pope; for these he grasped, leaving the future to take care of itself.

For Napoleon was personally undergoing a great trans-formation. Gradually his mind had filled with dreams of empire. The cannon of Marengo had hardly ceased to echo before he began to speak of "My beautiful France." Between himself and those about him he steadily increased the distance. His tone was that of Master. Tuscany having been taken from Austria, he made a kingdom out of it, put a feeble Bourbon upon its throne, dubbed the puppet King of Etruria, and brought him to Paris where the people of France could behold a king playing courtier to a French consul. At the Tuileries the ceremony and royalty encroached constantly upon republican forms, and the lip service of flatterers began to displace military frankness and democratic independence.

Looking forward to supreme power, Napoleon was too astute a politician to neglect the priest. As Alexander had bent his head in seeming reverence at altars, and listened with apparent faith to Grecian oracles ; as Cæsar had posed as Roman chief priest, and leagued himself to paganism; so Napoleon, who had been a Mussulman at Cairo, would now become a Catholic in Paris. It was a matter of policy, nothing more.

"Ah, General," said Lafayette to him, "what you want is that the little vial should be broken over your head."

It all led up to that.

Monarchy was to be restored, and its natural supports — the aristocrat and the priest — were needed to give it strength. By coming to terms with the Pope, Napoleon would win, and the Bourbons lose, the disciplined hosts of the Catholic Church.

Therefore the Concordat was negotiated, and the French Church, which even under the Bourbons had enjoyed a

x

certain amount of independence, was put under the feet of the Italian priest, under the tyranny of Rome.

By this compact the Pope held to himself the right to approve the clerical nominees of the State, while the tax-payers were annually to furnish $10,000,000 to pay clerical salaries. By this compact was brought back into France the subtle, resistless power of a corporation which, identifying itself with God, demands supreme control.

Napoleon himself soon felt the strength of this released giant, and the France of to-day is in a death grapple with it.

The time may come when the Concordat will be considered Napoleon's greatest blunder, his unpardonable political sin. It was not faith, it was not even philanthropy which governed his conduct. It was cold calculation. It was merely a move in the game of ambition. At the very moment that he claimed the gratitude of Christians for the restoration of religion, he sought to soothe the non-believers by telling them that under his system religion would disappear from France within fifty years.

It is not true that a majority of the French clamored for a return of the old forms of worship. On the contrary, the vast majority were indifferent, if not hostile. In the army it caused a dangerous conspiracy among the officers, against Napoleon's life.

When the Concordat came to be celebrated by a pompous pagan ceremonial in the cathedral of Notre Dame, it required all of his authority to compel a respectful attendance, as it had required the utmost exercise of his power to secure the sanction of the state authorities to the Concordat itself. More than one saddened Frenchman thought what General Delmas is reported to have said, when Napoleon asked his opinion of the ceremonial at Notre Dame; "It is a fine harlequinade, needing only the presence of the million men who died to do away with all that."

Yes, a million Frenchmen had died to do away with that, — the worst feature of the Old Order, — and now it had all come back again.   Once more the children of France were to have their brains put under the spell of superstition.   They were to be taught the loveliness of swallowing every marvel the priest might utter, and the damnation of thinking for oneself upon any subject ecclesiastical.   They were to be crammed from the cradle, on one narrow creed, and incessantly told that hell yawned for the luckless wight who doubted or demurred.

With a line of writing, with a spurt of the pen, Napoleon reënslaved the nation.   So well had the image breakers of the Convention done their work that it appeared to be only a question of time when France, "having by her own exertions freed herself, would, by the force of her example, free the world."   As Meneval states, "Catholicism seemed at its last gasp."   Rapidly Europe was being weaned from a worn-out creed, a threadbare paganism.   Idols had been broken, miracles laughed out of countenance, the bones of alleged saints allowed to rest, and the mummeries of heathen ceremonial mocked till even the performers were ashamed.

A few bigots or fanatics, chained by an education which had left them no room for unfettered thought, longed for the return of the old forms; but the mass of the French people had no more wish for their reëstablishment than for the restoration of the Bourbons.   France was religiously free : every citizen could believe or not believe, worship or not worship, just as he pleased.

Of all rulers, Napoleon had the best opportunity to give mental independence an open field and a fair fight. No ruler less strong than he could have achieved the task of lifting the Church from the dust, and frowning down the ridicule which had covered with discredit idol, shrine, creed, and ceremonial rite.

He did it — he alone ! And verily he reaped his reward. The forlorn prisoner of St. Helena, sitting in misery beside the cheerless hearth in the night of endless despair, cursed himself bitterly for his huge mistake.

Some who defend the Concordat say that it enabled Napoleon to make alliances which otherwise he could not have made. The facts do not support the assertion. He was at peace with Continental Europe already, and Great Britain was certainly not influenced to peace by France's agreement with the Pope. No alliances which Napoleon ever made after the Concordat were stronger than those he had made before ; and as the restorer of Catholicism in France, he was not nearer the sincere friendships of monarchs and aristocracies abroad than he had been previous to that time.

In the murk of modern politics the truth is hard to find, but even a timid man might venture to say that the question of religion is the last of all questions to influence international relations. Comparing the prolonged security which Turkey has enjoyed with the fate which recently befell Catholic Spain and Protestant South African republics, the casual observer might hazard the statement that it is at least as safe to be Mahometan as Christian, so far as winning international friendship is concerned.

"Don't strike ! I am of the same faith as you —
both of us hope for salvation in the blood of the same
Savior !" is a plea which is so worthless among Christians that the weaker brother never even wastes breath
to make it.

CHAPTER XXIV

TO say that the French were pleased with the consular government, would convey no idea of the facts. France was delighted, France was in raptures. Excepting the inevitable few, — some royalists, some Jacobins and some lineal descendants of the Athenians who grew tired of hearing Aristides called *The Just*, — all Frenchmen heartily united in praise of Bonaparte.

As proudly as Richelieu, in Bulwer's play, stands before his king and tells what he has done for France, — a nation found lying in poverty, shame, defeat, deathly decay, and lifted by the magic touch of genius to wealth, pride, victory, and radiant strength, — so the First Consul could have pointed to what France had been and what she had become, and justly claim the love and admiration of his people.

What reward should be given such a magistrate? In 1802 his consulship, which had already been lengthened by ten years, was, by the almost unanimous vote of the people, changed into a life tenure.

Consul for life (August, 1802), with the power to name his own successor, Napoleon was now virtually the king of France.

*   *   *   *   *   *

In St. Domingo, the Revolution in France had borne bitter fruit. The blacks rose against the whites, and a war of extermination ensued.

The negroes, immensely superior in numbers, overcame the whites, and established their independence. Toussaint L'Ouverture, the leader of the blacks, and a great man, became president of the black republic, which he patterned somewhat after Napoleon's consulate.

The rich French planters, who had the ear of Napoleon in Paris, urged him to put down the revolt, or to bring the island back under French dominion. Thus these Bourbon nobles led Napoleon into one of his worst mistakes. He aligned himself with those who wished to reëstablish slavery, put himself at enmity with the trend of liberalism everywhere, and plunged himself into a ruinous war.

Mainly from the army of the Rhine, which was republican and unfriendly to himself, he drew out of France twenty thousand of her best troops, put them under command of Leclerc, his brother-in-law, and despatched them to St. Domingo, to reconquer the island.

Here again it is impossible to escape the conclusion that Napoleon had not duly considered what he was doing. There is evidence of haste, want of investigation, lack of foresight and precaution. The whole plan, from inception to end, bears the marks of that rashness which is forever punishing the man who tries to do everything.

The negroes gave way before Leclerc's overwhelming numbers; and, by treachery, Toussaint was captured and sent to France to die in a dungeon; but the yellow fever soon came to the rescue of the blacks, and the expedition, after causing great loss of life, ended in shameful failure. Leclerc died, the remnants of the French army were brought back to Europe in English ships, and the negroes established their semi-barbarous Republic of Hayti (1804).

This much may be said by way of defence for
Napoleon's treatment of San Domingo : it had been one
of the choicest possessions of the French crown, and he
wished to regain it for his country, just as he regained
Louisiana, and just as he yearned for the lost territories
in Hindustan.   Visions of a vast colonial empire haunted
his imagination, and the spirit which influenced him in
his efforts in the West Indies was, perhaps, the same
which lured him to Egypt, which caused him to attach
such extreme importance to Malta, and which caused
him to send men-of-war to South Australia to survey
the coast for settlement.

Meantime the Peace of Amiens was becoming a very
frail thing, indeed.   To all men, war in the near future
seemed inevitable.   Very positively England had pledged
herself to restore Malta to the Knights of St. John ; very
emphatically she now refused to do so.   By way of excuse
she alleged that France had violated the spirit of the
treaty by her aggressions on the Continent.   In reply,
Napoleon insisted that France had done nothing which
it was not well known she intended at the time peace was
made.   He also reminded England that she had taken
India.   And this was true, but truth sometimes cuts a
poor figure in debate.   In vain such splendid types of
English manhood as Charles Fox stood forth boldly in the
British Parliament, and defended the First Consul.   England was determined not to give up the Mediterranean
fortress.   France had no navy, no sailor with a spark of
Nelson's genius, and Malta was safe.   On the Continent
Napoleon might rage and might destroy ; but England had

proved how easy it was for her to hear the losses inflicted upon Continental Europe, and she was prepared to prove it again. Safe in her sea-girt isle, she was not to be intimidated by armies hurled against her allies.

In this crisis, when conciliatory measures might have availed to avert war, Lord Whitworth was sent to Paris as British ambassador. With his coming all hope of accommodation vanished. He was a typical English aristocrat, the very worst man who could have been sent if peace was desired. From the first, his letters to his government show that he was intensely hostile to Napoleon and to the consular government. To his superiors at home he misrepresented the situation in France, and where he did not misrepresent, he exaggerated. Finally, when Napoleon went out of his way to have a long conference with him, and to urge that England should keep her contract, he showed himself coldly irresponsive, and hinted that Malta would not be given up. Following this private and urgent conference came the public reception, in which Napoleon, with some natural display of temper and with the frankness of a soldier, asked Whitworth why England wanted war, and why she would not respect treaties. Whereupon Whitworth represented to his court that he had been grossly insulted, and all England rang with indignation. A falser statement never caused more woe to the human race. Bismarck cynically confessed that he it was who changed the form, the wording, and the tone of " the Ems telegram " which caused the Franco-German War of 1870-1. It is not too much to say that Whitworth's exaggerated report, and the changes for the worse which the British ministry made in it when making it public, was one of the controlling causes of the wars, the bloodshed, and the misery which followed the year 1804.

During all this while the English newspapers were filled with the bitterest abuse of Napoleon. The most shameful lies that were ever published against a human being were constantly repeated against him in the British journals. That he should be subjected to such treatment during years of peace, and while he was giving most cordial welcome to the thousands of Englishmen who were now visiting France, filled Napoleon with wrath. He knew that by law the press of Great Britain was free; but he also knew that these papers, especially the ministerial papers, would not be filled with scurrilous personal abuse of him unless the government encouraged it. He knew that the political press reflects the views of the political party, and that when ministerial journals hounded him with libels, the ministers had given the signal. In vain he protested to the English ministry; he was told that in England the press was free. Then, as all his admirers must regret, he, also, stooped to libels and began to fill the official organs in France with outrageous attacks upon England.

Another grievance Napoleon had against Great Britain — she harbored men who openly declared their intention of assassinating him. English protection, English ships, English money, were ever at the command of the royalists who wished to stir up revolt in France, or to land assassins who wished to creep to Paris. On this subject, also, the English government would give no satisfaction. It coldly denied the accusation, disavowed the assassins, and continued to encourage assassination.

While relations were thus strained, a report of General

Sébastiani on the eastern situation was published. In the paper, Sébastiani had ventured to say that six thousand French troops might reconquer Egypt. Here was another insult to England. Here was another excuse for editorial thunder, another provocative of parliamentary eloquence. England did not choose to remember that Sir Robert Wilson had just published a book, also on the eastern situation, and that in this publication Napoleon had been represented as the murderer of prisoners at Jaffa, and the poisoner of his own sick in the hospitals. This book had been dedicated to the Duke of York by permission, and had been presented by the author to George III., at a public levee.

England was bent on war; no explanations or remonstrances would soothe her, and on May 18 war was declared. But she had already seized, without the slightest warning, hundreds of French ships laden with millions of merchandise — ships which had come to English harbors trusting to her faith pledged in the treaty. This capture and confiscation excited almost no comment, but when Napoleon retaliated by throwing into prison thousands of Englishmen who were travelling in France, England could find no words harsh enough to condemn the outrage. Even so intelligent a historian as Lockhart is aghast at Napoleon's perfidy. For, mark you, England had *always* seized what she could of the enemy's property previous to a declaration of war, whereas Napoleon's counterstroke was a novelty. It had never been done before, therefore it was an unspeakable atrocity — "It moved universal sympathy, indignation, and disgust." So says Lockhart, repeating dutifully what his father-in-law, Sir Walter Scott, had already said. And the most recent

British historian, J. H. Rose, writing of that period, falls into the well-worn path of Tory prejudice, and ambles along composedly in the hallowed footprints of Lockhart and Sir Walter.

Their style of putting the case is like this: It was wrong to seize an enemy's ships and sailors previous to a declaration of war, but Great Britain had always done it, and, consequently, she had a right to do it again. It was right for France to retaliate, but France had never retaliated, and, consequently, she had no right to do it now. Thus England's hoary wrong had become a saintly precedent, while Napoleon's novelty of retaliation was a damnable innovation. In this neat manner, entirely satisfactory to itself, Tory logic makes mesmeric passes over facts, and wrongs become rights while rights become wrongs.

The eminent J. H. Rose, Master of Arts, and " Late Scholar of Christ's College, Cambridge," remarks:

" Napoleon showed his rancour by ordering some eight or ten thousand English travellers in France to be kept prisoners." Why the eminent Master of Arts and " Late Scholar of Christ's College " did so studiously omit to state that England had already seized French ships and sailors before Napoleon seized the travellers, can be explained by no one but a master of the art of writing partisan history.

" Napoleon showed his rancour " — by hitting back when Britain dealt him a sudden unprovoked and dastardly blow. Showed his rancour! " Sir, the phrase is neat," as Mirabeau said to Mounier upon a certain historic occasion.

Napoleon hastened to put Louisiana beyond England's

reach.   This imperial, but undeveloped, province had been lost to France by the Bourbon, Louis XV. and had only recently been recovered.   Napoleon profoundly regretted the necessity which compelled him to sell it to the United States, for he realized its value.

The war recommenced with vigor on both sides.   Great Britain seized again upon all the colonies which she had released by treaty, and French armies in Italy or Germany added territory to France.

Spain refusing to join the league against Napoleon, Great Britain made war upon her, captured her treasure ships upon the high seas, and thus forced her into the arms of France.   She not only put her fleet at Napoleon's disposal, but agreed to furnish him a monthly subsidy of more than $1,000,000.

Definitely threatening to invade Great Britain, Napoleon made preparations for that purpose on a scale equal to the mighty task.   Along the French and Dutch coasts 160,000 men were assembled, and vast flotillas built to take them across the Channel.   So great was the alarm felt in England that her coasts were watched by every available ship, and almost the entire manhood of the island enrolled itself in the militia, and prepared for a desperate struggle.

So prominently did Napoleon stand forth as the embodiment of all that monarchical Europe detested, so completely did he represent all that England and the Bourbons most dreaded, that a mad determination to kill him took possession of his enemies.   The head of the conspiracy was the Count of Artois, afterward king of France under the name of Charles X.   The meetings of the conspirators were held in London.   The plan adopted was that Pichegru (who had escaped from South America) and Moreau should be brought together to head the malcontents in the army; Georges Cadoudal, and a band of royalists equally resolute, should be landed on the Norman coast, should proceed to Paris, and should kill the First Consul; a royalist revolt should follow, and the Count of Artois should then himself land on the Norman coast to head the insurrection. The English minister to Bavaria, Mr. Drake, was actively at work in the plot, and in one of his letters to a correspondent, wrote: "All plots against the First Consul must be forwarded; for it is a matter of little consequence by whom the animal be stricken down, provided you are all in the hunt." Among others who were in the background and winding sonorous horns to those who were "in the hunt," were certain British agents, — Spencer Smith at Stuttgard, Taylor at Cassel, and Wickham at Berne. Directly in communication with the heads of the conspiracy in London was the under secretary of state, Hammond, the same who was so intolerably insolent to the United States during the second term of President Jefferson.

Lavishly supplied with money by the English government, a ship of the royal navy was put at their service, — Captain Wright, an officer of that navy, being in command.

The assassins were landed at the foot of a sea-washed cliff on the coast of Normandy in the night. Using a secret path and the rope-ladder of smugglers, they climbed the precipice and made their way secretly to Paris. Here they spent some weeks in organizing the conspiracy. The danger to Napoleon became so urgent that those who had the care of his personal safety felt that no precautions could be too great. De Ségur, captain of the body-guard, relates how Caulaincourt, Grand Marshal of the palace *pro tem*, woke him up after twelve o'clock at night toward the end of January, 1804, with: "Get up! Change the parole and the countersign immediately. There is not an instant to lose. The duties must be carried out as if in the presence of the enemy!"

Napoleon himself remained cool, but gradually became very stern. Asked by one of his councillors if he were afraid, he replied: "I, afraid! Ah, if I were afraid, it would be a bad day for France."

The first great object of the conspirators was to bring Pichegru and Moreau together. It was hoped and believed that this could be readily done. It was remembered that Moreau had concealed the treasonable correspondence of Pichegru which had fallen into his hands in 1796. It was known that Moreau heartily disliked Napoleon. It was known that Moreau, sulking in his tent, and bitterly regretting his share in Napoleon's elevation to power, was in that frame of mind which leads men into desperate enterprises.

Nevertheless, the conspirators found him very shy. By nature he was irresolute and weak, strong only when in command of an army. He consented to meet Pichegru, and did meet him at night, and have a few words with .him in the street. Afterward Pichegru visited Moreau's house, but the proof that Moreau agreed to take any part in the conspiracy is not satisfactory. It seems that Moreau had no objection to the "removal" of Napoleon and the overthrow of the government. He even spoke vaguely of the support which he and his friends in authority might bring to those who were conspiring; but Moreau was a republican, — one of those ardent young men of 1789 who had left school to fight for the Republic, and he was not ready to aid in the restoration of the Bourbons. Willing to countenance the overthrow of Napoleon, he was not willing to undo the work of the Revolution. According to one account, he himself aspired to succeed Bonaparte. This disgusted Cadoudal, who in scornful anger declared that he preferred Napoleon "to this brainless, heartless Moreau." Inasmuch as Moreau had already become disgusted with Cadoudal, the conspiracy could not knit itself together.

Meanwhile, repeated conferences were held between the assassins and various royalists of Paris who were in the plot, the most prominent of these being the brothers Polignac and De La Rivière. Napoleon knew in a general way that his life was being threatened, knowing just enough to be convinced that he must learn more or perish. His police seemed powerless, and as a last resort he tried a plan of his own. Causing a list of the suspected persons to be brought to him, his attention became fixed upon the name of a surgeon, Querel. In the belief that this man must be less of a fanatic than the others, he ordered that the surgeon should be brought to trial, and the attempt made to wring a confession from him. Tried accordingly, condemned, sentenced, and about to be shot, Querel broke down and confessed.

Learning from him that the most dangerous of the conspirators were even then in Paris, a cordon of troops was thrown around the city, and a vigilant search begun. Pichegu, after dodging from house to house, was at length betrayed by an old friend with whom he had sought shelter. Georges was taken after a desperate fight in the street. Captain Wright was seized at the coast and sent to Paris. Moreau had already been

arrested.   Many other of the Georges band were in
prison.   Napoleon's fury was extreme, and not unnat-
ural.   He had been lenient, liberal, conciliatory to his
political foes.   He had pushed to the verge of imprudence
the policy of reconciliation.   Vendeans, royalists, priests
— all had felt his kindness.   Some of the very men who
were now threatening him with assassination were émigrés
whom he had relieved from sentence of death and had
restored to fortune.   What had he done to England or
to the Bourbons that they should put him beyond the
pale of humanity?   Had he not almost gone upon his
knees in his efforts to secure peace?   Had he ever lifted
his hand against a Bourbon save in open war which they
themselves had commenced?   And now what was he to
do to put a stop to these plots hatched in London?
To what court could he appeal?   With the Bourbons
safely housed in England and supplied with British money,
ever ready to arm against him the fanatics of royalism,
what was he to do to protect his life?   Was he to await
the attack, living in constant apprehension, never knowing
when the blow would fall, uncertain how the attack would
be made, ignorant who the assassin might be, and in eternal
doubt as to whether he could escape the peril?   Can mortal man be placed in a position more trying than that of
one who knows that sworn murderers are upon his track,
and that some one moment of every day and every night
may give the opportunity to the unsleeping vigilance of
the assassin?

Roused as he had never been, Napoleon determined not
to wait, not to stand upon literal self-defence.   He would
strike back, would anticipate his enemies, would paralyze
their plans by carrying terror into their own ranks.

The head of the conspiracy, Artois, could not be reached. Expected on the French coast, he had not come. But his cousin, the Duke d'Enghien was at Etten-heim, close to the French border.

What was he doing there? He had borne arms against France, a crime which under the law of nations is treason, and which under the law of all lands is punishable with death. By French law, existing at the time, he had for-feited his life as a traitor. He was in the pay of England, the enemy of France. He was closely related by blood and by interest to the two brothers, Provence and Artois, who were making desperate efforts to recover the crown for the Bourbon family. What was the young Bourbon duke doing so near to the French border at this particu-lar time?

Royalist authors say that he was there to enjoy the pleasures of the chase ; also to enjoy the society of the Princess de Rohan, to whom they now say, without evi-dence, that he was secretly married.

Sir Walter Scott, a most unfriendly witness for Napoleon, admits that d'Enghien " fixed himself on the frontier for the purpose of being ready to put himself at the head of the royalists in East France, or Paris itself."

That he was on the Rhine awaiting some event, some change in France in which he would have " a part to play," was confessed, and cannot be denied.

What was the movement at whose head he was waiting to place himself? What other plan did the royalists have in progress at the time other than the Georges-Pichegru plot? If d'Enghien was waiting on the Rhine until they should have dealt the blow in Paris, was he not an accomplice, a principal in the second degree? It does not matter whether he knew the details of the Georges-Pichegru conspiracy or not. If he had been instructed to hold himself in readiness on the French frontier to enter the country and "act a part" therein, his common sense told him that a plot was on foot, and if he did not wish to be treated as an accomplice, he should not have acted as one. The cowardly d'Artois had not left London, and the Duke d'Enghien was to enter France as representative of the Bourbon family after the First Consul should have been killed.

The rule in law and equity is that where one is put upon notice of a transaction, he is to be held as knowing all that he could have learned by reasonable inquiry. The instructions issued to d'Enghien put him upon notice that something unusual was in progress, that it concerned him, and that he had a part to play. Prudent inquiry made by him of his Bourbon relatives in London would have put him in possession of the facts. This inquiry he either made or he did not: if he made it, he learned of the plot; if he did not make it, his was the negligence of being ignorant of the plan in which he was to "act a part."

It is very improbable that the Count of Artois, who had sent word to the Count of Provence at Warsaw asking his adhesion to the conspiracy, should have given his cousin, d'Enghien, a "part to act" in it without informing him of the nature of the drama itself.

The police reports made to Napoleon led him to believe that the young duke was privy to the plot, and was waiting at Ettenheim ready to take part in it. Here was a Bourbon he could reach. Through this one, he would strike terror into the others. "Neither is my blood ditch-water! I will teach these Bourbons a lesson they will not soon forget. Am I a dog to be shot down in the street?"

After deliberating with his councillors, Talleyrand and all the rest, the First Consul issued his orders. A French squadron rode rapidly to the Rhine, crossed over to Etten-heim, seized the Duke, who had been warned in vain, and hurried him to Paris. Stopped at the barrier, he was sent to Vincennes, tried by court-martial that night, condemned upon his own confession, sentenced to death, shot at day-break, and buried in the moat of the castle.

This harsh act of retaliation had met the approval of Talleyrand — an approval given in a written paper which he was quick to seize and destroy upon Napoleon's fall in 1814. During the day upon which the Duke was being taken to Vincennes, Talleyrand was asked, "What is to be done with the Duke d'Enghien?" and had replied to the questioner, "He is to be shot."

The Consul Cambacérès, who had voted for death at the trial of Louis XVI., opposed the arrest, giving his reasons at length. Napoleon replied: "I know your motive for speaking — your devotion to me. I thank you for it; but I will not allow myself put to death without defending myself. I will make these people tremble, and teach them to keep quiet for all time to come."

Poor Josephine, who could never meet a member of the old noblesse without a collapse of spirit, a gush of adulation, and a yielding sensation at the knees, made a feeble effort to turn her husband from his purpose; but when Napoleon reminded her that she was a mere child in politics, and had better attend to her own small affairs, she dried her tears, and went into the garden to amuse herself with her flower-beds.

Napoleon himself made a thorough study of the papers, taken with the Duke at Ettenheim, and drew up a series of questions which were to be put to the prisoner by Réal, state councillor. The messenger sent by the First Consul did not see Réal, and the paper was not handed him till five o'clock next morning. Worn out by continuous toil, the councillor had gone to bed the evening before, leaving instructions with his household that he was not to be disturbed. Next morning when he was posting along the highway to Vincennes, he met Savary on his way back to Paris. Savary had already carried out the death-sentence, and the victim was in his grave.

It seems that the young Duke had not realized his danger. A term of imprisonment, at most, was all he feared. In vain the court-martial endeavored to hint at the fatal consequence of the admissions he was making. Unconscious of the fact that he was convicting himself, he repeated the statements that he had borne arms against France, that he had been in the pay of England, that he had tampered with French soldiers on the Rhine, that he had been instructed to place himself near the Rhine where he could enter France, arms in hand, and be ready for the part he was to play; and that he intended to continue to bear arms against the government of France which he regarded as a usurpation.

It must not be forgotten that in sending the Duke d'Enghien before a court-martial, Napoleon had before him certain documentary evidence which we do not now possess. The Duke's own papers, Talleyrand's opinion, and the reports of certain officials disappeared from the archives after the Bourbons returned in 1814 — just as the documentary evidence against Marie Antoinette was

destroyed, and the letters which crowned heads of Europe
had written Napoleon stolen and carried away.

Peculiarly awful must have been the vision of sudden
death to this youthful prince of the blood-royal, as he
was dragged from bed in the dismal darkness of early
morning, and hurried to face a file of silent soldiers beside
an open grave. After the first shock and outcry of amazement, the courage in which his race has rarely been wanting came to the condemned, and he met his fate with a
soldier's nerve.

In 1805, during the march upon Vienna, Napoleon received at his bivouac M. de Thiard, who had known
d'Enghien well. For a long while the Emperor sat talking with this officer, asking many questions about the
Duke, and listening with interest to all that was told him.

"He was really a man, then, that prince?" he asked,
and this casual remark was his sole comment.

Among all those who believe that the life of a prince
is more sacred than that of a plebeian, among aristocrats
of all countries, and among the crowned heads of Europe,
there was a burst of grief and rage when it became known
that Napoleon had shot a Bourbon duke. Thousands of
pages were written then, thousands have been written
since, in denunciation of this so-called murder. Men who
had never uttered a word in condemnation of Lord Nelson's treatment of Carraccioli, could find no words harsh
enough for Napoleon's usage of d'Enghien. Alexander
of Russia, who had whimpered in the palace while his
father was being stamped, choked, and smothered to death
in the adjoining room, and who had promoted the assassins
to high trusts in his own service, took Napoleon's conduct
more to heart than did any of the royal fraternity. As-

suming the lofty moral attitude of one who is missioned
to rebuke sin, he broke off diplomatic relations with
France and put the Russian court in mourning. Napoleon launched at the Czar a crushing reminder on the
subject of Paul's death, and Alexander suffered the subject to drop.

Paris, stunned at first by the tragedy, recovered itself
immediately; and when Napoleon appeared at the theatre
a few nights afterward, he was acclaimed as usual. Talleyrand gave a ball, and society was there with the same old
stereotyped smile upon its vacuous face.

Nevertheless, it is certain that the death of this young
Duke injured Napoleon in public esteem, was of no political service to him, armed his enemies with a terrible
weapon against him, and gave to the exiled Bourbons a
sympathy they had not enjoyed since the Revolution. Said
Fouché, "It is worse than a crime; it is a blunder."
But there is no evidence that Napoleon ever regretted it.
It is true that he became enraged when Talleyrand denied
his share in the transaction, and that he always maintained
that Talleyrand had advised it; but he never shirked his
own responsibility.

When he lay upon his death-bed at St. Helena, an
attendant read to him from an English publication a
bitter attack upon those guilty of the alleged murder of
d'Enghien. The dying Emperor had already made his
will; but he roused himself, had the paper brought, and
interlined with his own hands these final words in which
he assumed full responsibility: —

"I had the Duke d'Enghien arrested and tried because
it was necessary to do so for the safety, the honor, and the
interest of the French people at a time when the Count

of Artois openly admitted that he had sixty paid assassins in Paris. Under similar circumstances I would do so again."

The trials of Moreau, Georges, and the other conspirators did not take place until Napoleon had become emperor. The prosecution was clumsily managed; and as to Moreau, public opinion was divided. His services, so recent and so great, gave some color to the story that Napoleon was actuated by jealousy in having him classed with criminals. However, Moreau weakened his defence by an exculpatory letter he wrote Napoleon, and this together with such proofs as the government could furnish, and such influence as it could bring to bear on the court, resulted in a conviction and a sentence of two years in confinement. This penalty Napoleon changed into one of banishment. Georges and a number of others were shot. Pichegru and Wright committed suicide. The Polignacs and Rivière, as guilty as the guiltiest, were pardoned — they being of gentle birth, and being fortunate in having the friendship of some who stood near Napoleon.

CHAPTER XXV

DURING the years of the peace (1801–1804), French influence upon the Continent kept marching on. Napoleon's diplomacy was as effective as his cannon. Holland became a subject state, with a new constitution dictated by France, and a governing council which took guidance from France (1801).

Lombardy dropped its title of the Cisalpine, and became the Italian republic, with Napoleon for President. French troops entered Switzerland, put down civil strife, and the country for ten years enjoyed peace and prosperity under a constitution given it by Napoleon, he being virtually its ruler under the name of Mediator of the Helvetic League.

In Germany, a general shaking up and breaking up of political fossils and governmental dry bones occurred. The territory ceded to France by the treaty of Lunéville needed to be reorganized. The German princes, who were dispossessed, required compensation. Prussia had to be paid for her neutrality. Austria wished to recoup her losses. How was it possible for diplomacy to satisfy at the same time France, which had fought and won; Austria which had fought and lost ; and Prussia, which had not fought at all ?

Napoleon was ready with his answer. Let the strong help themselves to the territories of the weak. At Rastadt, Napoleon had remarked to Marten, "Does not public law nowadays consist simply in the right of the stronger?" Evidently it did, as it does yet, and ever has done. Upon this theory the German complication was worked out. There were fifty so-called Free Cities which, being weak and in debt, might be forcibly absorbed. There were a number of ecclesiastical princes, ruling wretchedly over wide and rich domains, whose tempting wealth might be confiscated. There were hundreds of knights of the German Empire, decayed relics of mediævalism, each holding as private property a snug territory, whose people the knight taxed, judged, and outraged at his own good pleasure. The Congress of Rastadt had been laboring upon this German problem at the time Austria murdered the French envoys (1798). The task was now resumed (1801) nominally by the Congress at Ratisbon, but really by French diplomats in Paris. Talleyrand, as Minister of Foreign Affairs, had a magnificent opportunity to feather his nest with bribes, and he made the most of it. German diplomatists posted to Paris, paid court to the corrupt minister, laughed at all his good sayings, fondled his poodle, petted his supposed bastard, and lavished their gold upon him to win his influence.

When the process of reorganization was completed, Germany had been revolutionized. Most of the Free Cities were no longer free, but were incorporated with the territory of the government in which they were located. The ecclesiastical princes were reduced to the condition of salaried priests, their domains confiscated to the governments. Bavaria, Baden, Würtemberg, were given large increase of territory; Prussia was not left unrewarded; France got all she was entitled to; and Austria, the defeated nation, lost almost nothing. The happy combination of France, Prussia, Austria, and Russia, to settle their differences at the expense of the Free Cities and the Princes of the German Catholic Church, had been blessed with brilliant success.

Following the redistribution of German lands came changes yet more vital. The wretched little feudal sovereignties disappeared. The imperial knights lost their out-of-date principalities. The leaven of the French Revolution penetrated far beyond the Rhine. Offices ceased to be bought, sold, and inherited. Regular systems of taxation, police, and legal procedure came into use. The trades and professions were thrown open to all : caste was breached, the peasant freed from some of his heaviest burdens. Education, in some parts of Germany, was taken out of the hands of the Church, and the clergy made amenable to the law.

In this manner Napoleon had, unconsciously perhaps, laid the foundation for the union of the German peoples into one great empire, by the suppression of so many of those small, jealous, and hide-bound principalities which had divided the land, and which nothing but overwhelming pressure from without could have reformed.

Thus, while still wearing the modest title of First Consul, the ruler of France had grown to proportions which were imperial. To the French, he was the necessary man without whom they might relapse into chaotic conditions. The wondrous structure he had reared seemed to rest upon his strength alone. His life was the sole guarantee of law and order. Should assassins strike him down, what would be the situation in France ? To avoid such a danger, **and** to deprive royalist fanatics of such a temptation, would it not be better to make Napoleon monarch, and to settle the succession? In that event his death would not bring about endless confusion and violent convulsions. Reasoning of this kind seems to have moved the Senate to propose that the First Consul accept a new title, and on May 18, 1804, he proclaimed himself Emperor of the French.

Partly by the force of circumstances, partly by sincere conviction, partly by the exertion of Napoleon's wonderful gift for the management of men, France had been so well prepared for this change in her form of government that she indorsed it by a practically unanimous vote. Only such stalwart exponents of a principle as Carnot and Lafayette protested.

With the Empire came all things imperial : a change of constitution ; a creation of high dignitaries ; the ennobling of the Bonaparte family, Lucien excepted ; the creation of marshals in the army ; the establishment of court forms and etiquette in the palace.

Gorgeous and imposing were the ceremonies which ushered in the New Order. Paris, France, Europe, were dazzled by the lavish expenditures, the magnificent parade, with which the Consul became Emperor. He spared no expense, no pains, no personal discomfort, to make the pageant a success. Historians have sneered at the rehearsals by means of which he prepared each actor in the coronation for his part ; but the ridicule would seem to be misplaced. His example has set the fashion ; and not only are private marriages rehearsed in our day, but royal funerals and royal coronations perfect their functions by the same prudent process.

That nothing might be wanting to the solemnity and

impressiveness of the occasion, Napoleon insisted that the Pope should come from Rome to Paris and officiate. So recent and so immense had been Napoleon's services to the Church that the Pontiff could not refuse, more especially as he had other favors to ask.

Brilliant as a dream was the coronation in the great cathedral of Notre Dame. Paris never witnessed a civic and military display more splendid. The Church, the State, princes foreign and native, grandees old and new, blazed forth in the utmost that wealth and pride and vanity could display. In a coach heavy with gold Napoleon and Josephine rode, amid soldiers, to the church where the Pope had long awaited their coming; and when the great Corsican had been conducted through the proper forms, had prayed, had sworn, had been oiled and blessed, he proudly took the crown out of the Pope's hands, crowned himself, and then crowned the kneeling Josephine (December, 1804). His mother was not there, she was in Rome with the revolted Lucien; but when the artist David painted the picture of the coronation, Napoleon, with his never failing eye for effect, had Madame Letitia put in. Just as he wished for his mother on this the great day of his life, he did not forget his father.

"Joseph, what would father have said!"

One who had lifted himself from a cottage to the White House in these United States drew all hearts to himself when, after having taken the oath of office, he turned to his old mother and kissed her. Not far distant from the same creditable feeling was Napoleon's regret for his father.

Mother Letitia could not be persuaded to leave Rome

and the insurgent Lucien; but the old nurse journeyed from Corsica to see her nursling crowned. Napoleon hugged and kissed the old woman, lavished every attention upon her, and kept her in Paris a couple of months. When she returned to Ajaccio, she was laden with gifts.

Nor could Brienne be overlooked in these sunny days of triumph and of happiness. The Emperor must return to the school grounds of his boyhood, view the old familiar scenes, talk of old times with such former acquaintances as might still be there. Behold him, then, soon after his coronation, arriving at the château of Brienne, at six in the evening, where Madame de Brienne and Madame Loménie await him at the foot of the steps. He spends the night at the château, whose kind mistress had so often made him welcome in the forlorn days of his youth. He walks about the place, pointing out every spot familiar to him when at school. He visits the field of La Rothière, a favorite strolling place of his youth. He is so affable, so animated, so interested, that his movements seem to say, See where I started from, and where I have arrived. "And what has become of Mother Marguerite, the peasant woman who used to sell milk, eggs, and bread to the boys?" Mother Marguerite is still living, still to be found at the thatched cottage in the woods. By all means, the Emperor must quit the fine circle at the château and visit the old peasant in the hut. A man so gifted with eye to effect could never miss a point like that. So the horse is saddled and brought; the Emperor mounts and rides; and at the cottage in the wood his Majesty alights and enters.

"Good day, Mother Marguerite!" The aged eyes are dim, and they gleam with no recognition. She knows that the Emperor is in the neighborhood; she expects to go to the château to see him; she will carry him a basket of eggs to remind him of old times. Suddenly his Majesty puts himself where the dim eyes can see him better, draws nearer to her, and mimicking in voice and manner his schoolboy tone, and rubbing his hands as he had used to do : "Come, Mother Marguerite! Some milk and fresh eggs; we are dying of hunger."

A little more jogging of the memory, and the ancient dame, knowing now who it is, falls at the Emperor's feet. He lifts her, and still insists on the eggs and milk. She serves, he eats, both of them happy, and both of them full of reminiscences of the years long ago. Though he left her a purse of gold, Mother Marguerite probably was prouder of the fact that he came to her house and ate.

One more visit the great Emperor will pay Brienne, the year of the last visit being 1814. Foreign invaders will be encamped all round about the playgrounds of his boyhood. Prussian Blücher will be taking his ease and his dinner in the château. Prussian Blücher will give him battle at Brienne, and will rout him at La Rothière. And to his companions, the falling Emperor will again point out places of interest in the old schoolground, but not in the happy vein of 1804.

What should be done with Italy? French arms had wrested her from Austria and defended her from Russia. She was too weak to stand alone. Take away the support of France, and she would again be cut up and devoured by the stronger powers. On all sides she was threatened. The English were at Malta, the Russians at Corfu, the

Austrians in Venice, while in Naples and Rome were apparent allies, but actual foes. Reasons of state made it
imperative that Napoleon's imperial system should embrace
Italy, and the Italians themselves favored the change.

Napoleon tendered the crown to his brother Joseph.
To the amazement of the world that preposterous egotist
refused upon two grounds : first, Italy was too near to
France for its king to enjoy that complete independence
which Joseph felt necessary to his self-respect ; second,
the crown of France belonged to him, in prospect, as heir
of the childless Napoleon ; and Joseph would not exchange
this selfish, shadowy claim for the certainty offered him
by his too partial brother ! Surely there never lived a
man more be-cursed with ingrates of his own blood than
Napoleon !

" I am sometimes tempted to believe," said he, " that
Joseph thinks I have robbed my elder brother of his share
of the inheritance of the late king, our father ! "

It was only after Joseph had resisted all persuasions
that Napoleon decided to make himself king of Italy
"until the peace."

In April, 1805, taking Josephine with him, he crossed
the Alps. Everywhere he was greeted with enthusiasm.
On the field of Marengo he and Josephine sat upon a
throne and viewed the splendid rehearsal of the battle
in which the young hero had crushed Austria and rescued
Italy at a blow.

In May, 1805, he placed upon his head, amid pomps and
ceremonies in the cathedral of Milan, the iron crown of
the Lombards. Josephine looked on from the gallery;
she was not crowned queen of Italy ; but her son, the
loyal and gallant Eugène Beauharnais, was made Viceroy

of the new kingdom. His Holiness, the Pope, was not present at the ceremony; his Holiness was chagrined and unfriendly; he had left Paris a disappointed man; he had asked many favors of Napoleon, " my son in Christ Jesus," which had been denied, and already was to be seen the slender line of the rift between Napoleon and the Papacy which was to grow and grow, widening year by year, until the yawning chasm was to ingulf much of the strength of the Empire.

But, for the time being, the Pope went his way almost unnoticed, meekly implacable, humbly vindictive, waiting his chance to strike the ruler he had so recently oiled and blessed, while the vaulting Corsican, using an archbishop to manipulate the clerical machinery instead of a pope, inflated himself with pride as he felt upon his head the crown of Charlemagne.

And had he no cause to be proud? Did the history of the world disclose a more dazzling record than his? Not born to the throne, a stranger to the purple and the gold of rank, the greatest Empire of modern times was his; and, as heir to the Cæsars, he had now caught upon his arms the grandeur and the glory of old Rome. Emperor of the West! — another Theodosius, another Charles the Great! And only a few years ago he had meekly stopped to scrape the mud of the streets off his coarse boots to avoid offence to the nose of Madame Permon: had pawned his watch for food; had moodily thought of drowning himself in the Seine because his mother had pleaded for help which he was too poor to give!

If ever mortal was justly proud, it was he, — Napoleon, the penniless son of the lawyer; Napoleon, tireless student, unwearied worker. unconquerable adventurer,

z

resistless soldier of Fortune, — Napoleon, Emperor of France and King of Italy, whose crowns had come to him unstained of blood ! He was the strongest, the wisest, the best in fight, in work, in council ; and they had raised him aloft on their bucklers as the strongest had been lifted in the valiant days of old.

Nothing in Napoleon's career was more brilliant than his triumphal progress through the Italian cities. Everything which a passionate, imaginative people could do to testify their admiration and affection, they did ; and during these brief, sunny weeks when he moved amid ovations and splendors, amid rejoicings and blessings, amid music and flowers, with Josephine by his side, he probably came as near to happiness as his restless, craving nature could come. Everywhere he left indelible footprints, — roads, canals, public buildings of all sorts, mighty and useful works which made his tour memorable for all time.

Genoa, following the lead of Italy, and friendly suggestions from France, voted to unite her fortunes with those of the new Empire. The Doge and the Senate went in state to Milan, were received by Napoleon on his throne, and prayed that he would accept the ancient republic as a part of France. Graciously the modern Cæsar consented ; the Doge became a French senator, and out of the territories of the republic were carved three French departments.

The little republic of Lucca caught the general infection, sent a deputation to Milan, begged at Napoleon's hands a government and a constitution, was warmly welcomed by the Emperor, and was bestowed as an imperial fief upon his sister Elisa, wife of a Corsican fiddler named Bacciochi.

JOSEPHINE in 1809

From a water-color by Isabey

The horror and indignation with which European kings and cabinets looked upon these encroachments can easily be imagined. With one accord they began to cry out against Napoleon's "insatiable ambition." England did not consider how she had despoiled France in Canada, on the Ohio, in Hindustan. Russia and Austria made no account of provinces taken from Poland or Turkey. All the great nations were growing greater; the general balance of power had been disturbed: was France alone to be denied the right to extend her system over states which asked for it, and which were dependent upon her for protection?

In January, 1805, Napoleon had written directly to the King of England, as he had done once before, asking for peace. As before, his advances had been repelled. Great Britain had already begun to knit together the threads of another coalition. An understanding existed between England, Russia, Austria, and Sweden. Naples, through her Bourbon rulers, was fawning at Napoleon's feet, flattering and servile, while secretly she was plotting his downfall. Well aware of the storm which was gathering on the Continent, Napoleon prepared for it, but did not for an instant relax his efforts at Boulogne.

His plan was to send his fleet to sea, decoy Nelson into pursuit, and then, while his own ships doubled and came back to the Channel, to cross his army over to England, under its protection, in his flat-bottomed boats. "Masters of the Channel for six hours, we are masters of the world."

It was not to be. Wind and waves fought against him. The incapacity of his navy fought against him. Into soldiers on land he could infuse courage, confidence, sympathetic coöperation. But the navy baffled him: all his efforts were vain. His admirals could not, or would not, have faith; could not, or would not, obey orders; could not, or would not, coöperate. Utterly wasted were all his labors, all his expenditures. Austrian armies were marching against Bavaria, Napoleon's ally; Russian hordes were moving down from the north; Prussia's magnificent army of fifty thousand men was in the balance, wavering ominously, and threatening to unite with the coalition.

Such was the situation on the Continent when the despatches reached Napoleon that all his great plans for the invasion of England had gone to wreck and ruin; that his admiral had misconceived or had disobeyed positive orders; that the French fleet would not only be unable to give him aid, but was so scattered and so placed that it must inevitably fall a prey to the English.

"It was about four o'clock in the morning of August 13, that the news was brought to the Emperor," says Ségur. "Daru was summoned, and on entering gazed on his chief in utter astonishment." The Emperor "looked perfectly wild"; his hat jammed down over his eyes, "his whole aspect terrible." As soon as he saw Daru, he rushed up, and poured out a torrent of pent-up wrath. He railed at his admiral, his imbecile admiral, "that damned fool of a Villeneuve!" He paced "up and down the room, with great strides for about an hour," venting his rage, his disappointment, his reproaches. Then stopping suddenly and pointing to a desk, he exclaimed: "Sit down there, Daru, and write!" And with marvellous self-control, wresting his thoughts away from Villeneuve, the fleet, the blasted plans of invasion, he dictated to the secretary, hour after hour, as fast as pen could catch the rushing words, the whole campaign of Ulm in its largest outline, in its smallest detail, embracing, as it did, the movement of his own vast legions lying along the coast for two hundred leagues, the movement of Masséna from Italy, of Marmont from Holland, and of Bernadotte from Hanover. Four hundred thousand soldiers were moving against the French; less than half that number of French rushed to repel the attack. The vast camps on the Boulogne coast vanished, the eagles set Rhineward, other legions marched as they had never marched before — thousands speeding along the roads in coaches. The Austrians had not waited for the Russians; Bavaria had been overrun; and Mack, the Austrian general, was now dawdling about Ulm. Before he suspected what was happening, Napoleon's combination had been made, a circle of steel drawn about his adversary; and the French armies, closing in upon front, rear, and flanks, held the Austrians as in a mighty trap. With the exception of a few squadrons which broke through the gaps in the French lines as they advanced, the whole Austrian army laid down its arms (October 20, 1805). In the *Memoirs* of de Ségur we are given a personal glimpse of the Emperor which is perhaps more interesting to the average reader than the dreary narrative of march, counter-march, manœuvre, and battle.

During the combats around Elchingen, Napoleon, soaked with rain, went to a farmhouse at Hasslach to wait for Lannes and the Guard to come up. There was a stove which threw out its comfortable heat, and before it sat a drummer boy, wet, cold, and wounded. Napoleon's staff officers told the boy to get out, and go somewhere else. The drummer would not hear of it. The room was big

enough for both the Emperor and himself, he said, and
he meant to stay. Napoleon laughed, and told them to
let the boy alone, "since he made such a point of it."
In a few moments the Emperor was dozing on one side
of the stove and the drummer lad on the other. Around
the two sleepers were grouped the staff officers, standing,
and awaiting orders.

Louder roared the cannon, and every few minutes
Napoleon would rouse himself and send off messengers
to hasten Lannes. While the Emperor was thus napping, Lannes came up, entered the room abruptly, and
exclaimed: "Sire! What are you thinking about? You
are sleeping while Ney, single-handed, is fighting against
the whole Austrian army!"—"That's just like Ney,
I told him to wait," said Napoleon, and springing on
his horse, he galloped off so fast that Lannes, afraid now
that the Emperor would rush into danger, roughly seized
the bridle rein and forced him back in a less dangerous
position. Ney was reënforced, and the Austrians routed.

In the midst of his own successes, Napoleon received
the tidings from Trafalgar. Nelson had fought the combined fleets of France and Spain, had lost his own life,
but had won so complete a triumph that England's
supremacy at sea was not disputed again throughout
the Napoleonic wars. The shock to Napoleon must
have been stunning, but he only said, "I cannot be
everywhere."

Continuing his advance, he entered Vienna, November
13, 1805, and lost no time in throwing his army across
the Danube, in hot pursuit of the retreating enemy.

By a trick and a falsehood, Murat and Lannes secured the great bridge, and much precious time was saved. By a similar trick, the Russians deceived Murat a few days later, and escaped the net Napoleon had thrown around them, and thus "the fruits of a campaign were lost." Murat gained the bridge by pretending that an armistice. had been agreed on; the Russians made good their escape by duping Murat with the same falsehood.   Napoleon's anger was extreme, the more so as a blunder of Murat's had come within a hair's-breadth of spoiling the campaign of Ulm.

Failing to trap the Russians as he had trapped the Austrians, there was nothing for Napoleon to do but to press the pursuit.   League after league the French penetrated a hostile country, new armies mustering on all sides to rush in upon them, until they were in the heart of Moravia.   The Emperor Francis of Austria had joined the Czar Alexander, and the combined Russo-Austrian forces, outnumbering the French, confronted Napoleon at Austerlitz.   The position of the French, far from home and surrounded by populations rushing to arms, was critical.   Napoleon realized it, and so did his foe. There is no doubt that he would have welcomed an honorable peace, but the terms offered by the Czar were so insulting that he indignantly rejected them.   Hastily concentrating his army, he made ready to fight.   He artfully cultivated the self-confidence of the enemy, and put them under the impression that he was trying to escape.   They had the hardihood to believe that they could turn his position, cut him off from his line of retreat, and do to him at Austerlitz as he had done to Mack at Ulm.

Indeed, the position of the French army demanded all
of Napoleon's firmness, all of his genius. He had about
eighty thousand men; the Emperors in his front had
ninety thousand. His right was threatened by the Archduke Charles with an army of forty thousand; his rear
by the Archduke Ferdinand with twenty thousand; on
his left flank was unfriendly Prussia with a magnificent
force of one hundred and fifty thousand. The combined armies in his front, taking the offensive, attacked
the French advance guard at Wischau, and routed it.
Napoleon was uneasy. He sent envoys to the Czar and
sought a personal interview. Surrounded by young hotheads, Alexander repulsed the overture, sending Dolgorouki to meet the Emperor of the French. Full of the idea
that the French were frightened and would pay hand-
somely for the privilege of getting back home, young
Dolgorouki demanded of Napoleon the surrender of Italy,
Belgium, and the Rhine provinces.

"What more could you ask if you were in France?"
exclaimed the indignant Napoleon. The envoy's manner
was as offensive as his language, and Napoleon finally
ordered him off. Violently irritated, Napoleon stood
talking to Savary for some time, striking the ground with
his riding-whip, as he dwelt upon the insolence of the
Russians. "Please God, in forty-eight hours I will give
them a lesson!"

An old grenadier stood near, filling his pipe for a smoke.
Napoleon walked up to him and said, "Those fellows think
they are going to swallow us up." — "If they try it," said
the veteran, "we'll stick in their craws." Napoleon
laughed, and his brow cleared.

Drawing his army back to a still better position, Napo-

leon studied the ground thoroughly, reconnoitred diligently, and waited. He soon guessed the plan of the
enemy, to turn his right flank. But to do this they must
expose their own flank to him, and he would strike them
as they marched. So confident was Napoleon that he
could destroy his enemy if the turning movement across
his front were attempted, that he lured them still farther
by withdrawing from the high-ground, the Pratzen plateau — "a grand position," from which he could easily
have inflicted upon the Russians an ordinary defeat. But
an ordinary defeat was not what he wanted ; he manœuvred
to lead his foes into a false movement where they could
be annihilated.

On December 1, 1805, about four in the afternoon,
Napoleon could see through his field-glass that the great
turning movement of the Russians had commenced. He
clapped his hands and exclaimed, "They are walking into
a trap; before to-morrow night that army will be mine ! "

Ordering Murat to make a sham attack and then retire
so as to confirm the enemy in his delusion of a French
retreat, Napoleon dictated a stirring address to his troops,
pointing out to them the Russian mistake and the advantage the French could take of it. Everything done that
could be done, the great captain called his staff about
him, and sat down to dinner in the hut which served him
for a bivouac. Seated around the table on wooden
benches were Murat, Caulaincourt, Junot, Rapp, Ségur,
Mouton, Thiard, and others. As serenely as though he
were in Paris, Napoleon led the conversation to literary
topics, dramatic poetry especially, and commented at length
on the merits of various authors and plays. From these
subjects he passed on to Egypt, and again spoke of the

wonderful things he would have done had he taken
Acre. He would have gained a battle on the Issus, become Emperor of the East, and returned to Paris by
way of Constantinople. Junot suggested that they might,
even now, be on the road to Constantinople. But Napoleon said: " No. The French do not love long marches.
They love France too well. The troops would prefer to return home." Junot questioned this; but Mouton bluntly
declared that the Emperor was right, that the army was
tired out, it had had enough : it would fight, but would
do so because it wished to win a battle which would end
the war and allow the men to return home.

Throwing himself upon some straw in his hut, Napoleon
slept till far into the night. Then he mounted his horse,
and once more went the rounds to see that all was right.
He went too near the Russian lines : roused some Cossacks,
and escaped capture by the speed of his horse. Getting
back into his own lines, he was stumbling along on foot in
the darkness when he fell over a log. A grenadier, to
light his way, made a torch of some straw. The blaze
showed to other soldiers the Emperor. Upon a sudden
impulse, more torches were made of straw, while the shout
arose, " Live the Emperor ! " It was the anniversary of
the coronation, and the troops remembered. The one
torch became a score, the score a hundred, then thousands,
until a blaze of light ran along the line for miles, while
the shout of " Live the Emperor!" roused even the Russian hordes. It was such an ovation as only a Cæsar
could inspire. It was so unstudied, so heartfelt, so martial and dramatic, that Napoleon was profoundly moved.
" It is the grandest evening of my life," he exclaimed.

At dawn he called his staff to the hut, ate with them

standing, and then, buckling on his sword, said, " Now, gentlemen, let us go and begin a great day! " A moment later he sat his horse on a hill that overlooked the field, his staff and his marshals around him. As the sun cleared itself of the mists, " the sun of Austerlitz," the final orders were given, the marshals galloped to their posts, and the famous battle began. By four o'clock that evening the Russo-Austrian army was a wreck — outgeneralled, outfought, knocked to pieces. Napoleon had ended " *this* war by a clap of thunder." The Czar fled with the remnant of his host, escaping capture at the hands of Davoust by the well-worn falsehood of an armistice. The Emperor Francis came in person to Napoleon to sue for peace, was kindly received, and was granted terms far more liberal than he had any right to expect.

On December 27, 1805, the Treaty of Presburg was signed. Austria ceded Venice, Friuli, Istria, and Dalmatia to Italy ; Tyrol to Bavaria, which Napoleon erected into an independent kingdom ; Würtemberg and Baden received cities and territory as rewards for adherence to France. Austria sanctioned all of Napoleon's recent encroachments in Italy, and agreed to pay an indemnity of $8,000,000.

In the battle of Austerlitz the Allies lost about fifteen thousand men, killed and wounded, besides twenty thousand prisoners. The French loss was about twelve thousand.

Marbot relates an incident which illustrates the character of Napoleon.

One of the familiar episodes of the battle of Austerlitz was the retreat of the Russians over the frozen lakes. Napoleon himself ordered the cannoneers to cease shooting

at the fugitives, and to elevate their pieces so that the
balls would fall upon the ice. The balls fell, the ice
cracked, and some two thousand Russians sank to watery
graves.

Next day Napoleon, being near this spot, heard feeble
cries for help. It was a Russian sergeant, wounded, adrift
in the lake, supporting himself on an ice floe. Napoleon's
sympathies were at once aroused, and he called for volunteers to save the Russian. Many attempts were made,
several Frenchmen came near being drowned, and finally
Marbot and Roumestain stripped, swam to the man, and
brought him to the shore. Napoleon had every attention
shown to the poor fellow — the survivor of the host which
sank the day before under his pitiless orders.

CHAPTER XXVI

IN England the wonderful triumph of Napoleon spread consternation and bitter disappointment. So much hard cash had been wasted, so many well-laid plans smashed, so much blind hatred brought to nothing! Other faces besides Pitt's took on "the Austerlitz look." That most arrogant of ministers had offered money to all who would unite against France, had encouraged Austria to attack Bavaria because of the refusal of Bavaria to enter the coalition against France, had landed English troops in Calabria to stir up the priest-ridden peasantry to insurrection, and had pledged himself to the task of driving the French from Germany, from Switzerland, from Italy and Holland. A mightier ruin had never fallen upon haughtier plans. The French were now masters of more territory than ever; Napoleon's power greater than ever; England's allies were being dismembered to strengthen the friends of France; and the British troops which had been sent to Calabria, and which had won the battle of Maida (July, 1806), abandoned the enterprise, and left the peasantry to suffer all the vengeance of the French. Whether Mr. Pitt's last words were, "My country! How I leave my country!" or, as Mr. D'Israeli used to relate, "I think I could now eat one of Bellamy's pork pies," it is certain that he took the news of Austerlitz as Lord North took Saratoga, "like a ball in the breast."

On the Continent Napoleon was supreme, and he used his advantage vigorously. The Bourbons of Naples had played him false, and he dethroned them. In western Germany was organized the Confederation of the Rhine, composed of Bavaria, Baden, Würtemberg, and thirteen smaller principalities, and containing a population of eight million. Created by Napoleon, it looked to him for protection, put its military forces at his service, and became, practically, a part of his imperial system.

By these changes the Emperor of Austria was reduced to his hereditary dominions, and his shadowy Holy Roman Empire ceased to exist, August 6, 1806.

Following Austerlitz came a grand distribution of crowns and coronets. Brother Joseph condescended to become King of Naples, with the distinct understanding that he waived none of his "rights" to the throne of France, and that he should be treated as an "independent ally" of the Emperor.

Holland was turned into a subject kingdom, and Louis Bonaparte put upon its throne.

To his sister Elisa, Napoleon gave additional territory in Italy; and to Pauline, who had married Prince Borghese, was given Guastalla. Madame Bacciochi, who was morally another Caroline of Naples, was a good ruler, and her government of her little kingdom was excellent. As to Pauline, she cared for nothing but pleasure; and not knowing very well what else to do with her Guastalla, she sold it.

Caroline Bonaparte, importunate in her demands for imperial recognition, was offered the principality of Neufchâtel. She haughtily declined it. Such a petty kingdom was obviously, even glaringly, less than her share.

Yielding to this youthful and self-assertive sister, Napoleon had to create the Grand Duchy of Berg to satisfy her and her no less aspiring husband, Murat.

The scapegrace Jerome Bonaparte, one of whose numberless freaks was that of paying $3,000 for a shaving outfit long prior to the arrival of his beard, was made to renounce his beautiful young American wife, Miss Patterson ; and was kept in imperial tutelage till such time as he should be made king of Westphalia, with a Würtemberg princess for queen.

Eugene Beauharnais, Viceroy of Italy, was married to the daughter of the king of Bavaria ; and Stephanie Beauharnais, Josephine's niece, was wedded to the son of the Elector of Baden.

In these grand arrangements for the Bonaparte family, Lucien was left out. He and Napoleon had quarrelled, the cause being, chiefly, that Lucien would not discard his wife, as the pusillanimous Jerome had done. Napoleon was offended because Lucien at his second marriage had selected a woman whose virtue was far from being above suspicion. " Divorce her," demanded Napoleon ; "she is a strumpet."

"Mine is at least young and pretty," retorted Lucien, with sarcastic reference to Josephine, who was neither young nor pretty. Angrily the brothers parted: the elder insisting on the divorce, and offering a kingdom as a bribe: the younger scornfully spurning the bribe, and cleaving to his wife. This manly and independent attitude was the easier to maintain since Lucien had already amassed a fortune in Napoleon's service. Taking up his residence in a grand palace in Rome, surrounded by rare books, paintings, and statuary, comforted by the prefer-

ence and the presence of Madame Letitia, a favorite of
the Pope because an enemy of Napoleon, Lucien cultivated letters, wrote the longest and the dullest epic of
modern times, and called it *Charlemagne*.

While elevating to thrones the members of his family,
the Emperor could not forget those who had served him
in the army and in civil affairs.   From the conquered
territories he carved various principalities, duchies, and so
forth, for distribution among the Talleyrands, Bernadottes,
and Berthiers, who were to betray him later.   A new
order of nobility sprang up at the word, — a nobility based
upon service, and without special privilege, but richly endowed, and quick to arrogate to itself all the prestige ever
enjoyed by the old.

Surrounded as he was by hostile kings, Napoleon felt
the need of supports.   In creating the Confederation
of the Rhine, in putting his brothers upon adjacent
thrones, in bestowing fiefs upon his high officials, he
believed himself to be throwing out barriers against foreign foes, and propping his empire with the self-interest
and resources of all these subject princes whom he had
created, never dreaming that in the day of adversity his
own brothers and sisters would think of saving themselves
at his expense.

On the very night of Napoleon's return to Paris from
the army, he summoned his council.   The finances were
in confusion ; there had been something of a panic, and
only the victory of Austerlitz restored confidence.   The
minister, who had brought about this state of things by his
mismanagement, was Barbé-Marbois, a royalist whom Na-

poleon had recalled from banishment and elevated to high office. During the Emperor's absence the minister had allowed the contractors and speculators to become partners in the management of the treasury, had allowed these speculators to use public funds, and had carried his complaisance to such an extent that they now owed the government more than $25,000,000. Under the Old Régime it was quite the usual thing to allow contractors and speculators to use and misuse public funds. In our own day it is the universal rule. No well-regulated Christian government would think of issuing a loan, undertaking public improvements, or refunding its debt without giving to some clique of favored capitalists a huge share of the sum total : just as it would shock a modern government to its foundation if the principle were enforced that public funds should be rigidly kept in public depositories to be used for public purposes only.

Napoleon, however, was neither a ruler of the ancient Bourbon type, nor a Christian governor of the modern sort. He would not float loans, levy war taxes, nor allow his treasury to become the hunting-ground of the Bourse. England was fighting Napoleon with paper money, was floating loan after loan, was giving to speculators and contractors golden opportunities to enrich themselves. In the end, England's paper money, loans, and war taxes were to whip the fight ; but in the meantime Napoleon believed himself right and England wrong. He honestly believed that England would sink under her debt, taxes, and worthless currency. When he saw her grow in strength year by year, her manufactures increase, her trade increase, her wealth, power, and population increase, he was unable to comprehend the mystery. Mr.

2 ▲

Alison, the Tory historian, who chronicles the facts, explains, kindly, that this growth of England was illusive and fictitious. To Napoleon, sitting desolately on the rock at St. Helena, housed in a remodelled cow barn and tormented by rats, it must have seemed that this paper-money growth of English power was not quite so illusive as Mr. Alison declared.

Sternly adhering to his own system, Napoleon called the erring minister and the greedy speculators to account. Marbois was dismissed from office, the speculators thrown into jail, the property of the syndicate seized, and the debt due the treasury collected. The Bank of France was overhauled, the finances put into healthy condition, and the public funds advanced until they commanded a higher price than ever before, nearing par.

CHAPTER XXVII

AFTER the treaty of Presburg the Archduke Charles, in paying off the Austrian troops, said to them, "Go and rest yourselves until we begin again." Even at that early date the European powers were acting upon the fixed principle that the war against France was not to cease till she had been forced back into her ancient limits. No matter what battles might be fought, treaties made, and territories yielded, the one thing upon which England, Austria, and Russia were agreed, was that Napoleon must be crushed. He represented the New Order brought forth by the Revolution. He represented liberalism, civil and religious freedom, and progress in its modern sense of giving to every man a chance in life. Such principles were destructive to the repose of Europe, and the ruling classes in Europe were deeply attached to this repose. England's ruling class, supported in lordly preeminence by the patient millions below them, wanted no levelling tendencies to invade her caste-ridden isles. Germany, whose nobles and landowners clung to all the privileges and barbarities of feudalism, abhorred the Code Napoleon, and the democratic germs of the Napoleonic system. Russia, almost as benighted as Persia or Turkey, dreaded a trend of events which meant freedom for the serf and civil rights for the common people. The nobleman in Russia, the peer of Great Britain, the

petty lord in Germany, was at heart one and the same
man.   He had been born to wealth, privilege, and
power ; he meant to keep what birth had given him, and
he meant to pass it on to his son, "forever in fee simple.'
Of course he explained that God had ordained it so.
And what the nobleman asserted, the priest maintained.
If Napoleon foresaw that as Consul war would be made
upon him continually by the opposing systems of Europe,
how much less hope was there for peace now, when he
had begun to shatter the ancient feudalisms?

Let crimination and recrimination exhaust itself, let
Thiers write bulky volumes in Napoleon's favor, while
Lanfrey and Baring-Gould print heavy pamphlets against
him, the truth lies here : —

Napoleon represented principles which were considered
ruinous to the Old Order in Europe, and the beneficiaries
of that Old Order were determined not to surrender without a desperate fight.   Just as the Old Order in France
resisted all efforts at reform, so on a wider field the
kings and aristocracies of Europe resisted Napoleon.
They could not believe themselves safe while he was
aggressive and triumphant.   Therefore, while Austria
might bow to the storm, while the Emperor Francis
might come to Napoleon's tent, pleading for mercy, and
get it, the true sentiment of Austria was voiced by the
Archduke Charles, when he said to the troops, " Go rest
yourselves, my children, till we begin again.'   It was
only a question of time and opportunity when they would
begin again.

Prussia had been one of the first nations to arm against
revolutionary France.   Lugged in by Austria, she had
published the famous proclamation of Brunswick, had

invaded France, and had been beaten back at Valmy. In due time Prussia had become disgusted with the French royalists — tired of a contest in which, gaining no glory, she lost men, money, and prestige. She had made peace with the Republic, and had become honestly neutral. Harmonious relations had continued to exist between the two nations until the rupture of the Peace of Amiens. England had then done her utmost to draw Prussia into the third Coalition, but had not quite succeeded. In the grand strategy leading to the climax at Ulm, it had become necessary to march some French troops through Anspach, a Prussian province. This violation of his territory gave great offence to the young King Frederick William IV., and he threatened war.

Napoleon's crushing blows on Austria intimidated Prussia and made her hesitate; but when the French risked themselves in Moravia, and the outlook for Napoleon began to grow gloomy, Prussia sent him her minister, Haugwitz, bearing an ultimatum. Napoleon realized his peril, postponed immediate action, and fought the battle of Austerlitz. His victory released him from danger, and Haugwitz, forgetting his ultimatum, poured forth congratulations. Napoleon heard them with a sardonic amusement he did not conceal, bluntly declaring that Austerlitz had changed the Prussian tone.

When the Confederation of the Rhine was about to be formed, Napoleon, by the treaty of Vienna, ceded Hanover to Prussia partly in return for Anspach and Bayreuth. Hanover being the personal domain of the King of England, its cession to Prussia was a fair guarantee against Prussian and English coöperation. That he gave so rich a bribe to Prussia proves his earnestness in seeking her friendship. Those who criticise Napoleon's politics, dwell on his imprudence in not separating England from the Continent. The critics say that he ought to have known that he was not strong enough to combat combined Europe. The probabilities are that Napoleon understood the situation quite as well as those divines and college professors who now criticise him. How was he to get Continental Europe on his side save by force of arms? Had he not tried treaties with Naples and Austria? Had he not exhausted conciliation with Russia and Prussia? In what way was he to cripple England if not by shutting her out of the Continent, and how could he do that without using force? His navy was gone; England had rejected his repeated overtures for peace; her gold bribed European diplomats and cabinets to wage war upon him : how was he to deal with armies hurled against him if he did not fight them? Unite the Continent against England! That was precisely what he was trying to do, and England knew it. Hence her bribes, hence successive wars. Ever and ever it was Napoleon's hope to win his way to a Continental league against England, forcing her to peace, and to the terms she had made at Amiens.

The inherent antagonism of the European monarchs to Napoleon was shown when the Czar visited Berlin in 1805, and at the tomb of Frederick the Great vowed alliance and friendship to the Prussian king.

In 1806 that pledge was solemnly repeated, the Czar and the King having broken it a good deal in the interval. Whether the last oath would amount to more than the first, would depend upon circumstances; but the formal act proved at least how instinctive and vehement was their antagonism to Napoleon.

After Mr. Pitt's death, Fox succeeded him in the min·
istry, and almost immediately Napoleon again made overtures for peace.   There was much less hope of it now, for
the situation had greatly changed.   Passions on both sides
the Channel were at white heat, territorial distributions
had been made which it would be difficult to unmake, and
Fox, as a known friend of Napoleon, might find himself
unable to make concessions which Pitt could safely have
offered.

Of course, England would demand that Hanover be restored; Malta, she would certainly keep.   In the temper
which the newspapers had created in England, no minister would have dared now to surrender that island.   But
still peace was possible.   Equivalents for Malta might be
arranged.   As to Hanover, Napoleon might take it from
Prussia, giving her something just as good in exchange.
The negotiations were set on foot, through Lord Yar-
mouth, one of the Englishmen who had been held in
France at the beginning of the war.   When Prussia
learned that Napoleon was using Hanover as a bait to
England, her smothered ill-will burst into flames.   Violent talk, violent pamphlets, broke out in Prussia, and
Davoust intensified matters by having Palm, the bookseller of Naumberg, shot, because he had circulated incendiary documents against the French.

The war feeling rose irresistibly.   Even had the King
been inclined to oppose it, he could not have done so.   His
Queen, his army chiefs, his nobles, his troops, his people
— they all clamored for war.

The young officers at Berlin whetted their swords on
the steps of the French embassy, and broke the windows
of Prussian ministers who favored peace.

Napoleon was at Paris when the news came that the
Prussian hotheads had been sharpening their blades in
front of his embassy. His hand went to his sword-hilt:
"They will learn that our swords need no whetting — the
insolent braggarts!"

So confident were the Prussians, so impatient were
they to hurl themselves into the struggle, that they
would not wait for Russian aid. Apparently they
feared that Prussia might have to divide the glory.
Was not theirs the army of Frederick the Great? Was
not their cavalry the finest in Europe? Had not General
Rüchel announced on parade that the army of his Majesty
of Prussia possessed several commanders who were the
equals of Bonaparte? Why await Russia? The delay
would put Napoleon on his guard. At present he was
unsuspicious of immediate attack. Prussian diplomats
had lulled him with assurances that their preparations
were a mere pretence. There were a few scattered French
forces in Bavaria; Prussia could hurl her two hundred
thousand veterans upon Saxony, absorb the Saxon forces,
and brush the French out of Germany before Napoleon
could help himself. So thought the Prussian war party,
at the head of which was the Queen and Prince Louis,
brother of the King. On horseback, clad in uniform,
Queen Louisa appeared at the head of the army, fanning
the war fever into flames. Prince Louis took high command for active service, and the old Duke of Brunswick
(he of the famous manifesto of 1792 and of Valmy) tot-
tered forth under the weight of his fourscore years to
suggest bold plans which he lacked the vigor to prosecute.
While Prussian cohorts were mustering and marching
upon Saxony, the Prussian ambassador in Paris was still

playing a confidence game on Napoleon. At last Prussia launched an ultimatum giving the Emperor of the French until October 8 to save himself by submission. The Prussian army, one hundred and thirty thousand strong, concentrated near Jena; the French seemed at their mercy, the chief dispute among the Prussian commanders being whether they should wait till after the date fixed by the ultimatum to pass the Thuringian Forest and attack the enemy. When the ultimatum reached Paris, Napoleon was gone, was on the Rhine, was ready to launch two hundred thousand men upon the now amazed and bewildered Prussians. The great Emperor had not for a moment been deceived. All the time that he had been listening with placid face to the lies of the Prussian diplomat, he had been massing troops where they were needed. When the courier caught up with him and delivered the ultimatum, he laughed at it. With masterly speed he threw himself upon the Prussian flank and rear. Prussia had repeated the mistake of Austria; her losses were even more ruinous. Prince Louis, attacking Lannes at Saalfeld (October 10), was routed and killed.

When Napoleon reached Jena with his main army of ninety thousand men, he supposed that the bulk of the Prussians were before him. Cautious as ever, he sought the advantage of position, and secured it. A Saxon parson showed him a secret path to the heights commanding the Prussian position, and during the night this path was made practicable for artillery. When day dawned (October 14, 1806), the unequal battle commenced, the French outnumbering the enemy two to one. Hohenlohe, the Prussian commander, was almost annihilated, the remnants of his army fleeing in wild disorder.

At the same time Davoust with twenty-seven thousand French fought the main Prussian force, about double his own, at Auerstädt. Badly commanded by the Duke of Brunswick and the King of Prussia, the Germans fought with desperate valor, but were utterly beaten. Broken and driven, they fled from the field, making for Weimar, and ran into the masses of fugitives who were flying from the field of Jena. Murat's dreaded cavalry were in hot pursuit, and a scene of the wildest confusion followed. To the beaten army all hope was lost. There was no fixed line of retreat, no rallying-point, no master-mind in control. In hopeless fragments the fugitive host fell apart, and the relentless pursuit was never slackened until the last one of these bands had been captured. With in- credible ease and rapidity the Prussian monarchy had been brought to the dust.

CHAPTER XXVIII

THERE is no doubt that Napoleon had more personal feeling against Prussia than against any foe he had heretofore met, England excepted. In fact, the manner in which Prussia had acted justified much of this enmity. She had tried to blow hot and cold, run with the hare and hold with the hounds in so shameless a manner that even Charles Fox, the sweetest tempered of men, had denounced her to the English Parliament in the bitterest of terms. She had toyed with England, sworn and broke faith with Russia, dallied with and deluded Austria, trifled with and played false to Napoleon, and finally, after taking the Hanover bribe from him, had sent the Duke of Brunswick to St. Petersburg to assure Alexander that Frederick William III. was still his friend, and that the apparent alliance with Napoleon meant no more than that Prussia was glad to get Hanover.

It is no wonder that Napoleon had declared that Prussia was for sale to the highest bidder, and that she would be his because he would pay most. He had paid the price, — Hanover. When he saw that Prussia meant to keep the price, and not the contract, his feeling was that of the average man who finds that where he thought he had made a good trade, he has been swindled.

Therefore, when the Queen of Prussia, Prince Louis, the Duke of Brunswick, and the war party generally,

showed their determination to break faith with him;
when the young officers insulted his embassy; when the
Prussian army launched themselves against a member of
his Confederation of the Rhine, Napoleon was genuinely
incensed.   They had shown him no consideration, and he
was inclined to show them none.

He roughly denounced the conduct of the Duke of
Weimar, when speaking to the Duchess in her own palace; but when she courageously defended her absent husband, Napoleon's better nature prevailed, he praised her
spirit, and became her friend.

The Duke of Brunswick, mortally wounded at Auerstädt, sent a messenger to Napoleon praying that his
rights as Duke of Brunswick might be respected.   Napoleon answered that he would not spare the *duke*, but
would respect the general; that Brunswick would be
treated as a conquered province, but that the Duke himself should have that consideration shown him which, as an
old man and a brave soldier, he deserved.   At the same
time, and as additional reason for not sparing the Duke as
a feudal lord, Napoleon reminded him of the time when he
had advanced into France with fire and sword, and had proclaimed the purpose of laying Paris in ashes.   The son of
the dying Duke took this natural reply much to heart, and
swore eternal vengeance against the man who sent it.

Napoleon understood very well that the war had been
brought on by the feudal powers in Germany, — those
petty lords who had dukedoms and principalities scattered throughout the land, miniature kingdoms in which
these lords lived a luxurious life at the expense of the
peasantry.   These feudal chiefs were desperately opposed
to French principles, and dreaded the Confederation of

the Rhine. Every elector, prince, duke, or what not, expected, with trembling, the day when he might be "mediatized," and his little monopoly of a kingdom thrown into the modernized confederation. Hence their eagerness for war, and hence Napoleon's bitterness toward them. It went abroad that he said that he would make the nobles of Prussia beg their bread. He may have said it, for by this time he was no longer a mute, all-concealing sphinx. He had become one of the most talkative of men; therefore, one of the most imprudent. Unfortunately, he did nothing to separate the cause of the German people from that of the German nobles. His heavy hand fell upon all alike; and it was his own fault that the national spirit of Germany rose against him finally, and helped to overthrow him. Not only did he speak harshly, imprudently of the Prussian nobles, he committed the greater blunder of reviling the Queen. True, she had well-nigh said, as a French empress said later, " This shall be *my* war ! " She had inspired the war party by word and by example. In every way known to a beautiful young sovereign, she had made the war craze the fashion. She had done for Prussia what Eugénie afterward did for France, — led thousands of brave men to sudden death, led her country into a colossal smash-up. Eugénie's husband, swayed by an unwomanly wife, lost his liberty and his throne. By a mere scratch did Louisa's husband, as blindly led, escape the same fate. A brazen but patriotic lie, told by old Blücher to the French general, Klein, — " an armistice has been signed," — saved Frederick William III. from playing Bajazet to the French Tamerlane. A political woman was ever Napoleon's " pet aversion." In his creed the place held by women was that of mothers of numerous children, breeders of stout soldiers, wearers of dainty toilets, companions of a lustful or an idle hour, nymphs of the garden walks, sirens of the boudoir, nurses of the sick, comforters of grief, censer bearers in the triumphal progress of great men. A woman who would talk war, put on a uniform, mount a horse, and parade at the head of an army, aroused his anger and excited his disgust. This feeling was the secret of his dislike to the Queen of Prussia, and of his ungentlemanly references to her in his bulletins.   But while those references were such as no gentleman should have made, they were infinitely more delicate than those in which the royalist gentlemen of Europe were constantly alluding to Napoleon's mother, his sisters, his wife, his step-daughter, and himself.   It is only fair, in trying to reach just conclusions, to remember the circumstances and the provocations under which a certain thing is said or done.   If we constantly keep in view this standard in weighing the acts and words of Napoleon, it will make all the difference in the world in our verdict.   Napoleon was no passionless god or devil. His blood was warm like ours; his skin was thin like ours ; a blow gave him pain as it pains us; slanders hurt him as they hurt us ; infamous lies told about his wife, sisters, and mother wrung from him the same passionate outcries they would wring from us.   And this fact also must be kept in mind : before Napoleon stooped to make any personal war upon his sworn enemies, he had appealed to them, time and again, to cease their personal abuse of him and his family.

On October 27, 1806, Napoleon made his triumphal entry into Berlin, giving to the corps of Davoust the place of honor in the march.   It was a brilliant spectacle, and the people of Berlin who quietly looked upon the scene were astonished to see the contrast between the Emperor's plain hat and coat, and the dazzling uniforms of his staff.

Says Constant : " We came to the square, in the middle of which a bust of Frederick the Great had been erected. On arriving in front of the bust, the Emperor galloped half around it, followed by his staff, and, lowering the point of his sword, he removed his hat and saluted the image of Frederick. His staff imitated his example, and all the general officers ranged themselves in semicircle around the monument, with the Emperor. His Majesty gave orders that each regiment as it marched past should present arms."

The Prince Hatzfeldt brought the keys of the city to the conqueror, and Napoleon at once organized a new municipal government, putting Hatzfeldt at the head of it. The Prince, instead of being faithful to the confidence Napoleon placed in him, used his position to gather information about French forces and movements. This information he forwarded to the fugitive king, Frederick William. Hatzfeldt may not have realized that his conduct was that of a spy; may not have understood that holding an office by Napoleon's appointment he must be loyal to Napoleon. Serving two masters under such circumstances was a risky business, and Hatzfeldt found it so. His letter to the King was intercepted, and brought to Napoleon. The Prince was about to be court-martialled and shot. Already the necessary orders had been given, when the Princess Hatzfeldt, wife of the accused, gained access to the palace, and threw herself at Napoleon's feet. A woman in tears — a genuine woman and genuine tears — Napoleon could never resist; and Hatzfeldt was saved,

as the Polignacs had been, by the pleadings of a devoted
woman.

After Waterloo, the Duke of Wellington, confident now
that he was the greatest man that ever walked upon the
earth, bought Canova's statue of Napoleon, carried it to
London, stood it up in his hall, and made of it a hat-rack,
umbrella-stand, and cloak-holder. It would seem that
the men who say that Napoleon had no generous, chivalrous
instincts have failed to see in Wellington's conduct any
evidence of indelicacy of feeling. These critics, however,
are confident that, in seizing as trophies the sword and
sash of Frederick the Great, as Napoleon did at this time,
he committed a most outrageous act. It may fairly be
argued that the rule as to trophies is not so clear as it
might be. The law seems to be obscure, and the decisions
conflicting. So far as can be gathered from a reading of a
number of authorities, the rule seems to be that after a
conqueror has overthrown his enemy, he can take whatever his taste, fancy, and greed suggest.

Of course we are here speaking of Christians — civilized, complacent, watch-me-and-do-as-I-do Christians.
It will be found that they have taken any sort of plunder
which can be carted away. All over England is the loot
of India; all over Spain that of South America and
Mexico; and in sundry portions of these United States
may be found articles of more or less value which used
to belong to China or the Philippines. They — the Christians — have taken the ornaments from the bodies of
the wounded and the dead; have wrenched from arms,
and fingers, and necks, and ears, the jewels of man,
woman, and child; have robbed the temple and the
shrine; have not spared the idol, nor the diamonds

that blazed in its eyes; have taken sceptre, and sword, and golden throne; have stripped the palace, and robbed the grave. A dead man of to-day and a dead man of thousands of years ago, are as one to the remorseless greed of the Christians. In the name of science the mummy is despoiled; in the cause of "advancing civilization" the warm corse of the Chinaman or the Filipino is rifled. When we find among the crown jewels of Great Britain the "trophies" wrenched from the living and the dead in Hindustan; when we see the proud people of the high places wearing the spoil of Egyptian sepulchres, it is difficult to know where the line is which separates legitimate from illegitimate loot. Consequently, we are not certain whether Napoleon was right or wrong in robbing the tomb of Frederick the Great of the sash and sword.

While at Berlin, Napoleon issued his famous Berlin Decree. The English, repeating the blow they had aimed at France during the Revolution, had (1806), by an "Order in Council," declared the entire coast of France in a state of blockade. In other words, Great Britain arrogated to herself the right to bottle up Napoleon's Empire, the purpose being to starve him out.

By way of retaliation, he, in the Berlin Decree, declared Great Britain to be in a state of blockade. It is curious to notice in the books how much abuse Napoleon gets for his blockade, and how little England gets for hers. Usually in trying to get at the merits of a fight for the purpose of fixing the blame, the question is, "Who struck the first blow?" This simple rule, based on plain common sense, seems to be lost sight of here entirely.

When England struck at Napoleon with a sweeping

2 B

blockade which affected eight hundred miles of his coast, had he no right to strike back? The Berlin Decree was no more than blow for blow.

There can be no doubt that in this commercial war Napoleon got the worst of it. England suffered, but it was for the want of markets. Continental Europe suffered, but it was for the want of goods.

Napoleon's Continental system, about which so much has been said, was, after all, nothing more than a prohibitory tariff. In course of time it would have produced the same effect as a prohibitory tariff. The Continent would have begun to manufacture those goods for whose supply it had heretofore depended upon England. In other words, the blockade, shutting off the supply of certain cloths, leather goods, hardware, etc., would have forced their production on the Continent. A moderate tariff stimulates home production in the ratio that it keeps out foreign competition. A prohibitive tariff, shutting off foreign wares entirely, *compels* the home production of the prohibited articles. Napoleon's Continental system, prohibiting all English goods, would inevitably have built up manufactories of these goods on the Continent. During the years when these enterprises would have been getting under way, the people of the Continent would have suffered immense loss and inconvenience; but in the long run the Continent would have become the producer of its own goods, and Great Britain would have been commercially ruined. This Napoleon saw; this the English Cabinet saw: hence the increasing bitterness with which this death struggle between the two went on.

The great advantage of England was that she had the goods ready for market, and the Continent wanted them.

The enormous disadvantage of Napoleon was that he neither had the goods nor the men ready to take hold and manufacture them. The all-important *now* was on the side of England. The ink was hardly dry on the Berlin Decree before Napoleon himself had to violate it. He needed enormous supplies for his army in the winter campaign he was about to begin. Continental manufactories did not produce what he wanted, England did, and Napoleon's troops were supplied with English goods. What the master did, his minions could imitate. All along the coast French officials violated the law, sold licenses, winked at smuggling at so much per wink, and feathered their nests in the most approved and gorgeous style. The Continental system did great damage to England, since it drove her trade into tortuous, limited channels. It did great damage to the Continent, since it worked inconvenience to so many who needed English goods, and so many who had Continental produce to sell to England. But it never had a fair test, did not have time to do its work, and therefore has been hastily called Napoleon's crowning mistake. Failing to get a fair trial for his system, it collapsed, and must therefore be called a blunder; but it must be remembered that its author believed he could get a fair trial for it; that he worked with tremendous tenacity of purpose for many years to bring Continental Europe to accept and enforce it. Could he have done so, the candid reader must admit that he would have smitten England's manufactures, her commercial life, as with a thunderbolt. It should also be remembered that to Napoleon's policy, so much resisted then, France owes many of those manufactures which constitute her wealth at the present day.

CHAPTER XXIX

AFTER allowing his army a brief rest, Napoleon set out against the Russians. His troops entered Poland, and on November 28, 1806, Murat took possession of Warsaw. The Poles received the French as deliverers. They believed that the dismemberment of their country by Austria, Prussia, and Russia was to be at last avenged, and Poland once more to take its place among the nations. By thousands the bravest flocked to the French standards, as enthusiastic for Napoleon as were the French themselves.

It may be that in his treatment of Poland the Emperor made one of his huge mistakes. It may be that he here lost his one great opportunity of permanently curbing the three Continental powers, whose combined strength finally wore him out. Had Poland's resurrection as a nation been promptly proclaimed, had her crown been given to some born soldier, like Murat, Lannes, Soult, or Poniatowski, he would have drawn to his physical support every man of Polish blood, and to his moral support the active approval of every liberal in the world.

Across the path of Russia he would have thrown the living rampart of a gallant nation, fired by love of country and a passion for revenge. With Turkey on one frontier, and united Poland on another, and the mighty power of Napoleon ready to aid both, Russia's position would, apparently, have been desperate. In like manner, a united Poland, on the flanks of Austria and Prussia, would, apparently, have been the very best guarantee that those two nations would not invade France.

In brief, had Napoleon decreed the liberty of Poland, he would have secured an ally whose strength and position were of vast importance to him, and whose need of his support would have kept her loyal. On the other hand, he would have incurred the lasting hatred of the three robber powers, and they would have had a common cause of union against him. This is what he realized, and this is what held him back; but in the end his temporizing, inconsistent, I-will-and-I-won't policy did exactly that — brought upon him the lasting hatred of the three robber powers, and lost him the united support of Poland. For in order that his ranks might be recruited with Polish volunteers, he constantly dangled before the eyes of the unfortunate nation the prospect of independence. "Show yourselves worthy and then—." In other words, rush to my eagles, fight my battles, die in my service, lavish your blood and your treasures upon me, and I will then consider whether Poland shall once more become a nation! It is a sorry picture — this of the greatest man of history sporting with Polish hopes, rights, lives, destiny.

Gallant men of this heroic nation gave him their lives — for Poland. At least one beautiful Polish woman gave him her honor — for Poland. He won part of the country because of his vague promises. He failed to win united Poland because his promises *were* vague. But the mere fact that Poland looked to Napoleon as its liberator, the fact that Poles trooped by thousands to fight for him, the fact that he erected Prussian Poland into the Grand Duchy of Warsaw, bore just the bitter fruit which Napoleon was so anxious the tree should not bear — the union of the three powers which had despoiled Poland, and whose suspicion and hatred had been aroused past all remedy by his dalliance with the Poles.

But these final results were all in the future as yet. For the time, Napoleon's plan worked well enough. He got all the help he needed from Poland without burning any bridges between him and the three powers. His attitude seemed to say to Russia, Austria, and Prussia, "See what I can do with these Poles if you provoke me too far!" Polish independence was artfully utilized in two ways; to the Poles it was an aspiration rousing them to rush to the French eagles; to the three powers it was a threat, warning them to come to terms with Napoleon.

In the game of national chess, Poland thus became a mere pawn on the board. From any moral point of view such a policy is infamous. And the indignation of the historian is deepened when he is forced to add that Napoleon's conduct was but an imitation of the statecraft of former times, just as similar infamies of the present day are imitations of time-honored precedents of kings and cabinets. Cavour one day exclaimed, "What rascals we should be if we did for ourselves what we are doing for our country!" He was referring to some especially dirty work (dirt and blood being copiously mixed), which he had been doing in copartnership with Napoleon III. in bringing about Italian independence. The confession is worth remembering. Christian civilization has certainly reached a curious pass when its leading statesmen admit that in statecraft they are continually doing things which would disgrace them as private citizens.

In the *Memoirs* of the Princess Potocka there is a vivid picture of the Polish situation in the winter of 1807, the writer being in Warsaw at the time.

" The 21st of November, in the morning, the arrival of a French regiment was announced. How shall I describe the enthusiasm with which it was received? To understand such emotions properly one must have lost everything and believe in the possibility of hoping for everything — like ourselves. This handful of warriors, when they set feet on our soil, seemed to us a guarantee of the independence we were expecting at the hands of the great man whom nothing could resist.

" The popular intoxication was at its height : the whole town was lit up as if by magic. That day, forsooth, the town authorities had no need to allot quarters to the new arrivals. People fought for them, carried them off, vied with each other in treating them best. Those of the citizens who knew no French, not being able to make themselves understood, borrowed the dumb language which belongs to all countries, and by signs of delight, handshakings, and bursts of glee made their guests comprehend that they freely offered all their houses contained, *cellars included.*

" Tables were even laid in the streets and squares. Toasts were drunk to Napoleon, to his Grand Army, to the Independence of Poland. There was hugging and kissing, and a little too much drinking." Next day came dashing Murat and his brilliant staff, with braided uniforms, gold and silver lace, nodding plumes of red, white, and blue, and a good deal of rattle and bang, fuss and

bustle, generally.   A noisy cavalier was Murat, ostenta-
tious, boastful, full of the reminiscences of his own me-
teorie career.

Lodged at the Hotel Raczynski, where there was a vile
chimney which smoked, the Grand Duke of Berg left it, and
quartered himself "in our house,' —'the palace Potocki,—
where he bored the inmates with his loud manners, his
theatrical airs, and his too frequent reference to his most
recent feat of arms, — the storming and taking of Lubeck at
the head of his cavalry.   Murat gave the Warsaw people
to understand that the Emperor would soon arrive, and
would enter the city with a certain degree of pomp.   The
authorities bestirred themselves ; reared triumphal arches,
composed inscriptions, ordered fireworks, plaited wreaths,
and gave the usual warnings to poets and orators.   The
whole town was thrown into the private agony which is
the prelude to a public and joyful reception.

And after all the toil and suffering of preparing for
the Emperor's triumphal entrance, what should he do but
come riding into Warsaw on a shabby little post-horse,
between midnight and day, with no one in attendance
save Roustan, the Mameluke 1   The imperial carriage had
mired on the road, and Napoleon had left it sticking in
the mud.   When he reached Warsaw, all were asleep, and
" the Emperor went to the sentry box himself to wake up
the sentinel."

That same evening the authorities of the city were
received by the Liberator, who talked to them graciously
and volubly upon all topics excepting that of liberation.
Upon this all-important subject he uttered nothing more
than what are called "glittering generalities."   Poland,
it appeared, had not yet done enough.   Poland must rouse

herself. " There must be devotion, sacrifices, blood."
Otherwise Poland would never come to anything. Running on in his nervous, rapid way, Napoleon alluded to the
great exertions he would have to make to bring the campaign to a prosperous end. But he was sure that France
would do all he demanded of her. Putting his hands in
his pockets, he exclaimed : "I have the French *there*. By
appealing to their imagination I can do what I like with
them ! "

The Polish magnates listened to this statement with
considerable surprise, which pictured itself upon their
faces. Observing this, Napoleon added, " Yes, yes, it is
just as I tell you," and took snuff.

Keenly disappointed as many of the Polish nobles were
at Napoleon's doubtful attitude, the country generally
was enthusiastic in its faith that he would, at the proper
time, do the proper thing. Every want of the French
was supplied. Where voluntary offerings fell short,
forced contributions made good the difference.

Warsaw had never been more brilliant. The heart of
the doomed nation beat again. There were smiles, open
hands, glad festivities. There were brilliant balls at
Murat's ; brilliant balls at Talleyrand's ; brilliant balls
at the palace of Prince Borghese ; brilliant receptions
held by the Emperor. It must have been a spectacle
worth seeing, — a ballroom in reawakened Warsaw, where
the loveliest ladies of Poland and the bravest warriors
of France danced the happy hours away. It must have
been a sight worth seeing, — Talleyrand entering a grand
reception hall filled with the notables of Poland and
gravely announcing, " The Emperor ! "

Well worth seeing was the stout, stunted figure,

crowned by the pale, set, marble-like face and large head, which came into view at Talleyrand's announcement, and which stood within the doorway a moment to see and to be seen.

Did lovely Polish women crowd about the mighty Emperor, listening for the least word in favor of Poland's independence? Did fair patriots appeal by look and word to him, yearning for the magic names, Liberty, Freedom? Vain the ardent, beseeching look; vain the tender, seductive voice. It would not do at all. He had suspected that — had steeled himself against it; and eager patriotism, voiced by women never so bewitching, could not break through that watchful guard. But as he leaves the room, he pauses again, and says to Talleyrand in a tone loud enough to be heard by all, "What pretty women!" Then the imperial hand salutes the company, and the Liberator is gone!

It must have been a sight worth seeing, — that ball at Talleyrand's where Napoleon danced, and cultivated Madame Walewski, and where the imposing Talleyrand, with folded napkin under his arm, and gilt tray in his hand, humbly served his imperial master with a glass of lemonade.

Army affairs called Napoleon to the front; but after the bloody struggle at Pultusk, the weather stopped military movements. Continual rains had ruined the roads. Cannon stuck in the mire, soldiers perished in the bogs. Even Polanders had never seen anything equal to it.

Napoleon returned to Warsaw quite serene, remarking, "Well, your mud has saved the Russians; let us wait for the frost."

Busy with French affairs, Polish and Russian affairs, busy also and above all at this time with army affairs, the

Emperor relaxed himself socially to a greater extent than usual, and made himself exceedingly agreeable.

He entered into all the amusements, gossiped familiarly with all comers to his receptions, played whist, danced square dances, attended the concerts of his Italian orchestra, and led the applause with zest and good taste.

" How do you think I dance? " he smilingly inquired of the young Princess Potocka. " I suspect you have been laughing at me."

" In truth, sire," answered the adroit lady, " for a great man your dancing is perfect."

Sitting down to whist, Napoleon turned to Princess Potocka at the moment the cards were dealt and asked : —

" What shall the stake be ? "

" Oh, sire, some town, some province, some kingdom."

He laughed, looking at her slyly.

" And supposing you should lose ? "

" Your Majesty is in funds and will perhaps deign to pay for me."

The answer pleased. He loved bold talk, prompt replies, definite answers. Halting, uncertain, indefinite people he could never endure.

Answer quick and answer positively, and your reply, though untrue, might please him better than if you hesitatingly told him the truth.

The same lively writer gives another lifelike picture of Napoleon in one of his fits of ill temper.

One day at Warsaw he received information that General Victor, bearing important despatches, had been captured by the Prussians. This piece of news enraged the Emperor. It chanced that upon the same day a Dutch delegation arrived to congratulate him upon the victory of Jena. They were admitted to audience just before the Emperor's regular reception.

" It was near ten o'clock, and we (those in the reception room) had been awaiting a long time . . . when, the door being noisily thrown open, we saw the fat Dutchmen, in their scarlet robes, roll rather than walk in. The Emperor was prodding them, exclaiming in rather loud tones, ' Go on ! go on ! ' The poor envoys lost their heads, and tumbled all over each other."

Princess Potocka says that she felt like laughing ; but when she looked at the Emperor's face, she did not dare.

" The music soothed him quickly ; toward the end of the concert his gracious smile returned, and he addressed pleasant words to the ladies he liked best, before sitting down to his whist table.

" Excepting foreign ministers, and some of the high functionaries at play, all stood while Napoleon sat. This did not displease Prince Murat, who lost no opportunity to pose and to strike attitudes which he judged appropriate to show off the beauty of his figure. But little Prince Borghese was enraged and still had not the courage to sit down."

But the Emperor's amusements did not confine themselves to such things as whist and quadrilles alone. A certain Madame Walewski, " exquisitely pretty," " her laugh fresh, her eyes soft, her face seductive," caught the attention of the imperial visitor. " Married at sixteen to an octogenarian who never appeared in public, Madame Walewski's position in society was that of a young widow." She was " lovely and dull," tempting and not unyielding. Talleyrand's diplomacy is said to have done some very humble work as go-between, and the Madame was soon known to be the Emperor's favorite.

Josephine, hearing vague rumors of high-doings at the Polish capital, generously offered to brave the rigors of travel and season to join her absent spouse. In the gentlest manner in the world he insisted that she stay where she was.

The gay time at Warsaw ended abruptly. Ney having made a dash at the Russians, without orders, Bennigsen roused himself to general action, and Napoleon went forth to one of the bloodiest battles in history — Eylau, February 8, 1807. Fought in a blinding snowstorm, the losses on both sides were frightful. So doubtfully hung the result that the Emperor himself escaped capture because he was concealed from view in the old churchyard. Augereau's corps, caught in the snow-drift, blinded by wind-driven sleet, and exposed point blank to deadly Russian fire, was annihilated. Only a desperate cavalry charge, led in person by Murat, checked the Russian advance. When darkness fell, the French were about to retreat when Davoust, laying ear to ground, heard the retiring rumble of Russian guns. So the French held their position and claimed the victory. The Russians, in retreat, also claimed it.

On each side rose hymns and prayers of thanks and praise to God : Russians grateful that they had won; French rejoicing that they had prevailed. Bennigsen continued to retire; Napoleon went back into winter-quarters; and the only distinct and undisputed result of the battle was that some twenty-five thousand men lay dead under the snow.

Napoleon did not return to Warsaw, but made his head-

quarters at Osterode, where he shared all the discomforts of
his soldiers while doing more work than any hundred men
in the army.   In spite of the dreadful weather and boggy
roads, he was constantly on horseback, going at full speed
from one outpost to another.   Frequently he rode ninety
miles during the day.   With his own eyes he inspected the
military situation down to the smallest details, untiring
in his efforts to have his men well placed, well clothed,
well fed.   The sick and the wounded were indeed "his
children."   He spared no efforts in their behalf, and this
was one of the secrets of the cheerfulness with which his
soldiers made such sacrifices for him.   Sometimes in the
march when the weary legions were weltering through
the mud, drenched with rain or pelted by sleet, or blinded
by snow, hungry and homesick, murmurs would be heard
in the ranks, complaints would even be thrown at the
Emperor as he passed.   But when the enemy was in
sight, murmurs ceased.   " Live the Emperor ! " was all
the cry.   They shouted it wherever they caught a
glimpse of him on the field ; they shouted it as they
rushed to battle ; and after the fight was over those
who came forth unharmed, and those who were mangled, and those who were about to die — all shouted,
" Live the Emperor ! "   Nothing like the devotion of the
French soldier to Napoleon had ever been known before, and not till another Napoleon comes will be seen
again.

The care of his army by no means filled all of the Emperor's time : he ruled France from Poland, just as
though he were at St. Cloud.   Couriers brought and
carried ministerial portfolios, brought and carried official reports and orders.   Every detail of government

passed under the eye of the master, all initiative rested with him.

Madame Walewski was brought secretly to headquarters, an indulgence Napoleon had never allowed himself before. While at Finckenstein, he received envoys from Persia and Turkey, and gravely discussed plans for an invasion of India.

In June the Russians again took the offensive. Their commander-in-chief, Bennigsen, one of the murderers of the Czar Paul, had shown great courage and ability. At Pultusk he had beaten Lannes and Davoust; at Eylau he had fought the Emperor to a standstill, and had carried away from that field twelve of the French eagles.

Bennigsen renewed the war by an attack on Ney, whom he hoped to cut off. A hasty retreat of the French saved them. Then Napoleon came up, and the Russians retired. At Heilsberg they stood and fought, both sides losing heavily. At length the superiority of the French leader made itself felt. He lured Bennigsen into a false position, closed on him, and wellnigh crushed him, at the battle of Friedland, June 14, 1807. This victory ended the campaign. The Russians asked for an armistice, which was promptly granted. The two emperors, Napoleon and Alexander, met on a raft, moored in the Niemen, near Tilsit, June 25, 1807, embraced each other cordially, and, amid the rapturous shouts of the two armies drawn up on opposite sides of the river, commenced those friendly, informal conferences which led to peace.

The town of Tilsit, having been made neutral ground, became the headquarters of the two emperors, who established their courts there, and lived together like devoted

personal friends. The poor fugitive, Frederick William
of Prussia, was invited to come, and he came. Later
came also his queen.

On the 7th of July, 1807, the Treaty of Tilsit was signed.

Prussia lost her Polish provinces, which were erected
into the grand duchy of Warsaw, and given to the Elector
of Saxony. A slice of this Polish Prussia, however, was
bestowed on Alexander. Dantzic, which the French had
taken, was declared a free city, to be garrisoned with
French troops till maritime peace should be ratified.
The Prussian dominions in lower Saxony and on the
Rhine, with Hanover, Hesse-Cassel, and other small states
were formed into the kingdom of Westphalia for the
profligate Jerome Bonaparte.

Ancient Prussia, as well as Silesia, was restored to
Frederick William.

Much ado has been made over Napoleon's alleged harshness to Queen Louisa at Tilsit; but a careful reading of
the authorities proves that his only harshness consisted in
declining to give to her that for which she asked. She
went there to influence Napoleon by a beautiful woman's
persuasions; and she failed. In the nature of things, it
could not have been otherwise. Having provoked the
war, and having lost in the trial of arms, Prussia had to
pay the penalty. The tears or cajoleries of Queen Louisa
could not of course obliterate the hard political necessities
of the case. Suppose the Empress Eugénie, in 1871, had
gone in tears to Bismarck or to the Emperor William,
could she have saved for France the provinces of Alsace
and Lorraine? Could she have reduced the war penalty
from $1,000,000,000 to $1,000,000? Just such a task
Queen Louisa undertook in 1807.

Beyond his refusal to be influenced, Napoleon was not guilty of any discourtesy to the Queen. On the contrary, he honored her with the most studious politeness and deference.

By the Treaty of Tilsit, Russia bound herself to mediate between France and Great Britain. On his part, Napoleon agreed to mediate between Russia and Turkey.

In secret articles, Russia bound herself to adopt Napoleon's Continental system in the event that Great Britain refused to make peace.

Furthermore, in that case, there was to be a northern confederation against England for the purpose of shutting her out of the Continent and of breaking her tyranny over the seas.

Russia, in return for this promise, was to be allowed to conquer Finland, a province of vast importance to her.

It is also stated by some authorities that Alexander agreed that Napoleon should do as he liked with Spain and Portugal ; while Napoleon consented that Alexander should be allowed to strip Turkey of Moldavia and Wallachia, provided Turkey refused his mediation.

CHAPTER XXX

A^T this period (1807) Napoleon was a strikingly handsome man. The "wan and livid complexion, bowed shoulders, and weak, sickly appearance" of the Vendémiaire period were things of long ago. The skin disease of the Italian campaign had been cured. Not yet fat and paunchy as he became toward the end, his form had rounded to a comely fulness, which did not impair his activity. The face was classic in profile, and in complexion a clear, healthy white. His chin was prominent, the jaw powerful, the head massive, being twenty-two inches round, according to Constant. The chestnut-colored hair was now thin, inclining to baldness on the crown. Worn long in his youth, he cut it short in the Egyptian campaign, and ever afterward continued to wear it so. His ears, hands, feet, were small and finely shaped. The nose was long, straight, well proportioned. His teeth were white and sound; the lips beautifully moulded; the expression about the mouth, when he smiled, being peculiarly sweet and winning. His eyes were gray-blue, and formed the striking feature of his face. All accounts agree that his glance was uncomfortably steady and penetrating; or, at other times, intolerably fierce and intimidating; or, again, irresistibly soft, tender, magnetic. One is struck with the fact that so many who knew him, and loved him or hated him, feared him or defied him, should emphasize the impression made upon them by his eyes. Before that steady gaze, which seized and held attention, Lavalette said that he felt himself turning pale ; Decrés lost all desire to be familiar ; Vandamme became a coward ; Augereau and Masséna admitted they were afraid ; Madame de Staël grew embarrassed ; and Barras faltered into silence at his own table. Not many years ago there lived in Michigan a battered veteran of the Italian wars, one who had been with Napoleon the day he reconnoitred Fort Bard, which had checked the army ; and this old soldier's recollection of Napoleon had dwindled down to the wonderful eyes which had fixed him as though they would pierce the very innermost fibre. During the year 1900 there died in London an aged man, who as a boy had seen Napoleon at St. Helena ; and his recollection of the fallen Emperor hung upon the same feature, — the eyes.

Generally, the expression of Napoleon's face was that of a student, — mild, pensive, meditative, intellectual. In moments of good humor, his smile, glance, voice, were caressing, genial, even fascinating. In anger, his look became terrible ; a rotary movement took place between the eyes, and the nostrils distended. All agree that in conversation there was such a play of feature, such quick changes of expression, such mirroring of the mind upon the face, that no description or portrait could convey an idea of it. Only those who had talked with him could realize it. But it is also agreed that when he wished to banish all expression, he could do that also, and his face then became a mask.

His voice was sonorous and strong. In anger it became harsh and cruelly cutting. In his best mood it was as soft and wooing as a woman's. His general appearance, then, at this time, was that of a well-built man, below the medium height, but powerfully moulded, the bust, neck, and head being massive, and the legs somewhat short for the trunk. Unfriendly critics called him stunted, his stature being about five feet, three inches.

He was inclined to be round-shouldered, and, when walking meditatively, he slightly stooped. In talking he gesticulated freely, sometimes violently; when in repose the hands were folded behind him, or across the breast, or one would rest within the waistcoat and the other behind him.

It is doubtful whether any true portrait of Napoleon exists. He has been idealized and caricatured until the real Napoleon may have been lost. If the death mask claimed to have been taken by Antommarchi is genuine, one must surrender the belief that Napoleon's head was massive, his brow imperial, his profile perfeet; for this mask exhibits a forehead which recedes, and which narrows above the temples. It shows the high cheek-bones of the American Indian, and the skull itself is commonplace. But this is not the Napoleon pictured in the portraits and *Memoirs* of his contemporaries. According to friend and foe, his head was massive, in fact too large to be in symmetry with his body. Madame Junot speaks of that "brow fit to bear the crowns of the world." Bourrienne, Méneval, and numbers of others speak of the magnificent forehead and classic face. And yet there are two or three fugitive portraits of Napoleon which are so different from the orthodox copies, and so much like the Antommarchi's death-mask, that one knows not what to believe.

Napoleon was very temperate in eating and drinking. He preferred the simplest dishes, drank but little wine, and that weakened with water. Coffee he drank, but not to excess. He ate fast, and used his fingers oftener than his fork. He was very sensitive to cold, and could not bear the least light in his room at night. He slept a good deal, from six to eight hours per day; and usually took a nap during the afternoon or evening. His standing order to his private secretary was a model of wisdom, "Never wake me to hear good news, that will wait; but in case of bad news wake me at once, for there is no time to be lost." Another rule of his was to sleep over a matter of doubt. "Night is a good counsellor."

While his nerves were very irritable, his pulse was slow and regular. He declared that he had never felt his heart beat. Medicine he detested and would not take. When ill, he left off food, drank barley water, and took violent exercise. He could not bear the least tightness in his clothing. His garments were of the softest, finest material, and cut loose. His hats were padded, his boots lined with silk, and both hats and boots were "broken" for him before he wore them. His favorite trousers were white cassimere, and a habit he had of wiping his pen on his breeches made a new pair necessary every morning. His taking of snuff consisted merely in smelling it. He used tobacco in no other form.

Extremely careful in business matters, he was disorderly in some personal details. In undressing he flung his clothes all about the room, and sometimes broke his watch in this way. Newspapers and books which he had been reading were scattered around in confusion. In shaving, he would never allow both sides of his face to be lathered at the same time: one cheek was finished before the other was touched. He had a habit of poking the fire with his foot, and burnt out many a pair of boots in so doing. Excessively fond of the hot water bath, he opened letters, read newspapers, and received callers while splashing around in the tub. On leaving the bath, his valet rubbed him down, using the flesh brush and coarse cloths, and then dressed him. The most self-helpful of men in matters of importance, he was one of the least so in this. He depended upon servants for almost everything connected with the care of his person. " Rub me hard ! Scrub me as though I were an ass ! " he would call to his valet, while he stood almost naked, and with a red bandanna handkerchief knotted about his head. He loved cologne-water and drenched himself with quantities of it. One of the privations he keenly felt at St. Helena was the lack of cologne. Other perfumes he detested, and Constant relates a curious incident of Napoleon calling to him one night to take out of his room a certain young lady who had been brought there, and who was " killing me with her perfume."

With his elevation to empire, Napoleon became more stately, reserved, dignified, and imposing ; but perfect ease and repose of manner he never acquired. The indolent, calm, and studied air of languor and fatigue which, according to a well-known standard, constitutes good-breeding, he did not have. Perhaps he did not realize its tremendous value. Nervous, intense, electrical, pulsing with vital power, tossed by colossal ideas, ambitions, purposes, it was never possible for him to become a self-complacent formality, posing with studiously indolent grace, and uttering with laborious ease the dialect of polite platitude.

But the man never lived who knew better how to talk, how to write, how to say what he meant. He could address mobs, committees, state councils, senates, armies, peoples, and kings. Who that ever lived excelled him in speaking to soldiers? Verily the lines are yet hot in his proclamations, and he who reads them even now will feel the magnetic thrill. How they must have inspired the soldiers *then!*

His speeches to the councils and the Senate were models in their way; his state papers have not been excelled; his diplomatic correspondence measures up the loftiest standards. In truth, his language varied with the subject and the occasion. He could be as elegantly gracious as any Bourbon, if the occasion required it. If it became needful to call a spade a spade, he could do it, and with a vim which left the ears tingling. In all of his talk, however, there was character, individuality, and greatness. Wrong he might often be, weak never. Whatever view he expressed, in youth or age, was stated clearly, and with strength. Even when sifted through the recollections of others, his sayings stand out as incomparably finer than those of any talker of that age. Compare the few little jests and epigrams of Talleyrand, for instance, with the numberless comments of Napoleon on men and things, on matters social, political, industrial, financial, military, and religious. It is like a comparison between a few lamps in a hallway and the myriad stars of the firmament. On every topic he discussed he said the best things that can be said on that side ; and there is no subject connected with human affairs in a state that he has not touched. Upon every subject he had a word which shot to the core of the matter. His talent for throwing into one dazzling sentence the pith of a long discussion was unexcelled. Some of the best sayings attributed to Talleyrand were really the sayings of Napoleon. It often happened that these terse expressions were coarse, the language of men on the street. At such sayings the "Lady Clara" tribe of men arched their eyebrows in delicate protest, and said to one another, "This Bonaparte is no gentleman; he was not so well brought up as we were, — we, the Talleyrands, Metternichs, and Whitworths!"

In one humor, Napoleon was brusque, coarse, overbearing, and pitiless; in another he was caressing, elegantly dignified, imperially generous and gracious. Between these extremes ran the current of his life : hence the varied impressions he made upon others. Charles Fox and Lord Holland knew him personally, and they risked political and social influence in England by defending him from the abuse which had become the fashion there. Almost without exception the men who came into personal relations with him loved him. The rare exceptions are such people as Bourrienne and Rémusat, whom Napoleon had to rebuke for ways that were crooked. Even to his valets he was a hero.

As Charles Fox said, "The First Consul at Malmaison, at St. Cloud, and at the Tuileries are three different men, forming together the *beau ideal* of human greatness."

To these three Napoleons should be added at least one other, — Napoleon at the head of his army.

In public, Napoleon trained himself to that majestic dignity, grace, and thoughtfulness which his imposing position required. The Pope did not act his part better at the coronation, nor Alexander at Tilsit. He rarely, if ever, overacted or underacted a public part, but in private there was a difference. In familiar converse he would pace up and down the room, or twitch in his chair, or throw his feet up on the desk, and open his penknife and whittle the chair arm, or sprawl on the floor studying his big maps, or sit down in the lap of his secretary.

With the rough good humor of a soldier, he would call his intimates "simpleton," "ninny," or even "fool"; he would pinch their ears, and lightly flick them on the cheek with his open hand. Whereupon the oversensitive biographers have unanimously shuddered, and exclaimed, "See what a vulgar creature this Napoleon was!"

In his personal habits he was neat to the point of being fastidious. If ever he wasted any time at all, it was the hours he spent in the bath. Simple in his dress and in his tastes, no gentleman was ever more scrupulously clean. Generally he wore the uniform of a colonel of his guard; and his plain gray overcoat, and plain little hat with its cheap tricolor cockade, formed a vivid contrast to the gaudy dress of foreign diplomats, or of his own officers.

He pretended that anger with him never reached his head, that he had his passions under perfect control. This was all nonsense. His temper frequently burst all bounds, and for the moment he was as insane as other men in a passion. Madame Junot states that when he fell into one of these fits of anger, he was frightful.

Upon at least one occasion of this kind he kicked the dinner table over, and smashed the crockery; at another he put his foot, in a violent and tumultuous manner, against the belly of Senator Volney.

It was rumored around the palace, on his return from

Spain in 1809, that he gave Talleyrand a "punch on the
nose"; and once when the jealous and watchful Josephine came upon him as he was enjoying himself with
another woman, he sprang at her in such a fury that she
fled the room in terror.

At Moscow while the Emperor was in his blackest
mood, everything going wrong, and a general crash
impending, Roustan, kneeling before him to put on his
boots, carelessly got the left boot on the right foot.   The
next instant he was sprawling on his back on the floor.
Napoleon had kicked him over.

It is said that he threatened Berthier once with the
tongs, and Admiral Bruix with his riding-whip.   On the
road to Moscow he rode furiously into the midst of some
pillaging soldiers, striking them right and left with his
whip, and knocking them down with his horse.

But these occasions were rare.   His control of himself
was almost incredible, and he learned to endure the most
startling and calamitous events without a word or a
change of expression.

If you would see far, far into the heart of Napoleon,
study his relations with Junot.   Not much brain had this
Junot, not much steadiness of character; but he was as
brave as a mad bull, and he had shared his purse with Napoleon in the old days of poverty and gloom.   More than
this, he had believed in Napoleon at a time when Napoleon himself had well-nigh lost heart.   So it came to pass
that Junot was the beloved of the chief, and remained so
in spite of grievous faults and sins.   Junot gambled, and
Napoleon abhorred gaming; Junot drank to excess, and
Napoleon detested drunkards; Junot was a rowdy, and Napolcou shrank from rowdyism; Napoleon loved order, and

Junot was most disorderly ; Napoleon loved a strict relation between income and outgo, and Junot was a marvel
of extravagant prodigality. Napoleon loved success, and
Junot brought failure upon him where it hurt dreadfully
— in Portugal, in Russia. Yet through it all Napoleon
never flagged in his indulgence to Junot. He made the
hot-headed grenadier Governor of Paris, Duke of Abrantes,
lapping him in honors and wealth. Sometimes Junot would
be angry at his chief, and Napoleon would coax him back
to good humor, as a father would a child. Sometimes
Junot would run to Napoleon with his griefs ; and the
busiest man in the world would drop everything, take his
suffering friend by the arm, walk him up and down some
quiet room or corridor, soothing him with soft words, with
caresses. One day when Junot had taken to his bed, because of a fancied slight at the palace, Napoleon, hearing
of it, slipped away from the Tuileries, went to the bedside
of his old comrade, comforted him, reassured him, and
stood by him until he was himself again.

When Madame Junot is in the throes of child-birth, it
is to Napoleon that the distracted husband flies. At the
Tuileries he is soothed by Napoleon himself, who sends off
messengers to inquire after the wife ; and when the ordeal
is safely over, it is Napoleon who congratulates the now
radiant Junot, finds his hat for him, and sends him off
home to the mother and babe.

At last there did come something like a rupture between these two — and why? Junot had brought scandal on Napoleon's sister while the brother was off with
his army in Germany. "To bring shame upon my sister
— *you*, Junot ! " and the great Emperor fell into a chair,
overcome with grief.

In his relations with Duroc, Berthier, Lannes, La Salle, Rapp, Méneval, Eugène Beauharnais, we find the same traits. The indulgence with which he treated those he liked, the pains he took to keep them in good humor, his care not to wound their feelings, and his caressing way of coaxing them out of their occasional sulks, shows a phase of Napoleon's own character which is usually overlooked.

He had many boyish ways which never left him. He would hum a song and whistle a tune to the last. During moments of abstraction he fell to whittling his desk or chair, sat upon a table and swung his leg back and forth, or softly whistled or hummed some favorite air. During the great disaster at Leipsic, when all had been done and all had failed, Napoleon, in a kind of daze, stood in the street and whistled "Malbrook has gone to the wars."

He was fond of playing pranks. He tried to drive a four-in-hand at Malmaison, struck a gate-post, and got thrown headlong to the ground, narrowly escaping fatal injuries to himself and Josephine. He would disguise himself, and go about Paris to hear the people talk, coming back delighted if he had provoked angry rebuke by some criticism of his on Napoleon. He would throw off his coat at Malmaison, and romp and play like a schoolboy. After dinner, if the weather was fine, he would call out, " Let's play barriers ! " and off would go his coat, and in a moment he would be racing about the grounds.

One afternoon while amusing himself in this way, two rough-looking men were seen near the gate, loitering and gazing at the romping group. The ladies saw fit to become frightened, and to make the usual hysterical outcry. Gallant young officers sprung forward to drive off the intruders, as gallant young officers should. But it turned out that one of the men was a maimed veteran of the wars, come with his brother, in the hope of catching a glimpse of the beloved form of his general — Napoleon. Having seen, having heard, the First Consul put his arm around Josephine, drew her toward the two men, gave them gracious welcome, introduced them to his wife, and sent them under Eugène's escort to the house to drink his health in a glass of wine. So promptly was the thing done, so naturally, so warmly, so tactfully, that the one-armed soldier was melted to tears.

In his rude horse-play, Napoleon taught his gazelle to chase the ladies of the court, and when the animal caught and tore a dress, or caught and pinched a leg, his delight was precisely that of the mischievous, slightly malicious boy. In playing barriers he cheated, as he did at all games, and violated all the rules. When he was unbent, when he was at Malmaison, he could take a joke as well as any. One very rough piece of horse-play he took a good deal more placidly than many a private citizen would have done. Passing through a gallery at Malmaison, he stopped to examine some engravings which were lying upon a table. Young Isabey happening to come into the gallery behind Napoleon, and seeing the back of the stooping figure, took it to be Eugène Beauharnais. Slipping up softly, Isabey gave a jump, and leaped upon Napoleon's shoulders, astraddle of his neck. Napoleon recovered from the shock, threw Isabey to the ground, asking, "What does this mean?"

"I thought it was Eugène," cried Isabey.

"Well, suppose it was Eugène — must you needs break his shoulder bones?" Without further rebuke Napoleon walked out of the gallery. Through the folly of Isabey, the secret leaked out, and there was just enough of the ludicious about it to embarrass both the actors, and Isabey went to play leap-frog elsewhere.

Napoleon was fond of children, knew how to talk to them, play with them, and win their confidence. The man never lived who knew better than he the route to the heart of a soldier, a peasant, or an ambitious boy. With these he could ever use exactly the right word, look, smile, and deed. He was familiar with his friends, joked them, put his arms around them, and walked with them leaning upon them : he never joked with men like Fouché, Talleyrand, Bernadotte, Moreau, and St. Cyr. These men he used, but understood and disliked.

Fat women he could not endure, and a pregnant woman showing herself when she should have been in seclusion, excited his disgust. One of the pictures he most liked to gaze upon was that of a tall, slender woman, robed in white, and walking beneath the shade of noble trees.

A fastidious, exacting busybody, he was forever on the lookout for violations of good taste on the part of the ladies of his court. He detested the low dresses which exposed the bosom to the vulgar gaze ; and if he saw some one dressed in peculiarly unbecoming style, he was rude enough to give words to his irritation. "Dear me ! are you never going to change that gown?" This was very, very impolite, but the costume was one which he abhorred, and the wearer had inflicted it upon him "more than twenty times."

Possibly if there were a greater number of outspoken Napoleons, there would be fewer absurdities in fashionable female attire.

To some of Napoleon's sharp sayings, the haughty

dames and damsels of the old aristocracy made some crushing replies — according to their *Memoirs*. It is fairly safe to say that these crushing retorts were made in the seclusion of the homes of the fair retorters. The man whose stern look and bitter tongue awed into embarrassed silence such a veteran in word-play as Madame de Staël, was not likely to be crushed by such pert and shallow beings as Madame de Chevreuse and her kind. .

For facts, events, his memory was prodigious; for names and dates, it was not good. Sometimes he would ask the same man about court three or four different times what his name was. In his later years his memory became very fickle, and he was known to forget having given the most important orders. He could not remember a charge he ordered Ségur to make in Spain; nor could he recall that he had ordered the charge of the heavy cavalry at Waterloo.

Noted at school for his skill in mathematics, and using that science constantly in his military operations, it is said that he could rarely add up a column of figures correctly.

He could not spell, nor could he write grammatically; and he took no pains to learn. A busy man, according to his idea, had no time to waste on such matters.

He loved music, especially Italian music; was fond of poetry of the higher sort, and appreciated painting, sculpture, and architecture. He loved the beauty and quietude of such country places as Malmaison, never wearied of adding to their attractions, and was happy when free from business, and taking a solitary stroll along garden walks amid flowers and under the shade of trees.

In his work, Napoleon was all system. No clerk

could keep papers in better order. No head of a department could turn off business with such regularity and despatch. He knew all about his army, down to the last cannon ; knew just what his forces numbered, where they were, and what their condition. He was master of the state finances, of every branch of the internal administration, of every detail of foreign affairs. He kept up with everything, systematized everything, took the initiative in everything. An extra plate of soup could not be served in the palace without a written order from Duroc, the proper officer. An army contractor could not render a false account without being exposed and punished. An overcharge could not be made in the palace furnishings without his finding it out. "He is a devil," said many a quaking Beugnot.

One day, says Constant, the pontoon men were marching with about forty wagons. The Emperor came along, and cried, "Halt ! "

Pointing to one of the wagons, Napoleon asked of the officer in charge: —

"What is in that ? "

The officer answered, " Some bolts, nails, ropes, hatchets, saws — "

" How many of all that ? "

The officer gave the number.

"Empty the wagon and let me see ! "

The order was obeyed, bolts, nails, ropes, saws, everything taken out and counted. But the Emperor was not satisfied. He got off his horse, climbed into the wagon over the spoke to see that it had been emptied.

The troops shouted: "Bravo ! That's right ! That is the way to find out ! "

He compared his mind to a chest of drawers, where each subject occupied its separate space. In turn he opened each drawer. No one subject ever got mixed with another. When all the drawers were shut, he fell asleep. Of course this was not literally true, but during his best years it came as near being literally true as is possible to the human brain.

After the day's work was done, he would enter into the amusements of his domestic circle, would play and dance with the young people, would read or listen to music, or would entertain the circle by telling some romantic story which he composed as he talked. In the evening he loved to have the room darkened while he threw the ladies into a gentle state of terror with a ghost-story.

Napoleon's penetration in some directions was wonderfully keen; in others remarkably dull. For instance, it was almost impossible to deceive him in matters of account, the number of men in a mass, or the plan of battle of a foe. He would converse with an engineer in reference to a bridge he had been sent to build and which Napoleon supposed he had built; after a few words he would turn away and say to the prefect, "That man did not build the bridge — who did it?" The truth would come out: an obscure genius had planned the work, and Napoleon would say to this genius, obscure no more, "Come up higher."

He could scan a list of political prisoners, pounce upon the name of a surgeon, decide at a flash that this man could not be a fanatic. "Bring him to trial, order him to be shot, and he will confess." And it so happened.

But it is marvellous that Napoleon, who revolutionized

2 D

the strategy of war, improved nothing, invented nothing, in the instruments of warfare. A Prussian offered to him the original of the needle-gun, and he totally failed to grasp the terrible effectiveness of the weapon. True, he experimented with it, ordering that specimens should be made and shown him. But when his armories turned out clumsy models, as at first they were almost sure to do, he seemingly lost interest. The Prussian carried his invention to Germany; and the Austrians and French of a later day melted like snow before this new and fearful gun.

When Fulton came to France with his steam-boat discovery, offering a means by which Napoleon might have destroyed with ease England's all-powerful navy, his invention was not appreciated. True, Napoleon gave him encouragement and money, and urged the wise men of the Institute to look into the thing; but Napoleon himself did not " take hold." When the sages of the Institute reported adversely to the new invention, as sages almost always do, Napoleon let the subject drop, apparently forgetting that it is usually the ignorant " crank " and the untutored " tenderfoot " who stumbles upon great inventions and the richest mines. So far-sighted in some directions, it seems unaccountable that he did not realize immediately the vast importance of the breech-loading gun, and the steam-propelled vessel. With the same muzzle-loading muskets he fought the first battle and the last. The same little cannon which could not batter down the old walls of Acre, sent balls which rebounded from the farmyard enclosures at Waterloo.

During all of his campaigns prior to 1812, Napoleon

gave personal attention to everything ; no detail was
neglected. He saw with his own eyes, taking nothing
for granted, nothing on trust. As far as possible he
followed up his orders, seeing to it that they were
executed. Thus on the night before Jena he risked his
life and came near being shot reconnoitring the Prussian
position, and after he had selected positions for his
batteries, and marked out the path up which the guns
were to be drawn to the heights, he could not rest
until he had gone in person and seen how his orders were
being executed. It was fortunate that he did so. The
foremost cannon carriage had got jammed between the
rocks of the passage and had blocked the way of all the
others. The whole battery was at a halt, and nothing
being done to forward the guns. Angry as he was, Napoleon at once took command, ordered up the sappers, held
a lantern while they were at work, and showed them how
to widen the road. Not until the first gun had passed
through did he leave the place. The failure to look after
such things was one cause of the disasters of his later
years.

He spared himself no fatigue in war. Sensitive to
cold, to evil smells, to ugly scenes, to physical discomfort
of all sorts, the Sybarite of the palace became the Spartan
on the campaign. He could stand as much cold, or heat,
or hunger, or thirst, camp hardships and camp nastiness
as any private. He could stay in the saddle day and
night, could march on foot by the hour in snow or mud,
could stand the storms of rain, sleet, and wind, made no
complaint of filthy beds and disgusting surroundings, and
could eat a soldier's bread out of the knapsack with all
of a soldier's relish.

In later years he carried his habits of luxury to the army, and with them came defeats. The general who in Italy could have taken all his baggage in a cart was followed in 1812 by a train of seventy wagons. He went to war then like Louis XIV., and the luck of Louis XIV. overtook him.

On the field of battle his aspect was one of perfect composure. No turn of the tide broke through his absolute self-control.

At Marengo, when the great plain was covered with the flying fragments of his army, and fugitives were crying: "All is lost! Save himself who can!" he was as calm as at a review. Berthier galloping up with more bad news, Napoleon rebuked him with, "You do not tell me that with sufficient coolness." When Desaix arrived, Napoleon took all the time that was necessary to make proper dispositions for the attack, exhibiting not the slightest nervousness under the galling Austrian fire.

In the retreat from Russia he was stoically serene, save on the rarest occasions. Only a few intimates knew how much, in private, he gave way to his immense burden of care, of grief, of impotent rage. To the army he appeared as cold, as hard, as unyielding as granite. When a general brought him some unusually appalling news, Napoleon turned away as though he did not wish to hear. The officer persisted; Napoleon asked, "Why do you wish to disturb my equanimity?"

If his fatigues had been excessive in the preparation for battle, and his dispositions had been made, and all was going as he had foreseen, he could slumber restfully while the combat raged. Thus at Jena, Ségur speaks of Napoleon asleep on the ground where his great map was unrolled — asleep with the grenadiers standing in hollow square about him.

Lord Brougham writes : " Lying under some cover in fire, he would remain for an hour or two, receiving reports and issuing his orders, sometimes with a plan before him, sometimes with the face of the ground in his mind only.

" There he is with his watch in one hand, while the other moves constantly from his pocket, where his snuff-box, or rather his snuff, lies.   An aide-de-camp arrives ; tells of a movement ; answers shortly, some questions rapidly, perhaps impatiently, put ; is despatched with the order that is to solve the difficulty of some general of division.   Another is ordered to attend, and sent off with directions to make some distant corps support an operation. The watch is again consulted ; more impatient symptoms ; the name of one aide-de-camp is constantly pronounced ; question after question is put whether any one is coming from a certain quarter ; an event is expected ; it ought to have happened ; at length the wished-for messenger arrives.   ' Well ! what has been done yonder ? ' — ' The height is gained ; the Marshal is there.' — ' Let him stand firm — not to move a step.'   Another aide-de-camp is ordered to bring up the guard.

" ' Let the Marshal march upon the steeple, defiling by his left — and all on his right are his prisoners.'   Now the watch is consulted and the snuff is taken no more ; the great captain indulges in pleasantry ; nor doubts any more of the certainty and of the extent of his victory than if he had already seen its details in the bulletin."

Cruelty and kindness, selfishness and generosity, loyalty and treachery, honesty and perfidy, are almost unmeaning terms if applied without qualification to Napoleon.

Where his plans were not involved, he frequently manifested the human virtues in their highest form ; where
those plans were involved, he practised all the vices without scruple or pity. Naturally he was humane, charitable,
kind, indulgent, sympathetic, generous ; if policy required
it, he became as hard as steel. He left no debt of gratitude
unpaid ; ignored none of the claims, however slight, of
kindred and old association. See how he behaves toward
Madame Permon, how tolerant he is of that intolerable
woman, how he forgets her snubs, how he forgives her a
public insult, how he follows her with respectful consideration all the days of her life — and why ? She had
been kind to him when he was a poor boy, had nursed
his father on the death-bed. "It is a devil of a temper,
but a noble heart; " and the noble heart makes him forget the devil of a temper.

He gave place and pension to early sweetheart, to boyhood friends, to schoolmates, to teachers. The son and
daughter of General Marbeuf found him delighted to
serve them in remembrance of their father. The widow
of the Duke of Orleans who had chanced to be the giver of
a prize to him at Brienne, and who had forgotten all about
it, was happily surprised to find that he had remembered.
He restored her confiscated pension, and gave a relative
of hers a place in the Senate. To the daughter of Madame
de Brienne he proved himself a vigilant guardian. So the
record runs throughout his life, and his last will is little
more than a monument of gratitude to those who had at
any time done him a service.

He was not free from superstition. What people called
"omens" made an impression upon him. He sometimes
made the sign of the cross, as though to ward off impend-

ing evil. When in Italy the glass over Josephine's portrait was broken, Marmont says that he turned frightfully pale, and exclaimed that his wife was either dead or unfaithful.

He was a man of insatiable curiosity. He wished to know everything, and to have a hand in everything. His police infested every nook and corner, and over his police he set spies, and over the spies he set the informer. Thus he had two or three systems going at the same time. He not only sought to know all about public affairs, but private matters also. He delighted in gossip and scandal, hugely enjoying his ability to twit some man or some woman with an amour which he had discovered. Theatre talk, street talk, drawing-room talk, were reported to him regularly. Copying the Bourbon example, he opened private letters to ascertain what correspondents were saying to each other. He allowed no freedom of the press, and no real freedom of speech. Journals which showed the least independence he suppressed. Authors, actors, orators, who ventured upon forbidden ground, felt the curb at once.

Lavish as he was in expenditures, there was method and economy throughout. He was good at a bargain, exacted the worth of his money, would tolerate no imposition or overcharge. His imperial displays were more magnificent than those of the Grand Monarch, but they cost him less than one-tenth as much.

It is not possible to dogmatize about a man like Napoleon, saying positively just what he was. A more contradictory mortal never lived.

The man who massacred the prisoners at Jaffa was the same who perhaps lost his crown because he would not

consent to excite civil war in Russia or in France. He
who had just sent tens of thousands to death at Borodino,
angrily reproved a careless member of his staff for allowing the hoof of his horse to strike one of the wounded,
causing a cry of pain.

" It was only a Russian," said the negligent rider.

" Russian or French, it's all the same," cried Napoleon,
furiously ; " I want them all cared for."

His temper was despotic; he could not brook opposition, nor tolerate independence.   Hence he banished
Madame de Staël, suppressed the tribunate which had
the power of debate, and frowned upon voluntary movements of all kinds, whether clubs or schools.   His
treatment of Toussaint was atrocious, filling the honest
biographer with anger, disgust, and shame : but, after all,
Toussaint was a rebel, and the way of the rebel is hard.
In his own eyes the insurgent, striving for national independence, is a hero : in the eyes of the world he is an
incendiary, unless he whips his master and becomes free.

From the grave of Robert Emmett, Ireland can speak
of England's treatment of rebels : from Cuba comes a
voice choked with blood, which vainly tries to do justice
to Spain's treatment of the rebel ; and from Siberia,
Hungary, Poland, Finland, Hindustan, Crete, Italy, South
Africa, come awful reminders of the well-known fact, —
the way of the rebel is hard.   Toussaint L'Ouverture,
regarded as a rebel, was cast into prison : Jefferson
Davis, regarded as a rebel, was cast into prison : Davis,
the white man, was put in irons and came near dying :
Toussaint, the black man, was ironed, and died.   In each
case the motive was the same, — to degrade and to punish
an alleged rebel.

Great has been the outcry made by the literary Scribes and Pharisees against Napoleon because of his cruelty to the hero of St. Domingo and to Andreas Hofer, the hero of the Tyrol; until these indignant people indict also the kings and cabinets who have slain their hundreds where Napoleon slew his dozens, we cannot feel much sympathy for the prosecution.

Relentlessly selfish in the pursuit of power, it will be admitted by those who impartially study his career that he used his power, not for personal and selfish pleasures, but for the future welfare of the peoples over whose destinies he presided. The laborious manner in which he worked out the revolutionary principle of lifting the despised Jew into full citizenship, will always be a striking illustration of the liberality of his statesmanship.

He loved to tour the country, to see with his own eyes, to hear with his own ears. He loved to meet the people face to face, to talk with them familiarly, to get at the real facts about everything. The man never lived who had such a passion for making things better. Harbors must be widened, deepened, made more secure. Trade routes must be improved, rivers linked to rivers, or rivers connected with seas. Mountains must be conquered by broad, easy-grade roads; and villages must be planted along the route for the convenience of the traveller. He tore out old buildings to make way for new ones, — larger, better, grander. Crooked streets — narrow, nasty, the homes of squalor, of crime, and of pestilence — he replaced by broad avenues and handsome buildings. Churches, schools, town-halls, arsenals, dockyards, canals, highways, bridges, fortifications, manufactories, harbor works, new industries, sprang up at his touch throughout the realms he ruled. Had he never been known as a warrior, his work as administrator and as a legislator would have made his name immortal. Had he never been heard of as a legislator, his work in Europe as a developer of material resources would have made it impossible for the world to forget him. The manufactories which he encouraged were but the beginnings of a mighty evolution which would have transferred to the Continent the vast profits England had so long reaped. At every seaport, on every canal, on all the highways, in every town from Venice to Brest and Cherbourg, the traveller of the present day sees the footprints of Napoleon the Great.

He rid Paris of the periodical nuisance of the Seine overflow, and along the river ran his magnificent embankments. At St. Helena he expressed a wonder that the Thames had never been thus controlled, and England afterward embanked her river as the great Emperor suggested.

His natural instinct was to make improvements. The first thing he did in Spain was to establish free-trade between her provinces, abolish feudal burdens, suppress one-third of the monasteries where "those lazy beasts of monks" lived in idleness at public expense, and to give the people the right to be heard in fixing taxes and making laws. The first thing the Bourbons did, on their return, was to restore all the abuses Napoleon had abolished.

In Italy, the first thing he did, after overturning the temporal power of the Pope, was to suppress the papal monopolies by which the Albani family had the sole right to manufacture pins, Andrea Novelli the exclusive privilege of selling oil for lamps, Alexandro Betti the monopoly of ferry boats, and so forth. To these benighted Romans he gave the Code Napoléon, trial by jury, home rule in local affairs, equality before the law, and relief from all feudal abuses.

The first thing the Pope did when in 1814 he was restored to temporal power was to abolish all things Napoleonic, and to reëstablish the hateful monopolies, feudal burdens, and papal customs.

In Egypt he projected the mighty work of adding millions of acres to the cultivable area by the construction of vast storage basins on the Nile. England has but recently carried to successful completion the magnificent plan he suggested.

In Milan he finished the gorgeous cathedral which had been commenced hundreds of years before. To stagnant, pestilential Venice he gave new life, dredging her lagoons, decreeing a Grand Canal, deepening her harbor, overhauling her sanitary system — spending $1,000,000 during his one visit. And the story is the same for almost every portion of his huge empire.

Bad? Lord Wolseley says he was not only bad, but "superlatively" so. Perhaps he was; but here is one publican and sinner who dares to say that were the good men to work half as hard as Napoleon did to improve the condition of *this* world, its moral and material situation would more nearly approximate the imagined perfection of that heavenly abode in whose behalf *this* poor planet and its poor humanity are so often neglected.

CHAPTER XXXI

TILSIT is generally considered the high-water mark of Napoleon's power. Not yet forty years of age, he was lord of lords and king of kings. With Russia for an ally, Continental Europe was at his mercy. Adding Westphalia and, also, enlarged Saxony to the Confederation of the Rhine, the Empire was guarded upon the west, from the North Sea to the Mediterranean, by an unbroken line of feudatory states. In all these subject lands the principles of the French Revolution took the form of law. The Code Napoléon, with its civil equality, jury trials, uniformity of taxes, publicity of legal proceedings, drove out the mediæval abuses which had so long robbed the people in the name of government. To his brother Jerome Napoleon wrote: "Be a constitutional king. Your people ought to enjoy a liberty, an equality, a well-being unknown heretofore to the Germans." And the Emperor reminded Jerome that if he gave his people the benefits of a wise and liberal administration, they would never wish to return to the barbarous rule of Prussia. Rule your kingdom wisely and liberally, said Napoleon, and "this kind of government will protect it more powerfully than fortresses or the armies of France."

Far-reaching as was the sweep of Napoleon's sword, that of his Code went farther. The soldier of the Revolution could never go as far as its principles. In the hour

412

of its deepest humiliation Prussia dropped the system of
Frederick, a worn-out garment, and clad itself anew.   She
freed the serf, abolished caste, opened all careers to merit,
made military service universal, and gave partial self-
government to towns and cities.   Under the ministry of
Stein, Prussia was born again, and the greatness of modern
Germany dates from the reorganization which followed
Jena — a greatness which, when analyzed, is seen to consist in calling in the Prussian people to resurrect a nation
which class legislation and the privileged nobles had led
to perdition.

In measuring the results of the French Revolution and
of Napoleon's victories, let us remember what Germany
was in the eighteenth century.   Let us not forget that
the great mass of the people were serfs chained to the
soil, mere implements of husbandry, burdened with the
duty of feeding the nation in time of peace, and fighting
for it in time of war, but uncheered by the hope of ever
becoming more than serfs.   Let us remember that the
great rights of the citizen had no legal existence, that
the arbitrary will of the lord was the peasant's law.   In
the very provinces out of which Napoleon fashioned the
kingdom of Westphalia a legitimate, divine-right prince
had sold to an equally God-appointed king of Great Britain
some thousands of soldiers to fight against the revolted
colonists in North America.   In the very cities which the
Code Napoléon now entered and ruled, might still be seen
the foul dungeons where alleged culprits were secretly
tried, secretly tortured, and secretly done to death with
atrocities which might have shamed a savage.

With Napoleon himself, however, imperialism had become a fixed creed.   Ever since Austerlitz, he had affected

greater reserve, exacted a greater deference, obeyed and
enforced a more rigid etiquette. Oriental baseness of flat-
tery pampered his pride; opposition to his will was not
dreamt of in his empire; pestiferous intriguers like
Madame de Staël lived in exile; pert maids of honor like
Mademoiselle de Chevreuse were sent away and silenced;
secret enemies, embryo traitors like Talleyrand and Bernadotte, fawned and flattered like the others, greedily clutch-
ing at all he flung to them, — money, titles, estates. The
Grand Monarch himself never lived in greater pomp than
this "Corsican upstart." The formulas of divine right
usurped the old popular phrases, and "Napoleon by the
grace of God Emperor, etc.," was the style of imperial
proclamations. "Religious veneration" was claimed for
the eagles of the army ; and the priests taught the children that "to honor and serve the Emperor is to honor
and serve God." No toil was spared to make the ceremonial at the palace conform to Bourbon precedent. The
hero of Austerlitz and Jena consented to be tutored by
the Campans, De Ségurs, Narbonnes, and De Brézés of
etiquette. When Louis XVIII. came to the throne in
1814, he apparently discovered but one serious fault in all
of Napoleon's imitation Bourbonism — his dinner had not
been escorted from kitchen to dining room by a squad of
soldiers.

Turkey had not nursed any very great degree of wrath
against Napoleon, on account of his attempt upon Egypt;
she had recognized his greatness and had become his ally.
During the campaign in Poland, while Napoleon's army
was weltering in the mud, which caused indignant French

soldiers to exclaim, " Is this what the Poles have the impudence to call their country?" England had sent a fleet to Constantinople to bully the Sultan into joining the league against France.

The terror of the unprepared Turk was profound, and he was about to submit; but it so happened that Napoleon was represented there by a man of courage and ability — General Sébastiani. Through his advice, and inspired by his confidence, the Sultan parleyed with the English, temporized, gained time, manned defences, and prepared for a struggle. A letter from Napoleon came at the right moment, exhorting and promising, as no one but Napoleon could exhort and promise. French diplomats steadied the nerves of the Commander of the Faithful, while French officers directed the work on the fortresses, so that when the English admiral was finally told that Turkey would resist his insolent demands, the Turks were all ready for battle, and the English were not. They had forced their way into Turkish waters, killing and wounding as they came; they now sailed away, pursued and bombarded, losing many in killed and wounded as they escaped.

Failing here, they determined to make sure of Denmark. By the Treaty of Tilsit the two Emperors contemplated a union of all the Continental powers against English commerce. Great Britain believed that Denmark would be forced to enter this league — but she had no proofs, so far as historians know. At any rate, no hostile steps had been taken by either Emperor: Napoleon had merely instructed Talleyrand to enter into negotiations with Denmark. Upon the plea that Napoleon meant to seize the Danish fleet, Great Britain determined to take charge of it herself, despite the fact that Denmark was at peace with her, had given no cause for war, and was even then represented at London by a resident, friendly minister. Concealing her purpose, smiling upon this duped minister to the last, Great Britain launched fleet and army against an unsuspecting people. Appearing before Copenhagen in force, the British demanded that the Danish fleet be given up to England in pledge, "until the peace."

Taken at disadvantage though they were, the Danes could not at once yield to so shameful a humiliation, and the English opened fire. For three days and nights the devoted city was shelled, and all the horrors of war inflicted upon it. For three days the British guns roared, strewing the streets with dead men, dead women, dead children; while eight hundred homes were in ruins or on fire. Then the Danes yielded, their city was looted, their ships taken away, and the exulting marauders sailed back to England towing their prizes, to be welcomed with rapturous enthusiasm.

To the Berlin Decree of Napoleon, Great Britain retorted with another "Order in Council." She declared that she would search all merchant vessels, and that neutrals should not be allowed to trade unless they had touched at a British port and paid duties there. Here was another violation of all law, — an insolent invasion of the right of neutrals to do business, save in contraband of war. Napoleon's counter shot was the Milan Decree, in which he very naturally declared that any ship submitting to such demands as England had made, should be treated as an English ship. Why not? It is apparent enough, that if neutral ships did business under English rules, paying duties at English ports, such ships were practically doing business as English ships.

Strange are the verdicts of history. Napoleon gets almost all the blame for this commercial war, in which he was first struck by England, and in which each of his decrees was but an attempt to ward off the blows England aimed at him.

To make a success of his Continental system, it was necessary that the entire seacoast of the Continent should be closed to English goods. In theory, the system was in force throughout the Continent, with the important exceptions of Spain and Portugal. To close the long line of seaboard these countries presented, was Napoleon's first purpose in meddling with their affairs.

Spain had been his ally, but had, perhaps, never had her heart in the alliance. At all events, when the great Bourbon conspiracy against Napoleon's life was on foot, in 1803, some of the accomplices of Georges had entered France under the protection of Spanish passports. Nevertheless, Spain had paid rich subsidies into Napoleon's coffers, and had sent her ships to be destroyed by Nelson at Trafalgar. So burdensome had become the alliance that Spain had grown tired of it. While Napoleon was involved with Prussia, and previous to Jena, the Spaniards had been called to arms by Godoy, the Prince of The Peace, real ruler of the kingdom. Napoleon believed that this call to arms was a measure of hostility to the French. The victory of Jena, however, changed the situation, and Godoy humbly came to terms with the winner.

Now again, in 1808, a treaty was made between France and Spain. Portugal, virtually an English colony, and

ruled from London, was to be conquered, and divided
between France and Spain. A French army, under Junot,
marched through Spain into Portugal, and captured Lis-
bon (November, 1807). The royal house of Braganza
made its escape to Brazil. Its throne was declared vacant
by Napoleon, and the French took full possession of the
country. But for Junot's rashness and rapacity, it seems
that the Portuguese, as a general thing, would have been
quite contented with the change of masters.

In Spain itself fateful events were on foot. The
old king, Charles IV. was a Bourbon, densely ignorant, extremely religious, and devoid of any real character.
His queen was a woman of some ability and force of character, but she had become infatuated with a common soldier, Manuel Godoy, and both she and her husband were
governed by the favorite.

The heir to the throne, Ferdinand, prince of the Astu-
rias, was a young man of obstinate temper, full of duplicity and cruelty. He was loved by the Spanish people,
partly because he was their handsome young prince-royal,
and partly because it was known that he hated Godoy.

The old king was made to believe that his son meant to
have him assassinated. He appealed to Napoleon for protection against Ferdinand. At the same time this prince
requested of Napoleon the hand of a Bonaparte princess
in marriage. Thus both factions looked to France, and
the French Emperor used each against the other.

The Spaniards rose against Godoy, a mob wrecked his
palace, and he fled for his life, hiding himself in a roll
of matting in a loft. Forced out by hunger, he was seen,
captured, and about to be torn to pieces when he was
rescued by the guards of Ferdinand, and taken, amid

blows and curses, to the barracks. The terrified old king abdicated in favor of his son; and on March 20, 1808, Ferdinand entered Madrid in triumph, to the frantic delight of the people.

French armies had already been massed in Spain, and some of the strongest fortresses seized by unscrupulous trickery. Murat was in chief command, and he marched upon the Spanish capital in overwhelming numbers — unresisted because the French were believed to be coming as friends of Ferdinand.

The old king, Charles IV., protested to Napoleon that his abdication had been made under duress; he prayed for help against his son. To Napoleon applied Ferdinand, also; for Murat held Madrid with forty thousand troops, and he had not yet recognized the title of the new king.

In April, 1808, the Emperor himself came to Bayonne, moving soon into the château of Marrac, which was surrounded by a lovely park "on the banks of the silver Nive." The place is now a ruin, the house having been gutted by fire in 1825, and the park being now used for the artillery of the garrison. But when Napoleon came there in 1808, soon to be joined by Josephine and the court, it was a place of beauty. Biarritz, the fashionable watering-place of to-day, was then unknown; but along the same shore where summer visitors now stroll, Napoleon romped with Josephine, "chasing her along the sands, and pushing her into the sea at the edge of the tide, until she was up to her knees in water." They bathed and played together, "and the great Emperor, England's ' Corsican Ogre,' used to hide her satin shoes on the sands while she was in the water, and not allow us to bring them to her, but made her walk from the beach to the carriage barefooted, which gave him immense delight."

All was very gay at the château of Marrao, everything free, easy, joyous, etiquette somewhat shelved. For instance, it is related that Josephine's harpsichord needed tuning, that a man was called in to tune it, that Josephine, who was unknown to the tuner, leaned her arms on the harpsichord, chatting very familiarly with the tuner, that her dress was so plain (and perhaps slovenly) that the amorous tuner took her to be a lady's-maid, accessible to kisses, that he assured her she was much prettier than the Empress, and that he was just about to kiss her, when the door opened and in walked the Emperor! Josephine laughed, Napoleon laughed, the tuner fled, — leaving his tools, — deaf to Napoleon's call for him to come back.

Equally true, perhaps, is another story of the same date. There was a ball at the château of Marrac, the windows were open, the night being warm. At a pause in the music, a lady stepped out upon the balcony, seen by the sentinels, who likewise saw an officer follow her and kiss her. The sentinels knew him — it was the Little Corporal. But he saw them also, and his sharp word of command rang out, "Shoulder arms!" "Right about turn!" They turned, and they stayed turned, fixed and immovable, until the relief came an hour or so later.

So much for the bright side of this famous picture.

*

By the most astonishing series of duplicities and perfidies, Napoleon gathered into his snare at Bayonne *all* the contending parties of the Spanish trouble, — King Charles, the Queen, Godoy, Ferdinand, and Don Carlos, Ferdinand's younger brother.

These Bourbons washed their dirty family linen in his presence, appealing to him against each other. Ferdinand's royal father shook a cane over his head and cursed him; Ferdinand's royal mother reviled him, and told him that the king, her husband, was not his father; and Godoy, the paramour of the wife and mother, sat down to meat with King and Queen, indispensably necessary to both. Charles IV., fond of pleasure and ease, resigned the crown of Spain to Napoleon; Ferdinand was asked to do likewise. He refused, and it was not till there had been an uprising in Madrid, cruelly suppressed by Murat, who lost nearly a thousand men, that he yielded. The revolt had been laid at his door, and Napoleon had threatened to treat him as a rebel.

Charles and Ferdinand became grandees of France, with princely revenues; in return Napoleon received Spain and its magnificent dependencies (May, 1808).

Calling Joseph Bonaparte from Naples to wear this new crown, Napoleon wished to give to the transfer some show of national consent. He summoned an assembly of Spanish prelates and grandees to Bayonne (June, 1808). They came, but as they came the ground upon which they walked was hot with revolt. All Spain was spontaneously and furiously running to arms. The assembly at Bayonne accepted Joseph and the constitution which Napoleon had prepared.

In all courts and cabinets Napoleon's conduct was hotly discussed; in most of them it was furiously condemned. True, he had not used Spain much more unscrupulously than he had treated Venice; nor, indeed, more perfidiously.

than England had dealt with India, Russia with Poland,
Prussia with Silesia. But there were two considerations
which weighed heavily against Napoleon : he was not a
legitimate king, and he was getting more than his share.
The small men began to ask, one the other, concerning the
meat upon which this our Cæsar fed ; and to say, one to
the other, that they, the small men, might, by union and
patience and perseverance, pull the big man down.

The more closely his statecraft is studied, the more
clearly will it be seen that in all things he conformed to
orthodox standards. He was neither better nor worse
than others. His march to power was bridged with broken
promises, pitiless deeds, utter disregard of human life, and
the rights of other peoples. A foe was an obstacle, which
must be got out of the way. If fair means would answer,
well and good; if fair means would not answer, then foul
methods would be used. Precisely the same principles
have been constantly practised by all conquerors, all conquering nations. Russia, England, Prussia, France — the
same policy built empires for each. The Russian Czar,
Alexander, fawned upon the Swedish minister, swearing
friendship and good intentions when the Russian legions
were already on the march to seize Finland. Russian
faith was solemnly pledged afterward to the Finns themselves, that their autonomy, their local institutions, should
never be destroyed. In our own day, we have seen a
most Christian Czar violate this written contract and
pitilessly Russianize helpless Finland.

England's empire is built on force and fraud; Prussia's
greatness rests on Frederick's crime against Silesia:
France under Napoleon merely conformed to the well-
known precedents. Ambitious and despotic, he made

war upon the weak, to shut out English goods, to cripple English commerce, and to bring her to terms of peace. This was bad enough, but we have lived to see things that were worse. We have seen England make war upon China to compel her to open her ports to the deadly opium trade — deadly to the Chinese, but most profitable to the English trader. We have lived to see a Dutch republic trampled out of existence because it would not allow English gold-miners to rule it.

Let us put away cant and lies and hypocrisy; let us frankly admit that Napoleon was a colossal mixture of the good and the bad, just as Cromwell was, just as Richelieu, Frederick, and Bismarck were. Those retained attorneys of royalism, clericalism, and absolutism, who gravely compile huge books to prove that Napoleon was a fiend, an evil spirit struggling against light, are the absurdest mortals extant. Even Spain now knows better; and the national revolt there at this era is against the very system the great democratic despot would have overthrown. "Down with the Jesuits!" they cry in all the cities of Spain in this year 1901. They are just a century behind time. Napoleon, a hundred years ago, put down the Jesuit and his Inquisition, swept feudalism away, gave just laws and representative government to a priest-ridden, king-accursed people. They were not ready for the boon, and repelled it. With mad infatuation Spaniards listened to monk and grandee and English marplot. Passion flamed, and reason fled. Blind hatred of all things French took possession of men, women, and children throughout the land. Peasants were even more frantic than princes and peers. Deeds of heroism, of self-sacrifice, of cruelty were done which amazed the world.

By desperate persistence, the Spaniards succeeded in getting back their good old system — Bourbon king, privileged aristocracy, priestly tyranny, feudal extortions. Great Britain kindly sent armies and subsidies to aid the good work. Spain got the old system back, and much good has it done her. It has eaten the heart out of a great people, made her name a byword among nations, stranded her in the race of human progress. To-day she comprehends what she lost a hundred years ago.

CHAPTER XXXII

WHEN Captain Marbot, bearing despatches from Murat announcing the riot in Madrid, reached the château of Marrac, he found the Emperor in the park, taking his after-dinner walk, with the Queen of Spain on his arm and Charles IV. beside him, followed by the Empress Josephine, Prince Ferdinand, Don Carlos, Marshal Duroc, and some ladies.

"What news from Madrid?" cried Napoleon, as Marbot, covered with dust, drew near. The despatches were delivered in silence, and Napoleon drew to one side to read them, and to overwhelm the officer with questions. In vivid terms, Marbot described the despair of the Spanish people, the fury with which they had fought, the threatening aspect of the populace even after the revolt had been put down.

"Bah!" exclaimed Napoleon, cutting him short; "they will calm down and will bless me as soon as they see their country freed from the discredit and disorder into which it has been thrown by the weakest and most corrupt administration that ever existed!"

When the Emperor had explained to the King and Queen of Spain what had occurred in Madrid, they turned upon Ferdinand with an outburst of rage. "Wretch!" cried the old King, "you may now be satisfied. Madrid has been bathed in the blood of my subjects shed in consequence of your rebellion against your father; their blood be on your head!" The Queen was no less bitter, and even offered to strike her son. Napoleon put a stop to the painful scene.

"Bah! they will soon calm down." So Napoleon thought, having no fear whatever that a tumultuous rising of peasants would make head against his troops. What his army had done in Italy and in Egypt, it could do in Spain. It only annoyed him, and somewhat puzzled him, to see that the people should reject his liberal constitution, and devote themselves with such frantic zeal to the most worthless of Bourbon kings. That Joseph would soon be in peaceful possession of the peninsula, that his generals would soon sweep the peasant bands out of the field, he did not doubt. Had he lacked faith as to this, he would probably not have given the crown to Joseph, — the placid, self-satisfied, comprehensively incapable Joseph. Had he dreamed of the long years of war that were to follow, he might have hearkened to the pleadings of Murat, and left that brilliant soldier to defend the crown which he so ardently coveted.

Amid ovations the Emperor and Josephine toured the provinces, on the return trip to Paris, everywhere welcomed with joy and admiration, while in the peninsula the great storm was muttering. Throughout Spain, in the highways and byways, from pulpit to market-place, Napoleon was denounced, defied, and resisted. Priests led the crusade, cursing the man of the Concordat as anti-Christ, minister of the devil, worthy of death and damnation. Committees of defence, juntas, sprang up everywhere; armies mustered almost at the stamp of the foot.

Wherever a Frenchman could be stabbed, shot from am-
bush, or taken and sawn asunder, it was done. Roads
were lined with ambuscades, stragglers and detached
parties cut off, and the French generals were soon thrown
on the defensive by this despised uprising of the people.
At Saragossa and Valencia the French troops were
repulsed; in Andalusia hordes of Spaniards surrounded
Dupont's army of twenty thousand, beat it in battle, and
forced it to capitulate (Baylen, July, 1808).

In August the English landed troops in Portugal; and
Junot, whose forces were scattered, fought with only
thirteen thousand men against Wellington with sixteen
thousand, was worsted at Vimeiro (August 21, 1808)
and by the convention of Cintra (August 30, 1808)
agreed to evacuate Portugal. He, too, had wanted to
become a king; he, too, had thought of himself rather
than of his master; he, too, had wrecked a splendid plan
by sheer mismanagement and monstrous rapacity.

The disaster in Spain and Portugal came upon Napoleon like a thunderbolt; his grief and indignation knew
no bounds; cries of rage and pain were wrung from him;
pointing to his uniform, he said, "There is a stain here."
At Aboukir, Brueys had at least fought and died like a
soldier; at Trafalgar Frenchmen had shown desperate
valor; but at Baylen an army of twenty thousand imperial troops had laid down their arms to gangs of insurgents! Oh, the shame of it! Who could estimate its
effect in Europe? When the Emperor spoke of Baylen
to his council of state, his voice trembled, and his eyes
were full of tears.

Conscious of the peril which menaced his supremacy,
Napoleon determined to go in person and put down the

Spanish revolt. But before doing so it was necessary that he and the Czar should have another conference, smooth over certain points of difference which had arisen, and come to a better understanding — hence the famous gathering at Erfurth (October, 1808). This time Alexander was Napoleon's guest, and very royally was he entertained. A more brilliant assembly was never seen in Europe. Subject kings, vassals, lords of the Empire, civil and military dignitaries, courtiers, ambassadors, diplomats, eminent men of letters, surrounded the two great Emperors, and rendered homage. Business and pleasure intermingled; and while frontiers of empire were being arranged, there were banquets, balls, grand hunts, orchestral music, and the drama. Actors brought from Paris played to the Emperors and their trains, and the Czar stood up one night and took Napoleon's hand at the line "the friendship of a great man is a gift from the gods." Davoust used to say that Napoleon had been nodding till the Czar improvised this little by-play.

If Napoleon was anxious for the future of his power, he concealed it well; his face showed nothing but serenity, good nature, and confidence. He found time to converse at length with Goethe and Wieland; he found time to act the suave host to lords and ladies; he was as firm with Alexander as he had been at Tilsit; and when the conference broke up, he had arranged everything as completely to his satisfaction.

In the *Memoirs* of Marshal Oudinot, we find the following anecdote of the Erfurth meeting : —

"Napoleon had occasional fits of forgetfulness which prevented him from displaying, in his relations with the sovereigns, all the forethought expected in a host.

"One day we were riding into the country, the two
Emperors, Napoleon and Alexander, riding side by side.
At a given moment, the former, carried away by his
thoughts, took the lead, whistling, and seeming to forget those he was leaving behind. I shall always remember Alexander, turning stiffly toward his neighbor,
and asking, 'Are we to follow?' 'Yes, sire.' I rejoined
Napoleon and told him of this little scene. He fell back,
offered an explanation, and that was the end of it."

So Marshal Oudinot thought, but as the compiler of the
Memoirs asks, who knows what influence this trifling incident may have had upon the proud, sensitive, suspicious,
and wavering Czar?

By the terms of the new agreement, Alexander was to
have a free hand on the Danube to take Moldavia and
Wallachia; that much had been understood at Tilsit, perhaps, but "Constantinople, never! That is the empire
of the world!" In return for the liberty to seize the
Danubian provinces, the Czar was to keep central Europe
quiet, while Napoleon conquered Spain and Portugal.
Prussia was notified by the Czar that she must remain
quiet, bow to Napoleon's will, and agree to his demands,
one of which was that Stein should be dismissed.

To Germans, generally, the heavy hand of the Czar,
coming down upon Frederick William in this imperative
fashion, must have suggested the thought that it was
high time the Lord's Anointed autocrat of Russia was
being sworn to friendship to Prussia, once more, at the
tomb of the great Frederick. The two oaths already taken
seemed to have slipped their hold.

Suppose that Napoleon had solemnly gone in state to
the Escorial and there, at night, had taken in his own the

hand of the Spanish king, and had, over the bones of dead
Spanish monarchs, sworn eternal friendship to Spain; suppose he had broken this vow as soon as made; suppose he
had gone the second time and sworn it all over again;
suppose he had violated his oath a second time: — would
royalist and clerical authors *ever* have found ink black
enough to fill their righteously indignant pens?

If we would correctly judge Napoleon, let us keep our
equilibrium and our standards of comparison; let us
throw him into contrast, not with the ideal man, but
with other rulers of his own time. By so doing we may
hope to come, in the humblest spirit and manner, to know
the great Corsican as he actually was.

Once more an effort was made to put an end to war.
The two Emperors sent couriers, — one French and the other
Russian, — to England, bearing offers of peace. These couriers were treated almost as spies by the English, were kept
under surveillance, and were finally sent back with a note
which gave no encouragement to the monarchs who sent
them.

King Joseph had been driven out of Madrid, was now
at Vittoria, and the insurgents controlled the country with
the exception of the soil occupied by the French armies.

Losing no time after the Erfurth interview, Napoleon
hastened to Spain, took command of the troops at Vittoria
(November 5, 1808), and moved forward. In a few days the
entire military situation was changed. The Spaniards were
out-generalled, beaten at all points, and escaped complete
annihilation by the too great haste of some of the French
generals. Within four weeks after the commencement of
the campaign, Madrid was retaken, and once more put
into the possession of the feeble Joseph.

On his march to the Spanish capital, Napoleon found his road blocked at the mountain pass of Sommo-Sierra. The insurgents had fortified the heights, their cannon completely controlling the defile. So strong was the position that a handful of veterans there might have checked an army.

But the impudence of these Spanish bands in presuming to resist his march threw Napoleon into a fury. He would not wait till his infantry could advance upon either side, turn the enemy, and almost certainly secure a bloodless victory. He raged and stormed, "What! my army stopped by armed bands, wretched peasants!"

"Patience, sire, I pray," pleaded General Walthour, who assured him that in a few minutes the pass would be cleared by infantry, which was even then advancing on either side. But no; the enemy must be charged with cavalry — a bristling battery, on the crest of a mountain gorge, must be swept out of the way by a cavalry dash.

"Go, Ségur! Go at once; make my Poles charge, make them take everything!"

There was astonishment — but the order had to be obeyed. At full speed the splendid soldiers of the Polish squadron dashed up the pass, to melt away in an awful fire from the battery above. Historians say that the cavalry charge succeeded. Ségur, who led the dash and was shot down in it, relates that the flanking infantry columns did the work.

"Does anybody know how Ségur came to be hurt? Was he carrying an order?" Napoleon asked, after the battle.

When reminded that he had himself given Ségur the order, he was silent, and "fell into a very thoughtful mood."

An English army under Sir John Moore had entered Spain and was advancing toward Madrid. When it learned that Napoleon was in the field, it began a retreat to the coast, which is famous in military history. The French, led by the Emperor, set out in hot pursuit; and it would be hard to say with certainty which party suffered the more frightful hardships, — the pursuers or the pursued. The weather was bitterly cold, with cutting winds, chilly rains, blinding snowstorms. In crossing the Gaudamara Mountains the storm was so fierce, the cold and the snow so terrible, that the advance guard of Napoleon actually began to retreat. It required all the Emperor's personal influence and example to encourage the men onwards. Dismounting, he trudged along on foot, Lannes and Duroc on either side, and hour after hour he plodded thus through the snow, up the mountain, at the head of his men. Near the summit, on account of the jackboots the officers wore, they could go no farther. Napoleon was lifted on to a gun carriage, and riding on a cannon, he reached the top, his generals similarly mounted. By forced marches the French were pushed on in the hope of cutting off the English retreat, but it could not be done. Horribly as they suffered, the English were not wholly demoralized. There were always some gallant thousands who would turn and fight when the French pressed them too hard. In this way the pursuers met bloody repulses. Many frightful scenes took place among the English; but General Marbot relates an incident of the French pursuit which throws a vivid light over the hideous character of this whole campaign. He saw three French grenadiers kill themselves because they were tired out, could no longer keep up, and chose death rather than the tortures which awaited them if they fell into the hands of the Spanish peasants.

Napoleon was so deeply impressed by the suicide of his grenadiers that in spite of the drenching rain and bitter cold he went the rounds of the bivouac that night, speaking to the wretched soldiers and trying to restore their courage.

At Astorga a courier arrived, bringing despatches from Paris which warned Napoleon that Austria was ready now "to begin again." She had completely reorganized her army, had patiently waited for the right moment, and was sure that it had come. The veteran troops of France were scattered over the Spanish peninsula; England had made good her grip on Portugal; Austria had about five hundred thousand soldiers ready, and now was the time to strike. The pursuit of the English was turned over to Soult, and the race for the seacoast continued as before. When the French could overtake the English at all, it was with an advance guard too small to crush the English rear-guard. If there was a clash, the French were repulsed. If the French came up in force, the English continued the retreat. At last the coast was made. There was a bloody fight, the battle of Corunna. Sir John Moore was killed, but his army, or what remained of it, got on board the English ships and sailed away.

As to Napoleon, he returned to Valladolid, where he busied himself for several days regulating the affairs of Spain, and in sending off innumerable despatches. Then springing upon his horse, he spurred away for Bayonne, in perhaps the wildest ride an emperor ever made. His escort clattered after him, strung out behind, and the

2 F

wondering peasants of Spain long remembered that meteoric vision. They heard in the distance a faint noise as of frantic racing; there burst into view a breathless cavalcade; it came on like a wind-driven cloud; there was a rush, and a noise like thunder, a fleeting glimpse of bent riders and straining steeds; there was, perhaps, a shout in passing; then it went as it came, and in a moment it was gone.

General Thiébault, on his way to Vittoria, was in the road, with carriage, aides, escort, and servants, when one of his attendants said, "Here comes the Emperor, I think." The General was about to alight from the carriage when he heard some one call : —

"Who is in that carriage?"

The servant hardly had time to answer " General Thiébault " before the imperial party tore by. "Savary was first, after him the Emperor, lashing Savary's horse, and digging the spurs into his own. . . . A good minute afterward Duroc and the Emperor's Mameluke galloped by, and at a like distance from them came a guide, exhausted with his efforts to make up lost ground, and four more brought up the rear as best they could."

From Valladolid to Burgos, some seventy-five miles, Napoleon rode in three hours and a half (January, 1809).

CHAPTER XXXIII

WHEN the Emperor reached Paris, he was in one of his worst moods. Many causes had combined to mar his serenity. His brother Joseph had violently found fault with him because he, Napoleon, had remodelled the government, making it better for the people, and not quite so good for the nobles and priests. Joseph resented this deeply. He, Joseph, was King of Spain. He, Joseph, was the proper person to remodel government, change laws, and manage the country. Napoleon was present merely as a military expert, a general whose service was temporarily needed to pull Joseph from beneath the enemy, and lead him by the hand back to the throne; but when this had been done, Napoleon should have gone away, leaving Joseph to do in Spain just as he thought best. This view was not only held by Joseph at the time, but as long as his worthless life lasted he never wearied of explaining to his friends how Napoleon had lost him the crown of Spain by "interfering in his affairs" in 1809.

Not less high than this was the estimate which Louis Bonaparte placed on his "rights" as King of Holland. No sooner had that morose, jealous, ill-conditioned dolt been placed on a throne by his elder brother than he arrogated to himself all the prerogatives of a dynastic

king.   The "divine right" virus got into *his* sluggish
veins, and he began to shift on to God the responsibility
for such a creature as himself being a king at all.   He
wished to rule Holland, not as a fief of the Empire, not
as part of the Napoleonic system, but as a piece of independent property which had come to him, Louis, through
a long line of ancestors.   When Napoleon gave him the
crown, the conditions were made plain.   Holland was a
part of France; must be governed with reference to
France; the friends and enemies of the one must be
those of the other.   In other words, Holland was a planet
in the French system, and Louis a subordinate king.
If Louis was too proud to rule as a lesser light in the
system of his great brother, he should have been as
frank as Lucien : he should have refused the crown.
But he accepted the splendid gift, and then violated
the conditions.   English goods poured into his markets.
To all intents and purposes he became the ally of Great
Britain, for it was her policy which he favored.   It was
her dearest object to break down the Continental system,
and Louis was aiding her to the best of his slight ability.
Could Napoleon be otherwise than furious?   Had Holland
been won merely that England should be enriched?   Had
he set his brother on a throne merely to weaken his own
empire, and to set an example of disloyalty to other
allies?   At a time when Prussia, Austria, and even Russia
were under contract to enforce the Continental system,
was it tolerable that his own brother, in all-important
Holland, should be throwing his ports open to the common foe?

This cause of trouble, also, was worrying Napoleon and
making it hard to maintain good humor.   And even this

was far from being all. Murat, his brother-in-law, was acting almost as badly as his brother. Murat, who was grand duke, wanted to be king, had coveted the crown of Poland, had claimed the Spanish throne, and in his disappointment, in both instances, had fallen into a rebellious mood.

Napoleon had given him Joseph's vacant throne in Naples; but it was rumored that he was still discontented, and had been holding communications with conspirators in Paris. And who were these conspirators? Talleyrand and Fouché, of course. These restless, overrated, and chronic traitors had been sagely conferring in Paris, as they had done previous to Marengo, for the purpose of agreeing upon a successor to Napoleon, in case he should be killed in battle or hopelessly defeated.

Nor was even this all : the funds had fallen, the treasury was drained, murmurs had begun to be heard in France against the expansion of the Empire ; conscriptions, which had been called for in advance of the legal time, began to be unpopular, desertions were frequent, and " the refractory " grew ever more numerous. The Spanish war was not relished. Generals ordered to Spain went, but went reluctantly. They carried no zeal, none of that buoyant confidence which is half the battle. Troops ordered there marched, but without enthusiasm. Compared with Italy and Germany Spain was a barren land. Against armed peasant bands no glory was to be won ; little booty could be expected. Even the Guard grumbled at such service. As Napoleon was holding a review at Valladolid just before quitting Spain, the murmurs in the ranks grew so loud that he lost control of himself, snatched the musket from one of the growlers, jerked the man out

of the line, threatened to have him shot, and then pushed
him back to his place while he sharply lectured the whole
troop.

Once more at Paris, Napoleon's courtiers grouped themselves around him with the same blandishments as before.
A few, a very few, might venture to speak frankly to him
and to tell him the truth, but the many had fallen into
the ways natural to all courts: they spoke, not to inform,
but to please. And foremost among those who came to
fawn and to flatter was " that cripple " whom Josephine
said she dreaded, Talleyrand.

Only dangerous to the weak, gifted with no constructive
talent whatever, incapable of sustained labor of any sort,
strong only in sudden emergencies, in the crises of political changes, Talleyrand was known to Napoleon like an
open book. Scorning him, rather than fearing him,
Napoleon's anger against him now was inflamed to the
highest pitch, not so much because of anything he had
done, as because of what his treachery implied. That so
keen-eyed a time-server as Talleyrand should begin to
plot, meant that confidence was shaken in the Napoleonic
power. That the funds should fall, conscripts dodge the
law, allies shirk their obligations, and domestic enemies
conspire, were but various symptoms of the same malady.

When Talleyrand appeared at the levee, Napoleon boiled
over. He began to rebuke the false courtier, began in a
moderate tone, but the more he talked the less he could
control himself. All the past perfidies of this most perfidious of men came to mind, and in bitter words were
hurled at Talleyrand's head. His venalities, his bribe-
takings, his betrayal of state secrets — they all swelled the
torrent of Napoleon's excoriation. " You base wretch, you

false-hearted minister. *You* pretend that you advised against the trial of the Duke d'Enghien when you urged it in writing; *you* pretend that you advised against the Spanish war when you urged me into it ! "

And at each sentence Napoleon advanced, face distorted with passion, hand raised in menace, while the guilty courtier slunk back step by step as the Emperor advanced, until he reached the wall. There he stood, with Napoleon's clenched hand in his face and Napoleon's blazing eyes threatening death, warning him, as he loved life, to say nothing, and let the storm pass.

When Talleyrand reached home, "he fell into a kind of fit," and the doctors had to be called in. Only a few days elapsed, however, before he was again at the levee, bending humbly before his master, and ready again with his fawnings and flatteries. Napoleon's anger had passed : he listened to the courtier's suave phrases with a smile of contemptuous indifference.

France had given Austria no cause for war. It was not even claimed that she had. Austria had causelessly provoked two wars already, had got whipped in both, had lost much territory, much money, much prestige. She now believed she was strong enough to win back all she had lost—hence she had mustered her forces and commenced the march into Bavaria. Her readiness to " begin again " had been accelerated by a bribe of $20,000,000 paid her by England.

Napoleon had massed troops at the point of danger, but had trusted to Berthier the direction of their movements. This officer had bungled matters so badly that the different divisions were widely scattered ; and the troops, conscious that something was wrong, were becoming

demoralized. Summoned by the signal telegraph, Napoleon made all haste to headquarters. He found the army
so ill-posted that he said to Berthier, "If I did not know
you to be true to me, I should suspect that you were a
traitor."

The Archduke Charles, commanding the Austrians, had
seen his advantage clearly, and was hastening to throw himself between the separate divisions of the French, to beat
them in detail. He commenced his campaign well, and it
appeared certain that he would crush the corps of Davoust
before it could be supported. But the Archduke was
almost superstitiously afraid of Napoleon, and no sooner
did he learn that the Emperor was now in command of the
French than the Austrians seemed paralyzed. Time was
given for Masséna and Davoust to support each other,
the one having been ordered to fall back while the other
moved forward. Calculating to the hour when these two
wings could support the centre, the great soldier fell
upon his enemy. The risk was great ; for should his two
lieutenants fail to come up, all would be lost. But
Davoust and Masséna were not Grouchys : they came, and
the campaign was saved. Never was Napoleon greater in
plan and execution than in 1809 ; not even in the Italian
campaign did he work harder. For a week he was almost
constantly in the saddle, never having time to undress. But
in that week he wrought utter confusion among his enemies,
and saved his empire. At Abensberg, at Landshut, at Eckmühl, at Ratisbonne, he struck the Austrians blow after
blow, and shattered their army, killing and wounding thirty
thousand men, capturing an equal number, and taking vast
spoil in guns, ammunition, stores, war material of all sorts.
The Archduke drew off his broken army on Bohemia ;

Napoleon marched upon Vienna, which fell May 12, 1809. The royal family fled to Hungary; the French Emperor, quartered at the palace of Schönbrunn, made preparations to cross the Danube.   There were no bridges this time for Lannes and Murat to win by stratagem; the river rolled broad and deep between French and Austrians; bridges would have to be built, and the French put across in face of an army ready to dispute the passage.

Had not victory declared for Napoleon, promptly and emphatically at the opening of the campaign, his ruin would have come in 1809 as it did in 1814.   The national spirit was declaring against him in Germany, as it had done in Spain.   Prussia was honeycombed with patriotic secret societies, pledged against him; and in anticipation of Austrian success, the young Duke of Brunswick and Colonel Schill had raised the standard of revolt.   The decisive victory of the French at Eckmühl alone prevented this abortive effort at a national uprising from being a success.   In the Tyrol, also, the people, intensely Catholic and opposed to the reforms Bavaria had introduced, rose against the Napoleonic power, and failed only because the French had been so prompt in scattering the strength of Austria.

In the crisis, Napoleon's ally, Russia, had shown little zeal.   She sent a very small army where she had promised a large one; and a general of their army wrote to the Austrian commander that he hoped they would soon be acting in concert.   Napoleon forwarded this letter to Alexander, who contented himself with the recall of the writer. But for the heroic conduct of Poniatowski and the Poles, it seems that the Austrian army would have succeeded in wresting the Grand Duchy of Warsaw from Saxony.

But Napoleon's triumphs at the opening of the campaign changed the aspect of affairs all around. Austrian armies had to be called in from Warsaw, from Italy, from Bohemia, to concentrate and oppose Napoleon on the Danube.

Choosing a position below Vienna, where the large island of Lobau divides the stream into two unequal channels, the French threw bridges across, and on May 20 commenced passing over, taking possession of the villages of Aspern and Essling, almost without opposition. Next day the Archduke Charles made a furious attack, first on Aspern, then on Essling also. The struggle was very bloody. Only a portion of the French had passed the river; the Austrians outnumbered them heavily; and, realizing this vast advantage, pushed it with splendid energy. Aspern was taken and retaken time after time; and when night put an end to the carnage, the French held only a portion of the smouldering ruins. Next day the battle was renewed, the French army still cut in two by the Danube. The corps of Davoust had not passed, and the Austrians were doing their utmost to break the bridges, which a sudden rise in the river already threatened to carry away.

So strong had been the efforts of the enemy to carry Aspern on their right, that Napoleon guessed they had weakened their centre too much. He therefore massed heavy columns against it, and began to drive it back. At this moment came the dreaded message, — " The bridges are gone ! "

He might have pressed on and beaten his foe, but Napoleon thought the risk too great. His columns halted, their fire slackened, and the orders to retire were given.

The wondering Austrians took fresh courage, and followed the retiring French with terrible effect. Masséna must hold Aspern, Lannes Essling, until the Emperor could get the army back to the island of Lobau. Aspern was everything; it must be held at all hazards.

"Hold your position! It is a question of saving the army — the bridges are gone!" So ran the despatch, and the grim soldier who held Genoa while Napoleon planned Marengo, now held Aspern while his Emperor prepared for Wagram.

Poor Lannes! Brave, unselfish, plain-spoken, leonine Lannes! Here his long march was to end. The same year that Madame Letitia in Corsica had begun to rock the cradle of Napoleon, the wife of an humble dyer in Gascony had begun to nurse the babe who became the Roland of Bonaparte's army. He had little education, no influential friends; but when the Revolution began to sound its tocsin and beat its drum, the Gascon lad went forth to the wars. From 1791, when he volunteered as grenadier, he had served without pause and with unsurpassed courage. Augereau made him colonel for bravery in the Pyrenees; and Napoleon made him general for brilliant service in Italy. He followed his chief to Egypt, and was shot through the neck at Acre. On the famous Sunday of Brumaire he aided in Napoleon's seizure of supreme power, and at Montebello fought the prelude to Marengo. He had loved Caroline Bonaparte, whom Murat won; and had Lannes instead of Murat been the imperial brother-in-law, much disaster might have been averted. Raised in rank, made marshal of the Empire, and Duke of Montebello, he was the same intrepid, ever growing, ever loyal soldier. Great at Austerlitz, great at Jena, great at Friedland, he was greater yet at Saragossa where he overcame a resistance which challenged the wonder of the world.

From that ruined city in Spain he had hastened to Germany, and had been again the right hand of the great captain who so well knew his worth. Better courtiers there were than Lannes, gallants who better graced a ballroom, flatterers who could better please the ear. But who of all the brave men of France could walk the battle-field with surer, steadier step than he?

Who at heart was more loyal to the chief — who so ready to forsake ease and comfort and go forth at the call of the chief into rain or snow, heat or cold, exhausting march or desperate battle? In all the long record of French heroism, who had done deeds more lionlike than Lannes?

Who was first over the bridge at Lodi, outstripping Napoleon and all, and slaying six Austrians with his own hand? Who led the vanguard across the frozen Alps and held the rout at Marengo till Desaix could come? Who, in this last campaign, had rallied the grenadiers beneath the blazing walls of Ratisbonne, seized a scaling ladder, when the bravest held back, and had rushed toward the battlements under a withering fire, shouting to his halting men, "I'll show you that I've not forgotten I was once a grenadier!" Who but Lannes had electrified these troops by his fearless example, and had carried them over the walls?

At Essling he had been in the thick of the fight, holding his ground with old-time grip. The slaughter had been immense, and the sight of the mangled body of General Pouzet, shot down at his side, had affected him painfully.

Sick of the hideous spectacle, he had gone a little to one side, and had seated himself on the embankment of a trench.

A quarter of an hour later, four soldiers, laboriously carrying in a cloak a dead officer whose face could not be seen, stopped in front of Lannes. The cloak fell open, and he recognized Pouzet. "Oh!" he cried, "is this terrible sight going to pursue me everywhere?" Getting up, he went and sat down at the edge of another ditch, his hand over his eyes, and his legs crossed. As he sat there a three-pounder shot struck him just where his legs crossed. The knee-pan of one was smashed, and the back sinews of the other torn. General Marbot ran to him; he tried to rise, but could not. He was borne back to the bridge, and one of his limbs amputated. Hardly was the operation over when Napoleon came up. "The interview," says Marbot, from whose *Memoirs* this account is literally taken, "was most touching. The Emperor, kneeling beside the stretcher, wept as he embraced the marshal, whose blood soon stained the Emperor's white kerseymere waistcoat."

"You will live, my friend, you will live!" cried the Emperor, pressing the hand of Lannes. "I trust I may, if I can still be of service to France and to your Majesty."

The weather was terribly hot, and fever set in with Lannes; on May 30th he died. In spite of the cares and dangers of his position, Napoleon had found time to visit the wounded man every day. A few moments after daybreak on the 30th, the Emperor came as usual, when Marbot met him and told him of the sad event. The amputated limb had mortified, and the stench was so strong that Marbot warned Napoleon against going in.

Pushing Marbot aside, the Emperor advanced to the dead body, embraced it, wept over it, remained more than an hour, and only left when Berthier reminded him that officers were waiting for orders.

"What a loss for France and for me!" Well may Napoleon have grieved and wept: here was a gap in his line that could never be filled. Said the Emperor at St. Helena, "I found him a pygmy; I lost him a giant."

The bridges connecting the island of Lobau with the bank of the Danube upon which the army had been fighting were not broken : hence the troops could be led back to the island. Once there, the position could be fortified and held, until the Vienna arm of the river could be rebridged.

This was done. Several weeks were spent in preparations, reënforcements brought up, larger, better bridges built, and all made ready for another attempt to cross.

The Archduke Charles, believing that Napoleon would direct his march upon Aspern and Essling, as before, calmly waited, confident that he could beat the French as before. On the night of July 4, 1809, while a terrible thunderstorm was raging, Napoleon began his attack upon the Austrian position at Essling and Aspern. This was a feint to hide his purpose of crossing at another place, in front of Enzersdorf.

While the Archduke's attention was fixed on the two villages first named, the French made a dash at Enzersdorf, and took it. Several bridges, ready-made, had been thrown across the river here, and Napoleon's army had passed almost before the Austrian knew what he was

about. Then the Archduke drew back into the vast
plain of the Marchfeld, and three hundred thousand
men lined up for the great battle of Wagram. From the
roofs and ramparts of Vienna, excited thousands gazed
upon that vast wheat field, yellow in the summer sun,
where the harvester Death was to reap where humble
peasants had sown.

For two days the tremendous struggle lasted. The
Austrians never fought better. In sight of fathers and
sons, of wives, daughters, sisters, sweethearts, who would
not fight well for home and native land? What did
the Austrian soldier know of the cause of the war? He
knew as much as his masters chose to tell him; and in
his heart he believed the French to be aggressors, tyrants, marauders, come to loot and ruin and enslave.

So they stood amid the burning wheat in the golden
grain fields, beneath the torrid sun, and fought as Napoleon had never seen them fight — fought as men fight
only when their souls are in it. And far off on the
housetops, steeples, and battlements of old Vienna were
straining eyes, beating hearts, hungry prayers, and the
wild hope that these marauders from France would be
scattered as the Turks had been scattered in that dread
time long ago.

But in those olden days Christians could hear the cry
of Christians, could fly to the relief of Christians. What
bannered host was that which had burst like a storm upon
the Moslem rear, scattering infidels like so much dust,
bringing salvation to the beleaguered town? Who but the
Polanders and John Sobieski had smitten the Turk and
sent the crescent backward in flight before the cross?
That was many and many a year ago. There would be

no "Poland to the rescue!" this time. Poland had been
devoured — by Moslems? No; by Christians. And at
the feast Austria had sat, greedily eating her share.

The shells set fire to the wheat; the smoke and the
flame from the burning grain mingled with the smoke and
flame of batteries. Troops moving to the charge were
halted or turned from their course; the wounded fell in
the midst of the blazing stubble, and were burnt to death
or suffocated.

Nothing could withstand the French. The Austrian
leader outclassed by his antagonist, the long trial of
strength yielded victory at length to the better soldier.
The efforts made on the wings had weakened the Archduke's centre. Masséna, though terribly shaken, was
able to hold the right, while Napoleon massed all his
available force to hurl it upon the Austrian centre.
But he must wait. Nothing could be done until Davoust
on the enemy's left had succeeded. Motionless as a
rock, Napoleon kept his eyes riveted on Neusiedel, a
village "which lies high and is surmounted by a tall
tower visible from all parts of the field." Davoust must
fling the Austrians back behind this village before the
attack on the centre could be made. "At last we suddenly saw the smoke of Davoust's guns beyond the tower."
Now the enemy's left was beaten. "Quick! quick!"
cried the Emperor to Aide-de-camp Marbot, who had come
from Masséna to ask instructions. "Tell Masséna to fall
upon whatever is in front of him, and the battle is won!"
All along the line flashed similar orders, while Macdonald, a hundred cannon blazing along his front, made
the famous charge which broke the Austrian centre.

It was a great fight, a great victory, and great were its

results.   Austria sued for peace, and Napoleon, ready as
he ever was to end a war, granted her terms as generous
as she had any right to expect.   She lost territory, and
had to pay an indemnity; but out of wreck which she
herself had made, her empire came forth practically intact.

As indemnity, she was asked to pay $20,000,000.   This
was the amount of the bribe she had taken from England
to begin the war.

An indemnity of $20,000,000!   How trivial this amount
when compared to the *one thousand millions* which Bismarck levied upon France.   How modest it looks beside
the $330,000,000 which China had to pay to Christian
missionaries and their supporting nations for the riots of
the year 1900 l

CHAPTER XXXIV

AFTER the French defeat at Aspern (May 22, 1809), and while they were shut up in the island of Lobau, it had seemed that Napoleon's position was almost desperate. The Tyrolese were in revolt, and had expelled the French and Bavarians; the young Duke of Brunswick had invaded Saxony and driven Napoleon's vassal king from his capital. Popular insurrections broke out in Würtemberg and Westphalia; England was holding her ground in Portugal, and was preparing an armament to fall upon the Dutch coast. Prussian statesmen, officers, preachers, poets, and patriots were clamoring for war. In this anxious crisis the courage and confidence of Napoleon were perfect. To beat the Austrians in his front was the one thing he must do. Succeeding in that, resistance elsewhere would disappear. Failing in that, all was lost. Thus Napoleon had reasoned, and he had judged rightly. After Wagram his peril passed. Austria, after having pledged faith to the Tyrolese, coldly deserted them, and they were crushed. Brunswick's effort failed as Schill's had failed; popular insurrections were stamped out; Prussia dared not move; and England's "Walcheren expedition" against Flushing and Antwerp ended in utter failure and heavy loss. Everywhere Napoleon's Empire stood the test: Eugène beat the Austrians in

Italy; and Wellington, after defeating Victor at Talavera, was driven back into Portugal by Soult. Out of the storm which had threatened his very existence, Napoleon came forth with frontiers extended to the borders of Turkey, cutting off Austria from the sea — an empire stretching in unbroken line from Bosnia to the straits of Calais.

Never had Napoleon's power seemed so great, nor his court so splendid. His vassal kings came to Paris with brilliant retinues, the kings of Saxony, Bavaria, Westphalia, Würtemberg, and Naples, the Viceroy of Italy, the Queen of Holland, besides princes and dukes by the dozen. Paris had become the capital of Continental Europe, and from Paris went forth the law to eighty million people. All Frenchmen realized the grandeur of this huge empire; but many a wise Frenchman was oppressed by anxieties. What if the Emperor should suddenly die? Would the succession go quietly to his brothers, or would the mighty fabric fall to pieces? All this power, all this splendor, hung as by a single hair upon the life of Napoleon; and there were others besides Talleyrand and Fouché who speculated upon what should be done if the Emperor should fall in battle. When the bullet struck his toe at Ratisbonne, the troops broke ranks and crowded toward him in their breathless eagerness to know whether he were seriously hurt; and the far-seeing said, "Suppose the ball had struck two feet higher!" When it became known that a young German fanatic, Staps, bent on assassinating the Emperor, had almost reached him with his knife when stopped, the same uneasy feeling prevailed. Too much depended on this one life. The Emperor had no bodily heir; by Josephine he would never have one;

the favorite nephew, Hortense's son, the little Napoleon,
might have been adopted, but he died of croup in Holland.

His power in the north being now secure, it was expected
that Napoleon would take charge of the war in the south,
and end it.   He could easily have done so.   England had
less than thirty thousand troops there, and the native soldiers, Spaniards and Portuguese, could not have stood
against French veterans led by the greatest soldiers of
all time.   Besides, he could have crushed resistance by
the mere weight of numbers.   Why did he never return
to Spain?   Joseph was blundering as stupidly as mortal
could; the French commanders were not acting in concert, but were pulling against each other; things were
going as badly as the English could reasonably expect;
and nowhere in the Empire was its Emperor needed worse
than here.   But Napoleon, once so quick to rush to the
point of danger, let the " Spanish ulcer " run, year in and
year out, with an apathy for which it is impossible to
account.   Either he had grown fonder of his personal
ease, or the dreary kind of warfare necessary to reduce a
national uprising did not appeal to his imagination, or he
feared that in his absence the north might again give
trouble, or he took an imperial pride in seeming to say
to the world that the insurrection in the south was too
trifling a matter for his personal attention and could be
left to his lieutenants.

Whatever the motive, he astonished his enemies no less
than his friends by failing to follow up Wagram with the
complete conquest of the peninsula.   Three hundred thousand French soldiers in Spain propped feeble Joseph on

his throne; but they were never able to put down resistance or expel the English.

Another serious matter which might have been settled at this time was his quarrel with the Pope.

The Concordat had accomplished great results for both contracting parties, and at first both were highly satisfied. Napoleon complacently rubbed his hands and declared, " With my soldiers, my prefects, and my priests I can do as I like."

But, after all, the Concordat was a compromise. Neither party got quite what was wanted. Napoleon expected that there would result a clergy wholly dependent upon his will ; a Pope who would be a sort of clerical lieutenant obeying imperial orders, content to move as a lesser light in the Napoleonic system. The Pope, on the other hand, eagerly expected a restoration, gradually, of the former spiritual prestige of the Church. When Napoleon was seen to attend Mass, and kneel for blessing or prayer, clerical fancy readily pictured the return of the good old times when pious Bourbon kings and their official mistresses had fallen on their knees at the feet of Jesuit confessors, and allowed the reins of government to be pulled by the Church. Especially did the Pope look for the restoration of his full temporal power, the return of the lost legations in Italy.

Both parties found themselves in grievous error. Napoleon not only believed he had done quite enough for the Church, but was inclined to think he had done too much. At any rate, he flatly declined to do more. He would not put priests in charge of the state schools ; he would not restore the legations. He was ready to lavish respectful attentions upon the head of the Church, ready to aid him in restoring public worship, ready to fill his coffers with cash ; but in the Concordat, the solemn contract already agreed on, he would make no change.

So the Pope had left Paris after the coronation in ill-humor. He refused to crown Napoleon at Milan ; refused to annul Jerome's marriage ; refused to recognize Joseph Bonaparte as King of Naples ; refused to close his ports to English commerce. Professing neutrality, he became as much the enemy of France as he had been when an avowed member of the European league against the Revolution. Enemies of Napoleon flocked to Rome and found friendly welcome there. Fugitives from French justice took refuge under papal immunity, and were protected. The Roman court, as in the time of the Revolution, became a nucleus of anti-French sentiment and intrigue. Papal animosity to the French did not cool its ire when it saw him do in Spain what he had wished to do in Italy — abolish the Inquisition. Napoleon complained, remonstrated, threatened — all to no purpose. Meekly obstinate, piously implacable, the Pope refused to come to terms, using God's name, of course, as a sanction to his own line of conduct.

During the campaign of 1809 Napoleon proclaimed the abolition of the temporal power of the Pope, and the papal territories were incorporated in the kingdom of Italy. The Pope's spiritual powers were not challenged : his revenues were largely increased. The Pope protested, as usual, that the temporal power, lands, cities, rich revenues, were the patrimony of St. Peter, of God, and that he, the Pope, had no right to give them up. Napoleon, in effect, replied that what a French emperor had given, a French emperor could take away ; and that it ill became the successor of Peter and the vicar of the homeless, moneyless Christ to be making such eternal clamor about money, wealth, lands, and earthly power and splendor. The situation at Rome, where French authorities and papal authorities were in conflict, became so embarrassing that the Pope was finally arrested, carried to Savona, and lodged in a palace there.   Later, he was transferred to the magnificent château of Fontainebleau in France, where he was luxuriously lodged and treated as a prince.

This complete rupture between Napoleon and the Church might never have been more than an annoyance, a crab nibbling at the toe of Hercules, had Napoleon continued fortunate.   But when disasters thickened, and his powers began to totter, the papal legions were not the weakest of those who assaulted his wavering lines.

Well had it been for France had Napoleon, in 1810, given personal attention to the Spanish war ; equally well had he come to some terms with the Pope, who had excommunicated him.   The longer each trouble was neglected, the more difficult its treatment became.

Napoleon would not go to Spain, he would not settle his differences with the Pope ; but he made up his mind to bring to an issue another long-deferred and vitally important matter — that of divorcing Josephine.

The Emperor must have an heir, the question of succession must not be left open longer : political necessity was inexorable : ambition would tolerate no obstacle.

Great as a man may become, he is human after all; and Napoleon flinched from saying the fateful word to Josephine.   From time to time he shrank from the pitiful task, and the way in which he led up to it is full of the pathos which sometimes lies in small things. Whenever Napoleon was at home, it was the custom for a page to bring in coffee for the Emperor after dinner. Every day Josephine herself would take the tray, pour the coffee, sweeten it, cool it, taste it, and hand it to Napoleon. Years had come and gone, and the little domestic custom had become as fixed as the relation of man and wife.

At length came the day of days for them both, the dismal evening upon which Napoleon had resolved to speak. He was gloomy and sad; she was red-eyed with weeping, wretched, waiting the word she dreaded and expected. Dinner was served, but neither ate, neither spoke. The Emperor rose from the table, she followed "with slow steps, her handkerchief over her mouth, as if to stifle her sobs." The page came with the coffee, offering the tray to the Empress, as he had always done. But Napoleon, looking steadily at Josephine, took the tray, poured the coffee, sweetened it, and drank; and Josephine knew that they had reached the parting of the ways. The tray was handed back to the page, the attendants withdrew at a sign from the master, Napoleon closed the door, and then with face as cold and sad as death he spoke of the divorce.

Constant, the valet, dreading "some terrible event," had sat down outside by the door. He heard shrieks, and rushed forward. The Emperor opened the door, the Empress was on the floor, "weeping and crying enough to break one's heart." They lifted her and bore her to her room, Napoleon assisting. There were tears in his eyes, and his voice was broken and trembling. It was a bitter night to them both, and Napoleon visited her room several times to inquire after her condition.

He did not sleep; he did not utter a word to his attendants. "I have never seen him," writes Constant, "in such affliction."

But his resolution stood, and on December 16, 1809, the divorce was formally pronounced. There was a final heart-breaking interview in Napoleon's bedchamber, to which the stricken wife had come to say good-by; there were sobs and tears and tender, regretful words; then Josephine, weeping, went back to her room, leaving Napoleon "silent as the grave, and so buried in his bed that it was impossible for one to see his face."

The ex-Empress's humiliation was softened in every manner possible. She was regally endowed with pensions and estates; she was treated with the most delicate respect; the friendship between herself and Napoleon remained uninterrupted; he delighted to do her honor; and her place in the Empire remained one of dignity and grandeur. Once the Emperor, returning from the chase with the kings of Bavaria, Baden, and Würtemberg, stopped at Malmaison to pay the ex-Empress a visit, and spent an hour in the château with her while the three little kings waited and lunched at her gate.

Napoleon's first thought was to wed a sister of the Czar of Russia, and proposals to that effect were made. The mother of the princess, however, was bitterly opposed to Napoleon, and alleged that her daughter was too young. Alexander, greatly embarrassed, asked for time. To the impatient Emperor of the French this evasion seemed to cover a refusal, and he would not grant the delay. In the meantime the Austrian Cabinet, dreading

the increased strength which such a marriage would give
to the Franco-Russian alliance, let it be known to Napoleon
that if he asked for the daughter of the Emperor Francis,
she would be promptly delivered.   Irritated by the hesitation of the Romanoffs, and flattered by the advances of the
Hapsburgs, Napoleon put his foot upon the "abyss covered with flowers."   On March 11, 1810, he was married
by proxy to Maria Louisa in Vienna, and the bride set
out at once for Paris.   "Take as your standpoint that
children are wanted," Napoleon had frankly written to
his negotiator at St. Petersburg : and the Austrian princess understood the situation thoroughly.   After a triumphal progress through the provinces of the Empire, she
reached the French frontier, was formally received, her
clothing all changed, her Austrian attendants relieved,
and France, taking her precious person in custody, re-
clothed her, surrounded her with a fresh lot of attendants,
and hastened with her in the direction of Compiègne,
where by appointment she was to meet her imperial
spouse.   Napoleon had himself dictated, to the minutest
detail, every movement of the bridal party, and he awaited
its coming with the utmost impatience, "cursing the ceremonial and the fêtes which delayed the arrival of his
young bride."

At length when Maria was within ten leagues of Soissons, Napoleon broke from all restraint.

At the top of his voice he shouted to his valet : "Heigho,
Constant !   Order a carriage without livery, and come
and dress me ! "

He bathed, he perfumed, he dressed, laughing all the
time like a boy at the effect which the surprise he was
planning would produce on his bride.   Over his uniform

he drew the gray overcoat he had worn at Wagram; and calling Murat to go with him, he secretly left the park of Compiègne, entered the plain carriage, and dashed along the road beyond Soissons. The rain was pouring down when he and Murat reached Courcelles, where they left the carriage and stood in the porch of the church for the bridal train to come up. Signing to the postilions to stop, Napoleon had intended to reach Maria Louisa unannounced; but the equerry, recognizing him, let down the step and called out, " His Majesty ! "

" Didn't you see that I signed you to be silent ? " exclaimed Napoleon, in a pet. But his ill-humor vanished at once, he hastened into the carriage, and flung his arms around the neck of his bride, who, nicely tutored, was all graceful submission, and who, looking from his face to his portrait which she held in her hand, remembered to say, " Your portrait does not flatter you."

Napoleon was in ecstasies. He was a boy again, amorous, rapturous, seeing everything with the eyes of a lover. Soissons had prepared a magnificent reception and banquet, but Napoleon could not think of tarrying. He must hasten on to Compiègne with the blushing Maria that very night. " He made love like a hussar ! " some have sneered. So he did, and most men who are not invalids or frigid decadents make love like hussars. Furthermore, most women who are young, healthy, and sane, have a stealthy preference for the hussar style of love-making.

Etiquette had prepared a bed for Maria at the Chancellor's, and one for Napoleon at the palace. Etiquette insisted that this separation was decorous, was most essential, was demanded by precedent and custom. " Not so," maintained Napoleon; "Henry IV. breached the custom, and so will I."

Had not the marriage already taken place in Vienna? If that ceremony, solemnized by the Archbishop of Vienna was valid, were not Napoleon and Maria man and wife? Why, then, separate apartments? He decided that a husband's rights were already his, and Maria made no strenuous objection, — so well had she been tutored in Vienna. Read what the imperial *valet-de-chambre*, Constant, writes : —

" The next morning at his toilet the Emperor asked me if any one had noticed his change of the programme." Constant lied, like a good servant, and "I told him, no." At that moment entered one of the Emperor's intimates who was unmarried. Pinching his ears, his Majesty said to him: " Marry a German, my dear fellow. They are the best women in the world : gentle, good, artless and as fresh as roses." And Constant states that Napoleon " was charmingly gay all the remainder of the day."

With imperial pomp the civil and religious marriage was solemnized at St. Cloud and Paris, April 1 and 2, 1810. The illuminations, the processions, the festivities, were gorgeous beyond description. After these were ended, there was a grand tour of the provinces by the imperial couple. Returning to Paris, the Austrian ambassador, Prince Schwarzenberg, tendered them the magnificent fête during which the tapestries in the vast temporary ballroom caught on fire, the building burned to the ground, and some of the revellers met fiery death.

As to Maria Louisa it may be said, once for all, that she was a commonplace woman, with no talent, no charac-

MARIA LOUISA

From the portrait by Gérard in the Louvre

ter, no graces of manner, and no beauty. She was strong, healthy, physically fresh and buxom, therefore admirably suited to Napoleon's immediate purpose. She was never a companion to him, never had any influence over him, never had any love for him, never understood or appreciated him. Dull, indolent, sensual, capable of no warm attachment, she simply yielded to her father's policy, married where she was told to marry, obeyed Napoleon as she was told to obey him, accepted his caresses, ate four or five times per day, bore him a child, pleaded her health against the bearing of more, gave herself little concern about his reverses, left him when her father called for her to leave him, took up with another man whom her father selected, lived with him in much contentment, and bore him several children.

Increasingly heavy became to Napoleon the burden of his family. Joseph in Spain required huge armies and huge subsidies to uphold him there, and his correspondence with his brother was one long, lugubrious howl for "more." Jerome's reckless dissipations and extravagance in Westphalia scandalized Germany, bringing reproach upon the Empire. Lucien contributed his share of mischief by encouraging the ill-temper of the Pope. Pauline, Caroline, Elisa were so many thorns in the flesh, so many annoyances more or less acute. Brother-in-law Murat, by his pride and boasting and complaints, disgusted friends of the Emperor, arousing jealousies among old comrades who had not been made kings. Mother Letitia, like the mother of Washington, complained that the illustrious son had not done enough for the author of his being. Uncle

Fesch, now a cardinal, had absorbed all the essence of his clerical order, and maddened his nephew by opposition in the quarrel with Rome.

And to cap a climax and advertise family feuds to the world, Louis Bonaparte vacated the throne of Holland, left the country privately, and went, almost as a fugitive, to " drink the waters " at Teplitz in Bohemia. For some days it was not even known what had become of him.

The Emperor's grief, anger, and mortification were extreme. Stunned by the blow dealt him by his brother, he said in broken voice : " To think that Louis should make me this return ! When I was a poor lieutenant of artillery, I divided my slender pay with him, fed him, taught him as though he were my son." And this cross-grained, thankless Louis had brought shame upon Emperor and Empire! Why? Because the brother who had put the sceptre in his hand wished him to rule Holland as a province of the Empire, in line with the policy of the Empire, sharing all the benefits of the Empire, and sharing likewise its burdens ! Because Napoleon would not consent that Holland should violate the Continental system, and become practically the ally of England in the great struggle for national supremacy, Louis had dropped the crown and gone away to drink mineral water in Bohemia.

A very aggravating mortal must have been this Louis, on general principles. Yielding to his brother's influence, he had wedded Hortense, the daughter of Josephine. There was no love prior to this marriage, and none afterward. Despite Napoleon's repeated, patient efforts, the two could never harmonize. With or without reason, Louis suspected the virtue of his wife. Ugly rumor reported that the first child of Hortense was not begotten by Louis, but by Napoleon. The younger brother may not have believed the story, but the fondness of the childless elder brother for the son of the younger, attracted attention and excited remark. The child was a promising boy; he was named after his uncle Napoleon, and he was devotedly fond of this uncle. The little fellow would come into Napoleon's room, put on the Emperor's hat, catch up his sword, put the belt over his shoulders, and, whistling a military air, go marching about in military style, with the sword dragging along on the floor. And Napoleon would be thrown into ecstasy, and would cry out, rubbing his hands: "Look at him! See the pretty picture!"

His love for the boy growing with the boy's growth, Napoleon had offered to make him King of Italy, preparatory, doubtless, to adopting him as heir to the Empire. Louis would not hear of it. Put his son above *him?* Give his child a throne, when he himself had none? Never in the world! So he objected flatly, saying to his brother with unparalleled impudence, "Such a favor from you to this child would revive the rumors that you are his father."

Is it any wonder that Napoleon's temper escaped control, and that he caught Louis about the body and flung him out at the door?

The little Napoleon had died, Hortense had separated from her impossible spouse, and was going a rapid pace of her own, with a certain Duc de Flahaut, famous for his shapely legs, — so much so that they wrung from the Emperor an exclamation on the subject of Flahaut and "his eternal legs." Holland's throne was vacant: what was Napoleon to do? Give it to some one else who

would be as ungrateful as Louis had been? Abandon
it entirely, and see England get a foothold there?

To escape the dilemma, Holland was annexed to the
Empire (July, 1810).

The royal line of Sweden was about to become extinct.
It became necessary to provide for the succession. The
Swedes decided to choose a Crown Prince from among
the illustrious Frenchmen who stood around Napoleon's
throne. They wished to win Napoleon's good-will and
protection by selecting one of his favorites, and they were
made to believe that they could not please him better than
by the choice of Bernadotte.

Were not this a matter so gravely serious, it would be
comical to the last degree. The marshal whom Napoleon
most detested and distrusted was Bernadotte. The marshal who most envied the Emperor, most hated him, most
longed to betray him, was Bernadotte. He had plotted
against his chief during the Consulate, and escaped court-
martial because he and Joseph Bonaparte had married
sisters. He had left Davoust in the lurch at Auerstadt,
imperilled the army, coldly leaving thirty thousand
French to combat sixty thousand Prussians, without lifting a hand to help the French. Again he had escaped ;
he was a member of the Bonaparte family.

At Wagram his conduct had been so darkly suspicious,
his proclamation claiming a victory where he had failed
miserably to do his duty, had been so insolent, that
Napoleon ordered him home in disgrace. But again
family influence prevailed, and he was made Governor of
Rome.

The Swedes had not kept the run of these events, and when Bernadotte's agents plied them with the argument that he was a member of the Bonaparte family, and a favorite with the Emperor, there were none to deny. Napoleon knew what was going on. He alone could have set the Swedes right, and nipped the intrigue in the bud. Why did he not do so? Absolutely no satisfactory answer can be given. A word from him would have made some other man Prince Royal of Sweden, but he would not speak. With apathetic scorn he looked on while Bernadotte worked the wires, feeling all the while that Bernadotte's success would be a misfortune to France. He not only refused to interfere, not only refused to correct the false representations upon which the Swedes acted, but gave his formal consent when it was asked, and furnished Bernadotte with $400,000 to equip himself in a suitable way in setting out to take possession of his new dignity.

Some months after Napoleon's second marriage, he and the Empress stood sponsors at the baptism of several infants of his great officers. When the baptismal ceremony had been finished, the Emperor turned to some of his intimate friends and said rubbing his hands together as he did when well pleased, " Before long, gentlemen, I hope we shall have another baby to baptize."

This joyful intelligence gradually spreading, the whole French nation began to look forward with a feeling of hope and satisfaction to the birth of Napoleon's heir.

On March 19, 1811, the Empress felt the first pains, and " the palace was in a flutter." Next morning early the crisis came. Napoleon sprang out of his bath, and covered with a dressing-gown hastened to his wife's room, saying to the excited doctor in charge, "Come, now, Dubois, don't lose your head." He embraced the suffering Empress tenderly, but, unable to endure the sight of her anguish, went to another room, where he stood, pale and trembling, awaiting the event. When the physician reported that an operation might be necessary, and that one or the other, mother or child, might have to be sacrificed Napoleon answered, without hesitation, "Save the mother, it is her right."

To calm them, he said : "Forget that you are operating upon an Empress. Treat her as though she were some shopkeeper's wife."

At length the cruel ordeal was over, the child safely delivered, and the mother relieved. The Emperor sprang to her couch and covered her with caresses. He was overwhelmed with joy; his face shone with delight. "Well, Constant, we have a big boy ! " he cried to his valet ; and to all others as he met them he continued to repeat rapturously, "We have a big boy ! " Very, very human was this "Corsican ogre," Napoleon Bonaparte.

If words and looks go for evidence, the warrior of Austerlitz, the giver of crowns and kingdoms, was never so happy as when he took his son in his arms, kissed it tenderly, and holding it toward his courtiers, said proudly, "Gentlemen, the King of Rome ! "

All Paris listened, eagerly attentive, to the great bells of Notre Dame ; steeple answered steeple, until every church had joined in the chorus. All Paris hearkened to the cannon, counting report after report : for if the child were a girl, the shots would stop at twenty-one ; if a boy, there would be one hundred. At the sound of the twenty-second gun there burst out a universal shout of joy and congratulation. " Hats flew up into the air, people ran to meet entire strangers, and with mutual embraces shouted, *Long live the Emperor!* Old soldiers shed tears of joy."

Behind a curtain at the window of the palace stood Napoleon, looking out upon this display of enthusiastic gladness. " His eyes swam with tears, and he came in that condition to kiss his son."

Never were national rejoicings greater at the birth of an heir to the throne. Cities, towns, private dwellings, illuminated not only in France, but throughout the Empire. Couriers rode with the news to foreign courts. Congratulations poured into the Tuileries from the four quarters of the earth. The Emperor seemed to be " walking in the midst of a delicious dream." He was the mightiest monarch of earth ; his wife " a daughter of the Cæsars " ; his son, his long-yearned-for son, had come, was strong and fair, — the " King of Rome ! " Napoleon's imagination was aflame ; human grandeur he had pushed to its limit.

His memory may have swept back to far-off Corsica, and to that day of 1769 when his mother had brought him into the world, lying on the floor " upon a wretched rug." From that dim period to this, what a march onward !

If Napoleon had been kind and indulgent to the barren Josephine, what was his tenderness to the fruitful Maria ! He almost smothered her with caresses, and almost, if not quite, wearied her with attentions. As to his boy, nothing could have been more touching than his boundless pride in him, his infinite patience with him, his intense paternal fondness for him.

Nothing would satisfy the Emperor but that Josephine must see his boy. Maria must not know; Maria being jealous of the ex-Empress. One day Napoleon had his child carried privately out to Bagatelle. Josephine was there. The little King of Rome was presented to her. Was she envious and jealous? Not so. She took the child in her arms, pressed it, kissed it, wept over it, prattled "baby talk" to it, fondling it with "unutterable tenderness" as though it were her own. Poor Josephine! Sternly truthful historians have told us about the infidelities and the want of honesty and scruple. With pain and sorrow we must tell the story of these as it is told to us; but let us turn the picture as quickly as we may, and look upon the other side — for there is another and a brighter.

It was true womanhood at its best when the barren, discarded wife continued to love the husband who had put her away; who loved and fondled the offspring of the other marriage with a greater tenderness than the child's own mother ever showed it; who remained faithful to Napoleon in the dark days when the second wife was false; who grieved brokenly over his fall, and wished to share his exile.

Evermore will this record speak for Josephine; evermore will it speak for Napoleon also.

Constant relates: "One day when Bonaparte came back very much fatigued from hunting, he sent to ask Maria Louisa to come and see him. She came. The Emperor took her in his arms and gave her a hearty kiss on the cheek. Maria took her handkerchief and wiped it off.

" ' Well, Louise,' said the Emperor, ' so I disgust thee ? '

" ' No,' replied the Empress, ' I have a habit of wiping myself like that.   I do the same with the King of Rome.' The Emperor seemed dissatisfied."

A wife and mother wiping off the kisses of husband and child reveals her own character so fully by the act that comment is unnecessary.

CHAPTER XXXV

"MY taskmaster has no bowels; it is the nature of things." This remark, made by Napoleon long prior to the divorce, was now to be verified with results calamitous to Europe and to himself. The war of 1812 was one for which he had no enthusiasm, and into which he was drawn by almost irresistible circumstances. To Metternich he said, "I shall have war with Russia on grounds which lie beyond human possibilities, because they are rooted in the case itself."

The French Emperor felt himself committed to his Continental system. His pride, his pledge, his self-preservation, were at stake. As long as England could make war upon him, and league against him the kings and cabinets of the Continent, his empire would never be secure. He might weather the storm for his own life; but the same endless antagonism, the same implacable hatred, would pursue his successor. To steady his throne, he must have peace with Great Britain: this peace he could not get till he conquered it; having no navy, he could only "conquer the sea on the land," and his only hope of doing this was to make good the Continental boycott against English manufactures. If he could close all Continental ports to British goods, he would starve England into peace. But as long as Continental ports were but partially closed, his policy would be a failure. Command of the seaboard was his great aim, hence the invasion of Spain and Portugal, the annexation of Holland, the Illyrian provinces, and the Duchy of Oldenberg.

The motive of Napoleon in granting Alexander such liberal terms at Tilsit was to get another adherent to the Continental system. The Czar took the benefits of the treaty and shirked its burdens. His coöperation with Napoleon in the war of 1809 was nothing less than a mockery, and when the Russian landlords clamored against the Continental system, Alexander began to relax it. When the Emperor complained of this violation of the treaty, the Czar retorted that Napoleon himself did not enforce his system, that he licensed violations of it — a retort in which there was truth enough to sting.

By a vast system of smuggling, misuse of the neutral flag, and the forging of neutral papers, English goods continued to pour into the Continent. Unless Napoleon could put a stop to this, he might as well give up the contest. In October, 1810, he wrote to the Czar urging him to seize these so-called neutral ships, alleging that they were English. " Whatever papers they carry, your Majesty may be sure they are English." It is now admitted that this statement of the Emperor was substantially correct. The Czar refused, and, to make his refusal the more galling, he issued a ukase, allowing the admission of colonial goods while it virtually prohibited French wines and silks. A plainer declaration of commercial war he could not have made. That it would lead to a clash of arms, he must have known. At any rate the Czar's entire line of conduct from 1810 was that of a monarch preparing for a great war. It was in 1810 he sounded the Poles, seeking to know whether they would side with Russia in a contest with Napoleon. His armies were increased, his fortresses strengthened, and he made secret approaches to England and to Austria.

In addition to the Continental system there were other grievances. Napoleon had added Galicia to the Grand Duchy of Warsaw, after the Treaty of Vienna in 1809, in violation of his agreement with the Czar. He had taken possession of Oldenberg, whose Duke had married a sister of the Czar. In each of these cases the Emperor had offered explanations, and he had offered an equivalent in Germany for Oldenberg ; but the transactions themselves rankled in the Russian memory — although she had really no right to object to Napoleon's treatment of Oldenberg which was a member of his Confederation of the Rhine; and although she had accepted at his hands a valuable increase of territory as the price of her lukewarm support in the war of 1809.

In the matter of the marriage, there had been irritation, Napoleon suspecting that Alexander meant to procrastinate and then refuse, while the Czar believed that the Emperor was wooing two princesses at the same time, and coolly balancing the Russian against the Austrian. This was not the truth, but was near it. A Napoleonic family council had debated the two alliances, upon the assumption that the Emperor could choose either, and had decided in favor of the Hapsburg. Alexander, the Romanoff, therefore felt insulted. In fact, after this second marriage of Napoleon, the Czar had believed that war was inevitable. Nevertheless, the fault even here was with the Czar. Napoleon had asked for his sister, and was entitled to a positive answer. Indefinite adjournment, without a promise, was, to a man in Napoleon's position, a polite way of refusing.

Still there was no rupture. Diplomatic relations were strained, war began to be talked of, preparations got under way, but diplomacy yet hoped to solve the problem. The final quarrel seems to have taken place over the wording of a new treaty. Alexander wanted Napoleon to say that "Poland shall never be restored." How could the Emperor guarantee such a thing? He was not Destiny. He could not foresee what might be done by others and by Time. He was willing to promise that *he* would never restore Poland, nor aid in its restoration. He wrote this promise in the strongest terms. The Czar struck out the amendment, rewrote the original, " Poland shall never be restored," and demanded Napoleon's signature.

Was this an affront, or not? There the case, so far as the actual rupture goes, rests. Napoleon considered it a humiliation to sign such an indefinite, peremptory guarantee; he thought it an insult for the Czar to show so plainly that he doubted his word.

England, of course, was buzzing at the Russian ear all this while. Her agents moved heaven and earth to make the " two bullies " fight. No matter which was worsted, Great Britain would be the gainer. She feared France on the Continent, Russia on the Indian frontier. A duel between these colossal powers would exhaust both, leaving England all the stronger by comparison.

Russia and Turkey were at war on the Danube. The Christians were doing their utmost to relieve the heathen of several thousand square miles of land. England exerted herself to bring about peace between Turk and

Russian, in order that the Czar might not have a war in his rear as Napoleon had in Spain.

It is said that a forged letter, in which Napoleon was made to state that he agreed to a partition of Turkey, was shown at Constantinople. The Turk had his suspicions of this letter; but an Englishman swore that he recognized Napoleon's writing. By some strange neglect, France had no ambassador in Turkey at this critical moment. Andréossy had been appointed, had set out, but had waited at Laybach for his credentials. When they at length arrived, and he proceeded to Constantinople, it was too late.

Before any declaration of war, and while diplomatic relations were still maintained by the two governments, the Czar sent an agent to Paris to pose as envoy and to work as spy. This man, Czernischeff, bribed a clerk in the French war office to steal a complete statement of the French forces, dispositions, equipments, etc. The clerk was shot; the noble Russian escaped by sudden, secret, and rapid flight.

At practically the same time, Napoleon was equally well served at St. Petersburg by a spy who stole the "states" of the Russian armies, and the plates from which the great maps of Russia were printed. From these plates Napoleon furnished his generals with maps for the Russian campaign.

Napoleon fully realized the nature of the task he had before him in a contest with Russia. To defend himself in Italy, Germany, or even Poland against the Czar was one thing; to invade that vast empire with the purpose of seizing its capital and compelling it to sign such treaties as he had imposed upon Austria and Prussia, was

another task altogether — a task colossal, if not appalling.
No one knew this better than Napoleon, and his preparations were made on a scale such as Europe had never
seen.

In advance of the work of the soldier came that of the
diplomat.   Both Russia and France sought alliances.
Great Britain was, of course, heartily with the Czar.
Sweden, controlled by Bernadotte, took the same side.
He had demanded, as the price of his alliance, that Napoleon give him Norway, thus despoiling the Danes.   The
Emperor refused, but offered Finland, which Russia had
seized.   The Czar promised Norway, and thus the Frenchman, Bernadotte, who probably had not yet spent all the
money Napoleon had supplied him with when he went to
Sweden, pledged his support to the enemies of France.
For all practical purposes, Russia likewise made an ally
of Turkey.   So utterly improbable did it seem that
Turkey would make peace with its hereditary enemy at
the very moment when it had the best opportunity fate
had ever offered in all the long struggle, that Napoleon
had not even calculated upon such an event.   It took him
completely by surprise.

Turkish recollections of Tilsit and Erfurth, Turkish
fears of other bargains of the same sort, and Turkish
dread of an English bombardment of Constantinople,
which was threatened, brought about the unlooked-for
treaty which gave Russia an army to throw upon Napoleon's flank.

In addition to these advantages the Czar had another,
and of vast importance — the war in Spain.   Three hundred thousand French troops were held in the peninsula,
and scores of the best officers the Empire could boast.

To Alexander it must have seemed that it would indeed be a miracle if Napoleon could sustain two such immense contests so far apart, one at the extreme south the other in the extreme north. Even Napoleon had appeared to grow weary of his huge tasks, and had been heard to say, " The bow is overbent."

But in getting ready for the contest he certainly accomplished wonders. So imposing were his armaments that Austria and Prussia both believed he would succeed, and they cast in their lot with the French. Each agreed to furnish contingents : the Emperor Francis assured his son-in-law that he might " fully rely upon Austria for the triumph of the common cause,' and the King of Prussia pledged his " unswerving fidelity." Upon these broken reeds the astute Emperor did not, in all probability, intend to lean very heavily. Events were soon to prove that they would bear no weight at all.

Before putting himself at the head of his army, Napoleon held a grand assemblage of his allies at Dresden (May, 1812). It was the most imposing, as it was the last, of the Napoleonic pageants, wherein vassal princes gathered about him and did him homage. Accompanied by the Empress Maria Louisa, he left St. Cloud May 9, reached Mayence on the 14th, and from thence made a triumphal progress to the Saxon capital. Princes of the Confederation of the Rhine hastened to receive their suzerain ; " many even came to wait for them on the road, amongst others the King of Würtemberg and the Grand Duke of Baden." The King and Queen of Saxony came forth from Dresden to meet them ; and a torchlight procession escorted them into the city. On the morrow came the Emperor and Empress of Austria, and the archdukes ;

following these came the King and Crown Prince of
Prussia, the Queen of Westphalia, and scores of princes,
noblemen, and dignitaries. "The splendor of the Court,"
says an eye-witness, "gave Napoleon the air of some
legendary Grand Mogul. As at Tilsit, he showered magnificent presents on all sides. At his levees, reigning
princes danced attendance for hours in the hope of being
honored with an audience. Every country sent its contingent. There were no eyes but for Napoleon. The
populace gathered in crowds outside the palaces, following
his every movement, and dogging his progress through
the streets, in hourly expectation of some great event."

The Crown Prince of Prussia begged for the privilege
of serving on the Emperor's staff, and was denied. Napoleon doubtless thought the campaign before him was
risky enough without the presence of a possible spy in his
military family.

Napoleon was no longer the man he had been in his
earlier campaigns. He had grown fat, subject to fits of
lassitude, and to a painful disease, dysuria. His plans
were as fine as ever, but the execution was nothing like
what it had been. He no longer gave such personal
attention to detail ; irresolution sometimes paralyzed his
combinations.

Nor were his generals up to their former standard. He
had made them too rich. They had pampered themselves
and grown lazy. They had no stomach for the Russian
war, joined their commands reluctantly, and worked without zeal. Neither was the army to be compared to those
of Austerlitz, Jena, and Wagram. In his host of six hundred thousand, there were but two hundred thousand
Frenchmen, the remainder being composed of Germans

from the Confederation of the Rhine, Prussians, Austrians, Italians, Poles, Swiss, Dutch, and even Spaniards and Portuguese. In such a motley array there could be no cohesion, no strength of common purpose which could stand a serious strain. Even the French soldiers, splendid as they undoubtedly were, were not animated by the same spirit as formerly. The causes of the war were beyond their grasp, even the generals felt that the Continental system was not worth fighting about. England, on the verge of commercial ruin, might know better : Napoleon certainly knew better; but to the average Frenchman the grievances on both sides were too vague and abstract to justify so huge a conflict.

No declaration of war had been published, neither Czar nor Emperor had yet fully committed himself, and hopes were entertained that even yet terms might be arranged. But when the travel-stained carriage of Count Narbonne rolled into Dresden, and he announced that Alexander had refused to make any change in his attitude, it became with Napoleon a question of back down or fight. The Czar was determined not to begin the war ; he was equally determined not to keep the contract made at Tilsit. Just as England had held Malta after pledging herself to give it up, Russia was resolved to repudiate and oppose the Continental system which she had promised to support.

At St. Helena Napoleon said that he and Alexander were like two bullies, each trying to frighten the other, and neither wishing to fight. From the manner in which Napoleon continued to hesitate and to send messengers, after all his preparations were complete, it would seem that he, at least, had hoped to the last that an aecommodation might be reached. Narbonne's report put an end to doubt.

Either Alexander's breach of the Continental system must be borne, to the ruin of Napoleon's whole policy, or there must be war. The Emperor had gone too far to stop. What would the world say if, after having made such gigantic preparations, he abandoned the enterprise without having extorted a single concession? The very "nature of things" drove him on, and, dismissing the Dresden conference, he put his host in motion for the Niemen.

Says General Marbot: "When the sun rose on June 24 we witnessed a most imposing spectacle. On the highest point near the left bank were seen the Emperor's tents. Around them the slopes of every hill, and the valleys between, were gay with men and horses flashing with arms." Amid strains of music from the military bands, the eagles were borne forward, and, under the eye of the master, a quarter of a million soldiers began to tramp over the bridges, shouting, "Live the Emperor!" Soon Napoleon himself crossed the bridge, and galloped through the forest at full speed on his Arab, as though it exhilarated him to be upon Russian soil.

The Russians made no attempt to check the invaders. Deceived as to Napoleon's plan of campaign, their armies were scattered, and soon became involved in the gravest peril. Had it not been for the terrible blunders of Jerome Bonaparte and Junot, the Russian force under Barclay de Tolly must have been cut off and destroyed. Had this been done, it might, like Ulm, have proved decisive. But Napoleon found it impossible to perfect his combinations: the Russian armies escaped, united, and the long campaign began.

Crops had failed in this part of Russia the year before, and the land was scantily supplied with provisions. The troops of the Czar laid waste the country as they retreated ; hence the invaders almost immediately began to suffer, for their commissariat could not sustain so tremendous a burden as the feeding of the half million men and one hundred thousand horses. The summer heat was stifling. Men and horses sank under it. One writer gives us a picture of Napoleon himself, stripped to his shirt and lying across a bed, panting and inert with heat. Torrents of rain followed. The roads were cut up, becoming mere sinks of mud. Desertions, straggling, mortalities, marauding, became frightful, so much so that an officer who came up with reserves stated that the route over which the Grand Army had passed looked like that of a defeated foe. Ten thousand horses died for want of forage between the Niemen and Wilna. After the floods came sultry weather again and the suffocating dust of the roads. The hospitals were crowded with the sick. Discipline was lax, movements slow and uncertain. There was a babel of languages, growing confusion, quarrels among officers, and much vacillation in the Emperor himself.

At Wilna the Polish question faced him again. Once more he temporized. He had mortally offended the Czar by enlarging the Grand Duchy of Warsaw, perpetually menacing Russia with a resurrected and vengeful Poland. He now froze the ardor of the Poles by indefinitely postponing the day of their deliverance. When he afterward realized how tremendously effective a united Poland would have been in the death struggle with the Czar, he must have inwardly cursed the bonds which tied his hands — the alliances with Prussia and Austria. Very

frankly, very honorably, he told the Polish delegation
that his engagements with these two powers made it
impossible for him to reëstablish their national independence.

While at Wilna Napoleon received an envoy from the
Czar, who proposed that if the French would recross the
Niemen, terms of peace might be agreed on. Such an
offer seemed to be altogether one-sided, giving substantial
advantages to Alexander, and assuring nothing to Napoleon. Therefore it was rejected.

After having lingered at Wilna from June 28 to July
16, a loss of time which Lord Wolseley thinks " it is impossible to explain away when we remember how late
it was in the year when he opened the campaign," the
Emperor marched upon Vitebsk. It was here that he
learned that Russia had come to terms with Sweden and
Turkey.

It was at this place that, according to Ségur, the Emperor exclaimed, " Here I am, and here I will stay,"
taking off his sword and throwing it upon the table. He
had pursued the Russians some distance beyond the town,
had failed to force them into a pitched battle, and had
now returned to headquarters. " I will stay here for
the winter, complete my army, give it a rest, and organize
Poland. The campaign of 1812 is at an end." Turning
to the King of Naples, he continued : " Murat, the first
Russian campaign is over. We will plant our standards
here. We will intrench and quarter the troops. The
year 1813 will see us in Moscow ; 1814 in St. Petersburg — the war with Russia is one of three years ! "

But he soon became irresolute. The thought of eight
months of inaction, with the Grand Army on the defensive,

2 1

became unbearable. What would the world say? " Europe will say, 'He stayed at Vitebsk because he *dared* not advance.' Am I to give Russia time to arm? How can we go into winter quarters in July? Let us forestall the winter! Peace is at Moscow. Why should we remain here eight months, idle and exposed to treacherous intrigues in the rear, when we can reach our goal in twenty days?"

He did not convince his marshals; they opposed the advance; but he angrily swept their objections aside.

To Duroc he said he would go to Smolensk and there winter. Complaining that his generals were sick of war, that he had made them too rich, that they could think of nothing but the pleasures of the chase on their estates, and the display of themselves in fine carriages in Paris, he ordered the advance upon Smolensk. Once more he failed to secure his much-desired pitched battle. The Russians fought his advance guard stubbornly, and inflicted heavy losses, but during the night they continued their retreat. The French found Smolensk a heap of smoking ruins; French shells and Russian patriots had fired it.

Much has been said about the alleged plan of Russia to lure Napoleon into the country and to destroy him by starvation. The fact seems to be that the Russians retreated because they could not help it. They fought often and desperately. The Czar himself came to the army for the express purpose of inspiring it to fight. Outnumbered and beaten, it fell back, desolating the country as it went; but the plain facts show that the Russians did all that was in their power to put a stop to the invasion. The alleged campaign policy of " luring Napoleon to his doom " is fiction.

At Smolensk, Napoleon was no more willing to stop than he had been at Vitebsk. Peace was at Moscow; he must press on; he must beat the enemy in a great pitched battle, and give his friend, the Czar, the excuse to his people without which he would not dare to come to terms. Again there were hot words between the Emperor and his marshals. Murat, in great anger, predicted that if the army was forced on to Moscow, it would be lost. But the order was imperative: "On to Moscow!" — and the army marched.

The Czar, or those who controlled him, were dissatisfied with the manner in which their side of the campaign had been conducted. There had been too much retreat, and not enough fight. Kutusoff was put in command with the understanding that he must give battle — a fact which, of itself, would seem to dispose of the theory that Napoleon was "lured" into the interior as a matter of policy.

At Borodino the Russians barred the road to "Mother Moscow": and here the pitched battle was fought. With a cannonade that was heard for eighty miles, a quarter of a million men here butchered each other all day long on September 7, until seventy thousand lay dead or wounded. Night ended the carnage, and next morning the Russians were again in retreat.

During this famous battle, Napoleon remained sitting, or slowly walking up and down at one place, where he received reports and sent orders. He spoke but little, and seemed ill. In fact, he was a sick man, suffering with a severe cold and with his bladder complaint. He showed no activity, and left the battle to his marshals. At three in the afternoon the Russians had put in their last reserves, and were in distress everywhere — driven from their intrenchment, and threatened with ruin should the French reserves now attack. Ney, Murat, Davoust, all clamored for the Guard, the Emperor's reserve. He hesitated. They sent again, and still he wavered. "Sire!" said Bessières, commander of the Guard, "remember that you are eight hundred leagues from your capital." Napoleon refused the Guard. Ney was amazed, furious: "What does this mean? What is the Emperor doing in the rear? If he is tired of fighting, let him go back to his d—d Tuileries, and leave us to do what is necessary!"

Thus the Guard never fired a shot, the battle remained unfinished, and the Russians retired in good order, when they might have been destroyed. Military critics say that the Emperor made two capital blunders at Borodino: first, in vetoing Davoust's offer to turn the Russian flank and come upon their rear; and, second, in not using his reserves.

That night the Emperor tried to dictate orders, but could not. He was too hoarse to talk. He was obliged to write; and he fell to it, writing rapidly, and throwing the scraps of paper on the table. Secretaries deciphered these scrawls slowly, and copied them, as fast as they could. As the papers accumulated, Napoleon would rap on his table for the secretaries to remove them. For twelve hours he labored, not a sound to be heard save the scratching of Napoleon's pen and the rapping of his hammer.

The French continued their march onward, and at last neared Moscow. Napoleon left his carriage, mounted his horse, and rode forward. "In the distance could be seen the long columns of Russian cavalry retiring in good order before the French troops." The French marched on, and at last Moscow was in sight. It was a proud moment for Napoleon when he stood on Pilgrim's Hill, surrounded by a brilliant staff, and gazed upon the towers, the golden domes of the vast city, while his lieutenants and his troops shouted, in wild enthusiasm, "Moscow! Moscow!"

The Emperor was heard to mutter, "It was time." Apparently his greatest enterprise had been crowned with success. His long triumphant march toward Asia would rank with Alexander's. Russia would now sue for peace, terms would be easily arranged, Continental unity would follow, and England would find herself an island once more — not an empire.

But it was soon apparent that Moscow was not like Berlin or Vienna. Here were no crowds of spectators to gaze upon the victors. The streets were silent, empty. The houses were deserted. Here was a vast city without citizens. The French were dumfounded. Napoleon refused at first to believe: "the thing was preposterous." The conquerors marched through the streets, the military bands playing, "To us is the victory," but the vast solitude awed them as they marched.

The sight of the Kremlin, however, gave the conqueror a thrill of exultation. "Here I am at last! Here I am in Moscow, in the ancient palace of the Czars! in the Kremlin itself!"

Almost immediately, and in spite of all Napoleon could do, commenced the wholesale pillage of the city. Discipline relaxed, and marauders stormed the vacant houses on the hunt for loot. In the middle of the night of the 16th of September, the sleeping Napoleon was roused and brought running to the window of the Kremlin by the cry of " Fire ! " The flames, feeding on wooden houses and fanned by high winds, defied control, and struck the conquerors with terror. As described by Napoleon himself, at St. Helena, " It was the spectacle of a sea and billows of fire, a sky and clouds of fire, mountains of red, rolling fire, like immense ocean waves, alternately bursting forth and lifting themselves to skies of fire, and then sinking into an ocean of fire below. Oh, it was the grandest, sublimest, most terrible sight the world ever saw ! "

Russians say that the French burnt the city ; the French say the Russians did it. French officers allege most positively that Russian incendiaries were caught in the act. It is certain that numbers of persons so taken were shot, as a punishment. On the other hand, so eminent a Russian as Tolstoï maintains that the carelessness of the French soldiers was the cause of the fires. The Russians who had burned Smolensk to deprive the French of its use, who made the line of their retreat a desert to deprive the French of supplies, were probably the burners of Moscow. They burnt it as they burnt Smolensk and every village on their line of march, as a war measure which would injure the invaders. The fact that Rostopchin, the mayor, had carried away all appliances for putting out fires, would seem to be a conclusive piece of circumstantial evidence.

This awful calamity, unexpected, unexampled, upset Napoleon's calculations. To destroy a town like Smolensk was one thing, to make of Moscow, one of the great cities of the world, an ocean of flame, a desert of ashes, was quite another. It was appalling : it stupefied, benumbed, bewildered Napoleon as no event in his career had done. He realized the frightful extent of the disaster, and saw himself hurled from the pinnacle to the abyss.

Indecision had already made sad havoc in the campaign : indecision now completed the ruin. Napoleon had loitered at Wilna eighteen days ; had halted sixteen days at Vitebsk. He had hesitated at Borodino, practically leaving the battle to his marshals, refusing them the reserves. Now at Moscow, he dawdled for five weeks, when every day brought nearer the march of two enemies that hitherto had not hindered him, — the Russian army, from the Danube, and *Winter !*

At the Kremlin was the most wretched man in existence. The Emperor had reached his Moscow only to find it a prison. Inexorable conditions shut him in with unpitying grip. He could not rest, could not sleep, would not talk, lingered long at table, lolled for hours on a sofa, — in his hand a novel which he did not read. He, the profoundest of calculators, who had from boyhood calculated everything, had for once miscalculated in everything. He had misjudged his friends and his foes ; had erred as to the Russian temper ; had fatally misconceived the character of the Czar. He knew Alexander to be weak, vain, vacillating ; he did not allow for the strength which strong advisers like Stein and Sir Robert Wilson and dozens of others might give to this wavering monarch. He had calculated upon finding peace at Moscow, and had not found it. He had felt assured that, at the worst, Moscow would furnish abundant food and excellent winter quarters. It did neither. At fault in so many matters of vital concern, the Emperor was a prey to the most gloomy reflections. He set up a theatre for his troops, but did not attend it. He rode daily through the streets on his little white Arab, but spoke to no one. Sometimes in the evening he would play a game of cards with Duroc. There were a few concerts at the palace; some singing by Italian artists, some piano music; but the Emperor listened moodily, "with heavy heart." He held his reviews, distributed rewards, but looked pale and stern, saying almost nothing. He duped himself with hopes of peace. He sent envoys and letters to Alexander — envoys who were not received, letters which were not answered. With an obstinacy which was fatal, he refused to see the truth of his situation. A lethargy, a failure of power to decide, mastered him. Even a light fall of snow was not warning sufficient to rouse him.

"At the Kremlin," says Constant, "the days were long and tedious." The Emperor was waiting for the Czar's answer, which never came. His morbid irritability was stirred by the great flocks of crows and jackdaws that hovered about the city. "My God," he cried, "do they mean to follow us everywhere!"

On October 3 he summoned a council of his marshals and proposed to march upon St. Petersburg. His officers listened coldly, and opposed him.

In a sort of desperation he then sent Lauriston to Kutusoff to ask for an interview with Alexander, saying to his envoy: "I want peace; you hear me. Get me peace. But save my honor if you can!"

The wily Kutusoff humored Lauriston, and Lauriston, in turn, nursed the infatuation of the Emperor. Thus precious days slipped away, the French were still at Moscow, winter was coming, and two other Russian armies, one from the north and one from the south, were marching steadily on to strike the French line of communication.

Napoleon wished to attack Kutusoff, drive him or destroy him, and then fall back on Smolensk. His officers counselled against this.

"Then what am I to do?"

"Stay here,' advised Count Daru. "Turn Moscow into a fortified camp, and so pass the winter. There is plenty of bread and salt. We can forage, we can salt down the horses which we cannot feed. As for quarters, if there are not houses enough here, there are plenty of cellars. We can hold out till spring, when our reënforcements, backed by Lithuania in arms, will come to the rescue and complete our success."

"Counsel of the lion!" exclaimed the Emperor. "But what will Paris say? what will they do? No; France is not accustomed to my absence. Prussia and Austria will take advantage of it."

At length a rabbit, fleeing for dear life from a Cossack, put an end to hesitation, and put two great armies in motion.

Tolstoï relates: "On October 14 a Cossack, Shapovalof, while on patrol duty, shot at a rabbit, and, entering the woods in pursuit of the wounded animal, stumbled upon the unguarded left flank of Murat's army"—Napoleon's advance guard.

Shapovalof, on his return to camp, told what he had seen, the news reached headquarters, a reconnoissance confirmed the statement, and the Russians, sorely tempted, broke the armistice, fell upon the unwary Murat, and did him immense damage. But for a difference between the Russian generals, it appears that Murat's entire force might have been captured.

The Emperor was holding a review in the courtyard of the Kremlin when members of his suite began to say to one another that they heard cannon firing in the direction of the advance guard. At first no one dared speak of it to Napoleon. Duroc finally did so, and the Emperor was seen to be seriously disturbed. The review had not been recommenced before an aide-de-camp from Murat came at full speed to report that the truce had been broken, the French taken by surprise, and routed with heavy loss.

This was October 18. At last Napoleon was a soldier again: the news of the battle had roused him to action. His decision was taken, orders flew, and before night the whole army was in motion.

CHAPTER XXXVI

ENCUMBERED by a vast amount of booty, a host of camp-followers, and a huge train of vehicles of all sorts, the Grand Army left Moscow, upward of one hundred thousand strong and with some fifty thousand horses. Neither men nor horses had been shod for a winter campaign. The clothing worn by the troops was mostly that of summer. The movement of the troops was slow, because of the enormous baggage. The Emperor wished to retreat by the Kalonga road which would carry him over a country able to support him with provisions. The Russians barred the way, and at Malo-Yaroslavitz the French, under Eugène Beauharnais, attacked and beat them. Falling back to a stronger position, the Russians still barred the way. Military critics say that had not Napoleon's retreat been so sluggish, he would have outstripped these Russians in their efforts to head him off. Had he burned all that plunder which his army was carrying away, he might have saved his army.

Marshal Bessières and others, sent forward to reconnoitre, reported that the enemy was too strongly intrenched to be dislodged; the army must get back to the old road by which it had come. Napoleon hesitated, listened to reports and advice, lost time, and finally gave the word to retreat by the old route — a fatal decision. What Bessières had seen, according to some authorities, was but a rear-guard : Kutusoff had retreated, and the new route by Kalonga could have been taken by the French.

With heavy heart the Emperor led the way to the other road — that which had already been swept bare in the advance to Moscow.

The Russians did not press the pursuit with any great vigor, but the Grand Army, nevertheless, melted like snow. Men and horses died of starvation, demoralization set in, bands of stragglers were cut off by Cossacks, so that after a battle at Wiasma, and previous to any snow or severe cold, only fifty-five thousand men and twelve thousand horses were fit for active service.

On November 6 the weather changed, and wintry horrors accumulated. The snow, the freezing winds, the icy rains, the lack of food, the want of shelter, the ferocity of pursuing foes, the inhumanity of comrades and friends, the immense plains to be crossed, the deep rivers to be bridged, the enormous burden of despair to be borne, — these were the factors of the most hideous drama war ever presented.

The Grand Army reeled in tattered fragments toward home, fighting, starving, freezing, meeting death in every shape known to man. The French marched in four divisions, commanded by the Emperor, Eugène, Davoust, and Ney. Terrible as was the daily loss by disease, death, and straggling, each of these divisions held its formation, and never failed to stand and fight when the Russians attacked. The unbending courage shown by these commanders, the steadiness of subordinate officers, the despairing gallantry

of the remnants of the Grand Army, stand out in bold relief to the general gloom of this mightiest of shipwrecks.
Much of the time Napoleon was on foot, clad in furs, staff
in hand to help him through the drifts, marching stolidly,
silently, with his men.   Nothing that he could do was
left undone; but that which he could do had little influence on general results as they tramped along.   Until
they reached Smolensk, he was almost as powerless as the
others; after that his superiority saved what was left of
the army.

The hardships of the retreat increased after November
14, when Smolensk was left behind.   Men fell by the road
exhausted, men were blinded by the glare of the light on
limitless fields of snow, men were maddened by the intolerable anxieties and woes of the march.   In the day
the ice cut their rag-covered or naked feet, the wind and
freezing rain tortured their hungry, tattered bodies.   At
night — nights of sixteen fearful hours — bivouac fires
were scant and insufficient, and when morning dawned,
the circle of sleeping forms around these dismal bivouacs
would sometimes remain forever unbroken — the sleep of
the soldier was the long one, the final one.

In October the Russian prisoners had said to the
French, " In a fortnight the nails will drop from your
fingers; you will not be able to hold your guns."   The
cold was even worse; not only did nails drop off, the
hands dropped off.   The time soon came when a benumbed
Frenchman, who had fallen into a ditch, and who had
piteously begged a passing comrade to lend a helping
hand, was answered, " I haven't any ! "   There were only
the stumps of the arms; the poor fellow's hands had been
frozen off.   " But here, catch hold of my cloak," he con-

tinued, and the man in the ditch having caught hold, was
dragged to his feet.

Conditions like these made savages of the men. In
the rush for food and fire and shelter, the strong tramped
down the weak. Frantic with cold and hunger, they
fought each other like wolves for place and provisions.
The weaker were shut out and died. Horse-flesh was common diet; it is even said that cannibalism occurred. For
warmth, artillerymen could be seen holding their hands at
the noses of their horses; for food, a soldier was considered lucky who found a little flour, half dirt and chaff,
in the cracks of a floor. But in the worst stages of this
awful retreat there was human heroism; there was human
sympathy and unselfishness. There is nothing finer in
the fine character of Eugène Beauharnais than the gallantry with which he set the good example of patience,
courage, loyalty, and self-sacrifice. From the time he beat
Kutusoff in the first fight after Moscow, to his taking
the chief command, which Murat abandoned, his conduct
was heroic. Rugged Davoust, the best of the marshals
now serving, who would have saved his master at Borodino, and who did snatch him from the burning streets
of Moscow, was a tower of strength after the retreat
began.

Other marshals did not love Davoust; they quarrelled
with him, said he was slow, and accused him of not maintaining discipline. On the retreat Ney, whom Davoust
had left behind, charged him with something like treachery. But Napoleon knew the value of Davoust, and history knows it. To the careful student of this eventful
epoch the conclusion comes home, irresistibly, that Napoleon might have remained till his death the mightiest

monarch of the world had he listened to two men, — in civil affairs, Cambacérès ; in military matters, Davoust.

As to Murat, he fought all along the front with such conspicuous gallantry, superbly mounted and gorgeously dressed, that he extorted the admiration of the Russians themselves. The Cossacks, especially, looked upon him as the bravest, the most martial of men. Murat fought the cavalry till the horses were all dead, and then he spent most of his time in Napoleon's carriage.

But Ney, rugged, lionlike Ney, surpassed them all, winning in this campaign the Emperor's proud title, " The brave of the braves." Such grandeur of courage, such steadiness, such loyalty, the world never surpassed. Separated from Davoust, beset by overwhelming numbers, he seemed a lost man. The Emperor, hard pressed himself, but determined to make a final effort to save his marshals, halted at Krasnoi, facing sixty thousand Russians with six thousand French. Nothing in Napoleon's own career is finer than this. Russian shells began to fly, screaming through the air and along the snow. Lebrun spoke of it as of something unusually terrible. " Bah ! " said the Emperor with contempt ; " balls have been whistling about our legs these twenty years." His desperate courage in standing at bay so impressed Kutusoff that he drew back, and Davoust came through. But Ney was still behind, and in the face of the tremendous odds the French were forced onward. In deep grief for his marshal, the Emperor reproached himself for having exposed Ney too much. From time to time he would inquire if any one had heard from him. On the 20th of November General Gourgaud came in haste to announce that Ney was only a few leagues away and would soon join. With a cry of joy, Napoleon ex·

claimed, "Is it true?" When Gourgaud explained how
Ney had marched and fought : how he had defied a belea-
guring host ten times his own number ; how, summoned to
surrender, he had replied, "A marshal of France has never
surrendered!" and how he had, partly by stratagem, and
partly by force, escaped with a small remnant of his command, Napoleon was delighted. "There are 200,000,000
francs in my vaults in the Tuileries, and I would give
them all to have Ney at my side!"

When the heroic survivors of this column joined the
main army, there were shouts and tears of joy.

It was Ney who held the Cossacks at bay toward the
final stages of the retreat ; it was Ney who fired the last
shot of the war as he recrossed the Niemen : it was Ney
who became almost literally the rear-guard of the Grand
Army.

Well might the Bourbon Duchess of Angoulême say, in
1815, when told the story of this man's antique heroism
in the Russian campaign, "Had we known all that, we
would not have had him shot!"

In the disorder, savagery, elemental chaos of this historic retreat, human nature flew to the extremes. There
were soldiers who slew each other in struggles for food,
and soldiers who risked starvation to share with others.
In some instances comradeship was mocked, in some it
was stronger than ever. There were instances where the
strong laughed at the weak who pleaded for aid. There
were cases where the strong braved all to save the weak.
Wounded officers were seen drawn on sledges to which
their comrades had harnessed themselves, brother officers
taking the place of horses. A child, abandoned by its
mother, was saved by Marshal Ney, and escaped all the

hardships of the retreat. Another mother drowning in the Beresina held her babe aloft in her arms, the child alive, the mother as good as dead.

One of the most touching and purely unselfish acts of devotion was that of the Hessian contingent in its protection of their hereditary prince. The people of Hesse had little cause to reverence their rulers — petty tyrants who had sold them into military servitude at so much a head to England, and who had misgoverned them with the worst of feudal methods. But on the coldest night of the retreat, when it seemed that the young Prince Emil would freeze to death, the remnant of the Hessians closed around him, " wrapped in their great white cloaks pressed tightly against one another, protecting him from wind and cold. The next morning three-fourths of them were dead, and buried beneath the snow."

By the time the French came near the Beresina, the two Russian armies, which had been released by the treaties the Czar had made with Turkey and Sweden, had reached the scene of war, and threatened the line of retreat. Kutusoff in overwhelming force in the rear, Wittgenstein and Tchitchagoff in front and flank, the French seemed doomed. When the Russians were driven by Oudinot from Borissow, they burnt the bridge over the Beresina. The ice had melted, the river was swollen, it was wide and deep, and the Russians were on the opposite bank ready to dispute the passage. To bridge and cross the river in the face of these Russians — such was the French necessity : either that or surrender, for Kutusoff was close behind.

Already the Emperor had destroyed his papers and burned his eagles to save them from capture ; already

2 K

had provided himself with poison, resolved to die rather than be taken prisoner.

Standing up to their lips in the freezing current of the river, soldiers worked all night, fixing the timbers for the bridge. It was a terrible labor, and several lost their lives, drowned or frozen. Those who toiled on, had to keep the masses of ice pushed away while they worked.

The Emperor sat in a wretched hovel, waiting for day. Great tears rolled down his cheeks. " Berthier, how are we to get out of this?" Murat urged him to take an escort of a few Poles, cross the river higher up, and escape. The Emperor silently shook his head, and Murat said no more.

Suddenly came news that was almost too good for belief : the Russians had disappeared! Tchitchagoff, deceived by Napoleon's feint to cross elsewhere, or misled by Kutusoff's despatches, had led his army away. The line of retreat was now open, the bridges were rapidly finished, and with shouts of " Live the Emperor!" the jubilant French began to cross. When in their hurry a jam occurred in the passage, and artillery teams got blocked, Napoleon himself sprang on the bridge, caught the horses, and helped to free the pieces.

The bridges, constructed under so many difficulties and in such haste, were frail, the crush of the crowd in going over became greater and greater. Finally the bridges gave way. They were repaired, but broke again. Beginning with this, the tumult, the terror, the frantic struggle for place, the loss of life, became frightful. The weak fell, they were trampled by men and horses, and ground to pulp by wheels. Some perished on the bridges, others were pushed off and drowned in the river. There were no side-rails or ledges, nothing to keep those on the outer edge from being crowded off — and they went over by hundreds, by thousands. The Russians under Wittgenstein having come up, a fierce battle ensued between them and the French rear-guard. Amid wild confusion, the passage of the river continued, while a storm raged and the cannon roared. In the evening the large bridge, crushed by the weight upon it, gave way, and with a fearful cry, which rose above the storm and the battle, the multitude that was crossing sank forever. Next day the battle raged again, while the crossing continued. Early in the night, Victor's rear-guard began to cross, the Russians cannonading the bridge, and covering it with the dead. Next morning the bridge was burned, and all the thousands of stragglers and camp-followers were cut off, and perished miserably.

Beyond the Beresina, the regulars of the Russian army did not press the pursuit, but the Cossacks hung on, inflicting heavy losses. From cold, from hunger, from disease, the French continued to lose fearfully; but the broken remnant of the Grand Army was now comparatively safe from the enemy.

Full details of the Malet conspiracy having reached Napoleon, he became anxious and restless. He believed he could render greater service to himself and the Empire by being in Paris. Turning over the command to Murat, at Smorgoni, the Emperor entered a covered sleigh, and set out for France.

Accompanied by Duroc, Caulaincourt and Lobau, Roustan the Mameluke, and a Polish officer, the Emperor sped across the snow on his way homeward. Almost captured by Cossacks, he reached Warsaw on the 15th of December, 1812, where he put up at the English Hotel, and sent for the Abbé de Pradt, his minister to the Grand Duchy. Here, in a small room of the hotel, moving about restlessly, stamping his feet for circulation while a servant girl bent over the hearth trying to make a fire from green wood, he gave his instructions to his treacherous minister, and announced that in the following spring he would be back in the Niemen at the head of three hundred thousand men. Then he sped onward toward Saxony.

Late at night, December 14, 1812, the sledge of the flying Emperor reached Dresden, where there was a brief conference between Napoleon and his faithful ally. Bitter beyond description must have been the reflections of the lonely fugitive in hurrying through those streets, where a few months before kings had crowded to his antechamber!

Escaping the conspiracies aimed at his life in Germany, he safely entered France, and reached Paris, late at night, December 18, 1812, arriving at the Tuileries almost alone, in a hackney coach.

There was an outburst of indignation in the Grand Army remnants when it was known that the Emperor had gone. "The same trick he played us in Egypt," said one General to another. Murat had on his hands a thankless task at best, and under his management the situation did not improve. At Wilna the Cossack "Hourra!" stampeded the French, who fled, loosing six thousand prisoners. At the steep hill, a few miles beyond, the horses could not drag the artillery up the ice-covered road, and it was abandoned.

Sick of such a responsibility, Murat bethought himself

that he also had a kingdom that might need his presence, and on January 16, 1813, he made over the command to Eugène Beauharnais.

There were seventeen thousand men in the army when Murat left it ; Eugène increased its numbers until, by the 9th of March, 1813, it was an effective force of forty thousand. Taking a strong position, his line stretching from Magdeburg to Dresden, the loyal Eugène waited for his Emperor to bring up reënforcements.

CHAPTER XXXVII

THERE is no convincing evidence that the Russian war
of 1812 was generally unpopular in France. There is
no proof whatever that any national calamity growing out
of it was expected or feared. So great was the confidence
which the Emperor's uninterrupted success had inspired,
that the current belief was that Russia would be beaten
and brought to terms. The glamour of the Dresden conference was sufficient to dazzle the French people, and the
magnificent host which gathered under the eagles of the
Empire left them no room for doubts. Led by such a captain as Napoleon, this army of half a million men would
bear down all opposition. Bulletins from the front, dictated by the Emperor, did not fail to produce the impression desired; and when at length the victory of Borodino
was followed by the French entry into Moscow, national
enthusiasm and pride reached its height.

The first shadow that fell upon France, the first thrill
of fear, was caused by the news that the Russians had
given their capital to the flames. Still, when it became
known that the Emperor was quartering the army amid
the ruins, that there was shelter and food for all, that
communications between Paris and Moscow were so well
guarded that not a courier or convoy had been cut off,
that Napoleon, seemingly quite at ease, was giving his

attention to the internal affairs of France, was drawing
up regulations for schools and theatres, was corresponding
with his son's governess upon the subject of the child's
teething, the French convinced themselves that the invasion had proved another triumph. They could not put
their eyes upon that sombre figure in the Kremlin, the
chief who had not a word to say to those about him, who
lay listless upon the sofa day by day, — a leader without
a plan, — wrapping himself in the delusion that even yet
the Czar would accept his peaceful overtures.

So strong was the system which Napoleon had organized
in France that it went on in his absence just as regularly
as when he was present. Even when the daring General
Malet, encouraged by the Emperor's great distance from
his capital, conspired with the priest, Abbé Lafon, to overthrow the government, the attempts never had the slightest chance of success. By means of a forged decree of
the Senate, and the announcement that the Emperor was
dead, the conspirators were for a moment enabled to secure
control of a small body of troops, arrest the minister and
the prefect of police, and to take possession of the city
hall. But almost immediately the authorities asserted
themselves, seized the conspirators, and put them to death.

The true significance of this episode lay in the fact that
so violent a revolutionist as Malet, who had plotted to kill
Napoleon because of the Concordat, was found in league
with the Abbé Lafon, a royalist and clerical fanatic, and
that they had agreed upon a programme which was so eminently sane as to be formidable.

According to their plan, Napoleon's family were to be
set aside, the conscription abolished, and the most oppressive taxes lifted. The Pope was to be restored to his tem-

poral power, and France was to secure peace with the
world by consenting to be reduced to her old boundaries
of Rhine, Alps, and Pyrenees. Those who had purchased
the confiscated property of the Church and the nobles were
to be quieted with the assurance that their titles should
not be questioned.

When we remember that peace was finally established in
France upon substantially the same lines as those marked
out by the Abbé Lafon, it becomes evident that he was in
touch with those royalist clericals who, failing miserably
in 1812, succeeded completely two years later. Napoleon's uneasiness when he heard of the conspiracy, and
his curiosity in asking for the minutest details, can well be
understood.

The twenty-fifth bulletin from the Grand Army told
France that the retreat from Moscow had begun. The
twenty-eighth bulletin, dated from Smolensk, and made
public in Paris on November 29, 1812, announced that
winter had set in. After this, France was left for eighteen
days without news — eighteen days filled with dread.
Then on December 17 came the avalanche. The twenty-
ninth bulletin, revealing much, suggested all — the Grand
Army was no more! The consternation, the dismay, the
stupor of grief and terror which overspread the stricken
land, can be imagined ; it passes the power of words.

And the home-coming of the Emperor — what was it
like, this time?

It was midnight in Paris, the 18th of December, 1812.
The Empress Maria Louisa, at the Tuileries, sad and un
well, had gone to bed. The imperial babe, the infant

King of Rome, was asleep. It was a mournful time in
France. Where was the hut from one end of the Empire to the other which did not hear sobs this bitter, bitter
night? How many women, at cheerless firesides, wept
and prayed for sons, husbands, lovers, shrouded in motionless snow on far Russian plains! Even the Empress was
sorrowful. She knew nothing of the fate of the army or
its chief. Napoleon himself might get rest for his unrest-
ing spirit from Cossack lance or Russian gun — in which
event the Empress Maria might find untold calamity for
her imperial self.

A common cab rolled into the courtyard below, and
steps were heard hastily ascending the stairs. Two men
hooded and wrapped up in furs, pushed their way into
the anteroom to the Empress's bedchamber. Voices were
heard in this anteroom, and the Empress, frightened, was
just getting out of bed, when Napoleon burst in, rushed
up to her, and caught her in his arms.

On the following day, according to Pasquier, the Emperor admitted no one but his archchancellor, his ministers, and his intimates. On the 20th, which was Sunday,
he attended divine service, and then held the usual levee;
after which he formally received the Senate and the
Council. Seated upon his throne, enveloped in his
robes of state, this wonderful man, so recently a fugitive fleeing almost alone through the wilds of Poland,
never presented a serener face to the world, nor looked
down upon the grandees who bowed before him with
haughtier glance, than upon this memorable Sabbath.
Loyal addresses were listened to with dignity and composure; imperial responses were made in a tone which convinced France and Europe that Napoleon remained

unconquered. Such was the grandeur of his attitude, so
powerfully did his fortitude, courage, magnetic audacity
appeal to this gallant nation, that it rallied to him with
almost universal sympathy and enthusiasm. Towns,
cities, corporate bodies, imperial dependencies, sent in
loyal addresses, offers of cordial support. From Italy,
Holland, the Rhine provinces, poured in warm expressions of attachment and fidelity. Rome, Milan, Florence,
Turin, Hamburg, Amsterdam, Mayence, testified their
sense of the benefits his rule had conferred upon them,
and tendered him " arms, armies, gold, fidelity, and constancy."

Napoleon had said that he would be back in Germany
in the spring with three hundred thousand men. He lost
no time in getting ready to keep his promise. It was an
awful task — this creation of a new army; but he set about
it with a grim resolution, a patient persistence, which
accomplished wonders. Skeleton regiments of veterans
were filled in with youthful recruits, and hurriedly drilled.
The twelve hundred cannon lost in Russia were replaced
by old guns from the arsenals, or new ones from the
foundries. The enormous loss of war material was made
good from the reserves in the military depots. But where
could the Emperor get horses to supply the mighty number frozen or starved in Russia? He could not get them.
His utmost exertions could but supply teams for the
artillery. Of cavalry he could mount almost none.

Meditate a moment on the situation. The civilized
world stood arrayed against one man, one people. England on the seas, in Portugal, in Spain; Russia marching
on with a victorious host; Sweden (having been promised
Norway and English money) uniting with the Czar;

Prussia and Austria leaving the side of France, — Prussia joining in the crusade, and Austria preparing to do so, — smaller German powers threatened with ruin if they did not declare war upon Napoleon; Murat at Naples betraying the man who had given him the crown; the Pope doing his utmost to sow disaffection by troubling the conscience of Catholics throughout the Empire; royalists in France beginning to stir, covertly and stealthily, in the tortuous ways of intrigue and conspiracy. All this we see upon one side. And upon the other, what? One man of supreme genius and courage, — backed by one gallant nation, — preparing to lead forth, to meet a world in arms, an army composed largely of boys, almost without cavalry, and almost without drill.

"I noticed at this epoch," says Constant, "that the Emperor had never hunted so frequently." Two or three times a week the hunting suit was donned, and the imperial party would seek the pleasures of the chase. As Napoleon had no real fondness for hunting, his valet was surprised. One day he learned the explanation. English newspapers, as the Emperor told Duroc, had been repeating that he was ill, could not stir, and was no longer good for anything. "I'll soon make them see that I am as sound in body as in mind!"

One of these hunts, Napoleon endeavored to turn to a particularly good account. The Pope was at Fontainebleau, to which place he had been removed from Savona at the opening of the Russian campaign. His quarrel with the Emperor had become most annoying in its consequences. Disaffection, because of it, had found its way into the very Council of State. All attempt at negotiation had been fruitless. On the eve of another great war,

here was a question which demanded settlement; and the
Emperor determined to go in person to the Pope.

On January 19, 1813, the hunt was directed to Gros-
bois, the fine estate which had belonged to Barras, then to
Moreau, and then to Berthier, Prince of Neufchâtel.   At
Grosbois, accordingly, the imperial party hunted.   "But
what was the surprise of all his suite when, at the moment
of reëntering the carriages, his Majesty ordered them to
be driven toward Fontainebleau."

The Empress and the ladies, having no raiment with
them other than hunting costumes, were in some confusion
at the prospect.   The Emperor teased them for a while, and
then let them know that by his orders the necessary change
of clothes had been sent from Paris beforehand and would
be ready for them at Fontainebleau.   Taking up his quarters in the ancient palace, Napoleon and Maria Louisa
went informally to call upon the Pope.   The meeting was
affectionate.   Again there were buggings and kissings;
again it was "My father!"   "My son!"   And again the
magnetism, the adroit winsomness of Napoleon, swept the
aged pontiff off his feet.   He signed a new compact with
his "son"; and once more there came to them both the
bliss due to the peacemakers.

Radiant with pleasure, Napoleon returned to Paris; and,
quick as couriers could speed, went the good news to all
parts of the Empire.   But he had been too fast .   He had
given permission that the rebellious cardinals — "the black
cardinals," who, refusing to attend the celebration of the
religious marriage with Maria Louisa, had been forbidden
to wear the red robes — might attend the Pope.   And these
black cardinals had not changed their color, — were still
black, — and they began immediately to urge the Holy

Father to break his plighted word. The Holy Father did so, pleading by way of excuse, that the paper he had signed was not a contract or treaty, but only the basis of one; and that Napoleon had acted in bad faith in making it public. But the Emperor inserted the treaty in the official gazette, keeping up the pretence that all was peace between him and the Pope; so that the French people at large knew no better until a much later date.

There are critics who say that Napoleon was too hasty in setting out to join his army in April, 1813. But the plain facts of the case would seem to show that Napoleon knew what he was about. Prussia had issued her declaration of war on March 17, 1813, and Blücher pushed forward to the Elbe. Russian troops had likewise reached the Elbe, and Cossacks raided in the vicinity of Dresden, which the French, under Davoust, evacuated. Blücher entered the Saxon capitol; the Saxon king was a fugitive; and the Prussians passed on toward Leipsic.

By the 24th of April the Czar of Russia and the King of Prussia were in Dresden. Bernadotte, at the head of thirty thousand Swedes, had joined Bülow, and was covering Berlin.

In view of these events, how can it be said with assurance that Napoleon was overhasty in taking the field?

Remembering that the Allies had threatened war upon those minor German powers who would not join them, and that Saxony was already in their grasp, it seems that Napoleon's conduct admits of easy explanation. Unless he checked the Allies, and that speedily, the Rhine Confederation would go to pieces; the French garrisons in various German cities would be lost. Eugène and his army would be cut off at Magdeburg, and the fabric of Napoleonic Empire would fall without a blow having been struck in its defence.

To accomplish these very purposes, the Allies had pressed forward; and great must have been the confusion in both armies; for Napoleon, as well as his enemies, was surprised when the two armies struck each other at Lützen, May 2, 1813. A bloody struggle followed; the Allies were outgeneralled, and they retreated from the field. Having no cavalry, the Emperor lost the usual fruits of victory; but the mere fact that he, so recently the fugitive from a lost army, now appeared at the head of another host, and had driven Russians and Prussians back in defeat, produced a moral effect which was immense. The enemy was driven beyond the Elbe; all hopes of breaking up the Rhine Confederation were at an end; Eugène and Napoleon would now unite; Saxony was redeemed. Napoleon entered Dresden in triumph. His friend and ally, the Saxon king, returned to his capital. The French army was full of confidence: the Allies made no effort to stand their ground till they reached Bautzen, on the Spree. Here, on May 21 and 22, they were assailed by the French, and again overthrown.

So competent a judge as Lord Wolseley is of the opinion that a mistake of Marshal Ney in this battle saved the allied army from total ruin. The Russians and Prussians held a strong fortified position resting on the Bohemian Mountains, from which there was only one line of retreat. Napoleon's quick eye took in the situation, and he sent Ney to the rear of the enemy with seventy thousand men, while he assailed their front with eighty thousand. In executing this turning movement, Ney became en-

gaged with a small force of Prussians, which Blücher
had detached to protect his rear. "Instead of pressing
his march along the rear of the allied army to cut off
its retreat, and attack it in the rear, whilst Napoleon
assailed it in front, Ney allowed his movements to be
checked, and his direction diverted by this insignificant
Prussian detachment. This fighting soon roused Blücher
to a sense of his extreme danger, and he at once fell back
and made good his retreat." The Russians made the
best of a bad situation till dark, and then escaped during
the night. "Ney had, in fact, only succeeded in manœuvring the Allies out of a position in which Napoleon intended
to destroy them, and where they must have been destroyed had his orders been skilfully obeyed."

As it was, the Allies drew off without losing a gun, and
Napoleon, looking over the thousands of dead that cumbered the field, exclaimed in rage and grief, "What a massacre for nothing!"

It was at this stage of the campaign that Napoleon is
thought to have made the crowning mistake of his later
years. He halted his victorious columns, and signed the
armistice of Pleiswitz (June 4, 1813).

Austria had, since her defeats in 1809, fully recovered
her strength. Her armies reorganized, her people animated by a patriotic spirit which had been intensified by
promises of constitutional reforms, she had come unhurt
out of the war of 1812, and was now determined to recover
her lost provinces and her position as an independent
power of the first class. With Russia and France both
severely crippled by the late struggle, Austria realized
her advantage too well to allow the opportunity to pass.
Either from Napoleon or the Allies the position lost in 1809

must be recovered. With this end in view, Metternich negotiated with all parties, — Prussia, England, France, and Russia. The amount of lying this able and eminent Christian did at this critical time would probably have taxed the conscience of even such veterans in deception as Fouché and Talleyrand.

Whether Napoleon could have won the friendship of Austria by frankly surrendering to her demands for the restitution of her lost territory, must always remain a matter of doubt. Inasmuch as the Austrian army was not quite ready to take the field, and her treasury was empty, and she had no complaint against Napoleon, excepting that she had made an unprovoked attack upon him in 1809 and had been thoroughly whipped, the probability is that a prompt concession of her demands would have gained her neutrality in the war of 1813. But this is by no means certain. When we remember the strength of dynastic prejudices, the influence of British money, the rising tide of German nationality and of hatred of Napoleon, the intense antagonism to French principles, the activity of royalist and clerical intrigue — it is difficult to escape the conclusion that had Napoleon yielded up what he had taken from Austria, he could have stopped at nothing short of a full surrender all along the line. And had he returned to France shorn of all that French blood had won, the storm of indignation there would have driven him from the throne. Napoleon himself expressed substantially this view at St. Helena; it may have been sound. Why, then; did he grant the truce? What did he mean by saying, after he had signed it, "If the Allies do not sincerely wish for peace, this armistice may prove our ruin"? No one can say. There are facts which appear to prove conclusively that he ardently wished for an honorable peace. Other facts seem to indicate that he was playing for time, that he never did mean to give up anything, and that he was beaten in a grand game of duplicity, where, intending to deceive, he was duped.

CHAPTER XXXVIII

THE guiding hand of Austrian diplomacy at this time being Metternich's, and that astute person having left behind him certain *Memoirs* which his family have arranged and published, it may be fairly presumed that any revelation of Metternich's own perfidy made in these *Memoirs* can be credited.

According to his own story, Metternich sought an interview with the Czar (June 17, 1813) and urged him to trust implicitly to the Austrian mediation which had been tendered to the belligerents. Alexander had his misgivings, and inquired: —

"What will become of *our cause* if Napoleon accepts the mediation?"

Metternich replied: —

"If he declines, the truce will come to an end, and you will find us among the number of your allies; if he accepts, *the negotiations will most certainly* show that Napoleon is neither wise nor just, and then *the result will be the same.* In any case, we shall have gained time to bring up our armies for combined attack."

What did Alexander mean by "our cause," which might be ruined by Napoleon's consent to allow Austria to mediate? If peace was all that the Allies wanted, why demur to Austria's offer?

514

And what did Metternich mean by assuring the Czar that it made no difference whether Napoleon declined or accepted, the results would be the same?

Evidently he meant to convince Alexander that "our cause" was as dear to Austria as to Russia; and that if Napoleon trusted to Austrian mediation, he would be deceived and despoiled. The Czar so understood it, and he "seemed exceedingly well pleased."

The political meaning of "our cause" was this: English diplomats had been unusually busy, and had (June 14 and 15, 1813) negotiated new treaties with Russia and Prussia whereby Great Britain agreed to pay heavy subsidies to those powers to prosecute the war, which was not to be ended without England's consent.

Inasmuch as England was no party to the negotiations then pending between Napoleon and the Allies, one of two things is obvious: the Allies were intent upon betraying England, or of duping France. As to which of the two it was meant to deceive, the language used by Metternich to Alexander, and by Alexander to Metternich, leaves no doubt.

What, on the other hand, were the thoughts of Napoleon? On June 2, 1813, he wrote to Eugène, who had been sent back to Italy, "I shall grant a truce on account of the armaments of Austria, and in order to gain time to bring up the Italian army to Laybach to threaten Vienna."

There are those who see in this a proof that Napoleon did not desire peace. Read in the light of the surrounding circumstances, it is just as easy to see in the letter an evidence that Napoleon merely wished to escape Austrian dictation.

He had already offered to treat for peace with Russia

and Prussia; and they, controlled by English influence, had refused to treat, save through Austria.

Anxious, suspicious, harassed by all sorts of cares, Napoleon summoned Metternich to Dresden.

Napoleon understood Metternich thoroughly, and despised him. With this man, as with Fouché, Talleyrand, and Bernadotte, the proud Corsican had too lightly indulged in the perilous license of contempt.

"Sire, why do you not send Metternich away?" Duroc inquired one day at the Tuileries.

"Ah, well," answered Napoleon, "if Austria sent me a new minister, I should have him to study; as to Metternich, he can no longer deceive me."

Summoned to Dresden, the Austrian diplomat went, and on June 27, 1813, held his famous interview with Napoleon. It was not then known to any save the parties to the treaty that Lord Aberdeen, acting for England, had already made his bargain with Austria, whereby the latter power agreed to accept an enormous bribe to enter the coalition against France. On the very day of Metternich's interview with Napoleon, Austria was actually signing the Reichenbach treaty which, affirmed by the Emperor Francis on August 1, 1813, placed Austria's two hundred thousand men at the service of "our cause."

Napoleon knew nothing of this; he suspected it, dreaded it, desperately sought to avert it. Hence his call to Metternich.

In his *Memoirs*, the Austrian statesman relates that he found the French Emperor at the Marcolini Garden, near the Elster meadows. "The French army sighed for peace. The generals had little confidence in the issue of the war." "The appearance of the Austrian minister at Napoleon's headquarters could only be regarded by the French generals as decisive in its results." Bursting with self-importance was this Metternich, of whom Napoleon said that he was always believing that he controlled everything, whereas he was eternally being controlled by others. In this instance he walked toward Napoleon's rooms with the majestic port of an arbiter of nations, whereas the whole thing had already been determined by Lord Aberdeen's negotiations at Vienna, not to mention the masterful influence of Sir Charles Stewart and Lord Cathcart in the counsels of Russia and Prussia.

" It would be difficult to describe," says Metternich, " the expression of painful anxiety shown on the faces of the crowd of men in uniform who were assembled in the waiting rooms of the Emperor. The Prince of Neufchâtel (Berthier) said to me in a low voice, " Do not forget that Europe requires peace, and especially France, which will have nothing but peace."

Of Berthier, Napoleon himself said that, in anything outside his specialty of writing despatches, " he was a mere goose." If Berthier made at this juncture any such remark to Metternich as that important man records, it would be a charity to let Berthier escape with so light a reproach as that of being a mere goose. Such a remark to such a man, by such a man, and at such a time is rankly odorous of disaffection, disloyalty, and the incipient treason which broke out openly a few months later.

Metternich, referring to Berthier's remark, complacently states, "Not seeing myself called upon to answer this, I at once entered the Emperor's reception room." Great was Metternich in this crisis, too great to bandy words with a mere mushroom, Prince de Neufchâtel!

"Napoleon waited for me, standing in the middle of the room with his sword at his side, and his hat under his arm. He came up in a studied manner and inquired after the health of the Emperor Francis. His countenance soon clouded over, and he spoke, standing in front of me, as follows: —

"'So you *too* want war; well, you shall have it. Three times have I replaced the Emperor Francis on his throne. I have promised always to live in peace with him. I have married his daughter. To-day I repent of it.'"

Metternich says that at this crisis he felt himself the representative of all European society. He felt the strength of his position, felt that the mighty Napoleon lay in the hollow of his hand.

"If I may say so, Napoleon seemed to me small!"

"If I may say so" — why the modest doubt? Where is the limit of what one may say in one's *Memoirs?* Do the writers of *Memoirs* ever by any possibility get worsted in discussion, or fail to say and do the very best thing that could have been said and done?

Metternich proceeds to relate how he read Napoleon a paternal lecture; how he explained to the French Emperor that France as well as Europe required peace; how he intimated that Austria would throw her aid to the coalition; how he predicted that the French army would be swept away, and how he asked the Emperor, "If this juvenile army that you levied but yesterday should be destroyed, what then?" "When Napoleon heard these words he was overcome with rage, he turned pale, and his features were distorted. 'You are no soldier,' said he, 'and you do not know what goes on in the mind of a soldier. I was brought up in the field, and a man· such as I am does not concern himself much about the lives of a million of men.' With this exclamation he threw his hat into the corner of the room."

Of course the *Memoirs* represent Metternich as promptly taking advantage of this imprudent outbreak, and as throwing Napoleon quite upon the defensive. It is noticeable that in the *Memoirs* of Napoleon's enemies, the authors invariably got the better of him in trials of wit. Some very dull people gave him some very crushing conversational blows — in their *Memoirs*.

But this much is known of the Dresden interview, — it lasted half a day, and Metternich reports less than half an hour's talk. The Austrian does not record how unerringly Napoleon guessed the riddle, and how directly he put the question, — " Metternich, how much has England paid you to act this part against me?" Nor does he record the fact that Napoleon, in his extremity, offered to buy Austria off by ceding the Illyrian provinces, and that the bargain could not be made because the Emperor Francis advanced his demands as often as Napoleon enlarged his concessions. Austria, sold to England, was perfectly willing to be bought by France; but the price demanded was so excessive, that Napoleon indignantly cried out, " I will die under the ruins of my throne before I will consent to strip France of all her possessions, and dishonor myself in the eyes of the world!"

Metternich records that he said to Napoleon: " You are lost. I thought it when I came here; now I know it." The Emperor's reply to this remarkable observation is not on the Metternich tablets. The writers of *Memoirs* have a habit of getting in the last word.

Not satisfied with having crushed Napoleon, Metter-

nich dealt a parting blow to Berthier, the Emperor's
goose.

" In the anterooms I found the same generals whom I
had seen on entering. They crowded round me to read
in my face the impression of nearly nine hours' conversation. I did not stop, and I do not think I satisfied their
curiosity. Berthier accompanied me to my carriage. He
seized a moment when no one was near to ask me whether
I had been satisfied with the Emperor." To this humblest
of questions, " Were you satisfied with the Emperor ? " the
important Metternich replied, with a loftiness which must
have painfully bruised the Emperor's goose : —

" Yes, yes ! It is all over with the man. He has lost
his wits."

It is all over with the man ; he has lost his mind —
great Metternich, small Napoleon, and poor Berthier, the
Emperor's assiduous goose!

One other important fact the Metternich *Memoirs* record:
the Archduke Charles needed twenty additional days to
bring up the Austrian reserves, and Metternich undertook
to decoy Napoleon into an extension of the armistice. The
Memoirs record how Napoleon vainly endeavored through
the Duke of Bassano to come to terms of peace ; how Metternich stubbornly stood his ground, refusing to budge an
inch ; how Napoleon kept up the contest until the Austrian
ordered his carriage and was about to leave Dresden ; how
Napoleon then yielded, calling Metternich back, and signing an agreement to accept Austrian mediation, to prolong
the armistice till August 10, and to submit the issues to a
congress of the powers to be assembled at Prague on the
10th of July.

In Thiers's *History of the Consulate and Empire* we read

that Napoleon by his cleverness and diplomacy lured the Allies into granting him precious delays most necessary to his welfare.   In Metternich's *Memoirs* we read that the Austrian, by his adroitness and implied threats, led Napoleon to the exact time which the Archduke Charles said was needed to get his forces just where he wanted them. Which of these contradictory stories is the truth? which is history?

The Congress of Prague assembled, and it soon became apparent that peace would not be made.   British influence dominated it from the first.   By consenting, once for all, to surrender his empire and become King of France, — France with the old boundaries, — Napoleon could doubtless have rid himself of the Allies.   But what then? Could he have held the throne in France after so complete a submission to foreign dictation?   Could he thus have secured internal peace for France itself?   Would not England have pressed home the advantage, restored the Bourbons, and destroyed the work of the Revolution?

When we recall what took place in 1814 and afterward, — the steady progress of reaction and counter-revolution until absolutism and aristocratic privilege had completely triumphed again throughout Europe, — we can but honor the sagacity and the unquailing courage of Napoleon in standing his ground, indomitably, against combinations without and disaffection within, rather than make craven surrender to a coalition which meant nothing less than death to democratic principles and institutions, as well as to his own supremacy.

In Spain the fortunes of war were going heavily against France.   King Joseph was in everybody's way, hampering military movements by his absurdities; the marshals were at odds with each other, and no coöperation could be had. Wellington, whose progress in the peninsula had been slow and fluctuating, now advanced into Spain, and won a decisive battle. Just as the victory of Salamanca had influenced Russian councils in 1812, that of Vittoria bore heavily against Napoleon at the Congress of Prague.

Napoleon himself had no confidence in the negotiations, and was painfully aware of the manifold perils which beset him. He returned to Mayence, and bent all his energies to the improvement of his situation. One day he called upon Beugnot to write at his dictation, and Beugnot, flurried at the unexpected summons, twice took the Emperor's chair. Napoleon said: "So you are determined to sit in my seat! You have chosen a bad time for it."

Soult was sent off to Spain to hold Wellington in check, Fouché and Talleyrand were summoned to aid in fathoming the Austrian intrigue, and influences were set to work to bring Murat back to the army.

CHAPTER XXXIX

TO Mayence the Empress Maria Louisa came, to spend a few days pending the peace negotiations. If Napoleon cherished the belief that her presence would have any bearing upon her father's policy, the illusion soon vanished. Austrian diplomats were already saying, "Politics made the marriage; politics can unmake it."

So confident was Austria that the Congress at Prague would accomplish nothing, that she had drawn up her declaration of war and held it ready, as the last day of the truce wore on toward midnight. At the stroke of the clock, the paper was delivered for publication, and the war signals were lit along the Bohemian mountains. When Napoleon's courier arrived, a few hours later, bringing to the French envoys authority to sign the terms demanded, the Allies declined to consider the matter at all. It was too late. Technically they were acting within their rights; but if we really wish to know the truth about the negotiations, the conduct of those diplomats, watching the midnight clock, sending out midnight declarations of war, and lighting midnight fires to proclaim the failure of the Congress, belongs to the class of actions which speaks louder than words. If their real purpose had been to stop the shedding of blood and to liberate Europe from

Napoleon's " cruel yoke," they would never have made so great a difference between midnight of the 10th and early morning of the 11th. Nothing was to be gained by such extreme rigor, beyond the ending of the Congress; for, by the terms of the treaty, six days' notice was necessary before the resumption of hostilities.

Says Metternich : " As the clock struck twelve on the night of August 10, I despatched the declaration of war. Then I had the beacons lighted which had been prepared from Prague to the Silesian frontier, as a sign of the breach of the negotiations.'

Pasquier relates an interesting story which he had from Daru.

One day toward the end of July, Sébastiani, a Corsican, and a life-long friend of Napoleon, came to make a report, and was asked by the Emperor what was being said about the military situation. Sébastiani replied that the current opinion was that Austria would join the Allies, in which event Dresden could no longer be made the central point of the French line of defence.

" You are all right," said Napoleon, " and my mind is made up. I am going to return to the banks of the Saale; I will gather there some three hundred thousand men, and, with my rear resting on Mayence, my right flank covered by the extremity of the mountains of Bohemia, I will show the enemy the bull's horns. He will seek to manœuvre under my eyes; no sooner has he committed his first mistake than I will fall upon him, crush him, and the coalition will vanish more quickly than it appeared."

Daru was sent for and told to go at once and prepare the

necessary orders for this retrograde movement. As Daru was leaving the room, Bassano entered, and the Emperor put to him the usual question, " What is being said?" Bassano replied that certain persons who pretended to know everything were speaking of a backward movement, saying: " That your Majesty cannot remain here. They forget that the great Frederick, with forces vastly inferior to your own, held out all winter in the same position against the combined armies of Austria and Russia."

This comparison made so deep an impression upon Napoleon that when Daru returned a few hours later with all the orders he had been told to prepare, he found the Emperor in a pensive mood, and was dismissed with these words, " The matter requires more thought."

The result of this new meditation was that he persisted in his first system of operations: Dresden remained the central point of his line.

Napoleon's position at the renewal of hostilities was well-nigh desperate. He had grossly deceived himself. Keenly aware of the demoralized condition of his own forces, he had not realized how much worse had been the condition of the Allies. Calculating upon the reënforcements he could muster, he had not rightly estimated the strength which Russia and Austria could add to their resources. As to Austria, particularly, it seems that he miscalculated to the extent of one hundred thousand men.

In other important respects, the allied position became stronger. Marshal Ney's chief of staff, Jomini, deserted, and carried over to the enemy the general knowledge he had gained in Napoleonic warfare, as well as the special information he had obtained in the present campaign. General Moreau, leaving Baltimore in the United States, had landed at Stralsund, where Bernadotte received him with the highest military honors; and he was now in position to direct the allied forces. Thus with Bernadotte, Jomini, and Moreau to guide their counsels, the Allies would be able to combat Napoleon with advantages they had never possessed before. They would be advised by men who understood his system, men who could anticipate his plans and defeat his combinations.

"We are teaching them how to beat us!" Napoleon himself had already said, speaking to Lannes of the improved Russian tactics. In this campaign his enemies had agreed upon the best of policies, — to avoid battle when he commanded in person, and to crush his lieutenants wherever found.

In yet another respect events were telling heavily against the French. Marshal Bessières, commander of the cavalry of the Imperial Guard, had been killed in one of the first skirmishes; and, after Bautzen, a spent cannon ball had mortally wounded Duroc. Both these were officers of the highest merit, devotedly attached to the Emperor, and possessing his implicit confidence. He had singled them out at the beginning of his career, had lifted them from the ranks, and had raised them to imperial peerages. Their loss he felt to be irreparable, and his grief was almost overwhelming. For the first time in his career he was so prostrated, on the evening of Duroc's death, that he was unable to give orders. Alone in his tent, his head bowed to his breast, he sat in a stupor of sorrow; and to his officers coming for instructions, he said, "Everything to-morrow." Next morning, at breakfast, Constant noticed the big tears which rolled down his cheeks and fell upon his plate.

The Allies, having tricked the great trickster in the matter of the armistice, broke it to effect the junction between the Russian and Austrian forces. This much more won by fraud, the war began again.

Napoleon made a dash at Blücher, who did not forget to fall back out of reach, as agreed among the Allies. The dreaded Emperor, being at a distance, vainly chasing Blücher, the main army of the Allies marched upon Dresden, where St. Cyr was in command of the defence.

On the 25th of August, 1813, some two hundred thousand of the allied troops invested the city, whose garrison was about twenty thousand. If the French should lose it, ruin to their campaign would follow. In vain Jomini urged the Austrian commander, Schwarzenberg, to attack at once, while Napoleon was away. No. The leisurely Prince, being fatigued, or something else, must await the morning of another day; for Napoleon was in Silesia, too far off to be a source of disquiet. On August 26 the assault began, St. Cyr meeting it with heroism, but steadily losing ground.

Three hundred pieces of artillery rained shot and shell upon the crowded city. The dying and the dead, men, women, and children strewed the streets. The inhabitants of the town implored the French to surrender. Two regiments of Westphalian hussars, from Jerome Bonaparte's kingdom, went over to the enemy. But the Emperor had not lost sight of Dresden. When the news reached him that the allied army was crossing the Bohemian frontier, he guessed the point threatened, and hurried to its relief. As he marched, courier after courier from St. Cyr galloped up to hasten the coming of succor. Napoleon's horses were spurred on to their highest speed, till he reached the outskirts of the city, from which, with his field-glass, he could survey the battle. The road over which he must enter Dresden was swept by such a fire from the Austrian guns that it is said Napoleon went down upon all fours to crawl past. As he entered the city, its defenders went wild with joy. "There he is! There he is!" was shouted by thousands, as the Old Guard rushed forward to meet him. "Nothing was heard," says Caulaincourt, "but clapping of hands and shouts of enthusiasm. Men, women, and children mingled with the troops and escorted us to the palace. The consternation and alarm which had hitherto prevailed, were now succeeded by boundless joy and confidence."

The Emperor had marched his army one hundred and twenty miles in four days over roads which heavy rains had turned into bogs. He had arrived in time; those who had strained their eyes to catch the first glimpse of the relief columns had not looked in vain. "There he is! There he is!" roused all drooping spirits, gave life to dead hope, so mysteriously irresistible is the influence of a great man. The date was August, 1813. Just a few months were to roll by before the good city of Paris would find itself beleagued by these same Allies. Napoleon would again be away, but would again be devouring distance, moving heaven and earth to get back in time. Again anxious eyes would look out over walls and battlements, scanning the horizon to catch a glimpse of the white horse and the stunted rider, flying to the relief. Ardent patriots, seeing what they long to see, will mistake some other figure for his, and will raise the cry. "There he is!" But traitors and cowards will be busy in the great captain's chief city, his own brother will act the craven and fly, his best-beloved of the surviving marshals will fight the feeble fight of the dastard, his son will be torn screaming and struggling from the palace, and while the haggard eye of the war-worn Emperor, almost there, will strain to see the towers of Notre Dame, the white flag will fly over a surrendered town.

Too late! Just a few hours too late.

That night in Dresden, after having reconnoitred and made all his dispositions, Napoleon was walking up and down his room. Stopping suddenly, he turned to Caulaincourt and said : —

"Murat has arrived."

This brilliant soldier had wavered until the battles of Lützen and Bautzen had been gained; but he had now come to lead a few more matchless charges of cavalry, meteoric in splendor, before he should lose heart again, forsake Napoleon utterly, and take his wilful course to utter and shameful ruin.

"Murat has come. I have given him command of my guard. As long as I am successful, he will follow my fortune."

The Allies were not aware that either Napoleon or Murat had arrived. It is said that the battle had not been long in progress before Schwarzenberg turned to the Czar and remarked, "The Emperor must certainly be in Dresden."

Holding the allied centre in check by a concentrated fire of heavy artillery, Napoleon launched Ney at their right and Murat at their left. Both attacks were completely successful. The allied army broke at all points,

and retreated toward Bohemia, leaving some twenty thousand prisoners in the hands of the French.

Torrents of rain had poured down during the whole day,
and as Napoleon came riding back into the city that evening by the side of Murat, his clothes dripped water, and a
stream poured from his soaked hat. As Constant undressed him he had a slight chill, followed by fever, and he
took his bed.

Worn out as he was, the Emperor must have felt profoundly relieved. He had won a victory of the first
magnitude, infinitely greater than those of Lützen and
Bautzen, for he now had cavalry. His mistake in having
granted the armistice had perhaps been redeemed. If his
lieutenants now served him well, the coalition which had
put him in such extreme peril would dissolve. He would
emerge from the danger with glory undimmed, empire
strengthened. "This is nothing!" he said, referring to
his triumph at Dresden. "Wait till we hear from Vandamme. He is in their rear. It is there we must look for
the great results."

Alas for such calculations! His lieutenants were ruin-
ing the campaign faster than he could repair it. The
Prussians, led by Bülow (nominally under Bernadotte),
had beaten Oudinot at Grossbeeren, on August 23, driving
the French back upon the Elbe. Blücher had caught
Macdonald in the act of crossing a swollen river in Silesia,
had fallen upon him and destroyed him, in the battle of
Katzbach, August 26; and, to crown the climax of disaster, Vandamme, from whom so much had been expected,
was, partly through a false movement of his own, and
partly through the failure of Napoleon to support him,
crushed and captured at Kulm (August 29 and 30).

Thus, Dresden proved a barren triumph. The Czar of Russia and the King of Prussia should have been taken prisoners; the allied army should have been annihilated; the war should have ended with a glorious peace for France. How did it happen that the wrecked army escaped, and made havoc with Vandamme at Kulm?

The story goes that the Emperor, pressing eagerly forward in pursuit of the vanquished foe, was suddenly stricken with severe sickness; and instead of being carried on to Pirna, was hurried back to Dresden. The army, left without leadership, slackened in the pursuit; the Allies were left undisturbed; and when they came upon Vandamme, that rash officer, taken front and rear, was overwhelmed by superior numbers.

As to the cause of Napoleon's sudden illness, accounts differ widely. General Marbot states that it was "the result of the fatigue caused by five days in the saddle under incessant rain."

According to the Emperor himself, as reported by Daru to Pasquier, the illness was "nothing but an attack of indigestion caused by a wretched stew seasoned with garlic, which I cannot endure." But he had at the time believed himself to be poisoned. "And on such trifles," said he to Daru, "the greatest events hang! The present one is perhaps irreparable."

Virtually the same explanation of his sudden return to Dresden, and the abandonment of the pursuit, was given by Napoleon at St. Helena.

It is significant that Constant's *Memoirs* represent the Emperor as vomiting and having a chill, accompanied by utter exhaustion, upon his return from the battle-field on the evening of the 27th. Overwork, exposure, mental anxiety, the continual strain of mind and body had evidently brought on a collapse. The illness which recalled him back from Pirna may have originated in the same natural causes. The "stew seasoned with garlic," or the "leg of mutton stuffed with sage" (for each statement occurs), may have been merely the thing which precipitated the breakdown which was already inevitable.

Whatever the cause, the results were decisive. As at Borodino, he lost all control of events, let the campaign drift as it would, and recovered himself when it was too late to repair the mischief.

Dresden was to prove the last imperial victory. When Napoleon, drenched and dripping, his fine beaver aflop on his shoulder, was taken into the arms of the grateful King of Saxony, on the return from the battle-field of Dresden, he was receiving the last congratulation which he as Emperor would ever hear from subject monarch. To this limit had already shrunk the fortunes of the conqueror who, a few months back, had summoned Talma from Paris to play "to a parquet of kings."

A stray dog wandering about the battle-field of Dresden, with a collar on its neck, attracted some curiosity, and it was soon known in the French army that the collar bore the inscription, "I belong to General Moreau." It was soon known, likewise, that this misguided soldier had been mortally wounded early in the action, and had died amidst the enemies of his country.

Napoleon believed that he himself had directed the fatal shot; but one who was in Moreau's party at the time contended that the ball came from a different battery.

Remaining in the vicinity of Dresden till the last days of September, Napoleon found himself gradually growing weaker. His army was crumbling away through hard-ships, disease, and battle. Reënforcements as steadily added to the strength of the Allies. Operating in a country hostile to him as it had never been before, Napoleon had the utmost difficulty in keeping himself advised of the numbers and movements of the forces opposed to him. So intense was the patriotic spirit in Germany that the spy could do almost nothing for the French, while the Allies were kept informed of everything.

It was Blücher who took the offensive for the Allies, and boldly crossed the Elbe at Wartenburg. Napoleon rushed from Dresden to throw himself upon the Prussians; but as soon as Blücher learned that Napoleon was in his front he shunned battle and went to join Bernadotte (October 7, 1813). The huge iron girdle of the allied armies was slowly being formed around the French; it became evident that the line of the Elbe must be abandoned.

But before taking this decision it seems that Napoleon had contemplated a bold forward march upon Berlin, and had been thwarted by the opposition of his generals. Ever since the Russian disasters had broken the spell of his influence, the Emperor had encountered more or less surliness and independence among his higher officers. The marshals had taken a tone which was almost insubordinate, and the great captain was no longer able to ignore their opinions.

When it became known that he intended to make a dash at Berlin, regardless of the possibility that armies double the size of his own might throw themselves between him and France, there was almost universal dissatisfaction among the troops. Moscow was recalled. Nobody wanted a repetition of that hideous experience. "Have

not enough of us been killed? Must we all be left
here?"

To add to Napoleon's embarrassment, news came that
Bavaria had deserted and gone over to the Allies. Says
Constant, "An unheard-of thing happened: his staff
went in a body to the Emperor, entreating him to abandon
his plans on Berlin and march on Leipsic."

For two days the Emperor did nothing. Quartered in
the dismal château of Düben, he became as inert, as apathetic, as he had been at Borodino and at Moscow. "I
saw him," writes Constant, "during nearly an entire day,
lying on a sofa, with a table in front of him covered with
maps and papers which he did not look at, with no other
occupation for hours together than that of slowly tracing
large letters on sheets of white paper."

The Emperor yielded to the pressure of his officers, and
" the order to depart was given. There was an outburst
of almost immoderate joy. Every face was radiant.
Throughout the army could be heard the cry, 'We are
going to see France again, to embrace our children, our
parents, our friends.'"

Falling back upon Leipsic, Napoleon found Murat already engaged with the Austrians. In the hope that
he could crush Schwarzenberg before Blücher and Bernadotte came up, the Emperor prepared for battle. There
were about one hundred and fifty thousand of the Austrians, while the French numbered about one hundred
and seventy thousand; but it was necessary to place the
divisions of Ney and Marmont on the north, where the
Russians and Prussians and Swedes were expected. The
great "Battle of the Nations" began on the morning of
the 16th of October, 1813, and raged all day. The ad-

vantage was with the French, for they fought from positions more or less sheltered; but the Emperor appears to have made one serious mistake. Blücher not having yet arrived, Ney and Marmont were ordered to Napoleon's aid in the effort to destroy the Austrians before the coming of reënforcements. Ney moved, but Marmont was already engaged with Blücher when he received the Emperor's order. Holding his ground and assaulted by overwhelming numbers, Marmont's corps was almost destroyed; while Ney, divided between his old position and the new, rendered no effective service in either place. Just as d'Erlon's corps, swinging like a pendulum between Quatre-Bras and Ligny did not strike at either point, so Ney lost his force on the fatal field of Leipsic.

General Marbot states, moreover, that Ney left his original position without orders from the Emperor. Blücher, getting up before Napoleon expected him, and worsting the French on the north, turned the scales in favor of the Allies.

Why it was that Napoleon had not called St. Cyr from Dresden, and thus added thirty thousand to his own forces, cannot now be known. He himself said at St. Helena that he sent despatches to this effect, but that they were intercepted. Taking into account the swarms of Cossacks and Bashkirs which were flying over the country, and also the intensely hostile spirit of the native populations, the capture of a French courier would seem to have been a natural event.

However, there are those who say that St. Cyr was left at Dresden on purpose, because Napoleon was unwilling that the Saxon capital should fall into the hands of the enemy. In other words, he left his garrison caged at

Dresden, just as he left cooped up within similar fortresses a sufficient number of veteran troops to have made
his army as large as that of the Allies.

In the year 1797 the young Napoleon had driven the
Austrian armies from Italy, had chased them through the
mountains of the Tyrol, and had come almost in sight of
Vienna. Austria sent Count Meerfeldt into the French
lines to sue for peace, and her prayer was granted. In
1805 this same Napoleon had shattered the Russo-Austrian forces at Austerlitz, and was about to capture both
Czar and Emperor. Again Count Meerfeldt was sent to
Napoleon's tent to beg for mercy, and again the plea was
heard. Now it was 1813, the tide had turned, and it
was Napoleon's time to ask for peace. His messenger
was a released captive, Count Meerfeldt, he of Leoben and
Austerlitz ; and to the message neither Czar nor Austrian
emperor returned any answer whatever.

During the 17th there was no fighting, and the French
made no movement. They could probably have retired
unmolested, but Napoleon was awaiting a reply to his
propositions.

During the night, rockets blazed in the sky on the
north — the signal to Schwarzenberg and Blücher that
Bernadotte and Bennigsen had come. The Swedes, the
German bands, the Russian reserves, were all up, and the
Allies would now outnumber the French two to one.

With the light of the 18th began " the greatest battle
in all authentic history." Nearly half a million men threw
themselves upon each other with a fury like that of mani-
acs. Men from every quarter of Europe were there, from
Spain to Turkey, from the northern seas to the Adriatic
and Mediterranean, men from palaces and men from huts,

men who flashed like Murat in the gaudiest uniforms of modern Europe, and men like the Bashkirs who wore the dress and carried the bow and arrow of ancient Scythia.

The French never fought better than on this day, nor did the Allies; but the French soldier was not what he had been, nor were French officers the same. Shortly before this the Emperor had said to Augereau, " You are no longer the Augereau of Castiglione; " and the answer was, " Nor have I the troops of Castiglione." Ney had written, after his overthrow at Dennewitz: "I have been totally defeated, and do not know whether my army has reassembled. The spirit of the generals and officers is shattered. I had rather be a grenadier than to command under such conditions." Napoleon had exclaimed in bitterness of spirit, " The deserters will be my ruin."

Bavaria, threatened by the Allies and carried along by the torrent of German patriotism, was threatening Napoleon's rear. The King of Würtemberg had honorably given notice that he also would be compelled to turn against the French. Saxony was moved by the same influences, and, in spite of the presence of her king in Leipsic, the Saxon troops felt the impulse of national passion. In the very hottest of the fight on the great day of the 18th, the Saxon infantry went over to Bernadotte, and turned their batteries upon the French. The Würtemberg cavalry followed. Then all was lost. The courage of the bravest, the skill of the ablest, sink before such odds as these. One account represents Napoleon as lifting a rage-swept face to heaven, with a cry of " Infamous! " and then rushing at the head of the Old Guard to restore the broken line. Another story is that he sank into a wooden chair which some one handed him, and fell into the deep sleep of utter exhaustion.

Bernadotte had commanded the Saxon troops for Napoleon in the campaign of 1809. He had issued a proclamation, on his own motion, claiming credit for the victory of Wagram for these Saxons, and the Emperor reproved him for the untruth and the impertinence. Operating now against Napoleon, and in Saxony, Bernadotte had broadcasted the country with a proclamation calling upon the Saxons to join him. It is quite possible that the coincidence of these circumstances influenced the wavering troops, who had used half their ammunition against the Allies, to spend the other half against the French.

This desertion of about twenty-five thousand men furnished one imperative reason for retreat; but there seems to have been a second, equally good. Constant says, "In the evening the Emperor was sitting on a red morocco camp-stool amidst the bivouac fires, dictating orders for the night to Berthier, when two artillery commanders presented themselves to his Majesty, and told him that they were nearly out of ammunition." Some two hundred and twenty-five thousand cannon balls had been fired, the reserves were exhausted, and the nearest magazines were out of reach.

The retreat began that night; and troops continued to pour across the one bridge of the Elster as fast as they could go. Why was there but one bridge? No satisfactory answer can be made, unless we adopt the theory of sheer neglect. The stream was so small that any number of bridges might have been built during the idle day of the 17th; but no orders were issued, and the French army was left to fight awful odds, with a river at its back,

over which lay the only line of retreat, and across which
there was a single bridge. Did the Emperor forget the
terrible experience of Aspern? Was he no longer the
Napoleon of Rivoli, as Augereau was no longer the Augereau of Castiglione?

"Ordener is worn out," Napoleon remarked at Austerlitz. "One has but a short time for war. I am good for
another six years, and then I shall have to stop."

Austerlitz was fought at the close of 1805; Leipsic
toward the end of 1813: the great captain had already
gone two years beyond his limit.

The lean, wiry, tireless young general of the Italian
campaign, who had fought Alvinczy five days without closing his eyes or taking off his boots, could never be identified
in the dull-faced, slow-moving, corpulent, and soon-wearied
Emperor of 1813.

Next morning, October 19, the Allies discovered that
the French were in retreat, and this attack was renewed
at all points with passionate energy. Napoleon left his
bivouac, came into Leipsic, took up quarters in the hotel
called *The Prussian Arms*. He went to the palace to take
leave of the King and Queen of Saxony, who wished to
follow his fortunes still. He advised them to stay and
make the best terms possible with the Allies. He released
his remaining Saxon troops. All day the retreat went
on, the battle raging at the same time, the French rear-
guard maintaining itself with superb courage.

The magistrates of the town, fearing its utter destruction, begged the Allies to suspend the cannonade till the
French could get away. "Let Leipsic perish," answered
the "Saviors of Germany"; and the guns continued to
roar.

To protect his rear while the retreat was in progress, Napoleon was urged to fire the suburbs next to the allied lines. He nobly refused.

What a horrible day it must have been! The steady thunder of a thousand cannon; the crackle of four hundred thousand muskets; the shouts of onset; the shrieks of the wounded; the fierce crash of caissons and wagons; the stormlike hurly-burly of countless men and horses, all wild with passion, all excited to the highest pitch of action, all crowding desperately toward the maddened town, the gorged, blood-stained streets — to reach the all-important bridge!

The world seemed ablaze with hatred for the fleeing French. The very body-guard of the Saxon king whirled upon their stricken allies, and poured deadly volleys into the retreating ranks. Even the cowardly Baden troop, which had been left in Leipsic by the French, to chop wood for the bakehouses, now laid aside their axes, and from the shelter of the bakeries shot down the French soldiers as they passed.

The Emperor with difficulty had crossed the river, and given personal direction to the reunion of the various corps. The rear-guard was making heroic efforts to save the army; and all was going as well as defeats and retreats can be expected to go, when suddenly there came a deafening explosion which, for a moment, drowned the noise of battle. It roused Napoleon, who had fallen asleep; and when Murat and Augereau came running to tell him that the bridge had been blown up and the rear-guard cut off, he seized his head convulsively in his hands, stunned by the awful news.

The French officer, charged with the duty of destroying the bridge when the rear-guard should have passed, had touched off the mine too soon.

The twenty odd thousand heroes who had been protecting the retreat, found themselves hemmed in — a swollen river in front, and three hundred thousand of the enemy in flank and rear. Some few dashed into the water and swam across, among them Marshal Macdonald. Some in attempting to swim were drowned, among them the golden-hearted, hero-patriot of Poland, Poniatowski. But the bulk of the rear-guard laid down their arms to the enemy.

In the three days at Leipsic Napoleon lost 40,000 killed, 30,000 prisoners, and 260 guns. The Allies lost in killed and wounded 54,000.

The retreat from Leipsic was less horrible than that from Moscow, but it was dismal enough. Men died like flies from camp diseases; and those who kept the ranks were demoralized.

At Erfurth, Murat left the army. The brothers-in-law embraced each other in the fervid French fashion, which looks so much and means so little. In this case it meant considerably less than nothing, for Murat had already decided to join the Allies, and Napoleon had issued orders to his minister of police to clap Murat into prison if he should set foot in France. Murat avoided the danger by getting to Naples by way of the right bank of the Rhine, and through Switzerland.

Sadly shorn of his strength, Napoleon wended his way homeward, doing what he could to save the remnants of his army. So woe-begone was the condition of the French that Bavaria, upon which Napoleon had heaped immense favors, found itself unable to resist the temptation to give

the ass's kick to the expiring lion. At Hanau the kick was
delivered, with sorry results for the ass. The mortally
wounded lion swept the Bavarians out of his path and
passed on, dragging himself across the Rhine at Mayence,
November 2, 1813.

CHAPTER XL

FROM the Rhine to the Vistula the retreat of the French caused an outburst of joy. Nationalities and dynasties drew a mighty breath of relief. Peoples, as well as kings, had warred against French domination in 1813; and peoples, rather than kings, had been Napoleon's ruin. Quickened into life by the French Revolution, Germany had partially thrown feudalism off; and, whereas in 1807 there had been no such political factor as a German people, in 1813 it was the all-powerful element of resistance to Napoleon. The German statesman outlined a people's programme, the German pamphleteer and agitator propagated it, the German poet inspired it, the German pulpit consecrated it, the German secret society organized it. There was the weapon; Spain had shown what could be done with it; the kings had but to grasp and use it. Under its blows, Napoleon's strength steadily sank.

Inspired by the German spirit, the allied armies rose after each defeat ready to fight again. Carried away by the current, Napoleon's German allies left his ranks and turned their guns upon him. Intimidated by its power, his trusty officers lost heart, lost nerve, lost judgment. Buoyed by its confidence, the kings had no fears, and rejected all compromise. Napoleon was barely across the

Rhine before his Rhenish confederation was a thing of the past, the kingdom of Westphalia a recollection, Jerome Bonaparte a fugitive without a crown, the Saxon monarch a prisoner, Holland a revolted province, Polish independence and the Grand Duchy of Warsaw a vanished dream.

The "Saviors of Europe" had saved it. Napoleon's "cruel yoke" would vex Germany no more. To emphasize the fact, the "Saviors" levied upon the country a tribute of men and money, which just about doubled the weight of Napoleon's cruel yoke.

Very heavy had been the hand of France during her ascendency. Very freely Napoleon had helped himself to such things in Germany as he needed. Very harshly had he put down all opposition to his will. And the French officers, imitating their chief, had plundered the land with insolent disregard of moderation or morality. From Jerome Bonaparte downward, Napoleon's representatives in Germany had been, as a rule, a scandal, a burden, an intolerable offence to German pride, German patriotism, and German pockets. It was with a furious explosion of pent-up wrath that Germany at last arose and drove them out.

Who was there to warn the peoples of the European states that they were blindly beating back the pioneers of progress, blindly combating the cause of liberalism, blindly doing the work of absolutism and privilege? Who would have hearkened to such a warning, had there been those wise enough and brave enough to have spoken? Viewed upon the surface, the work Napoleon had done could not be separated from his mode of doing it. The methods were rough, sometimes brutal, always dictatorial.

People could see this, feel it, and resent it — just as they saw, felt, and resented his exactions of men, money, and war material. They could not, or did not, make due allowance for the man's ultimate purpose. They could not, or would not, realize how profoundly his code of laws and his system of administration worked for the final triumph of liberal principles. They could not, or would not, understand that there was *then* no way under heaven by which he could subdue the forces of feudalism, break the strength of aristocracy, and establish the equality of all men before the law, other than the method which he pursued.

So the peoples in their folly made common cause with the kings, who promised them constitutions, civil and political liberty, and representative government. In their haste and their zeal, they ran to arms and laid their treasures at the feet of the kings. In their ardor and devotion, they marched and fought, endured and persisted, with an unselfish constancy which no trials, sufferings, or defeats could vanquish.

They advanced to the attack with fierce shouts of joy; on the retreat they were not cast down; reverses did not dampen their hopes nor shake their resolution. When the truce of Pleiswitz was granted, they welcomed it only as it gave them time to recuperate. When the Congress of Prague convened, they regarded it with dread, fearing that peace might be made and Napoleon left part-master of Germany. When the beacon lights blazed along the heights at midnight of August 10, they were hailed as slaves might hail the signals of deliverance.

In his *Memoirs*, Metternich relates that when, after the battle of Leipsic, he entered the palace of the King of

2 N

Saxony to notify him of the pleasure of the Allies, the Queen reproached him bitterly for having deserted Napoleon's "sacred cause." Metternich states that he informed her that he had not come there to argue the question with her.

And yet, if Metternich had any reply to make, then was the time to make it. The Queen's side of the case was weaker then than it would ever be again; Metternich's stronger. Perfect as may have been the Queen's faith, it was beyond her power to pierce the curtain of the years, and see what lay in the future. Had the spirit of prophecy touched her lips, she would have been taken for a maniac, for this would have been her revelation : —

"The promises the kings have made to the people will be broken; the hope of the patriot will be dashed to the ground; counter-revolution will set in; and the shadow of absolutism will deepen over the world. The noble will again put on his boots and his spurs; the peasant will once more dread the frown of his lord. The king will follow no law but that of his pleasure; the priest will again avow that Jehovah is a Tory and a Jesuit. Reactionaries will drive out Napoleon's Code, and the revolutionary principles of civil equality. The prisons will be gorged with liberals; on hundreds of gibbets democrats will rot. The Inquisition will come again, and the shrieks of the heretic will soothe the troubled conscience of the orthodox. Constitutions promised to peoples, and solemnly sworn to by kings, will be coldly set aside, and the heroes who demanded them will, by way of traitor's deaths, become martyrs to liberty.

"Mediævalism will return; statues of the Virgin will

weep, or wink, or sweat; and miracles will refresh the faith of the righteous, bringing death to the scoffer who too boldly doubts. The press will be gagged, free speech denied, public assemblies made penal. The Jesuits will swarm as never before, monasteries and convents fill to overflowing, church wealth will multiply, and neither priest nor noble will pay tribute to the state. Clerical papers will demand the gallows for liberals, clericals will seize the schools, clericals will forbid all political writings.

" The time will come when the European doctrine will again be proclaimed that the sovereign has full power over the lives and the property of his subjects. The time will come when this same Emperor Francis will publicly admonish the Laybach professors that they are not to teach the youth of Germany too much : — ' I do not want learned men !   I want obedient men ! '

" The time will come when in Bourbon France the work of the Revolution will be set aside by the stroke of the pen, and absolute government decreed again.   Even in England, free speech attempted at a public meeting will bring out the troops who will charge upon a mixed and unarmed multitude, wounding and slaying with a brutality born of bigoted royalism and class-tyranny.   The cry for reform there will challenge such resistance that Wellington will hold his army ready to massacre English people.

" The time will come when these three kings — Alexander, Francis, and Frederick William — will form their Holy Alliance in the interest of aristocracy, hereditary privilege, clerical tyranny, and absolute royalty.   By force of arms they will crush democracy wherever it appears ; they will bring upon Europe a reign of terror; and the cause of human progress will seem to be lost forever.

"And as for you, Prince Metternich, the time will come when you will have been so identified with the oppressors of the people, so well known as their busy tool, their heartless advocate, their pitiless executioner, their polished liar, hypocrite, and comprehensive knave, that a minister of state will proclaim amid universal applause, ' I sum up the infamy of the last decades in the name of Metternich ! ' "

All this might the Queen of Saxony have said to her insolent tormentor; for all this is literal truth. In the light of history the woman was right: Napoleon's was the " sacred cause."

When the Emperor reached Paris, his situation was as trying as any mortal was ever called upon to face. Not a legitimate king like Alexander, Frederick William, or Francis, his power could not rally from shocks which theirs had so easily survived. Great as had been his genius for construction, he could not give to his empire the solidity and sanctity which comes from age. He could create orders of nobility, and judicial, legislative, and executive systems; he could erect a throne, establish a dynasty, and surround it with a court; but he could not so consecrate it with the mysterious benediction of time that it would defy adversity, and stand of its own strength amid storms which levelled all around it.

The great Frederick and the small Frederick William remained the centre of Prussian hopes, Prussian loyalty, Prussian efforts even when Berlin was in the hands of the enemy, the army scattered in defeat, and the King almost a fugitive. Prussia, in all her battles, fought for the King; in her defeats, mourned with the King; in her resurrection from disaster, rallied round the King.

Austria had done the same. Her Emperor Francis had as little real manhood in him as any potentate that ever complacently repeated the formula of "God and I." He was weak in war and in peace; in the head, empty; in the heart, waxy and cold; in the spirit, selfish, false, cowardly, and unscrupulous. Yet when this man's unprovoked attacks upon Napoleon had brought Austria to her shame and sorrow, — cities burnt, fields wasted, armies destroyed, woe in every house for lives lost in battle, — Austria knew no rallying-point other than Francis; and when the poor creature came back to Vienna, after Napoleon had granted him peace, all classes met him with admiration, love, loyalty, and enthusiasm. Napoleon, returning to France victorious, was not more joyously acclaimed by the French than was this defeated and despoiled Francis applauded in Vienna.

The one was a legitimate king, the other was not. On the side of Francis and the Fredericks were time, training, habit, and system. Germans were born into the system, educated to it, practised in it, and died out of it — to be succeeded by generations who knew nothing but to follow in the footsteps of those that had gone before.

In France the old order had been overthrown and the new had not so completely identified itself with Napoleon that he could exert the tremendous force which antiquity and custom lend to institutions.

Nevertheless, the truth seems to be that in his last struggles Napoleon had the masses with him. Had he made a direct appeal to the peasantry and to the workmen

of the cities, there is every reason to believe that he could
have enrolled a million men.   The population in France
was not at a standstill then as it is now.   It was steadily
on the increase ; and it was fairly prosperous, and fairly
contented.   The Emperor had given special attention to
agriculture and manufactures.   In every possible way he
had encouraged both, and his efforts had borne fruit.   He
had not increased the taxes, he had not burdened the
State with loans, he had not issued paper money, he had
not even changed the conscription laws.   In some of his
campaigns he had called for recruits before they were
legally due ; but, as the Senate had sanctioned the call,
the nation had acquiesced.   It is true that men and boys
had dodged the enrolling officers, and that the numbers
of those who defied and resisted the conscriptions had
increased to many thousands ; but the meaning of this
was nothing more than that the people were tired of distant wars.

A pledge from the Emperor that soldiers should not be
sent out of France would apparently have rallied to him
the full military support of the nation.   But Napoleon
could not get his own consent to arm the peasants and
the artisans.   Both in 1814 and in 1815 that one chance
of salvation was offered to him ; in each year he rejected
it.

The awful scenes of the Revolution which he had witnessed had left him the legacy of morbid dread of mobs.
The soldier who could gaze stolidly upon the frightful
rout at Leipsic, where men were perishing in the wild
storm of battle by the tens of thousands, could never free
himself from the recollection of the Parisian rabble which
had slaughtered a few hundreds.   At Moscow he refused

to arm the serfs against their masters ; in France he as
deliberately rejected all proposals to appeal to the lower
orders to support his throne.

The secret is revealed by his question, " Who can tell
me what spirit will animate these men ? " He feared for
his dynasty, dreading a republic in which free elections
would control the choice of the executive.

But while the mass of the French people remained
loyal to Napoleon, the upper classes were divided. There
had always been a leaven of royalism in the land, and
Napoleon himself had immensely strengthened its influence. Bringing back the émigrés, restoring hereditary estates, creating orders of nobility anew, and establishing
royal forms, he had been educating the country up to
monarchy as no one else could have done — had been
" making up the bed for the Bourbons." The ancient
nobility, as a rule, had secretly scorned him as a Corsican
parvenu, even while crowding his antechambers and load-
ing themselves with his favors. Now that reverses had
commenced, their eyes began to turn to their old masters,
the Bourbons, and the hopes of a restoration and a counter-revolution began to take distinct shape in Paris itself.

To the royalists, also, went the support of a large number of the rich — men who resented the income tax of
twenty-five per cent, which Napoleon at this time felt it
necessary to impose upon them. Another grudge, they,
the rich, had against him : he would not allow them to
loot his treasury, as the rich were doing in England.
Nor would he grant exemptions from any sort of public
burden, special privilege being in his eyes a thing
utterly abominable. Hence, such men as the great
banker Laffitte were not his friends.

There was another element of opposition which made itself felt at this crisis. There were various contractors, and other public employees, who had taken advantage of the decline of Napoleon's power to plunder, embezzle, and cheat. The Emperor was on the track of numbers of these men, and in his wrath had sworn to bring them to judgment. "Never will I pardon those who squander public funds!" These men moved in upper circles, and had many social, political, and financial allies. Dreading punishment if Napoleon held his throne, they became active partisans of the Bourbon restoration. Even his old schoolmate, Bourrienne, his private secretary of many years, betrayed him shamelessly. The Emperor had detected the fact that Bourrienne had been using his official position for private gain, and had dismissed him ; but on account of old association had softened the fall by appointing him Consul at Hamburg. At this place Bourrienne amassed a fortune by violating the Continental system, and he now hated the man he had betrayed, and from whom he feared punishment. This was but one case among hundreds.

Then, there was the Talleyrand, Fouché, Remusat, Abbé Louis, Abbé Montesquiou, Duc de Dalberg sort. Talleyrand had been enriched, ennobled, imperially pampered, but never trusted. Napoleon had borne with his venalities and treacheries until men marvelled at his forbearance. This minister of France was in the pay of Austria, of Russia, of England, of any foe of France who could pay the price. It was probably he who sold to England the secret of Tilsit. It was certainly he who conspired with the Czar against Napoleon, and took a bribe from Austria every time she needed mercy from

France. It was he who extorted tribute from Napoleon's allies at the same time that he sold state secrets to Napoleon's foes. Denounced and dismissed, and then employed again, this man was ripe for a greater betrayal than he had yet made, and he now believed that the opportunity was close at hand.

Fouché, also, had been Napoleon's minister, Napoleon's Duke of Otranto. Dabbling in conspiracies of all sorts, and venturing upon a direct intrigue with England, Napoleon had disgraced him, instead of having him shot. Needing him again, the Emperor had reëmployed him, thereby affording another rancorous foe his chance to strike when the time should come.

In the army there was the same grand division of sentiment, — the rank and file being devoted to Napoleon, the officers divided.

The marshals were tired of war, there being nothing further in it for them. They had been lifted as high as they could go ; they had been enriched to satiety ; their fame was established. Why should they continue to fight ? Were they never to be left in peace ? What was the good of having wealth if they were never to enjoy it ?

The marshals were human ; their grumblings and growlings most natural. They honestly believed that peace depended upon the Emperor alone, that he only had to stretch forth his hand to get it.

He himself knew better ; but it almost maddened him to realize that so few understood this as he did.

"Peace! peace!" he cried impatiently, to Berthier the goose. "You miserable——! Don't you know that I want peace more than any one ? How am I to get it ? The more I concede, the more they demand!"

This brings us squarely to the question : Did the Allies, in good faith, offer Napoleon peace, and did he recklessly refuse it?

Then and afterward he contended that he had done everything in his power to secure honorable terms. Almost with his dying breath he repeated this statement at St. Helena. What is the truth about it?

Let any one who wishes to know, study the *Memoirs* of the period; let him further study the despatches and treaties of the Allies; let him give due weight to the influence upon these Allies of the Bourbons, the ancient nobility, the higher priests of the Catholic Church, the dynastic prejudices of the allied kings, and the intense personal hatreds of such powerful counsellors of kings as Pozzo di Borgo, Stein, Bernadotte, Castlereagh, and Talleyrand. In addition to this, let such a student consider how the Allies violated the armistice of Pleiswitz, the capitulations of Dantzic and Dresden, the treaties they made with Napoleon in 1812, and that which they made with him at his abdication in 1814.

Let such a student furthermore consider that these Allies not only broke the treaty they made with Napoleon in 1814, but likewise violated the pledges which they had made to their own peoples in drawing them into the war.

If, after the study of these evidences of the bad faith of the Allies, there still remains doubt, the *Memoirs* of Metternich will remove it — if it be removable.

The world knows that the only avowed purpose of the Allies was to liberate Europe by driving Napoleon back beyond the Rhine, and that this end had now been attained. Hence, if the real objects the Allies had in view were those which had been made public, why should not the war have ceased? Europe was free, Napoleon's empire shattered, nothing remained to him but France — why should the Allies follow him there? It was necessary to hoodwink the world upon this point, and it was Metternich's task to do it; — for the allied kings were determined to invade France and put an end to Napoleon's political existence. Metternich avows this himself; yet he persuaded them to make to Napoleon the celebrated Frankfort Proposals. All the world knows that the allied kings, with an apparent excess of magnanimity, offered even then to come to such terms with Napoleon as would have left him in possession of the France of 1792, a larger realm than the greatest of Bourbon kings had ever ruled. What the world did not know was that these Frankfort Proposals were not sincere, and were made for effect only. It was necessary to the Allies to cover their own designs, to justify their departure from the declarations of 1813, to create the impression that they themselves favored peace while Napoleon persisted in war. Succeeding in this, they would cut the ground from under his feet, divide the French, and deprive him of enthusiastic and united national support. With profound policy and duplicity, they sought to create in France itself the impression that Napoleon was the only obstacle to peace, and that their efforts were aimed at him, and not at France, her institutions, her principles, or her glory. Not for a moment was France given cause to suspect that the Bourbons were to be forced upon her, and the great work of the Revolution partially undone. Not for a moment was she allowed to realize that offers of peace to Napoleon were deceptive — intended only to embarrass him and to divide his people. Yet Metternich himself admits that the Frankfort Proposals were made for effect — not only admits it, but takes credit for it. He states that he was compelled to exert all his influence with the allied sovereigns to secure their consent to these proposals, and that he overcame their resistance, as he had overcome Alexander's in 1813, by assuring them that the offers would come to nothing.

CHAPTER XLI

HAD Napoleon promptly accepted the Frankfort Proposals as they were made, would he have secured peace? Manifestly not, for Metternich had put two conditions to his offer which do not look pacific. First, the war was not to be suspended during negotiations. Second, the Frankfort Proposals were only to be taken as *bases* upon which diplomats could work. Does this look like a *bona fide* offer of peace? Napoleon thought not, and impartial history must hesitate long before saying he erred. When in December, 1813, he sent his envoy to the Allies, agreeing to all they demanded, he was once more told that he should have consented sooner. The Allies had gained their point in having made the offer, and their active interest in the matter was at an end. The French envoy was kept in hand, seeking audiences and positive replies, while the allied armies marched into France.

France in 1814 was a nation of about thirty million souls. During the years 1812 and 1813 she had furnished nearly six hundred thousand soldiers to Napoleon's armies. Of these about half were prisoners in Russia and Germany, or were shut up in distant garrisons; about two hundred thousands were dead or missing; about one hundred thousand remained subject to the Emperor's call. It was his hope that further conscription would yield him three hundred thousand recruits ; but it failed to do so.

So much war material had been lost in the campaigns in Russia and Saxony that he could not furnish muskets to volunteers ; some went to war armed with shot-guns. Neither could he mount any large force of cavalry ; horses could not be had. Nor were there uniforms for all ; some went to the front in sabots and blouse. Money was lacking, and the Emperor took more than $10,000,000 from his own private funds (saved from his Civil List), and threw them into the equipment of the troops, calling also upon the rich for voluntary contributions, on a sliding scale which he was thoughtful enough to furnish. A few of the taxes were increased, the communal lands taken for the public service, and paper money issued against the value of this particular property.

Competent judges have expressed the opinion that had Napoleon at this time liberated the Pope and Ferdinand of Spain, and done so unconditionally, he might have won in the campaign which was about to open. The release of the Pope might have brought back to allegiance many of the disaffected ; the release of Ferdinand might have made it necessary for the English to quit Spain, and in this manner Napoleon would have drawn to his own subport the veterans he still kept there. The Duke of Wellingtou is quoted as saying that had Ferdinand appeared in Spain in December, 1813, the English would have had to evacuate it. He, of all men, should have known.

But Napoleon would not consent to make unconditional surrender to the Pope or to Ferdinand. He patched up a peace with the latter, which, being a half-way measure, yielded no benefit ; and as to the Pope, the Holy Father refused to treat on any terms with his " son in Christ Jesus."   Restore him to Rome first ; then he would treat.

From the time Napoleon returned from Saxony till he left Paris to take charge of his last campaign, less than three months passed.

There was never a time when he labored with greater patience or exhibited greater fortitude, courage, and determination.   But the evidence seems to indicate that he had lost hope, that he was conscious of the fact that nothing less than a miracle could save him.

Ever since the Russian campaign, he had not had the same confidence in his star.   As he set out from St. Cloud for his campaign in Saxony he said to Caulaincourt : "I envy the lot of the meanest peasant of my empire.   At my age he has discharged his debts to the country and remains at home, enjoying the society of his wife and children ; while I — I must fly to the camp and throw myself into the struggles of war."

Méneval states that in private he found the Emperor " careworn, though he did his best to hide his anxiety."

" But in public his face was calm and reassured.   In our conversations he used to complain of feeling tired of war and of no longer being able to endure horse exercise.   He reproached me in jest with having fine times, whilst he painfully dragged his plough."

Is there anything which is more pathetic and which shows how grandly Napoleon towered above the small men who were tugging to pull him down than his rebuke to the intriguers of the legislative body ?

At the head of a disloyal faction there, M. Lainé — an old Girondin, now a royalist, who was soon to set up the

Bourbon standard at Bordeaux — started a movement which was meant to give aid to the Allies by showing that divisions existed in France, and by forming a nucleus of Bourbon opposition. A committee, which Lainé controlled, made a report in which Napoleon's government was impliedly censured, and reforms demanded. Following this lead, others in the legislative body clamored for the acceptance of the Frankfort Proposals.

This movement of opposition in the legislative body, at a time when half a million men were on the march to invade France, was nothing short of treason. At such a crisis, the dullest of Frenchmen must have understood that obstruction to Napoleon was comfort to the enemy.

Even the cold Pasquier admits that the Emperor's words to these men were "somewhat touching."

Having reproved the committee for allowing Lainé, the royalist, to lead them astray, Napoleon said : " I stood in need of something to console me, and you have sought to dishonor me. I was expecting that you would unite in mind and deed to drive out the foreigner. You have bidden him come ! Indeed, had I lost two battles, it would not have done France greater harm."

Somewhat touching, Chancellor Pasquier ? Ah, if ever the great man was heard to sob in public, it was here ! A nobler grief, and a nobler expression of it, history has seldom recorded.

In the course of the same talk, the indignant Emperor reminded the legislators that whatever differences existed between him and them should have been discussed in private. " Dirty linen should not be washed in public." Then hurried away by angry impatience at those who were forever prating about the sacrifices he exacted of

France, he exclaimed, "France has more need of me than I of France." This was true, but the statement was imprudent; and his enemies at once misconstrued his meaning, and used the remark to his damage. He dismissed the legislative body fearing, doubtless, that while he was at the head of the army the royalists of the chamber might become a danger in his rear.

Blow after blow fell upon the defeated Emperor during the closing weeks of 1813. St. Cyr gave up Dresden, and Rapp surrendered Dantzic, upon condition that their troops should be allowed to return to France. The Allies set aside the conditions, and held the garrisons as prisoners of war.

Constant relates two incidents which reveal Napoleon's melancholy more fully than his words to Méneval or to the legislative body.

The Emperor went about Paris more informally than he had ever done. Sometimes on horseback, sometimes on foot, he went to inspect his public works, schools, and hospitals. Apparently he was curious to feel the public pulse. Constant says that the people cheered him, and that sometimes great multitudes followed him back to the Tuileries. The time had been when the Emperor had not paid any special heed to the shouts of a street mob. Now the cry of enthusiasm was music to his ears. After one of these episodes the Emperor would return to the palace in high spirits, would have much to say to his valet that night, and would be " very gay."

In his visits to Saint-Denis (Girl's School of the Legion of Honor) the Emperor was usually accompanied by two pages. "Now it happened in the evening," writes Constant, "that the Emperor, after returning from Saint-

2 o

Denis, said to me with a laugh on entering his chamber, where I was waiting to undress him, ' Well, well, here are my pages trying to resemble the ancient pages. The little rogues ! Do you know what they do ? When I go to Saint-Denis they wrangle with each other as to who shall go with me.' As he spoke, the Emperor was laughing and rubbing his hands, and repeated in the same tone a number of times, ' The little rogues.' "

Would Chancellor Pasquier admit that this was also " somewhat touching " ?

The greatest man of all history had said with proud mournfulness, " I stood in need of something to console me," and we do not realize how infinitely sad he was till we read in Constant's artless narrative that the shouts of the mob made him " very gay," and that the dispute of the boys in the palace as to which two should go out into the town with him made him rub his hands with pleasure, and repeat time and again, " Ah, the little rogues."

At the beginning of 1814 positive information came that Murat had made a treaty with Austria, and had promised an army of thirty thousand men to coöperate with the Allies against France. Much as this defection must have wounded the Emperor, the worst part of it was that he knew his sister Caroline to be more to blame than Murat. She did not believe that the Allies meant to dethrone Napoleon ; she believed he could make peace on the basis of the Frankfort Proposals ; and to save her own crown she believed that a treaty with the Allies was necessary. To this extent her treachery can be palliated — excuse for it there is none.

This defection was the cruelest blow of all ; for Murat had been promising his support, and the Emperor had based his plan of campaign upon it. He had intended that Eugène should unite his forces to those of Murat, and that the two should fall upon the Austrian line of communications, threatening Vienna. From this plan he had expected the happiest results.

Murat had been negotiating with England and Austria, but had not definitely made terms. It is said that he was driven to a decision by a wound which Napoleon inflicted upon his vanity. Murat, having written the Emperor that he could bring thirty thousand men to the field to aid France, was told to send the troops to Pavia, where they would receive " the Emperor's orders." The King of Naples received this letter on a day when, with the Queen and others, he was making a visit to Pompeii. He was so much hurt by Napoleon's tone that he tore the despatch in pieces, trampled on the fragments, and returned to Naples to close with the Austrian offers.

One must pity this brave, vain, fickle Murat, urged on to his shame and ruin by his innate levity of character, the sting of wounded vanity, the selfish promptings of an ambitious wife, and the temptings of professional diplomats.

England dug the grave for Murat as she did for Napoleon, her agent at Naples being Lord Bentinck. Murat having sent the Englishman a sword of honor, the latter wrote to his government : —

"It is a severe violence to my feelings to incur any degree of obligation to an individual whom I so deeply despise."

On the same day he wrote to Murat : "The sword of a

great captain is the most flattering compliment which a soldier can receive. It is with the highest gratitude that I accept, sire, the gift which you have done me the honor to send."

Lord Bentinck belonged, we must presume, to what Lord Wolseley calls " the highest type of English gentleman "; hence his duplicity must not be spoken of in the terms we use in denouncing the vulgar.

Another piece of bad luck had happened to the Emperor since the Saxon campaign — his two brothers, Joseph and Jerome, were in France. Wellington had not left the former much to resign in Spain ; but whatever there was, Joseph had surrendered it, and he had come away. He was now in Paris, confident as ever of his own great merits, and most unfortunately exercising his former evil influence. Napoleon made this imbecile Lieutenant-General of the kingdom, and having made the Empress regent, Joseph became President of the Council of Regency. The disastrous consequences of putting such power into Joseph's hands will be seen presently.

At length everything which human effort and human genius could achieve for the national defence, in so short a time, was done ; and it became imperative that the Emperor should join his army.

On Sunday of January 23, 1814, it being known that he would leave Paris in a few hours, the officers of the twelve legions of the National Guard assembled in the hall of the marshals, at the Tuileries, to be presented as the Emperor should return from Mass. Presently he came ; and while the Empress stood at his side, he took his little son in his arms, and presented him to the brilliant throng. In a voice which revealed his deep feeling, he told them that he was about to leave Paris to put himself at the head of the army to drive the invaders from France, and he reckoned on the zeal of all good citizens. He appealed to them to be united, and to repel all insinuations which would tend to divisions. " Efforts will not be lacking to shake your fidelity to your duties ; I rely on you to reject these perfidious attempts. Gentlemen, officers of the National Guard, I put under your protection what, next to France, is dearest to me in all the world, — my wife and my son ! "

Even Pasquier records that these words were uttered in tones which went to the heart, and with an expression of face that was noble and touching. " I saw tears course down many a cheek. All swore by acclamation to be worthy of the confidence with which they were being honored, and every one of them took this oath in all sincerity." Warming up a little, in spite of himself, the Chancellor adds, " This powerful sovereign in the toils of adversity, this glorious soldier bearing up against the buffets of fortune, could but deeply stir souls when, appealing to the most cherished affections of the human heart, he placed himself under their protection." The learned Chancellor frostily adds that " the capital did not remain indifferent to this scene, and was more deeply moved by it than one might expect."

Let us get out of this draught of wind from the frozen summits of eminent respectability, and turn to a man whose heart-beat had not been chilled in any social or judicial ice-box.

Constant writes : —

" . . . The Emperor's glance rested on the Empress and

on the King of Rome.   He added in a voice that betrayed
emotion, indicating by look and gesture his son, ' I con-
fide him to you, gentlemen ! '   At these words, a thousand
cries, a thousand arms arose, swearing to guard this precious trust.   The Empress, bathed in tears, would have
fallen if the Emperor had not caught her in his arms.
At this sight the enthusiasm reached its climax ;   tears
fell from every eye, and there was not one of the spectators who did not seem ready to shed his blood for the
imperial family."

*   *   *   *   *   *

At the beginning of 1814 France was threatened by
four armies, aggregating half a million men.   Wellington
was at the Pyrenees in the south, Bernadotte was in the
Netherlands, while Blücher and Schwarzenberg, crossing
the Rhine higher up, but at different points, were marching upon Paris by the Seine and the Marne.

With a confidence which events justified, the Emperor
left Soult to oppose Wellington.   As to Bernadotte, he
was neither trusted by the Allies nor feared by Napoleon.
The recreant Frenchman had merely come to terms with
the Allies because they had promised to take Norway from
Denmark and give it to Sweden.   In addition to this, the
Czar of Russia had dangled before Bernadotte's eyes, as a
tempting bait, the crown of France — a fact which of
itself proves the hollowness of the overtures made to Napoleon from Frankfort.   So well was the crafty Prince-Royal
of Sweden understood by those who had bought him, that
he was kept under strict personal surveillance by each of
the four great allied powers, — Russia, Austria, Prussia,
and Great Britain.   From an army led by such a man,
Napoleon had little to fear ; and he gave his whole personal

energies to Blücher and Schwarzenberg, especially to Blücher. This old hussar who had served under Frederick the Great, and who was now more than seventy years of age, was the most energetic of all the officers arrayed against France ; and he gave Napoleon more trouble than all the others put together. He could easily be outgeneralled, he could be beaten any number of times by such a captain as Napoleon ; but there was no such thing as conquering him. Routed one day, he was ready to fight again the next. Outmanœuvred at one point, he turned up ready for battle at another. His marches were swift, his resources inexhaustible, his pluck and determination an inspiration, not only to the Prussians, but to all the allied armies. He was not much of a general, was a good deal of a brute ; but he was about as well fitted for the task of wearing down Napoleon's strength as any officer Europe could have put into the field.

Moving slowly from the Rhine toward Paris, meeting no resistance which could hinder their march, the Allies, who were making war upon Napoleon alone, and who had no grudge against France, and whose wish it was, as they proclaimed, to see France " great, prosperous, and happy," gave rein to such license, committed such havoc upon property, and such riotous outrage upon man, woman, and child, that the details cannot be printed. In Spain, Napoleon had shot his own soldiers to put an end to pillage ; in Russia he had done the same. At Leipsic he had refused to burn the suburbs to save his army. In his invasions of Prussia and Austria he had held his men so well in hand that non-combatants were almost as safe, personally, as they had been under their own king. At Berlin the French Emperor publicly disgraced a prominent French officer for having written an insulting letter to a German lady.

In France the sovereigns whose every proclamation and treaty ran under the sanctimonious heading, "In the name of the Holy and Indivisible Trinity," let loose upon the country savage hordes of Cossacks, Croats, and Prussian fanatics who wreaked their vengeance upon the noncombatant peasantry and villagers until the invasion of the " Saviors of Society " became a saturnalia of lust and blood and arson, which no language fit for books can describe.

The Prussians had almost reached Brienne when the Emperor took the field with a small force, and drove them from St. Dizier. He then came upon Blücher at Brienne, suddenly, while the Prussian general was feasting at the château, and captured one of the higher officers at the foot of the stairs. The Emperor believed he had nabbed Blücher himself, and he shouted, " We will hold on to that old fighter; the campaign will not last long ! "

But Blücher had fled through the back door, and had escaped. The battle raged over the school grounds and the park where Napoleon had read and meditated in his boyhood. During the fight he found himself storming the school buildings, where the Prussians were posted; and he pointed out to his companions the tree in the park under which he had read *Jerusalem Delivered*.

One of the guides in the movement about Brienne was a curé who had been a regent of the college while Napoleon was there. They recognized each other, the Emperor exclaiming : " What ! is this you, my dear master ? Then you have never quitted this region ? So much the better; you will be more able to serve the country's cause."

The curé saddled his mare and took his place cheerfully in the imperial staff, saying, "Sire, I could find my way over the neighborhood with my eyes shut."

The Emperor drove the Prussians from Brienne with heavy loss; but when Blücher joined Schwarzenberg, and Napoleon with his slender force attacked this huge mass at La Rothière, he was beaten off, after a desperate combat.

Riding back to the château of Brienne to spend the night, the Emperor was suddenly assailed by a swarm of Cossacks, and for a moment he was in great personal danger; so much so that he drew his sword to defend himself. A Cossack lunged at him with a lance, and was shot down by General Gourgaud.

This incident gave Gourgaud a claim upon Napoleon which was heard of frequently afterward, — rather too frequently, as the Emperor thought. At St. Helena Gourgaud, a fretful man and a jealous, tortured himself and his master by too many complaints of neglect; and reminded the Emperor once too often of the pistol-shot which had slain the Cossack.

"I saw nothing of it," said Napoleon, thus putting a quietus to that particularly frequent conversational nuisance.

It was now the 1st of February, 1814; the Emperor fell back to Nogent, the Austrians following. Blücher separated from Schwarzenberg, divided his army into small detachments, and made straight for Paris. In a flash Napoleon saw his advantage, and acted. At Champ-Aubert he fell upon one of these scattered divisions and destroyed it. At Montmirail he crushed another; and hurling his victorious little army upon Blücher himself, drove that astonished old warrior back upon Châlons. Putting his guard into carts and carriages, and posting at the highest speed night and day, Napoleon united with Marshals Oudinot, Victor, and Macdonald at Guignes. On February 18 he fell upon the huge army of Schwarzenberg at Montereau and actually drove it back toward Troyes, — the Austrians as they retired calling upon old Blücher to come and give them help !

When Caulaincourt, early in December, 1813, had appeared at Frankfort ready to accept those famous proposals unconditionally, Metternich had shuffled, evaded, and procrastinated. Finally, a Peace Congress was assembled at Châtillon (February 6, 1814); and while the soldiers marched and fought, the diplomats ate, drank and made themselves merry in the farce of trying to arrange a treaty. Caulaincourt, gallant and hospitable, supplied his brother diplomats at Châtillon with all the good things which Paris could furnish, — good eatables, good drinkables, and gay women. Hence, the Peace Congress was a very enjoyable affair, indeed. It was not expected to do anything, and it fully came up to expectations. As the tide of success veered, so shifted the diplomats. When the Allies won a victory, their demands advanced ; when Napoleon won, the demands moderated. There was no such thing as a coming together.

CHAPTER XLII

A FTER his defeat at La Rothière, the Emperor author-
ized Bassano to make peace, giving to Caulaincourt
unlimited powers. But before the necessary papers could
be signed, Blücher had made his false movement, and
Napoleon's hopes had risen. Bassano, entering his room
on the morning of February 9, found the Emperor lying
on his map and planting his wax-headed pins.

" Ah, it is you, is it ? " cried he to Bassano, who held the
papers in his hands ready for signing. " There is no more
question of that. See here, I want to thrash Blücher. He
has taken the Montmirail road. I shall fight him to-morrow
and next day. The face of affairs is about to change.
We will wait."

In the movements which followed the Bonaparte of the
Italian campaign was seen again, and for the last time.
He was everywhere, he was tireless, he was inspiring, he
was faultless, he was a terror to his foes. We see him
heading charges with reckless dash, see him aiming cannon in the batteries, see him showing his recruits how to
build bridges, see him check a panic by spurring his own
horse up to a live shell and holding him there till the
bomb exploded, see him rallying fugitives, on foot and
sword in hand. We hear him appeal to his tardy marshals
to " Pull on the boots and the resolution of 1793"; we

hear him address the people and the troops with the military eloquence of his best days; we see him writing all
night after marching or fighting all day — his care and his
efforts embracing everything, and achieving all that was
possible to man.

That was a pretty picture at the crossing of the river
Aube, where Napoleon was making a hasty bridge out
of ladders spliced together, floored with blinds taken
from the houses near by. Balls were tearing up the
ground where the Emperor stood; but yet when he
was about to quench his extreme thirst by dipping up in
his hands the water of the river, a little girl of the
village, seeing his need, ran to him with a glass of wine.
Empire was slipping away from him, and his mind
must have been weighed down by a thousand cares; but
he was so touched by the gallantry of the little maid that
he smiled down upon her, as he gratefully drank, and he
said : —

" Mademoiselle, you would make a brave soldier ! "

Then he added playfully, " Will you take the epaulets?
Will you be my aide-de-camp?"   He gave her his hand,
which she kissed, and as she turned to go he added, " Come
to Paris when the war is over, and remind me of what you
did to-day ; you will feel my gratitude."

He was no gentleman ; he had not a spark of generosity
in his nature ; he was mean and cruel ; he was a superlatively bad man.   So his enemies say, beginning at Lewis
Goldsmith and ending at Viscount Wolseley.   It may be
so ; but it is a little hard on the average citizen who
would like to love the good men and hate the bad ones
that a " superlatively evil man " like Napoleon Bonaparte
should be endowed by Providence with qualities which

make such men as Wellington, Metternich, Talleyrand, Czar Alexander, Emperor Francis, or Bourbon Louis seem small, seem paltry, seem prosaic and sordid beside him.

Another glimpse of the Emperor fixes attention in these last struggles. He was at the village of Méry where he rapidly reconnoitred over the marshy ground bordering the Aube. Getting out of the saddle, he sat down upon a bundle of reeds, resting his back against the hut of a night-watchman, and unrolled his map. Studying this a few moments, he sprang upon his horse, set off at a gallop, crying to his staff, "This time we have got them!"

It did indeed seem that Blücher was entrapped and would be annihilated; but after very heavy losses he managed to get across the marsh and the river. It is said that a sudden frost, hardening the mud, was all that saved him.

Having been reënforced by the corps of Bülow and Woronzoff, which England had compelled Bernadotte to send, Blücher advanced against Marmont on the Marne. The French fell back upon the position of Marshal Mortier; and the two French generals, with about twelve thousand, checked one hundred thousand Prussians.

Napoleon, with twenty-five thousand, hurried to the support of his marshals, and was in Blücher's rear by March 1. Once more the Prussian seemed doomed. His only line of retreat lay through Soissons and across the Aisne. With Napoleon hot upon his track, and in his rear a French fortress, how was he to escape destruction? A French weakling, or traitor, had opened the way by surrendering Soissons. Had he but held the town for a day longer, the war might have ended by a brilliant triumph of the French. Moreau was the name of the commandant at Soissons — a name of ill-omen to Napoleon, whose fury was extreme.

" Have that wretch arrested," he wrote, " and also the members of the council of defence ; have them arraigned before a military commission composed of general officers, and, in God's name, see that they are shot in twenty-four hours."

Here was lost the most splendid opportunity which came to the French during the campaign. Blücher safely crossed the Aisne (March 3) in the night, and was attacked by Marmont on March 9. During the day the French were successful ; but Blücher launched at the unwary Marmont a night attack which was completely successful. The French lost forty-five guns and twenty-five hundred prisoners. In a sort of desperation, Napoleon gave battle at Laon, but was so heavily outnumbered that he was forced to retreat.

Almost immediately, however, he fell upon the Russians at Rheims, March 13, killed their general, St. Priest, and destroyed their force. It was at this time that Langeron, one of Blücher's high officers, wrote : " We expect to see this terrible man everywhere. He has beaten us all, one after another; we dread the audacity of his enterprises, the swiftness of his movements, and the ability of his combinations. One has scarcely conceived any scheme of operations before he has destroyed it."

This tribute from an enemy is very significant of what "this terrible man " might have accomplished had he been seconded. Suppose Murat and Eugène had been operating on the allied line of communications ! Or suppose Augereau had done his duty in Switzerland, in the rear of the Allies ! Spite of the odds, it seems certain that Napoleon would have beaten the entire array had he not been shamefully betrayed — abandoned by creatures of his own making.

As if the stars in their courses were fighting against this struggling Titan, he learned that the relations between his wife and his brother Joseph were becoming suspicious. Chancellor Pasquier states that he himself saw the letters written by Napoleon on leaving Rheims in which Savary, minister of police, was censured for not having made known the facts to the Emperor, and in which Savary was ordered to watch closely the suspected parties. Pasquier adds that at first he thought the Emperor must be deranged; but that information which came to him afterward caused him to believe that Napoleon's suspicions "were only too well founded."

Did ever a tragedy show darker lines than this? All Europe marching against one man, his people divided, his lieutenants mutinous and inclining to treason, his senators ready to depose him, a sister and a brother-in-law stabbing him to the vitals, members of his Council of Regency in communication with the enemy, nobles whom he had restored and enriched plotting his destruction, and his favorite brother, his Lieutenant-General of the kingdom, using the opportunity which the trust afforded to debauch his wife!

Is it any wonder that even this indomitable spirit sometimes bent under the strain?

Referring to the battle of Craonne, Constant writes : —

"The Emperor who had fought bravely in this battle as in all others, and incurred the dangers of a common soldier, transferred his headquarters to Bray. Hardly had he entered the room when he called me, took his boots off while leaning on my shoulder, but without saying a word, threw his sword and hat on the table, and stretched himself on the bed with a sound which left one in doubt whether it was the profound sigh of fatigue or the groan of utter despair. His Majesty's countenance was sorrowful and anxious. He slept for several hours the sleep of exhaustion."

After the Emperor's repulse at Laon, Schwarzenberg took heart and advanced toward Paris; but Napoleon, leaving Rheims, marched to Épernay, and the Austrians fell back, pursued by the French. The allied armies, however, concentrated at Arcis on the Aube, and, with one hundred thousand men, beat off the Emperor when he attacked them with thirty thousand.

Napoleon now made his fatal mistake—fatal because he could count on no one but himself. He moved his army to the rear of the Allies to cut their line of communications. This was a move ruinous to them, if the French armies in front should do their duty. The despatches in which Napoleon explained his march to the Empress Regent at Paris fell into the hands of the enemy, owing to Marmont's disobedience of orders in abandoning the line of communications. They hesitated painfully, they had even turned and made a day's march following Napoleon, when the capture of a bundle of letters from Paris, and the receipt of invitations from traitors and royalists in Paris, revealed the true situation there, and convinced them that by a swift advance they could capture the city and end the war. Accordingly they turned about, detaching a trifling force to harass and deceive the Emperor.

These movements, Napoleon to the rear and the Allies toward Paris, decided the campaign. The small force of eight or ten thousand, which the Allies had sent to follow the Emperor, was cut to pieces by him at St. Dizier, and from the prisoners taken in the action he learned of rumors that the Allies were in full march upon Paris. He soon learned, also, that through Marmont's disobedience of orders a severe defeat had been inflicted upon the two marshals, and that Blücher and Schwarzenberg had united.

What should Napoleon now do? Should he continue his march, gather up the garrisons of his fortresses, enroll recruits, and, having cut the enemy's communications, return to give him battle? He wished to do so, urged it upon the council of war, and at St. Helena repeated his belief that this course would have saved him. It might have done so. The army of the Allies, when it reached Paris, only numbered about one hundred and twenty thousand. Half that number of troops were almost within the Emperor's reach, and there were indications that the peasantry, infuriated by the brutality of the invaders, were about to rise in mass. At this time they could have been armed, for Napoleon had captured muskets by the thousand from the enemy. If Marmont and Mortier would but exhaust the policy of obstruction and resistance; if Joseph and War-minister Clarke, at Paris, would but do their duty, the Allies would be caught between two fires, for the Emperor would not be long in marshalling his strength and coming back.

But the older and higher officers were opposed to the plan. They told Napoleon that he must march at once to the relief of Paris. After a night of meditation and misery at St. Dizier, he set out on the return (March 28, 1814). At Doulevent he received cipher despatches from

2 P

Lavalette, postmaster-general in Paris, warning him that if he would save the capital he had not a moment to lose. This message aroused him for the first time to the extremity of the peril. He had expected a stubborner resistance from Marmont, had relied upon greater effectiveness in Joseph and Clarke. But even now he did not realize the awful truth, the absolute necessity for his immediate presence to save Paris — else he would have mounted horse and spurred across France as he had once done, to smaller purpose, across Spain : as he had done the year before when Dresden was beleaguered. In this connection let us remember what he had told Méneval, — that he was no longer able to endure horse exercise. For a cause which may have been physical, he did not mount a horse himself, for the long life-and-death ride, but he sent General Dejean. Through this messenger he told Joseph that he was coming at full speed, and would reach Paris in two days. Let the Allies be resisted for only two days — he would answer for the balance. Away sped Dejean, and he reached the goal in time.

The Empress and the King of Rome had been sent from the capital by Joseph, and Joseph had taken horse to follow ; but Dejean spurred after him, and caught him up in the Bois de Boulogne. Brother's message was delivered to brother, Napoleon's appeal made to Joseph ; and the answer, coldly given and stubbornly repeated, was, " Too late."

The Allies had marched, dreading every hour to hear the returning Emperor come thundering on their rear ; Marmont had made one of the worst managed of retreats, and had allowed the enemy to advance far more rapidly than they had dared to hope ; Parisians had vainly clam-

ored for arms, that they might defend their city ; and
while thousands of citizens stood on the heights of Mont-
martre, looking expectantly for the Emperor, who was
known to be coming, and while the cry, "It is he! It is
he!" occasionally broke out as some figure on a white
horse was seen in the distance, the imbecile Joseph wrote
to the traitorous Marmont the permission to capitulate.
This note had not been delivered, the fight was still
going on, and Dejean prayed Joseph to recall the note.
"The Emperor will be here to-morrow! For God's
sake, give him one day!"

With a sullen refusal to wait, Joseph put spurs to his
horse, and set out to rejoin Maria Louisa.

In the dark corridors of human passion and prejudice,
who can read the truth? The rebukes of the outraged
husband to a recreant brother may have swayed Joseph,
just as the reproofs of an indignant chief to a disobe-
dient subordinate may have controlled Marmont.

The note from Joseph did its work. The defence
ceased, the French army marched out, and the chief city
of France fell, almost undefended.

Talleyrand and his clique had invited the Allies to
march upon the capital, and the same party of traitors
had paralyzed the spirit of the defence as far as they were
able. They had found unconscious but powerful accomplices in Napoleon's brothers.

That night the French troops marching away from
Paris, according to the terms of the capitulation, were met,
only a few miles from the city, by Napoleon. After having sent Dejean, he had hurried his troops on to Doulain-
court, where more bad news was picked up ; and, by
double marches, he reached Troyes (March 29), where he

rested. At daybreak he left his army to continue its
march, while he, with a small escort, flew on to Villeneuve. There he threw himself into a coach and, followed by a handful of officers, dashed forward — to Sens,
where he learned that the Allies were before Paris, — to
Fontainebleau, where he was told of the flight of the Empress, — to Essonnes, where they said that the fight of Paris
was raging, — and to La Cour de France, only ten miles
from his capital, where at midnight (March 30), as he
waited for a fresh team to be put to his carriage, he heard
the tramp of horses and the clank of arms. It was a
squadron of cavalry on the highroad from Paris. He
shouted to them from the dark, and to his challenge came
the terrible response, " Paris has fallen."

The scene which followed is one of those which haunt
the memory. The chilly gloom of the night, the little way-
side inn, the halted cavalry, the horseless carriage, the
rage of the maddened Emperor, his hoarse call for fresh
horses, his furious denunciation of those who had betrayed
him, his desperate efforts to hurry the post-boys at the
stables, the passion which carried him forward on foot a
mile along the road to Paris, and the remonstrances of
his few friends who urged him to go back — make a weird
and tragic picture one does not forget.

It was not until he met a body of French infantry, also
leaving Paris, that the frenzied Emperor would stop, and
even then he would not retrace his steps. He sent Caulaincourt to make a last appeal to Alexander of Russia,
he who had risen in the theatre at Erfurth to take Napoleon's hand when the actor recited, " The friendship of a
great man is a gift of the gods."

A messenger was sent also to Marmont, and the Emperor waited in the road to receive his answer; nine miles, and not much more than an hour, being the tantalizing margin upon which, again, fate had traced the words, "Too late." Only the river separated him from the outposts of the enemy; their campfires could be seen by reflection in the distance, and yonder to the west was the dull glare hanging over Paris — Paris where a hundred thousand men were ready to fight, if only a leader would show them how!

Leaden must have been the feet of those hours, infinite the woe of that most impatient of men, that haughtiest of men, that self-consciously ablest of men, as he tramped restlessly back and forth on the bleak hill in the dark, awaiting the answers from his messengers.

At last he was almost forced into his carriage and driven back to Fontainebleau. Making his way to one of the humblest rooms, he fell upon the bed, exhausted, heart-broken.

You go to France to-day, and you see around you everywhere, Napoleon. You hear, on all sides, Napoleon. Ask a Frenchman about other historic names, and he will reply with extravagant politeness. Leave him to speak for himself, and his raptures run to Napoleon. *He* is the Man; *he* is the ideal soldier, statesman, financier, developer, the creator of institutions, organizer of society, the inspiration of patriotism.

What Frenchman speaks of the little men who pulled Napoleon down? Who remembers them but to curse their infamous names? Who does not know that the very soul of French memory and veneration for the past centres at the Invalides, where the dead warrior lies in state?

We see this now.   Time works its reversals of judgment.
The pamphlet gives way to the book ; the caricature to
the portrait ; the discordant cry of passion to the calm
voice of reason.   Angels roll away sepulchral stones ; and
posterity sees the resurrected Cromwells, the Dantons,
the Napoleons, just as they were.   Great is the power
of lies—lies boldly told and stubbornly maintained, but
great, also, is the reaction of truth.   The cause, and
the man of the cause, may have been slain by the falsehood, and Truth may serve merely to show posterity
where the grave is ; but sometimes — not always—she
does more ; sometimes the cause, and the man of the
cause, are called back into the battle-field of the living ;
sometimes the great issues are joined again ; sometimes
the martyr remains triumphant, the victim holds the
victory.

CHAPTER XLIII

THE final resurrection and triumph of Napoleon no one could foresee on March 31, 1814, when he lay in a stupor of weariness and soul-sickness at Fontainebleau, while the Allies were entering Paris.

It was a sad day out there at the old palace ; in the capital was spasmodic jubilation. Talleyrand, of the Council of Regency, had managed to remain in Paris when the Empress fled. Talleyrand became the moving spirit of royalist intrigue. He may not have intended the return of the Bourbons, may have been tricked by Vitrolles as Lord Holland relates; but he had meant all the while to overthrow Napoleon, and had countenanced, if not suggested, plans for his assassination.

To prove to Czar Alexander that France hungered and thirsted for the Bourbons, Talleyrand got up cavalcades of young aristocrats who rode about shouting, " Down with the tyrant ! Long live Louis XVIII. ! " Highborn ladies, also, began to take active part in the business, it being an axiom with Talleyrand that if you wish to accomplish anything important, you "must set the women going." Ladies of the old nobility, elegantly dressed, were in the streets, distributing white cockades, and drumming up recruits. Royalism and clericalism bugled for all their forces ; and while Napoleon's friends,

disorganized, awaited leaders, the day was carried for the
Bourbons.

So that when the Allies marched into Paris, as masters,
on March 31, 1814, the royalist faction welcomed the
invaders as "Liberators."

How had these royalists got back to France, to freedom, and to wealth? Through the magnanimity of "the
tyrant" whom it was now so easy to abuse. How had
those high-priests of the Church, who were Talleyrand's
aides in treachery, regained their places, their influence,
their splendid importance? Through the leniency of the
man who was now abandoned, denounced, sold to the enemies of France.

And how had the wars commenced which Napoleon had
inherited, and which he had never been able to end? By
the determination of kings and aristocracies to check the
spread of French principles, to crush democracy in its
birth, and to restore to its old place organized superstition, class-privilege, and the divine right of kings.
In the long fight, the new doctrine had gone down; and
the old had risen again. Royalists, clericals, class-worship-
pers, fell into transports of joy. Glorious Easter, with a
sun-burst, flooded them with light. They thronged the
streets in gala dress; they filled the air with glad outcry;
they kissed the victor's bloody hand, and hailed him as a
god.

They followed Czar Alexander through the streets to
Talleyrand's house, with such extravagance of joyful
demonstration that you might have thought him a French
hero fresh from victories won over foreign foes. Cossacks, driving before them French prisoners, were enthu-
siastically cheered as they passed through the streets.

Aristocratic women, by the hundred, trooped after the foreigners who led the parade, threw themselves with embraces upon the horses, and kissed the very boots of the riders. And these troops, mark you, were those who had made havoc in the provinces of France, with a ferocity and a lust which had not only wreaked its fill upon helpless maid and matron, but had revelled in the sport of compelling fathers, husbands, and sons to witness what they could neither prevent nor revenge, and which had coldly slain the victims after the bestial appetite had been glutted.

Cheer the Cossack bands as they prod with lances the bleeding French captives who have seen their homes burnt, and their wives and daughters violated and butchered! Hug the horses, and kiss the feet of the foreigners who have come to beat down your people, change your government, quell your democracy, force back into power a king and a system that had led the nation to misery and shame!

Do all this, O high-born ladies of France, for the triumph of to-day is yours! But when passion has cooled and reason returned; when overwhelming pressure from without has been removed and France has become herself again, your excesses of servility to-day will but have hastened the speed of the To-morrow in which your precious Bourbons, and your precious feudalism will be driven forever forth from the land into which foreign bayonets have brought them. The man who lingers at Fontainebleau is to-day no longer Emperor to the high and mighty ones in Paris. To confederated monarchs he is "Bonaparte"; to banded conspirators he is "Bonaparte"; to recreant marshals, ungrateful nobles, grasping clericals, treacherous Dalbergs and Talleyrands, he is "Bonaparte." Foreign and domestic foes make their appointment at his triumphal column in the Place Vendome, tugging and pulling to drag his statue down, as they have dragged *him* down.

The Empire is a wreck, the Napoleonic spell broken for all time to come. Down with the Corsican and his works! Up with the Bourbon lilies, and the glories of the Old Régime!

So runs the current — the shouts of the honest devotee and of the time-server whose only aim in life is to find out which is the winning side. Far-seeing, indeed, would be the sage, — wise as well as brave, — who, in this hour of national degradation, should dare to say that all this carnival of royalism would pass like a dream; — would dare to say that the fallen Emperor would rise again and would sweep his enemies from his path, and would come once more to rule the land — with the majesty and the permanence which belongs to none but the immortal dead.

*   *   *   *   *   *

Troops had collected in the neighborhood of Fontainebleau to the number of forty or fifty thousand. The younger officers and the men of the rank and file were still devoted to the Emperor. Whenever he appeared he was met with the same old acclamations; and shouts of "To Paris" indicated the readiness of the army for the great battle which it was thought he would fight under the walls of Paris. After his first torpor, Napoleon had recovered himself, had formed his plans, and had convinced himself that the allied army could be cut off and destroyed. But in order for him to succeed it was necessary that treason in Paris should give him a chance to win, and treason gave him no such chance. The high-priests and the nobles whose hands Napoleon had strengthened by his Concordat and the recall of the émigrés, made the streets of Paris hot with the hurry of their feet as they ran here, there, and yonder, marshalling their partisans. The Abbés Montesquieu and Louis, the Archbishop of Malines, cordially working with Talleyrand and Dalberg, and assisted by banker Laffitte and others of that kind, honeycombed the Senate and the various public bodies with conspiracy, drawing into one common net those who merely wished to end the war by getting rid of Napoleon, as well as those who were original Bourbonites. In this crisis there was none to take the lead for Napoleon. He had deprived the masses of the people of all initiative; had given them civil liberty, but had taken away from them all political importance. Into the hands of the nobles and the priests he had replaced power, wealth, influence, class organization. When the Church and the aristocracy turned upon him, where was the power of resistance to come from? The army was a tower of strength to the Emperor, it is true; but even here there was mortal weakness, for the higher officers, who had been ennobled, were imbued with the spirit of their class. If the Senate, and the Church, and the aristocracy should declare against Napoleon, it soon became evident that his marshals would declare against him also. He had so bedizened them with titles, loaded them with honors, and gorged them with riches, that they could get nothing more by remaining loyal, even though he should finally triumph. Upon the other hand, should he fail, they would lose everything; hence to desert him was plainly the safe thing to do.

Napoleon was holding a review of his troops at Fontainebleau when Caulaincourt was seen to approach him, and whisper something in his ear. He drew back as though he had been struck, and bit his lips, while a slight flush passed over his face. Recovering himself at once, he continued the review. Caulaincourt's whispered news had been that the Senate had deposed him.

' The allied sovereigns will no longer treat with Bonaparte nor any member of his family." This declaration had cleared the way for the creation (April 1) of a provisional government by the French Senate, which provisional government was composed of Talleyrand and four other clerical and aristocratic conspirators.

The beginning having been made, the rest was easy. On April 3 the Senate decreed the Emperor's deposition, alleging against him certain breaches of the Constitution, which breaches the Senate had unmurmuringly sanctioned at the time of their commission. Various public bodies in and around Paris began to declare against him, having no more right to depose him than the Senate possessed, but adding very sensibly to the demoralization of his supporters. Even yet the army was true; even yet when he appealed to the troops, the answering cry was, " Live the Emperor ! " Thus while in Paris his petted civil functionaries, his restored clericals, and his nobles were jostling one another in the tumultuous rush of desertion, and while the swelling stream of the great treason was rolling onward as smoothly as Talleyrand could wish, there was one cause of anxiety to the traitors, — the attitude of the French army.

On April 4 the Emperor held his usual review; it proved to be the last. The younger officers and the troops were as enthusiastic as ever, but the marshals were cold. After the parade they followed Napoleon to his room. Only in a general way is known what passed at this conference. The marshals were tired of the war, and were determined that it should come to an end. Napoleon had formed his plans to march upon Paris and fight a great battle to save his crown. Marshal Macdonald had approved the plan and was ready to second his chief; the others would listen to no plans, and were resolute in their purpose to get rid of this chief. It seems to be certain that if a surrender could not be got from Napoleon by fair means, the marshals were ready to try those that were foul. If he could not be persuaded, he was to be intimidated; and if threats failed, he was to be assassinated. Talleyrand's provisional government was equally determined and unscrupulous. Napoleon was to be killed if he could not otherwise be managed. Foremost among the marshals demanding his abdication, and apparently threatening his life, was Marshal Ney, whose tone and bearing to his chief are said to have been brutally harsh.

After having exhausted argument and persuasion upon these officers, Napoleon dismissed them, and drew up his declaration that he resigned the throne in favor of his son.

"Here is my abdication!" he said to Caulaincourt; "carry it to Paris." He appeared to be laboring to control intense emotion, and Caulaincourt burst into tears as he took the paper.

As long as the French army appeared to be devoted to the Emperor, the Allies had not openly declared for the Bourbons. They had encouraged the idea that they would favor a regency in favor of Napoleon's son, con-

ceeding to its fullest extent the right of the French people
to select their own rulers.   It was by the skilful use of
this pretence that many of the French officers had been
led astray.   It was by this mingling of the sweet with
the bitter that Napoleon's first act of abdication had been
wrung from him by the marshals.   Succeeded by the son
he adored, France would not be wholly lost to him, since
it remained to his dynasty.

But here again Marmont ruined all.   Played upon by
Laffitte and Talleyrand's clique, — flattered, cajoled, and
adroitly seduced, — this marshal of France made a secret
bargain with the Allies which took from the Emperor the
strongest body of troops then at hand.

Thus it happened that when the Ney-Macdonald delegation, bearing the conditional abdication, returned to
Paris, and were urging upon the Czar the claims of
Napoleon's son, the conference was interrupted by an
excited messenger who had come to announce to Alexander that Marmont's corps had been led into the allied
lines.   This astounding intelligence ended the negotiations.   The Czar promptly dropped the veil, and disclosed
the real policy of the Allies.   The marshals went back to
Fontainebleau to demand an abdication freed from conditions.

Marmont had dealt the final blow to a tottering cause
— "Marmont, the friend of my youth, who was brought
up in my tent, whom I have loaded with honors and
riches ! " as the fallen Emperor exclaimed, in accents of
profound amazement and grief.   Yes, when the miserable
renegade sat down to plot with Talleyrand the complete
ruin of the Empire, it was in a luxurious palace which
Napoleon had given him.

What officer had ruined a campaign in Spain and thereby done grievous injury to the Emperor in Russia? Who had disobeyed orders, brought on the night surprise at Laon, and wrecked Napoleon's pursuit of Blücher? Who had lost the line of communications, by movements against orders, and had let Napoleon's most important despatches fall into the hands of the enemy? Who had caused the defeat at Fère-Champenoise; who had so feebly resisted the allied advance upon Paris that their progress astonished themselves? Who had surrendered a vast city of eight hundred thousand souls to foreigners, when he must have known that Napoleon was coming to the rescue as fast as horse could run? Marmont, the spoiled favorite; Marmont, the vainglorious weakling; Marmont, the false-hearted traitor! Verily he reaped his reward. To the Bourbons he became a hero, and so remained for a season. But France — the real France — hated him as North America hates Benedict Arnold. The time came when he who had betrayed Napoleon for the Bourbons, betrayed the elder Bourbons for the House of Orleans. Despised by all parties, he wandered about Europe as wretched as he deserved to be. And the day came when the gondoliers at Venice pointed him out scornfully to each other, and refused to bend an oar for the miscreant.

"You see him yonder! That is Marmont. Well, he was Napoleon's friend, and he betrayed him!"

Undaunted even by Marmont's defection, Napoleon issued a proclamation, and began his preparations to retire beyond the Loire, and fight it out. His conditional abdication rejected, war could not be worse than peace, and he explained his plan of campaign to his marshals. They cut him short, brusquely, menacingly. The Emperor stood alone, forsaken by all his lieutenants, and made an imploring address to them, pleading with them to make one final effort for France. His words fell on hearts that were turned to stone. They harshly declared that the confidence of the army was gone. Macdonald said that they must have unconditional abdication.

The Emperor promised to reply next day, and, as his marshals filed out, he said, in bitterness of spirit, — "Those men have neither heart nor bowels; I am conquered less by fortune than by the egotism and ingratitude of my companions-in-arms."

Who has not read of that panic of apostasy which now ran like a torrent? From the setting sun at Fontainebleau to that which was rising in Paris, all turned—turned with the haste of panic-stricken pardon-seekers, or of greed-devoured place-hunters. From the highest to the lowest, the fallen Emperor's attendants left him. Princes, dukes, marshals, generals, — all creations of his, — fled from him as from the contagion of pestilence. Even Berthier, the favorite, the confidant, the pampered and petted — even Berthier bit his nails for a brief season of hesitancy, and then abandoned his friend to his misery. Marmont's treason had hurt, had wrung a cry of amazement and pain from that tortured spirit; but Berthier's was a crueller stab. "Berthier, you see that I have need of consolation, that my true friends should surround me. Will you come back?" Berthier went, and he did not come back.

They left him, singly and in squads, till he and his faithful guard were almost all that remained. His very valets, the Mameluke he brought from Egypt, and Constant whose *Memoirs* portray his master so lovingly, could not resist the panic of the hour; they turned their backs upon their master, and, according to that master's statements in his instructions to his executors, they robbed him before they fled. But there were some who did not go, a few who stood the storm. May their glorious names live forever! Among these it is pleasant to find the name of his old schoolmate, Colonel Bussy.

Bertrand, Gourgaud, Montholon, Bassano, Cambronne, Caulaincourt, Lavalette, Druot, and some others did not blanch. Nor did the Old Guard falter. The "growlers" had followed the chief — murmuring sometimes, but following — all through the terrors of the last campaign; they were ready to follow him again.

And there were womanly hearts that warmed to the lonely monarch, and would have consoled him — first of all, Josephine. She had watched his every movement though the campaign with an agony of interest and apprehension. His name was ever in her thoughts and on her lips. Of all who came from the army she would ask: How does he look? Is he pale? Does he sleep? Does he believe his star has deserted him? Often the harassed Emperor found time to write to her, brief notes full of kindness and confidence. These she would take to her privacy, read, and weep over. She understood the great man, at the last; she had not done so at first. From Brienne he wrote her, "I have sought death in many battles, but could not find it. I would now hail it as a boon. Yet I should like to see Josephine once more." This note she carried in her bosom.

When she heard of the abdication, she was frantic with grief, and she would have flown to his side, only she thought of one who had the better right, — Maria Louisa. As the broken monarch sat in the gloom, his great head sunk on his breast, two other noble-hearted women appeared at Fontainebleau. One of them was the beautiful Polish lady, Madame Walewski ; the name of the other is not given. They were announced, and the Emperor promised to see them. After waiting many hours, they went away. Napoleon had fallen into revery again and had forgotten they were there. It is said that he took poison, intending to kill himself. This has been questioned; but it is certain that he swallowed some drug which brought on a sudden and alarming illness, during which he said he was going to die. " I cannot endure the torments I experience. They have dragged my eagles in the dirt ! They have misunderstood me ! Marmont gave me the last blow ! I loved him. Berthier's desertion has broken my heart ! My old friends, my old companions-in-arms ! "

Says Constant : " What a night ! what a night ! While I live I shall never think of it without a shudder."

On the morning after this attempted suicide, Napoleon "appeared much as usual," and met his marshals to give them his answer to their demand for unconditional abdication. Even yet he made one more attempt to inspire them to effort, to infuse into them something of his own courage. It was all in vain. Then he scrawled the few lines in which he laid down his great office, and handed them the paper.

" You claim that you need rest ! Very well, then, take it ! "

"What shall we demand of the Allies in your behalf?" the marshals inquired.

"Nothing. Do the best you can for France; for myself, I ask nothing."

They went away upon their errand, and once more the Emperor sank into a stupor of despondency. Much of the time he spent seated upon a stone bench, near the fountain, in the English garden which he had himself laid out at the back of the palace. Just as he had lain, novel in hand, upon the sofa at Moscow, silent and moody day by day; and just as he had sat in the château of Düben, in 1813, idly tracing big letters on white paper; so he now sat by the hour on the stone bench in the garden at Fontainebleau, saying nothing, and kicking his heel into the gravel until his boot had made a hole a foot deep in the earth.

Deserted as he had been, Napoleon was yet a man to be dreaded; and the Allies were most anxious to come to terms with him, and to get him out of the country. Partly from fear of what he might do if driven to despair, and partly out of generosity to a fallen foe, the Czar influenced the other powers to sign the treaty of Fontainebleau with Napoleon, whereby he was to retain his title of Emperor, to receive a yearly pension of $400,000 from France, and remain undisturbed as Emperor of Elba. His son, as successor to his wife, was to have a realm composed of Parma, Placentia, and Guastalla.

Resigning himself to his fate, Napoleon received the Commissioners whom the Allies sent to take charge of his journey to his new empire, and busied himself in the selection of the books and baggage he intended to take with him.

With assumed gayety he said to Constant, whom the Emperor evidently believed would follow him, " Eh, well, my son, get your cart ready : we will go and plant our cabbages."

But every now and then the full sweep of bitter reality would come over him, and he would clap his hand to his forehead, crying : —

" Great God ! Is it possible ? "

His departure was fixed for April 20, 1814. The Imperial Guard formed in the White Horse Court of the palace. The Emperor appeared upon the stairs, pale and firm. A dozen or more stanch friends waited to bid him farewell. He shook hands with them all. The line of carriages was waiting ; but he passed hastily by them, and advanced toward the soldiers drawn up in the court.

It was seen then that he would speak to the troops, and dead silence reigned. The old, proud bearing was there again, — pride softened by unutterable sadness, — and the voice was full and sonorous as he spoke the few words which reached all hearts that day, reach them now, and will reach them as long as human blood is warm.

" Soldiers of the Old Guard, I bid you farewell ! For twenty years I have led you in the path of honor and glory. In these last days, as in the days of our prosperity, you have never ceased to be models of fidelity and courage. With men such as you, our cause could never have been lost ; we could have maintained a civil war for years. But it would have rendered our country unhappy. I have therefore sacrificed all my interests to those of France. Her happiness is my only thought. It will still be the object of my wishes. Do not regret my fate. If I have consented to live, it is in order to promote your glory.

I trust to write the deeds we have achieved together.
Adieu, my children! I would that I could press you all
to my heart.   Let me embrace your general and your
eagle!"

He took General Petit, commander of the Guard, in his
arms, and he pressed the eagle to his lips.

The soldiers sobbed, even the Commissioners were
touched; and Napoleon, hurrying through the group
which had gathered round him, reached his carriage, fell
back on the cushions, and covered his face with his hands.

There was the word of command, the crunching and
grinding of wheels, and the carriages were soon lost to
sight.

CHAPTER XLIV

THE Count of Provence was living in England when Napoleon's Senate called him to the throne. He was one of those who had "digged the pit" for his brother, Louis XVI.; and who, when that brother was falling into it, discreetly ran away to foreign lands. After several changes of asylum on the Continent, he had gone to England as a last refuge. France had well-nigh forgotten him. A generation of Frenchmen who knew not the Bourbons had grown up; and the abuses of the Old Order were known to the younger generation only as an almost incredible story, told in the evenings by older people, as the family circled about the hearthstone. So completely had the Revolution swept away the foul wrongs of the Bourbon system, that the younger generation could never be made to understand why their fathers hated it with such bitterness. Reined in by the iron hand of Napoleon, the nobles and the clericals of the Empire seemed to be harmless enough. Why should the noble and the priest of the Old Order have been so much worse than these?

The graybeards in France knew; but the younger people could no more realize the former situation than could the children of Daniel Boone, George Rogers Clarke, John Sevier, or of the New England pioneers, understand

598

the horrors of Indian warfare. The story of Bourbon misrule, class tyranny, and church greed fell upon the ear with a sound deadened by the lapse of twenty odd years.

Bourbon emissaries had pledges and soft words for all parties. To Napoleon's nobles were given the assurance that they should remain noble ; to his generals, that they should retain their honors and their wealth. To the priests it was not necessary to say that they should have even more than the Concordat gave, for the priests knew how dearly the Bourbons loved the old pact between Church and State. To pacify men of liberal ideas, promises were made that the restored Bourbons would rule as constitutional kings, recognizing in good faith the changes wrought by the Revolution. Napoleon's Senate was not so forgetful of its own safety, and of the interests of France, that it failed to put the contract in writing. The Constitution of a limited monarchy was formulated, and the Count of Artois, brother and representative of Louis XVIII., accepted its conditions.

In England the new King was given an ovation upon his departure for France, and he took occasion to write to the Prince Regent that, next to God, he owed his crown to Great Britain. This statement was not good policy, for neither in France nor among the potentates of the Continent did it tend to popularize the speaker; but it was the truth, nevertheless. The settled purpose of Pitt had been the restoration of the Bourbons, and upon this basis it is now known that he built the first European coalition against republican France. Canning and Castlereagh had but inherited the principles of the abler Pitt. In a speech in Parliament (April 7, 1814), Lord Castlereagh proclaimed that his "object had long been to restore Europe to that ancient social system which her late convulsions had disjointed and overthrown."

As Hobhouse says, "When he talks so plainly, even Lord Castlereagh can be understood ; when he professes such principles, even Lord Castlereagh may be believed."

Fresh from his London ovation, and full of his ideas of divine right, Louis met the French legislative body at Compiègne, and evaded their request for a declaration of the royal policy. It became evident that he intended to set aside the pledges made in his name, and to rule as absolute sovereign. To this purpose he was urged by clericals, nobles, and his own inclinations, for, as Napoleon said, "the Bourbons had learned nothing and forgotten nothing." With a royal disregard of facts, he had mentally abolished Napoleon's empire, all of its glories, all of its shame, and had appropriated the entire era to himself. In his own mind he had become King of France at the death of the boy, Louis XVII.; and the year 1814 was the nineteenth year of his reign ! Here, indeed, was cause for tribulation among the eminent turncoats who had exchanged Napoleon for the Bourbon ! If the Empire had been but a hallucination, what would become of the nobles created by the Emperor, the honors conferred by him, the lands whose titles had been granted by him, the great institutions which had been founded by him? What would become of his peers, his judges, his marshals, his schools, hospitals, and public charities ? Where would the Legion of Honor be ? What was to become of the revolutionary principle that all Frenchmen were equals in law, and that all careers were open to merit ? Questions like these buzzed throughout the land, and the hum of inquiry soon grew into the murmurs of alarm, of anger. If Bourbons came back to power in any such temper as that, what would become of eminent statesmen who had overturned the ancient monarchy, abolished the nobility, confiscated the wealth of the Church, and guillotined the King? What would be the fate of Talleyrand, Fouché, and Company? Aghast at such a prospect as unhampered and vengeful Bourbonism threatened, eminent renegades who had negotiated Napoleon's downfall with the Czar Alexander appealed to the Russian monarch to stand between themselves and the danger. Like most mortals, the Czar had a strict code of morals for his neighbors. Ready to break pledges himself, it shocked him to see Louis ignore the conditions upon which he had been summoned to France. In courtly phrase the Bourbon was notified that until he confirmed the promises Artois had made to the Senate, there should be no royal entry into Paris. Even under this pressure, Louis would not yield an iota of the precious dogma of divine right. Refusing to concede that the people had any inherent powers whatever, and stubbornly maintaining that all power, privilege, and sovereignty rested in him alone, he graciously published a proclamation in which he granted to the people, of his own free will, certain civil and political rights, ignoring the Senate altogether. This " Charter " having been signed, the King made his triumphal entry into Paris, May 3, 1814.

On the evening of the same day, as the sun was sinking in the Mediterranean, the mountains of the island of Elba rose upon the sight of the crew of the British vessel, the *Undaunted*, and Napoleon had his first glimpse of his little realm in the sea.

His journey from Fontainebleau to Fréjus, on the French

coast, had been, at first, soothed by many expressions of
kindness and of sympathy from the people who thronged
the line of travel; but as the fallen Emperor reached the
province where the White Terror had once raged, and
was to rage again, popular expressions underwent a complete change.   Mobs of hooting royalists surrounded his
carriage, and dinned into his ears the most brutal in-
sults.   Only his escort saved him from being torn to
pieces.   At Avignon he missed, almost by miracle, the
dreadful fate which overtook Marshal Brune there, after
Waterloo.   Napoleon believed that these royalist mobs
were set upon him by Talleyrand's provisional government, and perhaps his suspicion was correct.   It is certain
that a certain nobleman, Maubreuil by name, afterward
charged Talleyrand with having employed him to kill
Napoleon; and when Talleyrand denied the story, Maubreuil took the first occasion to beat him — a beating
which Talleyrand was wise enough not to endeavor to
punish by prosecution.

Surrounded by savage mobs who jeered him, insulted
him, threatened him, and made desperate efforts to seize
him, Napoleon is said to have lost his nerve.   Unfriendly
witnesses allege that he trembled, paled, shed tears, and
cowered behind Bertrand, seeking to hide.   What is more
certain, is that he disguised himself in coat and cap of the
Austrian uniform, mounted the horse of one of the attendants, and rode in advance of the carriages to escape
recognition.   Courage, after all, seems to be somewhat
the slave of habit: a soldier may brave death a hundred
times in battle, and yet become unnerved at the prospect
of being torn to pieces by a lot of maddened human
wolves.   It should be remembered, however, that the

only real evidence we have of Napoleon's terror was the wearing of the disguise. If this makes him a coward, he falls into much distinguished company, for history is full of examples of similar conduct on the part of men who are admitted to have been brave.

Napoleon had banished from court his light sister Pauline, because of some impertinence of the latter to the Empress Maria Louisa. This light sister was now living at a château which was on his route to the coast, and he spent a day and a half with her. Shocked to see her imperial brother in the Austrian uniform, she refused to embrace him until he had put it off and put on his own.

While Napoleon was staying at the château, a crowd of people from the surrounding country gathered in the courtyard. He went down and mingled with them. Soon noticing an old man who wore a red ribbon in his button-hole, Napoleon went up to him and said : —

" Are you not Jacques Dumont ? "

Too much surprised to reply at once, the veteran at length faltered, " Yes, my lord ; yes, General ; yes, yes, sire ! "

" You were with me in Egypt ? "

" Yes, sire ! " and the hand was brought to the salute.

" You were wounded ; it seems to me a long while ago ? "

" At the battle of Trebbia, sire."

The veteran by this time was shaking with emotion, and all the crowd had clustered thickly about these two.

Taking off his cross of the Legion of Honor, Napoleon put it upon his old soldier ; and while the veteran wept, the crowd shouted, " Live the Emperor ! "

" My name! To remember my name after fifteen years!" the old man continued to repeat; and so great was the sensation this little incident was creating that the Commissioners who had charge of the exile grew alarmed, and hastened to get him back into the house.

The captain and the crew of the British frigate had never seen the French Emperor save through the glasses of the English editors. Any one who knows how great is the power of an unbridled press to blacken the fairest name, distort beyond recognition the loftiest character, and blast the hopes of the noblest career, can readily comprehend what was the current British opinion of Napoleon Bonaparte in 1814. Seen through the eyes of Tory editors and pamphleteers, he was a man contrasted with whom Lucifer might well hope to become a popular hero.

Great was the surprise of Captain Usher and his sailors to see a handsome, quiet, polite, and self-controlled gentleman, who talked easily with everybody, conformed without fuss to all the ship regulations, gave himself no airs of superhuman loftiness, and took an intelligent interest in the ship and in the folks about him. So great was the charm of his manner, and of his conversation, that English prejudice wore away; and the sailors began to say, " Boney is a good fellow, after all."

It is amusing to note that Sir Walter Scott records with pride the fact that there was one sturdy sailor who was not to be softened, who retained his surliness to the last, and whose gruff comment upon all the good-humored talk of the Emperor was the word, "*Humbug!*" The name of this unyielding Briton was Hinton; and both Sir Walter and his son-in-law Lockhart record his name

with a sort of Tory veneration. In spite of the unyielding Hinton, the sailors of the *Undaunted* grew fond
enough of Napoleon to accept a handsome gratuity from
him at the journey's end ; and the boatswain, addressing
him on the quarter-deck in the name of the crew,
"Thanked his honor, and wished him long life and
prosperity in the island of Elba, *and better luck next
time.*"

Neither Sir Walter Scott nor his son-in-law Lockhart,
report Hinton's remarks upon this occasion; and they
leave us in doubt as to whether his virtue held out
against the golden temptation, or whether he pocketed
his share, with a final snort of, " Humbug! "

On May 4, 1814, the Emperor made his official landing
in Elba, whose inhabitants (about thirteen thousand souls)
received him well. He made a thorough investigation of
his new empire, its industries, resources, etc., and sitting
his horse upon a height from which he could survey his
whole domain, remarked good-humoredly that he found
it rather small.

Soon joined by his mother and by his sister Pauline, also
by the seven hundred troops of the Old Guard assigned
him by the Treaty of Fontainebleau, Napoleon's establishment at Porto Ferrajo resembled the Tuileries in miniature. Imperial etiquette stiffened most of its joints, and
put on much of its formidable armor. Visitors poured
into Elba by the hundred, and with many of these Napoleon conversed with easy frankness, speaking of past events
with the tone of a man who was dead to the world.

His restless energies found some employment in the
affairs of his little kingdom, and in the planning of all
sorts of improvements upon which he lavished freely the

funds he had brought from France. With Pauline's money he bought a country-seat, where he spent much time, and where he could occasionally be seen helping to feed the chickens.

His mother had come and his sister, but where was wife and child? The allied sovereigns had pledged themselves by formal treaty to send Maria Louisa to him under escort, and the promise had been broken. Wife and child had been enveloped with hostile influences, kept well out of his reach, hastened from France, and carried to Vienna.

Historians gloss over the intrigue which followed — as foul a conspiracy against human virtue and sacred human relations as ever soiled the records of the human race.

The Emperor Francis of Austria and Metternich, his minister, were determined that Maria Louisa should never rejoin her husband, treaty or no treaty. They knew her character, and for his daughter the royal father laid the most infamous snare. He deliberately encouraged Neipperg, an Austrian libertine of high degree; and Napoleon's wife, entangled in the meshes of this filthy intrigue which had found her all too ready to yield, no longer wished to return to the husband she had betrayed.

No wonder the authors who gloat over Napoleon's sins find no comfort here; and hurry on to other topics. They have made horrible accusations against him and his sister Pauline, on the mere word of a spiteful Madame de Rémusat, and of an unscrupulous liar like Fouché. But the accusations might be true, and nevertheless Napoleon would shine like a superior being beside such an exemplar of divine right as the Emperor Francis, who coldly and deliberately, as a matter of state policy, pushed his own daughter into the arms of a libertine!

We have read of the crimes of the vulgar, the canaille, the Marats, and the Héberts; does any page of modern history hold a story more sickening than this? Did any criminal of the vulgar herd stoop to depths more loathsome than Francis, Emperor "by the grace of God," wallowed in?

After having broken their treaty upon the sacred subject of wife and child, the allied kings found it easy enough to violate it upon matters less important. They did not respect the property of the Bonaparte family as they had agreed; they did not pay the Bonaparte pensions; they did not bestow the principalities promised for Napoleon's son; and they paid no respect to that provision of the compact which secured to Napoleon inviolably the island of Elba. Bitter personal enemies of the fallen Emperor, Pozzo di Borgo, Lord Wellington, Talleyrand, and others, agreed that he must be removed to a greater distance from Europe, St. Helena being the place which met with most favor. The fact that the allied kings had pledged themselves to allow him to remain at Elba, seems not to have entered into the discussions at all. He who had broken no treaties was already an outlaw in the counsels of those who had broken all: they could deal with him as they chose. "In the name of the most Holy Trinity" they had pledged faith to him; they could as easily breach the last treaty as its predecessors, being kings by the grace of God, and owing no fealty to ordinary moralities.

The British ministry began to negotiate with the East India Company for the island of St. Helena; and the purpose of the allied kings to send him there as a prisoner of war not only reached Napoleon at Elba, but actually found its way into the *Moniteur*, the official gazette of France.

The fact that Louis XVIII. did not pay one cent of the $400,000 which the Treaty of Fontainebleau had provided for Napoleon's annual revenue, was of itself a source of serious embarrassment to him, justifying him in setting aside a contract which his enemies did not regard; but it had less to do with his movements, perhaps, than any other breach of the treaty. He cared nothing for money; little for personal luxury. "I can get along with one horse, and with a dollar a day," he declared with demo cratic independence. Besides, he could easily have secured from Europe the sums he needed, as he himself publicly declared on his return to France. But when he found that his wife and child would never be surrendered; that Talleyrand and the Bourbons were still bent upon having him assassinated; that if he could not be killed he was to be taken away to a distant rock and held as a prisoner of war, the impulse became irresistible to make one desperate effort to escape the impending doom. Those who watched over his personal safety had already stopped, disarmed, and sent away two would-be assassins: who could tell whether the third would be stopped? It came to him that the Allies had agreed to send him to St. Helena: who could say when a British man-of-war might bear down upon little Elba? Brooding over his wrongs, and over the perils of his situation, Napoleon gave way to occasional bursts of anger, declaring that he would die the death of a soldier, arms in hand, before he would submit to the proposed removal.

A Scotchman of rank who visited Elba at this time wrote: "Bonaparte is in perfect health, but lodged in a worse house than the worst description of dwellings appropriated to our clergy in Scotland, yet still keeping up the state of Emperor, that is, he has certain officers with grand official names about him. We were first shown into a room where the only furniture was an old sofa and two rush-bottom chairs, and a lamp with two burners, only one of which was lighted. An aide-de-camp received us, who called a servant and said that one of the lights had gone out. The servant said it had never been lighted. 'Light it, then,' said the aide-de-camp. Upon which the servant begged to be excused, saying that the Emperor had given no orders upon the subject. We were then received by Bonaparte in an inner room. The Emperor wore a very old French Guard uniform with three orders, and had on very dirty boots, being just come in from his country house."

Then the writer describes a conversation in which Napolcou spoke without apparent reserve of his past life. Referring to the doings of the Bourbons in France, he remarked that they had better mind what they were about, as there were still five hundred thousand excellent soldiers there. "But what is all that to me?" he exclaimed with a rapid turn; "I am to all intents and purposes dead."

"His manner," says the Scotchman, "was that of a blunt, honest, good-hearted soldier's, his smile, when he chose it, very insinuating. He never has anybody to dinner. Bertrand says that they are in the greatest distress for money, as the French court does not pay the stipulated salary to Bonaparte.

"The following day the Emperor set off for his country house. He was in an old coach with four half-starved horses ; on the wheel-horse sat a coachman of the ordinary size, and the bridles had the imperial eagle on them; on the leaders there was a mere child, and the bridles had the coronet of a British viscount on them.   He had General Bertrand in the carriage, and two or three officers behind on small ponies, which could not, by all the exertions of their riders, keep up with the carriage, emaciated as those poor horses were."

The Scotchman contrasts the wretched little establishment at Elba with the splendor of the Tuileries where he went to see Louis XVIII. dine in public, — separate table for king, separate tables for princes of the blood-royal; attendant courtiers standing in full dress, duchesses only being permitted to sit; everything served on gold plate; the dining hall, a hundred feet long, brilliantly lighted and hung with gobelin tapestries, " and a very fine concert going on all the time."

The contrast between these two pictures, striking as it was to the Scotchman, was no less so to Napoleon, who felt the squalor of Elba and longed for the lost grandeur of France.   If there had been a secret bargain between the fallen Emperor and the Bourbons that they should prepare the country for his speedy return, they could hardly have gone to work in a more effective manner to accomplish that result.   They had not been in possession of the throne six months before the nation was fairly seething with discontent.

NOTE. — While the Congress of Vienna was in session, Dr. Richard Bright, an Englishman, was visiting the city and saw the pageant. He describes many of the august sovereigns who were in attendance, and gives an account of the festivities, amusements, and polite dissipations which were in progress.   But perhaps the most interesting page the Doctor wrote was that in which he relates his visit to Napoleon's son, who was then with his mother at the palace of Schönbrunn. "We found that all the servants about the palace were Frenchmen, who still wore the liveries of Napoleon. . . . We . . . were ushered into a room where the infant [King of Rome] was sitting on the floor amusing himself amidst a profuse collection of playthings. . . . He was at that moment occupied with a toy which imitated a well-furnished kitchen. He was the sweetest child I ever beheld; his complexion light, with fine, white, silky hair, falling in curls upon his neck. He was dressed in the embroidered uniform of an hussar, and seemed to pay little attention to us as we entered, continuing to arrange the dishes in his little kitchen. I believe he was the least embarrassed of the party. He was rather too old to admit of loud praise of his beauty, and rather too young to enter into conversation. His appearance was so engaging that I longed to take him in my arms, but his situation forbade such familiarity. Under these circumstances, we contrived a few trifling questions, to which he gave such arch and bashful answers as we have all often received from children of his age."

Madame Montesquieu was still with the child, but, after a while, she and all the other French attendants were dismissed. The effort was made to wean the poor boy of all things French, and to transform him into an Austrian.

It may be proper here to add that he died of consumption at the early age of twenty-one. It is darkly hinted that the same malevolent influences which destroyed the respectability of Napoleon's wife led the son into excesses which undermined his constitution. To the last he was passionately fond of his father, and when Marmont visited Vienna in 1831 the Duke de Reichstadt (as the boy was called in Austria) eagerly drew from him all that he would tell of the great Emperor.

The cage in which Napoleon's only legitimate son was kept was gilded with pension and title and outward show of deference, but it was a cage, nevertheless, and he died in it (1832).

CHAPTER XLV

THE ink was hardly dry upon the Charter before Louis XVIII. began to break its conditions. It had served its purpose, he had ridden into office upon it: what further use had he for it? Why should he trammel his actions by treaty when the other kings of Europe were freeing themselves from such fetters? To the south of him was Spain, where the liberals had framed a constitution which Ferdinand, released by Napoleon early in 1814, had sworn to respect, and which he had set aside the moment he had taken again into his hands the reins of power. Instead of reform and limited monarchy on the peninsula, there was now a full restoration of the Old Order, feudalism, tithes, local tyrannies, clerical and royal absolutism, the jails full of democrats, and the Inquisition hungry for heretics. Nobles and priests struck their ancient bargain, mastered a willing king, and with the resistless strength of self-interest, class-prejudice, and corporate unity of purpose, acting upon the ignorance, the superstition, and the cultivated hatreds of the people, carried Spain back with a rush to the good old times of Bourbon and Roman absolutism.

Not only in the south was counter-revolution triumphant; in the north it was equally so. In Jerome

Bonaparte's kingdom of Westphalia, where the people had driven out the system of Napoleon, and called in their former rulers, old laws and customs rattled back to their rusty grooves; the Code Napoléon vanished; equality of civil right was seen no more, feudalism fell like a chain upon the astounded peasant, purchasers of state lands were ousted without compensation, special privilege and tax exemptions again gladdened the elect, aristocracy and clericalism swept away every vestige of Jerome's brief rule, the torture chamber again rang with the shrieks of victims, and the punishment of death by breaking upon the wheel emphasized the desperate efforts nobles and priests were making to stem the torrent of modern liberalism.

And the Holy Father at Rome, loosed by Napoleon from Fontainebleau at about the same time that Ferdinand of Spain had been released from Valençay, had wended his way back to Italy as Ferdinand had to Spain, and, seated again in St. Peter's chair, had laid his pious hands to the same work in Rome which Ferdinand was busy with in Madrid.

With absolutism and feudalism triumphing all around him, why should not Louis XVIII. follow the glorious examples? Did he not owe it to God and the ancient Bourbon kings to cast out from France the devil of democracy which had rended her, and to clothe her once more in her right mind — in the docile obedience to kingly word and clerical admonition? Apparently he did; and apparently he believed that the quicker he set about it the better.

He had guaranteed freedom of the press in his Charter; but this was a promise he could not venture to keep. He meant to violate the Charter and to restore the Old Order; and he knew that this could not be done if the press remained free. He had lived in England where he may have heard Richard Brinsley Sheridan when he thrilled the House of Commons with that famous burst of eloquence, "Give them a corrupt House of Lords, give them a venal House of Commons, give them a tyrannical Prince, give them a truckling Court, and let me have but an unfettered Press, I will defy them to encroach a hair's-breadth upon the liberties of England!" Therefore, one of his first acts was to gag the press with a censorship. With indecent haste, this royal ordinance breaching the Charter was published just six days after the official publication of the Charter itself.

Unbridled criticism by those organs which in our modern system control public opinion being thus made impossible, other measures of similar tendency followed swiftly.

Loudly condemning Napoleon's toleration of heretics, Jews, and non-believers, the clericals induced the King to compel Frenchmen of all creeds and races to suspend business not only on the Christian Sabbath, but on the festival days of the Catholic Church.

Not satisfied with a grand religious ceremony to "purify" the spot upon which Louis XVI. had been guillotined, nor with having dug up bones supposed to be his and given them magnificent sepulture, Louis solemnly devoted France to the Virgin Mary, and her image was borne through the streets in formal procession, wherein the great dignitaries ambled along with lighted candles in their hands.

By the Charter, the army had been specially protected.

Napoleon's soldiers still had guns in their hands and rage in their hearts when Talleyrand was writing out the pledges with which the returning Bourbons were to be fettered. It was highly important to soothe these troops, or to remove their fear that the Bourbons would deal with them unjustly. Hence the sixty-ninth article of the Charter, which declared that soldiers in active service, the officers and soldiers in retreat, the widows, the officers and soldiers on the pension list, should preserve their rank, honors, and pensions.

By royal ordinance (December 16, 1814) this clause of the Charter was violated.

Fourteen thousand officers and sergeants were dismissed on half-pay; and the places of these battle-scarred heroes of the Empire were filled by five thousand nobles who had never seen service save with the enemies of France. Naval officers who had deserted the ships of their own country, and had served against their native land, were put back into the French navy, and given the rank they had won abroad. Veterans who had fought for the French Republic and the French Empire, from Valmy and Jemappes to Laon and Montmirail, found themselves officered by insolent little noblemen who had never smelt gunpowder. General Dupont, known principally for his capitulation at Baylen, was made minister of war. The tricolor flag which French soldiers had borne victoriously into every capital on the Continent was put away. Many of the bullet-shredded banners were destroyed — they and their splendid memories being hateful to the Bourbon soul.

The white flag of the old monarchy—a flag which living French soldiers knew only as the rallying-point of treason

and rebellion in La Vendée — was made the national standard.   The numbers of the regiments were changed, and the
veterans of a dozen historic campaigns lost the names by
which they were known, and which they had made glorious
in the arduous test of battle.   The Imperial Guard was
banished from Paris; the Swiss were again enrolled to
defend the palace, and clad in the uniform of 1792; a
Bourbon military household was organized, filled with
young nobles who had never fired a shot, who were paid
fancy salaries, and decked out in a livery which made
all Paris titter.   To complete the burlesque, they resurrected and made chief officer of the palace the old
Marquis of Chansenets, who had been Governor of the
Tuileries on August 10, 1792, and had escaped massacre
that day by hiding under piles of dead.

The young Bourbon dukes, Berry and Angoulême, knew
nothing whatever of war, practically or otherwise; yet they
were put in highest military command; and they gave themselves airs which neither Wellington, Blücher, or Napoleon
ever assumed.   These young princes of the blood-royal
told French veterans on parade that their twenty years
of service under the Republic and under the Empire
were but twenty years of brigandage.   When Napoleon's Old Guard failed to manœuvre as the youthful
Duke of Angoulême would have them do, they were
sneeringly advised to go to England to learn their drill.
Does a colonel so displease the Duke of Berry that he must
be cashiered, disgraced?   The haughty Bourbon tears off
the epaulets with his own hand!   At another time the
same doughty warrior strikes a soldier on parade.   Word
goes out that a monument is to be raised to the invading
émigrés whom English vessels had landed at Quiberon in

1795, and whom the republicans had slaughtered there. Honors to these being granted, Pichegru and Georges Cadoudal were not forgotten. Their names were mentioned with honor, masses recited for the repose of their souls, and a patent of nobility granted to Cadoudal's family.

By the Charter, laws were to be made by king, peers, and deputies acting together. In actual practice the King made his own laws. From the mouths of such men as Lainé, whom Napoleon had thoroughly understood and denounced, the gospel of non-resistance was heard in all its ancient simplicity, "If the King wills it, the law wills it."

Incredible as it may seem, the members of the old Parliament of Paris met at a private house, and drew up a protest against the Charter. With one accord nobles and priests began to speak of the return of feudalism, of seignorial rights, of tithes, of benefices, of exclusive chase, and of the confiscated lands. The clergy of Paris, in their address to the King (August, 1814), expressed their earnest desire for the restoration of "that old France, in which were intermingled, without distinction, in every heart, those two sacred names, — God and King."

At least one sermon was preached in which those citizens who did not restore to the nobles and the Church the lands which the Revolution had taken away were threatened with the doom of Jezebel — *and they should be devoured by dogs.* Three hundred petitions were found at one time lying upon the table of the Bourbon minister of the interior, sent there by distressed Catholics who declared that their priests refused them absolution on account of their being owners of national properties. To the trembling devotee, the poor slave of superstition, the priest said, "Surrender to Church and nobles the land you bought and paid for, else the gates of heaven shall remain shut to you!" Under the spell of clerical duress many a middle-class and peasant proprietor swapped good land for a verbal free passage to the new Jerusalem. Many nobles, imitating a king who had mentally abolished all changes since 1789, began to claim forgotten dues and to exercise offensive feudal privileges. The Duke of Wellington himself acted the *grand seigneur* of the Old Régime; and with a cavalcade of friends and a pack of hounds went charging at his pleasure over the crops of the farmers around Paris, trampling their young grain with serene disregard of peasant rights. These nobles of old France, who had fled from the dangers of the Revolution, and who had been restored by Napoleon, or by foreign bayonets, were as proud, as intolerant, as though they had accomplished the Bourbon restoration by themselves. They regarded the nobles of Napoleon's creation with unconcealed contempt. The wives of men whose fathers had been ennobled for shady services to shadier Bourbon kings, looked with lofty scorn upon the ladies of such men as Marshal Ney, whom Napoleon had ennobled for service as gallant as any soldier ever rendered to France. To mark beyond all mistake the dividing line between the old nobility and the new, the military schools were reëstablished, in which a hundred years of nobility were necessary for admission — another violation of the Charter.

Louis XVIII. was not devoid of talent, nor of worldly wisdom; but he was not the man to contrast favorably with Napoleon. It was his misfortune to be personally repulsive. Like his brother, Louis XVI. he was swinish in tastes and habits. So fat that he could not mount a horse, so unwieldy that he could only waddle about in velvet gaiters, he was no man's hero — nor woman's either. Those who loved the ancient system were compelled to use him, not because they loved *him*, but because they adored the system.

Gifted with small talent for governing, how could he bring order out of the chaos Napoleon's fall had left? How could he reconcile the intemperate greed of the partisans of the Old Order with the advocates of liberal ideas in France? How could he harmonize emancipated peasants with lords of Church and State who were clamorous to reënslave them? How could he restore prosperity to the French manufacturer suddenly ruined by the flood of English goods, which flood Napoleon had so long dammed with his Continental system? And when the curé of St. Roch refused holy burial to an actress, how could the feeble Louis control either arrogant priest or indignant, riotous friends of the actress? And how could he prevent all France from remembering that once before when this same priest had refused Christian burial to an opera dancer, the iron hand of Napoleon Bonaparte had fallen upon the unchristian curé, inflicting chastisement, and the reproof that "Jesus Christ commanded us to pray even for our enemies"?

No wonder, then, that when Carnot published a memorial, arraigning the government for its breaches of faith, and pointing out its rapid progress to absolutism, the book had a vast circulation. Chateaubriand was brought forward to write a reply, and he wrote it; but even Chateaubriand could not slay facts with a pen, though the courtiers at the palace seem to have believed that he had done so.

Such was the Bourbon restoration. Undoing much of the work of the Revolution, it menaced all. Apparently it was only a question of time when France would be clothed again in the political and religious garb of 1789. Those who had flattered themselves that they were getting constitutional monarchy in exchange of Napoleon's despotism, soon realized that the Bourbon system had most of Napoleon's vices and none of his virtues. Talleyrand, Fouché, and Company had expected to rule the kingdom as constitutional ministers. They found that their influence was nothing when opposed by such royalist courtiers as the empty-headed Blacas. Three months did not elapse after Talleyrand and Fouché had plotted the downfall of Napoleon before they were plotting the overthrow of Louis XVIII.

*　　*　　*　　*　　*　　*

At length the Congress of Nations assembled at Vienna (September, 1814), and a very grand gathering of notabilities it was. The Czar of Russia, the kings of Prussia, Denmark, Bavaria, and Würtemberg, the Emperor Francis of Austria, were present in person; the kings of England and France were represented by Lord Castlereagh and Prince Talleyrand, respectively; Saxony, Naples, and other small states were represented by delegations more or less official, and more or less recognized.

Statesmen of many countries, diplomats, envoys, agents, male and female, attended in great numbers; and in fêtes, banquets, balls, excursions, and miscellaneous amusements some $50,000 each day were gayly consumed.

Faithless in their dealings with Napoleon, the allied kings had been distrustful of each other; behind public treaties secret agreements had lurked, and now at the

Congress of Vienna these underhand dealings began to
crop out. Ostensibly Napoleon had been overthrown by
a grand, brotherly coöperation of all the European monarchs. Ostensibly the motive of this grand, brotherly co-
operation had been to liberate the people of Europe from
the grinding tyranny of Napoleonic government.

No sooner had eminently wise heads begun to wag at
this congress, loosening eminently sage tongues, than it
appeared that Russia, Prussia, Austria, and England had
made a secret bargain, quite a while ago, to divide at their
own pleasure the territories of which they had stripped the
too ambitious Emperor of the French. Consequently, the
representatives of these four Christian powers began to
hold little meetings of their own, to readjust the map of
Europe, shutting the door in the face of the eminent Talleyrand and lesser lights who had come there to wield
influence on a variety of subjects. This concert of the
four Christian powers, to the utter ignoring of other
powers, likewise Christian, would have resulted in a new
map of Europe, just suited to their own views but for one
thing. In reaching their secret agreement to shut out the
other powers, they had failed to come to an agreement
among themselves.

If four royal and Christian victors secretly agree to
monopolize the spoils, it is obviously of the utmost importance that they should not fall out while dividing the loot.
Russia, Austria, Prussia, and England were in harmony
so far as agreeing that those four should take everything
which Napoleon had lost ; but the Congress of Vienna had
barely passed the stage of mutual congratulations, and a
solemn return of thanks to God, before the row between
the four robber powers began. The Czar demanded all of

Poland; Prussia all of Saxony; Austria's eager eyes were fixed upon Italy, and England stiffened her grip on colonies generally.

A great deal has been said in praise of the masterly manner in which Talleyrand forced open the door, and led France again to the council board of nations. His boasted diplomacy seems to have amounted to no more than this: the four powers mentioned quarrelled among themselves, and France found her opportunity to take sides. Talleyrand made good the opening thus offered, but surely he was not the only Frenchman who could have done so. France had not been obliterated : she was still the France of 1792, which had successfully resisted all Europe. If the four great powers found themselves about to fight, two against two, was it owing to Talleyrand's genius alone that France was courted by one party to the feud? Surely not. It was owing to the greatness of France — not the greatness of Talleyrand.

Louis XVIII. could have brought into the field not only the remnants of Napoleon's army in the late campaign, but also the army with which Soult had fought Wellington, as well as the troops which the Treaty of Paris had released from northern prisons and garrison towns.

In a war which enlisted the support of the French people, half a million men could easily have been armed; hence we can readily understand why Austria and England, enraged by the greed of Russia and Prussia, signed a secret treaty with France in January 1815.

However, the spirit of compromise worked with the Congress of Vienna; and to avoid such a dreadful war as was on the eve of breaking out among the allied kings, the

Czar was allowed to take nearly all of Poland; and Prussia had her way with Saxony; for while they gave her only half of Saxony itself, they made up for the other half by giving her more than an equivalent on the Rhine.

Juggling with the doctrine of "legitimacy," and claiming that all thrones must be restored to princes who were rulers "by the grace of God," and not by the choice of the people, Talleyrand seems to have brought the powers to agree that Murat should be ousted from Naples, and the Bourbons restored. Bernadotte could not be treated likewise, because he was the adopted son of the legitimate King of Sweden!

He was not only confirmed in his high office, but the English fleet had been sent to aid him in seizing the prey which had been promised him as the price of his waging war upon his mother-country. Norway, which Napoleon had refused to promise him, and which the Czar had promised, was torn from Denmark by force, and handed over to Sweden, in spite of all the Norwegians themselves could do.

Informed of all that was passing in France, in Italy, and at the Vienna Congress, Napoleon prepared to make a bold dash for his throne. He communicated secretly with Murat, with various Italian friends, with various friends in France. Vague rumors began to circulate among his old soldiers that he would reappear in the spring.

Did he make a secret treaty with Austria, detaching her from the European alliance? There is some reason to believe that he did. He repeatedly declared at St. Helena that such a treaty had been made; and the author of the *Private Memoirs of the Court of Louis XVIII.* corroborates him. In that curious, interesting book a copy of the alleged treaty is given.

Napoleon himself is reported to have said that the conspiracy which Fouché had been organizing among the army officers forced him to leave Elba three months earlier than he had intended. This is important, if true, for it is conceded that had he waited three months longer his chances of success would have been immensely improved — provided that he had not in the meantime been seized as a prisoner of war or assassinated.

Concealing his design to the last moment, Napoleon gathered up his little army of eleven hundred men, went on board a small flotilla at Porto Ferrajo, February 15, 1815, and set sail for France. His mother and his sister looked on in tears while the troops were embarking, and the Emperor himself was deeply affected. As he embraced his mother and bade her farewell, he said, "I must go now, or I shall never go."

At the Tuileries on the night of March 2, 1815, a curious scene was witnessed in the saloon of the Abbé d'André, director-general of the royal police.

Quite a number of people being present, conversation fell upon certain ugly rumors concerning Elba. A gentleman just from Italy spoke of the active movements of Napoleon's agents. It was said that the Emperor was engaged in some hostile preparations. The gentleman from Italy evidently made an impression upon the company, and created a feeling of uneasiness. The mere thought of Napoleon Bonaparte breaking loose from Elba,

and landing in France, was enough of itself to materially
increase the chilliness of a night in March to the Bourbon
group.

But the Abbé d'André was equal to the emergency.
As director-general of police it was his business to
know what Napoleon was doing, and he knew.

Rising from his chair, and striding to the fireplace, he
faced the company, and harangued them thus: —

"It is certainly a very extraordinary thing that right-
thinking people should be the first to find fault with the
government. For heaven's sake, ladies and gentlemen,
do give the ministers credit for common sense! If you
think them indifferent to passing events, you are strangely
mistaken. They watch everything, see everything, and take
precautions against everything. Do not be alarmed about
Elba. Every step Bonaparte takes is carefully noted. Elba
is surrounded by numerous cruisers. All who come and all
who go are carefully examined. Government receives a
daily report of all that takes place there. Now, to convince
you that your alarms are silly, I will read you the report
we received yesterday."

With this the complacent police minister drew from
his pocket the official bulletin, and read it. His agent
represented that Napoleon was reduced to a very low state
of health, that he had the scurvy, and was assailed by the
infirmities of premature old age; that he rarely went out,
and that he would sometimes be seen on the seashore
amusing himself by tossing pebbles into the sea — a sure
sign of approaching lunacy. And so forth.

Having read this valuable report, d'André looked down
upon his auditors with a glance of triumph. He had
demonstrated to his complete satisfaction that Napoleon

was not only in Elba, but that he was pitching idle pebbles into a listless sea, and was on the direct route to the lunatic asylum.

This was March 2; on the day previous Napoleon had landed at Cannes, and was marching upon Paris!

The shock which Europe felt when the signal telegraph flashed the news that the lion was loose again, was such as Europe had probably never felt before, and will probably never feel again. It paralyzed the King and the court at the Tuileries; it created consternation among the kings and statesmen at the Congress of Vienna. The royalist lady who wrote the *Memoirs of the Court of Louis XVIII.*, declares that the King's ministers looked like men who had seen a ghost. They were frightened into such imbecility that they were incapable of forming any plan or giving any sane advice.

On the other hand, Wellington's belief was that Napoleon had acted on false information, and that the King would "destroy him without difficulty, and in a short time."

How Wellington ever managed to conjure up the mental picture of Napoleon being destroyed by Louis XVIII. is one of the psychological mysteries.

The man who, of all men, best knew that Louis XVIII. could never stand his ground against Napoleon was Louis himself; and he began to arrange to go out at one gate while Napoleon came in at the other. Proclamations he issued, but no man read them. A price he set on Napoleon's head, but no man was eager to earn it. Generals and troops he sent to stop the daring intruder, but the troops cried "Live the Emperor!" and the officers had to flee, or join the Napoleonic procession. The

Duchess of Angoulême, daughter of Louis XVI., ex-
horted the soldiers at Bordeaux, but even her appeals
fell flat. The Count of Artois and Marshal Macdonald
were equally unsuccessful at Lyons; their troops deserted
them, and they were forced to gallop away. Marshal Ney
was quite sure that he could manage the soldiers committed to him, and that he could cage the monster from
Elba. Pledging his word to the quaking King, he set
forth upon his errand, drew up his troops, harangued
them, and proposed the capture of Napoleon. They
laughed at him, drowned his voice in cries of "Live the
Emperor!" and the inconstant Ney fell into the current,
surrendered to his men, proclaimed his adherence to the
man he had been sent to capture, and went in person to
lay his offer of service at the feet of his old master!

Sadly Louis XVIII. turned to Blacas upon whom he had
too trustfully leaned for guidance and counsel. "Blacas,
you are a good fellow, but I was grievously deceived when
I mistook your devotedness for talent." With nobody to
fight for him, it was time he was leaving; and on the
night of March 19 he left. With him on his doleful way
to the frontier went a terror-stricken renegade, who dreaded
of all things that Napoleon should lay hands upon him, —
Marmont, the Arnold of France.

CHAPTER XLVI

DURING the voyage from Elba to France, Napoleon had been in the best of spirits, moving about familiarly among his men, and chatting freely upon all subjects. He had not told them where they were going, but probably they little needed telling. All must have felt that they were bound for France.

The passage was full of peril, for French cruisers were often in sight. One of these came quite near, so much so that Napoleon ordered his guards to take off their bear-skin caps and to lie down upon the deck. The commander of the French vessel hailed Napoleon's brig, and recognizing it as from Elba, asked, "How's the Emperor?" Napoleon himself seized the speaking-trumpet and replied, "He is wonderfully well."

At length the companions of the Emperor were told that they were bound for France, and those who could write were called around him to copy two proclamations he intended to scatter abroad upon landing. He had himself written these in Elba, but nobody present could read them — not even himself.

Casting these into the sea, he dictated two others, — one for his old soldiers, the other for the nation at large. He revised these papers ten times before they satisfied him, and then he set all hands making copies. Engaged thus, they came within sight of France, and they greeted the shores with enthusiastic shouts.

It was about five o'clock in the evening of March 1, 1815, that Napoleon and his little army landed near Cannes, and bivouacked in a meadow surrounded by olive trees, close to the shore. A captain and twenty-five men, sent to Antibes to rouse the garrison and bring it over to Napoleon, entered the town crying, "Live the Emperor!" without explanation or further statement; and the people of the place, knowing nothing of Napoleon's landing, took these men, who had suddenly come screaming through their quiet town, to be lunatics. The royal commandant had sufficient presence of mind to shut the town gates; and so the gallant twenty-six, who went to surprise and capture, got surprised and captured.

"We have made a bad beginning," said Napoleon, when news of this mishap reached him. "We have nothing to do but to march as fast as we can, and get to the mountain passes before the news of our arrival."

The moon rose, and at midnight the Emperor began his march. He had brought a few horses from Elba, had bought a few more from peasants after landing, and thus some of his officers were mounted, while he himself rode in a carriage given him by his sister Pauline, and which he had brought from Elba. They marched all night, passing through silent, moonlit villages, where the people, roused by reports of something unusual afoot, — the pirates had come, some said, — stood gaping at the marching troops, responding with shrugs of the shoulders to the shouts of "Live the Emperor!" It was not until the

column had passed through Grasse, a town of six thousand inhabitants, and had halted on a hill beyond, that the
people seemed to realize what was happening. The pirate
alarm disappeared, the fires of enthusiasm began to glow,
and with glad shout of "Live the Emperor!" the town-
folk came running toward the camp, bearing provisions
for the troops. From this time the country people were
certain that Napoleon had really come back, and his
march became one of triumph. Leaving cannon and carriage at Grasse, the column pressed on toward Cérénon
by mountain paths still covered with snow, the Emperor
marching on foot among his grenadiers. When he stumbled and fell on the rough road, they laughed at him; and
he could hear them calling him, among themselves, "Our
little monk." Reaching Gap on the 5th, he printed his
proclamations; and he began to scatter them by thousands.
And never before did proclamations find such willing
readers, or win such popular favor. Advancing toward
Grenoble, the advance-guard under Cambronne enconn-
tered a battalion of six thousand troops, sent to stop the
march of the invaders. The royalist commander refused
to parley with Napoleon's officers, and threatened to fire.
Cambronne sent to inform the Emperor of what had
occurred. Napoleon was riding in an old carriage, picked
up at Gap, when this report reached him. Mounting his
horse, he galloped forward to within a hundred yards of the
hostile battalion. Not a cheer greeted him. Turning to
Bertrand, the disappointed Emperor remarked, "They
have deceived me, but no matter. Forward march!"
Throwing the bridle of his horse to Bertrand, he went on
foot toward the royal troops.

"Fire!" shouted the officer, drawing his sword. And

then Napoleon, unbuttoning that familiar gray overcoat, and fronting them with that familiar cocked hat, made the famous address which broke down all military oppositiou between Grenoble and Paris, sweeping thousands of bayonets out of his way with a word.

"What! My children, do you not recognize me? It is your Emperor. If there be one among you who would kill his general, he can do it. Here I am!"

"Live the Emperor!" came the answer of six thousand men, as they melted into tears, broke ranks, and crowded around him to fall at his feet, kiss his hands, and touch the hem of his garment.

The officer who had ordered them to fire had a good horse and a fair start; hence he managed to escape.

The six thousand who had come to capture Napoleon turned and marched with him. By this time the country was aroused on all sides, and crowds flocked around the column, shouting "Live the Emperor!" Advancing beyond Vizille, the Emperor was met by Colonel Labédoyère, who had brought his regiment to join Napoleon's ranks. With cries of joy the troops mingled, and Napoleon took the ardent young colonel in his arms, pressing him to his breast, and saying, "Colonel, it is you who replace me upon the throne!" Onward then to Grenoble, where the gates had been closed, and the defences manned to resist the invader.

It was dark when Napoleon arrived before the walls. He ordered Labédoyère to address the troops within. This was done, and there were cries of "Live the Emperor!" from within the city. But the royal commandant had the keys, and the gates could not be opened. "Room! room!" came the cry from within. It was the

shout of citizens of the town coming with beams to batter
down the gates.

The work was soon done, the way was open, and the
Emperor's column found itself surrounded by a multitude
as enthusiastic as any they had met. With uncontrollable transports they laid hold of Napoleon, pulled him
from his horse, and bore him forward in their arms.

That night was one long festival for soldiers, citizens,
and peasants; and next morning a great crowd followed
him when he set out for Lyons. There, upon an immenser
scale, was repeated the ovation of Grenoble. Royal officers lost all control of their troops. Marshal Macdonald
and the Count of Artois were utterly abandoned; and
when they fled, were followed by a solitary trooper, to
whom Napoleon afterward gave the cross of the Legion
of Honor. For four days, this great city of southern
France testified in every possible way its unbounded joy
at the Emperor's return. It is said that twenty thousand
people were constantly under his windows. It is certain
that he never forgot these glorious days — almost the last
days which he might name glorious. His journey was now
no longer an adventure; once more he was a great power
among the nations of earth. He had committed no violence, had shed no blood. The love and the admiration
of a gallant people were his again — balm for all those
wounds of last year. In his address, at his departure, his
closing words were simple and touching, " People of Lyons,
I love you! " and there can be no doubt that he did.

Moving onward, he came to Auxerre on the 17th; and
in the evening came Marshal Ney, with something in word
and manner which suggests that he felt what nothing so
well describes as the term " sheepish." Very rude had he

been to his Emperor in 1814 — rude, brutal, threatening. Now there was a change. Ney was contrite, apologetic, explanatory. He had been misrepresented, it seems; and the newspapers had told lies about him. But Napoleon relieved him with: "Embrace me, my dear Ney. To me you are still the *Bravest of the brave.*"

Halting briefly at Fontainebleau on March 20, Napoleon spent some solitary hours in the room where he had suffered such agonies the year before; and he went again into the garden which had been his Gethsemane. Pushing on to Paris, he arrived after dark and entered the Tuileries at nine o'clock, borne on the shoulders of his wildly enthusiastic friends. Five thousand young nobles of the royal body-guard had left Paris that morning to head the royal army, and oppose Napoleon's advance. The troops they expected to command joined their Emperor near Paris; and the noble officers, left without commands, were heard in the Parisian saloons that evening plausibly explaining the cause of their failure to stop the usurper's progress.

The great city of Paris did not go out to meet the returning Emperor as Grenoble and Lyons had done. Paris was rather indifferent. "They let me come as they let the other fellows go," remarked Napoleon that night. Thousands of soldiers had cheered him as he entered the capital, adoring friends had pressed him so ardently at the Tuileries that he had cried out, "My friends, you smother me!" Elegant ladies of the imperial court, Hortense in the lead, had made ready to welcome him to the palace; they had thrown arms about his neck and kissed him. But as the wifeless, childless Emperor sat by the fireside late in the night, almost alone, his feet up, resting on the mantelpiece, he looked very tired and very sad. Many old

friends had met him; many had stayed away. Paris had
not been so warm as Lyons. France was not so unanimous as he had hoped. Confidence in him, and his
fortune and final success, was very far indeed from being
universal.

Bourrienne records that one of the Paris newspapers
made note of the various stages of Napoleon's return in
this wise: —

"A report is circulated that the Corsican brigand has
landed at Cannes;" a few days later the same pen wrote:
"Do you know what news is circulated? They say the
rash usurper has been received at Grenoble;" then later
came the announcement, "I have it from a good source
that General Bonaparte has entered Lyons;" then, after a
few days, it was, "Napoleon, it appears, is at Fontaine-
'bleau;" and on March 20 came the final, "His Majesty
the Emperor and King alighted this evening at his palace
of the Tuileries."

CHAPTER XLVII

WHILE it is true that the return of the Emperor had not pleased the nobles, the ultramontane priests, the capitalists, and the intriguers who had been working for the Duke of Orleans, there appears to be no doubt that the army and the masses of the people were sincerely rejoiced. The only thing which had a tendency to cool the general enthusiasm was the apprehension of war. But Napoleon having taken great pains to make it known that he wished for peace, that he meant to respect the Treaty of Paris, and that he intended to rule as a constitutional king, the French could not fully realize the certainty of war. They had heard the allied kings declare that France had the right to choose her own ruler, and had been told that the Bourbons were restored simply because the Senate and other organs of public opinion had deposed Napoleon and selected Louis XVIII. If the allied kings were telling the truth in making such declarations, then the French, who had put Napoleon aside for the Bourbon, had as much right to put the Bourbon aside for Napoleon. Neither to the French people, nor to Louis XVIII., did it appear certain that the allied kings would march their armies back into France to drive out an emperor the nation had welcomed.

Consequently the beginning of the Hundred Days was

marked with what General Thiébault calls a "boundless enthusiasm." He was present on the night of Napoleon's entry into Paris; he was one of the officers sent by the King to stop the Emperor's advance; and Thiébault says that " at least twenty thousand persons were crowding about the Tuileries. Suddenly Napoleon reappeared. There was an instantaneous and irresistible outburst. At sight of him the transports rose to such a pitch that you would have thought the ceilings were coming down; then, as after a thunder-clap, every man came to himself, quivering with ecstasy, and stammering like a man intoxicated."

This first night of his return had barely passed before Napoleon was hard at work reorganizing his government; and he continued to labor sixteen hours a day, almost without rest, to create an administration, an army, and a thorough system of national defence.

As Dumas tersely states, " At his voice, France was covered with manufactories, workshops, founderies ; and the armorers of the capital alone furnished as many as three thousand guns in twenty-four hours ; whilst the tailors made in the same time as many as fifteen and even eighteen hundred coats. At the same time the lists of the regiments of the line were increased from two battalions to five ; those of the cavalry were reënforced by two squadrons ; two hundred battalions of the National Guard were organized ; twenty marine regiments and forty regiments of the Young Guard were put in condition for service ; the old disbanded soldiers were recalled to the standard ; the conscriptions of 1814 and 1815 were raised ; soldiers and officers in retirement were engaged to reënter the line. Six armies were formed under the names of the Army of the North, of the Moselle, of the Rhine, of the Jura, of the Alps, and of the Pyrenees; whilst a seventh, the Army of the Reserve, collected under the walls of Paris and of Lyons, which cities were to be fortified."

Politically, Napoleon's position in France itself was full of trouble. Though they had cast out the Bourbons, the people had no intention of returning to imperial despotism. Liberal ideas prevailed everywhere, and Napoleon himself must not now hope to rule by personal sway. He must become the mouthpiece and the public agent of the nation, else he would become king of a minority faction, with the bulk of the nation against him.

As an evidence of his good faith in accepting limited power, Napoleon called to his counsels Benjamin Constant, leader of the French liberals, a friend of Madame de Staël, and a very bitter enemy to the Emperor. Constant responded to the invitation, and prepared an amendment to the constitution of the Empire, which Madame de Staël believed was precisely the thing needed to rally all France to Napoleon's support, and to make certain the future of the cause of liberalism.

This famous document, known as "The Act Additional," did not vindicate Madame de Staël's judgment. It angered all parties, more or less, for it was what modern politicians would call "a straddle." It contained enough democracy to offend the imperialists; and enough imperialism to disgust the democrats.

Let it be remembered that the rallying cry of the people who had flocked to the returning Emperor had been: "Down with the nobles! Down with the priests!" So intense had been this feeling, this terrible antagonism to the abuses of the Old Order, that Napoleon himself, at Lyons, had whispered, "This is madness." In Paris he

had found the same spirit. Nobles and priests were furiously hated, not so much on personal grounds, as because
they stood for an abominable system.

By tens of thousands the workmen of Paris had paraded
before the Tuileries, making the air ring with the old
war cries of the Revolution, and chanting fiercely the
song whose burden is " With the guts of the last of the
priests we will strangle the last of the kings!"

Now, of all men, Napoleon was the least likely to
throw himself into the arms of men like these. He had
no objection to nobles if they were *his* nobles; nor to
priests if they were *his* priests; nor, indeed, to kings if
they were *his* kings. Perfectly willing that the opportunities of life should be offered to all men alike, whether
peasants or princes, and democrat enough to wish that all
men should be equal in the eye of the law, — free to
choose their vocations, their religion, and their political
creed, — he had not the slightest idea of opening the
flood-gates of that pent-up democracy, socialism, and
communism which had horrified him in the days of
his youth.

In the " Act Additional" provisions were made for a
representative government and for the responsibility of
ministers. Freedom of religion, freedom of the press,
security for person and property, were also guaranteed.

The good effects of these concessions were nullified by
the creation of a hereditary House of Lords, which, it is
said, Napoleon opposed, but which was adopted in spite of
him. General Thiébault thought that this unpopular
feature of the new Constitution lost the Emperor two
hundred thousand men, who, otherwise, would have joined
his army.

This "Act Additional" was submitted to the people, and adopted, but the vôte was light.

By a decree which he had issued from Lyons, he had abolished the Senate and the legislative body. In their place was to be put the new House of Lords, and a legislative assembly. Urged by Lafayette, and other Liberals whose support he could not throw away, Napoleon ordered the elections much earlier than he had intended — and much earlier than was good for him, as it afterward appeared.

One by one grievous disappointments fell upon Napoleon and his people. It became evident that his return meant war. The Congress of Vienna declared that he had broken the Treaty of Fontainebleau, and declared him an outlaw. The armies of the kings were ordered to halt in their homeward march, and to set out for France again. Napoleon's letters to the Allies could not even be delivered; his couriers were turned back at the frontier.

If Austria had made a secret agreement with him, it became apparent that nothing was to be hoped for in that quarter.

Murat had ruined everything by madly plunging into the papal states, proclaiming Italian unity and independence, and dashing himself to pieces in an attempt far beyond his means and his ability. Austria believed that Murat was acting at the instigation of Napoleon, and this unfounded suspicion led her to think, as Napoleon said, that he had played her false.

Murat's army melted away in the face of Austrian and English opposition; the Italians did not rise as he had hoped; and the rash, unfortunate King of Naples fled to France, and hid himself near Toulon. From this place of concealment he sent to Napoleon the offer of his services; but the great man who had forgiven Ney, and reëmployed Fouché, drew the line at Murat. More's the pity! In an army which had a general's place for the infamous Bourmont, there surely might have been found room for the finest cavalry leader in the world — a man who had sinned, but had bitterly repented; a man whose splendid sword might have made Ligny another Jena, and Waterloo another Dresden.

As it was, Murat's failure strengthened the Allies, and cast a gloom over France.

Two things Napoleon needed above all others, — time and money. He had only a few weeks in which to create means of defence against a world in arms; and the lack of money made it impossible for him to utilize to the best advantage even these few weeks. Supported only by silver and gold (arrant cowards in times of war), and the note currency of the Bank of France, he was combating nations which redoubled their resources by the issue of paper money. He received liberal voluntary contributions; Hobhouse relates that it was a frequent occurrence for rolls of bank notes to be handed the Emperor while he was reviewing the troops. But, after all, such a resource yields comparatively little; and the scarcity of money seriously crippled the great captain in preparing for his last fight.

Before he sets out to join the army we see Napoleon in two characters which will never fade from the memory: one as the successor of Charlemagne and Emperor of the French; the other as the private citizen with his personal griefs.

Time being so short, it was decided that the electoral

colleges of France should have a grand open-air meeting as in the days of Charles the Great — a *Champ de Mai*, to be held in the Field of Mars.

On the 1st of June, 1815, deputations from all the constituencies of the Empire, together with those from the army, and every public body, assembled in that historic amphitheatre where the first Festival of the Federation had been held twenty odd years before. Sixty thousand troops added to the pomp of the ceremony, and countless throngs of Parisians crowded the field. There was inspiring music, impressive religious forms, and a great taking of oaths to the new Constitution. Napoleon himself took the oath, distributed the eagles to his enthusiastic soldiers, and in a far-reaching, sharply pitched voice delivered one of his masterly addresses.

"Emperor, consul, soldier, I owe everything to the people. In prosperity, in adversity, on the field of battle, in the council room, on the throne, in exile, France has been the soul and constant object of my thought and my efforts."

How could Frenchmen listen to words like these and not burst into cheers? Had he been dressed that day in simple uniform instead of absurd court costume; had he kept his baleful brothers — Joseph, Lucien, and Jerome — in the background instead of at the forefront; had he made his appeal and trusted his cause more unreservedly to the people, the *Champ de Mai* might have been a colossal repetition of his triumph at Grenoble and Lyons. As it was, Paris regarded it as a fine spectacle, an exhibition to be seen and applauded — nothing more. It touched the heart of the army; it did not touch the larger heart of the French people.

2 T

When the chambers met, the Emperor delivered still a
more successful speech. Hobhouse, who was present, says
that when he had finished with the sentence, pronounced
in a louder tone and with a flourish of the right hand,
" The sacred cause of country will triumph ! " he rose
quickly from his throne, " bowed to the assembly, and
retired amidst thunders of applause, which accompanied
him from the throne to the door, and obliged him several
times to turn round and salute the assembly as he was
ascending the stairs of the area. He appeared highly delighted. Indeed, nothing could exceed the enthusiasm,
which was the more gratifying as it proceeded from such
an assembly." When we remember that this assembly of
notables was already hostile to Napoleon, was already cut
up into factions, only one of which was devoted to him,
and that it was an open secret that these notables would
openly oppose him the moment the fortunes of war should
go against him, his oratorical triumph becomes all the more
remarkable.

So much for the Emperor, his labors, his speeches, his
dangers, his mighty efforts to conquer an impossible situation; we can admire it all, marvel at his genius, courage,
resources, and versatility; but it is only when we go with
him to Malmaison that we draw near to the *man*, feel for
him, feel with him, and realize how greatly he has been
misunderstood. He had always been a good son; he had
been but too affectionate, too generous, to his sisters and
brothers; he had been to both his wives one of the most
tenderly indulgent of husbands.

It seems that he had continued to hope, almost to the
last, that Maria Louisa would come to him at Elba, and
bring his boy. A lot of fireworks, we are told, had fallen

into his possession, and he had kept them carefully, ready to be used when wife and child should come. He knew, at length, that neither would ever see him again. He had been told of Neipperg, and the true reason why Maria Louisa had ceased to write. "Méva, tell papa I am still very fond of him!" and this message, sent almost by stealth, was all that Méneval could bring to the father from the little son who was held at Vienna. No wonder that Napoleon should be found sitting before a portrait of his son, with tears coursing down his cheeks.

Josephine was dead. The fall of the Emperor, her hero, her Cid, had bewildered and unnerved her. Frightened at the din of war that shook the whole realm, she had lived in terror at Malmaison. The allied kings paid her every attention, and in showing the King of Prussia over her lovely grounds when she was ill, broken out with an eruption, she had, it is said, brought on a fatal relapse. Murmuring the words "Elba" — "Bonaparte" — she died, while her hero was yet in exile. It is a revelation of his true character that before setting out on his last campaign he should claim one day out of the few fate gave him, and devote it to memories, to regrets, to recollections of the frail, but tender-hearted woman who had warmed to him when all the world was growing cold. He went to Malmaison, almost alone, and, with Hortense, walked over the grounds, seeing the old familiar places, and thinking of the "old familiar faces." He lingered in the garden he himself had made, and in which he used to love to work when he was First Consul, surrounded by trees and flowers, and inhaling the breath of nature. He used to say that he could work better there than anywhere else. He wandered through the park, looking out on the trees he had planted in those brilliant days long ago.   Every spot had its silent reminder of glories that were gone, of friends he would see no more.

He had asked to be told everything about Josephine, —her last days, her sickness, her dying hours ; no details were too trivial to escape him.   And as they told the story he would break in with exclamations of interest, of fondness, of sorrow.   On this visit to the château he wanted to see everything that could remind him of her, and of their old life together — the death-chamber at the last. Here he would have no companion.   " My daughter, let me go in here alone ! " and he put Hortense back, entered, and closed the door.   He remained a long while, and when he came out his eyes showed that he had been weeping.

⁂   *

His personal appearance at this time is thus described by Hobhouse, who saw him at a military review at the Tuileries : " His face was deadly pale ; his jaws overhung, but not so much as I had heard ; his lips thin, but partially curling, so as to give his mouth an inexpressible sweetness. He had the habit of retracting the lips and apparently chewing.   His hair was dusky brown, scattered thinly over his temples; the crown of his head was bald.   One of the names of affection given him of late by his soldiers is ' Our little monk.'   He was not fat in the upper part of his body, but projected considerably in the abdomen, so much so, that his linen appeared beneath his waistcoat. He generally stood with his hands knit behind him, or folded before him, but sometimes unfolded them, played with his nose, took snuff three or four times, and looked at his watch.   He seemed to have a laboring in his chest,

sighing or swallowing.   He very seldom spoke, but when
he did, smiled, in some sort, agreeably.   He looked about
him, not knitting but joining his eyebrows, as if to see
more minutely, and went through the whole tedious ceremony with an air of sedate impatience."

Hobhouse speaks of Napoleon's reception at the opera
where Talma was to play Hector.   " The house was choked
with spectators, who crowded into the orchestra.   The airs
of La Victoire and the Marseillaise were called for, and
performed amidst thunders of applause, the spectators
joining in the burden of the song. . . .   Napoleon entered
at the third scene.   The whole mass rose with a shout
which still thunders in my ears.   The vivats continued
until the Emperor, bowing right and left, seated himself,
and the play recommenced.   The audience received every
speech which had the least reference to their returned hero
with unnumbered plaudits."

General Thiébault in his *Memoirs* declares that Napoleon was no longer the same man he had once been; that
his face wore a greenish tinge and had lost its expression;
that his mouth had lost its witchery; "his very head no
longer had the pose which used to characterize the conqueror of the world; and his gait was as perplexed as
his demeanor and gestures were undecided.   Everything
about him seemed to have lost its nature and to be broken
up."

The lady who composed the *Memoirs of the Court of
Louis XVIII.* saw Napoleon holding a review at the
Tuileries, and had a conversation with him afterward.

" Bonaparte was dressed that day in a green uniform.
I have been told that it was the same which he afterward
wore at Waterloo, and which he wore, almost in tatters,

at St. Helena. He had been reviewing some troops that morning at the Champ-de-Mars, and his coat, hat, and boots were still dusty. . . . I looked in vain for the fire which once beamed in his eyes. He stooped more than usual; his head almost hung upon his breast; his complexion was yellow, his countenance melancholy and thoughtful, and his little hat drawn almost over his eyes, gave him a gloomy expression. His movements were still abrupt, but this seemed merely the effect of habit. . . . He had altogether a wearied, harassed appearance, which seemed to indicate a great man extinct."

To the same effect is the testimony of Chancellor Pasquier.

Carnot said: "I do not know him again. He talks instead of acting; he the man of rapid decisions; he asks opinions, he the imperious dictator, who seemed insulted by advice; his mind wanders, though he used to have the power of attending to everything, when and as he would; he is sleepy, and he used to sleep and wake at pleasure."

CHAPTER XLVIII

A LL had been done that could be done — all that it was
in his nature to do. He had equipped two hundred
thousand men in arms, and had filled them with martial
fire. He had called back to the service every officer who
would come, saving Augereau, who had betrayed Lyons
in 1814, and Murat, who had joined the Allies. He had
courted the liberals, temporized with the Jacobins, toler-
ated the royalists, and shut his eyes to incipient treason.
To the Constants and La Fayettes he had said, " Gentlemen, don't waste time in debates on constitutional law
while the nation is in danger; unite with me to save her";
but he knew that his appeal was wasted. To the dangerous traitor Fouché he had said, " I ought to have you
shot "; but he left him minister, and knew that if battles
were lost, Fouché would be the first to plot for the return
of the Bourbons.

He listened to Jacobin songs, appreciated Jacobin
strength, and believed that he could win the fight if he
would put on the red bonnet. But he would not. In
Brumaire, 1799, he had said, "If I conquer with the
Jacobins, I would then have to conquer against them."
His opinions had not changed. If he put on the red cap
of the Jacobins, and put guns into their hands, he might
save his own crown; but how about his son? Democracy

once unchained, who would ever bind it again? Thus he would not nationalize the war — his one chance of success.

With two hundred thousand men, the Emperor, who might have enrolled a million, turned to face all Europe. The allied kings already had a million men in arms, and England was supplying $55,000,000 a month to pay them. In quality, Napoleon had led few better armies than that of his last campaign ; but while the troops were passionately devoted to the Emperor, they had lost confidence in many of the higher officers, and went to the front dreading treachery in their leaders.

The Russians and Austrians could not reach the Rhine before July; but the armies of Blücher and Wellington, about one hundred thousand each, were already in Belgium. Napoleon could strike at these with only about one hundred and twenty-five thousand. But as the enemy was widely scattered, and was not expecting immediate attack, he believed that he might best open the war by throwing himself between Wellington and Blücher, preventing their junction, crushing them in detail, and thus discourage the coalition to such an extent that he might detach at least some of its members.

Had he waited two weeks longer, he could have taken with him the twelve thousand troops who were putting down the royalists in La Vendée; but he could not foresee that the revolt would be quelled so soon. Other errors, however, were committed, for which he alone was responsible. He left his best officer, Davoust, in Paris, instead of employing him in the field. Had Davoust been put in Grouchy's place, the result of the campaign would almost certainly have been different. Again, he had given no confidence to Ney, had not even notified the marshal whether he was to be employed. It was so late when Ney got his orders that the campaign had already opened, and the fighting begun before he could arrive from Paris, without his horses, and accompanied by a single aide-de-camp.

Another thing: the Emperor gave the command of his right wing, which was to act independently, to an officer untried in that capacity, — Grouchy; and he did it over the protest of Soult and other general officers, who warned him that Grouchy was not the man for such a place.

A gross blunder was made as to Bourmont. This man had been one of the Chouan chiefs of 1800, to whom Napoleon extended clemency. Pardoned, then, by the First Consul, he had afterwards been implicated in the Georges conspiracy, and had fled to Portugal. Junot picked him up there, took a fancy to him, got him employed; and the man being a good officer, won rapid promotion. In 1814 he had been one of the traitors, and had gone over to the Bourbons. In 1815 he fell in with the Napoleonic tide, and professed the zeal of a sincere imperialist. Seeking employment in the army, he was contemptuously refused by Davoust, who told him that he must perform quarantine. Most unfortunately, Labédoyère and Gérard had faith in Bourmont, and the matter was carried to the Emperor. To Labédoyère, Napoleon could refuse nothing, and Bourmont was appointed to the command of one of the finest divisions.

Concentrating his army swiftly, Napoleon was near Charleroi, on the evening of June 14, 1815, and next day crossed the Sambre.

At daybreak, on the morning of the 15th, General Bourmont, two officers of his staff, and eight soldiers deserted.

As Bourmont had been present at the Council of War, he knew the secrets of the French, and these he carried with him to the Allies. This treason, on the eve of battle, demoralized, for a time, the entire division, and had a depressing effect throughout the army.

Another "deplorable mischance" happened on this morning. An order to Vandamme to advance was sent by a single courier, whose leg was broken by a fall of his horse. The order was not delivered, Vandamme did not make the movement, and Napoleon's manœuvre, by which he had expected to cut off and capture the Prussian corps of Ziethen, failed.

Blücher, acting much more promptly than Wellington, concentrated his army at Fleurus, from which he retired on Ligny. Wellington and many of his officers were at the Duchess of Richmond's ball, in Brussels, on the night of June 15, when Napoleon's guns were heard. At eleven o'clock a despatch arrived which told of the French capture of Charleroi and advance upon Brussels. Although Wellington knew that Napoleon's army was in motion, he was taken by surprise at the nearness of his approach. Withdrawing into a private room with the Duke of Richmond, he called for a map, saying, "That damned rascal Bonaparte has humbugged me!"

From midnight on to dawn, the English army was hurrying to the front, to concentrate and fight. Without waiting for Wellington or his orders, Prince Bernard, of Saxe-Wiemar, had already occupied Quatre-Bras. When Wellingtou arrived there, June 16, he passed on at once to a conference with Blücher, to whom he had written a letter which Blücher had received at noon. In this letter, Wellington had seemed to promise aid to Blücher if he would fight at Ligny, — mentioning the positions which the troops of the Anglo-Belgian army then occupied.

The curious feature of the case is that Wellington's troops were not where his letter said they were, and that he remarked to one of his staff as he was leaving Blücher, "If he fights here, he will be damnably whipped."

This letter in which Wellington promised to help Blücher only came to light in 1876, and Lord Wolseley says that Wellington, "an English gentleman of the highest type, wholly and absolutely incapable of anything bordering on untruth or deceit, must have been misled by his inefficient staff." Perhaps so. But it looks marvellously like a case where the English gentleman of the highest type had been caught napping by "that damned rascal Bonaparte," and wanted "old Blücher" to fight, in order that the British army might have time to concentrate. Blücher's chief of staff, Gneisenau, held this view at the time, and died in that belief. So little did the opening events of the campaign depend upon any generalship of Wellington, that some of his officers had to violate his orders before they could reach the positions which it was absolutely necessary they should occupy.

It was near five o'clock on the evening of June 15 that Ney, who had come from Paris to Beaumont in a post-chaise, and from Beaumont had travelled to Avesnes in a peasant's cart, bought horses from Marshal Mortier. At that late hour he was given command of the left wing of the French army, with verbal orders from Napoleon himself. Just what these orders were is a matter of dispute. The partisans of Ney contend that the Emperor said, "Go and drive back the enemy." Napoleon and his sympathizers allege that the orders were to seize

Quatre-Bras, and hold it. That the Emperor meant to give such orders, there can hardly be a doubt. On his way to Quatre-Bras, Ney encountered some Nassau troops at Frasnes, who fell back at once. Instead of advancing upon Quatre-Bras, Ney halted some two or three miles short of it, and reported to Napoleon for further orders. A small force of French cavalry actually entered Quatre-Bras, and then retired.

The Emperor, worn out with fatigue, and suffering from urinary, hemorrhoidal, and other ailments, had gone back to Charleroi to sleep and rest.

For reasons not fully explained, it was nine o'clock on the morning of the 16th before Ney was ordered positively to advance and capture Quatre-Bras. Had he moved promptly, he could even then have taken the place, for it was held by a few thousand Nassauers only. It was not until 2 P.M. that Ney attacked. A still greater delay marked Napoleon's own movements. It was between two and three o'clock in the evening before he struck the Prussians at Ligny.

Here, then, were two battles raging on the same day only a few miles apart. Ney was making a desperate onset at Quatre-Bras, which he could easily have taken on the 15th, or early on the 16th, but which was now held by ever increasing numbers of the enemy. And Napoleon was straining every nerve to defeat the Prussians, who had profited enormously by his delays.

It was at this crisis of his fortunes that he was tantalized by one of the most remarkable of military mishaps. A corps of twenty thousand men under D'Erlon, intended to act with Ney, was on its march to Quatre-Bras, when a staff-officer, Colonel de Forbin-Janson, delivered a pen-

cilled order from Napoleon to D'Erlon, which was totally
misconstrued, and which led D'Erlon to march to the
French left, when he should have struck the Prussians
cross-wise, while the Emperor pressed them in front.
D'Erlon set out, came in sight of Ligny, and created
consternation among the French, who thought it a Prussian reënforcement. Napoleon, not expecting troops on
his left, was forced to suspend his movements until he
could ascertain the facts, thus losing precious time.
Strange to say, this French corps, now that it was on the
field, was not used at Ligny, but was countermanded by
Ney, whom Forbin-Janson should have informed of the
Emperor's order, and was marched back to Quatre-Bras,
where it arrived too late to help Ney. Had it gone into
action at either place, its aid must have been decisive.
As it was, these twenty thousand troops were as completely lost to the French "as though the earth had swallowed them up."

Night found the Prussians beaten; and a vigorous pursuit, such as Murat, or La Salle, or Bessières could have
made, might have disorganized them for the campaign.
But there was no pursuit. They rallied at their leisure,
and the French did not even know next day what route
their retreat had taken.

After the battle Napoleon was again exhausted, and
nothing was done to improve the victory. The Emperor
slept, and the army waited. Next morning at seven his
generals stood around, idle, grumbling, discouraged. Vandamme was saying: "Gentlemen, the Napoleon of the
Italian campaign no longer lives. Our victory of yesterday will lead to nothing. You will see."

Mr. Houssaye contends that the Emperor was not in

poor condition, physically or mentally; and he enumer-
ates facts to prove what he says. It all depends upon
what his standard of comparison is. Does he compare
the French general with the English chief, — the one
launching a host of men so swiftly and surely that they
were upon the enemy before it was known that they had
moved; and the other idling in a ball-room, issuing
late and confused orders, naming the wrong place for
concentration, and saved only by the initiative of Prince
Bernard, the disobedience of his own officers, and the bad
luck which dogged the movements of the French? If
you compare Napoleon to Wellington, one must say that
the former was *not* in poor condition. But if we compare
the Bonaparte of 1815 with Blücher, the admission must
be made that in sustained energy and unwavering tenacity
of purpose, the German far exceeded his great antagonist.
And if we contrast the Bonaparte of 1815 with the Bonaparte of 1796, we at once exclaim with Vandamme, —"The
Napoleon we knew in Italy no longer lives."

Mr. Houssaye himself states that late in the morning
of June 17 the Emperor did not know what had taken
place at Quatre-Bras the day before; did not know
the true situation there; did not know that by swiftly
moving to the aid of Ney he would envelop Wellington
with overwhelming numbers and crush him! Even the
Napoleon of 1814 would have missed no such chance as
that. When the facts at length became known to him
he realized what he had lost, dashed on with the vanguard to Quatre-Bras, and led the headlong pursuit of
the English rear-guard — but it was too late. Wellington
was well on his way to Mont St. Jean, and Lord Uxbridge
was desperately hurrying the last of the British cavalry

out of the danger, with his " Gallop! for God's sake gallop, or you will be captured!"

Furthermore, Mr. Houssaye relates an incident which corroborates Carnot, Pasquier, and others who say that the Emperor was no longer able to endure prolonged labor : —

"It was now (June 14) a little past noon. The Emperor, amid the cheers of the inhabitants, passed through Charleroi, and halted at the foot of the crumbling glacis, near the little public-house called La Belle-Vue. He got off his horse, sent for a chair, and sat down by the side of the road. The troops defiled past him, cheering him lustily as they marched, their shouts deadening the roll of the drums and the shrill calls of the bugles. The enthusiasm of the troops bordered on frenzy; they broke ranks to embrace the horse of their Emperor."

And what of Napoleon amid this splendid ovation — an ovation spontaneous and thrilling like that of the eve of Austerlitz?

He sat there dozing, the cheers of the troops, which deadened drums and bugles, being powerless to rouse him! It was only noon, he had only been in the saddle half a day — was *this* the man of Eckmühl, of Friedland, of Wagram? Was *this* the chief who used to ride and ride till horse after horse fell in its tracks?

Turn from this dozing chief, exhausted by half a day's work, and look at old Blücher. At the age of seventy-three, he is full of pluck and dash and persistence. He hurries up his divisions to fight as soon as he knows that the French are moving. He is in the thick of the combat at Ligny. He heads charges like a common hussar. His horse is shot and he falls under the

feet of rushing squadrons, is drawn out almost dead and
borne off the field unconscious. Bruised and battered,
the old man no sooner "comes to himself" than he is up
again, beating down the cautious counsels of his chief-of-
staff, and determined to go to the help of Wellington, —
who had not come to *his* help, — although the chief-of-
staff, Gneisenau, believing Wellington to be a "master
knave," wished the Prussians to leave the English to take
care of themselves at Waterloo, as the Prussians had been
left to take care of *themselves* at Ligny. And on the ever
memorable 18th, while Napoleon will be waiting, hour by
hour, for the ground to dry so that he can move his artillery, old Blücher will be coming as fast as he can hurry
his troops through the mud, as fast as he can drag *his*
artillery; and the net result will be that, while miry
ground stops the great Napoleon, it does not stop the
impetuous and indomitable Blücher.

CHAPTER XLIX

WHEN Napoleon finally awoke on the 17th, he spent the morning talking politics to Gérard and Grouchy. It was midday when he gave the latter some thirty-three thousand men, and sent him after the Prussians. The spirit, if not the letter, of his instructions was that he was to penetrate Blücher's intentions: "whether he was separating from the English, or meant to unite, and fight again!" Davoust would have known how to interpret such an order, and how to act upon it; Grouchy, it seems, did not. For thirty years there was a dispute about the order itself, but at length it came to light; and since its text has been known there has been little difference of opinion on the subject of Grouchy's conduct. Detached from the main army to take care of Blücher, and to prevent the Prussians from coming to the aid of the English, he failed miserably to perform the task intrusted to him, and was of no more service to Napoleon in the movement which decided the campaign than D'Erlon had been at Ligny.

Through torrents of rain, through the mud and slush of the cut-up roads, the French followed the English toward Brussels.

On the crests of Mont St. Jean, with the forest of Soignes behind him, Wellington drew up his men for battle, relying upon Blücher's promise to arrive in time to coöperate. There were eighteen thousand troops at Hal, which might have been called up to his support; but Wellington, entirely misconceiving Napoleon's plans, had expected an attack upon his right, and this large force at Hal was left there in idleness to guard against an imaginary danger. By two o'clock in the morning of the 18th, Blücher sent a courier to Wellington, promising the support without which the English army would have continued its retreat.

When Napoleon's vanguard reached La Belle Alliance, and he saw that Wellington's army was in position on the opposite heights, he was happy. He had feared that the English would retire behind the forest of Soignes, unite with the Prussians, and thus be too strong for him. If he could but fight Wellington while Blücher was away, he did not doubt his ability to " give the Englishman a lesson ": for while the French numbered 74,000, there were but 67,000 of the Anglo-Belgian army.

The French army floundered through the mud of the soaked wheat-fields, the miry lowlands of the Dyle, and were late in the night of the 17th in reaching their positions at La Belle Alliance. Indeed, some of the troops did not reach the battle-field till late next morning. The floods of rain had rendered it impossible for the provision trains to keep up. The exhausted French lay down with empty stomachs, to rest as well as they could on the wet ground, without shelter or fire, whilst the English army, comfortably fed, kept themselves warm by campfires.

At dawn the rain ceased. Napoleon again reconnoitred, the ground being so soft that in places he "mired up," requiring help to lift his feet out of his tracks. Unconscious that even then old Blücher was wading through the bogs, across country, to get from Wavre to the English left at St. Lambert, Napoleon allowed hour after hour to slip by, stealing from him every chance of victory. The natural line of Prussian retreat was on Namur: he did not know that while Blücher lay unconscious, on the 16th, Gneisenau, chief of staff, had directed the retreat on Wavre. Therefore, Napoleon took his breakfast leisurely, chatting cheerfully with his general officers; and when he rode along the lines, saw all the splendor of his magnificent array, heard the bugles and the bands, and the sweeter music of seventy thousand voices shouting "Live the Emperor!" the great captain's face glowed with pride and joy. To him such a spectacle, such a greeting, was the nectar of the gods; he drank it now for the very last time.

It was eight o'clock when he made his plan of battle, nine when he issued orders, at ten he lay down and slept an hour.

Napoleon mounted his horse at eleven, and rode along the Brussels highroad to the farmhouse of La Belle Alliance; then he returned to the height of Rossomme. Between the crest upon which he sat his white Arabian mare, "Désirée," and that upon which Wellington awaited his attack, stretched the slopes of the ridges and the grain-covered valley between, about a mile in width. The Emperor was as calm and as confident as he had ever been in his life. Sitting his horse on the heights where all his army could see him, see the old gray overcoat and little cocked hat, see the square, pale face and the squat, sturdy figure, he swept every part of the field and of the horizon with his glass, and then gave the word. It was near noon on this fateful Sabbath day when the signal guns were heard; and the Prussians of Bülow's corps were already approaching St. Lambert. The battle commenced with an attack on the château of Hougomont, a stone building on the British right, protected by walls and moat and hedge. The French corps of Reillé, in the three divisions of Foy, Bachelu, and Jerome Bonaparte, threw itself furiously against this fortress; and desperate fighting, attack, and defence made the place literally run with blood — but the English, though driven from the woods, held the château.

The attack on Hougomont was a feint which the rash Jerome carried too far. The real attack was to be on the English centre, and to prepare for this the Emperor formed a battery of eighty guns. It was about one o'clock when Ney, who was to lead the charge, sent word that all was ready.

Before giving the signal, Napoleon swept the horizon with his glass, long and carefully. Away to the northeast he saw something which fixed his attention: it might be a clump of trees ; it might be a column of soldiers. Staff officers followed the Emperor's gaze, levelled their glasses, gave various opinions. " Trees," said some; " Troops," said others. If troops, what troops — Blücher's or Grouchy's? Such an awful doubt demanded instant action. Napoleon called for General Domon and ordered him to take a division of light cavalry and ride to St. Lambert; if the troops were Prussians, he must stop them.

Dumas describes the movement of the light cavalry: " Three thousand horsemen moved to the right, four abreast, unrolled themselves like an immense ribbon, winding a moment in the lines of the army, then breaking loose through our extreme right, rode rapidly and re-formed like a parade nearly three thousand toises from its extremity."

Soon the Emperor's fearful doubt became a terrible certainty. Not trees, but troops, stood over there in the distance; and the troops were Prussians!

Where was Grouchy?

A Prussian prisoner taken in the territory where no Prussians should have been, was brought to the Emperor, and at his replies to the questions asked him, the imperial staff was panic-stricken; and Napoleon himself filled with a storm of impotent rage. No French troops had been seen where Grouchy should have been, and the Prussian host was crowding toward the field of battle!

From this time onward the doomed Emperor was fighting two battles: Wellington at Mont St. Jean, and the Prussians at Plancenoit. About seven thousand of the best troops were sent to hold the Prussians off, while the attack on Wellington was being renewed. This was toward three o'clock in the afternoon.

With two battles on his hands, Napoleon in his despair sent another messenger to Grouchy. Bitterly remarking upon the conduct of his lieutenant, who had been "amusing himself at Gembloux," the Emperor exclaimed that if Grouchy but repaired his "horrible fault," and marched promptly, all would yet be well; for, be it remembered, Grouchy was only ten or twelve miles to the right.

Suffering from local ailment which made the saddle painful to him, the Emperor dismounted and seated himself at a small table upon which his maps were spread. Sometimes he got up and paced back and forth with his hands crossed behind him. Sometimes he folded his arms on the table and there rested his head, — in pain or slumber. The management of the actual fighting which was going on all this while, was left almost entirely to Ney

and D'Erlon, but especially to Ney, whose rashness at
Waterloo was as ruinous to the French as his caution had
been at Quatre-Bras.

Wellington, on the contrary, was as anxious a man as
ever bravely faced a foe. He had not believed himself
equal to the combat with Napoleon, man to man, and had
only resolved to give battle after having been assured of
Blücher's aid. Whether the Prussians could arrive in
time, was Wellington's great doubt. He felt that his only
salvation lay just there ; and it was not until Bülow's
corps, at 4.30 P.M., had drawn away from Napoleon at least
sixteen thousand of his best troops, that Wellington, feeling the French onset in his front relax, exclaimed : " By
God! I believe we will whip them yet."   Stronger evidence than that of the Prussian military expert, Muffling,
is this Wellington exclamation, that he was a lost man
had not " Old Blücher " come.

Against Wellington's left the corps of D'Erlon was
hurled; and at Papelotte and La Haye Sainte the struggle
was as bloody, as desperate, as full of quick turns of fortune, ebb and flow, success mingled with failure, as any
known to history. The English line was terribly shaken,
the losses frightful, but the French finally were driven back.

The Emperor had intended to support Reillé with Lobau's corps; that corps had been sent from the field to
meet the Prussians.

Ney asked for a cavalry division to support the renewed
attack he was about to make with D'Erlon's corps. Owing
to some mistake, Ney got not only the cavalry division
which he had asked for, but the entire cavalry reserve,
so that he took with him some twelve thousand horse.

This mighty mass was not launched at the weakened

English left, but at the centre. How the French host rode down into the valley, up the hill, and charged upon the English guns and the English squares, repeating the assault time and time again, all readers know. Made with a heroism which the world can but admire, these charges were repulsed with a courage which nothing could shake. The English squares stood unbroken against French horse, as the French themselves had stood against the Mamelukes. Twice, thrice, the British cannoneers were driven from their guns; twice the British artillery was in the hands of the French. Why were not the guns spiked? Why at least, were not the sponges broken, or the caissons destroyed? In the melée no one gave the order. So the cannon and its ammunition and its rammer was left there ready for the British gunner, when the retreat of the French cavalry made it possible for him to return to his battery. The attack had been premature. The Emperor himself exclaimed, " This is an hour too soon, but as it has been done I must support it. The day may be lost by this mistake."

It is true that Wellington's army was fearfully battered; that, between his rear and Brussels, the road was full of panic-stricken fugitives, not all of whom were Belgians or Hanoverians. It is true that English officers had almost despaired, and that frantic riders flew to Bülow imploring him to save the British army. It is true that there was a gap in the English line into which Ney frantically sought to throw infantry, and so win the day. But Napoleon had already been forced to send ten thousand other veteran troops to hold in check the thirty thousand Prussians. When, therefore, Ney's messenger came, asking for infantry, the Emperor petulantly answered, " Infantry! Where

does he expect me to get them? Can I make them?"
There are those who say that had he thrown in the few reserve battalions of the Guard, the day might have been won.

So the great opportunity passed. La Haye Sainte was
taken; but the English line was mended by reënforcements where it had been broken, and the Prussians,
under Ziethen, joined Wellington on his left. It was now
seven o'clock. The French were about to be taken in the
flank by the entire Prussian army. Napoleon might have
drawn off in good order, but the junction of Blücher and
Wellington would spoil all his plans. There was a chance
yet for him to crush the English by a final charge into
which every available man should be thrown. If it succeeded, all was won; if it failed, all was lost. It was the
superb risk of the daring gambler: everything upon a
single cast.

The orders flew, lines were formed, the great captain
rode among his men, and spoke to them. The sound of
their shouts of "Live the Emperor!" reached the English
lines where the charge was expected, a deserter from the
French ranks having brought warning. Ney was put at
the head of the columns, and the march began. Through
the mud of the valley, and up the slippery hill they went,
under the murderous fire of all the English guns. Through
the dense ranks, too closely crowded in that small space,
great lines were cut by cannon balls, and so hot was
the musket fire that they could not deploy. Ziethen's
Prussians were now in the fight, coming with full force
on the right. Ney's men, taken front and flank, had yet
advanced to within fifty yards of the English line; but
unable to open their ranks and charge, under such a
terrific fire, they fell into confusion. The Emperor was

watching them through his glass. "They are all mixed up; for the present, all is lost." At the moment when Napoleon was saying this, Wellington was ordering the advance of his whole line; the Prussian guns were thundering on the French flank; and over the lost field ran the cry: "The Guard recoils! We are betrayed! Save himself who can!"

In vain Ney struggled to hold the rout; in vain the Emperor hoarsely shouted to his men to rally: it was dark; confusion was everywhere; and the French army, a mighty wreck, was swept from its moorings. English cavalry made furious charges, crying "No quarter!" and Napoleon had no cavalry reserves to meet the shock.

NOTE. — In reference to the disputed incident of the British demand for the surrender of the Old Guard, and Cambronne's reply, the truth seems to be, that such a demand was made, and that Cambronne did reply, defiantly, though nastily; and that his language shot out in the disgust and exasperation of the moment, can more accurately be rendered into the English phrase, "Go to hell!" than in the classic terms, "The Guard dies: it does not surrender!"

Immediately after his scornful response, the heroic Cambronne was shot full in the face, and was left for dead on the field.

Readers of Thackeray will remember how he jeers and laughs at the defiance of the Old Guard; just as they will remember how he jeers and mocks at the second funeral of Napoleon, — so sure is the professional fun-maker to overreach himself, now and then.

The truth is, that the French troops were badly handled in the actual fighting at Waterloo; and that Napoleon stated no more than the fact when he charged Ney with having acted like a madman.

The troops, cavalry, and infantry were massed in such dense formation, on such contracted area, that they were in each other's way, had no fair chance to do what they should have done, and were sacrificed horribly to the British artillery. At the very moment when Ney was clamoring for reënforcements, he had forgotten a part of his own troops, — who were not engaged, who could have been used, and who might have decided the day in his favor.

The mismanagement of the troops still further demoralized them, as it tended to confirm their suspicions that they were being betrayed.

It has been claimed that Napoleon intentionally deceived his own troops, toward the last, by sending word along the line that Grouchy had come. This is by no means certain. The Emperor could hear the guns of Grouchy, who was engaged at Wavre, just as Grouchy had heard, during the afternoon, the guns at Waterloo. Napoleon doubtless believed that Grouchy was at last going to show up on his extreme right.

The old road of Ohain seems not to have wrecked the French cavalry in the tragic manner Victor Hugo alleges. Romance, tradition, and patriotic painting represents the Emperor's squadrons as being engulfed in the ravine made by the road where it passed through the high ground — over which ground the cavalry is alleged to have charged, in ignorance that the ravine, or "hollow way," was there. Mr. Houssaye who has studied the matter thoroughly says that there is no historic foundation for the story.

The remnants of the Old Guard formed squares, and for a while held off their pursuers; but the barrier was too frail, and it soon melted away. Napoleon, dazed and despairing, spurred his horse toward the English guns, but Soult, according to Gourgaud, caught the bridle reins, and the Emperor was forced off the field, protected by the last of the Old Guard squares. With a few horsemen he rode away, so crushed, so tired, that Bertrand and Monthyon had to hold him upright in the saddle. Several times on the retreat he attempted vainly to rally the fugitives: the panic was too complete.

The English rested at La Belle Alliance ; and Wellington, after meeting and hugging Blücher, rode to Waterloo to write his despatches. A Rothschild agent had already gone at speed to the coast, to reach England ahead of the news, and make additional millions for that enterprising house.

The Prussians pressed the pursuit with relentless vigor;

and the summer moon lit as wild a man-hunt as this blood-soaked planet ever knew.

What should Napoleon do, — stay, and attempt to rally the army, or hasten to Paris to check intriguers and organize resistance to the invaders? He did not know what had become of Grouchy, did not know how much of his own army was left. He dreaded the betrayal and the deposition of 1814, not fully realizing the deeper pits of 1815. As a matter of fact, Grouchy's army was intact. He had led it in most leisurely fashion to Wavre, and it had listened all day to the guns of Waterloo. Gérard, Vandamme, Exelmans, felt that the Emperor was in the midst of a great battle, and with the instinct of soldiers urged that they should "March to the guns!" They pleaded with Grouchy to go, Gérard insisting with such temper that Grouchy's precious self-love was pricked. In vain was all remonstrance; Grouchy would not move. He went to Wavre, fought the rearguard which Blücher had left there to detain him, made himself as utterly useless to his chief as though he had not existed, and then, after Waterloo, fell back, in admirable order, to Namur. Pluming himself upon the safety of his corps, the loss of the Empire did not ruffle his self-complacent satisfaction.

There was chaos in Paris when it was known that the army was no more, and that the Emperor was at the Élysée. palace. The tongue of faction fiercely wagged, and conspiracy stalked unmasked wherever it would. Lafayette babbled of constitutions and guarantees for liberty, when France needed every strong arm and every gun. Fouché,

duping both imperialists and republicans, plotted for the
Bourbons, and opened communications with Wellington.
Lucien Bonaparte gave wings to his conceit, and dreamed
of a new government in which he should be chief and
Napoleon lieutenant!

Carnot alone kept his head and saw clearly what was
needed. "Give Napoleon all he wants, make him temporary dictator, hold up the man's hands, and let him save
the country!"

Grand old republican! History puts upon his memory, as a wreath, Napoleon's own sad words, uttered in
these days of trial, "Carnot, I have known you too
late!"

Fouché sowed distrust in the chambers, making them
believe that Napoleon meant to dissolve them. This the
Emperor was advised to do; and should, perhaps, have
done. When they refused to vote him supplies, they ceased
to be of service; became, instead, a source of weakness
and danger. Why not cut down such a tree? Why tolerate politicians who at such a moment prated of constitutional limitations?

Napoleon ordered his carriage to go to the chambers;
but after the horses had idly pawed the ground for hours,
he changed his mind. He would not go.

Ney returned in a fury from the army. Napoleon's bulletins of the battle had censured him. The marshal
angrily replied in the *Moniteur*, and he now from his place
in the House of Peers struck back at his late master.
When Labédoyère, Davoust, and others told the chambers that Grouchy's army was intact, and that thirty or
forty thousand of Napoleon's own troops had rallied, — all
of which was true, — Ney hotly denied it. Passionate

and positive, he declared that the army no longer existed; that all talk of defence was idle; that terms must be made with the enemy. Unfortunate man, whom Bourbon hatred had marked for a traitor's death! His one chance for life was to continue the fight for the Emperor; his headstrong folly and falsehood ruined both Napoleon and himself.

Nothing would satisfy the Lafayette party but Napoleon's abdication. The ground must be cleared for a republic or a limited monarchy. Freed of Napoleon, Lafayette believed that France could make peace with the Allies, and would be suffered to choose her own ruler and form of government. Fouché slyly encouraged this dream of the man whom Napoleon justly termed "a political ninny." No one knew better than Fouché that Napoleon's vacant throne would be filled by the king whom Napoleon had driven from it.

The plots that were at work became known throughout Paris, and created an immense sensation. The masses of the people wanted no Bourbons, no Lafayette experiments. In the face of such national danger, they wanted Napoleon. Great crowds began to collect, and the streets rang with cries of "Live the Emperor!" The multitude thronged the avenues to the Élysée palace, and clamored for Napoleon to assert himself.

But at last the great man's energy was dead. He cared no longer for anything. He was sick in mind and body, disgusted, worn out, utterly discouraged. The enemies of France he could fight — yes, a world full of them! — but France itself he would not fight. He would head no faction; would wage no civil war for his crown. It had come to that, and his heart failed him. Let the factions

rage, let his French enemies combine: he would not stoop
to such a combat.　At last he was vanquished: this greater
Percy's spur was cold.

Behind the armies of Blücher and Wellington blazed
the campfires of more than five hundred thousand soldiers
marching under their kings upon France: how could any
human being combat half of France and the whole of
Europe besides?　The great head sank upon his breast,
and the beaten Emperor muttered, "Let them do as they
will."

He gave in his abdication in favor of his son, when
abdication was demanded.　He submitted when his son
was set aside.　He made no effort to prevent the formation
of Fouché's provisional government.　He warned the erring statesmen that they were playing Fouché's game, and
were making a huge mistake; but he lifted no hand to check
the movement.　Soldiers as well as citizens clamored for
him to lead them; he answered their shouts with lifted
hat and bowed head, but in no other way.　When Fouché,
fearing him, ordered him away, he went.

Stopping at Malmaison, it was the same.　He took no
interest in anything, was apathetic, slept much, talked at
random, and strolled idly about the grounds.　Soldiers,
passing in the road, cheered him with as much enthusiasm
as ever, but he merely said, "It would have been better
had they stood and fought at Waterloo."

There was one flash of his old spirit.　The armies of
Wellington and Blücher, marching upon Paris, had become
widely separated.　He saw that they could be beaten in
detail, and he offered his services as a general to the
Fouché government to drive back the invaders.　The offer
was refused.

The army which had been operating in La Vendée clamored for him to put himself at its head; the army of the Loire sent envoys; citizens thronged about him and besought him to rouse himself and fight. "No. It would only be civil war. I will not shed the blood of the French in a purely personal cause."

He formed no plans. He lingered at Malmaison when he could have escaped. Finally he went to the coast, and again he wasted time in uncertainty when he might have safely taken ship to America.[1]

When almost every other chance was gone, he trusted himself to Captain Maitland of the British navy, whom Napoleon had understood to promise asylum for him in England.

The armies of Wellington and Blücher continued their advance. There was some fighting before Paris; then came capitulation; and then came the Bourbons, skulking back to the throne in the rear of the enemies of France. Lafayette and the provisional government were quietly swept into the outer darkness. In after years he lamented his error of 1815, and in 1830 he did what he could to square accounts with his friends, the elder Bourbons.

[1] Talma was present at the last parting, at Malmaison, between the Emperor and his mother, and he said it was one of the most tragic scenes he ever witnessed. When the last moment arrived, the Empress-mother, prostrated with grief, and with tears streaming from her eyes, could only utter in a tremulous voice, "Adieu, my son! Adieu." And Napoleon was so affected that he caught hold of both her hands and cried, "Adieu, my mother!" and burst into tears as he left her.—(Gronow's *Anecdotes*.)

CHAPTER L

WHATEVER legal right Great Britain had to treat the French Emperor as prisoner of war, must necessarily have grown out of the manner in which she got possession of his person. In regard to this, the actual facts are that Lord Castlereagh in 1814 had suggested that he come to England, where he would be well received; and Captain Maitland of the *Bellerophon*, while disclaiming any authority to bind his government, had certainly not said anything which would warn the Emperor not to expect such treatment as Castlereagh, an English minister, had seemed to offer in 1814. Upon the contrary, Napoleon was received on board Captain Maitland's ship with formal honors; and when Napoleon said, "I come to place myself under the protection of the British laws," Captain Maitland gave him no hint that those laws had no protection for him. If Great Britain did not intend to accept him in the spirit in which he offered himself, should she have received him without giving him notice that he was acting under a delusion? Was it honorable, was it right? If she considered him a captive, why not tell him so? Why receive him on board with formal demonstrations of honor; why invite him to banquets where British admirals treated him as a sovereign? Why wait till the fleet was on the English coast before reading to him the cold lines which consigned him to St. Helena?

The entire episode reeks with dishonor. It will not do to say that he was certain to have been captured anyhow; for that statement cannot be true. There were three vessels offered him at Rochefort, in either of which he might have escaped to America; or he could have placed himself at the head of some of the French troops, near by, and have recommenced the war. With Napoleon's standard once more up, his sword in his hand, who can doubt that he could have wrung from his enemies some settlement better than hopeless captivity upon a barren rock? At all events, it seems a shocking thing to open one's door to a vanquished foe, after he has knocked thereon with the plea of a guest; and then, after having let him enter as a guest, to bar the door upon him as a prisoner. No amount of argument can hide the shame of such a transaction.

When Napoleon came on board Captain Maitland's ship, there is no doubt whatever that he was sincere in his belief that he would be permitted to live in England as a private citizen. Nor is there any doubt that Maitland thought so too. When Admiral Hotham, of the British man of war, *Superb*, visited the *Bellerophon*, Maitland's ship, on the evening of Napoleon's going on board, he asked permission to see, not a prisoner, but an Emperor. And the breakfast he gave in Napoleon's honor next morning on the *Superb* was given, not to a captive, but to a sovereign. Not only the admiral, but all the officers of the squadron, paid to the distinguished visitor every honor; and he was invited to continue his journey in the more commodious vessel, the *Superb*. He declined, out

2 x

of regard for Maitland's feelings; and it was Napoleon's preference, and not Hotham's, which prevailed.

These things being considered, who can doubt that Napoleon and the naval squadron which had possession of him were honestly acting in the belief that he was on his way to England as a guest, as a great man in misfortune, who was seeking asylum in the magnanimity of a great people?

The time had been when the word "chivalry" counted for something in Great Britain, though, to be sure, its influence had been fitful. A king like Edward III. and a prince like Edward's son, who were knights, might exhaust generosity in their dealings with a captive king of France, who was likewise a knight; but the severed limbs and gory head of Scottish Wallace were quite enough to have caused Napoleon to doubt whether John of France received the benefit of a rule or of an exception.

Between the Black Prince, to whom John trusted, and the Prince Regent, to whom Napoleon wrote his manly and touching appeal, the difference in character was considerably wider than the chasm of the years which separated them. To this Prince Regent, known to history as King George IV., the fallen Emperor of the French wrote: "My political career is ended, and I come to sit down at the fireside of the British people. I place myself under the protection of their laws, and I claim this protection from your Royal Highness as the most powerful, most constant, most generous of my foes!"

Surely a manly appeal! Surely a noble confidence! The soldier who had wielded what an Englishman has recently called "the most splendid of human swords," turned to the chief of his foes and said, "The battle has

ST. HELENA 675

gone against me; my public life is at an end; I offer you my sword; let me sit down under your protection and spend the evening of my life in peace!"

He was a broken man; he had refused to make any further strife in France when thousands of the people implored him, to the moment of his departure, to stay and fight again. "No. I am tired out — tired of myself and of the world." He was ill, could no longer ride horseback in comfort, could no longer concentrate his mind for prolonged effort. And he who had been so restless now lay abed, or lolled with a novel in his hand, and gossiped or dozed by the hour.

Never in Napoleon's career had the prayer of a vanquished foe fallen upon ears which heard not. The battle ended; he was ready for peace. He bore no malice, took no revenge. Splendid acts of generosity lit his progress from first to last. During the Hundred Days when he was so much occupied and in such straits for money, he had sought out the Dowager-Duchess of Orleans, and renewed her large pension; she had delivered him a prize when he was a schoolboy. In the dreadful strain of the hours between Ligny and Waterloo, he had remarked the critical condition of a captive English officer, Colonel Elphinstone, and had sent his own surgeon to give immediate attention to the wounded man, thus saving his life. To the Belgian peasants he had threatened the terrors of hell if they neglected to succor the Prussian wounded.

It is folly to say that noble deeds like these spring from hearts that are base. Natural kindness, inborn nobility, must be the source from which such conduct flows. Generous himself to the vanquished, magnanimous to those who threw themselves upon his generosity, it is easy to understand how it was that Napoleon trusted confidently to the liberality of Great Britain. Just as the pallid face of the dead is the flag of truce which hushes the angry voice of feud, just as the lowered point of lance or sword threw around the weaker man the invisible armor which no gallant knight would ever pierce, so this greatest captain of modern times believed that he had only to say to England: "Enough! I am beaten! I throw myself on your clemency!" in order to win the same immunity from insult, harsh treatment, and continued warfare.

So, when British officials at length came on board the ship and read to him the decision of the English ministry, that he was to be taken to St. Helena as prisoner of war; when British officials searched his trunks, took charge of his cash, and demanded his sword, his amazement, grief, horror, and indignation were profound. He had made for himself a Fool's Paradise; he had seen himself living in England, at one of her quiet, lovely homes; had surrounded himself with books and friends, and was to spend the remainder of life as a private gentleman whose passion was literature. When the horrible reality came upon him, he seemed desperate, and contemplated suicide.

Lord Liverpool, English Prime Minister, had, in official despatches, expressed the opinion that the very best way to deal with Napoleon was to treat him as a rebel and have him hanged or shot. Lord Wellington's opinion ran along on parallel lines to this, he being one of those warriors to whom generosity was a myth. In this spirit the British government conveyed Napoleon to St. Helena; in this spirit he was treated as long as he lived; and in this spirit his dead body was pursued to the grave. In the same spirit men who never met him personally, and who studied him from the point of view of Toryism only, have blackened his memory from that day to this, seeing his faults, and nothing but his faults; trumpeting his sins, and nothing but his sins, just as though Napoleon Bonaparte were not a son of Adam, like any other, and wonderfully made out of the mixed elements of good and bad.

Even yet, royalism, absolutism, fetichism in Church and State, have a horror of Napoleon Bonaparte, so rudely did he smash their idols, so truly did he clear the way for modern liberalism. One can hardly escape the conclusion that even yet books of a certain type, written against Napoleon, are little more than briefs for the defendants in the case which the modern world makes against the kings, the nobles, and the priests for the manner in which they crushed democracy for a time on the false plea of crushing Napoleon.

Passing from the custody of Captain Maitland to that of Sir George Cockburn, Napoleon was made to feel the change of status as well as the change of ship. Sir George was a typical commander of a battle-ship, — a small monarch, a despot on a limited scale. His own *Diary* exhibits him as no other writing could. It shows him to have felt that he must make " Bonaparte " know his real position; make " Bonaparte " come down from his lofty perch and look up to the eminence of Sir George. If " Bonaparte " presumed to put on airs around Sir George, Sir George would soon teach him better. If " Bonaparte " showed the slightest inclination to act the Emperor, Sir George would promptly convince him that "I cannot allow it." If " Bonaparte " grew tired of sitting at the dinner table an hour and a half, having never been accustomed to spend more than twenty minutes in that manner,

Sir George would resent his leaving the table while the others guzzled wine; and would, as Napoleon left the room, make sneering remarks to "Bonaparte's" friends about "Bonaparte's" manners.

One of the things of which Sir George said "I cannot allow it," was the proposed gift of a handsome gratuity from "Bonaparte" to the sailors of the ship. Sir George evidently feared that such a gift, adding to "Bonaparte's" already great popularity with the crew, might bear fruit unpleasant to the taste of Sir George.

Indeed, the manner in which all those who came in contact with Napoleon found their prejudice melt away, is very remarkable. Fouché had selected General Becker as Napoleon's custodian in France for the reason that Becker bore the Emperor a grudge; yet by the time Napoleon went on board Maitland's ship, Becker had become an ardent friend, and the parting between them left Becker in tears.

Captain Maitland liked him, Lord Keith liked him, the crews of the English ships liked him. Even Sir George Cockburn ceased to hate him. "Damn the fellow!" exclaimed Lord Keith; "I believe that if he and the Prince Regent should meet, the two would be the best of friends in half an hour."

One incident of the voyage to St. Helena could not be told in words more vivid than those of Lord Rosebery: —

" Once only in that voyage did his apathy forsake him. At dawn one morning when the ship was making Ushant, the watch, to their unspeakable surprise, saw the Emperor issue from his cabin and make his way, with some difficulty, to the poop. Arrived there, he asked the officer on duty if the coast were indeed Ushant, and then taking a telescope, he gazed fixedly at the land. From seven till near noon he thus remained motionless. Neither the officers of the ship nor his staff as they watched him, durst disturb that agony. At last, as the outlines faded from his sight, he turned his ghastly face, concealing it as best he could, and clutched at the arm of Bertrand, who supported him back to his cabin. It was his last sight of France."

Landed at St. Helena, he was given shabby quarters in a renovated, repaired, and amplified cow-house. The walls of it were thin, the rooms small; the rain and the wind pierced it, the heat made an oven of it, the rats infested it; no shade trees cast grateful shade about it; no fruits or flowers relieved its dismal repulsiveness.

To make sure that Napoleon should not escape from the isolated, precipitous rock of St. Helena, a considerable fleet of cruisers girdled the island, and nearly three thousand troops watched the prisoner. The eye could not range in any direction without resting upon a sentinel. During the daytime the Emperor had continual reminders of his fallen condition; and when night came on the line of sentries closed in, and no one could pass.

The prisoner and his friends were allowed to have books to read; and if Sir Hudson Lowe in browsing among the European newspapers and magazines happened upon some peculiarly bitter weed of abuse of Napoleon, that particular paper or magazine was sure to be sent up to Longwood, Napoleon's residence. If books, papers, or magazines arrived in which the captive was tenderly handled, such articles became contraband, upon one plea or another, and rarely reached the lonely man they would have cheered. The prisoner and his companions were

given enough to eat, generally, and a sufficiency of fuel
and water.   It was only occasionally that Napoleon had to
feed the fire in his damp room by breaking up his furniture ; nor was it often that the quality of the food was such
that appetites were lost because of grave suspicions as to
the manner in which the cow or sheep which supplied the
beef or mutton had come to its death.

Excepting the bare necessities of life, the prisoner was
given nothing to make captivity reasonably comfortable.
Ditches and trenches were dug all about him, guns
planted, soldiers posted, and absurdly minute, vexatious
regulations made. If Napoleon rode, a British soldier
must attend him ; if he stayed in the house, a British soldier
must have sight of him every day.   No letter could come
or go without having been opened and read by his jailer,
Sir Hudson Lowe.   Books sent him, pictures, and everything else had to come through the same channel.   If any
article sent him were addressed to him as Emperor, it was
impounded relentlessly.   A Mr. Barber who had come to
live in the island had brought with him two portraits of
Napoleon's son, intending, as a kindness which would certainly be appreciated, to present them to the bereaved
father.   Sir Hudson Lowe forbade the gift, and the
Emperor never laid eyes upon the treasures.   It was only
through Eugène that Napoleon finally received a portrait
of his son : it came packed in a box of books.   A marble
bust of the King of Rome came also, and this was long
held by Lowe, who threatened to break it in pieces.   A
letter from Napoleon's mother, in which she offered to
share his lot though blind and bending with age, was torn
open and read by the governor before its delivery.   The
captive refused to consent that either his mother or his

sister Pauline should come : he was unwilling to see them subjected to the insolence of his jailers.

The question of title gave more trouble at St. Helena than almost any other. It was vexatious, it was met at every turn, and it could never be settled. It angered Napoleon excessively when Sir Hudson Lowe persistently continued to shut off from him all letters, books, or other articles which came addressed to "The Emperor." Great Britain was resolved that he should not be known by the title he had worn so long, which a vote of the French people had confirmed, which the Pope had consecrated so far as a pope can consecrate, which every king on the Continent had recognized, and which England herself had recognized at the Congress of Chatillon, if not under the ministry of Charles Fox. "General Bonaparte" was the highest title that Great Britain could now allow; and her prisoner resisted her as stubbornly on this point as General George Washington resisted her right to send him letters addressed " Mr. George Washington."

A small thing in itself, the refusal of his title became important to him because of the spirit which actuated those who refused it. They meant to degrade him in the eyes of the world, to wound his pride by an exertion of authority; and he resented it as all self-respecting men must resent the smallest of affronts when inflicted with the meanest of motives.

"Let us compromise," urged Napoleon; "call me General Duroc or Colonel Muiron." "No!" said Great Britain; "we will call you General Bonaparte, for *that* hurts you." In simple words, such was England's attitude throughout his captivity to this lonely, broken, most wretched man. A book which an Englishman, Byron's friend Hobhouse, wrote on the Hundred Days, and which would have given the exile immense pleasure, was not delivered because in sending it the author had written on the fly-leaf "To the Emperor Napoleon." And when the prisoner died, and his friends wished to inscribe on his coffin-lid the word, "Napoleon," Great Britain, speaking through Sir Hudson Lowe, refused the privilege, — Napoleon was the imperial name; it could not be permitted. The white face of the dead man, the folded hands, the frozen sleep of Death, made no appeal to his captor which could soften this inexorable enmity. Hounding him to his very grave they demanded that "Bonaparte" be added to "Napoleon," to prove to all the world that England, ungenerous to the living captive who had come to her for generosity, had been implacable even unto death, and after death. So it was that the coffin of this greatest of men went unmarked to the tomb. Save in anonymous burial there was no escape from the malignancy which had made his last years one long period of torture.

Napoleon's household at St. Helena consisted of General Bertrand and wife and children, Count Montholon and wife, Las Casas and son, General Gourgaud, and Doctor O'Meara, the Irish surgeon of the English battleship *Bellerophon*, who had asked and been granted by his government permission to attach himself to the Emperor as his physician. Besides these, there was a staff of domestics, and, toward the end, a Corsican doctor Antommarchi and a couple of priests.

Organizing his little establishment with the same love of system which he had shown throughout his career,

Napoleon preserved at St. Helena the etiquette of the Tuileries. He had his great household officers, as at Elba; his servants wore the imperial livery; intercourse between himself and the friends who attended him was as ceremonious as it had ever been. Nobody was admitted to his presence save after audience asked and granted. In his shabby little room this fallen monarch imposed his will upon those about him to such an extent that none of his friends entered until summoned, or left until dismissed. Not till general conversation was in full current did any of his companions address him unless first spoken to by him. No matter how long he might feel inclined to talk, they stood throughout, never daring to sit unless he graciously invited them to do so. He would read to the company, and they were expected to listen attentively. A yawn was an offence, and was rebuked on the spot. A nod was an aggravation, and it would be broken into by such prompt admonitions as, " Madame Montholon, you sleep ! "

Those were dreary days at St. Helena, and the nights were drearier still. He ceased to ride, so hateful was the sight of his jailers. He tried to get some amusement out of planting trees, making a garden, and digging a fish pond. Sometimes he romped with the children; often he played chess, and cards, and billiards. In the pathetic attempt to get the benefit of horseback exercise without having to ride out in custody of an English officer, he rigged up a wooden contrivance in the house and worked away on this make-believe horse for a while.

But books and composition were his great resources. He read much, dictated a great deal; and when these tired him, he called in his companions and tried conversation.

As was natural, his talk touched every epoch of his past, — his home and family in Corsica, his childhood, his school days, his early struggles, his first triumphs, his campaigns and battles, his numberless plans and undertakings, his mistakes and failures. He spoke of himself, generally, in the third person, as of one long since dead; and spoke of the events of his career as some one, seated upon a mountain top, might calmly describe the panorama below.

In alluding to those who had served him, in any capacity, his was the tone of a chemist reporting the result of some analysis.

He rarely showed much temper either way, for or against, but spoke with a curious indifference, as of remote historical characters. Even when stating his bad opinion of Fouché, Talleyrand, Augereau, Emperor Francis, or Czar Alexander, he manifested no rancor.

Without any trace of bitterness, he referred to the harm his brothers and sisters had done him; of Marmont, Berthier, Murat, Ney, he spoke with as much absence of malice as was possible under the circumstances. He took to himself all the blame for his great errors, — his Russian campaign and the attempt on Spain.

More inclined to be severe on those who had failed him during the Hundred Days, he put the burden where history must say it belongs, — on Bourmont, on Ney, on the false movement of D'Erlon's column, on Grouchy, and on Fouché and Lafayette.

The anniversary of Waterloo was a yearly affliction. It was a day that oppressed him, a day which wrung from him anguished regrets.

" Ah, if it were to be done over again ! "

How did it happen? why was it that his left failed him at Ligny, and his right at Waterloo? Was there treachery, or merely misfortune?

Over this problem he would ponder, with a face which revealed deep emotion; a feeling akin to that which had caused him to raise his hand and strike his forehead on the day when he heard the guns of Blücher's army where he had expected to hear Grouchy's.

Wellington he frankly hated: partly because Wellington had commanded at Waterloo, and partly because Wellington had sent him to St. Helena. In his Will, the dying Emperor left an unworthy trace of this bitter feeling by devising a sum of money to a man who was charged with having attempted to assassinate the English duke. True, the Emperor states that the man had been acquitted, but the Will asserts that Cantillon had as much right to kill Wellington as the latter had "to send me to die on this rock." Here is vindictiveness and a departure from good morals; but if ever circumstances justified such an offence, it was in the case of Napoleon.

But the time, hard as he tried to kill it, hung heavy on his hands. He would lie in bed till late in the day, spend hours in the bath, lounge in undress on the sofa. If he could by any means keep himself pleasantly occupied till midnight, he was overjoyed: "We have got through one more day!" "When I wake at night, do you think my thoughts are pleasant, remembering what I have been, and what I am?" "How long the nights are!" was an exclamation which reveals an ocean of misery.

With more to grieve over than all of his companions put together, he made it a point to set an example of cheerfulness, of amiable comradeship, of intelligent consideration for others. "We are a little group, a little family, condemned to pass dreary years of exile here on this bleak rock ; let us try make the time pass as agreeably as possible." When there were jealousies and bickerings between members of his little court, it was the Emperor who soothed them away. When a fretful Gourgand would take offence at something Napoleon had said or done, he was coaxed out of his ill-humor, or paternally sent to bed to sleep it off.

NOTE. — Lord Rosebery in his "Napoleon," says, "As to his habitation, Longwood was a collection of huts which had been constructed as a cattle-shed. It was swept by an eternal wind; it was shadeless, and it was damp. Lowe himself can say no good of it, and may have felt the strange play of fortune by which he was allotted the one delightful residence on the island with twelve thousand a year [about $60,000], while Napoleon was living in an old cow-house on eight."

CHAPTER LI

MANY visitors, passengers in English vessels, called to see him. Generally, but not always, he received them. Generally, but not always, visitors so received went away converted into sympathetic friends, sometimes enthusiastic partisans. Only a few days ago (April, 1901) there died in London an aged man who, when a lad, saw the Emperor at St. Helena. The boy had been fascinated; never ceased to recall the placid countenance, gentle, sonorous voice, and wonderfully expressive eye; and spoke of Napoleon with enthusiasm to the last.

If the world possessed a faithful record of Napoleon's conversation at St. Helena, no book would be more interesting, for he discoursed freely on almost every subject of human interest, and on most topics he touched he said something worth hearing. But we have only an imperfect, fragmentary, unreliable record. Long conversations extending through several hours, and jotted down by a secretary afterward, necessarily lose most of their flavor. It would be a miracle if such a method of reporting so rapid a talker as Napoleon were accurate.

On the subjects of death, religion, the soul, the hereafter, he is differently reported, — or, rather, he held two lines of expression. When thinking of political effect and the interests of his son, he would of course remember the Catholic Church, its power, its creed, and would say things which put him on the plane of the Concordat — the restorer of religion, the believer in Christ. But when he was not posing for effect, when he blurted out his real thoughts, all this disappeared. He did not believe in the modern doctrine about the soul, and scouted the idea of immortality. "When we are dead, my dear Gourgaud, we are altogether dead."

Again he would ask: "What is a soul? Where is the soul of a sleeper, a madman, a babe?" In spite of that old-time pointing to the stars in the heavens and the oft-quoted question which we are told dumfounded the materialists, "Can you tell me who made all that?" Napoleon at St. Helena proclaimed himself a materialist. Long before Darwin's great book appeared, Napoleon announced his belief in the principle of evolution. His great difficulty in reconciling the dogma of a benevolent and just God with the universe as it exists, was that the facts seemed all against the dogma. In the days of his power he had said scornfully, "God fights on the side of the heavy battalions;" at St. Helena he declared that he could not believe in a just God punishing and rewarding, for good people are always unfortunate and scoundrels are always lucky. "Look at Talleyrand; he is sure to die in his bed!" And so he did; and if the Pope's blessing was a passport to heaven, this most villanous of all Frenchmen reached heaven by the best and shortest route. The manner in which the weak — no matter how good — go down before the strong, — no matter how bad, — in human affairs, as in the realms of animal life, staggered his belief in the benevolence of the plan of creation. "Were I obliged to have a religion, I would worship the Sun — the source of all life, the real god of earth."

"Why should punishment be eternal?" Why damn a man who was brought into the world, not of his own will, and who was stamped with certain qualities which almost inevitably determined his character and conduct — why punish such a man with the eternal torments of hell because of a few years of sin? What good could it accomplish to torture poor human beings forever and forever? Would God *never* grow sorry? No? Then he was crueller than the savagest of the human race. Justice! Could it be just to create men with certain passions, turn them loose for a few years to see what they would do, and then when they had done what the law of their nature made it almost inevitable that they would do, — and what God knew they would do before he created them, — was it just to burn these helpless wretches forever in the slow fires of hell? Napoleon could not bring himself to think so.

He said that, when in Egypt, the sheiks had disturbed him considerably by alleging that he was a pagan because he worshipped three gods. These sheiks, with tantalizing persistence, maintained that God the Father, God the Son, and God the Spirit made three gods. Of course Napoleon endeavored to explain to these benighted Arabs that our three gods were only one. The sheiks of Cairo, however, being men of primitive mind and stubborn habit, would not open their eyes to the truth, and they continued to say that Mahomet's creed was better than Christ's, because Mahometans believe in one God, only. All other celestial beings are angels, lower than God. Human beings, men born of women, may be prophets, martyrs, sublimely missioned reformers, but they are not gods.

"As for me," exclaimed Napoleon, on one occasion, "I do not believe in the divinity of Christ. He was put to

2 Y

death like any other fanatic who professed to be a prophet
or a messiah.   There were constantly people of this kind."
As, indeed, there are.   England crushed the last one in the
Soudan a few years ago.

The great sorrow of Napoleon in his captivity was the
absence of his wife and son.   He believed, or pretended
to believe, that Maria Louisa was still faithful to him.
He had been told of her shame, he had even hotly denounced the infamous manner in which her father had put
her into the power of Neipperg, but with singular persist-
ency he would return to the idea that she yet loved him,
and would join him if the Allies would permit.   He could
not know that the mother of his child had declared that
she did not love him, and never had loved him.

A striking refrain, running through all the discussions of
those acts of his reign which had been under hottest fire,
is this, "History will do me justice."   Time and again,
after stating his explanations, reasons, motives, or justi-
fication, he comes back to the words, "History will do me
justice."

Considering all the circumstances, the confidence was
sublime.   His was a blasted name throughout the world.
In France it was bad taste to mention him.   By formal
enactment of combined Europe he was an outlaw, beyond
the pale of humanity, a pariah whom all were privileged
to stone.   Only one newspaper of the free press of England
had dared to say a word for him when the government
was making a prisoner out of a man it had not captured;
only two members of Parliament dared protest against the
wrong.

THE KING OF ROME

From the painting by Sir T. Lawrence

In France his followers, Ney and Labédoyère, had been shot, and Lavalette condemned. Reaction was rushing like an avalanche, and sweeping all before it. Royalist Catholics were outdoing in the White Terror the atrocities of the Red. Italy was her old self again, and Murat had looked into the muzzles of the Bourbon muskets, and had said, with the last flash of the old courage and pride, "Save my face, aim at my heart — fire!" Every pander who could distort or create was adding to the piles of books in which the Corsican monster was devoted to damnation here and hereafter. Yet, in spite of all, the captive was serenely at ease about his future.

"History will do me justice. My work will speak for itself. I shall soon be gone; but what I did, and what I attempted, will live for ages. My public improvements, my canals, harbors, roads, monuments, churches, hospitals, my school system, my code, my organization of the civil service, my system of finance, the manufactures that sprang up at my touch, the arts and sciences encouraged, the libraries founded, the triumphs of democracy which I organized and made permanent — these are my witnesses, and to posterity they will testify. Your Wellingtons and your Metternichs may dam the stream of liberal ideas, checking the current for the time; but the torrent will be only the stronger when it breaks.

"From the passions of to-day, I appeal to the sober judgment of to-morrow. Future generations will remember my intentions, consider my difficulties, and judge me leniently."

This superb confidence sustained him so buoyantly that he was never more imperial in his pose than at St. Helena. When Lowe threatened to have his room forcibly entered

each day in order that the jailer might know his prisoner
was still there, the indomitable Corsican said, "I'll kill
the first man that tries it!" and before that courage of
despair even Hudson Lowe drew back. When England
demanded his sword, he had placed his hand upon it and
looked the British officer in the eye with an expression
that could not be misunderstood. The brave and generous Lord Keith, more chivalrous than his government,
bowed to his captive, and retired without the sword.

"Let him" (Lowe) "send all my friends away, if he
will; let him plant sentinels at the doors and windows,
and give me nothing but bread and water: I care not.
My soul is free. I am as independent as when I was at
the head of six hundred thousand men; as free as when
I gave laws to Europe!"

Mr. Taine with painstaking malevolence traces Napoleon back to Cæsar Borgia; but this granite formation of
character was not Italian, it was Corsican. The spirit
which here nerved the solitary captive to brave a world
in arms was not that of his Italian father who bent the
courtier's knee to the conquerors of his country; it was
that of his Corsican mother, whose firmness of character
resisted all fears and all temptations. In Napoleon, Italy
may have reached her highest type; but in him, also, Corsica saw the last and the greatest of the heroic race of
Sampiero.

"The atmosphere of modern ideas stifles the old feudal-
ists, for henceforth nothing can destroy or deface the grand
principles of our revolution. These great truths can never
cease to exist. Created in the French Tribune, cemented
by the blood of battles, adorned by the laurels of victory,
hailed by the acclamations of the people, they can never be

turned backward. They live in Great Britain, illuminate America, they are nationalized in France. Behold the tripod from whence issues the light of the world! They will yet triumph. They will be the faith, the religion, the morality of all peoples, and this era will be connected with my name. For, after all, I kindled the torch and couse-crated the principle, and now persecution makes me the Messiah of those principles. Friends and foes must acknowledge that of these principles I am the chief soldier, the grand representative. Thus, when I am in my grave, I shall still be, for the people, the polar star of their rights. My name will be the war-cry of their efforts."

Scores of other quotations might be made to the same effect, and they go far to explain why modern liberalism regarded Napoleon as The Man. He grew to hate democracy? Yes. He crushed opposition to his will rigorously, pitilessly? Yes. He stifled free speech and smothered representative government? Yes. He was more despotic than any Bourbon? Yes. Then how dared he predict that his name would become the war-cry of the people in their struggle for civil rights?

Because he knew that posterity would see at work, within the body of his despotism, the spirit of democracy. He knew that with his system of civil and social equality, and the absolute privilege of every citizen, however humbly born, to rise to the loftiest positions, no real despotism could be possible; and that history would say so. When he, the Emperor, chosen by the people, stood up in his carriage on the streets of Paris and pointed out to his Austrian bride the window of the room in which he had lodged when he came up from Brienne, — a poor boy with his career to make, — his pride in pointing to that milepost on the toilsome route of his promotion was that of all self-made men, was that of the man who scorns to win where he has not fought, was that of the robust conqueror who wants nothing for which he has not paid the price of manly effort.

It was the same spirit which flashed out of him when Metternich presented from the Emperor of Austria, in 1809, the proofs that he was descended from the nobility of Florence.

" I will have none of such tomfoolery. My patent of nobility dates from the battle of Montenotte ! "

It was the same spirit which moved him to chide Duroc, his beloved Duroc, when that highest officer of the palace had been rude to Constant, the valet, Constant being in tears about it.

The same spirit was on him when he stopped to talk with poor Toby, the Malay slave of St. Helena, and to give him money ; the same when he rebuked Madame Balcombe, who with angry voice ordered some heavily burdened slaves to give way to her, in a steep, narrow path, — " Respect the burden, Madame ! "

Thought, feelings, deeds like these are not born in hearts barren of human sympathy, dead to the sense of fraternity, or alien to the sentiment which inspires the mystic to strive for the good of all.

* *

Bertrand states that after 1820 Napoleon was a confirmed invalid. Sitting in his chair, clad in dressing-gown, he spent the days reading, being no longer able to work or dictate.

" What a delightful thing rest is. The bed has become

for me a place of luxury. How fallen am I. Once my activity was boundless; my mind never slumbered; I sometimes dictated to four or five secretaries, who wrote as fast as words could be uttered. But then I was Napoleon. Now I am nothing. I am sunk into a stupor, I can hardly raise my eyelids, my faculties forsake me. I do not live ; I merely exist."

Through March and April, 1821, he was slowly dying, and suffering torments from his ailment — cancer of the stomach. His patience and his kindness to those around him were perfect.

On one of the last days of April he said to Montholon, early in the morning on awakening from sleep: " I have just seen the good Josephine. I reached out my arms to embrace her, and she disappeared. She was seated there. It seemed to me that I had seen her yesterday evening. She is not changed; she loves me yet. Did you see her ? "

Burning fever and delirium marked these final days; but in the lucid intervals he was calm, fearless, and thoughtful for the friends about him. On May 4 Bertrand asked him if he would have a priest. " No, I want no man to teach me how to die." Nevertheless, he accepted the usual clerical services. And the picture of a densely ignorant and dull-minded priest, taking possession of Napoleon Bonaparte, hearing his confessions and granting him heavenly passports, is one of those things which makes the vocabulary of amazement seem to need enlargement and intensification.

It would not, perhaps, be difficult to explain why Napoleon, in his last illness, accepted the services of a priest, and died in the arms of the Church; but it puzzles one to

understand why he embalmed in his Will his delusion as
to Maria Louisa. He had long known of her infidelity, he
received no line or message from her during the whole
time of his captivity; yet he speaks of her in his will as
though she had ever been the true and loving wife. Was
this done from personal pride? Or did he do it for the
sake of his son? Both motives may have influenced him,
especially the latter.

A storm was raging over the island on May 4. "The
rain fell in torrents, and a fierce gale howled over the
drenched crags of St. Helena. Napoleon's favorite willow
was torn up by the roots, and every tree he had planted at
Longwood was blown down.

"The night was very bad," says Montholon. "Toward
two o'clock delirium set in, accompanied by nervous
contractions. Twice I thought I heard the words, *France
— armée — tête d'armée — Josephine*, at the same time the
Emperor sprang from the bed, in spite of my efforts to
restrain him. His strength was so great that he threw me
down, heavily falling to the floor."

Others, hearing the noise, ran in, and the Emperor was
put back upon the bed, where he became calm again. At
six in the morning the death-rattle was heard. As Montholon approached the bed, the dying man made a sign that
he wanted water. He was past swallowing; his thirst could
only be allayed by a sponge pressed to his lips. He then
lay all day with his eyes fixed, seemingly in deep meditation. As the sun was setting, he died — the evening gun
of the English fort booming across the sea as his life went
out.

"Ah," said Marchand, "he died in the arms of victory!
He called for Desaix, Lannes, Duroc. I heard him order

up the artillery, and then he cried: 'Deploy the eagles! Onward!'"

"I shall never forget," says Stewart, "Marshal Bertrand coming out of the room and announcing, in a hollow voice, 'The Emperor is dead,' the last word being accompanied by a deafening peal of thunder."

Napoleon had made his preparations for death with the composure of an ancient pagan. He had given minute instructions to all about him as to their duties when he should be gone, and had directed an autopsy of his body in order that the true character of his disease might be known, for the benefit of his son. He inquired of the young priest whether he knew how to arrange the death chapel; and he dictated the form of notice which should be sent Sir Hudson Lowe when he, Napoleon, should be dead. In his Will, written by his own hand, he set out an elaborate list of legacies, including those who had befriended his boyhood, and those who had been loyal to him in the days of his power, as well as those whose fidelity had been the comfort of his captivity and dying hours. From his mother and nurse to his teachers and schoolfellows, his companions-in-arms and the children of those who had died in battle at his side, to the Old Guard and the faithful few at St. Helena, he swelled the debt of gratitude, and honored himself in remembering others. In regard to this Will, it may be of interest to state that only a small portion of the vast assets Napoleon claimed to have left in Europe could be found by his executors, and that during the second Empire the State voted $1,600,000 toward the unpaid legacies.

Given the funeral of a general officer, his unmarked coffin was borne by soldiers down into the little valley,

where was the willow, under which he often rested, and
the spring whose waters had so refreshed him in the fever
of his long decline. Here he was buried, May 8, 1821.

One day, at St. Helena, there was a stormy interview
between prisoner and jailer, between Napoleon and Sir
Hudson Lowe. The book from Hobhouse had been kept
by the governor, and this and many other things the captive resented.

"I detained the book because it was addressed to the
Emperor," said Lowe.

"And who gave *you* the right to dispute that title?"
cried Napoleon, indignantly.

"In a few years your Lord Castlereagh and all the others,
and you yourself, will be buried in the dust of oblivion;
or, if your names be remembered at all, it will be only on
account of the indignity with which you have treated me;
but the Emperor Napoleon will continue forever the sub-
jcet, the ornament of history, and the star of civilized
nations. Your libels are of no avail against me. You
have expended millions on them; what have they produced? Truth pierces through the clouds; it shines like
the sun, and like the sun it cannot perish!"

To which proud boast, Sir Hudson Lowe replied, as he
records, "You make me smile, sir."

Sir Hudson may have smiled then, and may have kept on
smirking as long as Napoleon lived. Nothing seemed less
likely than that the prophetic words of the prisoner would
come true. But there came a time when Sir Hudson did
not smile. When death had released the prisoner, and the
faithful companions of his years of misery went home and

told their story, — O'Meara in England, Las Casas and
Montholon in France, — Sir Hudson did not smile; for
all Europe rang with his name, and all generous hearts
condemned him. He turned to British courts for vindi-
cation, and did not get it. He applied to the English
ministers for high, permanent employment and liberal pension, and he got neither the one nor the other. Young
Las Casas invited him to fight, and he did not fight. He
dropped into a contempt which was so deep and so universal that even Wellington, in effect, turned his back upon
the creature he had used, having no further need for just
such a man.

"You make me smile, sir," said amused Sir Hudson,
when the shabbily clad, prematurely decrepit man, standing on the hearth of his dismal room, prophesied his political resurrection and his final triumph over his enemies.
Had Castlereagh heard, he also would have smiled, not
foreseeing that ghastly climax to political prostitution,
when, after a lifetime of truckling to royalism, and of
doing its foulest work, he should find the whole world
turn black, should cut his own throat, and be followed
to his tomb by the hoots of an English mob!

Wellington, too, would have been amused at hearing
the prisoner's prophecy; would have thought Napoleon
insane, not foreseeing the perilous times in England
when the progress of liberalism would break the line of
his Tory opposition; would win triumphs for reform in
spite of his threat that he would have his dragoons
"sharp grind their sabres as at Waterloo." With the
windows of his London home smashed by a British mob,
with millions of liberals shouting demands for better laws,
so fiercely that even Wellington gave up trust in those

sharp-ground swords, there came a day when the Iron
Duke may have remembered the prophet of St. Helena,
and read the words again — without the smile.

"In a few years you and all the others will be buried
in the dust of oblivion; but the Emperor will live forever, the ornament of history, the star of civilized
nations!"

It was a proud boast, and proudly has time made it good.
In a few years the Bourbons had played out their shabby
parts on the throne of France, and had gone into final
and hopeless exile, "unwept, unhonored, and unsung."

Liberalism had risen from defeats, and made its will
supreme. Both in England and in France the Old Order
had passed away, principles more enlightened prevailed.
A new day had dawned, not cloudless nor free from
storm, but better and brighter than 1815 or 1821. In the
year of our Lord 1840, the thought of the two great
nations turned to the grave at St. Helena. France asked,
and England gave — whom? The Emperor! Not
"Bonaparte" nor "General Bonaparte," save in the
minds of the very small and the exceedingly venomous;
but Napoleon, "the Emperor and king."

The grave at St. Helena was opened; the perfectly
preserved face, beautiful in death, uncovered amid sighs and
tears; and then the body, taken away to be entombed
"upon the banks of the Seine in the midst of the people
I have so much loved," was received on board a royal ship,
by a prince of the Bourbon house of Orleans, with masts
squared, flags flying, cannon booming, drums beating, and
every note of triumph swelling the pomp of that imperial
reception. With a vast outpouring of the people, France
welcomed the greatest Frenchman home.

"Truth cuts through the clouds; shines like the sun; and like the sun it is immortal!" Sublime confidence, sublimely justified!

"You make me smile, sir," said Lowe; but that was many years since. It is 1840 now, and Napoleon's turn has come.

From king to peasant, all France starts up to meet her returning hero. He comes back to a throne which none dispute. He comes back to a dominion no Marmont can betray. Allied kings will league themselves in vain to break that imperial supremacy. No Talleyrand or Fouché or Bourmont can find for treachery a leverage to overthrow that majestic power. No. It is secure in a realm which envy and malice and ignoble passion may invade, but cannot conquer. It has linked itself with things immortal; and for this imperial career and fame there can be no death.

Let Cherbourg's thousand guns salute! Let triumphal arches span the Seine as he passes on his way! Let hill and slope and river bank hold their gazing hosts! Let flowers and garlands shower down on the bier from every bridge. Let aged peasants drop on reverent knees, fire the old musket in humble salute, and then cover the weeping faces with trembling hands! Cold is this December day; but winter cannot chill this vast enthusiasm. From the quay, where the funeral barge moors, to the Church of the Invalides, where the tomb waits, a million people throng the route. Streets, avenues, squares, balconies, windows, roofs, trees — all are full of people. Cannons, drums, military bands, the tramp of men and war-horses, the glitter of endless lines of soldiers, the songs which rouse the passions and the memories, the shouts of dense

crowds stirred by electrical emotions — all these mark this
December day as the gorgeous funeral car bears Napoleon
to his final rest.   There is the white war-horse, not
Marengo, but one like him ; and upon the horse is the
saddle and the bridle Napoleon had used.   There are his
old Marshals Moncey, and Soult, and Oudinot ; there is
Bertrand and Gourgaud and Las Casas, the faithful companions of his long exile.   But above all there are the
relics of his ancient wars to come weeping around the
bier ; and there is a remnant of his Old Guard to march
with him to his tomb.   Oh, the magic of the mighty dead !
No freezing December air can keep down the fervor which
makes the great city ring with cries of "Live the
Emperor ! "

Sixteen black horses, plumed and draped, draw the
lofty funeral car over which lies the purple velvet robe,
and in which is the coffin — marked, at last, in letters of
gold, "Napoleon."   Princes of the Church come forth to
meet the body ; a king and his court and the proudest
notables of France wait within to receive it.

"The Emperor ! " cries the herald at the door ; and the
brilliant assembly rises, as one man, and makes the reverent bow to the dead man who enters.

Over all is the spell of a master spirit ; over all the
spell of a deathless past.

The sword of Austerlitz is handed to King Louis
Philippe by Soult ; and the King gives it to the faithful
Bertrand ; and Bertrand lays it, reverently, upon his
master's coffin.   The awful stillness of the great temple
is broken by the sobs of gray-haired soldiers.

With a grand *Requiem* chant, the funeral ends ; but the
silent procession of mourners coming in endless lines to

view the coffin lasts more than a week, bringing people from all parts of France, from Belgium, and from other lands.

Nor has that procession ended yet. Around the great man, lying there in his splendid tomb, with his marshals near him and the battle-flags he made famous drooping about him, still flows the homage of the world. The steps of those who travel, like the thoughts of those who are students of human affairs, turn from the four quarters of the earth to the tomb of this mightiest of men.

His impress lies upon France forever, in her laws, her institutions, her individual and national life; but his empire does not stop with France, — is cramped by no "natural limits" of Rhine and Alps and Pyrenees.

By force of genius and of character, by superior fitness to do great things, he was the chief usurper of his time. He is the usurper yet, and for the same reasons. He did the work kings ought to have done, — doing it in spite of the kings. He does it yet, in spite of the kings.

His hand, as organizer of the Revolution, which was greater even than he, is at the loom where the life-garments of nations are woven. Listen to this voice, coming out of Italy: " Within the space of ten years we had made [under Napoleon] more progress than our ancestors had done in three centuries. We had acquired the French civil, criminal, and commercial codes; we had abolished the feudal system, and justice was administered with improved methods." So wrote General Pépé; and what he said of Italy was equally true of every other portion of Continental Europe which had come under the imperial sway. It was this work Napoleon was doing from the very first day he grasped the reins of power; it was this work

the allied kings dreaded; it was this work they meant
to stop.

In that he strove for himself and his dynasty, Napoleon
failed miserably, for to that extent he betrayed his trust,
was false to his mission, wandered from the road. But
so far as his toil was for others, for correct principles, for
better laws, better conditions, productive of happier homes
and better men and women, he did not fail. No Leipsic
or Waterloo could destroy what was best in his career:
no William Pitt could pile up sufficient gold to bribe into
the field kings strong enough to chain peoples as they had
once been chained. In vain was Metternich's Holy Alliance, his armed resistance to liberal ideas; his savage
laws, his inhuman dragoonings:— the immortal could not
be made to die.

INDEX

A

Abensberg, battle of, 440.

Aboukir, battle of, 219–220.

Acre, siege of, 215.

"Act Additional"—amendment to Constitution, 1814, 637–639.

Adige, French defence, 156–167.

Ajaccio—
Birthplace of Napoleon, 17.
Paoli, *see that title.*
Reception of Napoleon, 1799, 230–232.
Revolutionary movements, 1789, 49–60.
[*See also* Corsica.]

Alexander, Czar of Russia—
Erfurth conference, 428.
Successor of Paul, 291.
Vienna Congress, 620–623.
[*See also* Russia.]

Alexandria taken by Napoleon, 203.

Alps crossed, 1800, 280.

Alvinczy, General, defeated by Napoleon, 162–168.

Amiens, Peace of, 293; ruptured, 312.

Amnesty to political offenders during Consulate, 258.

Ancients, council of, *see* Council of Ancients.

André, Abbé d', rumors as to movements of Napoleon at Elba, 624–625.

Antommarchi, death mask of Napoleon, 388.

Aragon, aid in Corsican struggle for independence, 3, 4.

Arcis on the Aube, battle of, 576.

Army of France—
Creation of new army by Napoleon, 1800, 279–282; 1813, 506.

Army of France, *continued*—
Destruction in Russia, retreat from Moscow, 1812, 493–499, 504.
Napoleon in—
Commander, 112–114, 126.
Loss of position, name struck from list of generals, 60–64, 104.
Western transfer, order evaded, 94–96, 104.
Reorganization by Napoleon, 264, 636.

Artois, Count of, conspiracy against Napoleon, 317–328.

Aspern, battle of, 442–443, 450.

Aube River crossing, incident, 572.

Aubrey—
Exile, 258, 259.
Napoleon transferred to army of the West, 95, 96.

Auerstädt, battle of, 362, 364.

Augereau, General—
Coup d'état of 18th Brumaire, 245, 251.
Directory supported by, during royalist movement, 182–184, 236.
Italian campaign, 162–164, 168.

Austerlitz, battle of, 347, 349.

Austria—
1793, French booty, bargain with England, 83.
1796, Napoleon's Italian Campaign, 144–186.
1799–1800, operations in Italy, peace of Lunéville, 224, 279–290.
1805, coalition of powers, defeat at Austerlitz, 339–347, 355–357.
1809, renewal of war, Wagram, etc., 439–449.
1812, ally of France, 476, 477.
1813, rising in Germany, mediation offered, 507–521, 554–556.

THE STORY OF FRANCE

FROM THE EARLIEST TIMES TO THE CONSULATE OF NAPOLEON BONAPARTE

By the HON. THOMAS E. WATSON

In two volumes. Cloth 8vo. Gilt tops. Price $5.00

HENRY M. BAIRD says in Literature:

"He has given us a highly interesting book upon one of the most fascinating themes of history. 'The Story of France' is the fruit of great research, and is a conscientious and thoroughly readable presentation of a great theme."

GEORGE CARY EGGLESTON says:

"His style is terse, simple, and direct. In narration he is rapid and graphic. His diction is strong and his presentation of events and of social conditions is always picturesque and often dramatic. He has wit, humor, and much of that rhetorical fervor which in oral utterance we call eloquence."

The New York Times more than once called attention to:

". . . the manifold merits of the book, the distinctness of its rapid portrayal of the various epochs of which it treats, its imaginative force, and its frequently impassioned eloquence."

The Evening Telegraph, Philadelphia, says of the second volume:

"The public will await it impatiently. Therein, of course, the author will describe the period of the great Revolution, which will naturally be the crown of the entire work. We have every right to expect it to be *an exposition which will attract the notice of the world.*"

The Outlook describes it as:

"*An exceptionally entertaining narrative.* . . . The author touches nothing that has not a vital interest either as illustrating the life of the age he is describing, or as affecting the life of the ages that follow. By means of concrete pictures rather than abstract generalizations he depicts the history of civilization. His own intense sympathies with the cause of the oppressed, and his constant finding of parallels between the battles against privilege in ages gone by and those of to-day, make the description of the dead past read like a description of the living present."

The American, of Philadelphia:

"Many histories of France have been written, many in the English tongue, but *none that can compare with this.* A more *brief, direct, yet readable* history *leaving a vivid impression* upon the mind is scarcely imaginable. . . . For our part we look upon history as an art, by the study of which we may learn to govern ourselves in a way to avoid the pitfalls that have been the undoing of great peoples, of firmly established governments, . . . and it is so that Mr. Watson regards history, so in his own inimitable style that he has written the history of France."

Lightning Source UK Ltd.
Milton Keynes UK
UKHW010347281218
334537UK00008B/337/P